EUROPE

IN REVIEW

READINGS AND SOURCES SINCE 1500

EUROPE

IN REVIEW

REVISED

Edited, with introductions by

George L. Mosse, Rondo E. Cameron,

Henry Bertram Hill, and Michael B. Petrovich,

University of Wisconsin

RAND MCNALLY & COMPANY

Chicago

RAND McNALLY HISTORY SERIES

FRED HARVEY HARRINGTON, *Advisory Editor*

Borden, ed., *America's Ten Greatest Presidents*
Caughey and E. May, *A History of the United States*
Freidel and Pollack, eds., *Builders of American Institutions: Readings in United States History*
Gatzke, *The Present in Perspective,* 2nd edition
Jones, *Ancient Civilization*
Mosse, *The Culture of Western Europe: The Nineteenth and Twentieth Centuries*
Palmer, ed., *Atlas of World History*
Palmer, ed., *Historical Atlas of the World*
Sellers, ed., *The Berkeley Readings in American History*
Sellers and H. May, *A Synopsis of American History*
Shannon, *Twentieth Century America: The United States Since the 1890's*
Starr, Nowell, Lyon, Stearns, and Hamerow, *A History of the World* (2 vols.)
Treadgold, *Twentieth Century Russia*
Williams, ed., *The Shaping of American Diplomacy*
Wright, *France in Modern Times: 1760 to the Present*

Copyright © 1957, 1964 by Rand McNally & Company
All rights reserved
Printed in the U.S.A. by Rand McNally & Company
Library of Congress Catalog Card Number: 64-17637

PREFACE

JACOB BURCKHARDT once defined historical studies as contemplation based upon the sources. This book is meant to introduce the student to some of the raw materials of European history. Such a book cannot, by its very nature, be either comprehensive or definitive. Many excellent source collections exist for the use of scholars, but these are too unwieldy to serve as an introduction to the source material of modern European history and often require previous historical training for their proper use. The selections in this book are, therefore, more particularly chosen to illustrate some of the major developments of modern European history.

A sampling of this kind is necessarily both personal and arbitrary. We have chosen documents which we believe to be significant expressions of the trend to be illustrated, and we have often included hitherto neglected sources which convey the flavor of the times better than many of the so-called "standard" source materials. Moreover, we have confined ourselves mainly to sources contemporary with the period under discussion and have, by and large, not been concerned with the commentaries of later historians. Here it should be noted that in making translations we have tried to present in a readable fashion the essence of the original, rather than a word-for-word rendering of the text such as one might make for a detailed, scholarly examination of the documents. For such a study the reader is referred back to the sources themselves, which are everywhere indicated.

Because we realize that students may need additional aid in understanding the selections, we have provided three devices which we hope will prove helpful. First, we have given a short general introduction to each chapter. In that introduction we have referred to the extracts, in this way giving the student an idea of the general framework of the selection. Secondly, each selection is preceded by a short individual introduction, noting its specific importance and relevance to the subject of the chapter. Thirdly, the questions at the end of each chapter refer directly to the documents themselves. They are designed to guide the student to the relevant issues and to assist him in comprehending the source. As one final aid to the student, we have included pertinent cross references, inserted in parentheses, in a number of the introductions. The cross-reference numbers that are not preceded by "p." refer to the selection number that appears in boldface type in the margin at the beginning of each selection. Cross-reference numbers preceded by "p." of course refer to a specific page, rather than a selection number.

We are indebted to many persons in the preparation of this volume. Some of the extracts in this volume are taken from a book of readings by George L. Mosse and Philip Taylor, and we wish to thank Mr. Taylor, of the University of Birmingham, for the use of several extracts which he has collected. John Thayer has provided invaluable assistance in the preparation of this book, including several translations from the Italian. Miss Phyllis Abbott and Mrs. Elsie Crabb deserve our thanks for the tedious work of typing and retyping the manuscript.

MADISON, WISCONSIN   G. L. M.
FEBRUARY, 1957   R. E. C.
                                      H. B. H.
                                      M. B. P.

CONTENTS

CHAPTER I

THE RENAISSANCE

THE RENAISSANCE as a historical concept is difficult to define. To historians of an older generation it signified the "rebirth" of men after medieval slumber. Going to the other extreme, some historians have thought the Renaissance to be no rebirth at all but simply a continuation of medieval life and thought. The truth seems to lie between these interpretations.

During the Renaissance, interest became more vitally centered in this world and less so in the next. However, this did not mean that the revival of classical learning was ever wholly detached from the other-worldly Christian tradition. Petrarch's letter to Boccaccio (2) illustrates this fact. The greatest artists and writers combined their realism with Christian themes. When Pope Nicholas V founded the Vatican library (3), he did not think of classical antiquity and Christianity as opposed to each other.

Yet the greater impetus toward a realistic view of life in the Italy of the despots (1) made itself felt. Machiavelli, analyzing the politics of his time (6), wrote a classic of modern *Realpolitik*. Jacob Fugger "the Rich" was more interested in his purse than in his soul and did not bother to disguise the fact (7). Some literature and art came to rely more upon classical than upon Christian inspiration. Thus we can speak of a "Renaissance of secularism" even if the best humanistic spirits combined classics, appreciation of reality, and Christian themes.

Through this revival of learning, a new concept of the "gentleman" or the "courtier" emerges. His ideal, as shown by Castiglione (5), is no longer glory alone but also a wide learning. In this way, the Renaissance was to influence the whole outlook of the ruling and upper classes. For Renaissance ideas spread from Italy to the rest of Europe.

In the north, however, "humanism" became "Christian humanism." Here the classical inspiration was rarely divorced from Christian concerns. Erasmus, the most learned man of his time, was interested in using humanism to reform the church. His *Praise of Folly* (8) shows his disgust with outward ceremonies that tended to obscure the basic content of Christianity. He too wanted to get to the sources—not those of Greece or Rome but those of Christianity.

In these various ways the Renaissance gave a new impetus to the development of modern Europe.

During the fourteenth and fifteenth centuries, most Italian city-states fell under the rule of the despots. This was the political setting for much of the Renaissance in Italy. Here John Addington Symonds, a historian of the last century, gives a graphic description of this kind of rule.

1   . . . If we examine the constitution of these tyrannies, we find abundant proofs of their despotic nature. The succession from father to son was always uncertain. Legitimacy of birth was hardly respected. The last La Scalas were bastards. The house of Aragon in Naples descended from a bastard. Gabriello Visconti shared with his half-brothers the heritage of Gian Galeazzo. The line of the Medici was continued by princes of more than doubtful origin. Suspicion rested on the birth of Frederick of Urbino. The houses of Este and Malatesta honored their bastards in the same degree as their lawful progeny. The great family of the Bentivogli at Bologna owed their importance at the end of the fifteenth century to an obscure and probably spurious pretender, dragged from the wool-factories of Florence by the policy of Cosimo de'Medici. The sons of popes ranked with the proudest of aristocratic families. Nobility was less regarded in the choice of a ruler than personal ability. Power once acquired was maintained by force, and the history of the ruling families is one long catalogue of crimes. Yet the cities thus gov-

erned were orderly and prosperous. Police regulations were carefully established and maintained by governors whose interest it was to rule a quiet
state. Culture was widely diffused without regard to rank or wealth. Public
edifices of colossal grandeur were multiplied. Meanwhile the people at large
were being fashioned to that self-conscious and intelligent activity which is
fostered by the modes of life peculiar to political and social centers in a condition of continued rivalry and change. . . .

The life of the despot was usually one of prolonged terror. Immured in
strong places on high rocks, or confined to gloomy fortresses like the Mi-
lanese Castello, he surrounded his person with foreign troops, protected his
bed-chamber with a picked guard, and watched his meat and drink lest they
should be poisoned. His chief associates were artists, men of letters, astrolo-
gers, buffoons, and exiles. He had no real friends or equals, and against his
own family he adopted an attitude of fierce suspicion, justified by the frequent
intrigues to which he was exposed. His timidity verged on monomania. Like
Alfonso II of Naples, he was tortured with the ghosts of starved or strangled
victims; like Ezzelino, he felt the mysterious fascination of astrology; like
Filippo Maria Visconti, he trembled at the sound of thunder, and set one
band of bodyguards to watch another next his person. He dared not hope for
a quiet end. No one believed in the natural death of a prince: princes must
be poisoned or poignarded. Out of thirteen of the Carrara family, in little
more than a century (1318–1435), three were deposed or murdered by near
relatives, one was expelled by a rival from his state, four were executed by
the Venetians. Out of five of the La Scala family, three were killed by their
brothers, and a fourth was poisoned in exile. . . .

John Addington Symonds, *The Renaissance in Italy* (New York: Henry Holt & Co., n.d.),
pp. 102–3, 118–19.

In this letter Petrarch tells Boccaccio (1313–1375) how good it is
to expend one's life in learning, and how this relates to Christian piety.

. . . Neither love of virtue nor the thought of approaching death must   2
distract us from the study of literature which, if pursued with good intentions, stimulates love of virtue and either diminishes or destroys the fear of
death. . . . For literature is no hindrance to one who takes it in the proper
spirit; to him it is not an obstacle but a comfort and an aid in the difficulties
of the earthly voyage. And as it happens with many foods that the same prove
troublesome to a weak and queasy stomach which to one healthy and craving
offer grateful and timely nourishment, so it is with studies. Those which

might prove harmful to weak minds seem beneficial to a keen and well disposed intellect. This is particularly so if, in both cases, the propensity be used with moderation.

And were this not true, how could one explain that persevering and resolute zeal, so highly praised, which many kept to the end? Cato was beginning to grow old when he started to study Latin letters, and already aged when he learned Greek. Varro reached his hundredth year, always reading and writing, and had departed from life before he abandoned his love of study. Livius Drusus did not allow age and blindness to distract him from the interpretation of civil law, to the profit of the Republic. Appius Claudius showed the same steadfastness when burdened with the same discomforts. Homer among the Greeks, likewise blind and very old, did the same, and showed himself equally resolute in a different type of study. Socrates devoted himself to music when already weighted down by his years. . . . Isocrates composed a volume of orations at ninety-four, Sophocles a book of tragedies when about one hundred. . . .

But setting aside those ancients and others like them, since it would be impossible to name them all, and speaking of those of our faith whom we are more desirous of emulating, did not these as well expend their lives on literature? Did they not grow old and die amidst their books so that many of them were stricken with death while intent on reading or writing? And to none of them, as far as I know, was proficiency in the literary disciplines considered a fault, except Jerome, while to many it bore the fruits of glory, and especially to him. I am well aware that Gregory praised Benedict for having renounced his studies, recently begun, through love of a more austere and solitary life. However, Benedict until then had had no interest, not only in poetry, but in any kind of study. Do you think that his laudator would have been worthy of praise had he done the same? I am convinced not, for it is one thing to have already learned, and another to study in order to learn. There is a great difference between the matter of the boy who renounces the possibility and that of the older man who casts away the accomplishment. The former frees himself of difficulty, the latter despoils himself of an ornament; one is free from arduous toil and an uncertain quest, the other throws away the sweet fruits already assured by continual effort, thus scorning and wasting a precious treasure acquired by long labor.

In conclusion, many reach a lofty degree of piety without learning; learning, however, has never prevented anyone from being pious. It is true that the Apostle Paul was said to have gone mad due to study, but the worth of this charge has long been recognized by all. Now if I be permitted to speak freely my mind, I say that the journey that leads to virtue through ignorance is perchance easy and smooth, but properly for the sluggish and the idle. Single is the end of all blessings, but many and diverse are the roads which lead to it. One is slower, the other more swift; the latter proceeds in light, the former in darkness; this one is found low, that one takes the high ground. By all ways is the voyage happy, but that which, attended by light, reaches the higher is more glorious. Whence it is that to the devout piety of a man of letters that of the unlearned, although likewise devout, appears less in comparison. Cite me whatever great religious man you wish who was unlettered, and I guarantee that I will be able to match him with an even more religious scholar. . . .

Giuseppe Fracassetti, *Lettere senili di Francesco Petrarca* (Firenze, 1869), I, 45–49. (Trans. John Thayer.)

The following account of the founding of the Vatican library by Pope Nicholas V (1450) shows the way in which a patron of learning operated in the Renaissance.

. . . Owing to the jubilee of 1450, a great quantity of money came in by this means to the apostolic see, and with this the pope commenced building in many places, and sent for Greek and Latin books, wherever he was able to find them, without regard to price. He gathered together a large band of writers, the best that he could find, and kept them in constant employment. He also summoned a number of learned men, both for the purpose of composing new works and of translating such existing works as were not already translated, giving them most abundant provision for their needs meanwhile; and when the works were translated and brought to him, he gave them large sums of money, in order that they should do more willingly that which they undertook to do.

He made great provision for the needs of learned men. He gathered together great numbers of books upon every subject, both Greek and Latin, to the number of five thousand volumes. So at his death it was found by inventory that never since the time of Ptolemy had half that number of books of every kind been brought together. All books he caused to be copied, without regard to what it cost him, and there were few places where his Holiness had not copiers at work. When he could not procure a book for himself in any way, he had it copied.

After he had assembled at Rome, as I said above, many learned men at large salaries, he wrote to Florence to Messer Giannozzo Manetti, that he should come to Rome to translate and compose for him. And when Manetti left Florence and came to Rome, the pope, as was his custom, received him with honor, and assigned to him, in addition to his income as secretary, six hundred ducats, urging him to attempt the translation of the books of the Bible and of Aristotle, and to complete the book already commenced by him, *Contra Judaeos et gentes;* a wonderful work, if it had been completed, but he carried it only to the tenth book. Moreover he translated the New Testament, and the Psalter, . . . with five apologetical books in defense of this Psalter, showing that in the Holy Scriptures there is not one syllable that does not contain the greatest of mysteries.

It was Pope Nicholas' intention to found a library in St. Peters, for the general use of the whole Roman curia, which would have been an admirable thing indeed, if he had been able to carry it out, but death prevented his bringing it to completion. He illumined the Holy Scriptures through innumerable books, which he caused to be translated; and in the same way with the works of the pagans, including certain works upon grammar, of use in learning Latin,—the *Orthography* of Messer Giovanni Tortelle, who was of his Holiness' household and worked upon the library, a worthy book and useful to grammarians; the *Iliad* of Homer; Strabo's *De situ orbis* he caused to be translated by Guerrino, and gave him five hundred florins for each part,—that is to say, Asia, Africa and Europe; that was in all fifteen hundred florins. Herodotus and Thucydides he had translated by Lorenzo Valla, and rewarded him liberally for his trouble; Zenophon and Diodorus, by Messer Poggio; Polybius, by Nicolo Perotto, whom, when he handed it to him, he gave five hundred brand-new papal ducats in a purse, and said to him that it was not what he deserved, but that in time he would take care to satisfy him. . . .

James Harvey Robinson, *Readings in European History* (Boston: Ginn & Co., 1904). I, 529–30. From Vespasiano's *Lives of Illustrious Men* (1498). (Reprinted by permission of the publisher.)

The period of the Renaissance means a new emphasis on writing, not only in Latin but in the native Italian tongue. Using Italian, writers could reach a wider audience and give a broader meaning to the "revival of learning." Here Dante defends the use of Italian in his *Convivio* (*ca.* 1300–1308).

4 To the perpetual shame and abasement of the evil men of Italy who commend the mother tongue of other nations and depreciate their own, I say that their action proceeds from five abominable causes: the first is blindness of discretion; the second, mischievous self-justification; the third, greed of vainglory; the fourth, an invention of envy; the fifth and last, littleness of soul, that is, cowardice. And each one of these grave faults has a great following, for few are those who are free from them. . . .

There are many who would rather be thought masters than be such; and to avoid the opposite—that is, to be held not to be such—they always cast blame on the material they work on, or upon the instrument; as the clumsy smith blames the iron given to him, and the bad harpist the harp, thinking to cast the blame of the bad blade and of the bad music upon the iron and upon the harp, and to lift it from themselves. Thus there are some—and not a few—who desire that men may hold them to be orators; and to excuse themselves for not speaking, or for speaking badly, they accuse or throw blame on the material, that is, their own mother tongue, and praise that of other lands, which they are not required to employ. And he who wishes to see wherefore this iron is to be blamed, let him look at the work which good artificers make of it, and he will understand the malice of those who, in casting blame upon it, think thereby to excuse themselves. Against such as these Cicero exclaims in the beginning of his book, which he names *De Finibus,* because in his time they blamed the Roman Latin and praised the Greek grammar. And thus I say, for like reasons, that these men vilify the Italian tongue, and glorify that of Provence. . . .

There are many who, by describing certain things in some other language, and by praising that language, deem themselves to be more worthy of admiration than if they described them in their own. And undoubtedly to learn well a foreign tongue is deserving of some praise for intellect; but it is a blamable thing to applaud that language beyond truth, to glorify oneself for such an acquisition.

Ibid., I, 522–23. (Reprinted by permission of the publisher.)

In his *Book of the Courtier* (1528), Baldassare Castiglione set up an ideal of social and literary accomplishment for the perfect gentleman. His gentleman served as a model for his own times and for succeeding generations.

. . . I will have this our Courtier therefore to be a gentleman born and of **5** good house. For it is a great deal less dispraise for him that is not born a gentleman to fail in the acts of virtue than for a gentleman. If he swerve from the steps of his ancestors, he stains the name of his family, and does not only not get, but loses what is already gotten. For nobleness of birth is (as it were) a clear lamp that shows forth and brings into light, works both good and bad, and inflames and provokes unto virtue, as well with the fear of slander, as also with the hope of praise. . . .

To come therefore to the quality of the person, I say he is well if he be neither of the least, nor of the greatest size. For both the one and the other have with it a certain spiteful wonder, and such men are marveled at, almost as much as men marvel to behold monstrous things. Yet if there must needs be a default in one of the two extremes, it shall be less hurtful to be somewhat of the least than to exceed the common stature in height. For men so shut up of body, beside that many times they are of a dull wit, they are also unapt for all exercises of nimbleness, which I much desire to have in the Courtier. . . .

You know in great matters and adventures in wars, the true provocation is glory: and whoso for lucre's sake or for any other consideration takes it in hand (besides that he never does anything worthy of praise) deserves not the name of a gentleman but is a most vile merchant.

And every man may conceive it to be the true glory that is stored up in the holy treasure of letters, except such unlucky creatures as have had no taste thereof.

What mind is so faint, so bashful and of so base a courage, that in reading the acts and greatness of Caesar, Alexander, Scipio, Hannibal, and so many others, is not incensed with a most fervent longing to be like them: and does not prefer the getting of that perpetual fame before this rotten life that lasts two days? . . .

Therefore . . . return again unto our Courtier, whom in letters I will have to be more than indifferently well seen, at the least in those studies which they call Humanities, and to have not only the understanding of the Latin tongue, but also of the Greek, because of the many and sundry things that with great excellency are written in it.

Let him much exercise himself in poets, and no less in Orators and Historiographers, and also in writing both rhyme and prose, and especially in this our vulgar tongue. For beside the contentment that he shall receive thereby himself, he shall by this means never want pleasant entertainments with women which ordinarily love such matters.

And if by reason either of his other business or of his slender study, he shall not attain unto that perfection that his writings may be worthy much commendation; let him be circumspect in keeping them close, lest he make other men to laugh at him. . . .

Baldassare Castiglione, *The Book of the Courtier* (1561), trans. Thomas Hoby (Everyman's Library), pp. 33, 39, 70–71.

Niccolò Machiavelli's *Prince* (1513) reflects the greater appreciation of realism in the Renaissance. Machiavelli wished to analyze politics as they were, not as they should be, and to give advice accordingly. His book was for centuries the most famous political treatise. Even when it was condemned as immoral and atheistic, it was still read. The following extracts give the trend of his argument.

. . . It now remains to be seen what are the methods and rules for a   **6** prince as regards his subjects and friends. And as I know that many have written of this, I fear that my writing about it may be deemed presumptuous, differing as I do, especially in this matter, from the opinions of others. But my intention being to write something of use to those who understand, it appears to me more proper to go to the real truth of the matter than to its imagination; and many have imagined republics and principalities which have never been seen or known to exist in reality; for how we live is so far removed from how we ought to live, that he who abandons what is done for what ought to be done, will rather learn to bring about his own ruin than his preservation. A man who wishes to make a profession of goodness in everything must necessarily come to grief among so many who are not good. Therefore it is necessary for a prince, who wishes to maintain himself, to learn how not to be good, and to use this knowledge and not use it, according to the necessity of the case.

Leaving on one side, then, those things which concern only an imaginary prince, and speaking of those that are real, I state that all men, and especially princes, who are placed at a greater height, are reputed for certain qualities which bring them either praise or blame. Thus one is considered liberal, another *misero* or miserly (using a Tuscan term, seeing that *avaro* with us still means one who is rapaciously acquisitive and *misero* one who makes grudging use of his own); one a free giver, another rapacious; one cruel, another merciful; one a breaker of his word, another trustworthy; one effeminate and pusillanimous, another fierce and high-spirited; one humane, another haughty; one lascivious, another chaste; one frank, another astute; one hard, another easy; one serious, another frivolous; one religious, another an unbeliever, and so on. I know that everyone will admit that it would be highly praiseworthy in a prince to possess all the above-named qualities that are reputed good, but as they cannot all be possessed or observed, human conditions not permitting of it, it is necessary that he should be prudent enough to avoid the scandal of those vices which would lose him the state, and guard himself if possible against those which will not lose it to him, but if not able to, he can indulge them with less scruple. And yet he must not mind incurring the scandal of those vices, without which it would be difficult to save the state, for if one considers well, it will be found that some things which seem virtues would, if followed, lead to one's ruin, and some others which appear vices result in one's greater security and wellbeing. . . .

Niccolò Machiavelli, *The Prince and the Discourses,* trans. Luigi Ricci (New York: The Modern Library, n.d.), pp. 56, 57.

How much fortune can do in human affairs and how it may be opposed:
It is not unknown to me how many have been and are of the opinion that worldly events are so governed by fortune and by God that men cannot by their prudence change them, and that on the contrary there is no remedy whatever, and for this they may judge it useless to toil much about them, but let things be ruled by chance. This opinion has been more held in our day from the great changes that have been seen, and are daily seen, beyond every human conjecture. When I think about them, at times I am partly inclined to share this opinion. Nevertheless, that our free will may not be altogether extinguished, I think it may be true that fortune is the ruler of half our actions, but that she allows the other half to be governed by us. I would compare her to an impetuous river that, when turbulent, inundates the plains, casts down trees and buildings, removes earth from this side and places it on the other; everyone flees before it and everything yields to its fury without being able to oppose it; and yet though it is of such a kind, still when it is quiet, men can make provision against it by dykes and banks, so that when it rises it will either go into a canal or its rush will not be so wild and dangerous. So it is with fortune, which shows her power where no measures have been taken to resist her, and directs her fury where she knows that no dykes or barriers have been made to hold her. And if you regard Italy, which has been the seat of these changes and who has given the impulse to them, you will see her to be a country without dykes or banks of any kind. If she had been protected by proper measures like Germany, Spain, and France, this inundation [i.e., the invasion of Charles VIII of France] would not have caused the great changes that it has, or would not have happened at all.

This must suffice as regards opposition to fortune in general. But limiting myself more to particular cases, I would point out how one sees a certain prince today fortunate and tomorrow ruined, without seeing that he has changed in character or otherwise. I believe this arises in the first place from the causes that we have already discussed at length; that is to say, because the prince who bases himself entirely on fortune is ruined when fortune changes. I also believe that he is happy whose mode of procedure accords with the needs of the times, and similarly he is unfortunate whose mode of procedure is opposed to the times. For one sees that men in those things which lead them to the aim that each one has in view, namely, glory and riches, proceed in various ways; one with circumspection, another with impetuosity, one by violence, another by cunning, one with patience, another with the reverse; and each by these diverse ways may arrive at his aim. One sees also two cautious men, one of whom succeeds in his designs, and the other not, and in the same way two men succeed equally by different methods, one being cautious, the other impetuous, which arises only from the nature of the times, which does or does not conform to their method of procedure. From this it results, as I have said, that two men, acting differently, attain the same effect, and of two others acting in the same way, one attains his goal and not the other. On this depend also the changes in prosperity, for if it happens that time and circumstances are favorable to one who acts with caution and prudence, he will be successful, but if time and circumstances change, he will be ruined because he does not change his mode of procedure. No man is found so prudent as to be able to adapt himself to this, either because he cannot deviate from that to which his nature disposes him or else because having always prospered by walking in one path, he cannot persuade himself that it is well to leave it; and therefore the cautious man, when it is time to act suddenly, does not know how to do so and is consequently ruined; for if one could change one's nature with time and circumstances, fortune would never change. . . .

I conclude then that fortune varying and men remaining fixed in their ways, they are successful so long as these ways conform to circumstances, but when they are opposed, then they are unsuccessful. I certainly think that it is better to be impetuous than cautious, for fortune is a woman, and it is necessary if you wish to master her, to conquer her by force; and it can be seen that she lets herself be overcome by the bold rather than by those who proceed coldly. And therefore, like a woman, she is always a friend to the young because they are less cautious, fiercer, and master her with greater audacity. . . .

A prince, then, is to have no other design, nor thought nor study, but war, and the arts and disciplines of it. . . . He never, therefore, ought to relax his thoughts from the exercises of war . . . which may be done in two ways: by the application of the body, and the mind. As to his bodily application, or matter of action, besides that he is obliged to keep his armies in good discipline and exercise, he ought to inure by sports and by hunting and hawking, and such like recreation, accustom his body to hardship and hunger and thrift. . . . But as to the exercises of the mind, a prince is to do that by diligence in history, and solemn consideration of the actions of the most excellent men by observing how they demeaned themselves in the wars. . . .

There is no other remedy against flatterers than to let everybody understand that you are not disobliged by telling the truth; yet if you suffer everybody to tell it, you injure yourself and lessen your reverence. Wherefore a wise prince ought to go a third way and select out of his state certain discreet men to whom alone he is to commit that liberty of speaking truth, and that of such things as he demands, and nothing else. But then he is to inquire of everything, hear their opinions, and resolve afterwards as he pleases. . . . That besides them, he will hearken to nobody; that he considers well before he resolves; and that his resolutions once taken, are never to be altered.

It may seem wonderful to some people how it should come to pass that Agathocles, and such as he, after so many treacheries and acts of inhumanity, should live quietly in their own country so long. . . . I conceive it fell out according as their cruelty was well or ill applied: I say well applied (if that word may be added to an ill action) and it may be called so when committed but once, and that of necessity for one's own preservation, but never repeated afterwards, and even then converted as much as possible to the benefit of the subjects . . . so that injuries are to be committed all at once. . . .

And from hence arises a new question, whether it is better to be beloved than feared, or feared than beloved? It is answered, both would be convenient, but because that is hard to attain, it is better and more secure (if one must be wanting) to be feared than loved; for in the general, men are ungrateful, inconstant, hypocritical, fearful of danger, and covetous of gain. . . . Love is fastened only by a ligament of obligation, which the ill nature of mankind breaks upon every occasion that is presented to his profit; but fear depends upon an apprehension of punishment, which is never to be dispelled.

There are two ways of contending, by law and by force: the first is proper to man, the second to beasts; but because many times the first is insufficient, recourse must be had to the second. It belongs, therefore, to a prince to understand both, when he makes use of the rational and when of the brutal way. . . . So that he must be a fox to find out the snares, and a lion to frighten away the wolves, but they who keep wholly to the lion have no true notion of themselves. A prince, therefore, that is wise and prudent cannot, nor ought not to keep his word when the keeping of it is to his prejudice, and the causes for which he promised removed. Were men all good, this doctrine was not to be taught, but because they are wicked and not likely to be punctual with you, you are not obliged to any such strictness with them; nor was there ever any prince that wanted lawful pretence to justify his breach of promise. . . .

A prince therefore is not obliged to have all the forementioned good qualities in reality, but it is necessary he have them in appearance. . . . Let a prince therefore do all he can to preserve his life and continue his supremacy, the means which he uses shall be thought honorable and to be commended by everybody.

The Works of the Famous Nicholas Machiavelli (London, 1680), pp. 210–11, 218–19, 221, 222–23.

The increasing secularism that is exemplified in Renaissance art, literature, and political thought was nowhere more prevalent than in economic affairs. Men have always been covetous, greedy, and self-seeking, but these basic instincts were—in theory at least—held in check by the ideals of medieval Christendom. With the flowering of Renaissance civilization, they easily burst their rather fragile bonds. Jacob Fugger "the Rich," a native of Augsburg, Germany, was the foremost businessman of his time—merchant, industrialist, and banker to popes, princes, and emperors. He is reported to have replied to a plea that he retire from his business and devote his declining years to the nourishment of his immortal soul, "I will continue to earn money as long as I live." The following passage is an extract from one of his partnership agreements (1512).

. . . in order that the business begun by us three brothers might the longer   7
continue, and so that our family and name be properly carried on, and my two brothers' sons become familiar with the trade, I have determined to carry on and manage the business myself, and to take industriously in hand my two brothers' sons. . . . I therefore invite them to join me in my common trade and in the Hungarian trade . . . for the six years next following the date of this document, and according to the terms of this agreement, but under no other conditions than the following:

The abovenamed four, my nephews, shall leave with me in my trade, for profit and loss during the specified time all their capital which is due and owing to them on account of the distribution and of the gain and profit of the trade which their two fathers and I formerly carried on . . . they are also faithfully bound to be true and obedient in all things, in whatsoever form and whatever things this may be required, and to further the trade and business, and to avoid damage and injury to it to the best of their ability, and to hold the business in complete secrecy and tell no one. And the association shall be called "Jacob Fugger und seine Gebrüder Söhne," or in Italian, "Jacobo Fugger e nepoti" [i.e., Jacob Fugger and nephews]. . . . And what I alone arrange, or bind the association to, to that shall they also none the less be committed, and shall be bound to its accomplishment along with me.

And what the abovenamed my four nephews collectively or singly shall do, that shall they or he in no way keep secret from me. To that end shall none of them conceal from me the record books or other writings, or their acts, but shall show me all faithfully and without contradiction. . . .

These my nephews shall further, neither collectively nor singly, carry on any kind of trade, enterprise, or association for themselves, neither among themselves nor with anyone else, without my knowledge and consent.

Jacob Strieder, *Jacob Fugger the Rich* (New York: Greenberg, 1931), pp. 191–95. (Reprinted by permission of the publisher.)

Desiderius Erasmus used his humanism to castigate the blindness and ignorance that seemed to prevent the church from being its true spiritual self. He was a master in the use of satire, the favorite literary medium of the Christian humanists in their battles with the divines. Such attacks as those in his *Praise of Folly* (1511), given below, paved the way for reformation by their emphasis on a spiritual renewal as over against external observances or arguments. But Erasmus never broke with the church and wanted a Catholic Reformation rather than a split with the existing order.

8   Almost all Christians are wretchedly enslaved to blindness and ignorance, which the priests are so far from preventing or removing that they blacken the darkness and promote the delusion; wisely foreseeing that the people (like cows, which never give down their milk so well as when they are gently stroked) would part with less if they knew more, their bounty proceeding only from a mistake of charity. Now if any grave, wise man should stand up and unseasonably speak the truth, telling everyone that a pious life is the only way of securing a happy death; that the best title to a pardon of our sins is purchased by a hearty abhorrence of our guilt, and sincere resolutions of amendment; that the best devotion which can be paid to any saints is to imitate them in their exemplary life; if he should proceed thus to inform them of their several mistakes, there would be quite another estimate put upon tears, watchings, masses, fastings, and other severities, which before were so much prized, as persons will now be vexed to lose that satisfaction they formerly found in them. . . .

Next come the philosophers, with their long beards and short cloaks, who esteem themselves as the only favorites of wisdom, and look upon the rest of mankind as the dirt and rubbish of the creation; yet these men's happiness is only a frantic craziness of brain. They build castles in the air, and infinite worlds in a vacuum. They will give you to a hair's breadth the dimensions of the sun, moon, and stars, as easily as they would that of a flagon or pipkin; they will give an elaborate account of the cause of thunder, or the origin of the winds, of the nature of eclipses, and of the most abstruse difficulties in physics, without the least demur or hesitation, as if they had been admitted into the cabinet council of nature, or had been eye-witnesses to all the methods of creation; though in fact nature does but laugh at all their puny conjectures: for they never yet made one considerable discovery, as appears from the fact that on no single point of the smallest moment have they unanimously agreed; nothing being so plain or evident but that by someone it is opposed and contradicted. . . .

The divines present themselves next; but it may perhaps be most safe to pass them by, and not to touch upon so harsh a string as this subject would afford. Besides, the undertaking may be very hazardous, for they are a sort of men generally very hot and passionate; and should I provoke them, they would no doubt set upon me with a full cry and force me with shame to recant. If I stubbornly refused to do this, they would presently brand me for a heretic, and thunder out an excommunication, which is their spiritual weapon to wound such as lift up a hand against them.

Now as to the popes of Rome who pretend to be Christ's vicars: if they would but imitate his exemplary life in being employed in an unintermitting course of preaching; in being attended with poverty, nakedness, hunger, and a contempt of this world; if they did but consider the import of the word Pope, which signifies a father; or if they did but practice their surname of most holy, what order or degrees of men would be in a worse condition?

All their riches, all their honors, their jurisdictions, their Peter's patrimony, their offices, their dispensations, their licenses, their indulgences, their long train of attendants (see in how short a compass I have abbreviated all their marketing of religion); in a word, all their perquisites would be forfeited and lost; and in their room would succeed watchings, fasting, tears, prayers, sermons, hard studies, repenting sighs, and a thousand such like severe penalties: nay, what is still more deplorable, it would then follow that all their clerks, amanuenses, notaries, advocates, proctors, secretaries, the offices of grooms, hostlers, serving men (and something else, which for modesty's sake I shall not mention); in short, all these troops of attendants which depend on his holiness would all lose their respective employments. This indeed would be hard, but what remains would be more dreadful: the very Head of the Church, the spiritual prince, would then be brought from all his splendor to the poor equipage of a scrip and staff. But all this is upon the supposition only that they understood the circumstances they are placed in; whereas now, by a wholesome neglect of thinking, they live as well as heart can wish. Whatever toil and drudgery belongs to their office, that they assign over to St. Peter or St. Paul, who have time enough to mind it; but if there be any pleasure and grandeur, that they assume to themselves as being "hereunto called," so that through Folly's influence no sort of people live more to their own ease and content.

Desiderius Erasmus, *Praise of Folly,* reprinted in Albert Hyma, *Erasmus and the Humanists* (New York: F. S. Crofts & Co., 1930), pp. 82–83, 89–90, 102–3. (Reprinted by permission of the publisher, Appleton-Century-Crofts, Inc.)

QUESTIONS

1. What distinguished the Italian despots from the monarchs in the western countries?
2. What was the basis for the despot's political power?
3. Why does Petrarch think that learning makes a man more devout?
4. Is there any significance in the kind of literature Pope Nicholas V had copied for his library?
5. What attainments must the well-rounded man of the Renaissance possess?
6. How, according to Machiavelli, can a good man survive in an evil world?
7. What does Machiavelli mean by "fortune" and how can man cope with it?
8. Is Machiavelli's Prince really, basically, a bad man, or are there also good qualities which he must possess to rule successfully?
9. What is it about Machiavelli's ideas which so shocked his contemporaries and future generations?
10. What reforms, do you think, would Erasmus have instituted in the religion and church of his time?
11. Can you contrast the ideas of Erasmus and those of Machiavelli?

CHAPTER II

THE REFORMATION

THE REFORMATION began as a religious movement. Whatever far-reaching consequences it was to have for our civilization, the only concern of the Reformers themselves was with men's souls. However, while the individual Reformers were primarily concerned with the church rather than with the state, the movement as a whole became entangled with political questions. Thus, Luther's concept of "the liberty of a Christian man," as seen in his *Treatise on Christian Liberty* (11), found a political echo in the Twelve Articles of the peasants (12), while Calvin found himself forced to add a section on civil government to his *Institutes of the Christian Religion* (15). Moreover, Calvin's theologically-founded ideas on "election" (13) and "discipline" (14) aided in giving unity to those classes of the population excluded from political and economic power. Resistance to authority, however, was not something most Reformers desired, and the Reformation led, in most cases, to the formation of state churches with stress upon obedience to the monarch. Here the English Act of Supremacy (17) and the Homily on Obedience (19) serve as illustration.

I. THE BREAK FROM ROME

The following is an extract from Luther's Ninety-Five Theses (1517).

9   In the desire and with the purpose of elucidating the truth, a disputation will be held on the underwritten propositions at Wittenberg, under the presidency of the Reverend Father Martin Luther, Monk of the Order of St. Augustine, Master of Arts and of Sacred Theology, and ordinary Reader of the same in that place. He therefore asks those who cannot be present and discuss the subject with us orally, to do so by letter in their absence. In the name of our Lord Jesus Christ. Amen.

1. Our Lord and Master Jesus Christ in saying "Repent ye" (*poenitentiam agite*) etc., intended that the whole life of believers should be penitence (*poenitentia*).

2. This word cannot be understood as sacramental penance (*poenitentia*), that is, of the confession and satisfaction which are performed under the ministry of priests.

3. It does not, however, refer solely to inward penitence (*poenitentia*); nay such inward penitence is naught, unless it outwardly produces various mortifications of the flesh.

4. The penalty (*poena*) thus continues as long as the hatred of self (that is, true inward penitence); namely, till our entrance into the kingdom of heaven.

5. The Pope has neither the will nor the power to remit any penalties except those which he has imposed by his own authority, or by that of the canons.

6. The Pope has no power to remit any guilt except by declaring and warranting it to have been remitted by God; or at most by remitting cases reserved for himself; in which cases, if his power were despised, guilt would certainly remain.

Translations and Reprints from the Original Sources of European History, II, No. 6, 11–12. (Reprinted by permission of the University of Pennsylvania Press.)

The problem of what constitutes a "good work" for Christians was central to the Reformation. In his *Treatise on Good Works* (1520), Martin Luther tells us what he meant by good works.

10   1. We ought first to know that there are no good works except those which God has commanded, even as there is no sin except that which God

has forbidden. Therefore whoever wishes to know and to do good works needs nothing else than to know God's commandments. Thus Christ says, Matthew xix, "If thou wilt enter into life, keep the commandments." And when the young man asks Him, Matthew xix, what he shall do that he may inherit eternal life, Christ sets before him naught else but the Ten Commandments. Accordingly, we must learn how to distinguish among good works from the Commandments of God, and not from the appearance, the magnitude, or the number of the works themselves, nor from the judgment of men or of human law or custom, as we see has been done and still is done, because we are blind and despise the divine Commandments.

2. The first and highest, the most precious of all good works is faith in Christ, as He says, John vi. When the Jews asked Him: "What shall we do that we may work the works of God?" He answered: "This is the work of God, that ye believe on Him Whom He hath sent." When we hear or preach this word, we hasten over it and deem it a very little thing and easy to do, whereas we ought here to pause a long time and to ponder it well. For in this work all good works must be done and receive from it the inflow of their goodness, like a loan. This we must put bluntly, that men may understand it.

We find many who pray, fast, establish endowments, do this or that, lead a good life before men, and yet if you should ask them whether they are sure that what they do pleases God, they say "No"; they do not know, or they doubt. And there are some very learned men, who mislead them, and say that it is not necessary to be sure of this; and yet, on the other hand, these same men do nothing else but teach good works. Now all these works are done outside of faith, therefore they are nothing and altogether dead. For as their conscience stands toward God and as it believes, so also are the works which grow out of it. Now they have no faith, no good conscience toward God, therefore the works lack their head, and all their life and goodness is nothing. Hence it comes that when I exalt faith and reject such works done without faith, they accuse me of forbidding good works, when in truth I am trying hard to teach real good works of faith.

4. Now every one can note and tell for himself when he does what is good or what is not good; for if he finds his heart confident that it pleases God, the work is good, even if it were so small a thing as picking up a straw. If confidence is absent, or if he doubts, the work is not good, although it should raise all the dead and the man should give himself to be burned. This is the teaching of St. Paul, Romans xiv: "Whatsoever is not done of or in faith is sin." Faith, as the chief work, and no other work, has given us the name of "believers on Christ." For all other works a heathen, a Jew, a

Turk, a sinner, may also do; but to trust firmly that he pleases God, is possible only for a Christian who is enlightened and strengthened by grace.

That these words seem strange, and that some call me a heretic because of them, is due to the fact that men have followed blind reason and heathen ways, have set faith not above, but beside other virtues, and have given it a work of its own, apart from all works of the other virtues; although faith alone makes all other works good, acceptable, and worthy, in that it trusts God and does not doubt that for it all things that a man does are well done. Indeed, they have not let faith remain a work, but have made a habitus of it, as they say, although Scripture gives the name of a good, divine work to no work except to faith alone. Therefore it is no wonder that they have become blind and leaders of the blind. And this faith brings with it at once love, peace, joy and hope. For God gives His Spirit at once to him who trusts Him, as St. Paul says to the Galatians: "You received the Spirit not because of your good works, but when you believed the Word of God."

10. Now you see for yourself that all those who do not at all times trust God and do not in all their works or sufferings, life and death, trust in His favor, grace and good will, but seek His favor in other things or in themselves, do not keep this Commandment, and practise real idolatry, even if they were to do the works of all the other Commandments, and in addition had all the prayers, fasting, obedience, patience, chastity, and innocence of all the saints combined. For the chief work is not present, without which all the others are nothing but mere sham, show and pretence, with nothing back of them; against which Christ warns us, Matthew vii: "Beware of false prophets, which come to you in sheep's clothing." Such are all who wish with their many good works, as they say, to make God favorable to themselves, and to buy God's grace from Him, as if He were a huckster or a day-laborer, unwilling to give His grace and favor for nothing. These are the most perverse people on earth, who will hardly or never be converted to the right way. Such too are all who in adversity run hither and thither, and look for counsel and help everywhere except from God, from whom they are most urgently commanded to seek it; whom the Prophet Isaiah reproves thus, Isaiah ix: "The mad people turneth not to Him that smiteth them"; that is, God smote them and sent them sufferings and all kinds of adversity, that they should run to Him and trust Him. But they run away from Him to men, now to Egypt, now to Assyria, perchance also to the devil; and of such idolatry much is written in the same Prophet and in the Books of the Kings. This is also the way of all holy hypocrites when they are in trouble: they do not run to God, but flee from Him, and only think of how they may get rid of their trouble through their own efforts or through

human help, and yet they consider themselves and let others consider them pious people.

II. LUTHER AND CHRISTIAN LIBERTY

In his *Treatise on Christian Liberty* (1520), Luther sets forth his distinction between "inward" and "outward" freedom.

. . . I set down first these two propositions concerning the liberty and the **11** bondage of the spirit:

A Christian man is a perfectly free lord of all, subject to none.

A Christian man is a perfectly dutiful servant of all, subject to all. . . .

Man has a twofold nature, a spiritual and a bodily. According to the spiritual nature, which men call the soul, he is called a spiritual, or inner, or new man; according to the bodily nature, which men call the flesh, he is called a carnal, or outward, or old man. . . .

First, let us contemplate the inward man, to see how a righteous, free and truly Christian man, that is, a new spiritual, inward man, comes into being. It is evident that no external thing, whatsoever it be, has any influence whatever in producing Christian righteousness or liberty, nor in producing unrighteousness or bondage. A simple argument will furnish the proof. What can it profit the soul if the body fare well, be free and active, eat, drink and do as it pleases? For in these things even the most godless slaves of all the vices fare well. On the other hand, how will ill health or imprisonment or hunger or thirst or any other external misfortune hurt the soul? . . . The soul receives no benefit if the body is adorned with the sacred robes of the priesthood, or dwells in sacred places, or is occupied with sacred duties, or prays, fasts, abstains from certain kinds of food or does any work whatsoever that can be done by the body and in the body. The righteousness and the freedom of the soul demand something far different, since the things which have been mentioned could be done by any wicked man, and such works produce nothing but hypocrites. . . .

One thing and one only is necessary for Christian life, righteousness and liberty. That one thing is the most holy Word of God, the Gospel of Christ . . . the soul can do without all things except the Word of God, and that where this is not there is no help for the soul in anything else whatever. . . . Nor was Christ sent into the world for any other ministry but that of the Word, and the whole spiritual estate, apostles, bishops, and all the priests, has been called and instituted only for the ministry of the Word. . . . For to preach Christ means to feed the soul, to make it righteous, to set it free and to save it, if it believe the preaching. For faith alone is the saving and efficacious use of the Word of God . . . "The just shall live by his faith" (Romans I:17). The Word of God cannot be received and cherished by any works whatever, but only by faith. . . .

. . . Priesthood [of the Christian man] . . . we explain as follows: First, as to the kingship, every Christian is by faith so exalted above all things that by a spiritual power he is lord of all things without exception, so that nothing can do him any harm whatever, nay, all things are made subject to him and compelled to serve him to his salvation. . . . The power of which we speak is spiritual; it rules in the midst of enemies, and is mighty in the midst of oppression, which means nothing else than that strength is made perfect in weakness, and that in all things I can find profit unto salvation, so that the cross and death itself are compelled to serve me and to work together with me for my salvation. . . .

Let this suffice concerning the inward man, his liberty and its source, the righteousness of faith, which needs neither laws nor good works, nay, is rather injured by them, if a man trusts that he is justified by them.

Now let us turn to the second part, to the outward man. . . .

Although, as I have said, a man is abundantly justified by faith inwardly, in his spirit, and so has all that he ought to have, except in so far as this faith and riches must grow from day to day even unto the future life: yet he remains in this mortal life on earth, and in this life he must needs govern his own body and have dealings with men. Here the works begin; here a man cannot take his ease; here he must, indeed, take care to discipline his body by fastings, watchings, labors and other reasonable discipline, and to make it subject to the spirit so that it will obey and conform to the inward man and to faith, and not revolt against faith and hinder the inward man, as it is the body's nature to do if it be not held in check. . . .

Hence a man cannot be idle, because the need of his body drives him and he is compelled to do many good works to reduce it to subjection. Nevertheless the works themselves do not justify him before God, but he does the works out of spontaneous love in obedience to God, and considers nothing except the approval of God, Whom he would in all things most scrupulously obey. . . .

Christ also, in Matthew xvii, when the tribute money was demanded of His disciples, argued with St. Peter, whether the sons of the king were not free from the payment of tribute, and Peter affirmed that they were. None the less, Christ commanded Peter to go to the sea, and said, "Lest we should offend them, go, and take up the fish that first cometh up; and when thou hast opened his mouth, thou shalt find a piece of money: that take, and give unto them for me and thee." This incident fits beautifully to our subject, since Christ here calls Himself and those that are His, children and sons of the King, who need nothing; and yet He freely submits and pays the tribute. . . .

Of the same nature are the precepts which Paul gives, in Romans xiii and Titus iii, that Christians should be subject to the powers that be, and be ready to do every good work, not that they shall in this way be justified, since they already are righteous through faith, but that in the liberty of the Spirit they shall by so doing serve others and the powers themselves, and obey their will freely and out of love.

Ibid., II, 312–40. (Reprinted by permission of the A. J. Holman Co.) See copyright note on p. 21.

The Peasant's Revolt (1524–25), though its causes were economic rather than religious, drew its inspiration from Luther's beliefs in the "pure Gospel" and "Christian liberty." Luther claimed that the peasants had transformed his "inward" liberty into "outward" liberty. The most famous manifesto of the peasants are the Twelve Articles (1525) which stemmed from the peasants in Swabia.

The First Article. First, it is our humble petition and desire, as also our **12** will and resolution, that in the future we should have power and authority so that each community should choose and appoint a pastor, and that we should have the right to depose him should he conduct himself improperly. The pastor thus chosen should teach us the Gospel pure and simple, without any addition, doctrine, or ordinance of man. For to teach us continually the true faith will lead us to pray God that through His grace this faith may increase within us and become a part of us. For if His grace work not within us, we remain flesh and blood, which availeth nothing; since the Scripture clearly teaches that only through true faith can we come to God. Only through His mercy can we become holy. Hence such a guide and pastor is necessary, and in this fashion grounded upon the Scriptures. . . .

The Third Article. It has been the custom hitherto for men to hold us as their own property, which is pitiable enough, considering that Christ has delivered and redeemed us all, without exception, by the shedding of His precious blood, the lowly as well as the great. Accordingly, it is consistent with Scripture that we should be free and wish to be so. Not that we would wish to be absolutely free and under no authority. God does not teach us that we should lead a disorderly life in the lusts of the flesh, but that we should love the Lord our God and our neighbor. We would gladly observe all this as God has commanded us in the celebration of the communion. He has not commanded us not to obey the authorities, but rather that we should be humble, not only towards those in authority, but towards everyone. We are thus ready to yield obedience according to God's law to our elected and regular authorities in all proper things becoming to a Christian. We, therefore, take it for granted that you will release us from serfdom, as true Christians, unless it should be shown us from the Gospel that we are serfs. . . .

The Sixth Article. Our sixth complaint is in regard to the excessive services demanded of us, which are increased from day to day. We ask that this matter be properly looked into so that we shall not continue to be oppressed in this way, and that some gracious consideration be given us, since our forefathers were required only to serve according to the word of God.

The Seventh Article. Seventh, we will not hereafter allow ourselves to be farther oppressed by our lords, but will let them demand only what is just and proper according to the word of the agreement between the lord and the peasant. The lord should no longer try to force more services or other dues from the peasant without payment, but permit the peasant to enjoy his holding in peace and quiet. The peasant should, however, help the lord when it is necessary, and at proper times, when it will not be disadvantageous to the peasant, and for a suitable payment.

The Eighth Article. In the eighth place, we are greatly burdened by holdings which cannot support the rent exacted from them. The peasants suffer loss in this way and are ruined; and we ask that the lords may appoint persons of honor to inspect these holdings, and fix a rent in accordance with justice, so that the peasant shall not work for nothing, since the laborer is worthy of his hire.

The Ninth Article. In the ninth place, we are burdened with a great evil in the constant making of new laws. We are not judged according to the offence, but sometimes with great ill will, and sometimes much too leniently. In our opinion, we should be judged according to the old written law, so that the case shall be decided according to its merits, and not with partiality.

The Tenth Article. In the tenth place, we are aggrieved by the appropriation by individuals of meadows and fields which at one time belonged to a community. These we will take again into our own hands. It may, however, happen that the land was rightfully purchased, but when the land has unfortunately been purchased in this way, some brotherly arrangement should be made according to circumstances. . . .

Conclusion. In the twelfth place, it is our conclusion and final resolution, that if any one or more of the articles here set forth should not be in agreement with the word of God, as we think they are, such article we will willingly recede from, when it is proved really to be against the word of God by a clear explanation of the Scripture. Or if articles should now be conceded to us that are hereafter discovered to be unjust, from that hour they shall be dead and null and without force. Likewise, if more complaints should be discovered which are based upon truth and the Scriptures, and relate to offences against God and our neighbor, we have determined to reserve the right to present these also, and to exercise ourselves in all Christian teaching. For this we shall pray God, since He can grant this, and He alone. The peace of Christ abide with us all.

Translations and Reprints from the Original Sources of European History, II, No. 6, 26, 27–30. (Reprinted by permission of the University of Pennsylvania Press.)

III. JEAN CALVIN

The doctrine of "election" is at the root of Calvinism. What was involved in being of the "elect," of the "saints," is clearly set forth in the Calvinist (Presbyterian) *Westminster Confession of Faith* (1647).

13

By the decree of God, for the manifestation of His glory, some men and Angels are predestined unto everlasting life, and others fore-ordained to everlasting death. . . .

Those of mankind that are predestined unto life, God, before the foundation of the world was laid, according to His eternal and immutable purpose, and the counsel and good pleasure of His will, has chosen in Christ unto everlasting glory, out of His mere free grace and love, without any foresight of faith, or good works, or perseverance in either of them.

As God has appointed the Elect unto glory, has He, by the eternal and most free purpose of His will, foreordained all the means thereunto. Wherefore they who are elected, being fallen in Adam are redeemed in Christ.

This effectual Call is of God's free, and special grace alone, not from anything at all foreseen by man who is altogether passive therein, until being quickened and renewed by the holy Spirit, he is thereby enabled to answer his Call and to embrace the grace offered and convey it.

They whom God has accepted in His Beloved, effectually called, and sanctified in His Spirit, can neither totally, nor finally, fall away from the state of grace; but shall certainly persevere therein to the end, and be eternally saved.

They who are effectually called, and Regenerated, having a new heart and a new spirit created in them, are further sanctified really and personally through the virtue of Christ's death and resurrection, by His Word and *Spirit* dwelling in them: the dominion of the whole body of sin is destroyed, and the several lusts thereof are more and more weakened and mortified: and they more and more quickened and strengthened in all saving graces, to the practice of true holiness, without which no man shall see the Lord.

Good works are only such as God hath commanded in His holy word. . . . These good works, done in obedience to God's commandments are the fruits and evidences of a true and lively faith.

This sanctification is throughout, in the whole man, yet, *imperfect in this life,* there abideth still some remnant of corruption in every part: whence arises a continual and irreconcilable war; the flesh lusting against the spirit, and the spirit lusting against the flesh.

The Advice of the Assembly of Divines (London, 1647), pp. 7–8, 21, 24, 28–29.

Church discipline was to be one of the important characteristics of Calvinism. The following letter of Calvin tells why there is need for such discipline and how it should be established. It was written to the Duchess of Ferrara (1564) when her chaplain complained to Geneva that he had difficulty in executing his ministry.

14   . . . Now that God has sent you back to your town, you must redouble your efforts to well regulate your subjects as well as your house. I know, Madam, how cantankerous people are, and how much you have previously laboured to reduce them, and this without results. However this may be, I pray you to perfect in that place the doctrine of St. Paul: not to leave off to do good, however much malice there may exist to cool your ardour. Above all, let your household be an example to those who cannot be rendered amenable and who sow confusion among those who are incorrigible and hardened. In order to do that, Madam, stretch out your hand, for you know that there exists a good police for the suppression of vices and scandals. I do not speak of the civil police, but of that of the Consistory of the Church, for these men, who are established to watch over manners, are men who believe in God; men of saintly life and of such sincerity and frankness that nothing can keep them from executing their office, because they are zealous to keep safe the entire honour of God. And may no one, of whatever degree and estate, or however high in your estimation, or in whatever reputation you hold him, be afraid to submit himself to that discipline to which the Son of God himself submitted, and to bend his neck in order to receive his yoke.

For I assure you, Madam, without such a remedy there will exist unbounded licence to breed horrible confusion.

Those who make some profession of Christianity are for the most part dissolute. In short, it is as if the Scripture were a fickle thing, if one sees how each man flatters himself and pursues his appetites. It is curious that those who voluntarily withdrew themselves from the tyranny of the Pope will not suffer that Christ exercise an amiable domination over them and over their salvation. But, in truth, the Devil uses this artifice in order to disgrace the truth of God, vilify the pure religion and blaspheme the sacred name of our Saviour. Thus you can see, Madam, that to have a Church truly reformed, it is more than necessary to appoint officers who have the duty to watch over the life of each man. And in order that no one may be afraid to render an account before the elders to whom this charge is committed, they must be elected by the Church, and this is one good reason why this freedom should be preserved; also such election serves to assure the greatest discretion in the choice of those who are proper for this task, and that they be approved by the Church.

I have no doubt, Madam, that you have aided our brother de Coulonges with your authority in drafting such an order. But knowing the corruption to which the courts of Princes are subject, it has seemed to me not superfluous to exhort you to keep up the work. At the same time it seems good that you be advised of one thing: this is that at all times the devil works to make the ministers of the Gospel contemptible through sinister reports and detractions, in order that one should hate them or be disgusted with them. The faithful must well guard themselves against such policy . . . I do not say that if there be some scandals among your servants, you, who are the principal member of the Church, should not be told of this first in order to give advice on how these scandals may be corrected, but that your authority must never stand in the way of (Church) discipline, for if your domestics be exempt, the whole reverence due the Consistory will flow away like water.

Jules Bonnet, *Lettres de Jean Calvin* (Paris, 1854), II, 546–48. (Trans. George L. Mosse.)

In the twentieth chapter of his *Institutes of the Christian Religion,* Calvin sets forth his view on civil government (1559).

. . . civil government is designed, as long as we live in this world, to **15** cherish and support the external worship of God, to preserve the pure doctrine of religion, to defend the constitution of the Church, to regulate our lives in a manner requisite for the society of men, to form our manners to civil justice, to promote our concord with each other, and to establish general peace and tranquillity. . . .

. . . if we direct our attention to the word of God, it will carry us much further; even to submit to the government, not only of those princes who discharge their duty to us with becoming integrity and fidelity, but of all who possess the sovereignty, even though they perform none of the duties of their function. For, though the Lord testifies that the magistrate is an eminent gift of his liberality to preserve the safety of men, and prescribes to magistrates themselves the extent of their duty, yet He at the same time declares, that whatever be their characters, they have their government only from Him; that those who govern for the public good are true specimens and mirrors of His beneficence; and that those who rule in an unjust and tyrannical manner are raised up by Him to punish the iniquity of the people; that all equally possess that sacred majesty with which He has invested legitimate authority. . . .

But in the obedience which we have shown to be due to the authority of governors, it is always necessary to make one exception, and that is entitled to our first attention—that it do not seduce us from obedience to Him, to whose will the desires of all kings ought to be subject, to whose decrees all their commands ought to be subject, to whose decrees all their commands ought to yield, to whose majesty all their sceptres ought to submit. And, indeed, how preposterous it would be for us, with a view to satisfy men, to incur the displeasure of Him on whose account we yield obedience to men! The Lord, therefore, is the King of kings; who, when He has opened His sacred mouth, is to be heard alone, above all, for all, and before all: in the next place, we are subject to those men who preside over us; but not otherwise than in Him. If they command anything against Him, it ought not to have the least attention; nor, in this case, ought we to pay any regard to all that dignity attached to magistrates; to which no injury is done when it is subjected to the unrivalled and supreme power of God.

A Compend of the Institutes of the Christian Religion, ed. Hugh T. Kerr, Jr. (Philadelphia: The Westminster Press, 1939), pp. 203, 213–14. (Reprinted by permission of the publisher.)

IV. THE ENGLISH REFORMATION

One of the important acts taken by the Reformation Parliament was to forbid any appeals from ecclesiastical courts to Rome. The Act in Restraint of Appeals (1532), with its key phrase of England as an "empire," also shows the national basis for the English Reformation.

16   (1) Where by divers sundry old authentic histories and chronicles it is manifestly declared and expressed that this realm of England is an empire, and so has been accepted in the world, governed by one supreme head and king, having the dignity and royal estate of the imperial crown of the same; (2) unto whom a body politic, compact of all sorts and degrees of people, divided in terms, and by names of spiritualty and temporalty, been bounded and owen to bear, next to God, a natural and humble obedience; (3) he being also instituted and furnished, by the goodness and sufferance of Almighty God, with plenary, whole, and entire power, pre-eminence, authority, prerogative and jurisdiction to render and yield justice, and final determination to all manner of folk, residents, or subjects within this his realm, in all causes, matters, debates and contentions, happening to occur, insurge, or begin within the limits thereof, without restraint or provocation to any foreign princes or potentates of the world; (4) the body spiritual whereof having power, when any cause of the law divine happened to come in question, or of spiritual learning, than it was declared, interpreted, and showed by that part of the said body politic called the spiritualty, now being usually called the English church, which always has been reputed, and also found of that sort; that both for knowledge, integrity and sufficiency of number, it has been always thought, and is also at this hour, sufficient and meet of itself, without the intermeddling of any exterior person or persons, to declare and determine all such doubts, and to administer all such offices and duties as to their rooms spiritual do appertain; (5) for the due administration whereof, and to keep them from corruption and sinister affection, the King's most noble progenitors, and the ancestors of the nobles of this realm, have sufficiently endowed the said church, both with honor and possessions; (6) and the laws temporal, for trial of property of lands and goods, and for the conservation of the people of this realm in unity and peace, without rapine or spoil, was and yet is administered, adjudged and executed by sundry judges and ministers of the other part of the said body politic, called the temporalty; (7) and both their authorities and jurisdictions do conjoin together in the due administration of justice, the one to help the other.

Danby Pickering, *The Statutes at Large* (Cambridge, 1763), pp. 257–58.

The Act of Supremacy (1534) completed the break of King Henry VIII with the Catholic Church.

The King's Grace to be Authorized Supreme Head.   **17**

(1) Albeit the King's Majesty justly and rightfully is and ought to be the supreme head of the church of England and so is recognized by the clergy of this realm in their convocations, yet nevertheless for corroboration and confirmation thereof, and for increase of virtue in Christ's religion within this

realm of England, and to repress and extirpate all errors, heresies, and other enormities and abuses heretofore used in the same: be it enacted by authority of this present parliament, That the King our sovereign lord, his heirs and successors, kings of this realm, shall be taken, accepted and reputed the only supreme head in earth of the church of England, called *Anglicana Ecclesia;* (2) and shall have and enjoy, annexed and united to the imperial crown of this realm, as well the title and style thereof, as all honors, dignities, pre-eminences, jurisdictions, privileges, authorities, immunities, profits and commodities to the said dignity of supreme head of the same church belonging and appertaining; (3) and that our said sovereign lord, his heirs and successors, kings of this realm, shall have full power and authority from time to time to visit, repress, redress, reform order, correct, restrain and amend all such errors, heresies, abuses, offences, contempts and enormities, whatsoever they be, which by any manner, spiritual authority, or jurisdiction ought or may lawfully be reformed, repressed, ordered, redressed, corrected, restrained or amended, most to the pleasure of Almighty God, the increase of virtue in Christ's religion, and for the conservation of the peace, unity and tranquillity of this realm; any usage, custom, foreign laws, foreign authority, prescription, or any other thing or things to the contrary hereof notwithstanding.

Ibid., pp. 312–13.

The Thirty-Nine Articles (1571) defined the doctrine of the Elizabethan Church. Here is Article 32 on the civil magistrate.

18   The queen's majesty has the chief power in this realm of England, and other her dominions, unto whom the chief government of all estates of this realm, whether they be ecclesiastical or civil, in all cases do appertain, and is not, nor ought to be subject to any foreign jurisdiction.

Where we attribute to the queen's majesty the chief government, by which titles we understand the minds of some slanderous folks to be offended: we give not to our princes the ministering either of God's word or of the sacraments, the which thing the injunctions also lately set forth by Elizabeth our queen do most plainly testify; but that only prerogative which we see to have been given always to all godly princes in holy scriptures by God himself, that is, that they should rule all estates and degrees committed to their charge by God, whether they be ecclesiastical or temporal, and restrain with the civil sword the stubborn and evil doers.

The bishop of Rome has no jurisdiction in this realm of England.

The laws of this realm may punish Christian men with death for heinous and grievous offences.

It is lawful for Christian men, at the commandment of the magistrate, to wear weapons, and to serve in wars.

The Thirty-Nine Articles of Religion, etc. (London, 1745), p. 105.

The approval by the Convocation and the Queen of the *Second Book of Homilies* (1571) completed the constructive phase of the English Reformation. The Homily on Obedience became one of the most famous statements on this subject. It states clearly a theory of social and political hierarchy with which most men of the sixteenth century would have agreed. Here are the religious foundations for the doctrine of obedience of the Reformation age. Contrast this with Calvin's ideas on obeying God before kings (15), which were to be the foundation for sixteenth- and seventeenth-century doctrines of resistance to authority.

An Exhortation Concerning Good Order and Obedience to Rulers and **19** *Magistrates.*

Almighty God has created and appointed all things in heaven, earth, and waters in a most excellent and perfect order. In heaven He has appointed distinct and several orders and states of archangels and angels. In earth He has assigned and appointed kings, princes, with other governors under them, in all good and necessary order. The water above is kept, and raineth down in due time and season. The sun, moon, stars, rainbow, thunder, lightning, clouds, and all birds of the air do keep their order. The earth, trees, seeds, plants, herbs, corn, grass, and all manner of beasts keep themselves in order. All the parts of the whole year, as winter, summer, months, nights and days, continue in their order: All kinds of fishes in the sea, rivers, and waters; with all fountains, springs, yea the seas themselves keep their comely course and order. And man himself also has all his parts both within and without, as soul, heart, mind, memory, understanding, reason, speech, with all and singular corporal members of his body, in a profitable, necessary, and pleasant order. Every degree of people in their vocation, calling, and office, has appointed to them their duty and order. Some are in high degree, some in low, some kings and princes, some inferiors and subjects, priests and laymen, masters and servants, fathers and children, husbands and wives, rich and poor, and everyone have need of other, so that in all things is to be lauded and praised the goodly order of God, without the which no house, no city, no commonwealth can continue and endure or last. For where there is no right order, there reigns all abuse, carnal liberty, enormity, sin and babylonical confusion. Take away kings, princes, rulers, magistrates, judges,

and such estates of God's order, no man shall ride or go by the highway un-
robbed; no man shall sleep in his own house or bed unkilled; no man shall
keep his wife, children, and possessions in quietness; all things shall be common, and there must needs follow all mischief and utter destruction, both
of souls, bodies, goods and commonwealths. But blessed be God that we in
this realm of England feel not the horrible calamities, miseries and wretchedness which all they undoubtedly feel and suffer that lack this godly order.
And praised be God that we know the great excellent benefit of God showed
towards us in this behalf. . . .

Let us learn also here by the infallible and undeceivable word of God that
kings, and other supreme and higher officers are ordained of God, who is
most high; and therefore they are here taught diligently to apply and give
themselves to knowledge and wisdom, necessary for the ordering of God's
people to their governance committed, or whom to govern they are charged
of God. And they be here also taught by Almighty God that they should
acknowledge themselves to have all their power and strength not from
Rome, but immediately of God most high. We read in the book of Deuter-
onomy (Chapter xxxiii) that all punishment pertains to God by this sentence,
Vengeance is mine, and I will reward. But this sentence we must understand to pertain also to the magistrates which exercise God's room in judgment, and punishing by good and godly laws here on earth. And the places
of Scripture which seem to remove from among all Christian men, judgment,
punishment, or killing, ought to be understood, that no man of his own
private authority may be judge over others, may punish or may kill. But we
must refer all judgment to God, to kings and rulers, judges under them,
which be God's officers to execute justice; and by plain words of Scripture,
have their authority and use of the sword granted from God, as we are
taught by St. Paul, that dear and chosen apostle of our Saviour Christ, whom
we ought diligently to obey, even as we would obey our Saviour Christ if he
were present. Thus St. Paul writes to the Romans (Chapter xiii). Let every
soul submit himself unto the authority of the higher powers, for there is
no power but of God. The powers that be, be ordained of God. Whosoever
therefore withstandeth the power, withstandeth the ordinance of God. But
they that resist, or are against it, shall receive to themselves damnation. . . .

The Second Part of the Sermon of Obedience
Forasmuch as God has created and disposed all things in a comely order,
we have been taught in the first part of the sermon concerning good order
and obedience: that we ought also in all commonweals to observe and keep
a due order, and to be obedient to the powers, their ordinances and laws,

and that all rulers are appointed of God, for a goodly order to be kept in the world; and also how the magistrates ought to learn how to rule and govern according to God's laws, and that all subjects are bound to obey them as God's ministers, yea, although they be evil, not only for fear but also for conscience sake. And here, good people, let us all mark diligently, that it is not lawful for inferiors and subjects, in any case, to resist and stand against the superior powers, for St. Paul's words be plain, that whosoever withstandeth, shall get to themselves damnation, for whosoever withstandeth, withstandeth the ordinance of God. Our Saviour Christ himself, and his apostles, received many and divers injuries of the unfaithful and wicked men in authority, yet we never read that they, or any of them caused any sedition or rebellion against authority. We read oft that they patiently suffered all troubles, vexations, slanders, pangs, and pains, and death itself obediently without tumult or resistance. They committed their cause to him that judges righteously, and prayed for their enemies heartily and earnestly; they knew that the authority of the powers was God's ordinance, and therefore both in their words and deeds they taught ever obedience to it, and never taught nor did the contrary. The wicked judge Pilate said to Christ, Knowest thou not, that I have power to crucify thee, and have power also to loose thee? Jesus answered, thou couldest have no power at all against me, except it were given thee from above. Whereby Christ taught us plainly that even the wicked rulers have their power and authority from God, and therefore it is not lawful for their subjects to withstand them, although they abuse their power. Much less is it lawful for subjects to withstand their godly and Christian princes which do not abuse their authority but use the same to God's glory and to the profit and commodity of God's people. . . .

Certain Sermons or Homilies, etc. (London, 1754), pp. 101 ff.

QUESTIONS

1. What was Luther's concept of repentance in the ninety-five Theses?
2. What does Luther mean when he writes about "faith" as the chief "work"?
3. In what did Luther's distinction between the "inward" and the "outward" man consist, and what consequences for human action did he draw from his ideas?
4. What is the relationship between Luther's concept of Christian liberty and the Twelve Articles of the peasants?
5. On what grounds do the peasants ask for freedom from oppression?
6. What, for Calvin, makes a person to be of the "elect"?

7. Why does Calvin see a need for church discipline?

8. What kind of discipline does he advocate?

9. How can Calvin's ideas on civil government lead to a resistance to established authority?

10. How does the Act in Restraint of Appeals attempt to prove that it is an act made by the whole nation?

11. List the definite controls over the church given to the king as supreme head.

12. How does belief in order lead to an argument for royal authority in the Homily on Obedience?

13. Define the idea of "hierarchy" as it emerges from this Homily, and show how God and Christ enter the picture in order to preserve this hierarchy.

CHAPTER III

THE CATHOLIC REFORMATION

THE CATHOLIC REFORMATION began before the posting of Luther's Ninety-Five Theses. However, challenged by the Reformers, it gained increased momentum. The Papacy threw off the last vestiges of Renaissance secularism (20). New religious orders were founded to revitalize the spiritual life of the church. The foremost of these was the Society of Jesus, or the Jesuit order, (recognized by the pope in 1540), whose spirit of dedication to the church is reflected not only in its constitution (21) but also in the writings of men like Father Robert Persons (22). Like all Jesuits, Father Persons carried on missionary activities, in his case among the English Protestants. By the time of the Council of Trent (1545–63), the reformation of the Catholic Church was complete (23).

The figure of Pope Pius V (R. 1566–72), one of the last popes to be sainted by the church, typifies the new spiritual impetus of the Reformation Papacy. Leopold von Ranke, the German historian of the nineteenth century, describes this pope.

Michele Ghislieri—now Pius V—was born of poor parents at Bosco, not far from Alessandria, in the year 1504, and when only fourteen years of age   **20** entered a Dominican monastery. There he surrendered his body and soul to the poverty and piety of a monk, as the Dominican order required. From the alms which he received, he scarcely kept enough for himself to have a coat made, and against the heat of summer he thought that abstinence and frugality were the best weapons. In spite of the fact that he became father confessor to the governor of Milan, he traveled by foot and with a sack on his back. If he taught, he did so with kindness and precision; if he had to administer his monastery as prior, he was strict and frugal: more than one monastery did he rid of its debts. . . . Even as Pope, he lived within the strict rules of a monk: he kept the fast completely and unremittingly, he did not permit himself to wear clothes made of fine cloth, he read often, and every day he heard the mass. In spite of this, he took care that his spiritual exercises did not keep him from public business, he took no siesta and arose early.

If one were to doubt whether his piety had solid foundations, it would be proof for his sincerity that he voiced the opinion that the Papacy in itself was not conducive to piety, and did not add to the salvation of the soul or to the glories of Paradise. Without prayer, he would not be able to bear the burden. The happiness of sincere inward prayer . . . prayer which often moved him to tears, prayer from which he arose with the conviction that he had been uplifted, remained to him until the end. The people were transported when they saw him in processions: barefoot, head uncovered, with the pure expression of sincere piety on his face, with a long and snow-white beard. They thought that such a pious Pope had never existed, and they spoke amongst themselves how the mere sight of him had converted Protestants. . . .

Pius V was certain that he was traveling a straight road. That this road had brought him to the Papacy filled him with a self-confidence which elevated him above any other considerations. . . .

One noticed that he never mitigated criminal sentences; on the contrary he usually wished that they were more severe. It did not suffice for him that the Inquisition punish crimes newly discovered, he had a search made for crimes dating back ten or twenty years. . . .

One may imagine with what severity he insisted on ecclesiastical discipline . . . [one Bull] fixed the punishment for the desecration of the Sabbath and for blasphemy. The nobility were to pay money fines. "A common man, however, who cannot pay, shall at first offense stand for a day before the door of the churches, his hands tied behind his back. On the second offense he shall be whipped through the town, and the third time his tongue shall be pierced and he shall be sent to the galleys."

Thus is the tenor of his ordinances: how often did one have to tell him that he was dealing with men and not with angels!

Leopold von Ranke, "Die Roemischen Paepste," *Sämmtliche Werke* (Leipzig, 1889), XXXVII, 230, 231–32, 233. (Trans. George L. Mosse.)

This excerpt from the constitution of the Society of Jesus (1540) explains the principles upon which it was founded.

21

In our society, which we wish to be called by the name of Jesus, let whoever desires to fight under the sacred banner of the Cross, and to serve only God and the Roman pontiff, His vicar on earth, after a solemn vow of perpetual chastity, let him keep in mind that he is part of a society, instituted for the purpose of perfecting souls in life and in Christian doctrine, for the propagation of the faith through public preaching, ministering the word of God, works of charity, and especially through the teaching of the young and uninstructed in the Christian precepts; and lastly for giving consolation to believers in hearing their confessions. Let him think first of God, then of the rule of this order, which is the way to Him; and let him follow after the end proposed by God with all his strength.

Let all members know, and let it be not only at the beginning of their profession, but let them think over it daily as long as they live, that the society as a whole, and each of them, owes obedience to our most holy lord, the pope, and the other Roman pontiffs, his successors, and to fight with faithful obedience for God. And however much he may be learned in the Gospel, and however we may be taught in the orthodox faith, let all Christians profess themselves under the Roman pontiff as leader and vicar of Jesus Christ. For the greater humility of our society, and toward the complete self-mortification of each one, and in order to aid the abnegation of our own wills to the greatest extent, let each one, besides that common obligation, be devoted to this special vow. So that whatever the present or other Roman pontiffs order that concerns the saving of souls and the spread of the faith, and to whatever provinces he shall wish to send us, this let us strive to accomplish as far as in us lies, without any turning back or excuse, whether he shall send us to the Turks, or to any other infidels, even those living in the lands that are called the Indies; or to any heretics or schismatics, or unbelievers, whatever. Wherefore let those that are about to join us consider long and well, before they put their shoulders to this task, whether they have enough grace for good deeds to mount this citadel at the command of their superiors. . . .

Let each vow be obedient to the general of the society in all things that concern the fulfillment of these our regulations.

George L. Mosse and Philip Taylor, *Outline and Sources for a History of Western Civilization* (Dubuque: William C. Brown Co., 1951), p. 22.

In his open letter to the city of London (1580), Father Robert Persons tells of his conversion from Protestantism to Catholicism and the motive for his mission to England. The latter statement is typical of many Jesuits who risked their lives in Protestant countries.

22   . . . Now with regard to my faith and considered religious principles, although the description of "Catholic" has adequately indicated them, yet I desire to explain them more clearly, if possible. Let Your Worships then know that *as a young man I had for long been led hither and thither by the misleading utterances of false preachers,* and this was accentuated after I had come to the University. There for many years I desired to accept the attitude newly adopted by my country [i.e., Protestantism] and by degrees to reconcile my conscience which was very opposed to it; for I perceived that all promotion in the service of the kingdom had been made to depend on this. I have to thank God, however, that He never allowed my wavering soul, though I was daily listening to and reading the new teachers, to adhere to them so obstinately as to be infected with this plague which it was God's will to keep from me. Yet the more I kept reading, ever the more uncertain and restless I seemed to become. But after I had begun to peruse the sacred writings of the Fathers, I perceived that everything they contained was so repugnant to this new doctrine that I was ashamed any longer to tempt God and do violence to my own convictions. For in those writings not only was I finding almost every line quite contrary to the new doctrine of our times, but, when I looked at the titles of their works, I discovered also that what is now being impiously taught is condemned by entire volumes written by the Fathers of the primitive Church. . . . So when I had compared the teaching and piety of the former with the latters' blindness combined with impiety, I had been of no discernment if I had any further doubts which one of them should be followed. . . . And so be it known to you that I firmly believe all that which the Catholic Church of Christ in any way proposes for belief. And I mean by this that church which has always been acknowledged as the visible church of Christ on earth. Of this I hold the Roman church is to be the most honoured part, and I hold the holy Bishop of that See to have been constituted by God, next after Himself, as the universal Pastor and supreme Governor of the whole of it; and all heretics, both ancient and modern, who have left the Church or shall leave it in the time to come, inventing some new form of belief, I hate to the death, and especially the heresiarchs of our day, *Luther, Zwingli, Calvin, Béza,* and men of the same kidney . . . for I am firmly convinced that there can no more be a new faith or religion than there can be some new God, or a Christ other than Him in whom we conscientiously believe.

And now I will set down openly and truthfully what has been the motive of my coming to these parts at this time. It is not unknown to you, I imagine, that there is a certain Society called, from its imitating in a special way the life of our Saviour, the Society of Jesus; and you have heard perhaps that by its profession it incurs the liability of being sent to any part of the whole world to preach the gospel of Christ, without taking any account of danger. It is with this end in view that so many men in these last few years have flocked to it through the various Colleges in which they arm themselves with the weapons necessary for so great a conflict. Here they spend their time partly in giving earnest attention to letters, partly also in taking stock of the strength for so great a labour as this; thereby fulfilling the counsel of Christ, who exhorts him who will build a tower to reckon the expense necessary for it, and so, too, him who is entering on a battle, especially when it is a most bloody one, to hold an inspection of his forces. And when this has been done and they perceive that they have laid aside all sensual love and have won a complete victory over themselves, so as to be resolved to despise for Christ's sake even the greatest advancement in this world, and to give up their own liberty and yield themselves wholly to the disposition of their superiors, holding no danger to be an excuse from carrying out their commands, then at length, when they have put off all earthly affections, whatever mission may be assigned to them, they welcome it invariably for the honour of God (always after the customary outpouring of prayer) without any dread at all, nay more, subjugating to the service of Christ their intellects and all their inclinations, and promising themselves the favour and help of Him for whose sake they are undertaking this enterprise. And that God has not failed them up to now, the many glorious deeds they have done in nearly all parts of the world bear witness.

Letters and Memoirs of Father Robert Persons, S.J. (London: Catholic Record Society, 1942), pp. 36–38. (Reprinted by permission of the publisher.)

The following examples from the Canons of the Council of Trent are taken from its Twenty-Third Session and Twenty-Second Session (1563), from the Seventh (1549) and Thirteenth Sessions (1552).

23   *Twenty-Third Session, Chapter IV.* Inasmuch as in the sacrament of Order, as also in Baptism and Confirmation, a character is imprinted which can neither be effaced nor taken away, this holy council with reason condemns the opinions of those who assert that the priests of the New Testament have only a temporary power; and that those who have once been properly ordained can again become laymen, if they do not exercise the ministry of God. And if anyone affirm that all Christians indiscriminately are priests of the New Testament, or that they are all mutually endowed with an equal spiritual power, he clearly does nothing but confound the ecclesiastical hierarchy—which is "as an army set in array";—as if, contrary to the doctrine of blessed Paul, "all were apostles, all prophets, all evangelists, all pastors, all doctors." Wherefore this holy Synod declares that, besides the other ecclesiastical degrees, bishops, who have succeeded to the place of the apostles, especially belong to this hierarchical order; that they are placed, as the same apostle says, "by the Holy Ghost, to rule the Church of God," that they are superior to priests, administer the sacrament of Confirmation, ordain the ministers of the Church, and that they can perform very many other things, over which functions others of an inferior order have no power. Furthermore, the sacred and holy synod teaches that, in the ordination of bishops, priests, and of the other orders, neither the consent, nor vocation, nor authority, whether of the people or of any civil power or magistrate whatsoever, is required in such wise that, without this, the ordination is invalid: nay, rather doth it decree that all those who being once called and instituted by the people, or by the civil power and magistrate, ascend to the exercise of the ministrations, and those who of their own rashness assume them to themselves, are not ministers of the Church but are to be looked upon as "thieves and robbers, who have not entered by the door."

Twenty-Third Session, Canon I. If anyone shall say that the New Testament does not provide for a distinct, visible priesthood, or that this priesthood has no power to consecrate and offer up the true body and blood of the Lord, or remit or refuse to remit sins, but that its sole function is that of preaching the Gospel, and that those who do not preach are not priests, let him be anathema.

Seventh Session, Of the Sacraments, Canon I. If anyone saith that the sacraments of the New Law were not all instituted by Jesus Christ, our Lord; or that they are more or less than seven, to wit, Baptism, Confirmation, the Eucharist, Penance, Extreme Unction, Orders and Matrimony; or even that any one of these seven is not truly and properly a sacrament, let him be anathema.

Canon VI. If anyone saith that the sacraments of the New Law do not contain the grace which they signify; or that they do not confer that grace on those who do not place an obstacle thereunto; as though they were merely outward signs of grace or justice received through faith, and certain marks of the Christian profession, whereby believers are distinguished among men from unbelievers, let him be anathema.

Canon IX. If anyone saith that in the three sacraments, to wit, Baptism, Confirmation, and Orders, there is not imprinted in the soul a character, that is, a spiritual and indelible sign, on account of which they cannot be repeated, let him be anathema.

Canon X. If anyone saith that all Christians have power to administer the word and all the sacraments, let him be anathema.

Canon XII. If anyone saith that a minister, being in mortal sin—if so be that he observe all the essentials which belong to the effecting or conferring of the sacrament—neither effects nor confers the sacraments, let him be anathema.

Thirteenth Session, Chapter IV. Since Christ our Redeemer declared that it was truly his body which he offered up in the form [*sub specie*] of bread, and since the Church has moreover always accepted this belief, this holy council declares once more that by the consecration of the bread and the wine the whole substance of the bread is converted into the substance of the body of Christ our Lord, and the whole substance of the wine into the substance of his blood, which change is aptly and properly termed transubstantiation by the Catholic Church.

Thirteenth Session, Canon VI. If anyone shall say that Christ, the only begotten son of God, is not to be worshipped with the highest form of adoration [*Latria*] including external worship, in the holy sacrament of the Eucharist, or that the Eucharist should not be celebrated by a special festival, nor borne solemnly about in procession according to the praiseworthy and universal rite and custom of the holy Church, nor held up publicly for the veneration of the people and that those who adore it are idolaters, let him be anathema.

Twenty-Second Session, Canon III. If anyone shall say that the sacrifice of the mass is only a praiseworthy deed or act of edification, or that it is simply in commemoration of the sacrifice on the cross and is not in the nature of a propitiation; or that it can benefit only him who receives it, and ought not to be offered for the living and the dead, for sins, punishment, atonement, and other necessary things, let him be anathema.

Translations and Reprints from the Original Sources of European History, II, No. 6, 35–38.
(Reprinted by permission of the University of Pennsylvania Press.)

QUESTIONS

1. In what did the discipline of the Jesuits consist?
2. What were the reasons for Robert Persons' conversion to Protestantism?
3. What reasons did he give for his missionary work? Are there any connections between these reasons and the ideas which governed the Jesuit order?
4. How does the stand taken at the Council of Trent on the nature of the clergy and the church contrast with the ideas of Luther and Calvin?
5. What Protestant idea is the Council of Trent combatting when it denies that the sacraments enumerated are merely outward signs of grace? (See Luther, pp. 18–21.)

CHAPTER IV

EMPEROR CHARLES V (R. 1519–56)

IT WAS a series of fortunate marriages (see genealogical table) (24) which, after the rise of the nation states, almost succeeded in restoring a measure of unity to Europe. Yet the reign of Emperor Charles V showed that it was by now impossible to attain such unity. France was afraid of being swallowed up by this reconstruction of the old Holy Roman Empire and resisted vigorously; German princes did not want to lose their chaotic freedom. New factors appeared on the scene: the Turks invaded Europe from the East, the last of many invasions Europe had to bear; Protestantism menaced the established faith as well as Charles's Empire (25). Pressed from all sides, the Empire disintegrated before it was ever really established. However, for nearly forty decisive years, Charles V dominated Europe, providing the background for the age of the Reformation.

The genealogical table on the following page shows the inheritance of Charles V. From his father, Philip, he inherited Burgundy, the Netherlands, and a claim to the Empire. From his mother, Joanna, he inherited Aragon and Castile.

GENEALOGICAL TABLE

The Inheritance of Emperor Charles V*

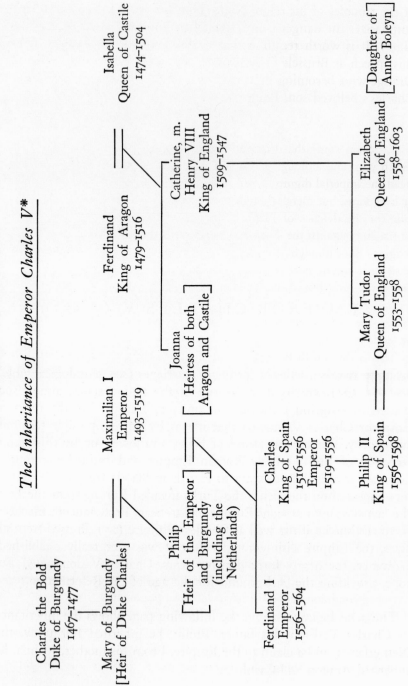

* The table has been simplified in order to show Habsburg relationships to the best advantage.

In his speech explaining his abdication, Charles V gave a review of the troubles of his reign. Notice both his piety and the fact that he emphasizes the danger from "sects of neighboring lands" (i.e., Protestants). It is worth recalling that, walking to the platform to deliver this speech at Brussels (1556), he leaned upon the arm of William of Orange who, becoming Protestant, was to lead the Dutch revolt against Charles's beloved son, Philip II.

. . . Soon came the death of my grandfather Maximilian, in my nine-   **25**
teenth year, and although I was still young, they conferred upon me in his stead the imperial dignity. I had no inordinate ambition to rule a multitude of kingdoms, but merely sought to secure the welfare of Germany, to provide for the defence of Flanders, to consecrate my forces to the safety of Christianity against the Turk and to labor for the extention of the Christian religion. But although such zeal was mine, I was unable to show so much of it as I might have wished, on account of the troubles raised by the heresies of Luther and the other innovators of Germany and on account of serious war into which the hostility and envy of neighboring princes had driven me, and from which I have safely emerged, thanks to the favor of God.

This is the fourth time that I go to Spain, there to bury myself. I wish to say to you that nothing I have ever experienced has given me so much pain or rested so heavily upon my soul as that which I experience in parting from you today, without leaving behind me that peace and quiet which I so much desired. . . . I am no longer able to attend to my affairs without great bodily fatigue and consequent detriment to the affairs of the state. The cares which so great a responsibility involves; the extreme dejection it causes; my health already ruined; all these leave me no longer the strength sufficient for governing the states which God has confided to me. The little strength that remains to me is rapidly disappearing. So I should long ago have put down the burden if my son's immaturity and my mother's incapacity had not forced both my spirit and my body to sustain its weight until this hour.

The last time that I went to Germany I had determined to do what you see me do today, but I could not bring myself to do it when I saw the wretched condition of the Christian state, a prey to such a multitude of disturbances, of innovations, of singular opinions as to faith, of worse than civil wars, and fallen finally into so many lamentable disorders. I was turned from my purpose because my ills were not yet so great, and I hoped to make an end of all these things and restore the peace. In order that I might not be wanting in my duty I risked my strength, my goods, my repose and my life for the safety of Christianity and the defence of my subjects. From this struggle I emerged with a portion of the things I desired. But the king of France and certain Germans, failing to preserve the peace and amity they had sworn, marched against me and were upon the point of seizing my person. The king of France took the city of Metz, and I, in the dead of winter, exposed to intense cold, in the midst of snow and blood, advanced with a powerful army raised at my own expense to retake the city and restore the Empire. The Germans saw that I had not yet laid aside the imperial crown and had no disposition to allow its majesty to be diminished.

I have carried out what God has permitted, since the outcome of our efforts depends upon the will of God. We human beings act according to our powers, our strength, our spirit, and God awards the victory and permits defeat. I have ever done as I was able, and God has aided me. I return to Him boundless thanks for having succored me in my greatest trials and in all my dangers.

I am determined then to retire to Spain, to yield to my son Philip the possession of all my states, and to my brother, the king of the Romans, the Empire. I particularly commend to you my son, and I ask of you in remembrance of me, that you extend to him the love which you have always borne towards me; moreover I ask you to preserve among yourselves the same affection and harmony. Be obedient towards justice, zealous in the observance of the laws, preserve respect for all that merits it, and do not refuse to grant to authority the support of which it stands in need.

Above all, beware of infection from the sects of neighboring lands. Extirpate at once the germs, if they appear in your midst, for fear lest they may spread abroad and utterly overthrow your state, and lest you may fall into the direst calamities. As to the manner in which I have governed you I confess that I have been more than once deceived, led astray by the inexperience of youth, by the hasty conclusions of young manhood, or by some other fault of human weakness. Nevertheless I make bold to assert that never of my knowledge or by my will has wrong or violence been done to any of my subjects. If then any can complain of having suffered such, I aver that it is unknown to me and against my will; I declare before all the world that I regret it from the bottom of my heart, and I beseech all present, and those who are not here as well, to wish me well and to pardon me.

Translations and Reprints from the Original Sources of European History, III, No. 3, 2–4. (Reprinted by permission of the University of Pennsylvania Press.)

The Turkish invasion of Europe brought the Turks into contact with the Christian population and politics. Here is a picture of the Christians as seen by the Turks, from about 1510.

. . . You know well the unwashed Gyaours [Christians] and their ways **26** and manners, which certainly are not fine. They are indolent, sleepy, easily shocked, inactive; they like to drink much and to eat much; in misfortunes they are impatient, and in times of good fortune proud and overbearing. They are lovers of repose, and do not like to sleep without soft feather-beds; when they have no women with them they are sad and gloomy; and without plenty of good wine they are unable to keep counsel among themselves. They are ignorant of any military strategems. They keep horses only to ride while hunting with their dogs; if one of them wishes to have a good war-horse, he sends to buy it from us. They are unable to bear hunger, or cold, or heat, effort and menial work. They let women follow them in the campaigns, and at their dinners give them the upper places, and they want always to have warm dishes. In short, there is no good in them. . . .

And then, the Christians fight constantly among themselves, because everyone desires to be a king, or a prince, or the first amongst them. One says to another: "Brother, help thou me today against this Prince, and tomorrow I will help thee against that one." Fear them not; there is no concord amongst them. Every one takes care of himself only; no one thinks of the common interest. They are quarrelsome, unruly, self-willed and disobedient. Obedience to their superiors and discipline they have none, and yet everything depends on that.

When they lose a battle, they always say: "We were not well prepared!" or "This or that traitor has betrayed us!" or "We were too few in number, and the Turks were far more numerous!" or "The Turks came upon us without previous declaration of war by misleading representations and treachery. They have occupied our country by turning our internal difficulties to their own advantage!"

Well, that is what they say, being not willing to confess truly and rightly: "God is on the side of the Turks! It is God who helps them, and therefore they conquer us."

Chedomil Mijatovich, *Constantine* (London, 1892), pp. 41–43.

QUESTIONS

1. Upon what were Charles V's claims on Burgundy and the Netherlands based?
2. On what causes did Charles blame his failures?

3. What is the importance of the religious element in Charles's concept of "empire?"

4. Did the Turks have any justification for their boasts of conquests?

5. What battles did the Christians lose to the Turks in the age of Charles V? What battles did they win against them?

CHAPTER V

THE EXPANSION OF EUROPE

MOTIVATED by the lust for wealth, religious enthusiasm, and the love of adventure; facilitated by improvements in ship-building and navigational techniques; and fortified with firearms and an unswerving belief in their own moral superiority (31), European peoples set out at the beginning of modern times to discover and conquer the world. Starting with the cautious explorations of the Portuguese in the fifteenth century (28) and the epoch-making voyage of Columbus in 1492, the "expansion of Europe" did not reach its completion until the cataclysmic wars of the twentieth century. The momentous and still unfolding consequences of these epic phenomena have affected and will continue to affect the lives of millions in every continent on the face of the globe.

The following selections illustrate merely the first century of expansion.

I. COMMERCIAL CURRENTS BEFORE 1500

Commercial and cultural contacts between Mediterranean Europe and Farther Asia are known to have existed at least as early as Roman times, and they have been more or less continuous ever since. The intensity of these relations, particularly in the field of commerce, picked up considerably about the time of the Crusades. The Italian city-states

—notably Venice—obtained great wealth and excited the envy of their neighbors as a result of their virtual monopoly of the business of distributing the produce of the East throughout Europe. (It is worthy of note that Portugal, being near the end of the line of this route of trade, paid the highest prices for the Eastern produce which they consumed.) The following extract, written by a member of the first European expedition to reach India by sea (1497–99), is an account of this commerce as it existed on the eve of the expansion of Europe.

27   From this country of Calecut, or Upper India, come the spices which are consumed in the East and the West, in Portugal, as in all other countries of the world, as also precious stones of every description. The following spices are to be found in this city of Calecut, being its own produce: much ginger and pepper and cinnamon, although the last is not of so fine a quality as that brought from an island called Cillan [Ceylon], which is eight days journey from Calecut. Calecut is the staple for all this cinnamon. Cloves are brought to this city from an island called Melequa [Malacca]. The Mecca vessels carry these spices from there to a city in Mecca called Judeâ [Jidda], and from the said island to Judeâ is a voyage of fifty days sailing before the wind, for the vessels of this country cannot tack. At Judeâ they discharge their cargoes, paying customs duties to the Grand Sultan. The merchandise is then transshipped to smaller vessels, which carry it through the Red Sea to a place close to Santa Catarina of Mount Sinai, called Tuuz, where customs dues are paid once more. From that place the merchants carry the spices on the back of camels, which they hire at the rate of four cruzados each, to Quayro [Cairo], a journey occupying ten days. At Quayro duties are paid again. On this road to Quayro they are frequently robbed by thieves, who live in that country, such as the Bedouins and others.

At Quayro the spices are embarked on the river Nile, which rises in Prester John's country in Lower India [Abyssinia], and descending that river for two days, they reach a place called Roxette [Rosetta], where duties have to be paid once more. There they are placed on camels, and are conveyed in one day to a city called Alexandria, which is a seaport. This city is visited by the galleys of Venice and Genoa, in search of these spices, which yield the Grand Sultan a revenue of 600,000 cruzados in customs duties, out of which he pays to a king called Cidadym an annual subsidy of 100,000 cruzados for making war upon Prester John. . . .

A Journal of the First Voyage of Vasco Da Gama, 1497–1499, trans. and ed. by E. G. Ravenstein (London: The Hakluyt Society, 1898), pp. 77–79. (Reprinted by permission of the publisher.)

II. THE PORTUGUESE IN THE EAST

Christopher Columbus, a Genoese sailing under the flag of Spain, attempted to reach the East by sailing west, thereby accidentally discovering the islands off the coast of a new continent in 1492. But Columbus persisted in believing until the end of his life that he had actually reached "the Indies." Meanwhile, the Portuguese, who for most of a century had been systematically exploring the west coast of Africa in an attempt to reach the East by rounding that continent, landed an expedition in India in 1498. The following letter from the King of Portugal to the King and Queen of Spain (1499) describes the success of that enterprise. The student will be able to judge for himself which of the two motives, the religious or the economic, was of greater weight with the explorers.

Most high and excellent Prince and Princess, most potent Lord and Lady! 28
Your Highnesses already know that we had ordered Vasco da Gama, a nobleman of our household, and his brother Paulo da Gama, with four vessels to make discoveries by sea, and that two years have now elapsed since their departure. And as the principal motive of this enterprise has been with our predecessors, the service of God our Lord, and our own advantage, it pleased Him in His mercy to speed them on their route. From a message which has now been brought to this city by one of the captains, we learn that they did reach and discover India and other kingdoms and lordships bordering upon it; that they entered and navigated its sea, finding large cities, large edifices and rivers, and great populations among whom is carried on all the trade in spices and precious stones, which are forwarded in ships (which these same explorers saw and met with in good numbers and of great size) to Mecca, and thence to Cairo, whence they are dispersed throughout the world. Of these [spices, etc.] they have brought a quantity, including cinnamon, cloves, ginger, nutmeg, and pepper, as well as other kinds, together with the boughs and leaves of the same; also many fine stones of all sorts, such as rubies and others. And they also came to a country in which there are mines of gold, of which [gold], as of the spices and precious stones, they did not bring as much as they could have done, for they took no merchandise with them.

As we are aware that your Highnesses will hear of these things with much pleasure and satisfaction, we thought well to give this information. And your Highnesses may believe, in accordance with what we have learnt concerning the Christian people whom these explorers reached [the Portuguese, handicapped by ignorance of the languages, mistook the Hindus for

Christians], that it will be possible notwithstanding that they are not as yet strong in the faith or possessed of a thorough knowledge of it, to do much in the service of God and the exaltation of the Holy Faith, once they shall have been converted and fully fortified [confirmed] in it. And when they shall have thus been fortified in the faith, there will be an opportunity for destroying the Moors [Moslems] of those parts. Moreover, we hope, with the help of God, that the great trade which now enriches the Moors of those parts, through whose hands it passes without the intervention of other persons or peoples, shall, in consequence of our regulations, be diverted to the natives and ships of our own kingdom, so that henceforth all Christendom, in this part of Europe, shall be able in a large measure to provide itself with these spices and precious stones. This, with the help of God, who in His mercy thus ordained it, will cause our designs and intentions to be pushed with more ardour [especially as respects] the war upon the Moors of the territories conquered by us in these parts, which your Highnesses are so firmly resolved upon, and in which we are equally zealous. . . .

Written at Lisbon, July 1499.

Ibid., pp. 113–14. (Reprinted by permission of the publisher.)

But the first impression which Da Gama and his company made on the inhabitants of India was not the overwhelming success which the King of Portugal intimated.

29   . . . The king, when he joined the captain [Da Gama], threw himself upon another couch, covered with various stuffs embroidered in gold, and asked the captain what he wanted.

And the captain told him he was the ambassador of the King of Portugal, who was Lord of many countries and the possessor of great wealth of every description, exceeding that of any king of these parts; that for a period of sixty years his ancestors had annually sent out vessels to make discoveries in the direction of India, as they knew that there were Christian kings there like themselves. This, he said, was the reason which induced them to order this country to be discovered, not because they sought gold or silver, for of this they had such abundance that they needed not what was to be found in this country. . . .

On Tuesday the captain got ready the following things to be sent to the king, viz., twelve pieces of "lambel" [a type of cloth], four scarlet hoods, six basins, a case of sugar, two casks of oil, and two of honey. And as it is the custom not to send anything to the king without the knowledge of the Moor, his Factor, and of the "bale," [bailiff] the captain informed them of his intention. They came, and when they saw the present they laughed at it, saying that it was not a thing to offer to a king, that the poorest merchant from Mecca, or any other part of India, gave more, and that if he wanted to make a present, it should be in gold, as the king would not accept such things. When the captain heard this he grew sad, and said that he had brought no gold, that, moreover, he was no merchant, but an ambassador. . . .

Ibid., pp. 58, 60. (Reprinted by permission of the publisher.)

The Moslems, mainly Arabs (but all Moslems were "Moors" to the Portuguese), were rightly suspicious of the intentions of the Europeans.

. . . We were well aware that the Moors of the place who knew us could **30** ill digest us. They had told the king that we were thieves, and if once we navigated to his country, no more ships from Mecca, nor from Quambaye [Cambay], nor from Imgros, nor from any other part, would visit him. They added that he would derive no profit from this [trade with Portugal] as we had nothing to give, but would rather take away, and that thus his country would be ruined. They, moreover, offered rich bribes to the king to capture and kill us, so that we should not return to Portugal.

Ibid., pp. 71–72. (Reprinted by permission of the publisher.)

The advice of the Moslems to the native ruler proved to be in the nature of prophecy. Da Gama and his company were lucky to return from the first voyage with their lives (about one third of the expedition perished on the voyage from disease) and a small cargo of spices and other commodities, but in succeeding years the Portuguese sent ever larger and more powerful expeditions to the Indian Ocean. Within fifteen years of their first voyage, the Portuguese were able—thanks to their superior weapons (firearms), ships, and organizational ability— to clear the ships of all other nations from the Indian Ocean and to establish a monopoly of its trade.

III. THE SPANISH IN THE NEW WORLD

Meanwhile, on the other side of the world the Spanish came to realize something of the true nature of their discoveries and set about systematically to exploit the commercial and colonial possibilities of the region. Hernando (Fernando) Cortes, a soldier of fortune who had settled in the islands which came to be known as the West Indies, led an expedition from Cuba to the coast of Mexico in 1519. One of his first encounters with the natives of that region is reported in the following passage.

31   . . . He made them understand how he had not come to do them any harm or evil, but only to speak to them on the part of Your Majesties; and that he, therefore, prayed that they would allow and approve of his landing. . . . The Indians answered to this that he could say all he wished from where he was, but that he should not talk of landing, neither he nor his people, for they would dispute his entrance; and, saying this, they menaced us with their arrows, bidding us to go away from there. . . .

. . . Seeing that it was the determination of the said Indians to resist his landing, and that they began to discharge arrows at us, he ordered that the charges of artillery be fired, and that we should charge them. When the shots were being fired and while landing they wounded some of us, but finally, in consequence of our rapid charges, and of the attack in the rear by those who had gone by the road, they fled, leaving us the town, and we took possession of that part of it which seemed to us the stronger.

The next day following, at the hour of vespers, two Indians, on the part of the caciques [chieftains], came to us, bringing certain jewels of very thin gold of little value. They told the Captain that they brought him those ornaments to induce him to go away, and, without doing them any harm or injury, to leave them their land where they had always been. The said Captain answered, saying that, as to doing them harm or injury, he had no such wish, and as to leaving them the land, they must understand that from henceforward they were to have for their Lords the greatest Princes of the earth, whose vassals they would be, and that they would have to serve them, and that, in acting thus, Your Majesties would grant them many mercies, and favours would grow upon them, and that they should be protected and defended from their enemies. They answered that they would be satisfied to do this, but still they required that their country should be left to them. Thus we all became friends, and, our friendship being established, the Captain told them that the Spaniards there with him had nothing to eat, as nothing had been brought from the ships, and he prayed them to bring us food during the time we remained on the Island; and they answered that the next day they would, and thus they went away, and remained away that day and the next, nor did they bring us any food.

Letters of Cortes, trans. and ed. Francis A. MacNutt (New York: C. P. Putnam's Sons, 1908), I, 146, 147–49. (Reprinted by permission of the publisher.)

In view of this reception, Cortes moved on to a more hospitable location.

. . . The next day a little before noon one of the caciques of that town came to whom the said Captain spoke, and made him understand through the interpreter that he had not come to do them any hurt nor injury but to inform them that they were to be vassals of Your Majesties, and how they were to serve them and to pay tribute of what they had in their country, as did all who are such. And the cacique answered that he was very satisfied to be such, and to obey, and that he would be much pleased to serve them, and to have such high Princes for lords as the Captain had made them understand Your Royal Majesties were. Immediately afterwards the Captain told him that, since he was so well disposed towards his King and Lord, he would see what great favours Your Majesties would grant him in the future; and, saying this, he made him put on a shirt of holland, and a robe of velvet, and a girdle of gold, with which the said cacique was much pleased and happy. He told the Captain then that he wanted to go to his country, and asked him to wait for him there, for the next day he would come back and bring him such things as he had, so that we might more fully understand his good will towards the service of Your Royal Highnesses. Thus he took his leave, and departed; and the next day the said cacique returned, as he had agreed, and spreading a white cloth before the Captain, he offered him certain precious jewels of gold, which he placed upon it. . . .

After the said cacique had taken leave of us . . . some of those noble persons who came in this armada . . . assembled and spoke with the Captain Fernando Cortes, saying that this land was good and that, judging by the sample of gold which that cacique had brought, it was reasonable to believe that it must be very rich, and that he and all his Indians were well disposed towards us. For these reasons, it seemed to us . . . that a town should be founded and peopled there in the name of Your Royal Highnesses. . . . Immediately, therefore, he began with great diligence to found and people a town, to which the name of Rica Villa de la Vera Cruz was given.

Ibid., I, 154–57. (Reprinted by permission of the publisher.)

Using the newly founded town of Vera Cruz as a base of operations, Cortes moved inland toward the Aztec Empire of Montezuma, concerning which he had heard stories of prosperous cities and great wealth. With a combination of Spanish cavalry, firearms, audacity, deceit, and treachery, he made alliances with native tribes hostile to Montezuma, and conquered and destroyed the Aztec civilization. In subsequent years, having received reinforcements from the islands and from across the sea, and vested with the title of "Captain-General of New Spain," he extended the Spanish dominions from Honduras on the south to California on the north. His attitude toward the country and his treatment of the natives is typified in the following passage.

33   . . . The country is very rich in gold mines, and, once these people are pacified, our settlers say that they will get possession of them and reduce to slavery the people who had once offered themselves to Your Majesty, and had afterwards rebelled and had killed the Spaniards, and done every mischief. I ordered that those who were captured should be branded with Your Highness's mark, and, after separating the part [i.e., of the slaves] belonging to Your Majesty, that the rest should be distributed among the members of the expedition.

    Ibid., II, 199. (Reprinted by permission of the publisher.)

IV. HOLLAND BECOMES A COLONIAL POWER

The riches of the Indies and of the New World, which Portugal and Spain tried to keep to themselves, excited the envy of the maritime powers to the north—France, the Low Countries, and England. Stimulated by religious strife, the Dutch Netherlands—which had formed a part of the empire of Charles V—broke away from the Spanish dominion in the second half of the sixteenth century. When Portugal fell under the sway of Spain after 1580, the Dutch mingled with their defensive tactics a bold offense by invading with their ships the formerly exclusive preserve of the Portuguese in the Indian Ocean. The following passage, a portion of a commercial newsletter to the famous Fugger banking house of Augsburg (Germany), illustrates the success which attended their efforts.

34   *From Amsterdam, the 24th day of July 1599.*
    Out of the eight Dutch ships which left fourteen and a half months ago for India to obtain spices, four arrived here this week. They are richly laden. Their most important consignment is nearly 300 loads of pepper, which should come to over 4,000 packets. The remaining cargo consists of other kinds of spices, such as cloves, nutmeg, cinnamon, etc. The four other ships with soldiery have been left at Banca. These have set sail for the Moluccas and are to follow in a few months. This is considered here as great tidings, and much wonder is expressed that they should have taken such a short time over the journey. It took them seven months to make the East Indies and they lay two months in Banca. There they procured all their cargo, and

have returned in five and a half months. Never have the Portuguese accomplished such a journey. . . .

In the meantime, the Portuguese attacked the town of Banca, but with the help of the Dutch, the Indians have killed 800 of these and captured the rest with the ships. Whereas the Dutch have succeeded so greatly in this sea journey they will undertake others, and if the King of Spain does not beware and put a stop to them, in time great harm will befall the kingdom of Portugal. . . .

The Fugger News-Letters, ed. Victor Von Klarwill, trans. Pauline de Chary (London: John Lane, 1924), I, 222.

V. ENGLAND JOINS IN

The English, meanwhile, had had but small success in their enterprises, despite the fact that John Cabot, a Venetian in the employ of Henry VII, had made a landfall on the North American continent as early as 1497. In the sixteenth century the English found their greatest profits from overseas activity in peaceful trade (e.g., the Muscovy Company) or in out-and-out piracy (e.g., Sir Francis Drake), rather than in colonial empires. But a harbinger of things to come is to be found in the writings of Richard Hakluyt, indefatigable exponent of maritime discovery and overseas settlement (1582).

    . . . I conceive great hope that the time approaches and now is, that we **35** of England may share and partake (if we will ourselves), both with the Spaniards and the Portuguese, in part of America and other regions as yet undiscovered. . . . Yea, if we would behold with the eye of pity how all our prisons are pestered and filled with able men to serve their country, which for small robberies are daily hanged up in great numbers . . . we would hasten and further every man to his power the deducting of [conveying] to some colonies of our superfluous people into those temperate and fertile parts of America, which, being within six weeks sailing of England, are yet unpossessed by any Christians. . . .

Richard Hakluyt, *Divers Voyages Touching the Discovery of America* (London: The Hakluyt Society, 1850), p. 8. (Reprinted by permission of the publisher.)

QUESTIONS

1. What Eastern produce was consumed in Europe before the great discoveries? By what routes did it reach Europe? Who were the "middlemen"?

2. What motives actuated the Portuguese and Spanish in their voyages of exploration? Which motives were of greater importance?

3. How were the Portuguese and Spanish received by the inhabitants of the countries which they discovered? What was their response to the reception they were accorded?

4. When did the Dutch enter the competition for empire? What factors favored their ambitions?

5. What arguments did Hakluyt advance in favor of English colonization?

CHAPTER VI

THE WARS OF RELIGION

BETWEEN 1562 and 1648 several nations of Western Europe were involved in civil wars, usually referred to as the Wars of Religion. Although political causes were just as important as the conflict between Catholics and Protestants (37), religious strife provided the ideological basis for these wars. The French religious wars (1562–98) resulted in the Edict of Nantes (1598) (36), which established a limited toleration for the Huguenots. The Thirty Years' War (1619–48) ended in the Treaty of Westphalia (40), which firmed both the political and religious division of Germany. At one point in that war it looked as if the Emperor and the Catholic faith might triumph. However, the Swedish King Gustavus Adolphus came to the rescue of the German Protestants (1630) (38). As a result of his victories, it became impossible to restore religious unity to Germany, even though the Swedish King himself was killed at the Battle of Luetzen (1632) (39). Germany suffered much during this long period of war, and the attitude of the population is well illustrated by the greatest literary work to come out of the conflict: Grimmelshausen's *Simplicissimus* (1699) (41).

The Wars of Religion also marked a crucial period in the development of modern political thought. On the one hand, those fighting against a hostile monarchy developed theories of resistance to authority. On the other hand, the hard-pressed monarchs countered with ideas of absolutism. John Knox tells us the reasons for opposing anointed kings (42); Jean Bodin formulated the theory of sovereignty which was to be used by monarchs to justify their increasing absolutism (43).

I. FRANCE

The following are some of the main provisions of the Edict of Nantes, proclaimed by King Henry IV in 1598.

36   III. We ordain that the Catholic Apostolic and Roman religion shall be restored and reëstablished in all places and localities of this our kingdom and countries subject to our sway, where the exercise of the same has been interrupted, in order that it may be peaceably and freely exercised, without any trouble or hindrance. Forbidding very expressly all persons of whatsoever estate, quality or condition, under the penalties recited above, from troubling, molesting or disturbing ecclesiastics in the celebration of divine service, in the enjoyment or perception of tithes, fruits or revenues of their benefices, and all other rights and dues belonging to them; and that all those who during the troubles have taken possession of churches, houses, goods or revenues belonging to the said ecclesiastics, and who retain and occupy the same, shall surrender to them entire possession and peaceable enjoyment of such rights, liberties and sureties as they had before they were deprived of them. Forbidding thus very expressly to those of the said religion called Reformed to have preaching or perform other exercise of the said religion in churches, houses and habitations of the said ecclesiastics.

VI. And in order to leave no occasion for troubles or differences between our subjects, we have permitted and herewith permit those of the said religion called Reformed to live and abide in all the cities and places of this our kingdom and countries of our sway, without being annoyed, molested or compelled to do anything in the matter of religion contrary to their consciences, nor for this reason to be subject to visitation in houses and places where they desire to dwell, upon condition that they comport themselves in other respects according to that which is contained in this our present edict.

VIII. In houses of fiefs, where those of the said religion have not . . . high justice or military tenure, the exercise of said religion may be enjoyed for the family alone. It is not however intended, in case there should happen to arrive other persons, up to the number of thirty outside of the family, whether it be upon the occasion of a baptism, visits of friends or otherwise, that this should be cause for investigation: provided also that the said houses shall not be within the cities, towns or villages belonging to Catholic lords other than ourselves, having the right of high justice, in which the said Catholic lords shall have their houses. In which case those of the said religion shall not be able to enjoy said exercise in said towns or villages, unless by permission and leave of said lords high justices, and not otherwise.

IX. We also permit those of the said religion to make and continue the exercise of the same in all villages and places of our dominion where it was established by them and publicly enjoyed several and divers times in the year 1597, up to the end of the month of August, notwithstanding all decrees and judgments to the contrary.

X. We very expressly forbid to all those of the said religion the exercise, either in respect to ministry, regulation, discipline or the public instruction of children, and otherwise, in this our kingdom and lands of our dominion, of all that concerns religion, otherwise than in the places permitted and granted by the present Edict.

XIV. As well from performing any function of the said religion in our court or retinue, or equally in our lands and territories beyond the mountains, or in our city of Paris, or within five leagues of the said city: at the same time those of the said religion who live in the said lands and territories beyond the mountains and in our said city, and for five leagues thereabout, may not be investigated in their houses, nor constrained to do anything in respect to religion contrary to their consciences, providing they comport themselves in other respects according to that which is contained in our present Edict.

XV. And it will not be allowed for the said religion to be practiced in the armies, except in the quarters of those chiefs who may be of that confession, not however in those quarters wherein our own person is lodged.

XVIII. We also forbid all our subjects of whatever quality and condition, from carrying off by force or persuasion, against the will of their parents, the children of the said religion, in order to cause them to be baptized or confirmed in the Catholic Apostolic and Roman church; and the same is forbidden to those of the said religion called Reformed, upon penalty of being punished with especial severity.

XXI. Books concerning the said religion called Reformed may not be printed and publicly sold except in cities and places where the public exercise of the said religion is permitted. And as for the other books, which may be printed in other cities, they shall be examined and investigated, as much by our officers as by theologians, according as it is prescribed in our ordinances; and we enjoin our judges and officers to carry out this order.

XXII. We ordain that there shall be no difference or distinction made in respect to the said religion in receiving pupils to be instructed in universities, colleges and schools; nor in receiving the sick and poor into hospitals, retreats and public charities.

XXIII. Those of the said religion called Reformed shall be obliged to respect the laws of the Catholic Apostolic and Roman church, recognized in this our kingdom, for the consummation of marriages contracted or to be contracted as regards the degrees of consanguinity and kinship.

Translations and Reprints from the Original Sources of European History, III, No. 3, 30–32. (Reprinted by permission of the University of Pennsylvania Press.)

Henry IV, speaking before his army at Ivry (1590), claimed that while his enemies were betraying their country under a religious pretext, he was defending France.

37   . . . My enemies, born for the shame and misfortune of France, seek their fatherland beyond her borders [i.e., Spain]. For what other aim can we imagine them to have, when we see them carrying on criminal intercourse with the mortal enemy of the French name, waging war under her auspices, marching under her ensigns, and slavishly obeying her orders, carrying their blindness to the extent of turning her arms against the bowels of France? Look at their army; see the standards of Spain before your eyes. Those are the people who for thirty years have been working for the ruin of France. All the disorders that have troubled the peace of this country have been excited and sustained by their artifices and their secret intrigues. Religion served as their pretext; in reality it was the crown at which they aimed. Can a more convincing proof be desired than the lamentable death of my predecessor [i.e., Henry III], the Prince to whom we owe so much, and who had heaped benefits on the very authors of this wretched war? In spite of the hatred that he bore toward those whom it pleased them to call heretics, did they not turn their arms against him, snatch from him the best part of his dominions and, finally, by the most terrible of all parricides, cut the thread of his life? It is to avenge such a frightful crime that you have come here. I need say no more. On the outcome of this day depend your lives, your honor and your goods. . . .

W. F. Reddaway, *Select Documents of European History* (New York: Henry Holt & Co., n.d.), II, 101–2. (Reprinted by permission of the publisher.)

II. GERMANY

Gustavus Adolphus, in a conversation with a representative of the Elector of Brandenburg (1630), tells his reasons for leading an army into Germany.

I have come hither for no other reason than to save the poor oppressed **38** Estates and their subjects from the terrible tyranny and oppression of those thieves and robbers who have tormented them hitherto and to help the Elector to escape a like fate. . . . Does he not know that the Emperor and his friends are resolved to go on until the Evangelical religion in the Empire is completely rooted out, and that his fate will be to deny his religion or to quit his countries? . . . for God's sake take resolves worthy of men. . . . I cannot go back: the die is cast: we have crossed the Rubicon. I am seeking no profit for myself except the safety of my realm. Else have I only expenses, toil and peril. They gave me cause enough by twice sending help to my foes in Prussia, and designing to seize the Baltic ports. . . . Let the Elector cease to be the Emperor's servant in his own countries: who makes himself a sheep, him the wolf devours. . . . I will not hear of neutrality: the Elector must be friend or foe. . . . God is fighting with the devil. If the Elector will hold to God, let him join me; if to the devil, he will have me to contend with; no third course will be allowed.

Max Schilling, *Quellenbuch zur Geschichte der Neuzeit* (Berlin, 1890), pp. 125–26. (Trans. George L. Mosse.)

The following is a contemporary description of Gustavus Adolphus going into the Battle of Luetzen (1632), in which he was killed.

"The Bride never longed for the wedding morning," says the *Swedish* **39** *Intelligencer,* "as the King longed for the day to break." But when dawn came, a thick mist overspread the field, and "the sun, as if his great eye had beforehand overread the fatality of the day, seemed very loath to begin it. . . . But the martial King, ever forcing himself to awaken time and hasten on mortality, would needs make his drums beat two hours before daylight." Prayers were then read at the head of each regiment and Luther's Psalm, "Eine feste Burg ist unser Gott," [i.e., A mighty fortress is our God] and the King's own battle hymn, "Versage nicht du Häuflein klein," [i.e., Do not despair, you small assembly] were sung as the men stood to their arms. The King went into the battle without armor as his custom was, and on his usual white charger, and without having tasted food. He made a short speech to his soldiers. To the Swedes he said: "There you have the enemy in front of you. He is not on a mountain or behind entrenchments this time, but on the open plain. You know well how eagerly he has sought to avoid fighting and that he is only fighting now because he cannot escape us. Fight then, my dear countrymen and friends, for God, your country, and your King. I will reward you all, and bravely: but if you flinch from the fight, you know well that not a man of you will ever see Sweden again." And to the Germans he spoke in a similar strain. Then he waved his sword over his head, crying: "Forward in God's name; Jesu! Jesu! Jesu! help us to strive today to the honor of thy Holy Name."

C. R. L. Fletcher, *Gustavus Adolphus* (New York: G. P. Putnam's Sons, 1890), pp. 281–82.

The Treaty of Westphalia is a long document which would cover over a hundred of our printed pages. The extract (from paragraph 8) given below illustrates the virtual independence from the Emperor and Empire which the treaty gave to the German princes. This is a landmark in the growing political disunity of Germany. From now on until unification (1870), Germany is little more than a geographical expression. (See p. 326.)

40   1. In order that for the future all political quarrels be avoided, all Electors, Princes and Estates of the Empire shall, through this treaty, be confirmed in their ancient rights and liberties in such a manner, as they can and should not be driven from them by anyone acting under his own authority, under any pretext whatsoever.

2. They shall, without contradiction, have a voice in all consultations and matters concerning the Empire; especially when new laws are to be made or to be interpreted, war is to be declared, contributions are to be made, soldiers are to be mustered and quartered, new fortresses are to be erected in the name of the Empire in the territories of the estates, or old ones are to be garrisoned, also where peace is to be made or alliances are to be contracted. Such matters shall not occur in the future without the diets and the free voice of all Estates; especially shall all Estates be free to form leagues among themselves or with foreign [powers], but in such a way that they are not directed against Emperor and Empire, the peace of their country or [against] this treaty and against the oath by which each is bound to Emperor and Empire.

Schilling, *op. cit.*, p. 162. (Trans. George L. Mosse.)

Grimmelshausen's *Simplicissimus* (1669), though written after the war, deals with "Simpleton's" adventures during the Thirty Years' War. It reflects both the horror of the war and the feeling of resignation that followed it.

Although I was not minded to take the peace-loving reader into the house **41** of my father, together with these looters, because horrible things will transpire there, yet my history, which I bequeath to dear posterity, requires it— to testify through my own example what cruelties were now and then perpetrated in our German war, that such evils have been necessary visitations, adjudged by God for our benefit. . . .

Before this I did not know or imagine anything else but that my mother, father, myself and the servants were alone in this world, as I did not know any other humans or habitation. . . . But soon after this I got to know the origins of men in this world and that they would have to leave it. Only in outward appearance was I a human being . . . otherwise little better than an animal.

The first thing which these looters did was that they stabled their horses, then each one went about his peculiar business, each leading to ruination and decay; though some began to cook and fry so that it looked as if a gay banquet was to be held—yet others stormed through the house from cellar to attic . . . others again made up parcels of cloth, dresses and other household goods as if they were going to hold a sale; what they did not want to take with them they destroyed; some of them pierced the hay with their swords as if they did not have enough sheep or swine to gore . . . others demolished ovens and windows as if they wanted to proclaim an eternal summer. . . . Only then did they start to remove the stones from the pistols and to use them as thumbscrews on the peasants, and to torture the poor devils as if they had wanted to burn them as witches . . . everyone had his invention for torturing the peasants and each peasant had his own personal torture . . . [my father] had a special honor because he was the head of the household . . . they bound him so that he could not move his feet or hands, and rubbed the soles of his feet with salt which our old goat licked off; thus tickled he was about to burst with laughter . . . in such laughter he confessed his guilt and opened up his hidden treasures, which contained more gold, pearls and valuable stones than one could have expected a peasant to possess. . . .

[After having become a servant to the governor of Hanau] my master wanted to have sport with me and said: I see that you do not want to be ennobled, that you despise all titles. I answered: Master, if I were to be

ennobled within the hour, I would not accept the title . . . I am happy without work! Master, you are the most miserable man in Hanau. . . . Look,
you are surrounded by enemies, you alone are responsible for the defense of
this fortress, you must see how your enemy can be thwarted and how your
plans can be kept secret. Beyond this you must see that there is here no
lack in money, provisions, munitions; thus you have to maintain the whole
countryside in vassalage through requisitions and levying of tributes . . . if
you send your people out for such work their best results come from stealing,
burning and murdering . . . you have incurred a grave responsibility towards
God. It is possible that the honor and pleasure [gained from this] gives you
satisfaction, but do you know who will have the use of the treasures which
you have thus gathered? And even if these riches remain yours you will
have to leave them in this world, and you can take nothing with you but
the sins which you acquired through the gaining of these treasures. . . . If
you are lucky in that you can make good use of your booty, then you are
[nevertheless] wasting the sweat and blood of the poor who now are lacking all in miserable poverty, and who are wasting away and dying of hunger.

H. J. Chr. von Grimmelshausen, *Der Abenteurliche Simplicissimus* (Halle, 1888), pp. 14–16,
121–23. (Trans. George L. Mosse.)

III. THE DOCTRINE OF RESISTANCE TO AUTHORITY

When Calvin wrote his chapter on civil government in his *Institutes*
(see p. 27), he stated that while obedience to rulers must be the general rule, there is one exception: when the ruler seduces us from obedience to God. Here was a doctrine of resistance which could be used
by the Protestants in fighting the religious war against Catholic monarchs. Thus the period of the religious wars sees important statements
of resistance to authority which went far toward advocating a limited
monarchy. John Knox (1505–1572), the leader of the Scottish Reformation and of the rebellion against Mary, Queen of Scots, provides a
good example when he defends the Presbyterian ministers, in a conversation with the Queen Regent (1559), against the charge of dis-
loyalty to the crown. Catholic writers were to use identical arguments against Protestant monarchs.

42   Where she [i.e., the Queen Regent] complains of our preachers, affirming
that irreverently they speak of princes in general and of her in particular,
inducing the people thereby to defection from their duty, etc., and therefore
that such thing cannot be suffered: because this accusation is had against

God's true ministers, we cannot but witness what trend and order of doctrine they have kept, and yet keep, in that point. In public prayers they commend to God all princes in general, and the magistrates of this our native realm in particular. In open audience they declare the authority of princes and magistrates to be of God; and therefore they affirm, that they ought to be honored, feared, obeyed, even for conscience's sake; provided that they command or require nothing expressly repugnant to God's commandment and plain will, revealed in His Holy Word. Moreover, they affirm, that if wicked persons, abusing the authority established by God, command things manifestly wicked, that such as may and do bridle [i.e., resist] the inordinate appetites of princes, cannot be accused as resisters of the authority, which is God's good ordinance. To bridle the fury and rage of princes in free kingdoms and realms, they affirm, it appertains to the nobility, sworn and born councilors of the same, and also to the barons and people whose voice and consent are to be required in all great and weighty matters of the commonwealth. Which if they do not, they declare themselves criminal with their princes, and so subject to the same vengeance of God, which they deserve, for that they pollute the seat of justice, and too, as it were, make God author of iniquity. They proclaim and they cry, that the same God who plagued Pharoah, repulsed Senacherib, struck Herod with worms, and made the bellies of dogs the grave and sepulcher of despiteful Jezebel, will not spare the cruel princes, murderers of Christ's members, in this our time. In this manner they speak of princes in general and of Your Grace in particular.

The Works of John Knox, ed. David Laing (Edinburgh, 1846), I, 410–11.

IV. THE EMERGING DOCTRINE OF ABSOLUTISM

Against the doctrines of resistance, the monarchs began to stress their absolute powers. The nature of such powers was defined in its classic form by Jean Bodin in his *République* (*ca.* 1576), written during the turmoil of the French religious wars. His doctrine of "sovereignty" laid the foundations for such full-fledged theories of "absolutism" as that of Thomas Hobbes (see p. 82). To Bodin, a king endowed with full sovereignty seemed the only way out of religious and political conflict.

In this we can recognize the power and majesty of a true sovereign **43** prince: When the estates of the people are assembled, persons request and supplicate to their prince in all humility, without [however] having any power to command, disclaim, or to deliberate, [or] to declare laws, edicts and ordinances [unless] it pleases the king to consent or to dissent, to command or to defend. . . . Those . . . who have written of the duty of magistrates and others, have gone out of their way to argue that the estates of the people are more illustrious than the prince; a thing which revolts true subjects in the obedience which they owe to their sovereign monarch. There is neither reason nor any foundation whatsoever for such an opinion. . . .

. . . Because there is nothing higher on earth after God than sovereign princes, and as they are established by Him as His lieutenants to command men, it is necessary to be aware of their station, to respect them and to revere their majesty in all obedience, to talk to them with all honor; because he who abuses his sovereign prince abuses God of Whom he is the image on earth. . . . In order that one can recognize him who is . . . the sovereign prince, one has to know his qualities which are not common to other subjects; because if they were common they could not be any part of a sovereign prince. . . .

He who has no [earthly] sovereign is he who gives law to all his subjects, who makes peace and war, who gives power to all the offices and magistrates of his country, who levies taxes, [who] enfranchises him who seems worthy, and who gives pardon to him who had deserved death: What more power could one desire in a sovereign prince? These are always the marks of sovereign power. . . . Just as the great sovereign God cannot create a god who is His equal because He is infinite, so we can say that the princes whom we have described as the image of God cannot elevate a subject to his station because then his [the Prince's] power would no longer exist. . . .

Because this is so, it follows that the prime mark of sovereignty is not to give justice, because that is common to the prince and to the subjects, just as is [the power] to institute or to abolish offices, because the prince and the subject [both] may share that power—especially as respects the officers serving justice or the police, or war or finance . . . [nor] is it the prime mark of sovereignty to give rewards to them who have merited them, because that is common to the prince and the magistrates, because the magistrates may receive that power from the prince; also, it is not a prime mark of sovereignty to take counsel of the affairs of a state, because that may be the charge of the privy council or the senate of the Republic. . . . We might say the same thing as regards the law [which] the magistrates can give to them who are within the power of their jurisdiction, but he [the magistrate] can do nothing against the edicts and ordinances of his sovereign prince, and to make this point clearer, we must presuppose that the word of the law signifies the right command of him, or of those who have power over all others without exception of person; and to go further . . . there is no one but the sovereign prince who can give law to all his subjects without exception, be it in general or in particular.

Jean Bodin, *Les six livres de la République* (Lyons, 1593), n.p. (Trans. George L. Mosse.)

QUESTIONS

1. What liberties did the Edict of Nantes give to the Huguenots in France?
2. What did the Edict of Nantes forbid the Huguenots to do?
3. Do you think Henry IV's accusations against his adversaries were justified?
4. Did Gustavus Adolphus think of his participation in the Thirty Years' War merely in terms of a "preventive" war? Why did he think Sweden endangered in 1630?
5. How exactly did the Treaty of Westphalia prevent German unity from coming about?
6. How exactly does *Simplicissimus* reflect the despair of the war?
7. What royal actions would warrant resistance, according to John Knox? What actions was he, in fact, resisting?
8. What is the prime mark of sovereignty, and why?
9. What are the marks by which we can recognize a sovereign prince?

CHAPTER VII

THE ENGLISH REVOLUTION

THE STRUGGLE between Parliament and the monarchy is the dominant feature of English life in the seventeenth century. The issues at stake were economic, religious, and constitutional. The Apology of 1604 shows the temper of the House of Commons (44). It is a lesson read to James I, who had come to the throne just one year before. The preservation of the privileges of Parliament meant not only such rights as free speech, but also participation in the determining of the religion of the state and power over the purse. To the claims of the Apology that the voice of the people is as the voice of God, James opposed his idea of the "divine right of kings" (45). Once the revolution took its course (1640-60), it was neither king nor Parliament, but the Puritan army under Oliver Cromwell, which emerged victoriously. This victory was won under the great religious impulse of Puritanism, as Cromwell's defense of his arbitrary actions against Parliament shows (46). The death of Cromwell and the excesses of the "Saints" facilitated the restoration of Charles II, but it was the King's own declaration of Breda (1660) which, by the forgiveness it promised, smoothed the way for the restoration (49). Another revolution (1688) was needed to assure the triumph of parliamentary government. The Bill of Rights (1688), to which William and Mary had to subscribe, was supposed to make royal absolutism impossible (50).

Two important political theories emerged from this long struggle. John Locke defended the revolution in his stress on the inalienable rights of subjects (51). Thomas Hobbes stressed the need for peace, which, he thought, could come about only under an absolutist government (52).

Meanwhile the triumph of Parliament in 1688 had meant the triumph of the Whigs. Drawn from those classes of the population who had opposed royal absolutism all along, they saw in parliamentary government the best assurance of economic progress, based upon the guarantee of property rights, free from any threats of arbitrary taxation or regulated economy. Under their auspices, England entered its great age of the Industrial Revolution (see p. 198).

The following is an extract from the Apology of 1604, presented by the House of Commons to King James I. It is a "classic" statement of the rights of subjects.

. . . Now concerning the ancient rights of the subjects of this realm, **44** chiefly consisting in the privileges of this house of parliament, the misinformation openly delivered to your Majesty has been in three things: first, that we held not privileges of right, but of grace only, renewed every parliament by way of donature upon petition, and so to be limited. Secondly, that we are no Court of Record, nor yet a court that can command view of records; but that our proceedings here are only to acts and memorials, and that the attendance with the records is courtesy, not duty. Thirdly and lastly, that the examination of the return of writs for knights and burgesses is without our compass, and due to the chancery.

Against which assertions, most gracious Sovereign, tending directly and apparently to the utter overthrow of the very fundamental privileges of our House, and therein of the rights and liberties of the whole Commons of your realm of England, which they and their ancestors from time immemorable have undoubtedly enjoyed under your Majesty's most noble progenitors, we the knights, citizens and burgesses of the House of Commons assembled in parliament and in the name of the whole Commons of the realm of England, with uniform consent for ourselves and our posterity, do expressly protest, as being derogatory in the highest degree to the true dignity, liberty, and authority of your Majesty's high court of parliament and consequently to the rights of all your Majesty's said subjects and the whole body of this your kingdom; and desire that this our protestation may be recorded to all posterity. And contrariwise, with all humble and due respect to your Majesty our sovereign lord and head, against these misinformations we most truly avouch, first, that our privileges and liberties are our right and due inheritance, no less than our very lands and goods. Secondly, that they cannot be withheld from us, denied or impaired, but with apparent wrong to the whole state of the realm. . . .

What cause we your poor Commons have to watch over our privileges, is manifest in itself to all men. The prerogatives of princes may easily, and do daily grow: the privileges of the subject are for the most part at an everlasting stand. They may be by good providence and care preserved, but being once lost are not recovered but with much disquiet.

The rights and liberties of the Commons of England consist chiefly in these three things: first, that the shires, cities and boroughs of England, by representation to be present, have free choice of such persons as they shall put in trust to represent them: secondly, that the persons chosen, during the time of the parliament, as also of their access and recess, be free from restraint, arrest and imprisonment: thirdly, that in parliament they may speak freely their consciences without check and controlment, doing the same with due reverence to the sovereign court of parliament, that is, to your Majesty and both the Houses, who all in this case make but one politic body, whereof your Highness is the head. . . .

. . . For matter of religion, it will appear, by examination of truth and right, that your Majesty should be misinformed, if any man should deliver that the kings of England have any absolute power in themselves, either to alter religion (which God defend should be in the power of any mortal man whatsoever) or to make any laws concerning the same, otherwise than as in temporal causes by consent of parliament. . . .

There remaineth, dread Sovereign, yet one part of our duty at this present, which faithfulness of heart, not presumption, doth press: we stand not in place to speak or do things pleasing. Our care is, and must be, to confirm the love and tie the hearts of your subjects, the commons, most firmly to your Majesty. Herein lies the means of our well deserving of both: there was never prince entered with greater love, with greater joy and applause of all his people. This love, this joy, let it flourish in their hearts for ever. Let no suspicion have access to their fearful thoughts, that their privileges, which they think by your Majesty should be protected, should now by sinister informations or counsel be violated or impaired; or that those, which with dutiful respects to your Majesty, speak freely for the right and good of their country, shall be oppressed or disgraced. Let your Majesty be pleased to receive public information from your Commons in parliament as to the civil estate and government; for private informations pass often by practice: the voice of the people, in the things of their knowledge, is said to be as the voice of God. And if your Majesty shall vouchsafe, at your best pleasure and leisure, to enter into your gracious consideration of our petition for the ease of these burdens, under which your whole people have of long time mourned, hoping for relief by your Majesty; then may you be assured to be possessed of their hearts, and, if of their hearts, of all they can do or have. And so we, your Majesty's most humble and loyal subjects, whose ancestors have with great loyalty, readiness and joyfulness served your famous progenitors, kings and queens of this realm, shall with like loyalty and joy, both we and our posterity, serve your Majesty and your most royal issue for ever, with our lives, lands and goods, and all other our abilities: and by all means endeavor to procure your Majesty's honor, with all plenty, tranquillity, content, joy and felicity.

G. W. Prothero, "Apology of the House of Commons," *Select Statutes and Other Constitutional Documents* (London: Oxford University Press, 1913), pp. 286–93. (Reprinted by permission of the publisher.)

James I stated his viewpoint on the divine right of kings (1610), an idea which was shared by most seventeenth-century monarchs like Louis XIV (see p. 100).

. . . The state of monarchy is the supremest thing upon earth, for kings **45** are not only God's lieutenants upon earth and sit upon God's throne, but even by God himself are called gods . . . in the scriptures kings are called gods and so their power after a certain relation compared to the divine power. Kings are also compared to fathers of families, for a king is truly *parens patriae,* the politic father of his people. And lastly, kings are compared to the head of this microcosm of the body of man. . . .

I conclude then this point touching the power of kings with this axiom of divinity, that as to dispute what God may do is blasphemy, . . . so is it sedition in subjects to dispute what a king may do in the height of his power. But just kings will ever be willing to declare what they will do, if they will not incur the curse of God. I will not be content that my power be disputed upon; but I shall ever be willing to make the reason appear of all my doings, and rule my actions according to my laws. . . . I would wish you to be careful . . . that you do not meddle with the main points of government; that is my craft. . . . It is an undutiful part in subjects to press their king wherein they know beforehand he will refuse them. . . .

Ibid., pp. 293–94. (Reprinted by permission of the publisher.)

Oliver Cromwell's justification of the army's attack on Parliament (1648) brings out the religious impulse which motivated the Puritan army. This is from a letter to Colonel Hammond (Robin).

46

. . . You say: "God hath appointed authorities among the nations, to which active or passive obedience is to be yielded. This resides in England in the Parliament. Therefore active or passive resistance," &c.

Authorities and powers are the ordinance of God. This or that species is of human institution, and limited, some with larger, others with stricter bands, each one according to its constitution. But I do not therefore think the Authorities may do *anything,* and yet such obedience be due. All agree that there are cases in which it is lawful to resist. If so, your ground fails, and so likewise the inference. Indeed, dear Robin, not to multiply words, the query is, Whether ours be such a case? This ingenuously is the true question.

To this I shall say nothing, though I could say very much; but only desire thee to see what thou findest in thy own heart to two or three plain considerations: *First,* Whether *Salus Populi* [the good of the people] be a sound position? *Secondly,* Whether in the way in hand, really and before the Lord, before whom conscience has to stand, this be provided for; or if the whole fruit of the war is not like to be frustrated, and all most like to turn to what it was, and worse? And this, contrary to Engagements, explicit Covenants with those who ventured their lives upon those Covenants and Engagements, without whom perhaps, in equity, relaxation ought not to be? *Thirdly,* Whether this Army be not a lawful Power, called by God to oppose and fight against the King upon some stated grounds; and being in power to such ends, may not oppose one Name of Authority, for those ends, as well as another Name—since it was not the outward Authority summoning them that by *its* power made the quarrel lawful but the quarrel was lawful in itself? If so, it may be, acting will be justified *in foro humano* [before men]. But truly this kind of reasonings may be but fleshly either with or against: only it is good to try what truth may be in them. And the Lord teach us.

My dear Friend, let us look into providences; surely they mean somewhat. They hang so together; have been so constant, so clear, unclouded. Malice, swollen malice against God's people, now called "Saints," to root out their name; and yet they, "these poor Saints," getting arms, and therein blessed with defence and more!—I desire, he that is for a principle of suffering [i.e., passive obedience] would not too much slight this. I slight not him who is so minded: but let us beware lest fleshly reasoning see more safety in making use of this principle than in acting! Who acts, if he resolve not through God to be willing to part with all? Our hearts are very deceitful, on the right and on the left.

What think you of Providence disposing the hearts of so many of God's people this way, especially in this poor Army, wherein the great God has vouchsafed to appear! I know not one officer among us but is on the increasing hand. And let me say, it is after much patience—here in the North. We trust, the same Lord who hath framed our minds in our actings is with us in this also. And all contrary to a natural tendency, and to those comforts *our* hearts could wish to enjoy as well as others. And the difficulties probably to be encountered with, and the enemies:—not few; even all that is glorious in this world. Appearance of united names, titles and authorities "all against us";—and yet not terrified "we": only desiring to fear our great God, that we do nothing against His will. Truly, this is our condition.

And to conclude. We in this Northern Army were in a waiting posture; desiring to see what the Lord would lead us to. . . . Dear Robin, beware of men; look up to the Lord. Let Him be free to speak and command in thy heart. Take heed of the things I fear thou has reasoned thyself into; and thou shall be able through Him, without consulting flesh and blood, to do valiantly for Him and His people. . . .

Oliver Cromwell, Letter to Colonel Robert Hammond, *Letters and Speeches,* ed. Thomas Carlyle (New York, 1847), pp. 108 ff.

Once the victory over Parliament had been won by the army, the Puritans themselves proved disunited in their ideas about religion and government. The following argument for toleration, by a follower of Roger Williams (1646), illustrates the emergence, during this period, of a more liberal religious viewpoint.

. . . Oh *Christ* arise, and *spread* thy *glorious* fame,   **47**
That all may *know,* the *sweetnesse* of thy *Name:*
As—' *Affric, Europe,* and *America*
Expect! and *waite* the *dawnings* of that *day,*
That *Papists, Greeks,* and we the *Protestants*
Of *Calvins Sect,* those too, the *Lutherans,*
And *they* that are a *streine* above them *all,*
At *Jesus* feet, at *length* may *humbly* fall,
That so such *Christs,* which *most* in fancy *make*
(Whence 'tis (Men think) that Christendome doth *shake*)
May at th' *appearing* of the *Lord* depart,
And *all* may *worship* him ev'n with *one heart:*

That so the *Nations* may this glory *see;*
And into *it,* at length *transformed* be:
This to *effect,* can't be by *sword* of *man,*
But *that* which to *with-stand,* no *Kingdomes* can,
For 'tis the *Lords* owne *might,* the *sword* that doth,
Ev'n with *two edges* flow out of *Gods* mouth,
By which are *slaine* the *wicked* of each *Land,*
And will sure *breake* each Persecutors *band:*

Then *England,* and *Yee Nations* round *about,*
That are now so lofty, and so *stout:*
At length *downe fall* to *him* that's *Lord* of you:
And *learne* with *him,* like *meeknesse* for to *show:*
If you with *iron Rods, Saints breake* and *bruise.*
Know then *your selves,* that *Christ* you *so* will *use.*

Tracts and Other Papers, Relating Principally to the Origin, Settlement, and Progress of the Colonies in North America, from the Discovery of the Country to the Year 1776, collected by Peter Force (New York: Peter Smith, 1947), IV, No. 6, 19–20.

However, the Puritans were not united in advocating toleration. Here the argument is made against tolerance by a prominent New England Puritan (1647).

48   . . . He that willingly assents [to toleration in religion], if he examines his heart by daylight, his conscience will tell him, he is either an Atheist, or an Heretic, or an Hypocrite. . . . Not to tolerate things merely indifferent to weak consciences, argues a conscience too strong; pressed uniformity in these causes much disunity. To tolerate more than indifference is not to deal indifferently with God; he that doth it takes His Scepter out of His hands and bids Him stand by. Who has to do to institute religion but God. The power of all religion and ordinances lies in their purity: their purity in their simplicity: then are mixtures pernicious. I lived in a city where a papist preached in one church, a Lutheran in another, a Calvinist in a third; a Lutheran one part of the day, the Calvinist the other, in the same pulpit. The religion in that place was but motley and meager, their affection leopard-like.

If the whole creature should conspire to do the Creator a mischief, or offer Him an insolency, it would be nothing more than in erecting untruths against His Truth, or by sophisticating His truth with human medleys. The removing of some one iota in Scripture may draw out all the life and traverse all the Truth of the Bible; but to authorize an untruth by a toleration of state, is to build a sconce against the walls of Heaven, to batter God out of His Chair. . . .

Nathaniel Ward, *The Simple Cobbler of Aggawam in America* (London, 1843), pp. 5–6.

The Declaration of Breda (1660), given by Charles II from his exile in Holland, smoothed the way for his restoration.

Charles R.   **49**

Charles, by the grace of God, King of England, Scotland, France and Ireland, Defender of the Faith, &c. To all our loving subjects, of what degree or quality soever, greeting.

If the general distraction and confusion which is spread over the whole kingdom doth not awaken all men to a desire and longing that those wounds which have so many years together been kept bleeding, may be bound up, all we can say will be to no purpose; however, after this long silence we have thought it our duty to declare how much we desire to contribute thereunto; and that as we can never give over the hope, in good time, to obtain the possession of that right which God and nature hath made our due, so we do make it our daily suit to the Divine Providence that He will, in compassion to us and our subjects, after so long misery and sufferings, remit and put us into a quiet and peaceable possession of that our right, with as little blood and damage to our people as is possible; nor do we desire more to enjoy what is ours than that all our subjects may enjoy what by law is theirs, by a full and entire administration of justice throughout the land, and by extending our mercy where it is wanted and deserved.

And to the end that the fear of punishment may not engage any, conscious to themselves of what is past, to a perseverance in guilt for the future, by opposing the quiet and happiness of their country, in the restoration of King, Peers and people to their just, ancient and fundamental rights, we do, by these presents, declare that we do grant a free and general pardon, which we are ready, upon demand, to pass under our Great Seal of England, to all our subjects, of what degree or quality soever, who, within forty days after the publishing hereof, shall lay hold upon this our grace and favor, and shall, by any public act, declare their doing so, and that they return to the loyalty and obedience of good subjects; excepting only such persons as shall hereafter be excepted by Parliament, those only to be excepted. Let all our subjects, how faulty soever, rely upon the work of a King, solemnly given by this present declaration, that no crime whatsoever, committed against us or our royal father before the publication of this, shall ever rise in judgment, or be brought in question, against any of them, to the least endamagement of them, either in their lives, liberties or estates, or (as far forth as lies in our power) so much as to the prejudice of their reputations, by any reproach or term of distinction from the rest of our best subjects; we desiring and ordaining that henceforth all notes of discord, separation and difference of parties be utterly abolished among all our subjects, whom we invite and conjure to a perfect union among themselves, under our protection, for the resettlement of our just rights and theirs in a free Parliament, by which, upon the word of a King, we will be advised.

And because the passion and uncharitableness of the times have produced several opinions in religion by which men are engaged in parties and animosities against each other (which, when they shall hereafter unite in a freedom of conversation, will be composed or better understood), we do declare a liberty to tender consciences, and that no man shall be disquieted or called in question for differences of opinion in matter of religion which do not disturb the peace of the kingdom; and that we shall be ready to consent to such an Act of Parliament as, upon mature deliberation, shall be offered to us, for the full granting that indulgence.

And because, in the continued distractions of so many years, and so many and great revolutions, many grants and purchases of estates have been made to and by many officers, soldiers and others who are now possessed of the same, and who may be liable to actions at law upon several titles, we are likewise willing that all such differences, and all things relating to such grants, sales and purchases, shall be determined in Parliament, which can best provide for the just satisfaction of all men who are concerned.

And we do further declare that we will be ready to consent to any Act or Acts of Parliament to the purposes aforesaid, and for the full satisfaction of all arrears due to the officers and soldiers of the army under the command of General Monk; and that they shall be received into our service upon as good pay and conditions as they now enjoy.

Given under our Sign Manual and Privy Signet, at Our Court at Breda, this 4 day of April, 1660, in the twelfth year of our reign.

S. R. Gardiner, *Constitutional Documents of the English Revolution* (*1628–1660*) (Oxford: Oxford University Press, 1889), pp. 351–52. (Reprinted by permission of the publisher.)

The Bill of Rights (1689) was supposed to make sure that royal absolutism would not recur at the expense of the Parliament, and to guarantee certain basic legal rights to the subjects. As such, it is the great document which closes the age of revolution in England.

50   . . . And thereupon the said lords spiritual and temporal, and Commons, pursuant to their respective letters and elections, being now assembled in a full and free representation of this nation, taking into their most serious consideration the best means for attaining the ends aforesaid, do in the first place (as their ancestors in like case have usually done), for the vindicating and asserting their ancient rights and liberties, declare:

1. That the pretended power of suspending laws, or the execution of laws, by regal authority, without consent of parliament, is illegal.

2. That the pretended power of dispensing with laws, or the execution of laws, by regal authority, as it has been assumed and exercised of late, is illegal.

3. That levying money for or to the use of the crown by pretense of prerogative, without grant of parliament, for longer time or in other manner, that the same is or shall be granted, is illegal.

4. That it is the right of subjects to petition the king, and all commitments and prosecutions for such petitioning are illegal.

5. That the raising or keeping a standing army within the kingdom in time of peace, unless it be with consent of parliament, is against law.

6. That the subjects which are Protestants may have arms for their defense suitable to their conditions, and as allowed by law.

7. That election of members of parliament ought to be free.

8. That the freedom of speech, and debates of proceedings in parliament, ought not to be impeached or questioned in any court or place out of parliament.

9. That excessive bail ought not to be required, nor excessive fines imposed, nor cruel and unusual punishments inflicted.

10. That jurors ought to be fully impaneled and returned, and jurors which pass upon men in trials for high treason ought to be freeholders.

11. That all grants and promises of fines and forfeitures of particular persons before conviction are illegal and void.

12. And that for redress of all grievances, and for the amending, strengthening, and preserving of the laws, parliament ought to be held frequently.

And they do claim, demand, and insist upon all and singular premises, as their undoubted rights and liberties; and that no declarations, judgments, doings, or proceedings, to the prejudice of the people in any of the said premises, ought in any wise to be drawn hereafter into consequence or example.

To which demand of their rights they are particularly encouraged by the declaration of his Highness the prince of Orange as being the only means for obtaining a full redress and remedy therein.

Statutes of Realm, VI.

John Locke (1632–1704) justified the rights of liberty and property as over against government and society. He advocated the kind of government which those who made the Bill of Rights hoped for. The following extract is from his *Of Civil Government* (1690).

51   If man in the state of Nature be so free as has been said, if he be absolute lord of his own person and possessions, equal to the greatest and subject to nobody, why will he part with his freedom . . . and subject himself to the dominion and control of any other Power? To which it is obvious to answer that though in the state of Nature he has such a right, yet the enjoyment of it is very uncertain and constantly exposed to the invasion of others; for all being kings as much as he, every man his equal, and the greater part no strict observers of equity and justice, the enjoyment of the property he has in this state is very unsafe, very insecure. This makes him willing to quit this condition which, however free, is full of fears and continual dangers; and it is not without reason that he seeks out and is willing to join in society with others who are already united, or have a mind to unite for the mutual preservation of their lives, liberties and estates, which I call by the general name—property.

The great and chief end, therefore, of men uniting into commonwealths and putting themselves under government, is the preservation of their property; to which in the state of Nature there are many other things wanting.

First, there wants an established, settled, known law, received and allowed by common consent to be the standard of right and wrong, and the common measure to decide all controversies between them. For though the law of Nature be plain and intelligible to all rational creatures, yet men, being biased by their interest, as well as ignorant for want of study of it, are apt to allow of it as a law binding to them in the application of it to their particular cases.

Secondly, in the state of Nature there wants a known and indifferent judge, with authority to determine all differences according to the established law. For every one in that state being both judge and executioner of the law of Nature, men being partial to themselves, passion and revenge is very apt to carry them too far, and with too much heat in their own cases, as well as negligence and unconcernedness, makes them too remiss in other men's.

Thirdly, in the state of Nature there often wants power to back and support the sentence when right and to give it due execution. They who by an injustice offended will seldom fail where they are able by force to make good their injustice. Such resistance many times makes the punishment dangerous, and frequently destructive to those who attempt it.

Thus mankind, notwithstanding all the privileges of the state of Nature, being but in an ill condition while they remain in it are quickly driven into society. . . . It is this makes them so willingly give up every one his single power of punishing to be exercised by such alone as shall be appointed to it amongst them, and by such rules as the community, or those authorized by them, to that purpose shall agree on. And in this we have the original right and rise of both the legislative and executive power as well of the governments and societies themselves.

For in the state of Nature, to omit the liberty he has of innocent delights, a man has two powers. The first is to do whatsoever he thinks fit for the preservation of himself and others within the permission of the law of Nature; by which law, common to them all, he and all the rest of mankind are one community, make up one society distinct from all other creatures, and were it not for the corruption and viciousness of degenerate men, there would be no need of any other, no necessity that men should separate from this great and natural community, and associate into lesser combinations. The other power a man has in the state of Nature is the power to punish the crimes committed against that law. Both these he gives up when he joins in a . . . particular political society, and incorporates into any commonwealth separate from the rest of mankind.

The first power—viz., of doing whatsoever he thought fit for the preservation of himself and the rest of mankind, he gives up to be regulated by laws made by the society, so far forth as the preservation of himself and the rest of that society shall require; which laws of the society in many things confine the liberty he had by the law of Nature.

Secondly, the power of punishing he wholly gives up, and engages his natural force, which he might before employ in the execution of the law of Nature, by his own single authority, as he thought fit, to assist the executive power of the society as the law thereof shall require. For being now in a new state, wherein he is to enjoy many conveniences from the labor, assistance, and society of others in the same community, as well as protection from its whole strength, he is to part also with as much of his natural liberty, in providing for himself, as the good, prosperity, and safety of the society shall require, which is not only necessary but just, since the other members of the society do the like.

But though men when they enter into society give up the equality, liberty, and executive power they had in the state of Nature into the hands of the society, to be so far disposed of by the legislative as the good of the

society shall require, yet it being only with an intention in every one to preserve himself, his liberty and property (for no rational creature can be supposed to change his condition with an intention to be worse), the power of
the society or legislative constituted by them can never be supposed to extend
farther than the common good, but is obliged to secure every one's property
by providing against those three defects above mentioned that made the
state of Nature so unsafe and uneasy. And so, whoever has the legislative
or supreme power of any commonwealth, is bound to govern by established
standing laws, promulgated and known to the people, and not by extempo-
rary decrees, by indifferent and upright judges, who are to decide controversies by those laws; and to employ the force of the community at home
only in the execution of such laws, or abroad to prevent or redress foreign
injuries and secure the community from inroads and invasion. And all this
to be directed to no other end but the peace, safety, and public good of the
people.

John Locke, *Of Civil Government* (London, 1690), II, 345–50.

The political theory of Thomas Hobbes (1588–1679) was much different from that of John Locke. The Revolution and the Civil War led
Hobbes to believe that absolutism was the way to overcome the evil of
man and that men would gladly contract away their "rights" for the
sake of peace. The following are extracts from his *Leviathan* (see Job
41 in the Bible), one of the first thoroughgoing and modern justifica-
tions for absolutism (1651).

52   . . . So that in the nature of man we find three principal causes of quarrel. First, competition; second, diffidence; thirdly, glory.

The first maketh men invade for gain; the second, for safety; and the
third, for reputation. The first use violence, to make themselves masters of
other men's persons, wives, children, and cattle; the second, to defend them;
the third, for trifles, as a word, a smile, a different opinion, and any other
sign of undervalue, either direct in their persons or by reflection in their
kindred, their friends, their nation, their profession, or their name.

Hereby it is manifest that during the time men live without a common
power to keep them all in awe, they are in that condition which is called
war; and such a war, as is of every man, against every man. For WAR
consisteth not in battle only, or the act of fighting; but in a tract of time,
wherein the will to contend by battle is sufficiently known: and therefore
the notion of *time* is to be considered in the nature of war, as it is in the nature of weather. For as the nature of foul weather lieth not in a shower or
two of rain but in an inclination thereto of many days together; so the nature

of war consisteth not in actual fighting, but in the known disposition thereto during all the time there is no assurance to the contrary. All other time is PEACE.

Whatsoever therefore is consequent to a time of war, where every man is enemy to every man; the same is consequent to the time, wherein men live without other security than what their own strength and their own invention shall furnish them withal. In such condition there is no place for industry because the fruit thereof is uncertain and consequently no culture of the earth; no navigation nor use of the commodities that may be imported by sea; no commodious building; no instruments of moving, and removing, such things as require much force; no knowledge of the face of the earth; no account of time; no arts, no letters, no society; and which is worst of all, continual fear, and danger of violent death; and the life of man, solitary, poor, nasty, brutish, and short.

A *commonwealth* is said to be *instituted* when a *multitude* of men do agree and *covenant, every one with every one,* that to whatsoever *man,* or *assembly of men,* shall be given by the major part, the *right* to *present* the person of them all, that is to say, to be their *representative;* every one, as well he that *voted for it* as he that *voted against it,* shall *authorize* all the actions and judgments of that man, or assembly of men, in the same manner as if they were his own, to the end to live peaceably amongst themselves, and be protected against other men.

From this institution of a commonwealth are derived all the *rights,* and *faculties* of him, or them, on whom sovereign power is conferred by the consent of the people assembled.

First, because they covenant, it is to be understood they are not obliged by former covenant to anything repugnant hereunto. And consequently they that have already instituted a commonwealth, being thereby bound by covenant, to own the action and judgments of one, cannot lawfully make a new covenant amongst themselves, to be obedient to any other in anything whatsoever, without his permission. And therefore, they that are subject to a monarch cannot without his leave cast off monarchy and return to the confusion of a disunited multitude nor transfer their person from him that beareth it to another man, or other assembly of men: for they are bound, every man to every man, to own and be reputed author of all that he that already is their sovereign shall do and judge fit to be done; so that any one man dissenting, all the rest should break their covenant made to that man, which is injustice; and they have also every man given the sovereignty to him that beareth their person; and therefore if they depose him, they take from him that which is his own, and so again it is injustice. . . .

That he which is made sovereign maketh no covenant with his subjects beforehand, is manifest; because either he must make it with the whole multitude, as one party to the covenant; or he must make a several covenant with every man. With the whole, as one part, it is impossible because as yet they are not one person: and if he make so many several covenants as there be men, those covenants after he hath the sovereignty are void, because what act soever can be pretended by any one of them for breach thereof is the act both of himself and of all the rest, because done in the person, and by the right of every one of them in particular. Besides, if any one, or more of them, pretend a breach of the covenant made by the sovereign at his institution, and others, or one other of his subjects, or himself alone, pretend there was no such breach, there is in this case no judge to decide the controversy; it returns therefore to the sword again and every man recovereth the right of protecting himself by his own strength, contrary to the design they had in the institution. It is therefore in vain to grant sovereignty by way of precedent covenant. The opinion that any monarch receiveth his power by covenant, that is to say, on condition, proceedeth from want of understanding this easy truth, that covenants being but words and breath, have no force to oblige, contain, constrain, or protect any man but what it has from the public sword. . . .

Thirdly, because the major part hath by consenting voices declared a sovereign; he that dissented must now consent with the rest. . . .

Fourthly, because every subject is by this institution author of all the action and judgments of the sovereign instituted; it follows that whatsoever he doth, it can be no injury to any of his subjects; nor ought he to be by any of them accused of injustice. . . .

Fifthly, and consequently to that which was said last, no man that hath sovereign power can justly be put to death. . . . For seeing every subject is author of the actions of his sovereign, he punisheth another for the actions committed by himself. . . .

Sixthly, it is annexed to the sovereignty to be judge of what opinions and doctrines are averse, and what conducive to peace. . . .

Seventhly, it is annexed to the sovereignty the whole power of prescribing the rules whereby every man may know what goods he may enjoy, and what actions he may do . . . and this is it men call *propriety*. . . . These rules of propriety . . . are the civil laws; that is to say, the laws of each commonwealth in particular. . . .

Eighthly, is annexed to the sovereignty the right of judicature; that is to say, of hearing and deciding all controversies which may arise concerning law, either civil or natural, or concerning fact. . . .

Ninthly, is annexed to the sovereignty the right of making war and peace with other nations and commonwealths; that is to say, of judging when it is for the public good. . . .

Tenthly, . . . the choosing of all counsellors, ministers, magistrates, and officers both in peace and war. . . .

Eleventhly, to the sovereign is committed the power of rewarding with riches, or honors, and of punishing with corporal or pecuniary punishment, or with ignominy, every subject according to the law he hath formerly made. . . .

Lastly, considering what value men are naturally apt to set upon themselves; what respect they look for from others; and how little they value other men; from whence continually arise amongst them emulation, quarrels, factions, and at last war, to the destroying of one another and diminution of their strength against a common enemy; it is necessary that there be laws of honor, and a public rate of the worth of such men as have deserved, or are able to deserve well of the commonwealth. . . . To the sovereign therefore it belongeth also to give titles of honor; and to appoint what order of place and dignity each man shall hold, and what signs of respect in public or private meetings they shall give to one another. . . .

The Works of Thomas Hobbes, ed. Sir William Molesworth (London, 1839), III, 111–13, 159–67.

The successful outcome of the "Glorious Revolution" resulted from the combined action of both Whigs and Tories, but the Whigs, who drew an important element of their support from the merchant class and the "city men" (financiers), gained political ascendancy in the years immediately following 1689. Their political opponents sought to show that the alliance of the Whigs with the "monied interests" was a source of corruption and fraud. The following selection, written after a decade of Whig rule, is a stinging satire which purports to relate a conversation between two ardent Whigs, "Mr. Whiglove" and "Mr. Double."

53

Do. I know 'em [the ministers of the government] inside and outside; I am Master of all their private Affairs; I am privy to all the Corruption in their respective Offices; most of their Bribes went through my Hands; I know the bottom of the Transaction with Michael Godfrey, when the Bank of England was set up; I was the Go-between when the New East-India Company was erected. . . . The Knowledge of these and many other Things makes me fear'd and vallu'd by the whole Party. And take this for a Rule, if you would be respected by Great Men, you must wind yourself into all their dangerous Secrets. Besides, I have good store of Mony in my Pocket; and he who has that shall be esteem'd and courted, let his Birth be never so mean, or his Life never so infamous.

Wh. This has been a happy Revolution to you, Mr. Double, for if I am not misinform'd, Matters are well mended with you of late Years.

Do. They are so, Thanks to my Industry. I am now worth Fifty thousand Pound, and fourteen years ago I had not Shoes to my Feet.

Wh. This is a strange and sudden Rise.

Do. Alas 'tis nothing, I can name you fifty of our Friends who have got much better Fortunes since the Revolution, and from as poor beginnings.

Wh. It would serve as a good Instruction if you would please to let me know how you did rise in the World. I am a Gentleman born to some Fortune and have good Relations, yet I can do nothing, and rather grow worse than better in my Estate, notwithstanding that all along I have been as hearty a Whig as the best of you.

Do. That's true, but you have always been a Whig out of Principle, and we have no regard for such People at all, they are Volunteers that will serve us for nothing; we value none but those who are Whigs out of Interest, and who . . . are ready to do anything, Good, Bad, or Indifferent, that may promote our Designs. . . . The Malt-Duty, the Window-Tax, and the Tax upon Births, Burials, and Marriages, were the Off-springs of my Brain. You had never had the Bank of England if I had not introduced Michael Godfrey to the Acquaintance of Charles M——e. Without me S——S——d had never got his New East-India Company. . . .

Wh. I always understood that we Whigs had been the Divisers of the new Taxes and remote Funds [public debts], but did not know till now the share you have had in it.

Do. I have done my Part, and I think I have reason to pretend to a great deal of Merit. For what had become of our Party if it had not been for these Projects? 'Tis true, we have run the Nation over Head and Ears in debt by our Funds, and new Devices, but mark what a Dependance upon our Noble Friends [the Government] this way of raising Mony has occasion'd. Who is it stick to 'em but those who are concerned in Tallies and the new Stocks? The plain Country Gentleman, who has nothing to trust to but his Estate, is for having em call'd to an Account for robbing the Nation, but we, who through their Means, have so many Years got fifteen and twenty per cent for our Mony, and who by their Help have had so many other ways of raising our Selves, Cry up their Innocence, and long to see 'em again at the Helm, that under their Countenance and Protection we may once more fleece the Kingdom. Take this for a Rule, if you see any

Man very hot for 'em in the Country, he or his Relations are engag'd in the Annuities; and they whom he hear roaring so for 'em in the City, are such as have Stock-jobb'd Tallies at 30, or 40 per Cent Profit. For we have taken Care to insinuate to all those who have dealt with the Exchequer that the Eighteen Millions England now owes will spread this about in the Country as you Travel. . . .

Wh. I must confess we are very much departed from the Principles we profess'd twenty Years ago. But pray tell me of what sort of Persons does our Party consist at present, for we still call our selves Whigs?

Do. 'Tis not so easy as you imagine to describe the strange Medly of which we are now compos'd, but I shall do my best to let you into the Secret. First, you must know there are some Men of true Worth and Honour that still continue among us; why I can't guess. . . . The Bulk of our Party consists of those who are of any Side where they can best make their Markets; such sort of Men naturally like the Whigs most, because ours was a negligent weak Administration. . . .

Charles Davenant, *The True Picture of a Modern Whig, Set forth in a Dialogue between Mr. Whiglove and Mr. Double, Two Under-Spur-Leathers to the Late Ministry* (London, 1701), pp. 14–15, 25–26, 37–38.

QUESTIONS

1. What rights were the Commons defending in their Apology of 1604?
2. What would have been James I's criticism of the demands of the House of Commons?
3. Compare James I's concept of the divine right of kings with Bishop Bossuet's (p. 102).
4. What made Oliver Cromwell so sure that God was with the army against Parliament?
5. Why did Cromwell think that the army was a lawful power to oppose the King?
6. List the points made in the arguments for and against toleration.
7. What concrete concessions does Charles II grant in his Declaration of Breda?
8. In what way does the Bill of Rights fulfill the aspirations which the House of Commons put forward in the Apology of 1604?
9. What rights of the state of nature does man give up, according to John Locke, when he enters into society? Why does he give up these rights?
10. What are the limits of government according to Locke? How does he justify limiting government in this way?

11. What is Hobbes's view of human nature and how does this fit in with his theory of government?

12. What does Hobbes mean when he says that every subject is the author of all the sovereign's actions?

13. When does every man recover the right to protect himself by the sword?

14. Contrast the ideas of Hobbes and Locke.

15. In what specific ways are the Whigs accused of making economic gain from the revolution?

CHAPTER VIII

THE RISE OF SCIENCE

DURING the sixteenth and seventeenth centuries the rise of science introduced a new directive force into our civilization. To be sure, there had been scientific endeavor during the Middle Ages and the Renaissance, but the stepped-up pace of scientific discoveries during these centuries begins the "Scientific Age."

These scientific discoveries were carried on through academies, or societies, which stood outside the established and more traditionally-minded universities. "The Royal Society of London, for the Improving of Natural Knowledge," became the most famous of these societies. Bishop Thomas Sprat, who was a member, describes its origins (54). He also shows us the attitude of mind which underlay this scientific endeavor, an attitude which struck him as "new" and opposed to older ways of searching for the truth. This new outlook was one of the most important results of the "Scientific Revolution," as it is sometimes called. It meant a new way of looking at religion; a new world view which found its culmination in the Enlightenment (see p. 151).

The man who, in the seventeenth century, best typifies the influence of the rise of science on man's thought is René Descartes. Disillusioned with the traditional search for truth, he wrote his *Discourse on Method*, which put forward a "system" of thought based on the radical search for "proof" (55). This "Cartesianism" was to be of lasting influence in translating the kind of scientific method which Sprat describes into a new view of man and the universe.

Thomas Sprat (1636–1713), Bishop of Rochester, wrote the first history of the Royal Society (1667). He describes how the Society started during the English Civil War with informal meetings at Oxford (1640). It was not until 1662 that the Society was officially incorporated.

54   Their first Purpose was no more than only the Satisfaction of breathing a freer Air, and of conversing in Quiet one with another, without being ingag'd in the Passions and Madness of that dismal Age. And from the Institution of that Assembly, it had been enough if no other Advantage had come but this: That by this means there was a Race of young Men provided against the next Age, whose Minds receiving from them their first Impressions of sober and generous Knowledge, were invincibly arm'd against all the Inchantments of Enthusiasm. . . . For such a candid and unpassionate Company, as that was, and for such a gloomy Season, what could have been a fitter Subject to pitch upon than Natural Philosophy? To have been always tossing about some Theological Question, would have been, to have made that their private Diversion, the Excess of which they themselves disliked in the publick: To have been eternally musing on Civil Business, and the Distresses of their country, was too melancholy a Reflexion: It was Nature alone, which could pleasantly entertain them in that estate. The contemplation of that, draws our Minds off from past, or present misfortunes, and makes them Conquerors over Things, in the greatest public Unhappiness: While the Consideration of Men and human Affairs, may affect us with a thousand various disquiets; that never separates us into moral Factions; that gives us room to differ, without anomosity; and permits us to raise contrary Imaginations upon it, without any Danger of a Civil War. . . .

Their Meetings were as frequent, as their Affairs permitted: their Proceedings rather by Action, than Discourse; chiefly attending some particular Trials, in Chemistry or Mechanics: they had no Rules nor Method fix'd: their Intention was more to communicate to each other their Discoveries, which they could make in so narrow a Compass, than as united, constant, or regular Inquisition. And me thinks, their Constitution did bear some resemblance to the Academy lately begun at Paris: where they have at last turn'd their Thoughts from Words to experimental Philosophy, and perhaps in Imitation of the Royal Society. Their Manner likewise, is to assemble in a private

House, to reason freely upon the Works of Nature; to pass conjectures, and propose Problems, on any Mathematical, or Philosophical Matter, which comes in their Way. And this is an Omen, on which I will build some Hope, that as they agree with us in what was done at Oxford, so they will go on farther, and come by the same degrees, to erect another Royal Society in France. I promise for these Gentlemen here (so well I know the Generosity of their Design) they will be most ready to accept their Assistance. To them, and to all the Learned World besides, they call for Aid. No difference of Country, Interest, or Profession of Religion, will make them backward from taking or affording Help in this Enterprise. And indeed all Europe, at this time, have two general Wars, which they ought in Honour to make; the one a holy, the other a philosophical: The one against the common Enemy of Christendom, the other also against powerful and barbarous Foes, that have not been fully subdued almost these six thousand Years, Ignorance, and false Opinions. Against these, it becomes us, to go forth in one common Expedition: All civil Nations joining their Armies against the one, and their Reason against the other; without any petty Contentions about Privileges, or Prudence. . . .

I will here, in the first place, contract into few Words, the whole Sum of their Resolutions; which I shall often have occasion to touch upon in Parcels. Their Purpose is, in short, to make faithful Records of all the Works of Nature, or Art, which can come within their Reach; that so the present Age, and Posterity, may be able to put a Mark on the Errors, which have been strengthened by long prescription; to restore the Truths, that have lain neglected; to push on those, which are already known, to more various Uses; and to make the way more passable, to what remains unrevealed. This is the Compass of their Design. And to accomplish this, they have endeavoured, to separate the Knowledge of Nature, from the Colours of Rhetoric, the Devices of Fancy, or the delightful Deceit of Fables. They have labour'd to enlarge it, from being confined to the Custody of a few, or from Servitude to private Interests. They have striven to preserve it from being overpress'd by a confus'd Heap of vain and useless Particulars; or from being straightened and bound too much up by general Doctrines. They have tried to put it into a Condition of perpetual Increasing; by settling an inviolable Correspondence between the Hand and the Brain. They have studied to make it not only an Enterprise of one Season, or of some lucky Opportunity; but a Business of Time; a steady, a lasting, a popular, an uninterrupted Work. They have attempted, to free it from the Artifice, and Humours, and Passions of Sects: to render it an Instrument, whereby Mankind may obtain a Dominion over Things, and not only over one another's judgments: And lastly, they have begun to establish these Reformations in Philosophy, not so much, by any solemnity of Laws, or Ostentation of Ceremonies, as by solid Practice and Examples; not by a glorious pomp of Words; but by the silent, effectual, and unanswerable Arguments of real Productions. . . .

And now, to come to a Close of the second Part of the Narration: The Society has reduc'd its principal Observations, into one common Stock; and laid them up in Public Registers, to be nakedly transmitted to the next Generation of Men; and so from them, to their Successors. And as their Purpose was, to heap up a mixed mass of Experiments, without digesting them into any perfect Model; so to this End, they confin'd themselves to no order of Subjects; and whatever they have recorded, they have done it, not as complete Schemes of Opinions, but as bare unfinish'd Histories. . . .

In the Order of their Inquisitions, they have been so free, that they have sometimes committed themselves to be guided, according to the Seasons of the Year; sometimes, according to what any Foreigner, or English Artificer, being present, has suggested; sometimes, according to any extraordinary Accident in the Nation, or any other Casualty, which has happened in their Way. By which roving and unsettled course, there being seldom any Reference of one Matter to the next; they have prevented others, nay even their own Hands, from corrupting or contracting the Work; they have made the raising of Rules and Propositions, to be a far more difficult Task, than it would have been, if their Registers had been more Methodical. Nor ought this Neglect of Consequence and Order, to be only thought to proceed from their carelessness; but from a mature and well grounded Premeditation. For it is certain, that a too sudden Striving to reduce the Sciences, in their Beginnings, into Method, and Shape, and Beauty, has very much retarded their Increase. And it happens to the Invention of Arts, as to Children in their younger Years; in whose Bodies, the same Applications, that serve to make them strait, slender, and comely, are often found very mischievous, to their Ease, their Strength, and their Growth. . . .

By their fair, and equal, and submissive way of Registering nothing but Histories, and Relations; they have left room for others, that shall succeed, to change, to augment, to approve, to contradict them at their discretion. By this, they have given Posterity a far greater Power of judging them, than ever they took over those that went before them. By this, they have made a firm Confederacy, between their own present Labours, and the Industry of future ages; which how beneficial it will prove hereafter, we cannot better guess, than by recollecting, what Wonders it would in all likelihood have produc'd e'er this, if it had been begun in the Times of the Greeks, or Romans, or Schoolmen; nay even in the last Resurrection of learning. What

Depth of Nature could by this Time have been hid from our View? What Faculty of the Soul would have been in the dark? What Part of human Infirmities not provided against? If our Predecessors, a thousand, nay even a hundred Years ago, had begun to add by little and little to the Store, if they would have endeavour'd to be Benefactors, and not Tyrants over our Reasons; if they would have communicated to us, more of their Works, and less of their Wit. . . .

Thomas Sprat, *The History of the Royal Society of London, for the Improving of Natural Knowledge* (London, 1734), pp. 53, 55–57, 61–62, 115–16.

René Descartes (1596–1650) wrote the *Discourse on the Method of Rightly Conducting the Reason and Seeking Truth in the Sciences* (1637). In this, his most famous work, he describes his important new method and how he came to adopt it.

. . . My present design, then, is not to teach the Method which each **55** ought to follow for the right conduct of his Reason, but solely to describe the way in which I have endeavoured to conduct my own. They who set themselves to give precepts must of course regard themselves as possessed of greater skill than those to whom they prescribe; and if they err in the slightest particular, they subject themselves to censure. But as this Tract is put forth merely as a history, or, if you will, as a tale, in which, amid some examples worthy of imitation, there will be found, perhaps, as many more which it were advisable not to follow, I hope it will prove useful to some without being hurtful to any, and that my openness will find some favour with all.

From my childhood, I have been familiar with letters; and as I was given to believe that by their help a clear and certain knowledge of all that is useful in life might be acquired, I was ardently desirous of instruction. But as soon as I had finished the entire course of study, at the close of which it is customary to be admitted into the order of the learned, I completely changed my opinion. For I found myself involved in so many doubts and errors, that I was convinced I had advanced no farther in all my attempts at learning, than the discovery at every turn of my own ignorance. And yet I was studying in one of the most celebrated Schools in Europe, in which I thought there must be learned men, if such were anywhere to be found. I had been taught all that others learned there; and not contented with the sciences actually taught us, I had, in addition, read all the books that had fallen into my hands, treating of such branches as are esteemed the most curious and rare. I knew the judgment which others had formed of me;

and I did not find that I was considered inferior to my fellows, although there were among them some who were already marked out to fill the places of our instructors. And, in fine, our age appeared to me as flourishing, and as fertile in powerful minds as any preceding one. I was thus led to take the liberty of judging of all other men by myself, and of concluding that there was no science in existence that was of such a nature as I had previously been given to believe. . . . And, in fine, of false Sciences I thought I knew the worth sufficiently to escape being deceived by the professions of an alchemist, the predictions of an astrologer, the impostures of a magician, or by the artifices and boasting of any of those who profess to know things of which they are ignorant.

For these reasons, as soon as my age permitted me to pass from under the control of my instructors, I entirely abandoned the study of letters, and resolved no longer to seek any other science than the knowledge of myself, or of the great book of the world. I spent the remainder of my youth in travelling, in visiting courts and armies, in holding intercourse with men of different dispositions and ranks, in collecting varied experience, in proving myself in the different situations into which fortune threw me, and, above all, in making such reflection on the matter of my experience as to secure my improvement. For it occurred to me that I should find much more truth in the reasonings of each individual with reference to the affairs in which he is personally interested, and the issue of which must presently punish him if he has judged amiss, than in those conducted by a man of letters in his study, regarding speculative matters that are of no practical moment, and followed by no consequences to himself, farther, perhaps, than that they foster his vanity the better the more remote they are from common sense; requiring, as they must in this case, the exercise of greater ingenuity and art to render them probable. In addition, I had always a most earnest desire to know how to distinguish the true from the false, in order that I might be able clearly to discriminate the right path in life, and proceed in it with confidence. . . .

It is true that, while busied only in considering the manners of other men, I found here, too, scarce any ground for settled conviction, and re-marked hardly less contradiction among them than in the opinions of the philosophers. So that the greatest advantage I derived from the study con-sisted in this, that, observing many things which, however extravagant and ridiculous to our apprehension, are yet by common consent received and approved by other great nations, I learned to entertain too decided a belief in regard to nothing of the truth of which I had been persuaded merely by example and custom: and thus I gradually extricated myself from many errors powerful enough to darken our Natural Intelligence, and incapacitate us in great measure from listening to Reason. But after I had been occupied several years in thus studying the book of the world, and in essaying to gather some experience, I at length resolved to make myself an object of study, and to employ all the powers of my mind in choosing the paths I ought to follow; an undertaking which was accompanied with greater suc- cess than it would have been had I never quitted my country or my books. . . .

And as a multitude of laws often only hampers justice, so that a state is best governed when, with few laws, these are rigidly administered; in like manner, instead of the great number of precepts of which Logic is composed, I believed that the four following would prove perfectly sufficient for me, provided I took the firm and unwavering resolution never in a single instance to fail in observing them. . . .

The *first* was never to accept anything for true which I did not clearly know to be such; that is to say, carefully to avoid precipitancy and prejudice, and to comprise nothing more in my judgment than what was presented to my mind so clearly and distinctly as to exclude all ground of doubt. . . .

The *second,* to divide each of the difficulties under examination into as many parts as possible, and as might be necessary for its adequate solution. . . .

The *third,* to conduct my thoughts in such order that, by commencing with objects the simplest and easiest to know, I might ascend by little and little, and, as it were, step by step, to the knowledge of the more complex; assigning in thought a certain order even to those objects which in their own nature do not stand in a relation of antecedence and sequence. . . .

And the *last,* in every case to make enumerations so complete, and re- views so general, that I might be assured that nothing was omitted. . . .

René Descartes, *Discourse on the Method of Rightly Conducting the Reason and Seeking Truth in the Sciences* (London: Blackwood and Son, 1873), pp. 47–48, 52–53, 61.

Descartes's argument for the existence of God was to be of great importance to future thinkers. Especially the men of the Enlighten- ment were to follow his reasoning which leads to "deism."

. . . Finally, if there be still persons who are not sufficiently persuaded of **56** the existence of God and of the soul, by the reasons I have adduced, I am desirous that they should know that all the other propositions, of the truth of which they deem themselves perhaps more assured, as that we have a body, and that there exist stars and an earth, and such like, are less certain;

for, although we have a moral assurance of these things, which is so strong that there is an appearance of extravagance in doubting of their existence, yet at the same time no one, unless his intellect is impaired, can deny, when the question relates to a metaphysical certitude, that there is sufficient reason to exclude entire assurance, in the observation that when asleep we can in the same way imagine ourselves possessed of another body and that we see other stars and another earth, when there is nothing of the kind. For how do we know that the thoughts which occur in dreaming are false rather than those other which we experience when awake, since the former are often not less vivid and distinct than the latter? And though men of the highest genius study this question as long as they please, I do not believe that they will be able to give any reason which can be sufficient to remove this doubt, unless they presuppose the existence of God. For, in the first place, even the principle which I have already taken as a rule, viz., that all the things which we clearly and distinctly conceive are true, is certain only because God is or exists, and because he is a Perfect Being, and because all that we possess is derived from him: whence it follows that our ideas or notions, which to the extent of their clearness and distinctness are real, and proceed from God, must to that extent be true. Accordingly, whereas we not infrequently have ideas or notions in which some falsity is contained, this can only be the case with such as are to some extent confused and obscure, and in this proceed from nothing, (participate of negation,) that is, exist in us thus confused because we are not wholly perfect. And it is evident that it is not less repugnant that falsity or imperfection, in so far as it is imperfection, should proceed from God, than that truth or perfection should proceed from nothing. But if we did not know that all which we possess of real and true proceeds from a Perfect and Infinite Being, however clear and distinct our ideas might be, we should have no ground on that account for the assurance that they possessed the perfection of being true.

Ibid., pp. 80–81.

QUESTIONS

1. What was the method by which the Royal Society hoped to "restore the Truths"?
2. Why did the men of the Royal Society neglect "consequence and order," and what did they hope to gain by this?
3. What criticism of general dogmas does Sprat imply?
4. What, for Descartes, is the only true method of arriving at a judgment?

5. Compare and contrast the method of Descartes with that adopted by the Royal Society as described by Sprat.
6. Why does Descartes think it less certain that we have a body than that God exists?
7. Why, for Descartes, does the presupposition of the existence of God remove doubt?

CHAPTER IX

LOUIS XIV (1638-1715)

LOUIS XIV (1638–1715) has always been regarded as the out-standing example of an absolute monarch. His own statements of political philosophy (58) (and those of Bossuet (59) which found favor at his court) show that he regarded himself as such.

Within France, the centralization symbolized by the Intendants of Richelieu (57) was tightened still further. The army and navy were strengthened. Under Colbert's direction new industries were built up and old ones regulated, while trade and colonies received much attention (60). The Huguenots, whose position had been guaranteed by the Edict of Nantes in 1598, now came to be regarded as a political menace and were actively persecuted in the interests of uniformity.

But the King was primarily interested in foreign affairs. With his powerful armed forces and an expert diplomatic corps as his instruments, he used every opportunity to aggrandize his country and increase his own fame. While he made some successful advances toward achieving Richelieu's ideal of "natural frontiers" for France, the scope of his ambitions and the nature of his methods made his aims seem to his contemporaries quite unlimited. There grew up against him successive coalitions, in which England and Holland came to play a leading part.

The extent of Louis's absolutism and of his success must not be exaggerated. His ambitions abroad suffered checks. At home, traditional institutions, local privileges, and inefficiency of administration hampered his policy and imposed practical limitations to his power. These, together with his overweening pride and spendthrift nature, contributed to the decline of France under his less able successors.

Much of the power and glory of the reign of Louis XIV came from the careful labors of Louis XIII's first great minister, Cardinal Richelieu (in office 1624–42)—a man with a nerve of steel in a frail and sickly body. His goals, outlined in the following document from his own pen and intended to guide his successors, became the dominant features of French internal and external policy.

When your Majesty resolved to admit me both to your council and to an important place in your confidence for the direction of your affairs, I may say that the Huguenots shared the state with you; that the nobles conducted themselves as if they were not your subjects, and the most powerful governors of the provinces as if they were sovereign in their offices. **57**

I may say that the bad example of all of these was so prejudicial to this realm that even the best courts were affected by it, and endeavored, in certain cases, to diminish your legitimate authority as far as it was possible in order to carry their own powers beyond the limits of reason.

I may say that every one measured his own merit by his audacity; that in place of estimating the benefits which they received from your Majesty at their proper worth, they all valued them only as they satisfied the demands of their imagination; that the most scheming were held to be the wisest, and often found themselves the most prosperous.

I may further say that the foreign alliances were unfortunate, particular interests being preferred to those of the public, and in a word, the dignity of the royal majesty was so disparaged, and so different from what it should be, because of the misdeeds of those who conducted your affairs, that it was almost impossible to recognize it. It was impossible, without losing all, to tolerate longer the conduct of those to whom your Majesty had intrusted the helm of state; and yet everything could not be changed at once without violating the laws of prudence, which do not permit the passing from one extreme to another without preparation.

The bad state of your affairs seemed to force you to precipitate decisions, without a choice of time or of means. And yet it was necessary to make a choice of both, in order to profit by the change which necessity demanded of your prudence.

The best minds did not think that it would be possible to pass without shipwreck all the rocks in such uncertain times. The court was full of people who censured the temerity of those who wished to undertake a reform, and all well knew that princes find it easy to impute to those who are near them the bad outcome of the undertakings upon which they have been well advised; few people consequently expected good results from the change which it was announced that I wished to make, and many held my fall assured even before your Majesty had elevated me.

Notwithstanding these difficulties which I explained to your Majesty, knowing how much kings may do when they make good use of their power, I dared to promise you, with assurance, that you would soon find remedies for the disorders in your state, and that your prudence, your courage, and the benediction of God would give a new aspect to this realm.

I promised your Majesty to employ all my industry and all the authority which it should please you to give me to ruin the Huguenot party, to abase the pride of the nobles, to bring back all your subjects to their duty, and to elevate your name among foreign nations to the point where it ought to be. . . .

Cardinal de Richelieu, *Testament politique,* ed. L. André (Paris, 1947), pp. 93-95. (Trans. H. B. Hill.)

Most divine-right, absolute monarchs took themselves and their tasks with complete seriousness. Louis XIV certainly did, as the following selections from his memoirs clearly indicate.

58   Kings are absolute lords and have a full and inherent right to dispose of all property, secular and ecclesiastical alike, and to employ them as wise stewards, namely, according to the needs of their State.

Those mysterious words, the franchises and liberties of the Church, with which they try to dazzle us, apply equally to all the faithful, whether lay or ecclesiastical, who are all equally sons of that common mother; but they do not exempt either class from subjection to kings, obedience to whom is laid down even in the Gospels. . . .

The fact that the clergy are allowed to hold assemblies and discuss what taxes they can pay, must not be ascribed to any special privilege, for the same freedom is granted to the inhabitants of several provinces, as a sign of the honesty of early times, when a sense of justice was enough to arouse every man to do his duty as far as lay in his power; yet that never prevented force from being applied against the clergy and laity when they refused to do their duty willingly. . . .

Although a prince's honor compels him to keep his word, prudence does not allow him to place absolute reliance on that of others; and because he is incapable of deceiving anyone, he must not believe himself incapable of being deceived.

As soon as a decision is taken to break an agreement, a pretext is easy to find: no treaty ever contained a clause that could not be interpreted to one's own advantage. In treaties everyone speaks according to his interests of the moment, but most people later try to interpret them according to new circumstances that have arisen; and when the original reason for making a promise no longer exists, there are few men whose promises will survive; but it should be added, and should be noted especially, that this mode of conduct is more to be feared in states that depend on the will of the many than in those that are ruled by one man. . . .

Certainly one of the surest cures against changes of fortune is to know how to change with fortune.

Consistency is not always doing the same things, but rather always doing such things as lead to the same goal.

Although this goal, which is no other than our glory and the greatness of our State, is essentially the same at all times, yet the means by which we may attain it are not always identical. It often happens that what is useful on one occasion is harmful on another. The world in which we live is subject to such various and sudden changes, that it is not in our power to keep the same policy for very long.

The clever ruler must therefore be like the clever pilot, who knows how to use all possible winds in order somehow to sail in the direction of the port where he wishes to be; and experience has shown over and over again two completely opposite courses of action becoming perfectly compatible merely through changes of circumstances, and everything working together harmoniously towards the same result.

Louis XIV, *Mémoires* (Paris, 1806), II, 208 ff.; I, 228, 165. (Trans. Philip Taylor.)

For the European world at large, the principal sanction for absolutism was religious—that it was God's will that one specially chosen man was divinely delegated to carry out on earth His holy purpose in its political aspects. Quite naturally this was to be done in close collaboration with the church, which therefore gave its firm support to the theory. One of the ablest exponents of this view was Louis XIV's court preacher, Bishop Bossuet (1627–1704), a gifted orator and persuasive polemical writer, from whose writings the following passages were taken.

59   . . . Princes, therefore, act as God's servants, and as His agents upon earth. . . .

It is clear, therefore, that their persons are sacred, and that to attack them is sacrilege. . . .

Since their power comes from above, they must not consider themselves entitled to use it as they please; they must employ it with fear and restraint, as something that comes to them from God, and for which God will require a reckoning. . . .

Kings therefore ought to tremble when making use of the power that God gives them, and should reflect how terrible is the sacrilege of using to bad ends a power that comes from God. . . .

Majesty is the reflection in the prince of the greatness of God.

God is infinite. God is all. The prince by his very nature, is not thought of as an individual but as a public person, the whole State resides in him; the people's whole will is included within his. As all perfection and every virtue is united in God, so the powers of all individuals are united in the prince. . . .

God's power makes itself felt from one end of the world to the other; the king's power operates simultaneously throughout all his kingdom. It regulates the whole kingdom as God regulates the whole world.

When God withdraws His hand the world relapses into chaos: when authority ends within a kingdom, all is confusion.

Think of the prince in his cabinet. Thence proceed the commands that make officials and captains, citizens and soldiers, provinces and armies on land and sea, all move in harmony. This is the reflection of God Himself who, seated on His throne high above the firmament, sets all Nature in motion. . . .

Royal power is sacred, and there is nothing more firmly grounded in the Word of God than the obedience due, as a matter of faith and conscience, to lawful authority.

When Jesus Christ told the Jews to render unto Caesar those things that were due unto Caesar, He did not scrutinize how the emperors' power had been established; it was enough that He found the emperors established and ruling: He required people to respect in their power the commandment of God and the basis of public peace. . . .

The violence of a prince can be met by his subjects only with respectful petitions, without rebellious murmuring, and by prayers for his change of heart.

(Concludes with a translation of a passage from St. Augustine: *City of God*, Book V). . . .

Kings are truly happy if they rule justly the peoples committed to their charge; if they do not become puffed up with pride amid the speeches of those who flatter, and amid the obsequiousness of their courtiers; if their lofty station does not prevent them from reflecting that they are still mortal men; if they use their power to expand God's religion and to cause His infinite majesty to be revered; if they fear God and love Him; if they put before that kingdom where they alone are masters the kingdom in which they will not be afraid to find equals; if they are slow to punish but quick to pardon; if they enforce public vengeance, not to please themselves, but solely for the welfare of the State, which requires such harshness; if such pardon as they give works towards the betterment of the wrongdoer and not towards letting crime go unpunished; and when they are forced to severity, take care to soften it with benefits and examples of benevolence; if their passions are held in check just as completely as they might be let loose; if they prefer to govern rather their own sinful desires than the most proud and formidable kingdoms; and if they are led to such actions not by a desire for some empty glory, but by the love of eternal joy; giving to God every day for their sins an acceptable offering of prayer, of heartfelt sympathy for the wrongs that mankind endures, and of deep humility before the majesty of the King of Kings. Emperors who live in such a way are happy in this life through faith; and they will be happy indeed on that day when the glory we expect is revealed. . . .

Oeuvres de Bossuet (Paris, 1841), I, 323, 324–25, 370, 376, 379, 481–82. (Trans. Philip Taylor.)

The economic policies of early modern times are known by the name of "mercantilism." Although specific policies varied widely from country to country, it may be said that, in general, their over-all aim was to increase the power of the national state, or more precisely, to increase the power of the ruling class within the national state. In France, these policies are so closely identified with the great minister of Louis XIV, Jean-Baptiste Colbert (1619–1683), that they are known as *"Colbertism."* In domestic affairs, Colbert labored to increase commerce and industry and to make the name of France renowned for the high quality of its industrial products; this he did by the establishment of new manufactures and by a strict regulation of industrial production. In his foreign economic policy, Colbert entertained the illusion that one nation could increase its commerce only at the expense of others, a fallacy known as the "lump of trade" theory. The following selections illustrate Colbert's views and policies on these two subjects.

60   *To the Police Officers* [*of the Kingdom*]

Paris, 18 March, 1669

The King having been informed that the majority of workers . . . are failing to observe strictly the rules and regulations which have been fixed in each of the cities where industries have been established, His Majesty has caused to be delivered, in his Royal Council of Commerce, the orders which you will find attached hereto, and at the same time he has commanded me to tell you that you should carefully publish and post them . . . throughout your jurisdiction, and that you should yourself see to their punctual execution, in order that all cloths should be of the length and width stated in the said rules and regulations; moreover, you should know in advance that His Majesty has given the necessary orders that the merchandise should be delivered directly to the markets in the cities where they are to be sold, that they should be inspected in conformity with the above mentioned orders, that those not of the required quality may be confiscated, and that His Majesty will administer the appropriate penalties to police officers who have neglected their duties.

Lettres, instructions et mémoires de Colbert (8 vols.; Paris, 1862–73), II, 459–60. (Trans. R. E. Cameron.)

60a   . . . Commerce is a perpetual, peaceful war of enterprise and industry among all nations.

It is carried on with 20,000 ships, and this number cannot be increased.

Each nation works incessantly to have its legitimate portion, or to gain at the expense of another.

The Dutch fight this war at the present time with 15 to 16,000 ships, a government of merchants whose whole aim and interest is to maintain or increase their commerce, and a great deal more application, industry, and economy than any other nation;

The English, with 3 to 4,000 ships, less industry and application, and more expense than the Dutch;

The French, with 5 or 600 [ships].

These last two cannot increase their commerce except by augmenting the number of their ships [and cannot do that except by] . . . taking them from the 15 or 16,000 belonging to the Dutch.

If they [France and England] remain divided, it will be difficult, not to say impossible, to succeed in this; but if they are joined by a strict alliance . . . one can say certainly and demonstrably that the feeble beginnings of commerce which they have in the four parts of the world will become great and considerable, and that they will have the satisfaction of seeing the number of their subjects' ships increase, perhaps by several hundred each year, and that is greatly to be desired for the well-being and advantage of the two kingdoms.

Ibid., VI, 269–70. (Trans. R. E. Cameron.)

One of the great memoir writers of the eighteenth century was the French courtier Saint-Simon (1675–1755), who produced an interminably long account of court life. It is studded, however, with brilliant sketches, especially of the kings. The following two of Louis XIV were written some years after the old monarch's death, but they are fresh and convincing.

The king's great qualities shone more brilliantly by reason of an exterior **61** so unique and incomparable as to lend infinite distinction to his slightest actions; the very figure of a hero, so impregnated with a natural but most imposing majesty that it appeared even in his most insignificant gestures and movements, without arrogance but with simple gravity; proportions such as a sculptor would choose to model; a perfect countenance and the grandest air and mien ever vouchsafed to man; all these advantages enhanced by a natural grace which enveloped all his actions with a singular charm which has never perhaps been equaled. He was as dignified and majestic in his dressing gown as when dressed in robes of state, or on horseback at the head of his troops.

He excelled in all sorts of exercise and liked to have every facility for it. No fatigue nor stress of weather made any impression on that heroic figure and bearing; drenched with rain or snow, pierced with cold, bathed in sweat or covered with dust, he was always the same. I have often observed with admiration that except in the most extreme and exceptional weather nothing prevented his spending considerable time out of doors every day.

A voice whose tones corresponded with the rest of his person; the ability to speak well and to listen with quick comprehension; much reserve of manner adjusted with exactness to the quality of different persons; a courtesy always grave, always dignified, always distinguished, and suited to the age, rank, and sex of each individual, and, for the ladies, always an air of natural gallantry. So much for his exterior, which has never been equaled nor even approached.

In whatever did not concern what he believed to be his rightful authority and prerogative, he showed a natural kindness of heart and a sense of justice which made one regret the education, the flatteries, the artifice which resulted in preventing him from being his real self except on the rare occasions when he gave way to some natural impulse and showed that,—prerogative aside, which choked and stifled everything,—he loved truth, justice, order, reason,—that he loved even to let himself be vanquished.

Nothing could be regulated with greater exactitude than were his days and hours. In spite of all his variety of places, affairs, and amusements, with an almanac and a watch one might tell, three hundred leagues away, exactly what he was doing. . . . Except at Marly, any man could have an opportunity to speak to him five or six times during the day; he listened, and almost always replied, "I will see," in order not to accord or decide anything lightly. Never a reply or a speech that would give pain; patient to the last degree in business and in matters of personal service; completely master of his face, manner, and bearing; never giving way to impatience or anger. If he administered reproof, it was rarely, in few words, and never hastily. He did not lose control of himself ten times in his whole life, and then only with inferior persons, and not more than four or five times seriously. . . .

Now for the reverse of the picture:

Louis XIV's vanity was without limit or restraint; it colored everything and convinced him that no one even approached him in military talents, in plans and enterprises, in government. Hence those pictures and inscriptions in the gallery at Versailles which disgust every foreigner; those opera prologues that he himself tried to sing; that flood of prose and verse in his praise for which his appetite was insatiable; those dedications of statues copied from pagan sculpture, and the insipid and sickening compliments that were continually offered to him in person and which he swallowed with unfailing relish; hence his distaste for all merit, intelligence, education, and, most of all, for all independence of character and sentiment in others; his mistakes of judgment in matters of importance; his familiarity and favor reserved entirely for those to whom he felt himself superior in acquirements and ability; and, above everything else, a jealousy of his own authority which determined and took precedence of every other sort of justice, reason, and consideration whatever.

James H. Robinson, *Readings in European History* (Boston: Ginn & Co., 1934), II, 285–87. (Reprinted by permission of the publisher.)

QUESTIONS

1. What, in the opinions of Louis XIV and Bossuet, were the necessary attributes of royal absolutism?
2. What is "Colbertism"?
3. What was the attitude of Louis XIV and Bossuet toward the church?
4. Could absolutism and mercantilism have stayed in harmony indefinitely?

CHAPTER X

THE RISE OF PRUSSIA

THE EIGHTEENTH CENTURY witnesses the rise of two powers to international prominence: Prussia and Russia. The rapid rise of Prussia to dominance in Northern Germany dates from the Thirty Years' War and was furthered by a series of rulers of great ability. Prussia was a modern centralized state in which the army, led by the nobility (or Junkers), became an integral part of the nation's organization. Frederick William I built the Prussian army into an effective fighting force, while stressing the duty of his subjects to strengthen the Prussian economy through hard work and simple living (62). His son, Frederick the Great, made Prussia a power of great international importance through his successful prosecution of the Seven Years' War. By the middle of the eighteenth century, a new first-class power had appeared in Europe, well organized and ably ruled. In internal affairs Frederick the Great continued his father's work. Though adopting ideas of the Enlightenment (see p. 151), he remained, nevertheless, a practical statesman devoted, above all, to what he conceived to be the national interests of Prussia (65).

Frederick William I (1688–1740), through wise economy, military severity, and the establishment of an excellent army, laid the foundations for Prussia's future greatness. Here the Austrian ambassador to the court of Prussia gives his impressions of the army and of the character of the king (1723).

It is certain that among troops one cannot see their equal in the world in **62** beauty, propriety and order; and although along with marching, parading, manual dexterity and the like, goes much that is affected and forced, these are accompanied by so many useful and proper things which belong to the craft itself, that one must say, all in all, that not the least thing is missing in the Army and the troops. . . . Their number is about 7,000 men, and no regiment is below 100 men; the armory is provided in abundance with siege and field artillery so that nothing remains save to harness the horses; and there is such a store of powder, shot and cannonball as if a real war were in the vicinity; similarly one sees in Berlin and the whole of Brandenburg as many [troop] movements as there were in Vienna when we were involved in the latest Turkish war.

All this the King directs, solely and by himself, and besides this he works on public affairs, private affairs, economic affairs and the affairs of his domain with such seriousness that no thaler [dollar] can be spent without his signature.

He who has not seen it can not believe that one man in the world, of whatever intelligence, could expedite and do by himself so many different things, as one sees this King expedite daily; for which he uses the morning from 3 o'clock to 10 o'clock, but then spends the rest of the day with military exercises, in Berlin. . . .

Max Schilling, *Quellenbuch zur Geschichte der Neuzeit* (Berlin, 1890), p. 299. (Trans. George L. Mosse.)

The following instructions, laid down by Frederick William I for the education of his son (1718), mirror his idea of kingship. They also show the kind of education against which Crown Prince Frederick (later Frederick the Great) rebelled.

1. My son must say his prayers, kneeling beside his servants, morning **63** and evening. . . .
7. [he is to be] kept away from Operas, Comedies and other worldly vanities and he should be made, as much as possible, to despise them; and because the veneration which children owe to their parents belongs to piety, the marshal of the household and the sub-governor must teach my son from the start, and in time, what he owes to me and my wife in respect and submission, which does not have to be servile and slavelike. . . . [they] must

encourage him to manage, save and to be humble, and to look to it that he becomes a good provider. . . .

As concerns Latin, my son shall not learn it, nor shall anyone talk to me about this, but both [governors] shall see to it only that he get used to a short and elegant way of writing in German and French. The art of calculating, Mathematics, Artillery and Economics he must learn from the bottom up; ancient history can be taught to him in passing only, but the history of our own times, since the last hundred years, he must be taught exactly. He must be completely conversant with *Ius Naturale* and *Gentium,* or the international law, as well as geography and that which is of note in every country; especially, however, must he be taught the history of his own [royal] house.

Most especially, both governors must make it a special project to instill into my son the true love for soldiering, and to bring home to him that nothing in this world can give to a prince fame and honor like the sword; and that he would be a man despised by all the world if he did not also love [the sword] and to see in it the only real glory. . . .

Ibid., 230, 231–32. (Trans. George L. Mosse.)

How Frederick reacted to his father's advice can be seen in this rebuke given to him by Frederick William I (1728). It mirrors the opposition of the old king to the entrance of the more "refined" French manners into Prussia.

64   His stubborn, evil mind does not love his father; for if one does everything, loving one's father especially, then one does what he wants, not when he is present only, but when he does not watch everything. Moreover he knows very well that I cannot stand an effeminate chap, one who has no human instincts, who is shy, who can neither ride nor shoot and who, besides all this inappropriately combs his hair on his body like a fool, and does not cut it; and I have reprimanded all this a thousand times, all in vain; there is no improvement. . . .

Ibid., p. 241. (Trans. George L. Mosse.)

Frederick II, "The Great," of Prussia (1712–1786) put down his thoughts on government in his *Political Testament* (1752). Here are some excerpts from this document.

65   Politics is the science of always using the most convenient means in accord with one's own interests. In order to act in conformity with one's interests one must know what these interests are, and in order to gain this knowledge

one must study their history and application. . . . One must attempt, above all, to know the special genius of the people which one wants to govern in order to know if one must treat them leniently or severely, if they are inclined to revolt . . . to intrigue. . . .

[The Prussian nobility] has sacrificed its life and goods for the service of the state, its loyalty and merit have earned it the protection of all its rulers, and it is one of the duties [of the ruler] to aid those [noble] families which have become impoverished in order to keep them in possession of their lands: for they are to be regarded as the pedestals and the pillars of the state. In such a state no factions or rebellions need be feared . . . it is one goal of the policy of this state to preserve the nobility.

A well conducted government must have an underlying concept so well integrated that it could be likened to a system of philosophy. All actions taken must be well reasoned, and all financial, political and military matters must flow towards one goal: which is the strengthening of the state and the furthering of its power. However, such a system can flow but from a single brain, and this must be that of the sovereign. Laziness, hedonism and imbecility, these are the causes which restrain princes in working at the noble task of bringing happiness to their subjects . . . a sovereign is not elevated to his high position, supreme power has not been confined to him in order that he may live in lazy luxury, enriching himself by the labor of the people, being happy while everyone else suffers. The sovereign is the first servant of the state. He is well paid in order that he may sustain the dignity of his office, but one demands that he work efficiently for the good of the state, and that he, at the very least, pay personal attention to the most important problems. . . .

You can see, without doubt, how important it is that the King of Prussia govern personally. Just as it would have been impossible for Newton to arrive at his system of attractions if he had worked in harness with Leibnitz and Descartes, so a system of politics cannot be arrived at and continued if it has not sprung from a single brain. . . . All parts of the government are inexorably linked with each other. Finance, politics and military affairs are inseparable; it does not suffice that one be well administered; they must all be . . . a Prince who governs personally, who has formed his [own] political system, will not be handicapped when occasions arise where he has to act swiftly: for he can guide all matters towards the end which he has set for himself. . . .

Catholics, Lutherans, Reformed, Jews and other Christian sects live in this state, and live together in peace: if the sovereign, actuated by a mistaken zeal, declares himself for one religion or another, parties will spring up, heated disputes ensue, little by little persecutions will commence and, in the end, the religion persecuted will leave the fatherland and millions of subjects will enrich our neighbors by their skill and industry.

It is of no concern in politics whether the ruler has a religion or whether he has none. All religions, if one examines them, are founded on superstitious systems, more or less absurd. It is impossible for a man of good sense, who dissects their contents, not to see their error; but these prejudices, these errors and mysteries were made for men, and one must know enough to respect the public and not to outrage its faith, whatever religion be involved.

Die Politischen Testamente Friedrichs des Grossen, ed. Volz (Berlin, 1920), pp. 27, 29, 31, 38, 39, 77. (Trans. George L. Mosse.)

QUESTIONS

1. From extracts 62 and 63, can you come to any definition of what is sometimes called the "Prussian spirit?"
2. Frederick is an "enlightened despot." What in his political thought is in tune with the Enlightenment?
3. How did Frederick put his thoughts on government into practice?

CHAPTER XI

THE RISE OF RUSSIA

RUSSIA emerged from Tartar domination and evolved into a national state under the rulers of Muscovy, especially Ivan III (1440–1505) and his grandson Ivan IV (1530–1584). Border wars and domestic crises, however, prevented Russia from participating in general European affairs until the eighteenth century. Although Western influences reached the Russians long before, Russia was pushed into the Western stream by Peter the Great (1672–1725) and his successors, notably Catherine II (1729–1796). These monarchs were crowned revolutionaries. Peter was a rebel by character (66), though his reforms arose from practical needs rather than from an idealistic admiration for Western culture (67). Catherine II actually came to the throne in a palace revolt against her husband Peter III (70). Acting in an age of enlightened despotism, these rulers of Russia brought out more sharply than anywhere else in Europe the essential contradiction between enlightenment and despotism (71, 72).

I. PETER THE GREAT (1672–1725)

Here is an evaluation of Peter's revolutionary character by the outstanding Russian historian of the nineteenth century, V. O. Kluchevsky (1841–1911).

In his spiritual composition, Peter the Great was one of those simple individuals who need only to be studied to be understood. **66**

In person a giant nearly three *arshini* [approximately seven feet] in stature, he towered a full head above those amongst whom it was his lot to move, and not infrequently found, when performing the ceremony of according the Easter Greeting, that his back ached with the necessity of having to bend forward so frequently. Also his strength was proportionate to his height, for a regular course of the axe and hammer developed the vigor and the dexterity of his muscles until he could twist a silver plate into a scroll with his fingers as easily as he could cleave a flying shred of cloth with a sword. . . . A foreign ambassador presented to the two young Tsars in 1683, tells us that Peter was then a lively, handsome lad, and formed a sharp contrast with his brother Ivan, who, seated on the great silver, ikon-surmounted throne with the Cap of Monomakh pulled down over lowering brows, and eyes looking at no one, almost resembled a lifeless statue, whereas the little Peter, by his side, was sporting jauntily the duplicate Cap manufactured to meet the occasion of the joint Tsarship, glancing cheerfully and trustfully about him, and with difficulty being kept in his seat at all. Later, however, this picture of Peter changes for the worse, when either the shock sustained by his childish intelligence through the horrors of 1682, or an injudicious mode of treating an immature constitution, or (most likely explanation of all) these two factors combined developed in him a nervous disorder which first showed itself during his twelfth year, and took the form of tremblings of the head, and of the circumstance that, on lapsing into profound thought, or into violent emotion, his features would assume a scowl which wholly marred their comeliness. And since there went with these a birthmark on his right cheek, and a habit of tossing his arms about when walking, he came to be such a remarkable figure that in 1697 the customers in a barber's shop at Saardam easily recognized the Tsar of All the Russias—though perhaps they did so the more easily in that there were present in the shop at the time some officious Dutch ex-residents of the Muscovite capital, and that in moments of forgetfulness Peter's large and restless eyes would be wearing a distraught stare, and his mien in general bidding fair to terrify anyone not possessed of the strongest of nerves. . . .

In his own home, Peter was never anything but a guest, for alike during adolescence and during manhood he was forever either on a journey or engaged in some out-of-doors occupation. In fact, if at about the age of fifty he could have halted for a moment and reviewed his past, he would have seen that his adult years had included few periods when he had not been bound for some destination, when he had not been journeying on one of the tours which took him from Archangel to Azov, and from Astrakhan to Derbent, and from the Neva to the Pruth. And an effect, amongst others, of these years of traveling was to develop, and to fix, in him a restlessness, an itch for changes of scene, a yearning for swift sequences of impressions, which converted haste into a habit and rendered him a man always in a hurry. In this connection we know even the length of his stride, and can see that, to keep pace with him, the ordinary man must either run or have progressed by a series of leaps. Besides, he never could remain seated for long: even when taking part in a Court festivity he would leave his chair at intervals, if the function proved protracted, dart into another room, and stretch his legs. And the same restlessness led him, during his earlier years, to cultivate the art of dancing, and to become a familiar and a welcome guest at the merrymakings equally of artisan, of aristocrat, and of tradesman. Nor was his tirelessness in the pursuit of the Terpsichorean art deterred by the fact that he was never able to take any regular course beyond what he picked up at the "eventide practisings of the Lefort establishment." Meanwhile, if not sleeping, traveling, feasting, or inspecting, he was constructing, for his hands were ever at work, and owing to the fact that he never lost an opportunity of applying them to manual labor, they never lost their horniness. Especially during his younger and more inexperienced days did he never visit a factory or a workshop without engaging in the special process to which it was devoted; in such places he simply could not remain an onlooker, and least of all, if he had not previously encountered the operation which he happened at the moment to be investigating. Instinctively his fingers itched for a tool, that he might fall to with the rest. It need hardly be added that this innate taste for the practice of handicrafts developed in him a manual dexterity which, added to his mental alertness, led to his needing merely to scrutinize an unfamiliar task for that task to become his own. In short, a taste originally only a precocious addiction to industrial pursuits and technical labor eventually became a permanent trait. Come what might, he felt that he must learn and master any new accomplishment encountered; and he would do so even before he had considered whether the accomplishment was likely ever to prove useful to him. All this, added to the truly marvelous stock of technical knowledge which he acquired, enabled him, as early in his career as his first foreign tour, to inform the Princes present at the banquet at Koppenburg that he was familiar with the working of fourteen trades. Nor was this an overstatement: never did he need to be present in a factory for long before he had made himself at home with its specialized appliances. One outcome of this was that when death had removed him, every place in which he had ever resided was found to be heaped with articles of his own manufacture, such as boots, and chairs, and crockery, and snuffboxes, and the rest, and heaped to a degree which renders it a marvel how he can have gained time for those articles' construction. Also, his mechanical prowess filled him with an immense belief in his own skill, and, amongst other things, he came to consider himself both a first-rate surgeon and a first-rate dentist. Yes, no matter what the horror which his prospective patients might display on realizing that they were to be attended by the Tsar in person, he would present himself before them with his instruments, and officiate then and there. And to his dental prowess in particular, and to the magnitude of his dental practice, he left behind him a memorial in the shape of a whole sackful of teeth! But above all other things, he loved shipbuilding, and no affair of State would detain him when, instead, there was an opportunity of plying an axe on a wharf. Even in his later years, in the years when he had come to live in his self-built capital of St. Petersburg, he never let a day pass without devoting at least two out of the twenty-four hours to the practice of some nautical pursuit. And naturally, he attained a proficiency in marine technique which led contemporary opinion to regard him as the best shipwright in Russia, seeing that, besides being able to design and sketchplan a seagoing craft, he could construct it with his own hands, from keel-laying to the last technical detail. The less wonder, therefore, that he took an immense pride in this manual dexterity, and stinted neither money nor efforts to extend and consolidate the country's shipbuilding industry. True, some may think it curious that a man who had been born in an inland city like Moscow should have come to be a sailor standing in as much need of the breath of the sea as a fish stands of water; but with that it must be remembered that it was to that breath, and to hard physical exercise, that he always attributed the ultimate recovery of his physical constitution, and the annulment of the damage wrought it through youthful excesses. And to the same cause, probably, was due his invincible, truly sailor-like appetite. At all events, we are told by contemporary writers that a meal never came amiss to him—that, on attending a reception, he could always, no matter whether he had dined or not, sit down again and fall to with the best. Usually his routine was that he rose at five, and after lunching from eleven until twelve, retired for a nap (never, even when guests were present, did he omit this item) before rejoining his tablemates for dinner, and with renewed vigor resuming the task of eating and drinking.

Hence there stand before us the factors (1) that early in his career certain untoward incidents of childhood and youth wrenched him clear of the finicking forms of the old Kremlin Court (2) that the society surrounding him during his later youth was of nondescript and nonexacting type (3) that the tenor of his early pursuits early made him handy with the axe, with the lathe, with the saw, and with the correctional cudgel, and (4) that his essentially non-sedentary life converted him into a foe to all ceremony. . . .

True, Peter in himself was honorable and sincere; towards his own personality he was as censorious and exacting as he was just and benevolent towards the personalities of others; but the unfortunate point was that the whole bent of his activity insensibly made him a better manipulator of inanimate objects and tools than a manager of living and breathing human beings. He looked upon the latter as so many mechanical instruments, and knew how to use those instruments to the best possible advantage, and had an instinctive sense for the task most suitable for each: yet all the time either inability or disinclination rendered him powerless to put himself in the human instrument's position, or to understand the instrument's nature as that nature really was. The sphere in which these psychological peculiarities found their supremely lamentable expression was the sphere of his own domestic relations. And so much was this the case that even his vast knowledge of his vast dominions never brought him enlightenment as to the one small corner represented by his home and family. Thus to the end of his life he remained a guest on his own hearth. With his first wife he never really lived. His second wife gave him only too much cause to complain. And so far did he fail ever to conciliate the Tsarevitch, his son, that when the time came he could not save that son from baleful influences, and for a while the very existence of his dynasty stood in danger.

To sum up: Peter became eventually a ruler wholly different from his predecessors, despite that a certain genetical connection, a certain historical sequence of type and career, is traceable between them all. For first and foremost, Peter was a Steward of State, and none of his forerunners had been able to excel him in grasp of, and in discernment of, the prime sources of a nation's wealth. True, the earlier Tsars, of the old dynasty as of the new, also had been Stewards of State; but they had been Stewards of sedentary habit only, soft-handed men, rulers who administered only through the agency of others; whereas Peter issued as a Steward-Laborer-Governor, as a Self-taught Dispenser, as an Emperor-Artisan.

V. O. Kluchevsky, *A History of Russia* (London and New York: E. P. Dutton & Co., 1926), IV, 25–26, 27–29, 44–45. (Reprinted by permission of the publisher.)

In this analysis of Peter's attitude toward the West and his reasons for undertaking reform, the Russian historian Kluchevsky emphasizes the Tsar's practicality rather than a mere idealistic admiration for Western culture.

What was Peter's attitude towards Western Europe? It was an attitude **67** largely governed by the fact that amongst the tasks which he inherited from his predecessors there was included the task of "performing all things according unto the example of strange lands," of, that is to say, Western Europe in particular, and that this task, again, entailed upon him at once a vast amount of labor, no little disappointment with regard to the national forces, and a constant exercise of self-denial. And how, precisely, did he understand the task? Did he see in Russia's relation to Western Europe a relation worthy of permanent retention as a model, or did he conceive that the world of the West need be used as a temporary instructor only, and could be dispensed with on the instruction's conclusion? Well, already we have seen that, in his view, seventeenth century Russia's greatest hurt had been her loss of the Baltic Provinces, and consequent alienation from Western culture. Yet how came it about that his country so greatly needed communication with that culture? It is the custom of some to portray the Reformer as a blind, irresponsible "Westerner," as a man who loved things Western less because they were better than the Russian article than because they were altogether unlike it, and to declare that he desired more than approximation of the two—that he desired their complete assimilation. Yet it is difficult to believe that a ruler so purposeful as Peter can really have leaned towards such a purely platonic affection. No, we see the prime end for which he needed Western Europe when in 1697 he organized, and under an assumed name, himself joined, a "Grand Embassy" designed to collect and import, for his country's benefit, every possible outcome of marine and general technical skill. For Peter nourished no blind indulgent passion for the Europe of the West. Rather, he never ceased to treat it with grave distrust, and had the less inducement to cultivate fanciful ideas about Russo-European spiritual relations in that he knew in advance the ill-wind and contempt likely to be encountered there by Russia. It was for this last reason that long afterwards, in 1724, when he was drafting a solemn ode with which to celebrate the first anniversary of the Peace of Nystadt, he wrote that consistently the nations of Europe had striven to exclude Russia from the light of reason, and, above all, to restrain her from advancing in the art of war, but that now those nations had had dust thrown in their eyes as regards Russia's military progress ("there are certain matters which they are powerless to discern"), and that might be ascribed to a divine miracle, and verily that obfuscation of the nations should therefore be given the more lyrical prominence during the forthcoming festival, "and set forth at large, as a matter of much purport"—as, that is to say, a matter of much promise for a furnishing of new ideas. Gladly, too, would one believe a tradition which has descended to us from different sources, and avers that Peter once uttered, and Ostermann once recorded, the words: "For a few score years only shall we need Europe. Then shall we be able to turn our backs upon her." All this makes it clear that Peter looked upon Russian approximation to the West as a means to an end rather than as an end in itself. And what did he hope to gain by that approximation? Before we can answer that question we must recall the purpose for which he sent his Russian youths abroad, and the species of foreigner whom he imported. The students dispatched abroad he dispatched thither for study of mathematics, natural science, shipbuilding, and navigation, and the foreigners hired thence he hired for service as military officers, shipbuilders, navigators, factory superintendents, and mining engineers (later, as in addition, jurisconsults, departmental officials, administrative experts, and above all, financial specialists) whose help might enable him to establish in Russia certain things which he had observed to be of utility in the West. For instance, Russia lacked a regular army, so he organized one. Russia lacked a fleet, so he built one. Russia lacked a sea route for her external trade, so Peter's army and fleet proceeded to reconquer the Baltic's eastern shores. Russia's industrial production was weak, and her industrial development almost non-existent, and technical knowledge imperatively needed, so Peter equipped his capital with a Marine Academy, Schools of Navigation and Medicine, a training college for gunners and sappers, and seminaries for acquisition of mathematics and Latin, whilst alloting to the chief towns of his *gubernii* and *provintzii* elementary "schools of ciphers," and schools for the children of soldiers doing garrison duty. Again, Russia needed funds to cover her State expenditure, so Peter set to work and tripled the State's revenue. Lastly, Russia needed a well-regulated administration which could manage his swarm of new and intricate institutions, so he engaged foreign specialists to organize a new central administrative system, and to put it into working order. Nor was this all, for the foregoing include only the tasks for which he sought Western European assistance, whereas, although technical training and skill in popular industrial and financial and administrative matters constituted the principal sphere of labor in which Peter invited Western Europe to come and work while teaching his Russian people to do the same (for his object was not so much to borrow the fruits of Western technique as a temporary loan than to adopt them permanently, and to transplant their products, and those products' prime lever, technical culture, to Russia for good), he also assimilated and developed as no other Tsar had done before or ever has since done, the idea to be seen flitting through more than one intellect of the seventeenth century, the idea that the productiveness of popular labor must be augmented before technical attainments can assist that labor to develop untouched natural resources, and to bear additional taxatory burdens. Wherein Peter stands alone in the history of our land, even as he stands alone there as regards his foreign policy, as regards the policy which made its chief end direction of the nation's forces to the question of the Baltic Provinces, as the question seeming most to bear upon the nation's economy. Yet, though he imported into the routine of popular labor an aggregate of new productivity almost beyond apprehension, beyond appraisement, such signs of a resultant enrichment of the country manifested themselves less in a heightened level of popular prosperity all round than in a generally heightened level of State revenue collection, in that any surplus earnings realized by the people very soon disappeared into the gullet of war. For the same reason it was that popular-industrial reform had, in turn, to give place to financial reform, and progress in general to become progress exclusively in fiscal matters, so that when Pososhkov told Peter that the problem of filling up the Imperial Treasury was insignificant as compared with the problem of "enriching the people, which is a great and a divine task indeed," he voiced not so much a politico-economic truth as a despondent deduction which he and other thinkers of the day drew from observed events. Peter's generation, therefore, never toiled for its own benefit, but always for the benefit of the State, and while performing more and better labor than preceding generations had ever done, issued from the task even poorer than they. But on the other hand, it may be said that Peter bequeathed to subsequent generations not a *kopek* of State indebtedness, nor squandered a single working day at their expense; also, that he devised for them a store of State resources which long relieved them of the necessity of adding anything on their own account. Indeed, the fact that he made himself the creditor rather than the debtor of the future was what, more than all else, constituted his superiority to his successors. But as this last is a subject more apposite to the results of his reforms than to the reforms themselves, we will leave it until later, and for the moment, say only that in estimating the sum of Peter's efforts to secure the external security of the country rather than the State's internal position or the popular welfare, we must look for the fundamental idea of his reforms in his popular-industrial undertakings, and consider the course of those reforms to have been marked out by their failures of accomplishment, and their principal result to have been what he achieved at least in the financial sphere.

Thus the State forces represented by Peter's form of supreme authority, dispensation of justice, and corporate-social system were derived by him from ancient Russia, and his technical means for organization of an army, a fleet, a State-economic order, a popular-economic order, and a new set of administrative institutions were borrowed from the West. Yet can we properly describe factors which communicated to the life of Russia new forms and principles (no matter whether those forms and principles were beneficent, or whether they were the reverse) as a revolution in that life, whether renovatory or destructive? That certain of Peter's contemporaries who helped to transmit his reforms to their successors regarded the phenomenon as a revolution lies beyond doubt, as also does the fact that, if the Petrine reforms did not renovate the country, they at least alarmed it, and stirred it to its depths. This they did, however, less through their novelty than through their conditions, and less through their character than through what I might call their "temperament," while the people whom they most of all affected were the people of the succeeding period—the people of the Reformer's own period mostly failed to apprehend their meaning, but realized sufficiently their practical conditions of working to derive thence an impression with which Peter more than once found himself forced to reckon. The conditions to which I refer developed even as Peter's character did, and ran both with the environment of his reforming activity and with his relation, arising out of that environment, towards his people's habits, circumstances, and ideas. In other words, Peter's reforms owed their peculiar setting to external warfare and internal discord. Yet though the former of these was their mainspring, it influenced both their course and their issue adversely, for it compelled them to be carried out amongst all the disorder and hubbub of military conflict, and, to meet the needs and difficulties which they evoked at every step, Peter had so to keep accelerating their pace as to communicate to them an unhealthy nervous, feverish pulse, and an excessive rate of progression. Only in his closing days, when at last he stood released from military cares, did he really find leisure to halt and survey the position, to weigh his projected measures, to consider those measures' possible development, and to await accomplished schemes' possible outcome.

Ibid., IV, 220–24. (Reprinted by permission of the publisher.)

Because they were so dramatic, Peter's reforms involving dress and the wearing of beards are sometimes better remembered than his more practical contributions. Here is a useful interpretation of these sartorial and tonsorial reforms, written by Eugene Schuyler, a former American minister to the Russian Court at the end of the nineteenth century.

To the orthodox, old-fashioned Russian, the beard was then as sacred **68** as it is now to a Turk, or as the queue is to a Chinaman. The Patriarch Adrian, shortly after his accession, had promulgated a fulminating edict against all who were so irreligious, unholy, and heretical as to shave or cut their beards, an ornament given by God, and which had been worn by all the holy prophets and apostles, and by the Saviour himself. Only such men as Julian the Apostate, Heraclius the Heretic, Constantine the Iconoclast, Olgerd the Idol-worshipper, and Amurath the Mussulman, had forced their subjects to shave, while Constantine the Great, Theodosius the Great, and Vladimir the Great had all worn beards. Peter, in his eagerness to adopt the usages of Western Europe, chose to consider the beard as the symbol of what was uncivilized and barbarous. He was not content with repealing the decree of Alexis, and saying that his subjects might shave, but he said that they *must* shave. For Peter himself it was easy; he had little beard, and even his moustache, which he allowed to grow, was always very thin. What had begun in jest was soon done in earnest. Decrees were issued that all Russians, the clergy excepted, should shave, but those who preferred to keep their beards were allowed to do so on condition of paying a yearly tax, fixed at a *kopek* (two cents) for the peasantry, and varying from thirty to a hundred rubles (from $60 to $200, a ruble being worth at that time about $2) for the other classes, the merchants, as being the richest and most conservative, paying the highest sum. On the payment of this duty they received a bronze token, which they were obliged always to wear about their necks, and to renew yearly. Many were willing to pay this very high tax in order to keep their beards, but most conformed to the Tsar's wishes, some through policy, some through "terror of having their beards (in a merry humor) pulled out by the roots, or taken so rough off, that some of the skin went with them." The Tsar would allow no one to be near him who did not shave. Perry [an English traveler] writes:

"About this time the Tsar came down to Vorónezh, where I was then on service, and a great many of my men who had worn their beards all their lives were now obliged to part with them, amongst whom one of the first that I met with, just coming from the hands of the barber, was an old Russ carpenter that had been with me at Camisbinka, who was a very good workman with his hatchet, and whom I always had a friendship for. I jested a little with him on this occasion, telling him that he was become a young man, and asked him what he had done with his beard. Upon which he put his hand in his bosom and pulled it out and showed it to me; further telling me that when he came home, he would lay it up to have it put in his coffin and buried along with him, that he might be able to give an account of it to St. Nicholas, when he came to the other world, and that all his brothers (meaning his fellow-workmen who had been shaved that day) had taken the same care."

Soon after compelling his courtiers to shave their beards, Peter began a crusade against the old Russian dress. On October 9, Lefort and Golovín, the only two members of the Great Embassy then in Moscow, entered the town in solemn state.

"No one was allowed to appear except in German dress, which was especially meant to irritate Prince Ramadanófsky with the sight of what he liked not, for when it was told to him that the ambassador Golovín had put on the German dress at Vienna, he answered: 'I do not believe Golovín to be such a brainless ass as to despise the garb of his fatherland.'"

A few months afterward, Peter himself gave a carnival entertainment, at which the boyár Sheremétief, who had just returned from his visit to Italy, appeared in full foreign dress, wearing the cross of Malta, which many envied him. The Tsar cut off, with his own hands, the sleeves of some of his officers which seemed to him to be too long. He said: "See, these things are in your way. You are safe nowhere with them. At one moment you upset a glass, then you forgetfully dip them in sauce. Get gaiters made of them." On January 14, 1700, appeared a decree commanding all the courtiers and the officials, as well in the capital as in the provinces, to wear nothing but foreign clothing, and to provide themselves with such suits before the end of the carnival. This decree had to be repeated frequently throughout the year, and models of the clothing were publicly exposed. According to Perry, these patterns and copies of the decree were hung up at all the gates of the towns, and all who disobeyed these orders were obliged either to pay a fine, or "to kneel down at the gates of the city, and have their coats cut off just even with the ground, so much as it was longer than to touch the ground when they kneeled down, of which there were many hundreds of coats that were cut accordingly; and being done with a good humour, it occasioned mirth among the people and soon broke the custom of their wearing long coats, especially in places near Moscow and those towns wherever the Tsar came." As this decree did not affect the peasantry, it was less difficult to put it into execution. Even the women were compelled to adopt foreign fashions, and to give up the old Russian costumes. Peter's sisters set the example. Here the women, as might perhaps be expected, were less conservative than the men. They saw, in the adoption of foreign fashions of dress, a great opening to variety of costume. Decrees were even issued against high Russian boots, against the use of Russian saddles, and even of long Russian knives.

There is no absolute and real connection between costume and civilization. Shaved faces and short garments made the Russians no more civilized and no more European than they were before, although they made them conform in one respect to the usages of civilized people. It is the natural spirit of imitation, the desire not to be different from the rest of the civilized world, that induces peoples rising in the scale of civilization to adopt the fashion of the garments of more highly cultured nations, even though the new costume may be both unbecoming and inconvenient. This we have seen in our own day among the Japanese. We see it also in the way peasant costumes constantly disappear, and even the neat white cap gives place to a tawdry imitation of a lady's bonnet, and the comfortable and convenient knee-breeches and long stockings to the awkward trousers. At the same time, there is often a tendency to see in European dress something necessary to modern and Western life; there is a tendency to the false reasoning that a man becomes civilized because he wears European garments. This tendency is sometimes seen in missionaries, who immediately put what they call Christian clothing on their new converts, to the great inconvenience of the latter; and this feeling seems to have had some influence on Peter when he changed the costume of Russia by an edict. Only in one way can such an arbitrary and forced change be defended—that it might, perhaps, render the people more ready to accept Western ideas. If they had violently broken with the traditions of their fathers in point of costume, they might be more easily led to break with them in other respects. Still, even without decrees of this kind, had people been left free to dress as they liked, as European notions and European habits crept into Russia, the change of dress would naturally follow.

Eugene Schuyler, *Peter the Great, Emperor of Russia* (New York: Charles Scribner's Sons, 1884), I, 338–42. (Reprinted by permission of the publisher.)

For ideas such as the ones expressed here, Peter Chaadaev, a leading Russian thinker in the second quarter of the nineteenth century, was declared legally insane by Emperor Nicholas I. The following essay is from a work Chaadaev wrote in 1837 entitled *Apology of a Madman*. It was an extreme retort to the equally extremist opinions of Russian conservatives who regarded the reforms of Peter the Great as a calamitous break with Russian tradition. The argument is still being waged today.

69   For three hundred years Russia has aspired to consort with Occidental Europe; for three hundred years she has taken her most serious ideas, her most fruitful teachings, and her most vivid delights from there. For over a century Russia has done better than that. One hundred and fifty years ago the greatest of our kings—the one who supposedly began a new era, and to whom, it is said, we owe our greatness, our glory, and all the goods which we own today—disavowed the old Russia in the face of the whole world. He swept away all our institutions with his powerful breath; he dug an abyss between our past and our present, and into it he threw pell-mell all our traditions. He himself went to the Occidental countries and made himself the smallest of men, and he came back to us so much the greater; he prostrated himself before the Occident, and he arose as our master and our ruler. He introduced Occidental idioms into our language; he called his new capital by an Occidental name; he rejected his hereditary title and took an Occidental title; finally, he almost gave up his own name, and more than once he signed his sovereign decrees with an Occidental name.

Since that time our eyes have been constantly turned towards the countries of the Occident; we did nothing more, so to speak, than to breathe in the emanations which reached us from there, and to nourish ourselves on them. We must admit that our princes almost always took us by the hand, almost always took the country in tow, and the country never had a hand in it; they themselves prescribed to us the customs, the language, and the clothing of the Occident. We learned to spell the names of the things in Occidental books. Our own history was taught to us by one of the Occidental countries. We translated the whole literature of the Occident, we learned it by heart, and we adorned ourselves with its tattered garment. And finally, we were happy to resemble the Occident, and proud when it consented to count us as one of its own.

We have to agree, it was beautiful, this creation of Peter the Great, this powerful thought that set us on the road we were to travel with so much fanfare. It was a profound wisdom which told us: That civilization over there is the fruit of so much labor; the sciences and the arts have cost so much sweat to so many generations! All that can be yours if you cast away your superstitions, if you repudiate your prejudices, if you are not jealous of your barbaric past, if you do not boast of your centuries of ignorance, if you direct your ambition to appropriating the works of all the peoples and the riches acquired by the human spirit in all latitudes of the globe. And it is not merely for his own nation that this great man worked. These men of Providence are always sent for the good of mankind as a whole. At first one people claims them, and later they are absorbed by the human race, like those great rivers which first fertilize the countryside and then pay their tribute to the waters of the ocean. Was the spectacle which he presented to the universe upon leaving his throne and his country to go into hiding among the last ranks of civilized society anything else but the renewed effort of the genius of this man to free himself from the narrow confines of his fatherland and to establish himself in the great sphere of humanity?

That was the lesson we were supposed to learn. In effect we have profited from it, and to this very day we have walked along the path which the great emperor traced for us. Our immense development is nothing more than the realization of that superb program. Never was a people less infatuated with itself than the Russian people, such as it has been shaped by Peter the Great, and never has a people been more successful and more glorious in its progress. The high intelligence of this extraordinary man guessed exactly the point of our departure on the highway of civilization and the intellectual movement of the world. He saw that lacking a fundamental historical idea, we should be unable to build our future on that impotent foundation. He understood very well that all we could do was to train ourselves, like the peoples of the Occident, to cut across the chaos of national prejudices, across the narrow paths of local ideas, and out of the rusty rut of native customs; that we had to raise ourselves, by one spontaneous outburst of our internal powers, by an energetic effort of the national conscience, to the destiny which has been reserved for us. Thus he freed us from previous history which encumbers ancient societies and impedes their progress; he opened our minds to all the great and beautiful ideas which are prevalent among men; he handed us the whole Occident, such as the centuries have fashioned it, and gave us all its history for our history, and all its future for our future.

Do you not believe that if he had found in his country a rich and fertile history, living traditions, and deep-rooted institutions, he would have hesitated to pour them into a new mold? Do you not believe that faced with a strongly outlined and pronounced nationality, his founding spirit would have demanded that that nationality itself become the necessary instrument for the regeneration of his country? On the other hand, would the country have suffered being robbed of its past and a new one, a European one, being put in its place? But that was not the case. Peter the Great found only a blank page when he came to power, and with a strong hand he wrote on it the words *Europe* and *Occident:* from that time on, we were part of Europe and of the Occident.

The Mind of Modern Russia, ed. Hans Kohn (New Brunswick, N. J.: Rutgers University Press, 1955), pp. 50–53. (Reprinted by permission of the publisher.)

II. CATHERINE II (1729–1796)

The Russian Empress' own description of how she took power by force from her husband Tsar Peter III tells the discerning reader even more about her character than about the events she describes with such disarming simplicity.

My advent to the throne had been planned for the last six months. **70** Peter III lost what little intelligence he ever had. He shocked and offended everyone; he wanted to disrupt the Guards and sent them campaigning for that purpose, and would have had them replaced by his Holstein troops that were ordered to remain in town. He wanted to change his religion, marry Elizabeth Worontsov, and arrest me. On the day of the peace celebrations, after insulting me publicly at table, he ordered my arrest in the evening. My uncle, Prince George, made him withdraw the order.

From that day I kept my ears open to the offers made to me since the Empress [Elizabeth's] death. The plan was to lock him up in his room, like Princess Anne and her children. He went to Oranienbaum. We had full confidence in a great number of captains in the Guards regiments. The ins and outs of the secret were in the hands of the three brothers Orlov, the eldest of whom, according to Osten, used to follow me everywhere and committed innumerable follies. His passion for me was openly acknowledged and that is why he undertook what he did. They are all three of them very determined men and loved by most soldiers, having served in the Guards. I have great obligations in regard to them, all Petersburg is witness of it.

The Guards were all prepared and at the end there were thirty or forty officers in the secret and about ten thousand subalterns. There was not one traitor during the three weeks, because the plotters were divided into four separate sections and only the leaders met for the execution of the plan, while the real secret remained in the hands of these three brothers. Panin wanted the declaration to be made in favor of my son, but all the others were against it.

I was in Peterhof. Peter III was living and drinking at Oranienbaum. It was agreed that in case of treason we would not wait for his return but assemble the Guards and proclaim me Empress. Devotion to me acted in place of treason. On the 27th the rumor spread that I had been arrested. A soldier came to a captain called Passek, the leader of a section, and told him that this was no doubt my end. He would not allow himself to be reassured and, still greatly alarmed, went to another officer and told him the same thing. The officer was not in the secret and, horrified that another officer had listened to this soldier without arresting him, reported to the Major, who ordered Passek's arrest. The whole regiment was astir. A report of what had happened reached Oranienbaum during the night and caused alarm among our confederates. They decided to send the second of the Orlov brothers to fetch me back to town while the other two spread the news that I was arriving. The Hetman Volkonski and Panin were in the secret.

I was sleeping peacefully in Peterhof at six in the morning of the 28th. The previous day had been disturbing as I was aware of what was going on. Alexei Orlov came in very calmly and said: "All is ready for the proclamation, you must get up"; I asked for details, he said: "Passek has been arrested." I hesitated no longer, dressed promptly, without further ado, and got into the carriage in which Orlov had arrived. Another officer was acting as groom at the carriage door, a third joined us a few miles away from Peterhof. A little further on, the eldest Orlov came to meet me with the younger Bariatinski, who gave me his seat in the coach, for my horses were exhausted. We went on to join the Ismailovski regiment, twelve men and a drummer, who started to beat the alarm. The soldiers rushed to kiss my hands, my feet, the hem of my dress, calling me their saviour. Two of them brought a priest with a cross and started to take the oath. After that I resumed my seat in the carriage, the priest with the cross walked in front, and we went on to the Semionovski regiment. They came to meet us, shouting *Vivat!* I alighted at the church of Kazan. Then the Preobrajenski regiment arrived, also shouting *Vivat* and saying: "Forgive us for being the last to come, our officers tried to arrest us, but here are four of them, whom we arrested to show you our zeal. We want what our brothers want."

The Horse Guards then came, in such a frenzy of joy as I have never seen before, weeping and shouting that the country was free at last. All this took place between the Hetman's garden and the Kazan Cathedral. The Horse Guards were led by their officers. As I knew that my uncle, to whom Peter III had given this regiment, was hated by his men, I sent word to him, begging him to stay at home, as I feared some accident to his person. But his regiment had already put him under arrest, pillaged his house, and manhandled him.

I then went to the Winter Palace where the Synod and Senate were assembled. A manifesto and the text of the oath were hastily composed. From there I walked to the troops, of which there were about 14,000 men, and was greeted with shouts of joy. Then on to the Old Winter Palace to make final arrangements. It was decided to go to Peterhof, where Peter III was to dine. I sent Admiral Talysin to Kronstadt. Chancellor Worontsov arrived loaded with reproaches. He was taken to the church to swear the oath. Then came Prince Trubetskoi and Count Shuvalov with the object of securing the regiments and killing me; they were also taken without offering resistance and made to swear the oath.

Having expedited our messengers and taken all necessary precautions, about ten in the morning I put on the Guards' uniform, having had myself proclaimed Colonel with great jubilations. I rode at the head of the troops to Peterhof and left a few men of every regiment to guard my son, who had remained in town. When we arrived at a little monastery half way along the road, Vice Chancellor Galitzine met us with a very flattering letter from Peter III (I forgot to say that as we left the town three soldiers from the Guards came up to me, sent from Peterhof to spread the manifesto among the people and said: "Take this, it is from Peter III but we are handing it to you and are glad to be able to join our brothers)." Then came a second letter brought by General Ismailov, who, throwing himself on his knees, asked me: "Do you consider me an honest man?" I replied that I did. "Well," he said, "it is a relief to be among intelligent people. The Emperor offers to abdicate. I will bring him to you and avoid a civil war for my country." I agreed to this and Peter III abdicated in perfect freedom at Oranienbaum, surrounded by 1590 Holstein men and then came with Elizabeth Worontsov, Gudovich and Ismailov to Peterhof where I gave him a guard of six officers and a few soldiers.

As it was St. Peter's Day, at midday we had to have dinner. While that was being prepared, the soldiers took it into their heads that Peter III had been brought by Field Marshal Prince Trubetskoi to try to work out a reconciliation between us. They began to whisper to anyone within earshot, including the Hetman, the Orlovs and others, that they had not seen me for three hours, that they were terrified that that old rogue Trubetskoi was pulling the wool over my eyes "by making a false peace between me and my husband and thus bringing about my ruin and theirs, too, in which case they would tear him to pieces." I went to Trubetskoi and told him to take the carriage, while I would go round the troops on foot alone. I told him what was being said. He went to town, extremely frightened, and I was received with frenzied cries, after which I sent the deposed Emperor to Ropsha, fifteen miles from Petersburg, under the command of Alexei Orlov, while respectable and comfortable rooms were being prepared for him in Schlüsselburg and also to give time to organize a relay of horses.

But God disposed differently. Fright had given him a colic that lasted three days and passed on the fourth. On that day he drank excessively—for he had everything he wanted except liberty. The illness affected his brain, it was followed by a great weakness and in spite of all the assistance of physicians, he gave up the ghost, after asking for a Lutheran priest. I had him opened up—but his stomach showed no traces of ill health. The cause of death was established as inflammation of the bowels and apoplexy. He had an inordinately small heart, quite withered.

The Memoirs of Catherine the Great, ed. Dominique Maroger (London: Hamish Hamilton, Ltd., 1955), pp. 341–45. (Reprinted by permission of the publisher.)

The following excerpts are from Catherine's celebrated Instructions (*Nakaz*) of 1767 to the Legislative Commission which she summoned to prepare a new law code for Russia. By her own admission Catherine borrowed most of the 566 articles from Montesquieu and Beccaria. "Like the raven in the fable," she wrote to Frederick II, "I have, you will perceive, decked myself out in peacock's feathers. Nothing in the composition is mine beyond just the ordering of the material, and an occasional word." Catherine's prudent foreign minister Panin remarked about this literary exercise in enlightenment, "It contains enough maxims to knock down a wall." Nothing much came of Catherine's instructions. Indeed, her horrified governors had to hide the document because it was so revolutionary.

71   *O Lord my God, hearken unto me, and instruct me; that I may administer Judgment unto thy People; as thy sacred Laws direct to judge with Righteousness!*

THE INSTRUCTIONS TO THE COMMISSIONERS
FOR COMPOSING A NEW CODE OF LAWS

1. The Christian Law teaches us to do mutual Good to one another, as much as possibly we can. . . .

9. The Sovereign is absolute; for there is no other Authority but that which centers in his single Person, that can act with a Vigour proportionate to the Extent of such a vast Dominion. . . .

11. Every other Form of Government whatsoever would not only have been prejudicial to Russia, but would even have proved its entire Ruin.

12. Another Reason is; That it is better to be subject to the Laws under one Master, than to be subservient to many.

13. What is the true End of Monarchy? Not to deprive People of their natural Liberty; but to correct their Actions, in order to attain the *supreme Good*. . . .

38. A Man ought to form in his own Mind an exact and clear Idea of what Liberty is. *Liberty is the Right of doing whatsoever the Laws allow:* And if any one Citizen could do what the Laws forbid, there would be no more Liberty; because others would have an equal Power of doing the same. . . .

41. Nothing ought to be forbidden by the Laws, but what may be prejudicial, either to every Individual in particular, or to the whole Community in general. . . .

67. Civil Liberty flourishes, when the Laws deduce every Punishment from the peculiar Nature of every Crime. The Application of Punishment ought not to proceed from the arbitrary Will, or mere Caprice of the Legislator, but from the Nature of the Crime; and it is not the Man, who ought to do Violence to a Man, but the proper Action of the Man himself. . . .

123. The Usage of Torture is contrary to all the Dictates of Nature and Reason; even Mankind itself cries out against it, and demands loudly the total Abolition of it. . . .

180. That Law, therefore, is highly beneficial to the Community where it is established, which ordains that every Man shall be judged by his Peers or Equals. For when the Fate of a Citizen is in Question, all Prejudices arising from the Difference of Rank or Fortune should be stifled; because they ought to have no Influence between the Judges and the Parties accused. . . .

194. (1) No Man ought to be looked upon as *guilty*, before he has received his judicial Sentence; nor can the Laws deprive him of *their* Protection, before it is proved that he has *forfeited all Right* to it. What Right therefore can Power give to any to inflict Punishment upon a Citizen at a Time, when it is yet dubious, whether he is *innocent* or *guilty?* Whether the Crime be known or unknown, it is not very difficult to gain a thorough Knowledge of the Affair by duly weighing all the Circumstances. If the Crime be known, the Criminal ought not to suffer any Punishment but what the Law ordains; consequently the Rack is quite unnecessary. If the Crime be not known, the Rack ought not to be applied to the Party accused; for this Reason, *That the innocent ought not to be tortured;* and, in the Eye of the Law, every Person is innocent whose Crime is not yet *proved.* . . .

205. The Intent of well-regulated Punishments, is not merely to torment a sensible Being: They are ordained for this wise End; which is, to prevent a Criminal from doing *farther* Injury to the Community for the future; and to *deter* his fellow Citizens from committing the *like* Offences. For this Reason, *such* Punishments, and *such* a *Mode* of inflicting them, ought to be selected, as will make the *deepest* and most *durable* Impression on the Minds of the People, and at the same Time with the *least* Cruelty to the Body of the Criminal. . . .

240. It is better to *prevent* Crimes, than to *punish* them. . . .

Conclusion

523. *Perhaps some Persons may object, after perusing these Instructions, that they will not be intelligible to every one. To this it may be an-*

swered: It is true, they will not be readily understood by every Person, after one slight Perusal only; but every Person may comprehend these Instructions, if he reads them with Care and Attention, and selects occasionally such Articles as may serve to direct him, as a Rule, in whatever he undertakes. These Instructions ought to be frequently perused, to render them more familiar: And every one may be firmly assured, that they will certainly be understood; because,

524. Assiduity *and* Care *will* conquer *every Difficulty; as, on the Contrary,* Indolence *and* Carelessness *will* deter *from every laudable Attempt.*

525. *To render this difficult Affair more easy; these Instructions are to be read over once, at the Beginning of every Month, in the Commission for composing the New Code of Laws, and in all the subordinate Committees, which depend upon it; particularly the respective Chapters and Articles intrusted to their Care, till the Conclusion of the Commission.*

526. *But as no perfect Work was ever yet composed by Man; therefore, if the Commissioners should discover, as they proceed, that any Rule for some particular Regulations has been omitted, they have leave, in such a Case, to report it to Us, and to ask for a Supplement.*

The Original signed with Her Imperial Majesty's *own Hand, thus*

Catherine.

Moscow, July 30, 1767.

Documents of Catherine the Great. "The Correspondence with Voltaire and the Instruction of 1767 in the English Text of 1768," ed. W. F. Reddaway (Cambridge, England: Cambridge University Press, 1931), pp. 215–94. (Reprinted by permission of the publisher.)

In the first half of her reign Catherine II delighted in the phrases of the Enlightenment. That she could not tolerate some of the practical consequences of the quest for liberty, equality, and fraternity is evident from her reaction to the news of the execution of Louis XVI of France in 1793, as noted by her secretary of state, A. V. Khrapovitskii, in his diary. The first entry shrewdly notes a parallel between the execution of the French king by his people and the execution of the popular peasant leader Pugachev in 1793 by Catherine.

72   January 31. This morning the news reached Her Majesty that the unfortunate Louis XVI had been decapitated on January 10 (21), 1793. A period of mourning of six weeks was ordered. A remarkable coincidence: it was on January 10, 1775, that Pugachev was executed in Moscow.

February 2. On receiving the news of the criminal murder of the French king, Her Majesty was forced to bed, ill and miserable. Thank God, she is better today. . . . Her Majesty spoke with me about the barbarity of the French and about the public injustice of concealing how the vote went at the judgment. "It is a crying injustice, even against a private individual. . . ."

February 5. A continuation of the conversation concerning the act of barbarism at Paris. . . . "Equality is a monster; it wishes to be king."

February 8. A decree to the Senate was signed breaking off political relations with France and banishing from Russia all the French of both sexes who do not take an oath on the model of the one issued in the decree. . . .

S. S. Dmitriev and M. V. Nechkina, *Khrestomatiia po istorii SSSR* (2nd ed.; Moscow, 1949), II, 335. (Trans. M. Petrovich.)

QUESTIONS

1. In extract 66 the Russian historian Kluchevsky asserts that Peter the Great was more adept in dealing with things than with people. What were the practical consequences of this character trait on his reign?
2. What were the practical needs which forced Peter the Great to carry out reforms in Russia?
3. Eugene Schuyler states in extract 68 that "there is no absolute and real connection between costume and civilization." Yet Peter's insistence that Russians abandon their beards and wear Western clothing had great symbolic significance in Russian history. Can you explain this?
4. In what specific ways do you think that a Russian conservative patriot of Chaadaev's time might find Chaadaev's praise of Peter's reforms extreme and unwarranted?
5. Why were Catherine's Instructions considered to be such a revolutionary document?
6. Having in mind the nature of Russian society in the eighteenth century, explain how, even with the best intentions, Catherine might have found it easier to be despotic rather than enlightened.

CHAPTER XII

COMMERCE AND CONQUEST

THE SIXTEENTH CENTURY witnessed the first phase of the expansion of Europe: the discovery by Europeans of most of the non-European world, the establishment of great colonial empires by Spain and Portugal, and the first faltering steps toward exploration, trade, and colonization by the inhabitants of England, France, and the Netherlands.

In the seventeenth and eighteenth centuries the second phase was accomplished. Overseas trade increased in amount and complexity, colonies assumed still greater importance, and the great powers engaged in a series of wars to win trade and mastery of the seas and colonial possessions. The Dutch, in the first half of the seventeenth century, were the first to challenge successfully the earlier mastery of Spain and Portugal; by the middle of the century their commerce was the marvel of Europe (73, 74). England reacted to the success of the Dutch with a series of laws known as the Navigation Acts, designed to deprive the Dutch of a large part of their carrying trade, and at the same time to strengthen the English merchant marine (75). The Navigation Acts also fitted neatly into the evolving English colonial policy (79-82).

France under Colbert likewise pursued a vigorous colonial and commercial policy (76; see also p. 104).

Following the three-cornered trade wars of the second half of the seventeenth century, which left the Netherlands an exhausted second-class power, France and England with their respective satellites squared off for the world wars of the eighteenth century (77–78). England had no sooner won the field than the successful revolt in her American colonies brought to an end the "old" colonial system (83).

I. THE RISE OF THE DUTCH

Josiah Child on the Causes of Dutch Pre-Eminence (1669)

The prodigious increase of the Netherlands in their domestic and foreign **73** trade, riches, and multitude of shipping, is the envy of the present, and may be the wonder of all future generations. And yet the means whereby they have thus advanced themselves are sufficiently obvious, and in a great measure imitable by most other nations, but more easily by us of this kingdom of England; which I shall endeavor to demonstrate in the following discourse.

Some of the said means by which they have advanced their trade, and thereby improved their estates, are the following:

First: they have in their greatest councils of state and war trading merchants that have lived abroad in most parts of the world; who have not only the theoretical knowledge, but the practical experience of trade; by whom laws and orders are contrived, and peaces with foreign princes projected, to the great advantage of their trade.

Secondly: their law of *gavelkind,* whereby all their children possess an equal share of their fathers' estates after their decease, and so are not left to wrestle with the world in their youth, with inconsiderable assistance of fortune, as most of our youngest sons of gentlemen in England are, who are bound apprentices to merchants.

Thirdly: their exact making of all their native commodities, and packing of their herrings, codfish, and all other commodities, which they send abroad in great quantities. . . .

Fourthly: their giving great encouragement and immunities to the inventors of new manufactures, and the discoverers of any new mysteries in trade, and to those that shall bring the commodities of other nations first in use and practice amongst them; for which the author never goes without his due reward allowed him at the public charge.

Fifthly: their contriving and building of great ships to sail with small charge, not above one third of what we are at for ships of the same burden in England; and compelling their said ships (being of small force) to sail always in fleets, to which in all times of danger they allow convoy.

Sixthly: their parsimonious and thrifty living, which is so extraordinary that a merchant of one hundred thousand pounds estate with them will scarce spend so much per annum as one of the fifteen hundred pounds estate in London.

Seventhly: the education of their children, as well daughters as sons; all which, be they of never so great quality or estate, they always take care to bring up to write perfect good hands, and to have the full knowledge and use of arithmetic and merchants' accounts. . . .

Eighthly: the lowness of their customs [taxes on imported goods] and the height of their excise [tax on retail sales], which is certainly the most equal and indifferent tax in the world, and least prejudicial to any people, as might be made appear, were it the subject of this discourse.

Ninthly: the careful providing for and employing their poor, which, it is easy to demonstrate, can never be done in England comparatively to what it is with them, while it is left to the care of every parish to look after their own only.

Tenthly: their use of banks, which are of so immense advantage to them that some, not without good grounds, have estimated the profit of them to the public to amount to at least one million of pounds sterling per annum.

Eleventhly: their toleration of different opinions in matters of religion; by reason whereof many industrious people of other countries that dissent from the established government of their own churches, resort to them with their families and estates, and after a few years cohabitation with them, become of the same common interest.

Twelfthly: their law-merchant, by which all controversies between merchants and tradesmen are decided in three or four days time, and that not at the fortieth part (I might say, in many cases not the hundredth part) of the charge they are with us.

Thirteenthly: the law that is in use among them for transference of bills for debt from one man to another. This is of extraordinary advantage to them in their commerce, by means whereof they can turn their stocks twice or thrice in trade, for once that we can in England. . . .

Fourteenthly: their keeping up public registers of all lands and houses sold or mortgaged; whereby many chargeable lawsuits are prevented, and the securities of lands and houses rendered indeed, such as we commonly call them, real securities.

Lastly: the lowness of interest of money with them, which in peaceable times exceeds not 3 per cent per annum; and is now, during this war with England, not above 4 per cent at most.

Sir Josiah Child, *A New Discourse of Trade* [*etc.*], (new ed.; London, 1804), pp. 3–4, 5–7.

William Temple on the Dutch East India Company (1673)

. . . The last I shall mention is the mighty advance that they have made **74** towards engrossing the whole commerce of the East Indies by their successes against the Portuguese, and by their many wars and victories against the natives, whereby they have forced them to treaties of commerce, exclusive to all other nations, and to the admission of forts to be built upon straits and passes that command the entrances into the traffic of such places. This has been achieved by the multitude of their people and mariners that have been able to furnish every year so many great ships for such voyages and to supply the loss of so many lives as the changes of climate have cost before they learnt the method of living in them: by the vastness of the stock that has been turned wholly to that trade; and by the conduct and application of the East Indy Company, who have managed it like a commonwealth rather than a trade; and thereby raised a state in the Indies, governed indeed by the Orders of the Company, but otherwise appearing to those nations like a sovereign state, making war and peace with their greatest kings, and able to bring to sea forty or fifty men of war and thirty thousand men at land, by the modestest computations.

Sir William Temple, *Observations upon the United Provinces of the Netherlands* (London, 1673), pp. 203–4.

II. ENGLAND'S CHALLENGE TO THE DUTCH

The English Acts of Trade and Navigation (1660)

For the increase of shipping and encouragement of the navigation of **75** this nation wherein, under the good providence and protection of God, the wealth, safety and strength of this kingdom is so much concerned; be it enacted by the King's most excellent majesty, and by the lords and commons in this present parliament assembled, and by the authority thereof, That from and after the first day of December, one thousand six hundred and sixty, and from thenceforward, no goods or commodities whatsoever shall be imported into or exported out of any lands, islands, plantations or territories to his Majesty belonging, or in his possession, or which may hereafter belong to or be in the possession of his Majesty, his heirs and successors, in Asia, Africa, or America, in any other ship or ships, vessel or vessels whatsoever, but in such ships or vessels as do truly and without fraud belong only to the people of England or Ireland, dominion of Wales or town of Berwick upon Tweed, or are of the build of and belonging to any the said lands, islands, plantations or territories, as the proprietors and right owners thereof, and whereof the master and three fourths of the mariners at least are English; under the penalty of the forfeiture and loss of all the goods and commodities which shall be imported into or exported out of any the aforesaid places in any other ship or vessel, as also of the ship or vessel, with all its guns, furniture, tackle, ammunition and apparel. . . .

II. And be it enacted, That no alien or person not born within the allegiance of our sovereign lord the King, his heirs and successors, or naturalized, or made a free denizen, shall from and after the first day of February, which will be in the year of our Lord one thousand six hundred sixty-one, exercise the trade or occupation of a merchant or factor in any the said places; upon pain of the forfeiture and loss of all his goods and chattels. . . .

III. And it is further enacted by the authority aforesaid, That no goods or commodities whatsoever, of the growth, production or manufacture of Africa, Asia or America, or of any part thereof, or which are described or laid down in the usual maps or cards of those places, be imported into England, Ireland, or Wales, islands of Guernsey and Jersey, or town of Berwick upon Tweed, in any other ship or ships, vessel or vessels whatsoever, but in such as do truly and without fraud belong only to the people of England or Ireland [etc.]. . . .

IV. And it is further enacted by the authority aforesaid, That no goods or commodities that are of foreign growth, production or manufacture, and which are to be brought into England, Ireland, Wales, the islands of Guernsey and Jersey, or town of Berwick upon Tweed, in English built shipping, or other shipping belonging to some of the aforesaid places, and navigated by English mariners, as aforesaid, shall be shipped or brought from any other place or places, country or countries, but only from those of the said growth, production or manufacture, or from those ports where the said goods and commodities can only, or are, or usually have been, first shipped for transportation, and from none other places or countries. . . .

V. And it is further enacted by the authority aforesaid, That any sort of ling, stockfish, pilchard, or any another kind of dried or salted fish, usually fished for and caught by the people of England, Ireland, Wales, or town of Berwick upon Tweed; or any sort of codfish or herring, or any oil or blubber made or that shall be made of any kind of fish whatsoever, or any whale-fins or whalebones, which shall be imported into England, Ireland, Wales, or town of Berwick upon Tweed, not having been caught in vessels truly and properly belonging thereunto as proprietors and right owners thereof, and the said fish cured, saved and dried, and the oil and blubber aforesaid (which shall be accounted and pay as oil) not made by the people thereof, and shall be imported into England, Ireland or Wales, or town of Berwick upon Tweed, shall pay double aliens custom.

VI. And be it further enacted by the authority aforesaid, That from henceforth it shall not be lawful to any person or persons whatsoever, to load or cause to be loaded and carried in any bottom or bottoms, ship or ships, vessel or vessels whatsoever, whereof any stranger or strangers born (unless such as shall be denizens or naturalized) be owners, part owners or master, and whereof three fourths of the mariners at least shall not be English, any fish, victual, wares, goods, commodities or things, of what kind or nature soever the same shall be, from one port or creek of England, Ireland, Wales, islands of Guernsey or Jersey, or town of Berwick upon Tweed, to another port or creek of the same, or of any of them; under penalty for everyone that shall offend contrary to the true meaning of this branch of this present act, to forfeit all such goods as shall be loaded and carried in any such ship or vessel, together with the ship or vessel, and all her guns, ammunition, tackle, furniture and apparel. . . .

VIII. And it is further enacted by the authority aforesaid, That no goods or commodities of the growth, production or manufacture of Muscovy, or to any the countries, dominions or territories to the great duke or emperor of Muscovy or Russia belonging, as also that no sort of masts, timber or boards, no foreign salt, pitch, tar, rosin, hemp or flax, raisins, figs, prunes, olive-oils, no sorts of corn or grain, sugar, potashes, wines, vinegar, or spirits called *aqua-vitae,* or brandy-wine, shall from and after the first day of April, which shall be in the year of our Lord one thousand six hundred sixty-one, be imported into England, Ireland, Wales, or town of Berwick upon Tweed, in any ship or ships, vessel or vessels whatsoever, but in such as do truly and without fraud belong to the people thereof, or some of them, as the true owners and proprietors thereof, and whereof the master and three fourths of the mariners at least are English; and that no currants nor commodities of the growth, production or manufacture of any the countries, islands, dominions or territories to the Ottoman or Turkish empire belonging, shall from and after the first day of September, which shall be in the year of our Lord one thousand six hundred sixty-one, be imported into any the aforementioned places in any ship or vessel but which is of English build, and navigated, as aforesaid, and in no other, except only such foreign ships and vessels as are of the build of that country or place of which the said goods are the growth, production or manufacture respectively, or of such port where the said goods can only be, or most usually are, first shipped for transportation. . . .

XVII. Provided also, and it is hereby enacted, That every ship or vessel belonging to any the subjects of the French King, which from and after the twentieth day of October in the year of our Lord one thousand six hundred and sixty shall come into any port, creek, harbor or road of England, Ireland, Wales, or town of Berwick upon Tweed, and shall there lade or unlade any goods or commodities, or take in or set on shore any passengers, shall pay to the collector of his Majesty's customs in such port, creek, harbor or road, for every ton of which the said ship or vessel is of burden, to be computed by such officer of the customs as shall be thereunto appointed, the sum of five shillings current money of England: And that no such ship or vessel be suffered to depart out of such port, creek, harbor or road, until the said duty be fully paid: And that this duty shall continue to be collected, levied and paid for such time as a certain duty of fifty solls [sous] per ton, lately imposed by the French King, or any part thereof, shall continue to be collected upon the shipping of England lading in France, and three months after, and no longer.

XVIII. And it is further enacted by the authority aforesaid, That from and after the first day of April, which shall be in the year of our Lord one thousand six hundred sixty-one, no sugars, tobacco, cotton-wool, indigos, ginger, fustic, or other dyeing wood, of the growth, production or manufacture of any English plantations in America, Asia or Africa, shall be shipped, carried, conveyed or transported from any of the said English plantations to any land, island, territory, dominion, port or place whatsoever, other than to such other English plantations as do belong to his Majesty, his heirs and successors, or to the kingdom of England or Ireland, or principality of Wales, or town of Berwick upon Tweed, there to be laid on shore. . . .

The Statutes at Large, ed. Danby Pickering (Cambridge, 1763), VII, 452, 453, 454–56, 458–59.

III. FRENCH COLONIAL POLICY

Instructions of Colbert to the French Commander in the West Indies (1667)

76   The King having resolved to send a squadron of his ships . . . to

America and the Antilles islands, His Majesty wishes to inform [the captain] of his purpose [in so doing]. . . .

He is, therefore, informed that the purpose of His Majesty is:

1. To insure the peace and tranquility of his subjects inhabiting said islands;

2. To insure their possession to the West Indies Company, created by His Majesty, to fortify its commerce, to exclude foreigners therefrom, and to oblige the inhabitants to submit themselves voluntarily to the rules and regulations of the Company.

3. To make the English of the island of Barbados understand that His Majesty intends to protect [his possessions] more strongly than ever, in order to convince them to live in peace and to execute in good faith the treaties of His Majesty with the King of England.

4. To reconnoiter all sea routes, fresh water islets, and even the coasts . . . and, above all, to prepare a very exact journal to serve the navigation of all the ships of His Majesty and his subjects;

5. To exclude all foreigners from the commerce of the said islands;

6. And, finally, to reconnoiter all the islands of the Gulf of Mexico, and [to determine] the entries, routes, and exits in the same of the Spanish fleets. . . .

Lettres, Instructions et Mémoires de Colbert, ed. Pierre Clément (Paris, 1865), III, ii, 398. (Trans. R. E. Cameron.)

IV. THE COLONIAL STRUGGLE BETWEEN FRANCE AND ENGLAND

The War of the Spanish Succession, the War of the Austrian Succession, and the Seven Years' War were at once European wars and world wars fought by the European powers. In the former aspect, the objectives were dynastic prestige and territorial aggrandizement; in the latter, the objectives were commerce and colonies. At the conclusion of the War of the Spanish Succession, the English, in return for recognizing the grandson of Louis XIV as King of Spain, gained among other valuable concessions the exclusive right of supplying the Spanish colonies in America with slaves, as well as the liberty of sending one trading ship a year to those same colonies, previously closed to all but Spanish ships. Under the terms of the Treaty of Paris, which ended the Seven Years' War, England obtained all but a few minor islands and trading posts of the once great French empire in North America, Africa, and Asia.

77   *The* Assiento, *or Contract for Allowing to the Subjects of Great Britain the Liberty of Importing Negroes into the Spanish America. Signed by the Catholic King at Madrid, the 26th day of March, 1713.*

THE KING

WHEREAS the Assiento agreed on with the royal Guinea Company, settled in France, for the introducing of Negro slaves into the Indies, is determined, and the Queen of Great Britain being desirous of coming into this commerce, and in her name the English Company, as is stipulated in the preliminaries of the peace, and that this Assiento should continue for the time and space of 30 years . . . it being my intention to conclude and finish this Assiento, with all possible condescension and complacency towards the Queen of Great Britain . . . I have of my own free will resolved to grant to the said Company by my said decree. All which is in the manner following:

I. First then to procure, by this means, a mutual and reciprocal advantage to the sovereigns and subjects of both crowns, her British Majesty does offer and undertake for the persons whom she shall name and appoint, that they shall oblige and charge themselves with the bringing into the West Indies of America, belonging to his Catholic Majesty, in the space of the said 30 years, to commence on the 1st day of May, 1713, and determine on the like day, which will be in the year 1743, viz., 144,000 Negroes of both sexes, and of all ages, at the rate of 4800 Negroes in each of the said 30 years, with this condition, That the persons who shall go to the West Indies to take care of the concerns of the Assiento, shall avoid giving any offence, for in such case they shall be prosecuted and punished in the same manner as they would have been in Spain, if the like misdemeanors had been committed there.

II. That for each Negro of the regular standard of seven quarters, not being old or defective, according to what has been practiced and established hitherto in the Indies, the Assientists shall pay 33 pieces of eight [*escudos*] and one third of a piece of eight [as a tax]. . . .

III. That the said Assientists shall advance to his Catholic Majesty, to supply the urgent occasions of the crown, two hundred thousand pieces of eight [*escudos*] in two even payments of one hundred thousand pieces of eight each, the first to be made two months after his Majesty shall have approved and signed this Assiento; and the second at the end of two other months next after the first payment; which sum so advanced, is not to be reimbursed before the end of the first twenty years of this Assiento, and then it may be deducted by equal portions in the ten last remaining years, after the rate of twenty thousand pieces of eight yearly, out of the produce of the duty upon Negroes, which they are to pay in those years. . . .

Additional Article

Besides the foregoing articles stipulated on behalf of the English Company, his Catholic Majesty, considering the losses which former Assientists have sustained, and upon this express condition, that the said company shall not carry on nor attempt any unlawful trade, directly nor indirectly, under any pretence whatsoever: and to manifest to her Britannic Majesty how much he desires to pleasure her, and to confirm more and more a strict and good correspondence, has been pleased, by his royal decree of the 12th of March, in this present year, to allow to the company of this Assiento, a ship of five hundred tons yearly, during the thirty years of its continuance, to trade therewith to the Indies, in which his Catholic Majesty is to partake a fourth part of the gain, as in the Assiento; besides which fourth, his Catholic Majesty is to receive five per cent out of the net gain of the other three parts which belong to England, upon this express condition, that they may not sell the goods and merchandises which each of those ships shall carry, but only at the time of the fair; and if any of these ships shall arrive in the Indies before the flotas and galleons, the factors of the Assiento shall be obliged to land the goods and merchandise (with which they shall be laden) and put them into warehouses that shall be locked with two keys, one of which to remain with the royal officers, and the other with the factors of the company, to the end the said goods and merchandise may be sold during the continuance of the said fair only; and they are to be free of all duties in the Indies. . . .

A Collection of all the Treaties of Peace, Alliance, and Commerce, between Great Britain and Other Powers, ed. Charles Jenkinson (London, 1785), I, 375, 376, 377, 397–98.

The Treaty of Paris (1763)

The definitive Treaty of Peace and Friendship between his Britannic **78**
Majesty, the Most Christian King, and the King of Spain. Concluded at Paris the 10th day of February, 1763. To which the King of Portugal acceded on the same day.
In the Name of the Most Holy and Undivided Trinity,
Father, Son, and Holy Ghost. So be it. . . .

Article I. There shall be a Christian, universal, and perpetual peace, as well by sea as by land, and a sincere and constant friendship shall be re-established between their Britannic, Most Christian, Catholic, and Most

Faithful Majesties, and between their heirs and successors, kingdoms, dominions, provinces, countries, subjects, and vassals, of what quality or condition soever they be, without exception of places or of persons. . . .

II. The treaties of Westphalia of 1648; those of Madrid between the Crowns of Great Britain and Spain of 1667 and 1670; the treaties of peace of Nimeguen of 1678 and 1679; of Ryswick of 1697; those of peace and of commerce of Utrecht of 1713; that of Baden of 1714; the treaty of the triple alliance of The Hague of 1717; that of the quadruple alliance of London of 1718; the treaty of peace of Vienna of 1738; the definitive treaty of Aix la Chapelle of 1748; and that of Madrid, between the Crowns of Great Britain and Spain of 1750; as well as the treaties between the Crowns of Spain and Portugal of the 13th of February, 1668; of the 6th of February, 1715; and of the 12th of February, 1761; and that of the 11th of April, 1713, between France and Portugal with the guaranties of Great Britain, serve as a basis and foundation to the peace, and to the present treaty: and for this purpose they are all renewed and confirmed in the best form, as well as all the general, which subsisted between the high contracting parties before the war, as if they were inserted here word for word, so that they are to be exactly observed for the future, in their whole tenor, and religiously executed on all sides, in all their points, which shall not be derogated from by the present treaty, notwithstanding all that may have been stipulated to the contrary by any of the high contracting parties; and all the said parties declare that they will not suffer any privilege, favour, or indulgence to subsist, contrary to the treaties above confirmed, except what shall have been agreed and stipulated by the present treaty. . . .

IV. His Most Christian Majesty [of France] renounces all pretensions which he has heretofore formed or might have formed to Nova Scotia or Acadia in all its parts, and guarantees the whole of it, and with all its dependencies, to the King of Great Britain. Moreover, his Most Christian Majesty cedes and guarantees to his said Britannic Majesty, in full right, Canada, with all its dependencies, as well as the island of Cape Breton, and all the other islands and coasts in the gulf and river of St. Lawrence, and in general, everything that depends on the said countries, lands, islands, and coasts, with the sovereignty, property, possession, and all rights acquired by treaty, or otherwise. . . .

V. The subjects of France shall have the liberty of fishing and drying on a part of the coasts of the island of Newfoundland, such as it is specified in the XIIIth article of the treaty of Utrecht. . . .

VI. The King of Great Britain cedes the islands of St. Pierre and Miquelon, in full right, to his Most Christian Majesty, to serve as a shelter to the French fishermen; and his said Most Christian Majesty engages not to fortify the said islands; to erect no buildings upon them but merely for the conveniency of the fishery; and to keep upon them a guard of fifty men only for the police. . . .

VIII. The King of Great Britain shall restore to France the islands of Guadaloupe, of Mariegalante, of Desirade, of Martinico, and of Belle Isle; and the fortresses of these islands shall be restored in the same condition they were in when they were conquered by the British arms. . . .

X. His Britannic Majesty shall restore to France the island of Goree in the condition it was in when conquered; and his Most Christian Majesty cedes, in full right, and guarantees to the King of Great Britain the river Senegal, with the forts and factories of St. Lewis, Podor, and Galam, and with all the rights and dependencies of the said river Senegal.

XI. In the East Indies Great Britain shall restore to France, in the condition they are now in, the different factories which that Crown possessed, as well as on the coast of Coromandel and Orixa as on that of Malabar, as also in Bengal, at the beginning of the year 1749. And his Most Christian Majesty renounces all pretension to the acquisitions which he has made on the coast of Coromandel and Orixa since the said beginning of the year 1749. His Most Christian Majesty shall restore, on his side, all that he may have conquered from Great Britain in the East Indies during the present war; and will expressly cause Nattal and Tapanoully, in the island of Sumatra, to be restored; he engages farther, not to erect fortifications, or to keep troops in any part of the dominions of the Subah of Bengal. . . .

XIX. The King of Great Britain shall restore to Spain all the territory which he has conquered in the island of Cuba, with the fortress of the Havana. . . .

XX. In consequence of the restitution stipulated in the preceding article, his Catholic Majesty cedes and guarantees, in full right, to his Britannic Majesty, Florida, with Fort St. Augustine, and the Bay of Pensacola, as well as all that Spain possesses on the continent of North America, to the east or to the southeast of the river Mississippi.

Ibid., III, 177–88.

V. ENGLISH COLONIAL POLICY

English colonial policies were designed primarily for the benefit of the mother country, only incidentally for that of the colonies. The Navigation Acts (see 75), which excluded all foreigners from trade with the colonies and required that certain enumerated products of the colonies be shipped only to England, are good examples of this. But, as Adam Smith observed, it was the greater liberty allowed to the English colonies in comparison with those of Spain, France, and other colonial nations, which permitted the English colonies to grow rapidly in wealth and population in the eighteenth century. Nevertheless, many of the colonists objected to even the comparatively mild restrictions and financial burdens levied on them by the Parliament sitting in London; eventually this discontent led to the Declaration of Independence and the successful War for Independence.

The Complex Pattern of Colonial Trade: New England Merchants

79   *Orders to Captain Burchmore*   *Beverly [Mass.], Nov. 26, 1774*

Captain Zachariah Burchmore: As you command our brigantine, we direct you to proceed immediately for Charleston, and there make sale of our rum if the market should be such as to pay the first cost and charges, but if otherwise, and you judge it prudent to proceed to Winyah for the benefit of getting rice cheaper, reserve 25 hogsheads rum to carry with you, as it helps ballast the vessel and with your cask may be put off at a tolerable price. The advantages, however, that arise from dispatch we esteem so great as to advise not to leave Charleston unless rice is higher than 57/6 per cwt. as the detention will be much longer in any other place, and perhaps be more than a balance for the saving of 10/ on each cask, which is the principal advantage gained at Winyah. These things would have you weigh well in your own mind and determine according to your judgment. When you have fixed on the place for loading, lay the whole of our interest out in rice and proceed with all possible dispatch for Cadiz [Spain]. If the market should be as high as 62 reals Vellon [a quarter of a peseta, about five cents] per cwt. clear on board, it would not be prudent to go further unless our friends Messrs. Bewick, Timmerman and Romero strongly advise to it. Bear it in mind that whoever receives your cargo must either advance the money or give bills on Malaga so as to enable you to load there with fruit and wine; and after the discharge of your rice, proceed directly for Malaga and apply to our friends Messrs. Kirkpatrick & Escott for 150 quarter casks wine, 20 fanegas [a bushel to a bushel and a half] of almonds, and if oil is cheap take 10 quarter casks, the balance in raisins unless they are much higher than usual, in which case you will take more wine and less fruit. But should they be at 75 or 80 reals Vellon, take only two or three hundred barrels with the other things above mentioned and desire them to give you a letter of credit to their friends at Lisbon for the balance in lemons. Call in there on your way to Falmouth and take the balance in fruit. When in England desire Mr. Banfield to get a licence for another voyage to load with rice and endeavour to sell so much of your cargo there as to pay the charges. It will not be worth while to wait any time for the licence, but as soon as you are reloaded, return immediately for Beverly where shall hope in due time to see you safely arrive.

English Historical Documents, ed. Merrill Jensen (New York: Oxford University Press, 1955), IX, 377. (Reprinted by permission of the publisher.)

Colonial Evasion of English Regulations

Governor William Shirley of Massachusetts to the Board of Trade of England　　**80**

Boston, New England
February 26, 1742/3

My Lords:

The seventh of the queries lately sent by your lordships to be answered is this, viz.:

What methods are used in the province under your government to prevent illegal trade; and are the same effectual?

I have singled out this query to answer in the first place because the illicit trade which appears to have been carried on in this province and some of the neighbouring colonies (within this last year more especially) is such as without the speedy interposition of the Parliament to stop it, must be highly destructive of the interests of Great Britain, by lessening the vent of her woolen and other manufactures and commodities in her own plantations, making her cease to be a staple of the European commodities for supplying them, letting foreigners into the profits of the plantation trade, and finally weakening the dependence which the British northern colonies ought to have upon their mother country. . . .

Ibid., IX, 371. (Reprinted by permission of the publisher.)

Colonial Regulations: The Iron Act of 1750

Whereas the importation of bar iron from his Majesty's colonies in　　**81**
America, into the port of London, and the importation of pig-iron from the said colonies into any port of Great Britain, and the manufacture of such bar and pig-iron in Great Britain, will be a great advantage not only to the said colonies, but also to this kingdom, by furnishing the manufacturers of iron with a supply of that useful and necessary commodity, and

by means thereof large sums of money, now annually paid for iron to foreigners, will be saved to this kingdom, and a greater quantity of the woollen, and other manufactures of Great Britain, will be exported to America in exchange for such iron so imported; be it therefore enacted by the king's most excellent Majesty, by and with the advice and consent of the Lords Spiritual and Temporal, and Commons, in this present Parliament assembled, and by the authority of the same, that from and after the twenty-fourth day of June, one thousand seven hundred and fifty, the several and respective subsidies, customs, impositions, rates, and duties, now payable on pig-iron, made in and imported from his Majesty's colonies in America, into any port of Great Britain, shall cease, determine, and be no longer paid; and that from and after the said twenty-fourth day of June, no subsidy, custom, imposition, rate, or duty whatsoever shall be payable upon bar-iron made in and imported from the said colonies into the port of London; any law statute, or usage to the contrary thereof in any wise notwithstanding.

IX. And, that pig and bar-iron made in his Majesty's colonies in America may be further manufactured in this kingdom, be it further enacted by the authority aforesaid, that from and after the twenty-fourth day of June, one thousand seven hundred and fifty, no mill or other engine for slitting or rolling of iron, or any plating-forge to work with a tilt hammer, or any furnace for making steel, shall be erected, or after such erection, continued, in any of his Majesty's colonies in America; and if any person or persons shall erect, or cause to be erected, or after such erection, continue, or cause to be continued, in any of the said colonies, any such mill, engine, forge, or furnace, every person or persons so offending, shall for every such mill, engine, forge, or furnace, forfeit the sum of two hundred pounds of lawful money of Great Britain.

Ibid., IX, 416–17. (Reprinted by permission of the publisher.)

Colonial Resistance to English Regulations: Boston Non-Importation Agreement, 1768

82   The merchants and traders in the town of Boston, having taken into consideration the deplorable situation of the trade and the many difficulties it at present labors under on account of the scarcity of money, which is daily decreasing for want of the other remittances to discharge our debts to Great Britain, and the large sums collected by the officers of the customs for duties on goods imported; the heavy taxes levied to discharge the debts contracted by the government in the late war; the embarrassments and restrictions laid on the trade by the several late Acts of Parliament; together with the bad success of our cod fishery this season, and the discouraging prospect of the whale fishery, by which our principal sources of remittances are like to be greatly diminished, and we thereby rendered unable to pay the debts we owe the merchants in Great Britain, and to continue the importation of goods from thence:

We, the subscribers, in order to relieve the trade under those discouragements, to promote industry, frugality, and economy, and to discourage luxury and every kind of extravagance, do promise and engage to and with each other as follows:

That we will not send for or import from Great Britain this fall, either on our own account, or on commission, any other goods than what are already ordered for the fall supply.

That we will not send for or import any kind of goods or merchandise from Great Britain, either on our own account, or on commissions, or any otherwise, from January 1, 1769, to January 1, 1770, except salt, coals, fish-hooks and lines, hemp, duck, bar lead and shot, wool-cards, and card-wire.

That we will not purchase of any factors, or others, any kind of goods imported from Great Britain from January 1, 1769, to January 1, 1770.

That we will not import on our own account, or on commission, or purchase from any who shall import from any other colony in America, from January 1, 1769, to January 1, 1770, any tea, glass, paper, or other goods commonly imported from Great Britain.

That we will not, from and after January 1, 1769, import into the province any tea, paper, glass, or painters' colours, until the Acts imposing duties on these articles have been repealed.

Ibid., IX, 724–25. (Reprinted by permission of the publisher.)

VI. THE END OF THE "OLD" COLONIAL SYSTEM

Definitive Treaty of Peace and Friendship between His Britannic Majesty and the United States of America. Signed at Paris, the 3rd of September, 1783. **83**

Art. I. His Britannic Majesty acknowledges the said United States . . . to be Free, Sovereign and Independent States; that he treats with them as such; and for himself, his Heirs and Successors, relinquishes all claims to the government, propriety and territorial rights of the same, and every part thereof.

Great Britain, Foreign Office, *British and Foreign State Papers* (London, 1841), I, Part I, 779–80.

QUESTIONS

1. What factors account for the great importance of the Dutch in commerce in the seventeenth century?
2. How did the English Navigation Acts affect the Dutch? The English colonies?
3. Indicate the similarities and differences in French, English, and Dutch colonial policies.
4. What advantages did the English derive from the Assiento? Why did the English desire the contract?
5. Indicate on a map of the world the colonial possessions that changed sovereignty according to the Treaty of Paris (1763).
6. What aspects of British colonial policy were objectionable to the American colonists?

CHAPTER XIII

THE ENLIGHTENMENT

ABSOLUTISM still dominated the scene in the eighteenth century, but beneath the structure of the absolute state new ideals of government were struggling slowly but surely to the surface. The rise of science suggested the application of scientific laws to human government, for the law of nature was seen as governing man as well as the physical world. The universe, including society, was like a clock. Once the mechanism had been wound up, it would run under its own power (85). God was merely the "first cause," the power which wound up the mechanism. In politics, men began to ask themselves why the absolute state was necessary when the laws of nature took care of man. In an expanding economy, the middle classes began to ask themselves the same question; they wanted the hand of the monarchy removed from private enterprise (84). In religion as well, this tendency was felt and resulted in the new and anti-theological faith of deism.

Yet *philosophes* like Voltaire did not want to destroy the absolute state. They were no democrats. Instead, they wanted to make the Leviathan (see p. 82) a more efficient monster. However, an antiquated bureaucracy would hardly reform itself. Only in Prussia, itself a new nation, was "enlightened despotism" really possible (see p. 108), although through great exertions, Austria too managed to accomplish some internal reforms (87).

The eighteenth-century Enlightenment was a crucial age in the development of both liberalism and materialism. Liberalism received added impetus through the eventual emphasis on individual freedom in a world governed by the scientific law of nature; materialism received its impetus through the receding power of religious ideas as typified by both deism and the growth of atheism.

Like every age the Enlightenment had its extremists. Men like Diderot went beyond deistic ideas to outright atheism. Rousseau reacted violently against the rational ideals of the Enlightenment and laid the foundations for both popular sovereignty and romanticism (86).

Baron de Montesquieu, although not wholly typical of the Enlightenment, was certainly one of its best-known writers. The following passages from his *Persian Letters* are more characteristic of the age than his greatest work, *The Spirit of the Laws*. First published anonymously in 1721 and presented as the naïve observations of wide-eyed Persian visitors to France, the book poked devastating fun at the targets of the *philosophes:* the abuses of churchly authority, the evils of misguided monarchy, and the pitfalls of aristocratic social life.

84 . . . The pope is the head of the Christians; an old idol, kept venerable by custom. Formerly he was feared even by princes; for he deposed them as easily as our glorious sultans depose the kings of Irimetta and Georgia. He is, however, no longer dreaded. He declares himself to be the successor of one of the first Christians, called Saint Peter; and it is certainly a rich succession, for he possesses immense treasure, and a large territory owns his sway.

The bishops are the administrators under his rule, and they exercise, as his subordinates, two very different functions. In their corporate capacity they have, like him, the right to make articles of faith. Individually, their sole duty is to dispense with the observance of these articles. For you must know that the Christian religion is burdened with an immense number of very tedious duties; and, as it is universally considered less easy to fulfil these than to have bishops who can dispense with their fulfilment, the latter method has been chosen for the benefit of the public. Thus, if anyone wishes to escape the fast of Rhamazan [lent], or is unwilling to submit to the formalities of marriage, or wishes to break his vows, or to marry within the prescribed degrees, or even to forswear himself, all he has to do is to apply to a bishop, or to the Pope, who will at once grant a dispensation.

The bishops do not make articles of faith for their own government. There are a very great number of learned men, for the most part dervishes [monks], who raise new questions in religion among themselves; they are left to discuss them for a long time, and the dispute lasts until a decision terminates it.

I can also assure you that there never was a realm in which so many civil wars have broken out, as in the kingdom of Christ.

Those who first propound some new doctrine are immediately called heretics. Each heresy receives a name which is the rallying cry of those who support it. But no one need be a heretic against his will; he only requires to split the difference, and allege some scholastic subtlety to those who accuse him of heresy, and, whether it be intelligible or not, that renders him as pure as snow, and he may insist upon being called orthodox. . . .

Other judges assume the innocence of the accused; . . . [others again] always deem them guilty. In dubious cases, their rule is to lean to the side of severity, apparently because they think mankind desperately wicked. And yet, when it suits them, they have such a high opinion of mankind, that they think them incapable of lying; for they accept as witnesses, mortal enemies, loose women, and people whose trade is infamous. In sentencing culprits, they pay them a little compliment. Having dressed them in brimstone shirts, they assure them that they are much grieved to see them in such a sorry attire; that they are tender-hearted, abhorring bloodshed, and are quite overcome at having to condemn them. Then these heart-broken judges console themselves by confiscating to their own use all the goods of their miserable victims. . . .

The king of France is old. We have no examples in our histories of such a long reign as his. It is said that he possesses in a very high degree the faculty of making himself obeyed; he governs with equal ability his family, his court, and his kingdom. He has often been heard to say, that, of all existing governments, that of the Turks . . . pleased him best—such is his high opinion of Oriental statecraft.

I have studied his character, and I have found certain contradictions which I cannot reconcile. For example, he has a minister who is only eighteen years old, and a mistress who is fourscore; . . . although he flies from the noise of cities, and is inclined to be reticent, from morning till night he is engaged in getting himself talked about; he is fond of trophies and victories, but he has as great a dread of seeing a good general at the head of his troops, as at the head of an army of his enemies. It has never I believe happened to anyone but himself, to be burdened with more wealth than even a prince could hope for, and yet at the same time steeped in such poverty as a private person could ill brook.

He delights to reward those who serve him, but he pays as liberally the assiduous indolence of his courtiers, as the labors in the field of his captains; often the man who undresses him, or who hands him his napkin at table, is preferred before him who has taken cities and gained battles. He does not believe that the greatness of a monarch is compatible with restriction in the distribution of favors, and, without examining the merit of a man, he will heap benefits upon him, believing that his selection makes the recipient worthy. Accordingly, he has been known to bestow a small pension upon a man who had run off two leagues from the enemy, and a good government on another who had gone four. . . .

My room is, as you know, separated from the others only by a slim partition, which is broken here and there, so that one can hear what is said next door. This morning I overheard a man, pacing rapidly up and down, and saying to another, "I don't know how it is, but everything seems to go against me. For more than three days I have said nothing which can do me honor, and I find myself entirely lost among the crowd of talkers; no one pays any attention to me, no one speaks to me twice. I had prepared some brilliant passages to lighten my conversation; not once was I allowed to get them off. I had a charming story to tell; but always when I found an opportunity for it, people evaded it, as if on purpose. I have nursed some witticisms in my head for four days without being able to make the least use of them. If this continues, it will end in my becoming a fool; I cannot avoid it, it seems to be my fate. . . ."

"I have an idea," replied the other. "Let us help each other to gain this reputation; suppose we form a partnership for the purpose. Every day we shall tell each other what we intend to say; and we shall help each other so well, that if any one attempts to interrupt the flow of our ideas, we shall inspire him with admiration; and if he refuses to be fascinated, then he will be coerced. We shall have the points fixed at which to approve; and where to smile, and where to burst out into a roar of laughter, will all be arranged beforehand. . . . Do as I have suggested, and I promise you, before six months, a place in the Academy. . . ."

Montesquieu, *The Persian Letters* (New York: Lincoln MacVeagh, 1929), pp. 68–69, 54–57, 100–102.

Voltaire, a middle-class poet, dramatist, historian, and—*par excellence*—polemical essayist, was far and away the best known and read of the *philosophes*. No philosopher at all in the formal sense, he had a brilliantly witty and satirical pen which he devoted to the cause of toleration, moderation, and reason. He believed the cause could be furthered by the propagation of "scientific" knowledge, of which he was a great popularizer. The first excerpt below illustrates this (1770). Another device he had frequent recourse to was a description of the basic principles of the natural social order, such as that in the second passage below (1745). By no stretch of the imagination could Voltaire be called a revolutionist. Indeed, to him the best form of government for most countries was enlightened despotism—especially if the despot was guided by the enlightenment of the "philosophers."

1. We are intelligent beings, and intelligent creatures cannot have been **85** created by a blind and unfeeling beast; there are certainly some differences between the ideas of a Newton and the braying of a mule. The intelligence of Newton springs, therefore, from another [higher] intelligence.

When we see a fine mechanism, we say that it was created by a good mechanic, and that that mechanic has a good understanding of such matters. The world is surely an admirable machine: therefore there must exist in this globe a wonderful intelligence, whatsoever it may be. This argument is not the worse for being old.

The movements of the stars, those of our little earth moving around the sun, all operate according to profound *mathematical* laws. Did not even Plato, who did not know one of these laws, the eloquent but mistaken Plato . . . who was even ignorant of the trigonometry of spheres, nevertheless have a genius good enough, and an instinct happy enough to call God the eternal geometrician; thus sensing that there exists a formative intelligence in the universe? . . . It is impossible to dispute this truth, which surrounds us and presses in upon us from all sides. . . .

2. It is impossible that there was ever on earth a state whose government was not, at first, that of a republic, for that is the natural working of human nature. Some families unite at first, against the bear and the wolf; he who has grain furnishes it in exchange for wood.

When we discovered America, we found all the people divided into republics, there were only two monarchies in that part of the world. Of [a] thousand nations we found only two oppressed.

And now what is better, that our fatherland should be a republican or a monarchial state? For four thousand years one has debated this question. Ask the rich for the solution, and they will love an aristocracy best, ask the people and they prefer a democracy; only the kings prefer a monarchy.

How then is it possible that almost the whole globe is governed by monarchs? . . . But, truly, the real reason is, as has been said, that men are very rarely worthy to govern themselves. . . .

Equality, the natural birthright of men, exists still among the Swiss to the extent to which it is possible. By that word you must not understand that absurd and impossible equality by means of which the servant and the master . . . the plaintiff and the judge are confounded with one another. But that equality instead by which the citizen only depends on the laws which protect the freedom of the feeble against the ambitions of the strong.

> *Dictionnaire Philosophique* (Paris, 1770) and *Essai sur les Moeurs* (Paris, 1745–1769). George L. Mosse and Philip Taylor, *Outline and Sources for a History of Western Civilization* (Dubuque: William C. Brown Co., 1951), pp. 51, 52.

Jean Jacques Rousseau, a man of tremendous sensitivity who declared war upon the society which had terrified and crushed his spirit, was one of the eighteenth century's greatest social critics. His moral observations (not his private life) remained quite consistent, but his intellectual observations did not, so that he frequently contradicted himself and, as well, offered solutions ill-suited to the nature of society. He had a warm interest, however, in the wants of men, all men, and if he could not speak to their minds he could speak to their hearts. People were amused and set to thinking by Voltaire and Montesquieu; they worshiped Rousseau. The most quoted of all during the Revolution, his words had an intoxicating effect not unlike the stirring phrases of "The Marseillaise."

from *Émile* (1762)

86   . . . All our wisdom is but slavish prejudice; all our customs are but subjection, torment and constraint. Man in society is born, lives and dies a slave. At his birth he is wrapped in swaddling clothes; at his death he is nailed in a coffin; as long as he retains human form he is chained by our institutions.

It is said that some midwives compress the heads of new-born children, claiming that this gives them a more seemly shape. And they are allowed to do it! Our heads would be ill-favored as the Author of our Being designed them. So they must be shaped on the outside by midwives and on the inside by philosophers. . . .

Liberty resides in no particular form of government, but in a free man's own heart. He carries it with him wherever he goes. The slavish man carries his slavery with him everywhere. The one would be a slave at Geneva, while the other would be free even in Paris. . . .

from *Considerations on the Government of Poland* (1771–72)

. . . All law-givers of olden times were governed by the same principles in the institutions they set up. All tried to find ties that would bind citizens to their country and one citizen to another; and they found these in special customs and in religious observances which were essentially and entirely national in character; in public games which often brought citizens together; in contests which increased their pride and self-respect as well as their vigor and strength; in pageants which called to mind the disasters, the triumphs, the fortitude of their ancestors, aroused their interest and inspired them to the same exploits, and bound them indissolubly to their country, which had been made their chief concern. It was Homer's poems declaimed in the open air to the Greeks in solemn assembly of the whole nation, and not on the commercial stage; it was the frequent playing of the tragedies of Aeschylus, Sophocles and Euripides; it was the garlands with which the victors in the games were crowned amid the cheers of all Greece, that by firing them incessantly to emulation and pride, raised their courage and fortitude to a pitch of intensity to which the modern world furnishes no parallel, and which we moderns find it hard even to credit. . . . If modern men meet together, it is in churches for a worship which has nothing national about it, which in no respect brings the fatherland to mind; it is in closed rooms which they pay to enter, and where on a licentious stage . . . they learn lessons of depravity, the only kind of lesson of which they ever take advantage; it is in debauched revels, where they make clandestine associations and seek all the pleasures that most divide mankind and most debase character. Are these incentives to a love of country? It is surprising that two such contrary modes of life lead to such different results, and that men to-day no longer find within them that energy of soul which everything combined to instil in the men of ancient times? . . .

Liberty is a strong food, but a difficult one to digest; it needs a healthy stomach. I laugh at those degraded people who, letting conspirators incite them to rise in arms, dare to speak of liberty, without having even a notion of what it is; who, with hearts a prey to all the vices of slaves, imagine that to be free they need only be rebels. Proud and holy liberty! if only these poor creatures could know you for what you are, if they knew what it costs to win and keep you, if they felt how much more harsh are your laws than the tyrant's yoke; their feeble souls, slaves to the very passions which free men would have to stifle, would fear you a hundred times more than servitude; they would fly from you as from a burden ready to crush them! . . .

from *The Social Contract* (1762)

. . . . To find a formula of association which defends the life and property of each with the united power of all and whereby each, making himself one with the whole, continues to owe obedience to himself alone and remains as free as before—such is the fundamental problem; its solution is furnished by the Social Contract.

Indeed, every individual, in his capacity as a man, may have a private will which conflicts with or differs from the general will which he has in his capacity as citizen. The appeal of his private interest may be quite different from that of the common interest. . . .

In order then that the social pact shall not be an empty formula, it embodies this tacit engagement, the sole sanction for all the others, that whosoever refuses to obey the general will shall be obliged to do so by the whole body: which means nothing else but that he shall be forced to be free. For such is the condition which, by sacrificing every citizen to his country, rescues him from all dependence upon persons; this condition is the movement of the political machine and the only justification of political obligations, which otherwise would be absurd, tyrannical and liable to the most dire abuse. . . .

A very striking change takes place in man when he leaves the state of nature for the social state; justice takes the place of instinct in his conduct and his actions receive the moral character which previously they lacked. Thus, and thus alone, the voice of duty takes the place of physical impulse, law succeeds to appetite and man, hitherto so self-centered, finds himself obliged to act upon different principles and to consult his reason before he obeys his desires. Although he thus deprives himself of some natural advantages, he gains other great ones in their place: his faculties expand with use, he finds a new breadth of idea, a new nobility of feeling, his whole soul rises to a point where, if the abuse of the new state did not often degrade him below the level of the old, he ought always to bless the happy hour which tore him irrevocably from it, and which made him no longer a narrow and brutish animal, but an intelligent being and a man. . . .

Oeuvres complètes de J. J. Rousseau (Paris, 1835), II, 404, 717; I, 705, 713, 644, 646. (Trans. Philip Taylor.)

Joseph II in 1765 joined his mother Maria Theresa as ruler of Austria, and shortly thereafter he issued a summary of his guiding principles, from which the following excerpts were taken. Joseph was not the most successful of the enlightened despots, but he may have been the most sincere. Of immensely complex character, his head-strong impracticality defeated many of his best plans, and he died a frustrated reformer, supposedly proposing that his epitaph read: "Here lies a sovereign who with the best of intentions never carried a single project into execution."

. . . Our present situation demands, as I see it, our undivided attention **87** and prompt measures of reform. Of course I am as yet a mere novice and can only express myself in accordance with general principles, relying upon hearsay and a little common sense. I am far from censuring what has been done, since I do not have such a high esteem for myself that I can believe that my wise predecessors would not have done the same thing as I, had they found themselves in the situation which prevails today, or had they seen things from the point of view that I regard them. . . .

I may say that all that I have observed or learned has forced me to the conclusion that there is nothing so dangerous as cleverness and subtlety in discussion. . . . Let us act then according to the dictates of good sense and reflection, for we shall have done enough if we reach our decisions in the light of such talents as the Creator has vouchsafed us, and execute them with confidence and determination when once we have made up our minds. I accordingly present here a sketch of the defects of our present system and set forth my pious desires for the future. . . .

The sovereign can, by giving employment and protection to workmen, especially to those dealing with raw materials and native products, not only prevent money from leaving the country but can even draw it in from abroad. But it is not money alone that promotes business, but the vigilance of the ruler, his personal inspection or at least that of a faithful minister, prompt justice, good police arrangements. The business men must be cajoled and protected, prizes must be offered, and the merchants must be comforted in their little troubles; but there must be no privileges granted, above all no exclusive rights or monopolies of any kind. . . .

As for education, I will say only a few words lest I find myself writing a whole volume. It is much neglected here. Fathers and mothers hope for nothing further than to see their children acquire an attitude of mind and general deportment like their own. The good souls believe that they have done everything and created a distinguished statesman when their son attends mass regularly, tells his beads, confesses every fortnight, and reads nothing except that which the narrow mind of his reverend priest permits him to think permissible. . . .

Touching the censorship, I believe that it should be very alert in dealing with everything that is printed or publicly sold; but to fumble in one's pockets or trunk, especially in those of a foreigner, is to carry zeal to an extreme; and it would be easy to prove that, in spite of the rigor used, there is no bad book which has been prohibited which is not to be found in Vienna, and that every one who is tempted by the prohibition can for twice its price get the book and read it. Accordingly any individual, in particular foreigners, who only bring in one copy, shall be left alone, since it is not the business of the sovereign to watch over individual consciences but only over the general good. . . .

Everything in this world can be made good if we diminish its faults and increase its advantages. The greatest prejudice of all and the least excusable is not to dare to attack or emancipate one's self from prejudice. We must have a great deal of courage and still more love of country to be a reformer in this world. No form of evil instinct is easier to inculcate, adopt, and follow than that which encourages ûs to leave things where we find them without giving any thought to the matter. But we shall have one day to give an account of the good that we should have sought for and then accomplished.

Maria Theresa und Joseph II, ihre Correspondenz, herausgegeben von Arneth (Vienna, 1868), as quoted in J. H. Robinson and C. A. Beard, *Readings in Modern European History* (Boston: Ginn & Co., 1908–09), I, 213–17. (Reprinted by permission of the publisher.)

QUESTIONS

1. What specifically does Montesquieu seem to be trying to accomplish in the selections from the *Persian Letters*?
2. What is Voltaire's concept of man and the universe?
3. How do the views of Rousseau differ from those of Voltaire?
4. What items of public affairs most attracted the attention of Joseph II? Why?

CHAPTER XIV

THE FRENCH REVOLUTION

THE FRENCH REVOLUTION warrants the closest study. No other single event in modern history so clearly epitomizes our times, with all its surging changes, frustrations, hopes, and dilemmas. Socially, the Revolution marked the passing of the aristocracy and the emergence of the middle class; economically, commerce and industry gained the right to supersede an agrarian-oriented system; politically, divine right absolutism gave way to representative government, with all its modern implications. In a particularly French sense the old aristocracy had outlived its usefulness and, unable to accommodate itself to the fundamental changes of the new age, was smashed down in blood. Paradoxically, it was easier to destroy than to build, and the resultant disillusionment paved the way for Napoleon (p. 176).

But before all this happened, the pressing need for reform found its theoretical justification in the ideas of the *philosophes* (see p. 151), who, if they were not revolutionaries, did preach that the rational bases for rational society could be found by rational men. A majority of the men who met in 1789 at Versailles in the National Assembly, convinced of the irrationality of the existing order, believed in that philosophy (88) and set forward on the path which led to limited monarchy, moderate republic (89, 90), and then the reign of terror (91, 92, 93).

As exciting as the drama of the Revolution was, it should not obscure two important things: First, despite the hecatomb that accompanied the Revolution's highest phase and the sordidness that characterized its initial outcome, the long-range benefits for society-at-large have been truly immense. Second, the violence of the Revolution, when looked at with a larger view of history in mind, is to be attributed less to a latent bestiality in man than to the deficiencies of the former ruling class, whose deplorable neglect of society's need for renovation reduced France to a dire condition, the very temper of which precluded rational solution.

After the first struggles between the aristocrats and the middle-class representatives in the National Assembly had resulted in the victory of the latter and the determination that there was to be a real revolution in the sense of deep social change, the general course to be followed was charted by the drafting of a blueprint. This was embodied in the Declaration of the Rights of Man and the Citizen, first published August 26, 1789. Obviously influenced by the American Declaration of Independence, it was a document straight out of the boundless optimism and rationalism of the eighteenth-century Enlightenment.

Declaration of the Rights of Man and the Citizen

88   The representatives of the French people, constituted in National Assembly, considering that ignorance, forgetfulness, or contempt of the rights of man are the sole causes of public misfortunes and the corruption of governments, have resolved to set forth in a solemn declaration the natural, inalienable, and sacred rights of man so that this declaration, being constantly before all members of the social body, may unceasingly recall to them their rights and their duties; so that the acts of the legislative power and those of the executive power may always be compared with the true aim of political organization and thus may be more respected; and so that the demands of the citizens, founded henceforth upon simple and incontestable principles, may always be aimed at maintaining the constitution and the happiness of all.

In consequence, the National Assembly recognizes and declares, in the presence and under the auspices of the Supreme Being, the following rights of man and citizen.

1. Men are born and remain free and equal in rights. Social distinctions can be based only upon the common good.

2. The aim of every political association is the preservation of the natural and imprescriptible rights of man. These rights are liberty, property, security, and resistance to oppression.

3. The source of all sovereignty is essentially in the nation; no body, no individual can exercise authority that does not emanate from it expressly.

4. Liberty consists in the power to do anything that does not injure others; accordingly, the exercise of the natural rights of each man has no limits except those that assure to the other members of society the enjoyment of these same rights. These limits can be determined only by law.

5. The law can forbid only such actions as are injurious to society. Nothing can be forbidden that is not forbidden by the law, and no one can be constrained to do that which it does not decree.

6. Law is the expression of the general will. All citizens have the right to take part personally, or by their representatives, in its enactment. It must be the same for all, whether it protects or punishes. All citizens being equal in its eyes, are equally eligible to all public dignities, places, and employments, according to their capacities, and without other distinction than that of their merits and their talents.

7. No man can be accused, arrested, or detained, except in the cases determined by the law and according to the forms which it has prescribed. Those who call for, expedite, execute, or cause to be executed arbitrary orders should be punished; but every citizen summoned or seized by virtue of the law ought to obey instantly; he makes himself culpable by resistance.

8. The law ought to establish only punishments that are strictly and obviously necessary, and no one should be punished except by virtue of a law established and promulgated prior to the offence and legally applied.

9. Every man being presumed innocent until he has been declared guilty, if it is judged indispensable to arrest him, all severity that may not be necessary to secure his person ought to be severely suppressed by law.

10. No one should be disturbed on account of his opinions, even religious, provided their manifestation does not trouble the public order as established by law.

11. The free communication of thoughts and opinions is one of the most precious of the rights of man; every citizen can then speak, write, and print freely, save for the responsibility for the abuse of this liberty in the cases determined by law.

12. The guarantee of the rights of man and citizen necessitates a public force; this force is then instituted for the advantage of all and not for the particular use of those to whom it is entrusted.

13. For the maintenance of the public force and for the expenses of

administration a general tax is indispensable; it should be equally apportioned among all the citizens according to their means.

14. All citizens have the right to ascertain, by themselves or through their representatives, the necessary amount of public taxation, to consent to it freely, to follow the use of it, and to determine the quota, the assessment, the collection, and the duration of it.

15. Society has the right to call for an account by every public agent of his administration.

16. Any society in which the guarantee of the rights is not assured, or the separation of powers not determined, has no constitution.

17. Property being a sacred and inviolable right, no one can be deprived of it, unless a legally established public necessity evidently requires it, under the condition of a just and prior indemnity.

> *Collection complète des lois, décrets, ordonnances, etc.,* ed. J. B. Duvergier (30 vols.; Paris, 1834 ff.), III, 240. (Trans. H. B. Hill.)

The rationalism of the revolutionary leaders, together with economic necessity and the moral vulnerability of much of the church hierarchy, led to an attack upon first the property and then the administrative organization and discipline of the Roman Catholic Church. This was perhaps the greatest tactical error of the revolutionists. As the following document (the papal bull *Charitas* of 1791), bearing the papal condemnation of French territorial seizures, indicates, henceforth all men had to make a mutually exclusive choice between revolution and the church. The break between Rome and France provided a "holy cloak" for all those who wished to oppose reform for whatever reasons. This break, together with the coming of war itself, were the two great events determining the course of the Revolution.

89 . . . Charity, which, as the Apostle Paul teaches, is long-suffering and benign, suffers and endures all things so long as any hope remains; with the result that, consequent upon its mildness, it is assailed by delusions such as are already beginning their covert approach. But if delusions increase daily and the time should be imminent where the situation threatens to collapse into one of schism, then the very laws of charity, linked with the duties of the apostolic office which we so unworthily exercise, demand and entreat that some fatherly but ready and efficacious remedy be applied to the growing affliction after the erring have been made aware of the enormity of their sin and of the full weight of the canonical penalties to which they are rendering themselves liable. For in this wise it will come to pass that those who have left the way of truth may return to their senses, and, having forsworn their delusions, may turn back to the Church which, like a loving mother, embraces the returning ones with open arms; it will come to pass, also, that the others who are true to the faith may speedily escape the wiles of false priests who, having made their way into the fold otherwise than by way of the proper gate, have no object other than to rage, slay, and destroy.

. . . we could scarcely credit the rumor . . . that the radical philosophers, joining forces and constituting the majority of the National Assembly in France, were stirring up feeling against the Catholic religion . . . In a letter dated 9 July, 1790, to Louis our son most dear in Christ, a most Christian King, we exhorted him again and again to refrain from confirming the *Civil Constitution of the Clergy* which would lead the nation into wrong and the kingdom into schism. For by no policy should it be made possible that a political assembly composed of mere men might change the universal discipline of the Church, the teachings of the holy Fathers, abolish the decrees of our councils, overthrow the hierarchical order, govern the elections of bishops at their own discretion, destroy the sees of our bishops, and banishing the higher form, impose the baser upon the Church. . . .

To be sure, the most Christian King refrained from giving the constitution his sanction; but, under the insistence and pressure of the National Assembly, he permitted himself to be carried away to the extent of lending his approval thereto. . . .

. . . Therefore, in order to establish a barrier to the growing schism at the very first opportunity, to recall the erring to their duties, to maintain the good in their resolution, we, abiding by the counsel of our reverend brothers, the cardinals of the Holy Roman Church, in deference to the prayers of all the bishops of the French Church, and following the precedents established by our predecessors, we, by virtue of the apostolic power which we exercise, and in view of the trend of events, declare first that all cardinals of the Holy Roman Church, . . . archbishops, bishops, abbots, vicars, canons, parish priests, presbyters, and all who are enlisted in the service of the church, whether secular or regular, *who have taken the civil oath* pure and simple as prescribed by the National Assembly, which oath is the poisoned fountainhead and source of all errors and preeminently a cause of mourning to the Catholic Church of France, shall be suspended from the tenure of any office whatsoever and liable to the charge of irregularity if they exercise such office, unless within forty days, dating from today, they have retracted said oath. . . .

We declare and decree likewise that the *consecrations* of same were and are criminal, and altogether illicit, illegitimate, sacrilegious, and performed in violation of the sanctions of the sacred canons; and . . . we declare them . . . *suspended* from all employment of the episcopal office. . . .

We equally . . . constrain, under similar *penalty of suspension,* not only the said consecrated clergy but also their consecrators not to venture to confer the sacrament of confirmation or orders, or to exercise in any way the episcopal office from which they have been suspended; and, similarly, those who may be initiated by them into ecclesiastical orders shall know that they are bound by the chains of suspension, and if they exercise the orders they have assumed they also shall be subject to the charge of irregularity.

Moreover, in order to anticipate a sequence of greater evils, . . . we decree and declare that *all other elections* to French churches . . . were, are, and shall be void, illegitimate, sacrilegious, and absolutely noneffective, and we rescind, cancel, and abrogate them now and forevermore; declaring in this connection that those falsely and illegally elected, and others elected in a similar manner, to churches, either cathedral or parish, are utterly devoid of spiritual jurisdiction in the governing of souls, and that the bishops thus far illicitly consecrated, . . . and those who may be consecrated hereafter, are and shall be suspended from all employment of the episcopal order, and that the parish priests . . . installed by the sacerdotal ministry are and shall be suspended; and, in addition, we expressly forbid the elect, or those who may be elected as bishops, to venture to accept either the episcopal consecration or order from anyone, whether metropolitan or bishop, and we forbid the pseudo bishops and their sacrilegious consecrators and all other bishops and archbishops to presume, under any pretext or excuse, to consecrate those vainly elected or to be elected; admonishing, moreover, the said elect and those to be elected not to act as archbishops, bishops, or parish priests, or vicars, nor to assume the title of any church, whether cathedral or parish, nor to arrogate unto themselves any jurisdiction or any authority for the governing of souls, or any faculty, *under penalty of suspension and nullification,* from which penalty none of those above mentioned will ever be able to gain absolution except through us or those whom the Apostolic See may have delegated.

. . . up to this point we have declared the infliction of these canonical penalties in order that the sins thus far committed may be corrected, and that henceforth there may be an obstacle in the way of their wider propagation. For we entrust the future to the Master, in the hope that those who perform consecrations, that the invaders of both cathedral and parish churches, that all the authors and partisans of the constitution which has been published will acknowledge the error of their ways, and through repentance will return to the fold from which they are torn away not without artifice and trickery. And thus we, urging them in fatherly terms, exhort and again exhort, and beseech in the Master's name, that they renounce their ministry, that they retract their steps from the road to perdition down which they have plunged, and that they at no time perform those monstrous acts of the doctrines spread abroad by men steeped in the philosophy of this age, acts which are opposed to the institutions of Christ, the traditions of the Fathers, and the regulations of the Church. But if it should ever come to pass that our present policy of temperate action and our fatherly admonitions should be of no avail—which God forbid!—let them realize that it is not our intention to exempt them from those more weighty penalties to which they are subject by the canons; let them convince themselves that they will be subjected by us to anathema, and that we will denounce them, stricken by the anathema of the Universal Church, as schismatic, and cut off from the communion of the Church and ourselves. For it is altogether appropriate that *each one should have chosen to wallow in the mire of his own folly, that the statutes should abide, and that each should cast in his lot with those whose error he has followed. . . .*

Finally, we beseech you in the Master's name, dear sons, Catholics everywhere in France, and reminding you of the religion and faith of your fathers, we, moved in our heart of hearts, urge you not to abandon your religion, inasmuch as it is the one and only true religion which bestows life eternal, and also preserves civil societies and causes them to prosper. Be steadily on guard lest you lend ear to the insidious voices of the philosophy of this century which lead to death. . . .

Dated at St. Peter's, Rome, April 13, 1791, in the 17th year of our pontificate (Pius VI).

J. H. Stewart, *A Documentary Survey of the French Revolution* (New York: The Macmillan Co., 1951), pp. 184–85, 186–89. (This document reprinted with the special permission of its translator, Norman J. DeWitt.)

The National Convention made several conflicting statements on the foreign policy of the Revolution, but none was so effective upon people abroad, both friends and enemies, as the following decree. Coming on the eve of the French military expansion into the rest of Europe that was to find no end in space short of flaming Moscow and no end in time until Napoleon's banishment to St. Helena in 1815, it contained the thoughts and emotional appeals which could strike with paralyzing fear the guardians of the old order, while simultaneously inflaming the hearts of legions of revolutionary "fifth columnists" among the oppressed and not-so-oppressed. The modern day of propaganda had dawned.

Decree for Proclaiming the Liberty and Sovereignty of All Peoples

90   *December 15, 1792*

The National Convention, after having heard the report of its united committees of finance, war, and diplomacy, faithful to the principles of the sovereignty of the people, which do not permit it to recognize any of the institutions that constitute an attack upon such, and wishing to fix the rules to be followed by the generals of the armies of the Republic in the countries where they shall carry its arms, decrees:

1. In the countries which are or shall be occupied by the armies of the Republic, the generals shall proclaim immediately, in the name of the French nation, the sovereignty of the people, the suppression of all the established authorities and of the existing imposts and taxes, the abolition of the tithe, of feudalism, of seignorial rights . . . of real and personal servitude, of the privileges of hunting and fishing, of forced labor . . . of nobility, and generally of all privileges.

2. They shall announce to the people that they bring them peace, assistance, fraternity, liberty and equality, and that they will convoke them shortly in primary or communal assemblies in order to create and organize administration and a provisional judiciary; they shall attend to the security of persons and property; they shall cause the present decree and the proclamation herewith annexed to be printed in the language or idiom of the country, and to be posted and executed without delay in each commune.

3. All the agents and civil and military officers of the former government, as well as individuals formerly reputed noble, or members of any formerly privileged corporation, shall be, for this time only, ineligible to vote in the primary or communal assemblies, and they shall not be elected to administrative positions or to the provisional judiciary.

4. The generals shall directly place under the safeguard and protection of the French Republic all the movable and immovable goods belonging to the public treasury, to the prince, to his abettors, adherents and voluntary satellites, to the public establishments, to the lay and ecclesiastical bodies and communities; they shall cause to be prepared without delay a detailed list thereof which they shall send to the executive council, and shall take

all the measures which are in their power so that these properties may be respected.

5. The provisional administration selected by the people shall be charged with the surveillance and control of the goods placed under the safeguard and protection of the French Republic; it shall look after the security of persons and property; it shall cause to be executed the laws in force relative to the trial of civil and criminal suits and to the police and the public security; it shall be charged to regulate and to cause the payment of the local expenses and those which shall be necessary for the common defence; it may establish taxes, provided that they shall never be borne by the indigent and laboring classes of the people.

6. When the provisional administration has been organized, the National Convention shall appoint commissioners from within its own body to go to fraternize with it.

7. The executive council shall also appoint national commissioners, who shall go directly to the people in order to act in concert with the generals and the provisional administration selected by the people upon the measures to be taken for the common defence, and upon the means employed to procure the clothing and provisions necessary to the armies, and to meet the expenses which they have incurred and shall incur during their sojourn upon its territory.

8. The national commissioners appointed by the executive council shall render an account to it of their operations every fifteen days. The executive council shall approve, modify or reject and shall render an account of its action directly to the Convention.

9. The provisional administration chosen by the people and the functions of the national commissioners shall cease as soon as the inhabitants, after having declared the sovereignty, liberty, equality, and independence of the people, shall have organized a free and popular form of government.

10. There shall be made a list of the expenses which the French Republic has incurred for the common defence and of the sums which it may have received, and the French nation shall make arrangements with the government which has been established for that which may be due; and in case the common interest requires that the troops of the Republic still remain upon the foreign territory, it shall take suitable measures to provide for their subsistence.

11. The French nation declares that it will treat as enemies the people who, refusing liberty and equality, or renouncing them, tries to preserve, recall, or treat with the prince and the privileged castes; it promises and engages not to subscribe to any treaty, and not to lay down its arms until

after the assurance of the sovereignty and independence of the people whose territory the troops of the Republic have entered and who shall have adopted the principles of equality, and established a free and popular government.

12. The executive council shall dispatch the present decree by extraordinary couriers to all the generals and shall take the necessary measures to assure its execution.

Duvergier, *op. cit.*, V, 82–83. (Trans. H. B. Hill.)

A nation which has enfranchised and freed its people belongs to them, and they to it. For its defense all people, all property may be called upon without limit. No longer do men in small numbers march off to war because paid to do so or ordered to do so by royal masters and aristocratic officers. Henceforth, as one of the signal counterparts of modern democracy, men fight for *their* country, and the hallmarks of the new age, so obviously a part of the pioneering document which follows, are national patriotism, universal military service, and total war.

Decree for the Levy en Masse (1793)

91   1. From this moment until that in which the enemy shall have been driven from the territory of the Republic, all Frenchmen are in permanent requisition for the service of the armies.

The young men shall go to battle; the married men shall forge arms and transport provisions; the women shall make tents and clothing and shall serve in the hospitals; the children shall make old linen into lint; the old men shall take themselves to the public places in order to arouse the courage of the warriors and preach the hatred of kings and the unity of the Republic.

2. The public buildings shall be converted into barracks, the public squares into workshops for arms, the soil of the cellars shall be washed in order to extract the saltpeter from them.

3. The arms of the military calibre shall be reserved exclusively for those who shall march upon the enemy; the service of the interior shall be provided with hunting pieces and side arms.

4. The saddle horses shall be requisitioned to equip the cavalry corps; the workhorses, other than those employed in agriculture, shall haul the artillery and the provisions.

5. The Committee of Public Safety is charged with the taking of all the necessary measures without delay for the establishment of an extraordinary manufacture of arms of every kind which corresponds with the zeal and

energy of the French people. It is authorized in consequence, to form all the establishments, factories, workshops and mills which shall be indeed necessary for the execution of these works, as well as to requisition for this objective within the entire extent of the Republic, the artisans and working-men who can contribute to their success. To this end there shall be put at the disposal of the Minister of War a sum of thirty millions, to be taken out of the four hundred ninety-eight million two hundred thousand livres in monies which are in reserve in the fund of the three keys. The central establishment of this extraordinary manufacture shall be at Paris.

6. The representatives of the people sent out for the execution of the present law shall have the same authority in their respective districts, and act in concert with the Committee of Public Safety; they are invested with the unlimited powers assigned to the representatives of the people to the armies.

7. Nobody can have a substitute for himself in the service for which he shall have been requisitioned. Civil service employees shall remain at their posts.

8. The levy shall be general. The unmarried citizens and widowers without children, from eighteen to twenty-five years of age shall march first; they shall assemble without delay at the head-towns of their districts, where they shall practice every day in the use of arms while awaiting the hour of departure.

Duvergier, *op. cit.,* VI, 107. (Trans. H. B. Hill.)

By the time of the Reign of Terror the almost blithe attitude of the early revolutionists had been seared away by the perplexing and complicated problems which had arisen to plague the progress of reform. What had appeared so easy in theory had proved so elusive in practice, and the Terror in large measure came from the resulting frustration. It was a desperate attempt to rephrase the objectives of the Revolution in harsh and clear form and to build the ideal society on the decapitated forms of its enemies, both at home and abroad. The following excerpt from the pen of Robespierre (1794), the very epitome of this epoch, is typical in both tone and content. It also might be called "Rousseau in action," although Rousseau, like so many revolutionary progenitors, would have been horrified by the Revolution he helped to create.

It is time to state clearly the goal of the Revolution. . . . It is time to **92** take stock, and face the obstacles which are still in our way, and the means which we must adopt to reach our goal. . . . What is our goal? The peaceful enjoyment of Liberty and Equality, the reign of that eternal justice whose laws are not engraved in stone and marble but in the hearts of all men, even in the heart of the slave who has forgotten these laws, and of the tyrant who denies them. We want a state of things where all cruel and base passions are enchained, all beneficial and generous passions are supported by the Laws, where ambition is the wish to deserve glory and to serve the fatherland, where social distinction rests on equality itself, where the Citizen obeys the Magistrate, the Magistrate obeys the people and the people obey the dictates of justice.

[We want a state] where the fatherland assures the well-being of each individual and where each individual proudly partakes of the prosperity and the glory of the fatherland . . . where commerce is the source of public wealth and not merely benefits the monstrous opulence of a few.

Democracy is a state where the sovereign people, guided by the laws which it has made does itself all that it can do, and delegates to its representatives all that which it can not do itself. . . . As the essence of a Democracy is equality, it follows that love of fatherland includes necessarily love of equality. . . .

It has been said that the terror belongs to a despotic government. Does our terror have anything in common with despotism? Yes, just as the sword which glitters in the hands of the heroes of liberty resembles that with which the henchmen of Tyranny are armed. . . . The Government of the Revolution is the Despotism of Liberty against Tyranny. Nature imposes on all physical and moral beings the duty to preserve themselves. . . . If Tyranny rules a single day there will not be a patriot alive the next morning. . . . How much one is concerned for the oppressors and how little for the oppressed. . . . One or the other must perish. Indulgence for the Royalists, cry some men. Mercy for the scoundrels. No: mercy and compassion for the innocents . . . for humanity.

The protection of society is due only to peaceful Citizens, and in a Republic there are no other citizens than republicans. The Royalists, the Conspirators, are to them . . . enemies. This terrible war of Liberty against Tyranny is it not one and indivisible? Our internal enemies, are they not the allies of our foreign foes? . . .

Discours et Rapports de Robespierre, ed. Vellay (Paris, 1908), pp. 324, 325–26, 327, 332–33. (Trans. George L. Mosse.)

The Reign of Terror, despite its wholesale bloodshed and flight from rational political procedure, was largely the sad result of the work of well-intentioned men. As the horror of it began to dawn on society, there came the inevitable reaction, and with the passing of the Terror there was a passing also of idealism. Note how, in the following document, there is an absence not only of the inflexible and doctrinaire idealism of Robespierre but also of the almost naïve optimism of the earlier Revolution. The author of this account, Clair Antoine Thibaudeau (1765–1854), was a provincial lawyer who had a distinguished legislative and administrative career extending throughout the period of the Revolution and Napoleon. Although as a confirmed republican he voted for the death of Louis XVI, he was recognized for his probity and good judgment. Many historians have exaggerated the corruptness that appeared in public life after the end of the Reign of Terror, yet note how different the tone has become in this account. The zeal of the earlier years is largely gone; the Revolution, in any real sense, is over.

. . . Individuals and families who had been driven into hiding by the **93** Terror began to see each other again and society re-emerged. People attended dinners, balls, and concerts. Riches were no longer a crime and luxurious appointments reappeared little by little, not with the prodigality of the days of the monarchy, but enough to provide the conveniences and amenities of life. In place of the old pomp and splendor there was now propriety and elegance. . . .

Participation in society . . . was a matter of inclination, not of duty. It fell largely to those with means, to bankers, contractors, and big businessmen. The families of those nobles who had not emigrated also had their salons. The one sought means of enjoying its wealth; the other to fill the need for seeing people—a most imperious need in France, and above all in Paris. The one looked for protection for its business ventures; the other, means for recovering its sequestrated fortunes or its exiled relatives and friends. All strove for that importance in the world of affairs which people of power and distinction can add. . . .

Many critics have decried the ostentation of the new rich and ridiculed their awkward and ignorant manners, as well as the bad taste which characterized the salons of the Republic. In the main, however, they appeared so only to the defenders of the old regime or to those with a narrow partisan spirit who twisted and exaggerated the truth. The title of *citizen* was actually worth more than that of *monsieur,* and despite the critics, our former marquises and countesses did not find our revolutionary officers too uncouth to marry. . . .

It was after the [fall of Robespierre] that I actually entered what was known as Parisian society. It was, like the society of all great capital cities, a casual assemblage of constantly changing composition, made up of people drawn from all conditions, ranks, and countries—quite unlike provincial society with its stable families and tight little groups. Along with other members of the Convention who had made names for themselves, I was much sought after. To accept one invitation was to encourage ten more. Once caught in this whirlwind of dinners and evenings, there was nothing to do but ride along with it, so I accepted all such kindnesses.

The gilded salons, as those of the unregenerate wing of the old nobility were called, did exercise an immense and evil influence. Revolutionary leaders were invited to these not because of their personal merits or in order to enjoy themselves; they were drawn in with the idea of flattering them in the hope of winning favors or corrupting their opinions. Outwardly they were showered with all kinds of seductions; behind their backs they were ridiculed. All this was obvious, but there were many who failed to see it. They thought that they increased their importance and standing by associating with the people of the old regime, and they let themselves be led astray by these deceitful approaches. First a few pleasantries at the expense of the Revolution would be tried. Did the listeners get angry? Perhaps the teller was a pretty lady. Their republicanism could not hold out against the fear of displeasing or appearing ridiculous. After having won them over by small talk, they could be insensibly molded in the hope of undermining institutions. They justified the old proverb: Tell me the company you keep, and I will tell you who you are. It is absolutely true that, no matter how firm your will may be, it is impossible not to be influenced by the society you frequent. You agree at first through politeness, then self-consciousness prevents a retracing of the false steps, and finally you accept the opinions of others in spite of yourself. So it was that the republican party provided many traitors, some by just making concessions, others by selling out completely to the royalists. . . .

C. A. Thibaudeau, *Mémoires sur la convention et le directoire* (2 vols.; Paris, 1824), I, 128–30, 137–39. (Trans. H. B. Hill.)

QUESTIONS

1. On the basis of the Declaration of the Rights of Man and the Citizen, what did Frenchmen want in 1789?
2. What aspects of the Revolution did the Pope most object to?
3. What is appealing about the propaganda decree? What was menacing?

4. What elements of nationalism do you find in the Levy en Masse?
5. What were Robespierre's ideals?
6. What changes have taken place in the political atmosphere by the time of Thibaudeau?

CHAPTER XV

NAPOLEON I (1769–1821)

IN A TIME of great turmoil and change there may appear a man who seems made for the moment, containing within himself an almost complete understanding and potential mastery of the forces which move and arouse people but which they are incapable of fully grasping, let alone controlling. Such a person was Napoleon Bonaparte, the frustrated Corsican rebel turned world conqueror, who found a revolution close to the end of its tether and turned its revived moral fervor into the marching cries of his legions. At once this magic formula produced brilliant results, but almost immediately Napoleon, not too secure emotionally, began to introduce most of the less original instruments of dictatorial control. Yet, with all that can be said of him, both for and against, he was the dramatic and living embodiment of his age, as his own words so well reveal.

Napoleon was first and foremost a soldier. Yet as a child of the Revolution he could make war seem like a people's war, and the army like a people's army, which, with him as its leader, had a rendezvous with destiny. His first spectacular victories were during his campaign in Italy in 1796–97. Success came at once, and less than a month after assuming command Napoleon issued the following proclamation to his troops:

Soldiers;

You have in a fortnight won six victories, taken twenty-one flags, fifty-five cannon, several strong places, and conquered the richest part of Piedmont; you have taken fifteen thousand prisoners and killed or wounded more than ten thousand men.

So far you had fought for barren rocks, made famous by your prowess, but useless to your country; now your services make you the equal of the army of Holland or of the Rhine.

Denied everything, you have supplied all that was necessary. You have won battles without cannon, crossed rivers without bridges, made forced marches without shoes, camped without brandy and often without bread. Only republican phalanxes, soldiers of liberty, would have been able to bear what you have born. Thanks be to you for this, my soldiers! Your country recognizes it owes its prosperity to you. As conquerors at Toulon you foreshadowed the immortal campaign of 1794; your present victories presage still greater.

The two armies which but recently attacked you with audacity are fleeing before you. Those perverse men who laughed at your misery and rejoiced in the thought of the triumph of your enemies have been confounded. . . .

Soldiers, your country is justified in expecting great things of you. Will you fulfill its hopes? The greatest obstacles undoubtedly have been overcome, but you still have battles to win, cities to take, rivers to cross. Is there anyone among you whose courage is weakening? Is there anyone who would prefer to return across the summits of the Apennines and the Alps and bear patiently the insults of that slavish soldiery? No, there is none such among the conquerors of Montenotte, of Millesimo, of Dego, of Mondovi. All of you are burning to carry far the glory of the French people; all wish to humiliate those proud kings who dare to think of placing us in fetters; all wish to dictate a glorious peace and one which will indemnify our country for the immense sacrifices which it has made; all would wish, as they go back to their native villages, to be able to say proudly, "I was with the victorious army of Italy!"

Friends, I can promise you this conquest, but there is one condition which you must swear to fulfill: It is to respect the peoples whom you deliver, it is to repress the horrible pillage which certain rascals committed, incited by our enemies. Without that, you will not be the deliverers of the people, but rather their scourge; you will not be an honor to the French people, which will disavow you. Your victories, your courage, your success, the blood of our brothers who have died in battle, will all be lost—even honor and glory. As for me and the generals who have your confidence, we should blush to command an army without discipline, without restraint, which recognizes no law but force. . . .

Peoples of Italy, the French army comes to break your chains; the French people is the friend of all peoples: Receive them with confidence. Your property, your religion, and your customs will be respected.

We are making war as generous enemies, and only against the tyrants who oppress you.

Bonaparte

Napoleon Bonaparte, *Correspondence de Napoleon Ier* (32 vols.; Paris, 1858–70), I, 187–88. (Trans. H. B. Hill.)

Napoleon may have wished to preserve many of the great reforms of the Revolution, but freedom of the press was not one of them. From the very day of his seizure of power he was extremely sensitive to what people said about him, especially in print. The circulation of books and pamphlets, particularly those printed abroad, could not be entirely controlled, although many attempts were made to suppress such voices of discontent. The regular newspapers, however, were another matter. The decree given below in effect meant that France had an official press, and no other. Such prevailed until after Napoleon's fall. It was only then, for example, that most Frenchmen first heard of the great naval defeat at Trafalgar, although some ten years had elapsed.

Decree Suppressing Newspapers, January 17, 1800

95   The consuls of the Republic, considering that a part of the newspapers which are printed in the department of the Seine are instruments in the hands of the enemies of the Republic; that the government is especially charged by the French people to watch over their security, decrees as follows:

1. The minister of police shall allow to be printed, published, and distributed during the course of the war only the following newspapers: . . . [The *Moniteur Universel* and twelve others are named], *and newspapers devoted exclusively to the sciences, arts, literature, commerce, and announcements and notices.*

2. The minister of the general police shall immediately make a report upon all the newspapers that are printed in the other departments.

3. The minister of the police shall see that no new newspaper is printed in the department of the Seine, as well as in the other departments of the Republic.

4. The proprietors and editors of the newspapers allowed by the present order shall present themselves to the minister of the police in order to justify themselves as French citizens, to give their residences and signatures, and to promise fidelity to the constitution.

5. All newspapers shall be immediately suppressed if they print articles contrary to the respect that is due to the social compact, to the sovereignty of the people and the glory of the armies, or which shall publish invectives against the governments and nations friendly or allied with the Republic, even if these articles are extracts from foreign periodicals.

6. The minister of the general police is charged with the execution of the present decree, which shall be printed in the *Bulletin of the Laws.*

Moniteur Universel (Paris), 29 nivôse am 8 [January 19, 1800], p. 2. (Trans. H. B. Hill.)

Just as Napoleon utilized those aspects of the Revolution beneficial to his rule, so he also revived any instruments of the old regime which could serve the same end. Thus it was that he returned to aristocracy and to a hierarchical social order. The close relationship between church and state had been an important feature of the old monarchy. The Revolution had ridden rough-shod over the church, submitting it to sufferings far in excess of the wishes of most Frenchmen. Napoleon in 1801, early in his career, made an advantageous peace with the pope. By 1807, as the following document indicates, the church had become an important adjunct to his rule.

IMPERIAL CATECHISM   **96**

Lesson VII. Continuation of the Fourth Commandment.

Q. What are the duties of Christians with respect to the princes who govern them, and what in particular are our duties towards Napoleon I, our Emperor?

A. Christians owe to the princes who govern them, and we owe in particular to Napoleon I, our Emperor, *love,* respect, obedience, fidelity, *military service* and the *tributes* prescribed for the preservation and defence of the Empire and of his throne; we also owe to him fervent prayers for his safety and the spiritual and temporal prosperity of the state.

Q. Why are we bound to all these duties towards our Emperor?

A. It is, first of all, because God, who creates empires and distributes them according to His will, in heaping gifts upon our Emperor, be it in peace or in war, has established him as our sovereign and has made him the minister of His power and His image upon the earth. *To honor and to serve our Emperor is then to honor and to serve God himself.* Secondly, because our Lord Jesus Christ by His doctrine as well as by His example, has Himself taught us what we owe to our sovereign: He was born the subject of Caesar Augustus; He paid the prescribed tax; and just as He ordered to render to God that which belongs to God, so He also ordered to render to Caesar that which belongs to Caesar.

Q. Are there not particular motives which ought to attach us more strongly to Napoleon I, our Emperor?

A. Yes; for it is he whom God has raised up under difficult circumstances to re-establish the public worship of the holy religion of our fathers and to be its protector. He has restored and preserved public order by his profound and active wisdom; he defends the state with his powerful arm; he has become the anointed of the Lord through the consecration which he received from the sovereign pontiff, head of the church universal.

Q. What ought to be thought of those who are lacking in their duty towards our Emperor?

A. According to the apostle Saint Paul, they would be resisting the order established by God himself and would render themselves *worthy of eternal damnation.*

Q. Will the duties to which we are held towards our Emperor be equally binding with respect to his legitimate successors in the order established by the constitutions of the Empire?

A. Yes, without doubt; for we read in the holy scriptures that God, Lord of heaven and earth, by an order of His supreme will and through His providence, gives empires not only to one person in particular, but also to his family. . . .

Grand Dictionnaire Universel du XIXe siècle [Larousse] (15 vols.; Paris, 1866–76), III, 567. (Trans H. B. Hill.)

Public education, first given impetus in France in the days of the Revolution, was immediately recognized by Napoleon as an agency of tremendous political significance which could, specifically, be used to free or to enslave men's minds. Napoleon was no person to leave such a potential weapon to its own devices. As the following decree indicates, he organized the educational system of France into a great pyramid, all under the control of a central body known as the University of France. No university in any common use of the word, it was an institution pointing toward those later refined in the twentieth century for "thought control" and public indoctrination.

Decree for Organizing the Imperial University, March 17, 1808

Title I. General Organization of the University.   **97**

1. Public instruction in the entire empire is intrusted exclusively to the University.

2. No school, no establishment for instruction whatsoever, can be formed outside the Imperial University and without the authorisation of its head.

3. No one can open a school nor give instruction publicly without being a member of the Imperial University and graduated by one of its faculties. Nevertheless, the instruction in the seminaries is under the control of the archbishops and bishops, each for his own diocese. They appoint and dismiss the directors and professors thereof. They are only required to comply with the regulations for the seminaries, approved by us.

4. The Imperial University shall be composed of as many academies as there are courts of appeal.

5. The schools belonging to each academy shall be placed in the following order:

1st. The faculties for the sciences of investigation and the bestowal of degrees;

2d. The *lycées* for the ancient languages, history, rhetoric, logic, and the elements of the mathematical and physical sciences;

3d. The colleges, secondary communal schools, for the elements of the ancient languages and the first principles of history and the sciences;

4th. The institutions and schools conducted by private instructors, in which the instruction is allied to that of the colleges;

5th. The schools and boarding-schools belonging to private masters and devoted to studies less advanced than those of the institutions;

6th. The petty schools and primary schools, in which reading, writing, and the first principles of arithmetic are taught. . . .

Title V. Of the Principles of Instruction in the Schools of the University.

38. All the schools of the Imperial University shall take for the basis of their instruction:

1st. The precepts of the Catholic religion;

2d. Fidelity to the Emperor, to the imperial monarchy, the depository of the welfare of the peoples, and to the Napoleonic dynasty, the conservator of the unity of France and of all the liberal ideas proclaimed by the constitutions;

3d. Obedience to the rules of the teaching corps, which have for their object the uniformity of instruction, and which tend to train for the state citizens attached to their religion, to their prince, to their fatherland, and to their family;

4th. All the professors of theology shall be required to conform themselves to the provisions of the edict of 1682, concerning the four propositions contained in the declaration of the clergy of France of the said year.

Title VI. Of the Obligations which the Members of the University Contract.

39. By the terms of article 2 of the law of May 10, 1806, the members of the Imperial University at the time of their installation shall contract by oath the civil obligations, special and temporary, which shall bind them to the instructional corps.

40. They shall bind themselves to the precise observance of the rules and regulations of the University.

41. They shall promise obedience to the grand master in all that he shall command them for our service and for the good of the instruction.

42. They shall bind themselves not to leave the instructional corps and their functions until after having obtained the consent of the grand master therefor in the forms which shall be prescribed.

43. The grand master can release a member of the University from his obligations and permit him to leave the corps: in case of refusal by the grand master, and of persistence on the part of the member of the University in the resolution to leave the corps, the grand master shall be required to deliver to him a letter of *exeat* after three consecutive demands repeated at intervals of two months.

44. Whoever shall have left the instructional body without having ful-

filled these formalities shall be removed from the roll of the University and shall incur the penalty attached to that removal.

45. The members of the University shall not be able to accept any salaried public or private position without the properly attested permission of the grand master.

46. The members of the University shall be required to inform the grand master and his officers of everything in the establishments of public instruction which may come to their knowledge that is contrary to the doctrine and the principles of the instructional corps.

47. The disciplinary penalties which the violation of the duties and obligations may entail shall be:

1st. Arrests;

2d. Reprimand in the presence of an academic council;

3d. Censure in the presence of the council of the University;

4th. Change to a subordinate employment;

5th. Suspension from duty for a fixed time, with or without total or partial deprivation of stipend;

6th. Reform or retirement given before the time of emeritation, with a stipend less than the pension of the emerited;

7th. Lastly, removal from the roll of the University.

48. Every person who shall have incurred removal shall be disqualified for employment in any public administration.

49. The relations between the penalties and the infraction of duties, as well as the grading of these penalties according to the different employments, shall be established by rules.

Title VII. Of the Functions and Prerogatives of the Grand Master of the University.

50. The Imperial University shall be administered and governed by the grand master, who shall be appointed and dismissed by us.

51. The grand master shall have the selection to the administrative places and to the chairs of the colleges and the *lycées;* he shall likewise appoint the officers of the academies and those of the University, and he shall make all the promotions in the instructional corps.

52. He shall install the persons who shall have obtained the chairs of the faculties, according to the competition whose method shall be determined by the council of the University. . . .

Title XIII. Of the Regulations to be Given to the Lycées, Colleges, Institutions, Boarding Schools and Primary Schools.

101. For the future, and after the complete organization of the University, the head-masters and critics of the *lycées,* the principals and regents of the colleges, as well as the masters of study of these schools, shall be bound to celibacy and to the life in common.

The professors of the *lycées* can be married and, in that case, they shall dwell outside of the *lycée.* The celibate professors can dwell therein, and take advantage of the life in common. . . .

104. There shall be nothing printed and published to announce the studies, the discipline, the boarding conditions, or upon the exercises of the pupils in the schools, unless the different programs have been submitted to the rectors and councils of the academies and approval has been obtained for them.

105. Upon the proposal of the rectors and the advice of the inspectors, and after an information made by the academic councils, the grand master, after having consulted with the council of the University, can cause the closing of the institutions and schools in which there shall have been discovered serious abuses and principles contrary to those which the University professes. . . .

Frank M. Anderson, *The Constitutions and Other Select Documents Illustrative of the History of France, 1789-1907* (New York: H. W. Wilson Co., 1908), pp. 314-22. (Reprinted by permission of the author.)

Secret state police were not new in the day of Napoleon, but this was the first time they were consciously built into a rational system and given all the elaboration and autonomy of a regular part of the public administration. Throughout most of Napoleon's career this system was headed by one man—Joseph Fouché, first religious educator, then revolutionary terrorist, before taking up the career of policeman. Fouché's memoirs, from which the passages below are quoted, must be taken with a grain of salt. Originally published in 1824, they were written by a literary hack, not by Fouché himself, and Fouché was a vain boaster anyway. They have, nevertheless, a ring of authenticity for the twentieth-century reader who recognizes here, in embryo, a characteristic instrument of totalitarianism.

98 . . . It was to the central focus of my cabinet that all the great affairs of state, of which I grasped the strings, finally converged. It will not be doubted that I had salaried spies in all ranks and all orders; I had them of both sexes, hired at the rate of a thousand or two thousand francs per month, according to their importance and their services. I received their reports directly in writing, having a conventional mark. Every three months I communicated my list to the Emperor, in order that there might be no double employment, and also in order that the nature of the service, occasionally permanent, often temporary, might be rewarded either by places or remunerations.

As to the department of foreign police, it had two essential objects; namely, to watch friendly powers and counteract hostile governments. In both cases it was composed of individuals purchased or pensioned, and commissioned to reside near each government or in each principal town, independent of numerous secret agents sent into all countries, either by the minister of foreign affairs or by the Emperor himself.

I also had my foreign spies. It was in my department also that the foreign gazettes prohibited to the perusal of the French people, and transcripts of which were sent to me, were treasured up. By that means I held in my hands the most important strings of foreign politics, and I discharged, in conjunction with the chief of the government, a task capable of controlling or balancing that of the minister charged with the function of foreign relations.

I was thus far from limiting my duties to espionage. All the state prisons were under my control, as well as the gendarmery. The delivery and the *visa* of passports belonged to me. To me was assigned the duty of overlooking amnestied individuals and foreigners. I established general commissariats in the principal towns of the kingdom, which extended the network of the police over the whole of France, and especially our frontiers.

My police acquired so high a renown that the world went so far as to pretend that I had, among my secret agents, three nobles of the *ancien régime,* distinguished by princely titles, and who daily communicated to me the result of their observations.

I confess that such an establishment was expensive; it swallowed up several millions, the funds of which were secretly provided from taxes laid upon gambling and prostitution and from the granting of passports. Notwithstanding all that has been said against gambling, reflecting and decided minds must allow that in the actual state of society the legal converting of vice into profit is a necessary evil. A proof that all the odium attendant upon the measure is not to be attributed exclusively to the republican governments, is that at the present day gambling taxes form part of the budget of the old government now re-established. Since it was an unavoidable evil, it became necessary to employ severe regulations, that the disorder might at least be under control. Under the Empire, the establishment of which cost nearly four hundred millions of francs, since there were thirty families to be provided with dignities and honors, it became necessary to organise the gambling-houses upon a much larger scale, for the produce of them was not solely destined to reward my moving phalanxes of spies. I nominated as superintendent-general of the gambling-houses in France, Perrein the elder, who already farmed them, and who, after the coronation, extended his privilege over all the chief towns of the Empire, upon condition of paying fourteen millions yearly, independent of three thousand francs daily to the minister of the police. All, however, did not remain in his hands.

All these elements of an immense power did not reach my cabinet there to expire without utility. As I was informed of all, it became my duty to centre in myself the public complaints, in order to make known to the head of the government the uneasiness and misfortunes of the state.

I will not therefore dissemble that it was in my power to act upon the fear or terror which either more or less constantly agitated the possessor of unlimited power. The great searcher into the state, I could complain, censure, and condemn for the whole of France. In this point of view, what evils have I not prevented? If I found myself unable to reduce, as was my wish, the general police to a mere scarecrow, or rather to a benevolent institution, I have at least the satisfaction of being able to assert that I have done more good than ill; that is to say, that I have avoided more evil than it was permitted me to do, having almost always to struggle with the prejudices, the passions, and the furious transports of the chief of the state.

In my second ministry I succeeded much more by the force of informations and of apprehension than by restraint and the employment of coercive measures. I revived the ancient police maxim—that three persons could not meet and speak indiscreetly upon public affairs without its coming the next day to the ears of the minister of police. Certain it is that I had the address to make it universally believed that wherever four persons assembled, there, in my pay, were eyes to see and ears to hear. Such a belief, no doubt, tended to general corruption and debasement; but, on the other hand, what evils, what wretchedness, what tears has it prevented! Such then was this vast and terrific machine called the general police of the Empire. . . .

The Memoirs of Joseph Fouché (London: H. S. Nichols, 1896), I, 233–36.

It is only fair to a figure as great as Napoleon to let him speak for himself. The quotations which follow, all written while in exile on St. Helena, show him in that essential greatness. Napoleon possessed to a unique degree the ability to feel the pulse of history in the making, to understand the nature of events and people, and to realize from both all that destiny had in store. This meant that he was capable of achieving much good, and he undoubtedly hastened the consolidation and dissemination of the social gains of the Revolution. At the same time he was utterly callous in regard to humanity as such, and while no sadism, no genocide marred his career, he shed few tears for the literally hundreds of thousands of men who immolated themselves before the altar of his fame. So while in one sense Napoleon served men, in another and morally more fundamental sense he used them— and he did it with an almost diabolical cunning.

[April 26, 1816]. Well, after all said and done, circumstances might have **99** led me to accept Islam, and as that excellent Queen of France used to say: How you do go on! But I should have wanted something worth my while, —at least up to the Euphrates. A change of religion, which is unpardonable for personal motives, may perhaps be accepted when immense political results depend on it. Henry IV rightly said: Paris is worth a mass. To think that the Empire of the East, perhaps the dominion of all Asia, was the matter of a turban and a pair of baggy trousers; for really that was all it came to.

Constantinople alone is an Empire; whoever possesses it can rule the world. . . .

[September 29, 1816]. You want to know the treasures of Napoleon? They are enormous, it is true, but in full view. Here they are: the splendid harbour of Antwerp, that of Flushing, capable of holding the largest fleets; the docks and dykes of Dunkirk, of Havre, of Nice; the gigantic harbour of Cherbourg; the harbour works at Venice; the great roads from Antwerp to Amsterdam, from Mainz to Metz, from Bordeaux to Bayonne; the passes of the Simplon, of Mont Cenis, of Mont Genèvre, of the Corniche, that give four openings through the Alps; in that alone you might reckon 800 millions. The roads from the Pyrenees to the Alps, from Parma to Spezzia, from Savona to Piedmont; the bridges of Jena, of Austerlitz, of the Arles, of Sèvres, of Tours, of Lyons, of Turin, of the Isère, of the Durance, of Bordeaux, of Rouen; the canal from the Rhine to the Rhone, joining the waters of Holland to the Mediterranean; the canal that joins the Scheldt and the Somme, connecting Amsterdam and Paris; that which joins the Rance and the Vilaine; the canal of Arles, of Pavia, of the Rhine; the draining of the marshes of Bourgoing, of the Cotentin, of Rochefort; the rebuilding of most of the churches pulled down during the Revolution, the building of new ones; the construction of many industrial establishments for putting an end to pauperism; the construction of the Louvre, of the public granaries, of the Bank, of the canal of the Ourcq; the water system of the city of Paris, the numerous sewers, the quays, the embellishments and monuments of that great city; the public improvements of Rome; the reëstablishment of the manufactories of Lyons. Fifty millions spent on repairing and improving the Crown residences; sixty millions' worth of furniture placed in the palaces of France and Holland, at Turin, at Rome; sixty millions' worth of Crown diamonds, all of it the money of Napoleon; even the Regent, the only missing one of the old diamonds of the Crown of France, purchased from Berlin Jews with whom it was pledged for three millions; the Napoleon Museum, valued at more than 400 millions.

These are monuments to confound calumny! History will relate that all this was accomplished in the midst of continuous wars, without raising a loan, and with the public debt actually decreasing day by day. . . .

[March 3, 1817]. In spite of all the libels, I have no fear whatever about my fame. Posterity will do me justice. The truth will be known; and the good I have done will be compared with the faults I have committed. I am not uneasy as to the result. Had I succeeded, I would have died with the reputation of the greatest man that ever existed. As it is, although I have failed, I shall be considered as an extraordinary man: my elevation was unparalleled, because unaccompanied by crime. I have fought fifty pitched battles, almost all of which I have won. I have framed and carried into effect a code of laws that will bear my name to the most distant posterity. I raised myself from nothing to be the most powerful monarch in the world. Europe was at my feet. I have always been of opinion that the sovereignty lay in the people. In fact, the imperial government was a kind of republic. Called to the head of it by the voice of the nation, my maxim was, *la carrière est ouverte aux talens* [career open to talent] without distinction of birth or fortune, and this system of equality is the reason that your oligarchy hates me so much. . . .

[June 2, 1817]. A singular thing about me is my memory. As a boy I knew the logarithms of thirty or forty numbers; in France I not only knew the names of the officers of all the regiments, but where the corps had been recruited, had distinguished themselves; I even knew their spirit.

3d. The 32d demi-brigade would have laid down its life for me because, after Lonato, I wrote: The 32d was there: I was easy.—The influence of words over men is astounding! . . .

[August 28, 1817]. Jesus was hanged, like so many a fanatic who posed as a prophet, a messiah; there were several every year. What is certain is that at that epoch opinion was setting towards a single God, and those who first preached the doctrine were well received: circumstances made for it. It is just as in my case, sprung from the lower ranks of society I became an emperor, because circumstances, opinion, were with me.

The Corsican, ed. R. M. Johnston(Boston: Houghton Mifflin Co., 1910), pp. 474–96.

QUESTIONS

1. To what things did Napoleon appeal in winning the hearts of his soldiers?
2. How did Napoleon not only suppress unfriendly newspapers but control friendly ones as well?
3. In what fashion did Napoleon enlist the church in his cause?
4. What specific features were involved in Napoleon's control of education?
5. What was the structure of Napoleon's secret police system?

CHAPTER XVI

THE CONGRESS OF VIENNA

THE CONGRESS OF VIENNA, which met in the Austrian capital in the fall of 1814, set out to establish a real and durable settlement after more than two decades of war. Napoleon had upset the map of Europe, and the Congress attempted to put it together again. The rivalries of the great powers and the presence of many interest groups at Vienna made this a formidable task. How this unwieldy Congress was organized is told in a letter from the British foreign secretary, Lord Castlereagh, to his prime minister, Lord Liverpool (100).

The rivalry of the big powers centered upon Poland and Saxony. Russia desired Poland, and Prussia was willing to be compensated by getting Saxony, which had, mistakenly, remained loyal to Napoleon. Neither Bavaria nor Great Britain wanted to see such aggrandizements. The ensuing deadlock enabled Prince Talleyrand to break the stalemate by throwing his weight to Austria, Bavaria, and Britain. Through this move he managed to insert France, the defeated nation, into the council of the victors. His letter to his king tells this story (101).

The final settlement was based largely on the principle of "legitimacy," symbolized by the Holy Alliance (102). This mystical organization did not control the actions of any ruler who signed it. It came to symbolize, however, the spirit of "reaction" against revolutions and national aspirations that was dominant in the years after Vienna. The political reality behind the Holy Alliance was the Quadruple Alliance by which Austria, Prussia, Russia, Great Britain and, later, France bound themselves to maintain the settlement at Vienna for two decades.

In the following letter, Lord Castlereagh tells his prime minister how the Congress of Vienna is being organized and points out some of the territorial problems that have arisen.

Castlereagh to Liverpool. Vienna **100**
November 21, 1814

. . . In framing the successive protocols herewith transmitted of the deliberations of the eight Powers who signed the Peace of Paris, you will perceive that it has not been deemed advisable, in the present state of the business, to assemble the plenipotentiaries at large in Congress, there being nothing as yet sufficiently matured to submit to them for their ultimate confirmation.

In proportion as the subject underwent consideration, it became apparent that the Congress was incompetent to act as a constituted and deliberative assembly, possessing the power of binding dissentient voices by the majority of the votes: that it could not delegate to commissions powers which it did not itself possess, and that the preparatory negotiations must originate with the parties naturally interested.

This has at last led to an arrangement which seems sufficient for every practical purpose and to which there seems no longer any objection. The plenipotentiaries of the eight Powers, in number twenty, vizt.: Austria two, Russia three, Great Britain four, France four, Prussia two, Portugal three, Spain one, and Sweden one, meet together occasionally as a directing body. In the interval the several subjects are treated of nearly under the following distribution.

The affairs of Poland are left to the three Powers locally interested, and the intervention of Great Britain: the Prince de Talleyrand and the other plenipotentiaries have always considered this as a suitable mode of discussing that subject, in the first instance, and he has confined himself to occasional explanations of the sentiments of his Court thereupon in his interviews with the sovereigns, and the parties interested. The details of these discussions have already been submitted to the Prince Regent.

At a very early period, a species of commission consisting of the five principal German Powers, viz.: Austria, Prussia, Bavaria, Hanover, and Württemberg, charged themselves with German affairs. They have made considerable progress in framing a project of confederation for Germany in pursuance of the principle laid down in the Treaty of Paris. The labors of these commissioners are exclusively confined to the constitutional organization of Germany, but its territorial distribution has been also a subject of frequent discussion between them and the other European Powers principally interested: and although nothing can definitely be settled till we know what is disposable in Poland to be assigned to the two great German Powers [Prussia and Austria], yet the whole has been examined so carefully, and in so many points of view, that I consider material progress has been made towards a final decision, if the principal Powers could agree upon the two fundamental questions of Saxony and Poland, which must in a great measure determine the quantum of means disposable to satisfy the various claims. . . .

British Diplomacy, 1813–1815, ed. C. K. Webster (London: Bell & Sons, Ltd., 1921), pp. 236–37. (Reprinted by permission of the publisher.)

The following letter from Talleyrand to Louis XVIII reports the important results of his diplomatic moves following the deadlock between the great powers over Saxony and Poland. Notice how it begins with a reference to another matter designed to support the legitimacy of Louis's cause.

101   *Vienna, 4th January, 1815*

Sire,

I have received the letter of the 23rd of last month, with which your Majesty has deigned to honor me.

On the 21st of the present month, the anniversary of a day of horror and eternal mourning [the guillotining of Louis XVI], a solemn expiatory service will be celebrated in one of the principal churches of Vienna. I am having the preparations made; and, in giving orders for them I have acted not only on the impulse of my feelings, but from a sense that it becomes the ambassadors of your Majesty, while acting as the interpreters of the sorrow of France, to proclaim that sorrow aloud in a foreign land and before the eyes of assembled Europe. All, in this sad ceremony, must bear proportion to the grandeur of its object, the splendor of the Crown of France, and the quality of those who are to witness it. All the members of the Congress will be invited, and I am assured that they will come. The Emperor of Austria has had me informed that he will be present, and no doubt his example will be followed by the other sovereigns. All that is most distinguished in Vienna, of both sexes, will feel it a duty to attend on the occasion. I do not yet know what it will cost, but the expense is a necessary one.

The news of the signature of peace between England and the United States of America was announced to me on New Year's Day by a note from Lord Castlereagh. I hastened to offer him my congratulations, and I also congratulated myself on the event, feeling that it may influence both the disposition of the minister and the resolutions of those with whose pretensions we have hitherto had to contend. Lord Castlereagh showed me the treaty. It does not affront the honor of either of the two parties concerned, and consequently it will satisfy both.

This happy intelligence was only the precursor of a still more fortunate event.

The spirit of the coalition and the coalition itself had survived the Peace of Paris. My correspondence has, up to the present time, supplied your Majesty with repeated proofs of this. If the plans which, on arriving here, I found had been formed, had been carried into execution, France might have stood alone in Europe without being in good relations with any one single Power for half a century to come. All my efforts were directed to the prevention of so great a misfortune, but my most ardent hopes did not reach the height of a complete success.

Now, Sire, the coalition is dissolved, and for ever. Not only does France no longer stand alone in Europe, but your Majesty already has a federate system such as it seemed that fifty years of negotiation could not have procured for her. France is in concert with two of the greatest Powers, and three States of the second order, and will soon be in concert with all the States which are guided by other than revolutionary principles and maxims. Your Majesty will be in reality the head and the soul of that union, formed for the defence of the principles which your Majesty has been the first to proclaim.

So great and happy a change is only to be attributed to that special favor of Providence which was so visibly marked by the restoration of your Majesty.

Under God, the efficient causes of this change have been—

My letters to M. de Metternich and Lord Castlereagh, and the impression which they have produced;

The suggestions which I gave Lord Castlereagh, relative to a union with France, and of which I gave your Majesty an account in my last letter;

The pains I have taken to lull his distrust by exhibiting perfect disinterestedness in the name of France;

The peace with America, which, by releasing him from difficulty on that side has left him more liberty of action, and given him greater courage;

Lastly, the pretensions of Russia and Prussia, as set forth in the Russian project . . . and especially the manner in which those pretensions were advanced and argued in a conference between their plenipotentiaries and those of Austria. The arrogant tone of that insolent and nonsensical document so deeply offended Lord Castlereagh that, departing from his habitual calmness, he declared that the Russians were claiming to lay down the law and that England was not disposed to accept it from anybody.

All this had influenced him, and I took advantage of the disposition of his mind to urge the union concerning which I had so often talked to him. He received all I said with animation and proposed that he should write to me his ideas on the subject. The day after this interview he called on me, and I was agreeably surprised when I saw that he had put his ideas into the form of articles. Up to the present he has been very little accustomed to praise from me, and he was therefore all the more pleased with the compliments which I bestowed upon his draft. He requested that M. de Metternich and I would read it with attention. I made an appointment for the evening and, after we had made a few slight alterations, we adopted it under the form of an agreement. In certain particulars it might have been more carefully drawn up, but in dealing with weak people delay is dangerous; so we have signed the document tonight. I hasten to forward it to your Majesty.

Your Majesty had authorized me by your letters in general, and by particular instructions of the 25th of October, to promise to Austria and Bavaria your Majesty's *most active co-operation,* and as a consequence to stipulate for such aid in favor of those two Powers as would probably be rendered necessary by the forces which would be opposed to them in case of war. Your Majesty has authorized me to do this, even supposing that England were to remain neutral; now, England has become an active party, and with her the United Provinces and Hanover; thus the position of France is a superb one.

General Dupont having written to me on the 9th of November that your Majesty would have a hundred and eighty thousand men available on the first of January, and a hundred thousand more in the month of March, without having recourse to a fresh levy, I thought that an auxiliary corps of a hundred and fifty thousand men might with propriety be stipulated, as England engages to furnish the same number of troops, and France could not do less. The agreement being made for defensive purposes only, the succors should not be furnished except in case of attack, and there is every reason to believe that Russia and Prussia will not run that chance.

Still, as this case might arise and render a military treaty necessary, I beg that your Majesty will be pleased to give orders for General Ricard's being sent here to assist me. He enjoys the confidence of Marshal Soult; and, having been for a long time in Poland, and especially at Warsaw, he has local knowledge which may be very useful in arrangements likely to occur. The report that has been made to me of his worth and ability leads me to prefer him to any other; but it is necessary that he should come incognito, and that the Minister of War, after having given him the requisite documents, should enjoin the profoundest secrecy upon him. According to what I have been told of him, he is a gentleman, one to whom your Majesty might, if you thought proper to do so, give your orders in person.

I entreat your Majesty to be pleased to command that the ratifications of the treaty be expedited, and sent to me as soon as possible. Your Majesty will no doubt think it well to impress upon M. de Jaucourt that none but men of well-tried discretion ought to be employed in that business. . . .

> I am, Sire, With the most profound respect,
> Your Majesty's most humble and obedient
> servant and subject,
>
> *Talleyrand*

The Correspondence of Prince Talleyrand and King Louis XVIII (New York: Charles Scribner's Sons, 1881), pp. 240–47.

The Holy Alliance was the brainchild of Tsar Alexander I of Russia. After the treaty had been signed by Russia, Austria, and Prussia, France gave her signature. Louis XVIII thus made his official repudiation of France's revolutionary and Napoleonic past.

The treaty called the Holy Alliance signed in Paris on the 14–26 September 1815 between the Emperors of Austria and Russia and the King of Prussia. **102**

In the Name of the most Holy and indivisible Trinity, Their Majesties the Emperor of Austria, the King of Prussia, and the Emperor of all the Russias, because of the great events which have transpired in Europe during the last three years, and principally because of the benefits which it has pleased Divine Providence to bestow upon those states whose governments have put their confidence and trust in Her only, having come to the innermost conviction that it is necessary to establish the course to be adopted by the great powers in their mutual relations to the sublime verities which the Eternal Religion of the God and Saviour teaches:

Declare solemnly that the present act has no other purpose than to manifest before the world their unshakable determination to take as the rules for their conduct, be it in the administration of their respective states or in their political relations with all other governments, solely the precepts of this holy religion; precepts of justice, charity and peace, which, far from being only applicable to private life, must, on the contrary, influence directly the decisions of Princes and guide all their measures as the only means of consolidating human institutions and of remedying their imperfections.

In consequence, their Majesties have agreed upon the following articles:

1. In conformity with the word of Holy Scripture, which commands all men to look upon themselves as brothers, the three contracting monarchs remain united by the links of a true and indissoluble fraternity; and, considering themselves as fellow citizens, they will give each other assistance, aid and relief on every occasion and in every place; considering themselves towards their subjects and their armies as fathers of one family, they will rule them in that same spirit of fraternity which prompts them to protect religion, peace and justice.

2. In consequence, the only principle in force, be it between these governments, be it between their subjects, is to render each other reciprocal services, to give testimony through an unalterable benevolence to the mutual affection with which they must be actuated, and not to consider themselves otherwise than members of the same Christian nation. The three allied Princes do not look upon themselves otherwise than delegated by Providence to rule three branches of the same family, to wit, Austria, Prussia, and Russia; confessing in this manner that the Christian nation, of which they and their people are a part, has in reality no other sovereign than Him to Whom alone, in reality, belongs the power; because in Him alone there are all the treasuries of love, of knowledge and of infinite wisdom, that is to say, God, our Divine Saviour Jesus Christ, the Word of the Highest, the word of life; Their Majesties therefore recommend with the greatest solicitude to their peoples, as the only means of enjoying that peace which comes from a good conscience and which alone is durable, to well fortify themselves increasingly each day in the principles and the exercise of the duties which the Divine Saviour has taught men.

3. All the Powers who want solemnly to affirm the sacred principles which have dictated the present act, and who recognize how important it is for the happiness of nations, too long disquieted, that these truths from now on exercise upon the destinies of men all the influence which belongs to them, will be received with as much eagerness as affection into this alliance. Made out in triplicate and signed in Paris in the year of grace 1815, the 26/14 September.

François   Frédéric-Guillaume   Alexandre

Act of accession of France to the Holy Alliance (19 November 1815): H. M. the Emperor of all the Russias having invited me, according to the article 3 of the above Treaty signed in Paris, the 26/14 September of the current year, between him and their Majesties the Emperor of Austria and the King of Prussia, to join in this act; I hereby solemnly declare that I affirm the sacred principles which have dictated it and that I engage myself to follow them, recognizing how important it is for the happiness of nations that these truths exercise from now on upon the destinies of men all the influence which belongs to them.

Given in Paris, the 19 November of the year of grace 1815.

Louis

M. de Clercq, *Recueil des traités de la France* (Paris, 1880), pp. 629–30. (Trans. George L. Mosse.)

QUESTIONS

1. What principal powers controlled the Congress of Vienna? How did they go about it, judging from Castlereagh's description of the organization of the Congress?
2. How did Talleyrand succeed in breaking up the coalition of victors in favor of France?
3. Through an approach to the representative of what nation did Talleyrand push his way into such a favorable position at Vienna?
4. Why was a promise of military aid to Austria and Bavaria of such importance? What powers did these nations fear would aggrandize themselves?
5. From the treaty of the Holy Alliance, what were the principles of the "reaction" in Europe?
6. What were the passages in this treaty which most clearly repudiated the age of the Revolution?

CHAPTER XVII

THE INDUSTRIAL REVOLUTION

THE TERM "industrial revolution" is misleading, denoting a sudden overturn in a previous state of affairs. In fact, the process of industrialization in England had deep historic roots, traceable in some industries as far back as the Middle Ages; by the time of Defoe (103) it had already proceeded a considerable distance. Nor was the "revolution" merely industrial; agricultural improvements were necessary to produce food for the growing urban population (104–6). Nevertheless, the popularity of the term stems from its association with the great inventions which multiplied rapidly after the middle of the eighteenth century and led to the substitution of machinery for hand labor and the introduction of the "factory system" (107–10).

Closely connected with the changes in technology and economic organization were other profound and far-reaching changes in social structure, politics, intellectual outlook, and even religion; the debate over the desirability of the social consequences of the process of industrialization began at once (111–26) and has continued to the present day.

I. MANUFACTURING BEFORE THE INDUSTRIAL REVOLUTION

England was already known as a manufacturing nation in the days when the word manufacture still meant "to make by hand." Although a few branches of industry used heavy machinery and a factory type of organization, the prevailing organization of industry, especially in textiles, was that known as the "putting out" or "domestic" system: the employer of labor distributed his material to workmen scattered about the countryside in their cottages where they worked it up by hand. In the following selection Daniel Defoe presents an impression of English industry in the first quarter of the eighteenth century.

. . . The manufactures of Great Britain are so prodigious in quantity **103** that the variety of kinds is scarce taken notice of; nay, some have their thoughts so engrossed by the woolen and clothing manufacture that when you name the word manufacture, they would understand nothing but the woolen manufacture; they would have it be called THE *Manufacture,* as if there were no manufacture, or that nothing was to be called a manufacture but what was made of wool; whereas Great Britain, as we shall see in its course, has her people employed in many very useful manufactures, and that such as make very considerable articles in our commerce as well our home trade as our foreign trade, giving business to the tradesman and to the merchant also, as it does likewise employment and wages to the poor. . . .

Daniel Defoe, *The Compleat English Tradesman* (London, 1727), II, Part II, 49-50.

II. IMPROVEMENTS IN AGRICULTURE

The rapidly growing population of England required a greatly increased food supply to support it, but English agriculture was handicapped by remnants of medieval practices in both technology and legal organization. It was a standing objective of agricultural reformers to introduce new crops, new methods of cultivation, improved breeds of livestock, etc. (104); but in order to do this it was necessary to enclose and consolidate the large open fields where small cultivators carried on their work in a sort of co-operative effort (105). The process of enclosure was not, however, without social cost in the form of displaced villagers who had not the capital necessary to take advantage of enclosure (106). Arthur Young, the author of the next two selections, was a well-known agricultural reformer and publicist whose writings were largely responsible for the introduction of improved methods of farming. Among his devoted readers were King George III, George Washington, Thomas Jefferson, and Queen Marie Antoinette of France.

Arthur Young on the Deficiencies of English Agriculture (1770)

104   The husbandry of the Marquis of Rockingham is much more worthy of attention than that of any palace; the effects which have and must continue to result from it are of the noblest and most truly national kind; a short sketch of his Lordship's operations will convince you how much an extensive tract of country is obliged to this patriotic nobleman for introducing a cultivation unknown before.

Upon turning his attention to agriculture, his Lordship found the husbandry of the West Riding of Yorkshire extremely deficient in numerous particulars. It was disgusting to him to view so vast a property cultivated in so slovenly a manner; eager to substitute better methods in the room of such unpleasing as well as unprofitable ones, he determined to exert himself with spirit in the attempt; and he executed the noble scheme in a manner that does honor to his penetration. A very few particulars, among many of the common practice, will show how much this country wanted a Rockingham to animate its cultivation.

1. Large tracts of land, both grass and arable, yielded but a trifling profit, for want of draining. In wet clays, the rushes and other aquatic rubbish usurped the place of corn and grass; the seasons of tilling were retarded, and even destroyed; and those pastures which ought to have fed an ox, scarcely maintained a sheep.

2. The pastures and meadows of this country were universally laid down in ridge and furrow, a practice highly destructive of profit, and detestable to the eye; and the manner of laying down such lands was as miserable as their product denoted poverty; for after many years ploughing of numerous crops but insufficient fallows, when the soil was so exhausted as to disappoint the expectation of corn, a parcel of rubbish called hay-seeds was scattered over the surface, and the field left to time for improvement. A villainous custom, and too much practiced in all parts of the kingdom.

3. The culture of turnips was become common, but in such a method that their introduction was undoubtedly a real mischief; *viz.,* without hoeing,

so that the year of fallow, in the general management, was the most capital year of slovenliness and bad husbandry.

4. The implements used in agriculture through this tract were insufficient for a vigorous culture, and consequently the husbandman sustained a constant loss.

These circumstances, among others, show how much the husbandry of this country wanted improvement. . . .

Arthur Young, *A Six Months Tour through the North of England* (London, 1770), I, 307–9.

The Necessity of Enclosure (1775)

. . . It may be laid down as a maxim, that without inclosures there can **105** be no good husbandry; while a county is laid out in open fields, every farmer tied down to the husbandry of his slovenly neighbour, it is simply impossible that agriculture should flourish. . . .

Arthur Young, *Political Arithmetic* (London, 1775), p. 198.

Some Social Consequences of Enclosure (1797)

A Petition of the hereunder-signed small Proprietors of Land and Persons **106**
entitled to Rights of Common [at Raunds, Northamptonshire].
That the petitioners beg leave to represent to the House that, under the pretence of improving lands in the same parish, the cottagers and other persons entitled to right of common on the lands intended to be enclosed, will be deprived of an inestimable privilege, which they now enjoy, of turning a certain number of their cows, calves, and sheep, on and over the said lands; a privilege that enables them not only to maintain themselves and their families in the depth of winter, when they cannot, even for their money, obtain from the occupiers of other lands the smallest portion of milk or whey for such necessary purpose, but in addition to this, they can now supply the grazier with young or lean stock at a reasonable price, to fatten and bring to market at a more moderate rate for general consumption, which they conceive to be the most rational and effectual way of establishing public plenty and cheapness of provision; and they further conceive, that a more ruinous effect of this enclosure will be the almost total depopulation of their town, now filled with bold and hardy husbandmen, from among whom, and the inhabitants of other open parishes, the nation has hitherto derived its greatest strength and glory, in the supply of its fleets and armies, and driving them, from necessity and want of employ, in vast crowds, into manufacturing towns, where the very nature of their employment, over the loom

or the forge, soon may waste their strength, and consequently debilitate their posterity, and by imperceptible degrees obliterate that great principle of obedience to the Laws of God and their country which forms the character of the simple and artless villagers, more equally distributed through the open counties, and on which so much depends the good order and government of the state. These are some of the injuries to themselves as individuals, and of the ill consequences to the public, which the petitioners conceive will follow from this, as they have already done from many enclosures, but which they did not think they were entitled to lay before the House (the constitutional patron and protector of the poor) until it unhappily came to their own lot to be exposed to them through the Bill now pending.

Great Britain, House of Commons, *Commons Journals*, July 19, 1797; as reprinted in A. E. Bland, P. A. Brown, and R. H. Tawney, *English Economic History: Select Documents* (London: Bell & Sons, Ltd., 1914), pp. 531–32.

III. THE GREAT INVENTIONS AND THE FACTORY SYSTEM

As previously pointed out (p. 198), the "industrial revolution," even in the narrow sense of the term, involved far more than the introduction of the factory system: canals, turnpikes, and eventually railways were constructed; mining output increased phenomenally, and new industries were undertaken or old ones reorganized—among them chemicals, glass, and pottery. But the most important and most spectacular technological advances were those having to do with the manufacture of iron (107), the steam engine (108), and cotton spinning (109); it was the latter industry which lent itself most readily to the factory system (110).

Innovation in the Iron Industry

107   *A letter of Abiah Darby, wife of the second Abraham Darby, a Quaker Ironmaster in the West of England (1775)*

. . . It was my Husband's Father, whose name he bore (Abraham Darby and who was the first that set on foot the Brass Works at or near Bristol) that attempted to mould and cast Iron pots, &c., in sand instead of Loam (as they were wont to do, which made it a tedious and more expensive process) in which he succeeded. This first attempt was tryed at an Air Furnace in Bristol. About the year 1709 he came into Shropshire to Coalbrookdale, and with other partners took a lease of the works, which only consisted of an old Blast Furnace and some Forges. He here cast Iron Goods in sand out of the Blast Furnace that blow'd with wood charcoal; for it was not yet thought of to blow with Pit Coal. Sometime after he suggested the thought, that it might be practable to smelt the Iron from the ore in the blast Furnace with Pit Coal: Upon this he first try'd with raw coal as it came out of the Mines, but it did not answer. He not discouraged, had the coal coak'd into Cynder, as is done for drying Malt, and it then succeeded to his satisfaction. But he found that only one sort of pit Coal would suit best for the purpose of making good Iron. . . .

My Husband's Father died early in life; a religious good man, and an Eminent Minister amongst the people call'd Quakers.

My Husband Abraham Darby was but Six years old when his Father died—but he inherited his genius—enlarg'd upon his plan, and made many improvements. . . .

But all this time the making of Barr Iron at Forges from Pit Coal pigs was not thought of. About 26 years ago my Husband conceived this happy thought—that it might be possible to make bar from pit coal pigs. Upon this he Sent some of our pigs to be tryed at the Forges, and that no prejudice might arise against them he did not discover from whence they came, or of what quality they were. And a good account being given of their working, he errected Blast Furnaces for Pig Iron for Forges. Edward Knight Esqr a capitol Iron Master urged my Husband to get a patent, that he might reap the benefit for years of this happy discovery; but he said he would not deprive the public of Such an Acquisition which he was Satisfyed it would be; and so it has proved, for it soon spread, and Many Furnaces both in this Neighbourhood and Several other places have been errected for this purpose.

Had not these discoveries been made the Iron trade of our own produce would have dwindled away, for woods for charcoal became very Scarce and landed Gentlemen rose the prices of cord wood exceeding high—indeed it would not have been to be got. But from pit coal being introduced in its stead the demand for wood charcoal is much lessen'd, and in a few years I apprehend will set the use of that article aside. . . .

T. S. Ashton, *Iron and Steel in the Industrial Revolution* (Manchester: The University Press, 1924), pp. 249–50, 251. (Reprinted by permission of the publisher.)

James Watt's Account of his Role in Developing the Steam Engine (1775, 1800)

My attention was first directed, in the year 1759, to the subject of steam-engines, by the late Dr. Robison, then a student in the University of Glasgow, and nearly of my own age. He at that time threw out an idea of applying **108** the power of the steam-engine to the moving of wheel-carriages, and to other purposes, but the scheme was not matured, and was soon abandoned on his going abroad. . . .

The attention necessary to the avocations of business prevented me from then prosecuting the subject further, but in the winter of 1763-4, having occasion to repair a model of Newcomen's engine belonging to the Natural Philosophy class of the University of Glasgow, my mind was again directed to it. At that period my knowledge was derived principally from Desaguliers, and partly from Belidor. I set about repairing it as a mere mechanician; and when that was done, and it was set to work, I was surprised to find that its boiler could not supply it with steam, though apparently quite large enough. . . .

[Thereupon followed numerous experiments, until Watt conceived the idea of a separate condenser:]

On reflecting further I perceived that, in order to make the best use of steam, it was necessary—first, that the cylinder should be maintained always as hot as the steam which entered it; and, secondly, that when the steam was condensed, the water of which it was composed, and the injection itself, should be cooled down to 100°, or lower, where that was possible. The means of accomplishing these points did not immediately present themselves, but early in 1765 it occurred to me that if a communication were opened between a cylinder containing steam and another vessel which was exhausted of air and other fluids, the steam, as an elastic fluid, would immediately rush into the empty vessel, and continue so to do until it had established an equilibrium, and if that vessel were kept very cool by an injection, or otherwise, more steam would continue to enter until the whole was condensed. . . .

When once the idea of the separate condensation was started, all these improvements followed as corollaries in quick succession, so that in the course of one or two days the invention was thus far complete in my mind, and I immediately set about an experiment to verify it practically. . . .

In 1768 I applied for letters patent for my "Methods of Lessening the Consumption of Steam, and, consequently, of Fuel, in Fire-Engines," which passed the seals in January, 1769; and my Specification was enrolled in Chancery in April following. . . .

After a series of various and violent opposition, I have at last got an Act of Parliament vesting the property of my new fire-engines in me and my assigns, throughout Great Britain and the Plantations, for twenty-five years to come, which I hope will be very beneficial to me, as there is already considerable demand for them. . . .

The title of the new patent, which passed the Great Seal on the 12th of March, 1782, was quite a general one; being "for certain new improvements upon steam or fire-engines, for raising water, and other mechanical purposes, and certain new pieces of mechanism applicable to the same." But in the specification, which was enrolled on the 4th of July, 1782, are comprehended the following "new improvements":

1. The use of steam on the expansive principle; together with various methods or contrivances (six in number, some of them comprising various modifications), for equalizing the expansive power.

2. The double-acting engine; in which steam is admitted to press the piston upwards as well as downwards; the piston being also aided in its ascent as well as in its descent by a vacuum produced by condensation on the other side.

3. The double-engine; consisting of two engines, primary and secondary, of which the steam-vessels and condensers communicate by pipes and valves, so that they can be worked either independently or in concert; and make their strokes either alternately or both together, as may be required.

4. The employment of a toothed rack and sector, instead of chains, for guiding the piston-rod.

5. A rotative engine, or steam-wheel. . . .

James P. Muirhead, *The Life of James Watt, with Selections from his Correspondence* (New York: D. Appleton & Co., 1859), pp. 59, 60, 64, 65, 67, 203, 232–33.

Arkwright's Inventions and the Introduction of the Factory System, by an Early Historian of the Cotton Industry (1835)

. . . Up to the year 1760, the machines used in the cotton manufacture in **109** England were nearly as simple as those of India; though the loom was more strongly and perfectly constructed, and cards for combing the cotton had been adopted from the woolen manufacture.

The cotton manufacture, though rapidly increasing, could never have received such an extension as to become of great national importance without the discovery of some method for producing a greater quantity and better quality of yarn with the same labor. . . .

On the 16th December, 1775, Mr. Arkwright took out a second patent for a series of machines comprising the carding, drawing, and roving machines, all used "in preparing silk, cotton, flax, and wool for spinning." The said machines were said to be "constructed on easy and simple principles, very different from any that had ever yet been contrived"; and Arkwright claimed to be "the first and sole inventor thereof," and asserted that "the same had never been practiced by any other person or persons whomsoever, to the best of his knowledge and belief." That this statement is to be received with some allowance the reader will perceive from the history we have given of the inventions.

When this admirable series of machines was made known, and by their means yarns were produced far superior in quality to any before spun in England, as well as lower in price, a mighty impulse was communicated to the cotton manufacture. Weavers could now obtain an unlimited quantity of yarn at a reasonable price; manufacturers could use warps of cotton, which were much cheaper than the linen warps formerly used. Cotton fabrics could be sold lower than had ever before been known. The demand for them consequently increased. The shuttle flew with fresh energy, and the weavers earned immoderately high wages. Spinning mills were erected to supply the requisite quantity of yarn. The fame of Arkwright resounded through the land; and capitalists flocked to him to buy his patent machines, or permission to use them. . . .

The factory system in England takes its rise from this period. Hitherto the cotton manufacture had been carried on almost entirely in the houses of the workmen: the hand or stock cards, the spinning wheel, and the loom, required no larger apartment than that of a cottage. A spinning jenny of small size might also be used in a cottage, and in many instances was so used: when the number of spindles was considerably increased, adjacent workshops were used. But the water-frame, the carding engine, and the other machines which Arkwright brought out in a finished state, required both more space than could be found in a cottage, and more power than could be applied by the human arm. Their weight also rendered it necessary to place them in strongly built mills, and they could not be advantageously turned by any power then known but that of water.

The use of machinery was accompanied by a greater division of labor than existed in the primitive state of the manufacture; the material went through many more processes; and of course the loss of time and the risk of waste would have been much increased if its removal from house to house at every stage of the manufacture had been necessary. It became obvious that there were several important advantages in carrying on the numerous operations of an extensive manufacture in the same building. Where water power was required, it was economy to build one mill, and put up one water-wheel, rather than several. This arrangement also enabled the master spinner himself to superintend every stage of the manufacture: it gave him a greater security against the wasteful or fraudulent consumption of the material: it saved time in the transference of the work from hand to hand: and it prevented the extreme inconvenience which would have resulted from the failure of one class of workmen to perform their part, when several other classes of workmen were dependent upon them. Another circumstance which made it advantageous to have a large number of machines in one manufactory was that mechanics must be employed on the spot, to construct and repair the machinery, and that their time could not be fully occupied with only a few machines.

All these considerations drove the cotton spinners to that important change in the economy of English manufactures, the introduction of the factory system; and when that system had once been adopted, such were its pecuniary advantages that mercantile competition would have rendered it impossible, even had it been desirable, to abandon it. The inquiry into the moral and social effects of the factory system will be made hereafter. . . .

Edward Baines, Jr., *History of the Cotton Manufacture in Great Britain* (London, 1835), pp. 115, 182–83, 184–85.

The Factory System and Factory Discipline, by a Contemporary Admirer (1835)

. . . The term *Factory System,* in technology, designates the combined **110** operation of many orders of work-people, adult and young, in tending with assiduous skill a series of productive machines continuously impelled by a central power. This definition includes such organizations as cotton-mills, flax-mills, silk-mills, woolen-mills, and certain engineering works; but it excludes those in which the mechanisms do not form a connected series, nor are dependent on one prime mover. Of the latter class, examples occur in ironworks, dye-works, soap-works, brass-foundries, &c. . . .

The main difficulty did not, to my apprehension, lie so much in the invention of a proper self-acting mechanism for drawing out and twisting cotton into a continuous thread, as in the distribution of the different members of the apparatus into one cooperative body, in impelling each organ with its appropriate delicacy and speed, and above all, in training human beings to renounce their desultory habits of work, and to identify themselves with the unvarying regularity of the complex automation. To devise and administer a successful code of factory discipline, suited to the necessities of factory diligence, was the Herculean enterprise, the noble achievement of Arkwright. Even at the present day, when the system is perfectly organized and its labor lightened to the utmost, it is found nearly impossible to convert persons past the age of puberty, whether drawn from rural or from handicraft occupations, into useful factory hands. After struggling for a while to conquer their listless or restive habits, they either renounce the employment spontaneously, or are dismissed by the overlookers on account of inattention. . . .

Andrew Ure, *The Philosophy of Manufactures; or, an Exposition of the Scientific, Moral, and Commercial Economy of the Factory System in Great Britain* (3rd ed.; London, 1861), pp. 13, 15–16.

IV. SOME SOCIAL CONSEQUENCES OF THE INDUSTRIAL REVOLUTION

The long-run effects of the process of industrialization included a progressive lightening of the burden of human labor and a progressive increase in the standards of comfort and material well-being. But a controversy, which still continues in the sixth decade of the twentieth century, broke out at once over the effects of industrialization on the workers. Critics pointed to the deadening effects on the workers' intellects of the mechanical repetition of motions, to the loss of security, to the unwholesome condition of the cities into which workers were crowded, to the evils of female and child labor, etc. Defenders of the new system praised its greater productivity and accused their opponents of using biased, unrepresentative, and even completely false evidence. Two of the principal early protagonists were Friedrich Engels, subsequently a collaborator of Karl Marx in formulating the doctrine of "scientific socialism," who published the first German edition of his *Condition of the Working Classes in England* in 1844, and Andrew Ure, a devoted advocate of the factory system, who published the first edition of his *Philosophy of Manufactures* in 1835. The following extracts give both sides of the argument, putting Engels' side by side with Ure's.

The Effects of Machinery

111   [Engels] . . . Before the introduction of machinery, the spinning and weaving of raw materials was carried on in the workingman's home. Wife and daughter spun the yarn that the father wove or that they sold, if he did not work it up himself. These weaver families lived in the country in the neighborhood of the towns, and could get on fairly well with their wages. . . . So it was that the weaver was usually in a position to lay by something and rent a little piece of land that he cultivated in his leisure

hours, of which he had as many as he chose to take, since he could weave whenever and as long as he pleased. True, he was a bad farmer and managed his land inefficiently, often obtaining but poor crops; nevertheless, he was no proletarian, he had a stake in the country, he was permanently settled, and stood one step higher in society than the English workman of today.

So the workers vegetated throughout a passably comfortable existence, leading a righteous and peaceful life in all piety and probity; and their material position was far better than that of their successors. They did not need to overwork; they did no more than they chose to do, and yet earned what they needed. They had leisure for healthful work in garden or field, work which, in itself, was recreation for them, and they could take part besides in the recreations and games of their neighbors, and all these games, bowling, cricket, football, etc., contributed to their physical health and vigor. They were, for the most part, strong, well-built people, in whose physique little or no difference from that of their peasant neighbors was discoverable. Their children grew up in the fresh country air and, if they could help their parents at work, it was only occasionally; while of eight or twelve hours work for them there was no question. . . .

Friederich Engels, *The Condition of the Working Class in England in 1844* (New York, 1887), pp. 3–4.

[Ure] . . . The blessings which physico-mechanical science has bestowed **112** on society, and the means it has still in store for ameliorating the lot of mankind, have been too little dwelt upon; while, on the other hand, it has been accused of lending itself to the rich capitalists as an instrument for harassing the poor, and of exacting from the operative an accelerated rate of work. It has been said, for example, that the steam-engine now drives the power-looms with such velocity as to urge on their attendant weavers at the same rapid pace; but that the hand-weaver, not being subjected to this restless agent, can throw his shuttle and move his treddles at his convenience. There is, however, this difference in the two cases; that in the factory, every member of the loom is so adjusted that the driving force leaves the attendant nearly nothing at all to do, certainly no muscular fatigue to sustain, while it procures for him good, unfailing wages, besides a healthy workshop *gratis:* whereas the nonfactory weaver, having everything to execute by muscular exertion, finds the labor irksome, makes in consequence innumerable short pauses, separately of little account, but great when added together; earns therefore proportionally low wages, while he loses his health by poor diet and the dampness of his hovel. Dr. Carbutt of Manchester says, "With regard to Sir Robert Peel's assertion a few evenings ago, that the hand-loom weavers are mostly small farmers, nothing can be a greater mistake; they live, or rather they just keep life together, in the most miserable manner, in the cellars and garrets of the town, working sixteen or eighteen hours for the merest pittance." . . .

Ure, *op. cit.*, pp. 6–7.

Competition and Labor Unions

113   [Engels] . . . Competition is the completest expression of the battle of all against all which rules in modern civil society. This battle, a battle for life, for existence, for everything, in case of need a battle of life and death, is fought not between the different classes of society only, but also between the individual members of these classes. Each is in the way of the other, and each seeks to crowd out all who are in his way, and to put himself in their place. The workers are in constant competition among themselves as the members of the bourgeoisie among themselves. The power loom weaver is in competition with the hand-loom weaver, the unemployed or ill-paid hand-loom weaver with him who has work or is better paid, each trying to supplant the other. But this competition of the workers among themselves is the worst side of the present state of things in its effect upon the worker, the sharpest weapon against the proletariat in the hands of the bourgeoisie. Hence the effort of the workers to nullify this competition by associations, hence the hatred of the bourgeoisie towards these associations, and its triumph in every defeat which befalls them. . . .

Engels, *op. cit.*, p. 51.

114   [Ure] . . . When the handicraftsman exchanges hard work with fluctuating employment and pay, for continuous labor of a lighter kind with steady wages, he must necessarily renounce his old prerogative of stopping when he pleases, because he would thereby throw the whole establishment into disorder. Of the amount of the injury resulting from the violation of the rules of automatic labor he can hardly ever be a proper judge; just as mankind at large can never fully estimate the evils consequent upon an infraction of God's moral law. Yet the factory operative, little versant in the great operations of political economy, currency, and trade, and actuated too often by an invidious feeling towards the capitalist who animates his otherwise torpid talents, is easily persuaded by artful demagogues, that his sacrifice of time and skill is beyond the proportion of his recompence, or that fewer hours of industry would be an ample equivalent for his wages. This notion seems to have taken an early and inveterate hold of the factory mind, and to have been riveted from time to time by the leaders of those secret combinations, so readily formed among a peculiar class of men, concentrated in masses within a narrow range of country. . . .

Ure, *op. cit.*, p. 279.

Conditions in the Cities

[Engels] . . . Every great city has one or more slums where the work- **115** ing class is crowded together. True, poverty often dwells in hidden alleys close to the palaces of the rich; but, in general, a separate territory has been assigned to it, where, removed from the sight of the happier classes, it may struggle along as it can. These slums are pretty equally arranged in all the great towns of England, the worst houses in the worst quarters of the towns; usually one or two-storied cottages in long rows, perhaps with cellars used as dwellings, almost always irregularly built. These houses of three or four rooms and a kitchen form, throughout England, some parts of London ex-cepted, the general dwellings of the working class. The streets are generally unpaved, rough, dirty, filled with vegetable and animal refuse, without sewers or gutters, but supplied with foul stagnant pools instead. Moreover, ventilation is impeded by the bad, confused method of building of the whole quarter, and since many human beings here live crowded into a small space, the atmosphere that prevails in these working-men's quarters may readily be imagined. . . .

The death rate is kept so high chiefly by the heavy mortality among young children in the working class. The tender frame of a child is least able to withstand the unfavorable influences of an inferior lot in life; the neglect to which they are often subjected, when both parents work or one is dead, avenges itself promptly, and no one need wonder that in Manchester, according to the report last quoted, more than fifty-seven per cent of the children of the working class . . . and not quite thirty-two per cent of the children of all classes in the country die under five years of age. . . .

Engels, *op. cit.*, pp. 19, 72.

[Pro] . . . I admit that the manufacturing districts have a repulsive exte- **116** rior. The smoke that hangs over them—their noisy, bustling, and dirty streets —the large proportion of the working classes seen there, many of whom have their persons and clothes blackened with their occupations—the hum and buzz of machinery in the factories—the flaming of furnaces—the rude earn-estness of the "unwashed artificers"—and their provincial dialect—are little calculated to gratify "ears polite," or to please the eye accustomed to parks and green fields.

But beneath this unpleasing exterior there moves steadily on that energetic and persevering industry which, combined with the highest mechanical skill, large capital, and mercantile intelligence and enterprise, constitutes *the main spring of all the foreign commerce of England*—which, by supplying 49/50 of all our exports, furnishes almost our *only* means of purchasing raw materials, luxuries, and necessaries from other countries—which is consequently the prop of the maritime power and greatness of England—which, by enabling our merchants to enter all foreign markets as buyers, animates the industry of every quarter of the globe, as well as enriches our own island—which has added more to the wealth, population, and power of England than at the close of the last century the boldest speculator could have thought possible—which has largely augmented the income of the landowner—and which, by the opulence it has created, has stimulated taste, rewarded genius, and promoted all the elegances that adorn the most advanced civilization.

Edward Baines, Jr., *The Social, Educational, and Religious State of the Manufacturing Districts* (3rd ed.; London, 1843), pp. 54–55.

117   [Ure] . . . The returns procured by Mr. Thorpe, of Leeds, justify the assertion that the mortality of that town has diminished since 1801, at which time there were scarcely any manufactories established in it. The population of the township was in 1801, 30,669; and the burials of the three years preceding being 2882, or 941 annually, the resulting rate of mortality is one in thirty-two and a half. In 1831 the population was 71,602, and the burials of the three years preceding were 5153, or 1718 annually, giving a rate of mortality of one in forty-one and a half. Thus, since the comfortable wages of factory labor have begun to be enjoyed, the mortality has diminished in the proportion of thirty-two and a half to forty-one and a half; that is, only three persons die now, where four died in the golden age of precarious rural or domestic employment. . . .

Ure, *op. cit.,* p. 396.

Living Conditions

118   [Engels] . . . When one remembers under what conditions the working people live, when one thinks how crowded their dwellings are, how every nook and corner swarms with human beings, how sick and well sleep in the same room, in the same bed, the only wonder is that a contagious disease like this fever does not spread yet further. . . .

Another category of diseases arises directly from the food rather than the dwellings of the workers. The food of the laborer, indigestible enough in itself, is utterly unfit for young children, and he has neither means nor time to get his children more suitable food. . . . Scrofula is almost universal among the working class, and scrofulous parents have scrofulous children, especially when the original influences continue in full force to operate upon the inherited tendency of the children. . . . How greatly all these evils are increased by the chances to which the workers are subject in consequence of fluctuations in trade, want of work, and the scanty wages of times of crisis, it is not necessary to dwell upon. Temporary want of sufficient food, to which almost every workingman is exposed at least once in the course of his life, only contributes to intensify the effects of his usual sufficient but bad diet. Children who are half starved just when they most need ample and nutritious food—and how many such there are during every crisis and even when trade is at its best—must inevitably become weak, scrofulous, and rachitic in a high degree. And that they do become so, their appearance amply shows. The neglect to which the great mass of workingmen's children are condemned leaves ineradicable traces and brings the enfeeblement of the whole race of workers with it. Add to this the unsuitable clothing of this class, the impossibility of precautions against colds, the necessity of toiling so long as health permits, want made more dire when sickness appears and the only too common lack of all medical assistance; and we have a rough idea of the sanitary condition of the English working class. . . .

One of the most injurious of these patent medicines is a drink prepared with opiates chiefly laudanum, under the name Godfrey's Cordial. Women who work at home, and have their own and other people's children to take care of, give them this drink to keep them quiet, and, as many believe, to strengthen them. They often begin to give this medicine to newly-born children and continue, without knowing the effects of this "heartsease," until the children die. The less susceptible the child's system to the action of the opium, the greater the quantities administered. . . .

Next to intemperance in the enjoyment of intoxicating liquors, one of the principal faults of English workingmen is sexual licence. But this, too, follows with relentless logic, with inevitable necessity out of the position of a class left to itself, with no means of making fitting use of its freedom. The bourgeoisie has left the working class only these two pleasures, while imposing upon it a multitude of labors and hardships, and the consequence is that the workingmen, in order to get something from life, concentrate their whole energy upon these two enjoyments, carry them to excess, surrender to them in the most unbridled manner. . . .

Thus the social order makes family life almost impossible for the worker. In a comfortless, filthy house, hardly good enough for mere nightly shelter, ill-furnished, often neither rain-tight nor warmed, a foul atmosphere filling rooms overcrowded with human beings, no domestic comfort is possible. The husband works the whole day through, perhaps the wife also and the elder children, all in different places; they meet night and morning only, all under perpetual temptation to drink; what family life is possible under such conditions? . . .

Engels, *op. cit.,* pp. 67, 68, 69–70, 85–86.

119 [Ure] . . . It seems established by a body of incontestable evidence that the wages of our factory work-people, if prudently spent, would enable them to live in a comfortable manner, and decidedly better than formerly, in consequence of the relative diminution in the price of food, fuel, lodgings, and clothing. . . .

. . . And as to the charge which has been made of the injury done to their constitutions by entering a factory in early life, the following refutation of it is most decisive. "There is one thing I feel convinced of from observation, that young persons, especially females, who have begun mill-work at from ten to twelve, independently of their becoming much more expert artists, preserve their health better, and possess sounder feet and legs at twenty-five than those who have commenced from thirteen to sixteen and upwards."

"At the Blantyre mills," says the same competent observer, " the spinners are all males. I visited the dwellings of nine of that class without making any selection. Found that every one of them was married, and that the wife had been in every instance a mill-girl, some of these women having begun factory work as early as at six and a half years of age. The number of children born to these nine couples was fifty-one; the number now living forty-six. As many of these children as are able to work, and can find vacancies, are employed in the mill. They all live in rooms rented from the owners, and are well lodged. I saw them at breakfast time, and the meal was composed of the following: viz., porridge and milk for the children; coffee, eggs, bread, oaten cake, and butter for the father. . . ."

Ure, *op. cit.,* pp. 306, 389–90.

Child Labor

[Con] . . . The most common age for boys to be taken to labour in **120** the coal-mines of this district [Oldham, in Lancashire] is at seven, eight, or nine. But in the 'mountain mines', or smaller collieries towards the hills, which have only thin strata, varying in thickness from 18 inches to 2 feet, they will go down as early as six, five, or even four years of age; some are so young they go in their bedgowns. One little fellow whom I endeavored to question could not even articulate, although his father, between whose legs he hid his little black face as he stood before me, answered for him that he was seven years old. . . .

House of Commons, Children's Employment Commission, *First Report of the Commissioners: Mines* (London, 1842), I, 15–16.

[Engels] . . . The report of the Central Commission relates that the **121** manufacturers began to employ children rarely of five years, often of six, very often of seven, usually of eight to nine years; that the working-day often lasted fourteen to sixteen hours, exclusive of meals and intervals; that the manufacturers permitted overlookers to flog and maltreat children, and often took an active part in so doing themselves. One case is related of a Scotch manufacturer who rode after a sixteen years old runaway, forced him to return running before the employer as fast as the master's horse trotted, and beat him the whole way with a long whip. . . .

Engels, *op. cit.*, p. 101.

[Ure] . . . Nothing shows in a clearer point of view the credulity of **122** mankind in general, and of the people of these islands in particular, than the ready faith which was given to the tales of cruelty exercised by proprietors of cotton-mills towards young children. The system of calumny somewhat resembles that brought by the Pagans against the primitive Christians, of enticing children into their meetings in order to murder and devour them. . . . The clamor for the ten-hour bill, and the subsidiary lamentation for the children, were confined among the operatives almost exclusively to the mule-spinners [i.e., who worked on the spinning mules]. . . . Since the said spinners are the sole employers of the younger children in cotton-mills, who are often their own offspring, and entirely at their disposal to hire or to turn away, they were the only persons capable of abusing them, the sole arbiters of their fate, and therefore amenable to the parents and the public for their good treatment. The millowner, in fact, could never interfere but beneficially for the children, to protect them against the occasional caprice of these friends to humanity, who alone could exercise tyranny over their dependents. . . .

I have visited many factories, both in Manchester and in the surrounding districts, during a period of several months, entering the spinning rooms unexpectedly, and often alone, at different times of the day, and I never saw a single instance of corporal chastisement inflicted on a child, nor indeed did I ever see children in ill-humor. They seemed to be always cheerful and alert, taking pleasure in the light play of their muscles—enjoying the mobility natural to their age. The scene of industry, so far from exciting sad emotions in my mind, was always exhilarating. It was delightful to observe the nimbleness with which they pieced the broken ends, as the mule-carriage began to recede from the fixed roller-beam, and to see them at leisure, after a few seconds' exercise of their tiny fingers, to amuse themselves in any attitude they chose, till the stretch and winding-on were once more completed. The work of these lively elves seemed to resemble a sport, in which habit gave them a pleasing dexterity. Conscious of their skill, they were delighted to show it off to any stranger. As to exhaustion by the day's work, they evinced no trace of it on emerging from the mill in the evening; for they immediately began to skip about any neighboring playground, and to commence their little amusements with the same alacrity as boys issuing from a school. It is moreover my firm convictions that if children are not ill-used by bad parents or guardians, but receive in food and raiment the full benefit of what they earn, they would thrive better when employed in our modern factories than if left at home in apartments too often ill aired, damp, and cold. . . .

Ure, *op. cit.*, pp. 290, 299, 301.

Education

123   [Engels] . . . It is true that the manufacturers boast of having enabled the majority to read, but the quality of the reading is appropriate to the source of the instruction as the Children's Employment Commission proves. According to this report, he who knows his letters can read enough to satisfy the conscience of the manufacturers. And when one reflects upon the confused orthography of the English language which makes reading one of the arts, learned only under long instruction, this ignorance is readily understood. Very few working people write readily; and writing orthographically is beyond the powers even of many "educated" persons. The Sunday schools of the State Church, of the Quakers, and, I think, of several other sects, do not teach writing "because it is too worldly an employment for Sunday." The quality of the instruction offered the workers in other directions may be judged from a specimen or two, taken from the Children's Employment Commission's Report, which unfortunately, does not embrace millwork proper. . . .

These children who are crammed with religious doctrines four or five years at a stretch, know as little at the end as at the beginning. One child "went to Sunday school regularly for five years; does not know who Jesus Christ is, but had heard the name; had never heard of the twelve Apostles, Samson, Moses, Aaron, etc." Another "attended Sunday school regularly six years; knows who Jesus Christ was; he died on the Cross to save our Saviour; had never heard of St. Peter or St. Paul." A third "attended different Sunday schools seven years; can read only the thin easy books with simple words of one syllable; has heard of the Apostles, but does not know whether St. Peter was one or St. John; the latter must have been St. John Wesley." To the question who Christ was, Horne received the following answers among others: "He was Adam," "He was an Apostle," "He was the Saviour's Lord's Son," and from a youth of sixteen: "He was a king of London long ago." . . .

Engels, *op. cit.*, pp. 74–75.

[Ure] . . . I believe there is an abundant increase of intelligence and **124** moral sentiment springing up among the factories, the fruits of Sunday Schools and other philanthropic establishments—planted and upreared chiefly by the work-people themselves, unaided by opulence, and unpatronized by power. It is a sublime spectacle to witness crowds of factory children arranged in a Sunday School. I would exhort the friends of humanity who may chance to pass through Cheshire or Lancashire, not to miss a Sunday's visit to the busy town of Stockport, which joins these two counties. It contains 67 factories, in which 21,489 operatives of all ages are employed comfortably for their families.

The Sunday School of this place was erected by the voluntary contributions chiefly of millowners in the year 1805. . . .

When I visited this school a few months ago, there were from 4,000 to 5,000 young people profiting by the instructions administered by 400 teachers, distributed into proper classes, and arranged in upwards of forty schoolrooms, besides the grand hall in the top of the building. I witnessed the very gratifying sight of about 1500 boys, and as many girls, regularly seated upon separate benches, the one set on the right side, and the other on the left. They were becomingly attired, decorous in deportment, and of healthy, even blooming complexions. Their hymn-singing thrilled through the heart like the festival chorus of Westminster. . . .

Ure, *op. cit.*, pp. 408, 411.

Morals

125　[Con] . . . In England, exclusive of Wales, it is only in some of the colliery districts of Yorkshire and Lancashire that female children of tender age and young and adult women are allowed to descend into the coal mines and regularly to perform the same kinds of underground work, and to work for the same number of hours as boys and men; but in the East of Scotland their employment in the pits is general; and in South Wales it is not uncommon. . . .

In great numbers of the coal-pits in this District [West Riding of Yorkshire] the men work in a state of perfect nakedness, and are in this state assisted in their labour by females of all ages, from girls of six years old to women of twenty-one, these females being themselves quite naked down to the waist. . . .

Betty Wardle: "I have worked in a pit since I was six years old. I have had four children, two of them were born while I worked in the pits. I worked in the pits whilst I was in the family way. I had a child born in the pits, and I brought it up the pit-shaft in my skirt; it was born the day after I were married—that makes me to know." . . .

House of Commons, Children's Employment Commission, *First Report of the Commissioners: Mines* (London, 1842), I, 23, 27.

126　[Pro] . . . When questioned as to the effect of factory employment on young females, he says: "It is fathers or friends who work in factories, and they have all a common interest in checking immorality among the younger assistants, both boys and girls. Suppose a cotton factory contains forty spinners, each of whom employs four piecers, making one hundred and sixty young persons of both sexes, and of ages varying from nine to twenty; I should say that thirty, at least, out of the forty spinners, were married men, and that many of them had large families. Now, even if none of their own children were working with them, yet they have all a common interest, as fathers, in discountenancing indecencies of conduct and language . . ."

Ure, *op. cit.*, pp. 420–21.

QUESTIONS

1. What were the conditions in England which permitted it to have an "industrial revolution"?
2. Why was agricultural reform necessary to permit the growth of industry? What forms did it take? What were its disadvantages?
3. What contributions did the Darbys make to the industrial revolution? James Watt? Richard Arkwright?
4. How did the "factory system" of industry differ from the "domestic system"?
5. What were some of the problems faced by the new industrialists?
6. How did the industrial revolution affect the working classes? How else, other than as a consequence of the industrial revolution, might the deplorable conditions in the industrial districts be explained?
7. Was the industrial revolution a "good" or a "bad" thing?

CHAPTER XVIII

REACTION AND ROMANTICISM

TWO KINDS of "reaction" dominated much of the thinking and the politics for three decades after the Congress of Vienna (see p. 190). Romanticism in a wide sense was a reaction against the forms and conventions of the eighteenth-century Enlightenment (see p. 151). It stressed not so much man's reason as his feeling and imagination. Romanticism revealed a new kind of appreciation for the beauties of nature and the "beauty" of religion. This appreciation was on an emotional plane, as the excerpts from Chateaubriand show (127, 128). In its political aspects romanticism tended, at first, to react against the French Revolution and all it stood for. But many romantics, like Chateaubriand, after first supporting political reaction turned toward liberalism and individualism. Because of its emphasis on the freedom of the emotions, romanticism is difficult to associate with any one political or social movement, for emotional freedom meant a variety of expression among the romanticists. Their chief reaction was against the formalism and rationalism of the previous era.

The conservatives reacted against the French Revolution. It was Edmund Burke who, in opposing the Revolution, laid the foundations of a conservative ideology (129). Metternich, after the Congress of Vienna, squarely opposed ideas of equality and liberalism (130). From Austria, he dominated the Quadruple Alliance, and indeed the times from 1815 to 1848 have been called the "Age of Metternich." How he applied his conservatism against the "new" trends of nationality and the urge toward radical activities can be seen in the Carlsbad Decrees (131).

I. ROMANTICISM

The following extract illustrates the romantic sense of beauty, bound up with the emotions and religious feeling. It is taken from François-René de Chateaubriand's *Genius of Christianity,* or *Beauties of the Christian Religion* (first published in 1813), and describes the author's impressions while at sea, bound for America.

The vessel in which we embarked for America, having passed the bear- **127** ing of any land, the space was soon occupied only by the twofold azure of the sea and of the sky. The color of the waters resembled that of liquid glass. A vast swell advanced from the west, though the wind blew from the east; enormous undulations extended from one horizon to the other, and opened in their valleys long vistas through the deserts of the deep. The fleeting landscapes changed with every minute: sometimes a multitude of verdant hillocks represented graves separated by furrows in an immense cemetery; sometimes the curling summits of the surges resembled white flocks scattered over a heath: now the space appeared small for want of an object of comparison; but if a billow reared its mountain crest, if a wave curved like a remote coast, or a squadron of sea-dogs passed by in the distance, the space suddenly opened before us. We were most powerfully impressed with an idea of magnitude when a light fog, creeping along the surface of the deep, seemed to increase immensity itself. O, how sublime, how awful, at such times, is the aspect of the ocean! Into what reveries it plunges you, either if imagination transports you to the seas of the north, into the midst of frosts and tempests, or wafts you to southern islands, blest with happiness and peace!

We often rose at midnight and sat down upon deck, where we found only the officer of the watch and a few sailors in profound silence. No noise was heard save the dashing of the prow through the billows, while sparks of fire ran with a white foam along the sides of the vessel. God of Christians! It is on the waters of the abyss, and on the expanded sky, that thou hast particularly engraven the characters of thy omnipotence! Millions of stars sparkling in the azure dome of heaven; the moon in the midst of the firmament; a sea unbounded by any shore; infinity in the skies and on the waves!

Never didst thou affect me more powerfully with thy greatness than in those nights when, suspended between the stars and the ocean, I had immensity over my head, and immensity beneath my feet!

I am nothing; I am only a simple, solitary wanderer: oft have I heard men of science disputing on the subject of a Supreme Being, and I have not understood them; but I have invariably remarked that it is in the prospect of the sublime scenes of nature that this unknown being manifests himself to the human heart. . . .

He who had not recognized in this prospect the beauty of the Deity had been greatly to be pitied. Religious tears involuntarily flowed from my eyes when my intrepid companions, taking off their tarred hats, began in a hoarse voice, to chant their simple song to that God who is the protector of mariners. How affecting were the prayers of these men who, from a frail plank in the midst of the ocean, contemplated a sun setting in the waves! How the invocation of the poor sailor to the Father of the distressed went to the heart! The consciousness of our insignificance, excited by the voice of infinity: our songs, resounding to a distance over the silent waves; the night approaching with its dangers; our vessel, itself a wonder, among so many wonders; a religious crew, penetrated with admiration and with awe; a priest, august in supplication; the Almighty diffused over the abyss, with one hand staying the sun at the portals of the west, with the other raising the moon in the eastern hemisphere, and lending, through immensity, an attentive ear to the feeble voice of his creatures—this is a scene which defies the art of the painter and the eloquence of the writer, and which the whole heart of man is scarcely sufficient to embrace! . . .

François-René de Chàteaubriand, *The Beauties of Christianity* [title under which *Genius of Christianity* was published in England] (London, 1813), I, 186-88, 189.

Chateaubriand, like most romantics, believed in the primacy of poetry and imaginative literary expression over scientific endeavor. The "heart" and "love" are stressed as indispensable elements in man's moral attainments, and religion is connected with these feelings. Contrast this extract with Voltaire (p. 155), and you will see what ideas the romantics were rejecting.

128   . . . A poet, by means of a few verses, lives to the remotest posterity, immortalizes his age, and transmits to future times those whom he deigns to celebrate in his compositions; the man of science, scarcely known during his lifetime, is forgotten the day after his death. Involuntarily ungrateful, he can do nothing for the great man, for the hero by whom he is patronized.

To no purpose will he place his name in a chemical furnace or a philosophical machine; estimable efforts, incapable, however, of reflecting any degree of luster: glory is born without wings; she is obliged to borrow those of the Muses when she would soar to the skies. It is Corneille, Racine, Boileau, the orators, the artists, who have contributed to immortalize Louis the Fourteenth much more than the celebrated men of science who flourished during his time. All ages, all countries, afford the same example. Let mathematicians then cease to complain if nations, by one general instinct, give to letters the precedence before the sciences. That man, in fact, who has bequeathed to the world one single moral precept, one single affecting sentiment, renders a greater service to society than the mathematician who discovered the beautiful properties of the triangle. . . .

To conclude, the vice of the day consists in separating abstract studies rather too much from literary studies. The one belongs to the understanding, the others to the heart; we should, therefore, beware of cultivating the former to the exclusion of the latter, and of sacrificing the part which *loves* to the part which *reasons*. It is by a happy combination of physical and moral attainments, and above all by the inculcation of religious ideas, that we shall succeed in again giving to our youth that education which of old produced so many great men. It must not be supposed that our soil is exhausted. The beautiful plains of France might again be made to yield abundant harvests, were they but cultivated somewhat in the manner of our forefathers: 'tis one of those happy regions where reign those tutelar *genii* of mankind, and that *divine breath* which, according to Plato, distinguish the climates favorable to virtue. . . .

Ibid., II, 267–68, 278–79.

II. CONSERVATISM AND THE POLITICAL "REACTION"

Edmund Burke is sometimes called the founder of modern conservatism. In his *Reflections on the Revolution in France* (1790) and in his *Speech on Reform of Representation of the Commons in Parliament* (1782), he put forward his contention that history and tradition are better guides for nations than that "reason" which the Enlightenment so much admired.

from *Reflections on the Revolution in France*

. . . If civil society be made for the advantage of man, all the advantages for which it is made become his right. It is an institution of beneficence; and the law itself is only beneficence acting by rule. Men have a **129** right to live by that rule; they have a right to do justice, as between their fellows, whether their fellows are in politic function or in ordinary occupation. They have a right to the fruits of their industry, and to the means of making their industry fruitful. They have a right to the acquisitions of their parents; to the nourishment and improvement of their offspring, to instruction in life, and to consolation in death. Whatever each man may separately do, without trespassing upon others, he has a right to do for himself; and he has a right to a fair portion of all which society, with all its combinations of skill and force, can do in his favor. In this partnership all men have equal rights; but not to equal things. He that has but five shillings in the partnership has as good a right to it as he that has five hundred pounds has to his larger proportion; but he has not a right to an equal dividend on the product of the joint stock. And as to the share of power, authority, and direction which each individual ought to have in the management of the state, that I must deny to be amongst the direct original rights of man in civil society; for I have in my contemplation the civil man, and no other. It is a thing to be settled by convention. . . .

But one of the first and most leading principles on which the commonwealth and the laws are consecrated is lest the temporary possessors and life-renters in it, unmindful of what they have received from their ancestors, and of what is due to their posterity, should act as if they were the entire masters; that they should not think it amongst their rights to cut off the entail and commit waste on the inheritance by destroying at their pleasure the whole original fabric of their society; hazarding to leave to these who come after them a ruin instead of a habitation,—and teaching these successors as little to respect their contrivances as they had themselves respected the institutions of their forefathers. By this unprincipled facility of changing the state as often, and as much, and in as many ways as there are floating fancies or fashions, the whole chain and continuity of the commonwealth would be broken; no one generation could link with the other; men would become little better than the flies of a summer. . . .

We are afraid to put men to live and trade each on his own private stock of reason; because we suspect that the stock of each man is small, and that the individuals would do better to avail themselves of the general bank and capital of nations and of ages.

To avoid, therefore, the evils of inconstancy and versatility, ten thousand times worse than those of obstinacy and the blindest prejudice, we have consecrated the state, so that no man should approach to look upon its defects and corruptions but with due caution; that he should never dream of beginning its reformation by its subversion; that he should approach to the faults of a state as to the wounds of a father, with pious awe and trembling solicitude. . . . Society is indeed a contract. . . . It is not a partnership in things subservient only to the gross animal existence of a temporary and perishable nature. It is a partnership in all science; a partnership in all art; a partnership in every virtue, and in all perfection. As the ends of such a partnership cannot be obtained in many generations, it becomes a partnership not only between those who are living, but between those who are living, those who are dead, and those who are to be born. Each contract of each particular state is but a clause in the great primeval contract of eternal society, linking the lower with the higher natures, connecting the visible and invisible world, according to a fixed compact sanctioned by the inviolable oath which holds all physical and all moral natures each in their appointed place. . . .

from *Speech on Reform of Representation of the Commons in Parliament*

. . . Prescription is the most solid of all titles, not only to property but, **129a** which is to secure that property, to government. They harmonize with each other and give mutual aid to one another. It is accompanied with another ground of authority in the constitution of the human mind, presumption. It is a presumption in favor of any settled scheme of government against any untried project, that a nation has long existed and flourished under it. It is a better presumption even of the *choice* of a nation,—far better than any sudden and temporary arrangement by actual election. Because a nation is not an idea only of local extent and individual momentary aggregation, but it is an idea of continuity which extends in time as well as in numbers and in space. And this is a choice, not of one day, or one set of people, nor a tumultuary and giddy choice; it is a deliberate election of ages and of generations; it is a constitution made by what is ten thousand times better than choice; it is made by the peculiar circumstances, occasions, tempers, dispositions, and moral, civil and social habitudes of the people, which disclose themselves only in a long space of time. . . .

Works of the Right Honourable Edmund Burke (Boston, 1871), III, 308–9, 356–57, 346, 358, 359; VII, 94–95.

In the next extract Metternich analyzes his career (1849) after he had fallen from power. He restates once more his opposition to the Revolution and Napoleon, as well as to the idea of nationality.

130   My public life started in the year 1794 and ended on the 13th of March 1848. . . . My first period [of public activity] was preceded by an age which had a profound influence upon me. It was the age of open revolution, since its outbreak in the year 1789. I was born and educated under the appearance of the old order of things and later, at an age in which youth gives its own force to the impressions it receives, I stood as eye witness on the field of battle where the old building was torn down and on which, even after sixty years, no new and durable one would be erected. From these facts, which did not pass me by, my actions of statesmanship developed in logical succession. Educated in a hospitalized world, I never lost sight of the illness which I observed from its first appearance to its transition, and I have never belonged to those who coupled the end of the French monarchy with the end of social upheavals. Napoleon quieted the Revolution in its most blatant manifestations. He did not destroy it, however, but used it for his own purposes. . . . It was clear to me that the Revolution had found a new form in Napoleon and it was clear to me also that when the man who had harnessed [the Revolution] vanished, she would, free once more, find renewed expression. This feeling had a decided influence on my actions in the peace talks and in the Congress of Vienna. . . . Penetrated by the feeling that society hovers in a period of transition, [I recognized] the obstacles which such a period puts in the way of government's attempt to lead the people from excitement to rest. . . .

The concept of nationality is of the same nature as Liberty, Equality, Fraternity which seem destined to replace the happy slogans of old, but which will not blot them out. After [1830] one satirist characterized the three slogans as the Liberty to hunger, the Equality of misery, and the Fraternity of Cain's brother. It is similar with the wrong application of the concept of nationality, such as equal rights of all nationalities within the political borders of one nation . . . all that goes beyond simple equality before the law leads into the blue yonder, and the blue yonder does not fit into the conditions of existence of the states and of the individuals within the states. If one stretches the concept of the equality of nationalities beyond its proper measure, it leads to suppression and therefore to struggle. . . .

We stand at the beginning of the last year of the first half of the nineteenth century. This half will leave to the second one an example of what is and what should be. In two sentences the result of this example is clear to my eyes. The future will outweigh by far what we have, but on the side of what we have the example will be more favorable in the realm of mistakes recognized. Among those bankruptcies which in the passage of the fifty year period will stand in a leading place, that of Liberalism is especially distinguished; its demise from the stage belongs to those blessings which an age gives to society without, and even against, its own co-operation.

Letter to Graf von Hartig, in *Metternich-Hartig Briefwechsel* (Wien: Literarische Anstalt, 1923), pp. 39, 40, 41, 44, 45. (Trans. George L. Mosse.)

At the instigation of Metternich, the representatives of the German princes convened at Carlsbad (1819) in order to devise repressive measures to check the spirit of discontent which was manifesting itself against the denial of unity to Germany. The decrees were directed at the universities and the press because it was here that the opposition against the "reaction" seemed to have found a home. The following extracts from these decrees show us Metternich's ideas in action.

Disciplines for the Universities 131

1. In every university there must be employed a special deputy of the ruler of the state, residing at the place of the University, provided with appropriate instructions and wide discretion, either in the person of the present curator or of another found capable by the government.

The task of this deputy should be to guard the strict execution of the existing laws and disciplinary regulations, to watch carefully over the spirit which academic teachers show in their public and private lectures, and, without direct interference in the scientific and teaching methods, to give [this] a beneficent direction, looking to the future destination of studying youth; finally [he must] give his unflagging attention to everything which can serve to further morality, good order, and external decency.

2. The federal governments promise each other to remove from the universities and other schools, university and public school teachers who through proven departure from their duty, through misuse of their rightful influence upon the character of youth, through spreading of evil teachings which are hostile to public quiet and order or which undermine the basis of the existing form of the state, and who have proved without doubt their unfitness to execute the important office which has been entrusted to them. . . .

A teacher who has been excluded in this way may not be employed by any other federal state in any public school whatsoever.

Against the Misuse of the Press

1. As long as this decision remains in force, writings which appear in the form of daily papers or as magazines, as well as such which are not

over twenty printed pages in length, may not be printed in any German federal state without the prior knowledge or the prior authorization of the authorities of the country. . . .

9. All printed matter appearing in Germany, should it be included under the decision of this act or not, must be furnished with the name of the publisher, and if belonging in the class of newspapers or magazines, also with the name of the editor; printed matter which does not follow these rules may not be circulated in any federal state and must, if this should be done in secret, be confiscated immediately on their appearance, the spreaders of them convicted to the proper payment of money or to prison, depending on the circumstances.

Max Schilling, *Quellenbuch zur Geschichte der Neuzeit* (Berlin, 1890), pp. 415–17. (Trans. George L. Mosse.)

QUESTIONS

1. What struck Chateaubriand as particularly Christian during his sea voyage?
2. Why does Chateaubriand think poetry more worthy than mathematics?
3. What is Edmund Burke's objection to basing a commonwealth on "reason" only?
4. Why, for Burke, is prescription the most solid of all titles?
5. What sort of commonwealth do you think Burke had in mind when he wrote his reflections?
6. What results of the French Revolution and Napoleon did Metternich abhor particularly, and why?
7. Do you think that the conditions for the removal of teachers in the Carlsbad Decrees could be accomplished without "direct interferences in the scientific and teaching methods"?

CHAPTER XIX

LIBERALISM

WITH THE END of the Napoleonic adventure, demands for independence and liberty were becoming ever more insistent in Europe. In opposition to the Reaction (see p. 223), liberalism took hold of this feeling for liberty and gave to it an ideological content taken from the past. Thus the natural-law ideas of the Enlightenment (see p. 151) became a system of "natural liberty." It is in the name of this natural liberty that Adam Smith drastically restricted the functions of the state (132). Benjamin Constant, in his address of 1813, further elaborates upon the nature of individual freedom. By stressing this freedom as more important than political freedom (though this, too, was to be desired), he shows us one of the political limits of liberal ideology (133).

In his *Autobiography* John Stuart Mill describes the beliefs of his father. Here we can see a more practical side of liberalism emerging. James Mill was associated with a group of men who were interested in political issues, and they justified their liberal arguments not through an appeal to phrases like "the rights of man" but through stress on good government (134). They became the "utilitarians" in the liberal camp, whose leader was to be Jeremy Bentham.

By the middle of the century Darwinism with its idea of "evolution" and "natural selection" (see p. 318) was coming into vogue, and here Herbert Spencer made one of the most celebrated applications of the scientific theory to liberal ideology (135).

The practical results of liberalism were many. The English Reform Bill (see p. 250) and the reign of King Louis Philippe in France represent but two examples. On the more popular level, Samuel Smiles's *Self-Help* gives us a good instance of liberalism applied to personal living (136). The morality put forward by this best seller is much the same morality which *The History of the Fairchild Family* (see p. 258) sought to instill in the younger generation.

In his famous *Wealth of Nations,* Adam Smith lays down the limitations on government that would preserve the natural system of liberty (1776).

132 . . . According to the system of natural liberty, the sovereign has only three duties to attend to; three duties of great importance, indeed, but plain and intelligible to common understandings: first, the duty of protecting the society from the violence and invasion of other independent societies; secondly, the duty of protecting, as far as possible, every member of the society from the injustice or oppression of every other member of it, or the duty of establishing an exact administration of justice; and, thirdly, the duty of erecting and maintaining certain public works and certain public institutions, which it can never be for the interest of any individual, or small number of individuals, to erect and maintain; because the profit could never repay the expense to any individual or small number of individuals, though it may frequently do much more than repay it to a great society.

Adam Smith, *An Inquiry into the Nature and Causes of the Wealth of Nations,* ed. Edwin Cannan (New York: Random House, 1937), p. 651. (Reprinted by permission of the publisher.)

The definition of liberty and freedom which motivated liberalism was stated clearly by Benjamin Constant in his address on "The Freedom of the Ancients Compared with That of the Moderns" (1813). Here Constant contrasted the two types of freedom and gives us a good example of the manner in which men, after the French Revolution, believed that their "freedom" was a new thing, not beholden to the past. Though this was not correct, Constant illustrates well the fervor for freedom which dominated the minds of many men at the beginning of the nineteenth century.

Ask yourselves first, gentlemen, what an Englishman, a Frenchman, or **133** an inhabitant of the United States in our day understands by the word freedom?

It means the right of each one to be subject to nothing but the laws, not to be arrested nor detained, nor put to death, nor to be maltreated in any manner through the arbitrary will of one or more individuals. It is the right of each one to tell his own opinions, to choose his profession and to exercise it; to dispose of his property, even to misuse it; to go and to come without obtaining permission, and without rendering an account of his motives or of his steps. It means for each one the right to associate with other individuals, be it to confer on his interests, be it to worship the religion which he and his associates prefer, be it simply to fill his hours and his days in a manner which conforms best to his inclinations, to his imagination. Finally, it is the right of each one to influence the administration of the government, be it through the nomination of all, or of certain officials, be it through representation, petitions, demands, which the authorities are more or less forced to take into consideration. Compare now the freedom of the ancients with this freedom.

That freedom consists in exercising collectively, but directly, many parts of the entire sovereignty, to deliberate, in the public square, of war and peace . . . to vote the laws, pronounce judgements, examine the accounts, the acts, the administration of the Magistrates. . . . But at the same that all this is what the ancients called freedom, they admit as compatible with this collective freedom the subjection of the individual to the authority of the whole. You find among them almost none of the possessions which, as we shall see, are a part of the freedom of the moderns. All private actions are submitted to severe scrutiny. Nothing is granted to individual independence, neither on account of opinions, nor on account of ingenuity, nor, above all, on account of religion. The power to choose one's own worship, a power which we regard as one of our most precious rights, would have seemed to the ancients a crime and sacrilege . . . the laws regulate the morals, and as morals affect everything, there is nothing which laws do not regulate.

Thus among the ancients, the individual, almost habitually sovereign in public affairs, is a slave in all his private concerns. . . . Among the moderns, on the contrary, the individual, independent in his private life, is not, even in the freest state, sovereign in more than appearance only. His sovereignty is limited, almost always suspended; and if there are fixed but rare times, during which he is still surrounded by precautions and fetters in which he exercises this sovereignty, it is always only to abdicate it. . . .

I have come, gentlemen, to share with you the opinion which, in my conviction, these facts must produce; you will recognize with me the truth of the following principles:

Individual independence is the first need of the moderns. In consequence we must never demand their sacrifice to establish political freedom. It follows that none of the numerous and much praised institutions which, in the ancient republics, hindered individual freedom are admissible in modern times. . . .

As modern liberty differs from ancient liberty, it follows that it is also menaced by a danger of a different nature.

The danger of ancient freedom was that solely mindful of assuring the division of social power, men might sell too cheaply individual rights and possessions.

The danger of modern freedom is, that absorbed in the pleasure of our personal independence, and in the pursuit of our individual interests, we renounce too easily our right to partake in political power. . . .

Political liberty gives to all citizens, without exception, the task to examine and study their most sacred interests, to broaden their spirit, ennoble their thoughts, and establishes among them a kind of intellectual equality which makes up the glory and the power of a people.

Benjamin Constant, *Cours de Politique Constitutionelle* (Paris, 1872), II, 541, 542, 552, 558. (Trans. George L. Mosse.)

John Stuart Mill here describes the views of James Mill, his father (d. 1836), who was a member of that liberal circle in England known as "Philosophic Radicalism." These men shared the ideas of other liberals but tended to be more practical and less theoretical in their approach toward the issue of human freedom. To them, this freedom was not a matter of abstract human rights but of good government. Their mentor was Jeremy Bentham, whose "utilitarianism" attempted to justify liberal reforms through "the greatest good for the greatest number" and not through abstract systems of natural liberty.

134   . . . But though none of us, probably, agreed in every respect with my father, his opinions, as I said before, were the principal element which gave its colour and character to the little group of young men who were the first propagators of what was afterwards called "Philosophic Radical-ism. . . ." Malthus's population principle was quite as much a banner, and point of union among us, as any opinion specially belonging to Bentham. This great doctrine, originally brought forward as an argument against the indefinite improvability of human affairs, we took up with ardent zeal in the contrary sense, as indicating the sole means of realizing that im-provability by securing full employment at high wages to the whole la-bouring population through a voluntary restriction of the increase of their numbers. The other leading characteristics of the creed, which we held in common with my father, may be stated as follows:

In politics, an almost unbounded confidence in the efficacy of two things: representative government, and complete freedom of discussion. So complete was my father's reliance on the influence of reason over the minds of mankind, whenever it is allowed to reach them, that he felt as if all would be gained if the whole population were taught to read, if all sorts of opinions were allowed to be addressed to them by word and in writing, and if by means of the suffrage they could nominate a legislature to give effect to the opinions they adopted. He thought that when the legislature no longer represented a class interest, it would aim at the general interest, honestly and with adequate wisdom; since the people would be sufficiently under the guidance of educated intelligence, to make in general a good choice of persons to represent them, and having done so, to leave to those whom they had chosen a liberal discretion. Accordingly aristocratic rule, the government of the Few in any of its shapes, being in his eyes the only thing which stood between mankind and an administration of their affairs by the best wisdom to be found among them, was the object of his sternest disapprobation, and a democratic suffrage the principal article of his politi-cal creed, not on the ground of liberty, Rights of Man, or any of the phrases, more or less significant, by which, up to that time, democracy had usually been defended, but as the most essential of "securities for good government." In this, too, he held fast only to what he deemed essentials; he was comparatively indifferent to monarchical or republican forms—far more so than Bentham, to whom a king, in the character of "corrupter-general," appeared necessarily very noxious. Next to aristocracy, an estab-lished church, or corporation of priests, as being by position the great depravers of religion, and interested in opposing the progress of the human mind, was the object of his greatest detestation; though he disliked no clergyman personally who did not deserve it, and was on terms of sincere friendship with several. In ethics, his moral feelings were energetic and rigid on all points which he deemed important to human well being, while he was supremely indifferent in opinion (though his indifference did not show itself in personal conduct) to all those doctrines of the common morality, which he thought had no foundation but in asceticism and priest-craft. . . .

All those to whom I looked up, were of opinion that the pleasure of sympathy with human beings, and the feelings which made the good of others, and especially of mankind on a large scale, the object of existence, were the greatest and surest sources of happiness. . . .

John Stuart Mill, *Autobiography* (New York: Henry Holt & Co., n. d.), pp. 105–7, 138.

Herbert Spencer in his *The Man Versus the State* makes use of the scientific arguments which Charles Darwin had put forward in his *Origin of the Species by Means of Natural Selection* (1859). (See p. 319.) By transferring the argument from the natural to the social sciences, Spencer was able to restate liberalism in an extreme form (1875).

135   Be it or be it not true that Man is shapen in iniquity and conceived in sin, it is unquestionably true that Government is begotten of aggression and by aggression . . . we find proofs that, at first recognized but temporarily during leadership in war, the authority of a chief is permanently estab-lished by continuity of war; and grows strong where successful war ends in subjection of neighboring tribes. And thence onwards, examples fur-nished by all races, put beyond doubt the truth, that the coercive power of the chief developing into king, and king of kings, (a frequent title in the ancient East), becomes great in proportion as conquest becomes habitual and the union of subdued nations extensive. Comparisons disclose a further truth which should be ever present to us—the truth that the aggressiveness of the ruling power inside a society increases with its aggressiveness outside the society. . . .

An obvious implication is that political ethics, originally identical with the ethics of war, must long remain akin to them; and can diverge from them only as warlike activities and preparations become less. Current evi-dence shows this. At present on the Continent, the citizen is free only when his services as a soldier are not demanded; and during the rest of his life he is largely enslaved in supporting the military organization. Even among ourselves a serious war would, by the necessitated conscription, suspend the liberties of large numbers and trench on the liberties of the rest by taking from them through taxes whatever supplies were needed—that is, forcing them to labour so many days more for the State. Inevitably the established code of conduct in the dealing of Governments with citizens must be allied to their code of conduct in their dealings with one another. . . .

. . . Among men's desires seeking gratifications, those which have prompted their private activities and their spontaneous cooperations, have done much more towards social development than those which have worked through governmental agencies. That abundant crops now grow where once only wild berries could be gathered is due to the pursuit of individual satisfactions through many centuries. . . . Perpetually, governments have thwarted and deranged the growth but have in no way furthered it; save by partially discharging their proper function and maintaining social order. So, too, with those advances of knowledge and those improvements of appliances by which these structural changes and these increasing activities have been made possible. It is not to the State that we owe the multitudinous useful inventions from the spade to the telephone; it was not the State which made possible extended navigation by a developed astronomy; it was not the State which made the discoveries in physics, chemistry, and the rest which guide modern manufacturers. . . . The world wide transactions conducted in merchants' offices, the rush of traffic filling our streets, the retail distributing system which brings everything within easy reach and delivers the necessaries of life daily at our doors, are not of governmental origin. All these are results of the spontaneous activities of citizens, separate or grouped. . . .

And then a truth to which the foregoing one introduces us, is that the spontaneously-formed social organization is so bound together that you cannot act on one part without acting more or less on all parts. We see this unmistakably when a cotton-famine, first paralyzing certain manufacturing districts and then affecting the doings of wholesale and retail distributors throughout the kingdom, as well as the people they supply, goes on to affect the makers and distributors, as well as the wearers of other fabrics—woolen, linen, etc. Or we see it when a rise in the price of coal, besides influencing domestic life everywhere, hinders many of our industries, raises the prices of the commodities produced, alters the consumption of them and changes the habits of consumers. What we see clearly in these marked cases happens in every case, in sensible or in insensible ways. And manifestly, Acts of Parliament, are among those factors which, beyond the effects directly produced, have countless other effects of multitudinous kinds. As I heard remarked by a distinguished professor, whose studies give ample means of judging—"When once you begin to interfere with the order of Nature there is no knowing where the results will end." And if this is true of that sub-human order of Nature to which he referred, still more is it true of that order of Nature existing in the social arrangements of human beings. . . .

One of the most familiar facts is that animals of superior types, comparatively slow in reaching maturity, are enabled when they have reached it, to give more aid to their offspring than animals of inferior types. The adults foster their young during periods more or less prolonged, while yet the young are unable to provide for themselves; and it is obvious that maintenance of the species can be secured only by this parental care. It requires no proving that the blind, unfledged hedge-bird, or the young puppy even after it has acquired sight, would forthwith die if it had to keep itself warm and obtain its own food. The gratuitous aid must be great in proportion as the young one is of little worth either to itself or to others; and it may diminish as fast as, by increasing development, the young one acquires worth, at first for self-sustentation and by and by for sustentation of others. That is to say, during immaturity benefits received must vary inversely as the power or ability of the receiver. Clearly if during the first part of life benefits were proportioned to merits, or rewards to deserts, the species would disappear in a generation.

From this *régime* of the family group, let us turn to the *régime* of that larger group formed by adult members of the species. Ask what happens when the new individual acquiring complete use of its powers and ceasing to have parental aid is left to itself. Now there comes into play a principle just the reverse to that above described. Throughout the rest of its life each adult gets benefit in proportion to merit—reward in proportion to desert: merit and desert in each case being understood as ability to fulfill all the requirements of life—to get food, to find shelter, to escape enemies. Placed in competition with members of its own species and in antagonism with members of other species, it dwindles and gets killed off or thrives and propagates, according as it is ill-endowed or well-endowed. Manifestly an opposite *régime,* could it be maintained, would, in course of time, be fatal. If the benefits received by each individual were proportionate to its inferiority—if, as a consequence, multiplication of the inferior was furthered and multiplication of the superior hindered, progressive degradation would result; and eventually the degenerate species would fail to hold its ground in presence of antagonistic species and competing species.

The broad fact then, here to be noted, is that Nature's modes of treatment inside the family group and outside the family group are diametrically opposed to one another; and that the intrusion of either mode into the sphere of the other, would be destructive either immediately or remotely.

Does any one think that the like does not hold of the human species? He cannot deny that within the human family, as within any inferior family, it would be fatal not to proportion benefits to merits. . . . Surely none can fail to see that were the principle of family to be adopted and fully carried out in social life—were reward always great in proportion as desert was small, fatal results to the society would quickly follow; and if so, then even a partial intrusion of the family *régime* into the *régime* of the State, will be slowly followed by fatal results. Society in its corporate capacity cannot without immediate or remoter disaster interfere with the play of these opposed principles under which every species has reached such fitness for its mode of life as it possesses, and under which it maintains that fitness. . . .

And yet, notwithstanding the conspicuousness of these truths, which should strike everyone who leaves his lexicons and his law-deeds, and his ledgers, and looks abroad into that natural order of things under which we exist, and to which we must conform, there is continual advocacy of paternal government. The intrusion of family ethics into the ethics of the State, instead of being regarded as socially injurious, is more and more demanded as the only efficient means to social benefits. So far has this delusion now gone, that it vitiates the beliefs of those who might, more than all others, be thought safe from it. In the essay to which the Cobden Club awarded its prize in 1880, there occurs the assertion that "the truth of Free Trade is clouded over by the laissez-faire fallacy"; and we are told that "we need a great deal more parental government—that bugbear of the old economists". . . .

The process of "natural selection," as Mr. Darwin called it, cooperating with a tendency to variation and to inheritance of variations, he has shown to be a chief cause (though not, I believe, the sole cause) of that evolution through which all living things, beginning with the lowest and diverging and rediverging as they evolved, have reached their present degree of organization and adaptation to their modes of life. So familiar has this truth become that some apology seems needed for naming it. And yet, strange to say, now that this truth is recognized by most cultivated people—now that the beneficent working of the survival of the fittest has so impressed on them that, much more than people in past times, they might be expected to hesitate before neutralizing its action—now more than ever before in the history of the world, are they doing all they can to further survival of the unfittest!

Herbert Spencer, *The Man Versus the State* (New York: Appleton & Co., 1897), pp. 334–35, 357, 358–61, 362–63, 365.

Samuel Smiles's *Self-Help* (1859) takes the ideas of liberalism and applies them to everyday life. This version of the ideology was immensely popular and has outlasted liberalism itself. Millions of copies of Smiles's book were sold, and it is still in demand.

136   "The worth of a State, in the long run, is the worth of the individuals composing it." J. S. Mill.

"We put too much faith in systems, and look too little to men." B. Disraeli.

"Heaven helps those who help themselves," is a well-tried maxim, embodying in a small compass the results of vast human experience. The spirit of self-help is the root of all genuine growth in the individuals; and, exhibited in the lives of many, it constitutes the true source of national vigor and strength. Help from without is often enfeebling in its effects, but help from within invariably invigorates. Whatever is done *for* men or classes, to a certain extent takes away the stimulus and necessity of doing for themselves; and where men are subjected to over-guidance and over-government, the inevitable tendency is to render them comparatively helpless.

Even the best institutions can give a man no active aid. Perhaps the utmost they can do is, to leave him *free* to develop himself and improve his individual condition. But in all times men have been prone to believe that their happiness and well-being were to be secured by means of institutions rather than by their own conduct. Hence the value of legislation as an agent in human advancement has always been greatly over-estimated. To constitute the millionth part of a legislature, by voting for one or two men once in three or five years, however conscientiously this duty may be performed, can exercise but little active influence upon any man's life and character. Moreover, it is every day becoming more clearly understood, that the function of government is negative and restrictive, rather than positive and active; being resolvable principally into protection,—protection of life, liberty, and property. Hence the chief "reforms" of the last fifty years have consisted mainly in abolitions and disenactments. But there is no power of law that can make the idle man industrious, the thriftless provident, or the drunken sober; though every individual can be each and all of these if he will, by the exercise of his own free powers of action and self-denial. Indeed, all experience serves to prove that the worth and strength of a state depend far less upon the form of its institutions than upon the character of its men. For the nation is only the aggregate of individual conditions, and civilization itself is but a question of personal improvement.

National progress is the sum of individual industry, energy, and up-rightness, as national decay is of individual idleness, selfishness, and vice. What we are accustomed to decry as great social evils, will, for the most part, be found to be only the outgrowth of our own perverted life; and though we may endeavor to cut them down and extirpate them by means of law, they will only spring up again with fresh luxuriance in some other form, unless the conditions of human life and character are radically improved. If this view be correct, then it follows that the highest patriotism and philanthropy consist, not so much in altering laws and modifying institutions, as in helping and stimulating men to elevate and improve themselves by their own free and independent action. . . .

Any class of men that lives from hand to mouth will ever be an inferior class. They will necessarily remain impotent and helpless, hanging onto the skirts of society, the sport of times and seasons. Having no respect for themselves, they will fail in securing the respect of others. In commercial crises, such men must inevitably go to the wall. Wanting that husbanded power which a store of savings, no matter how small, invariably gives them, they will be at every man's mercy, and, if possessed of right feelings, they cannot but regard with fear and trembling the future possible fate of their wives and children. "The world," once said Mr. Cobden to the working men of Huddersfield, "has always been divided into two classes,—those who have saved, and those who have spent,—the thrifty and the extravagant. The building of all the houses, the mills, the bridges, and the ships, and the accomplishment of all other great works which have rendered man civilized and happy, has been done by the savers, the thrifty; and those who have wasted their resources have always been their slaves. It has been the law of nature and of Providence, that this should be so; and I were an imposter if I promised any class that they would advance themselves if they were improvident, thoughtless, and idle."

Equally sound was the advice given by Mr. Bright to an assembly of working men at Rochdale, in 1847, when, after expressing his belief that "so far as honesty was concerned, it was to be found in pretty equal amount among all classes," he used the following words: "There is only one way that is safe for any man, or any number of men, by which they can maintain their present position if it be a good one, or raise themselves above it if it be a bad one,—that is, by the practice of the virtues of industry, frugality, temperance, and honesty. There is no royal road by which men can raise themselves from a position which they feel to be uncomfortable and unsatisfactory, as regards their mental or physical condition, except by the practice of those virtues by which they find numbers amongst them are continually advancing and bettering themselves. What is it that has made, that has in fact created, the middle class in this country, but the virtues to which I have alluded?"

Samuel Smiles, *Self-Help* (Boston: Fields, Osgood & Co., 1869), pp. 15–17, 282–83.

QUESTIONS

1. For both Smith and Constant, what areas of human life are definitely excluded from governmental interference?
2. What are Constant's main objections to ancient democracy?
3. Why does Constant put more emphasis on individual than on political freedom?
4. Can it be said that optimism about human nature underlies the ideas of James Mill?
5. What did James Mill deem the "essentials" to which he held fast?
6. How does the idea of the "survival of the fittest" emerge in the thought of Herbert Spencer?
7. What point is Spencer trying to make when he compares the family in the animal world with the human family?
8. Compare Smiles's view of the function of government with that of Adam Smith, and his view of man's free powers with Spencer's arguments.
9. What, for Smiles, makes an "inferior" class? Compare what he thinks of as "virtue" with *The History of the Fairchild Family* (p. 258).

CHAPTER XX

NATIONALISM

THE MODERN CONCEPT of nationalism is of relatively recent origin. Before the age of the French Revolution, the concept of nationality was based upon personal allegiance to a monarch. After the French Revolution, this personal allegiance was replaced by allegiance to an abstract idea: the Nation. Modern nationalism directed man's first loyalty to a community linked by common language, custom, and historical tradition.

Within this definition, nationalism tended to vary from country to country. In Germany, the Napoleonic occupation proved a great stimulus to a nationalism seeking that unity which the country had failed to attain earlier in its history. It was during the French occupation that Johann Gotlieb Fichte gave his *Addresses to the German Nation* (137), in which we can already see a self-assertion combined with the idea of national superiority. At the same time, partly under the influence of the Romantic movement (see p. 221), increased stress was put upon the common historical past of a nation, a stress which tended to make this nationalism exclusive, while implying that only valid "historical memories" could really produce a great nation (138). The doctrine of superior race (139) put the capstone on the development of a more aggressive nationalism. In Germany, then, nationalism tended toward ideas of racial and national superiority which the eventual attainment of German unity did not wipe out (see Treitschke, p. 329).

In France, nationalism was connected with the Revolutionary and Napoleonic past; with trying to prove that France's vitality was still a continuing thing in spite of the fact that this glorious epoch was over (140).

In Italy, nationalism again varied from other countries. Here the glorious Roman past played a major role and was combined with the republicanism of ancient times (see Mazzini, p. 334).

Johann Gotlieb Fichte gave his *Addresses to the German Nation* in a series of lectures at the University of Berlin (1807-8).

137   . . . I speak for Germans simply, of Germans simply, not recognizing, but setting aside completely and rejecting, all the dissociating distinctions which for centuries unhappy events have caused in this single nation. You, gentlemen, are indeed to my outward eye the first and immediate representatives who bring before my mind the beloved national characteristics, and are the visible spark at which the flame of my address is kindled. But my spirit gathers round it the educated part of the whole German nation, from all the lands in which they are scattered. It thinks of and considers our common position and relations; it longs for that part of the living force with which these addresses may chance to grip you, may also remain and breathe from the dumb printed page which alone will come to the eyes of the absent, and may in all places kindle German hearts to decision and action. Only of Germans and simply for Germans, I said. In due course we shall show that any other mark of unity or any other national bond either never had truth and meaning or, if it had, that owing to our present position these bonds of union have been destroyed and torn from us and can never recur; it is only by means of the common characteristic of being German that we can avert the downfall of our nation which is threatened by its fusion with foreign peoples, and win back again an individuality that is self-supporting and quite incapable of any dependence upon others. With our perception of the truth of this statement, its apparent conflict (feared now, perhaps, by many) with other duties and with matters that are considered sacred will completely vanish. . . .

Let us be on our guard against being taken unawares by this sweetness of servitude, for it robs even our posterity of the hope of future emancipation. . . . Let us not allow our spirit, as well as our body, to be bent and subjected and brought into captivity.

If you ask me how this is to be brought about, the only entirely comprehensive answer is this: We must at once become what we ought to be in any case, namely, Germans. We are not to subject our spirit; therefore we must before all things provide a spirit for ourselves, and a firm and certain spirit; we must become earnest in all things and not go on existing frivolously, as if life were a jest; we must form for ourselves enduring and unshakable principles which will serve as a sure guide for all the rest of our thoughts and actions. Life and thought with us must be of one piece and a solid and interpenetrating whole; in both we must live according to nature and truth, and throw away foreign contrivances; in a word, we must provide character for ourselves; for to have character and to be German undoubtedly mean the same; and the thing has no special name in our language, because it is intended to proceed immediately from our very existence without any knowledge or reflection on our part. . . .

If only Germany at any rate had remained one, it would have rested on itself in the center of the civilized world like the sun in the center of the universe; it would have kept itself at peace, and with itself the adjacent countries; and without any artificial measures it would have kept everything in equilibrium by the mere fact of its natural existence. It was only the deceit of foreign countries that dragged Germany into their own lawlessness and their own disputes; it was they who taught Germany the treacherous notion of the balance of power, for they knew it to be one of the most effective means of deluding Germany as to its own true advantage and of keeping it in that state of delusion. This aim is now sufficiently attained, and the result that was intended is now complete before our eyes. Even if we cannot do away with this result, why should we not at any rate extirpate the source of it in our own understanding, which is now almost the only thing over which we still have sovereign power? . . .

Now, at last, let us be bold enough to look at the deceptive vision of a universal monarchy, which people are beginning to hold up for public veneration in place of that equilibrium which for some time has been growing more and more preposterous, and let us perceive how hateful and contrary to reason that vision is. Spiritual nature was able to present the essence of humanity in extremely diverse gradations in individuals and in individuality as a whole, in peoples. Only when each people, left to itself, develops and forms itself in accordance with its own peculiar quality, and only when in every people each individual develops himself in accordance with that common quality, as well as in accordance with his own peculiar quality—

then, and then only, does the manifestation of divinity appear in its true mirror as it ought to be, and only a man who either entirely lacks the notion of the rule of law and divine order, or else is an obdurate enemy thereto, could take upon himself to want to interfere with that law, which is the highest law in the spiritual world. Only in the invisible qualities of nations, which are hidden from their own eyes—qualities as the means whereby these nations remain in touch with the source of original life—only therein is to be found the guarantee of their present and future worth, virtue, and merit. If these qualities are dulled by admixture and worn away by friction, the flatness that results will bring about a separation from spiritual nature, and this in its turn will cause all men to be fused together to their uniform and conjoint destruction. . . .

Johann Gotlieb Fichte, *Addresses to the German Nation,* trans. R. F. Jones and G. H. Turnbull (Chicago: The Open Court Publishing Co., 1922), pp. 3–4, 207–8, 229, 232. (Reprinted by permission of the publisher.)

Friedrich Schlegel was one of the chief figures in the German Romantic movement. In his history of ancient and modern literature (1812), he applies the romantic sentimentality about the past to the problem of nationalism. The result is the stress on "old national memories" which alone can produce a nation. Notice that here nationalism becomes something equated with "spiritual development," and that we are on the way to the exaltation of the nation as the highest good, not only in realistic terms, but in spiritual terms as well.

138   . . . Comparing the nations as to their values, it seems important above all things, from this historical point of view, for the far distant development, yes for the spiritual development of the nation, that a people possess great old national memories—which for the most part lose themselves in the dim past of its first origins, and which to maintain and glorify is the chief task of poetry. Such national memories, the greatest inheritance a people can have, are an advantage which cannot be replaced by anything else; and if a people finds itself elevated in its own spirit and, as it were, ennobled, by the fact that it has such memories from ancient pre-history, that it has, in one word, poetry, then just through this it will be put on a higher level in our own eye and judgment. It is not the far-reaching undertakings, not the peculiar events alone which determine the worth and dignity of a nation. Many nations which were unhappy have vanished without a name and have barely left a trace; others, happier, have left the memory of their expansion and their conquests, but we barely pay attention to the news of these matters if the spirit of the nation does not lend a higher purpose to such undertakings and events which repeat themselves only too often in world history. Curious deeds, great events and fates are by themselves not enough to retain our admiration and to decide the judgment of posterity; a people, if it is to have a value, must arrive at a clear consciousness of its own deeds and fate. History is this self-consciousness of a nation, speaking from contemplative or narrative works. . . .

Deutsche Vergangenheit und deutscher Staat, bearbeitet von Paul Kluckholn (Leipzig, 1935), pp. 162–63. (Trans. George L. Mosse.)

In his essay on *The Inequality of the Races* (1853) the Comte de Gobineau expounded the theory of the superiority of the Aryan race over all others. Of this Aryan race, the Germans were the inheritors. There is in the race theory something of the idea of the survival of the fittest (see p. 318), which had currency even before Darwin's famous *Origins of the Species* appeared in print. This racial theory gave a pseudo-scientific veneer to aggressive nationalism, and it became the core of National Socialist ideology in our century (see Alfred Rosenberg, p. 475).

. . . Since the last half of the previous century [eighteenth], one reasons **139** on the basis of general principles, and one pretended also to relate all phenomena . . . to fixed laws. . . . The prosperity or the misfortune of a nation, its greatness and decadence, were related to their obvious vices and virtues. An honest people were necessarily a famous people, and, on the contrary, a society which attracted too many easy consciences was doomed without mercy to the ruin of . . . an Athens or Rome. . . .

With such keys one sought to open all the mysteries; but in reality they remained unsolved. Those virtues necessary to big groups must have a peculiar collective egoism which is not parallel to individual virtue . . . One must recognize and avow that here those merits and demerits which concern Christian consciences are beside the point, but instead certain aptitudes of soul and body determine or paralyze the life of nations. This leads us to inquire why some nations can be powerful and others cannot, and thus one is forced to acknowledge that this is a matter resulting from the particular race. . . .

I reject those groups whose social system is not vigorous enough to impose itself, with the fusion of blood, upon great multitudes. I come to those whose constituting principle has such strength that it can embrace all others who are near to its center of operations, incorporate them, and lift them up to the great vistas of uncontested domination of [its] ideas and action . . . in one word, such a people can call themselves a civilization. . . .

Is there an inequality of forces? It goes without saying that the American savages as well as the Hindus are our inferiors on that score . . . but we must distinguish between muscular force and that power of resistance whose most remarkable feat is its staying power . . . even feeble races have muscular power. Among peoples in the matter of force, as in the matter of beauty, there is a difference . . . though not so obvious. The Italians are more beautiful than the Germans or the Swiss, more beautiful than are the Frenchmen and the Spaniards. Thus the English have a bodily beauty which is superior to that of the Slavs. . . .

The Germans made their appearance in the midst of Roman society. At the same time they occupied the extreme northwest of Europe which, little by little, became their base of operations. Successive marriages with Celts and Slavs . . . multiplied the expansion of the new arrivals without degrading too rapidly their force of initiative. Modern society was born; it began to perfect its members and to further the work of its creators. We have seen it discover America in practically our own day, uniting itself with the native society to lead it toward a new birth. . . .

The German people were filled with all the energy of the Aryan races. That was necessary so that it could fulfill the duty to which it was called. . . . It was indispensable that the last workers sent to the earth leave nothing difficult unaccomplished, as no one exists except themselves to accomplish such feats . . . they achieve the conquest of the globe. . . . Here we have the existence of the best human species of the whole white race . . . result of the evolution of faculties which is like a peak, like a summit, like the final goal of history.

But religion itself has not promised us eternity, only science in showing us what we have commenced to do seems to hold out hope that we might finish it. There is therefore no ground for astonishment to find once again confirmation of a fact no longer doubtful. The sad knowledge is not death; it is the certitude to arrive there degenerated; and perhaps that fear, reserved for our descendants, can leave us cold if we did not feel, with secret horror, that the hands of destiny are already upon us.

Comte Joseph-Arthur de Gobineau, *l'Essai sur l'inégalité des races humaines* (1853–1855), (Paris, 1862). (Trans. George L. Mosse.)

In the next extract the French poet and statesman Alphonse de Lamartine (1790–1869) discusses the progress of the French nation and introduces us to nationalism as it grew up in France.

The revolutions of the human mind are gradual like the periods in the **140** progress of nations. They resemble the process of vegetation, which enlarges the plant, though the eye is unable to measure that increase while it is being effected.

In all beings, God has proportioned this period of growth to the length of existence which he destines to them. Man, who is to live for a century, grows for five and twenty years, or even longer. Nations, which are to live through two or three thousand years, have revolutions of development—of childhood, youth, manhood, and at length old age, which last not less than two or three centuries. The difficulty with the vulgar [i.e., common people] is, amid those convulsive phenomena which mark the revolutions of a nation, to distinguish the crises of growth from those of decay, youth from old age, and life from death.

Superficial philosophers deceive themselves in this: they imagine a nation in decline because her ancient institutions are giving way. In their eyes she is about to expire, when in fact she is renewing her youth. This was said of France when, at the commencement of the first revolution, her absolute monarchy perished. It was said at the dissolution of the feudal system; it was said at the fall of theocracy; it is repeated this day on the extinction of constitutional monarchy.

But they are deceived. France is young. She may exhaust many modes of rule before she will have exhausted the vigorous intellectual life with which God has endowed her race.

There is one sure means of avoiding error respecting the character of such crises; it is to mark well the governing element in a revolution. Revolutions produced by a vice, by an individual, by the crimes or the isolated greatness of a man, by ambition, whether personal or national, by rivalry between two dynasties, by thirst of conquest or of blood, by unjust ideas of national glory, above all, by hatred between different classes of citizens; such revolutions are the preludes of decay, the signs of decomposition and death, in a nation or a race. But if revolutions are the product of a moral principle, of an idea, of a logical process, of conviction, of sentiment, of an aspiration, undefined and vague though it be, towards an improved order of government and society, of a desire to develop and perfect the relations between citizen and citizen, between people and people; if they embody a lofty ideal instead of an abject passion, such revolutions attest, even in their catastrophes and temporary aberrations, a youth and vitality which promises long and glorious seasons of growth.

Such was the character of the French revolution of 1789; and such is the character of the second French revolution of 1848.

The revolution of 1848 is nothing more than a continuation of the former, with fewer elements of disorder, and greater elements of progress. In both it was a moral idea which exploded on the world. This idea, this principle, is THE PEOPLE—the people who, in 1789, relieved themselves from the pressure of servitude and ignorance, from privileged classes and an absolute monarchy; the people which, in 1848, freed themselves from the oligarchy of the few, and a too stringent and exclusive constitutional monarchy;—the germination in the government of the rights and interests of the masses.

This principle or idea of the people, this accession of the masses to political power, whatever difficulties a democratic phenomenon so novel presents to statesmen, is a moral truth equally palpable to the understanding and the heart of the philosopher. The revolution which bears in its bosom such an idea is a vital, not a mortal revolution. With God's help, the nation shall come forth from it fortified in right, in might, and in virtue.

Its course may be impeded by the ignorance of the masses, by the impatience of the nation, by the factions or sophisms of men who desire to substitute their individualities for the people. But it will end in the removal of such men; it will fathom their sophisms, and will develop those germs of reason, justice, and virtue which God has implanted in the blood of the French race. . . .

Alphonse de Lamartine, *History of the French Revolution of 1848* (London, 1870), pp. 1–3.

QUESTIONS

1. Is there anything in Fichte's *Addresses* which foreshadows the doctrines of German national superiority?
2. How does Fichte criticize the idea of a universal monarchy?
3. How, according to Schlegel, can a people have "value"?
4. Do you see any connection between the nature of Schlegel's arguments and your reading on romanticism (see p. 221)?
5. What is Gobineau's criticism of the general principles and fixed laws of the eighteenth century?
6. What properties of the Aryan race are supposed to make it superior?
7. How did Lamartine think that revolutions renewed France's youth?
8. Compare Fichte and Treitschke (p. 329) as to their similarities and differences.

CHAPTER XXI

THE GROWTH OF DEMOCRACY IN BRITAIN

ALTHOUGH Britain had no revolution in the nineteenth century, she made steady progress in the direction of a greater popular participation in government. A landmark in this progress was the Parliamentary Reform Bill of 1832. The arguments about this broadening of the franchise pitted the Liberals (141, 142) against those who wanted to preserve the *status quo* (143). But although the Liberal point of view won out, this did not mean the enfranchisement of the working classes. Those excluded from the vote formed the Chartist movement and presented petitions to Parliament which showed the continuing discontent of the lower classes (144).

The next reform bill (1867) was passed not by the Liberals, but by the Conservatives. For under the leadership of Benjamin Disraeli, conservatism had become Tory democracy, adjusting to the need for greater democracy while keeping intact the Tory principles of aristocracy, church, and crown. Disraeli himself explained the principles of this new conservatism (145).

While the Conservatives tended to steal the issue of reform from the Liberals, liberalism (see p. 229) nevertheless continued to make itself felt. Above all, the strict Liberal ideas on morality, tempering the principles of freedom and self-advancement, left their imprint on

Victorian England. The extracts from *The History of the Fairchild Family* illustrate this aspect of English life in the nineteenth century (146).

Lord John Russell explains the principles of the Liberal reform of Parliament while introducing the Parliamentary Reform Bill to the House of Commons (1832).

141   It is my opinion, therefore, that the whole measure will add to the constituency of the Commons House of Parliament, about half a million of persons, and these all connected with the property of the country, having a valuable stake amongst us, and deeply interested in our institutions. They are the persons on whom we can depend in any future struggle in which this nation may be engaged, and who will maintain and support Parliament and the Throne in carrying that struggle to a successful termination. I think that those measures will produce a farther benefit to the people, by the great incitement which it will occasion to industry and good conduct. For when a man finds that by industrious exertion, and by punctuality, he will entitle himself to a place in the list of voters, he will have an additional motive to improve his circumstances, and to preserve his character amongst his neighbors. I think, therefore, that in adding to the constituency, we are providing for the moral as well as for the political improvement of the country. . . .

I arrive at last at the objections which may be made to the plan we propose. I shall be told, in the first place, that we overturn the institutions of our ancestors. I maintain, that in departing from the letter, we preserve the spirit of those institutions. Our opponents say, our ancestors gave Old Sarum Representatives, therefore we should give Old Sarum Representatives. We say, our ancestors gave Old Sarum Representatives because it *was* a large town; therefore we gave Representatives to Manchester, which *is* a large town. I think we are acting more as our ancestors would have acted, by letting in Representatives for our great commercial and manufacturing towns, than by excluding such Representatives. I may be told that the proposed Reform is contrary to the principle of Parliament, as settled at the time of the Revolution: and Mr. Burke may be quoted in support of the proposition, that as the same places continue to send Representatives, the principle of the Constitution must be the same. But whilst I acknowledge Mr. Burke's transcendant ability and unequalled powers of reasoning, I cannot approve of his mode of arguing this question. He might as well have held, that the principles of the Roman Empire in the time of Augustus were the same as the principles of the Roman Republic in the days of the first Brutus, as to say that because Old Sarum, from its size and importance in the time of Edward 3rd, sent Representatives to Parliament, it should continue to send those Representatives, or else we should no longer follow up the principle of our ancestors in forming the constitution of this House. It has been asserted also, if a Reform were to be effected, that many men of great talents who now get into this House for close boroughs, would not be able to procure seats. I have never entertained any apprehensions of the sort, for I believe that no Reform that can be introduced will have the effect of preventing wealth, probity, learning, and wit, from having their proper influence upon elections.

Hansard's Parliamentary Debates, 3rd series, II, 1083, 1085–86.

One member of Parliament here counters the argument which would delay reform in order to let popular agitation spend itself. He deals with the opinions of those who as Conservatives wanted to avoid such reform (1831).

What, then, it is said, would you legislate in haste? Would you legislate **142** in times of great excitement concerning matters of such deep concern? Yes, Sir, I would: and if any bad consequences should follow from the haste and the excitement, let those be held answerable who, when there was no need of haste, when there existed no excitement, refused to listen to any project of Reform—nay, who made it an argument against Reform, that the public mind was not excited. When few meetings were held, when few petitions were sent up to us, these politicians said, "Would you alter a Constitution with which the people are perfectly satisfied?" And now, when the kingdom from one end to the other is convulsed by the question of Reform, we hear it said by the very same persons, "Would you alter the Representative system in such agitated times as these?" Half the logic of misgovernment lies in this one sophistical dilemma: If the people are turbulent, they are unfit for liberty: if they are quiet, they do not want liberty. I allow that hasty legislation is an evil. I allow that there are great objections to legislating in troubled times. But Reformers are compelled to legislate fast because bigots will not legislate early. Reformers are compelled to legislate in times of excitement, because bigots will not legislate in times of tranquillity. If, ten years ago—nay, if only two years ago, there had been at the head of affairs, men who understand the signs of the times and the temper of the nation, we should not have been forced to hurry now. If we cannot take our time, it is because we have to make up their lost time. If they had reformed gradually, we might have reformed gradually; but we are compelled to move fast because they would not move at all. . . .

Ibid., IX, 381–82.

In this same debate in the House of Commons about the Reform Bill, Sir Harvey Inglis states the Conservative argument against the bill.

143   But I mean to contend that the influences which now exist, have existed from the time when the Constitution received its present character, namely, at the Revolution; I mean to contend that under this system the House of Commons has attracted all those varied and combined talents, and that mass of intelligence which are so essential to the discharge of our duties; and which, under any other system, would too probably be excluded from our deliberations. . . . The noble Lord says that we are restoring the constitution. I am, then, entitled to ask, to what period does he go back? When was the constitution of this House other than it now is; when, at least, was it better and more popular? To that year, and to that day, I am at once content that we shall return. But unless I shall be told in something more than vain declamation; until, indeed, I shall be convinced, by regular evidence, that there ever was a time when this House was independent alike of the Crown and of the Aristocracy, and represented purely and solely the will of the people, I, for one, will be content with that "old almanack"—history, and will continue to contend that such a state of things never did exist. . . .

I say, Sir, that in proportion as you add to the power of this House, and in proportion as you add to the power of the people upon this House, you risk the existence of the other branches of the Constitution. . . .

I oppose this change in the construction of this House (and consequent change in the Constitution of this country), because I do not believe that a majority of the people desire such change: and because, if I did believe it, I am sent here to legislate, not for their will, but for their interests. I oppose it because the principle upon which this Reform is to be made is unrecognized in any era of the history of this House. I oppose it, because it diminishes those influences here which have always existed, and which are at this day essential to the balance of the Constitution. I oppose it, because against the body so assembled no charge is proved, or even made; because the influence of the Crown was never less than at this day; the influence of the aristocracy was never less; the influence of corruption by money, by places, or by party, was never less:—on every consideration of all which we enjoy, and of all which we are to hazard, I oppose the object of the noble Lord. With these feelings, with the deep conviction that this country has long practically enjoyed a Constitution, which even by the testimony of the noble Lord, has been the envy of other nations, and which I believe to be the glory and the happiness of our own, I will never consent to a plan which, in my judgment, subverts it.

Ibid., II, 1112, 1122, 1126–27.

The dissatisfaction with the limits of the Reform Bill is expressed by this Chartist Petition to Parliament (1839). It is an argument for manhood suffrage.

. . . Your petitioners dwell in a land whose merchants are noted for **144** their enterprise, whose manufacturers are very skillful, and whose workmen are proverbial for their industry. The land itself is goodly, the soil rich, and the temperature wholesome. It is abundantly furnished with the materials of commerce and trade. It has numerous and convenient harbors. In facility of internal communication it exceeds all others. For three and twenty years we have enjoyed a profound peace.

Yet with all the elements of national prosperity, and with every disposition and capacity to take advantage of them, we find ourselves overwhelmed with public and private suffering. We are bowed down under a load of taxes, which, notwithstanding, fall greatly short of the wants of our rulers. Our traders are trembling on the verge of bankruptcy; our workmen are starving. Capital brings no profit, and labor no remuneration. The home of the artificer is desolate, and the warehouse of the pawnbroker is full. The workhouse is crowded, and the manufactory is deserted. We have looked on every side; we have searched diligently in order to find out the causes of distress so sore and so long continued. We can discover none in nature or in Providence.

It was the fond expectation of the friends of the people that a remedy for the greater part, if not for the whole, of their grievances would be found in the Reform Act of 1832. They regarded that act as a wise means to a worthy end, as the machinery of an improved legislation, where the will of the masses would be at length potential. They have been bitterly and basely deceived. . . . The Reform Act has effected a transfer of power from one domineering faction to another, and left the people as helpless as before. . . . We come before your honorable house to tell you, with all humility, that this state of things must not be permitted to continue. . . .

Required as we are universally, to support and obey the laws, nature and reason entitle us to demand that in making of the laws the universal voice shall be implicitly listened to. We perform the duties of freemen; we must have the privileges of freemen. Therefore we demand universal suffrage. The suffrage, to be exempt from the corruption of the wealthy and the violence of the powerful, must be secret. . . . We ask for the reality of a good, not for its semblance; therefore we demand the ballot. The connection between the representatives and the people, to be beneficial, must be intimate. The legislative and constituent powers, for correction and for instruction, ought to be brought into frequent contact. Errors which are comparatively light when susceptible of a speedy popular remedy may produce the most disastrous effects when permitted to grow inveterate through years of compulsory endurance.

George L. Mosse and Philip Taylor, *Outline and Sources for A History of Western Civilisation* (Dubuque: William C. Brown Co., 1951), II, 11.

Benjamin Disraeli, prime minister (1868, 1874–80), was the chief founder of Tory democracy. In his speech on "Conservative and Liberal Principles" (1872) he explains his point of view on some of the chief issues of the day.

145   . . . Now, I have always been of the opinion that the Tory party has three great objects. The first is to maintain the institutions of the country—not from any sentiment of political superstition, but because we believe that they embody the principles upon which a community like England can alone safely rest. The principles of liberty, of order, of law, and of religion ought not to be entrusted to individual opinion or to the caprice and passion of multitudes, but should be embodied in a form of permanence and power. We associate with the Monarchy the ideas which it represents—the majesty of law, the administration of justice, the fountain of mercy and of honour. We know that in the Estates of the Realm [i.e., Parliament] and the privileges they enjoy, is the best security for public liberty and good government. We believe that a national profession of faith can only be maintained by an Established Church, and that no society is safe unless there is a public recognition of the Providential government of the world, and of the future responsibility of man. Well, it is a curious circumstance that during all these same forty years of triumphant Liberalism, every one of these institutions has been attacked and assailed—I say, continuously attacked and assailed. And what, gentlemen, has been the result? For the last forty years the most depreciating comparisons have been instituted between the Sovereignty of England and the Sovereignty of a great Republic. We have been called upon in every way, in Parliament, in the Press, by articles in newspapers, by pamphlets, by every means which can influence opinion, to contrast the simplicity and economy of the Sovereignty of the United States with the cumbrous cost of the Sovereignty of England. . . .

The people of England have expressed, in a manner which cannot be mistaken, that they will uphold the ancient Monarchy of England, the Constitutional Monarchy of England, limited by the co-ordinate authority of the Estates of the Realm, but limited by nothing else. Now, if you consider the state of public opinion with regard to those Estates of the Realm, what do you find? Take the case of the House of Lords. The House of Lords has been assailed during this reign of Liberalism in every manner and unceasingly. Its constitution has been denounced as anomalous, its influence declared pernicious; but what has been the result of this assault and criticism for forty years? Why, the people of England, in my opinion, have discovered that the existence of a second Chamber is necessary to Constitutional Government; and, while necessary to Constitutional Government, is, at the same time, of all political inventions the most difficult. Therefore, the people of this country have congratulated themselves that, by the aid of an ancient and famous history, there has been developed in this country an Assembly which possesses all the virtues which a Senate should possess—independence, great local influence, eloquence, all the accomplishments of political life, and a public training which no theory could supply.

The assault of Liberalism upon the House of Lords has been mainly occasioned by the prejudice of Liberalism against the land laws of this country. But in my opinion, and in the opinion of wiser men than myself, and of men in other countries beside this, the liberty of England depends much upon the landed tenure of England—upon the fact that there is a class which can alike defy despots and mobs, around which the people may always rally, and which must be patriotic from its intimate connection with the soil. Well, gentlemen, so far as these institutions of the country—the Monarchy and the Lords Spiritual and Temporal—are concerned, I think we may fairly say, without exaggeration, that public opinion is in favour of those institutions, the maintenance of which is one of the principal tenets of the Tory party, and the existence of which has been unceasingly criticised for forty years by the Liberal party. Now, let me say a word about the other Estate of the Realm, which was first attacked by Liberalism.

One of the most distinguishing features of the great change effected in 1832 was that those who brought it about at once abolished all the franchises of the working classes. They were franchises as ancient as those of the Baronage of England; and, while they abolished them, they proposed no substitute. The discontent upon the subject of the representation which has from that time more or less pervaded our society dates from that period, and that discontent, all will admit, has now ceased. It was terminated by the Act of Parliamentary Reform of 1867-8. That Act was founded on a confidence that the great body of the people of this country were 'Conservative.' When I say 'Conservative,' I use the word in its purest and loftiest sense. I mean that the people of England, and especially the working classes of England, are proud of belonging to a great country, and wish to maintain its greatness—that they are proud of belonging to an Imperial country, and are resolved to maintain, if they can, their empire—that they believe, on the whole, that the greatness and the empire of England are to be attributed to the ancient institutions of the land. . . .

Gentlemen, there is another and second great object of the Tory party. If the first is to maintain the institutions of the country, the second is, in my opinion, to uphold the Empire of England. If you look to the history of this country since the advent of Liberalism—forty years ago—you will find that there has been no effort so continuous, so subtle, supported by so much energy, and carried on with so much ability and acumen, as the attempts of Liberalism to effect the disintegration of the Empire of England. . . .

Well, what has been the result of this attempt during the reign of Liberalism for the disintegration of the Empire? It has entirely failed. But how has it failed? Through the sympathy of the Colonies with the Mother Country. They have decided that the Empire shall not be destroyed, and in my opinion no minister in this country will do his duty who neglects any opportunity of reconstructing as much as possible our Colonial Empire, and of responding to those distant sympathies which may become the source of incalculable strength and happiness to this land. Therefore, gentlemen, with respect to the second great object of the Tory party also—the maintenance of the Empire—public opinion appears to be in favour of our principles—that public opinion which, I am bound to say, thirty years ago, was not favourable to our principles, and which, during a long interval of controversy, in the interval had been doubtful.

Gentlemen, another great object of the Tory party, and one not inferior to the maintenance of the Empire, or the upholding of our institutions, is the elevation of the condition of the people. Let us see in this great struggle between Toryism and Liberalism that has prevailed in this country during the last forty years what are the salient features. It must be obvious to all who consider the condition of the multitude with a desire to improve and elevate it, that no important step can be gained unless you can effect some reduction of their hours of labour and humanise their toil. The great problem is to be able to achieve such results without violating those principles of economic truth upon which the prosperity of all States depends. You recollect well that many years ago the Tory party believed that these two results might be obtained—that you might elevate the condition of the people by the reduction of their toil and the mitigation of their labour, and at the same time inflict no injury on the wealth of the nation. You know how that effort was encountered—how these views and principles were met by the triumphant statesmen of Liberalism. They told you that the inevitable consequence of your policy was to diminish capital, that this, again, would lead to the lowering of wages, to a great diminution of the employment of the people, and ultimately to the impoverishment of the kingdom. . . .

Yet they were carried; and what do we now find? That capital was never accumulated so quickly, that wages were never higher, that the employment of the people was never greater, and the country never wealthier. I ventured to say a short time ago, speaking in one of the great cities of this country, that the health of the people was the most important question for a statesman. It is, gentlemen, a large subject. It has many branches. It involves the state of the dwellings of the people, the moral consequences of which are not less considerable than the physical. It involves their enjoyment of some of the chief elements of nature—air, light, and water. It involves the regulation of their industry, the inspection of their toil. It involves the purity of their provisions, and it touches upon all the means by which you may wean them from habits of excess and of brutality. . . .

And I can tell you this, gentlemen, from personal conversation with some of the most intelligent of the labouring class—and I think there are many of them in this room who can bear witness to what I say—that the policy of the Tory party—the hereditary, the traditionary policy of the Tory party, that would improve the condition of the people—is more appreciated by the people than the ineffable mysteries and all the pains and penalties of the Ballot Bill. Gentlemen, is that wonderful? Consider the condition of the great body of the working classes of this country. They are in possession of personal privileges—of personal rights and liberties—which are not enjoyed by the aristocracies of other countries. Recently they have obtained— and wisely obtained—a great extension of political rights; and when the people of England see that under the constitution of this country, by means of the constitutional cause which my right honourable friend the Lord Mayor has proposed, they possess every personal right of freedom, and, according to the conviction of the whole country, also an adequate concession of political rights, is it at all wonderful that they should wish to elevate and improve their condition, and is it unreasonable that they should ask the Legislature to assist them in that behest as far as it is consistent with the general welfare of the realm?

Selected Speeches of the Late Right Honourable the Earl of Beaconsfield, ed. T. E. Kebbel (London: Longmans Green & Co., 1882), pp. 525–28.

The cult of respectability in Victorian England was based on two factors: the renewed religious impulse which came from the evangelical movement and the self-righteousness of the increasingly powerful middle classes. *The History of the Fairchild Family,* a book for children written by Martha Butt (Mrs. Sherwood) in 1818, can serve as an illustration. It was meant to teach the very young to live a "righteous life" and to recognize their own irremediable sinfulness. A striking self-righteousness grew out of this strict morality. Books like this dominated the tone of the English nursery for most of the nineteenth century.

146   Mr. and Mrs. Fairchild loved and feared God, and had done so, by the mercy of God, ever since their younger days. They knew that their hearts were very bad, and that they could not be saved by any good thing they could do: on the contrary, that they were by nature fitted only for everlasting punishment: but they believed in the Lord Jesus Christ, and loved him for having died for them; and they knew that he would save them, because he saves all those people who trust in him. They believed also in the Holy Spirit of God—that it enters into the wicked hearts of men, and makes them good: and they knew that they could not do any thing well without the help of this Holy Spirit; therefore they used to pray for the Holy Spirit every day: and their prayers were heard, for they were helped to be good every day.

Mr. and Mrs. Fairchild loved their little children dearly; but they did not wish them to be handsome, rich, or great: all they desired for them was that they might be the children of God, and go to heaven when they died. . . .

"Men can never leave off sinning, my dear," said Mr. Fairchild, "because sin is in our hearts, and will continue to trouble us to our dying day; but in proportion as the people of any town, or village, or house, believe on the Lord Jesus Christ, and love him, they will become more and more happy; and in proportion as people give way to sin, they become more miserable. In those heathen countries where God is not known at all, the people are poor, miserable, cruel, and dirty wretches: they do not know what it is to be happy: the fields look barren and desolate, and the very beasts share their misery. . . .

Lucy Fairchild's Journal, Written when she was Nine Years and a Half old.

"When I awoke this morning, Mamma called me to make my bed, and dust the room; and I felt cross and wished I was like Miss Augusta Noble, and had servants to wait upon me; and was proud, and wished for fine things, and that Lady Noble was my mamma, and not my own dear mamma.

Mamma gave Emily a bit of muslin and some pink ribbon; and I was envious, and hated Emily a little while, though I knew it was wicked.

When Papa gave Henry the strawberry I was angry again: and then I thought of Mrs. Giles, who loves one of her little girls and hates the other. I thought that my papa and mamma were like Mrs. Giles, and that they loved Henry and Emily more than me.

When Papa was reading and saying prayers I wanted to be at play; and was tired of the Bible, and did not wish to hear it.

And then I thought a very bad thought indeed! When Mrs. Barker came, I despised her for being ugly, though I knew that God had made her such as she is, and that he could make me ugly in one moment."

As soon as Lucy had finished writing these last words, she heard her mamma come up stairs and go into her room: she immediately ran to her, and, shewing her the book, "Oh, Mamma! Mamma!" she said "you cannot think what a wicked heart I have got! Here is my journal; I am ashamed to shew it to you: pray do not hate me for what is written in that book."

Mrs. Fairchild took the book and when she had read what was written, "My dear child," she said, "I thank God, who has by his Holy Spirit helped you to know a little of the wickedness of your heart. Your heart, my dear, is no worse, and no better, than the hearts of all human creatures; for there is none good, no not one. 'As in water face answereth to face, so the heart of man to man.' (Prov. xxvii. 19). And yet, as I told you before, there are many people who live to a very old age without knowing that their hearts are wicked: they think themselves very good, and they think that they shall go to heaven as a reward for their goodness. They do not see the need of a Saviour, and therefore never apply to him for help; thus they live and die in unbelief. But happy are those, my dear Lucy, who are brought to the knowledge of their own sinful nature whilst they are young."

Mrs. Sherwood (Martha Butt), *The History of the Fairchild Family* (London, 1818), pp. 2, 3, 12, 88–90.

QUESTIONS

1. Contrast the arguments of Lord John Russell and Sir Harvey Inglis. What are the main differences between them?
2. Referring to the section on liberalism (p. 229), how does Lord John Russell's argument reflect Liberal ideas?

3. What are the arguments used by the Chartists for manhood suffrage?
4. How, according to Benjamin Disraeli, could the ancient institutions of England best serve to satisfy popular aspirations?
5. In what way could Disraeli's Tory principles lead toward social reform?
6. What are the chief points of morality which Lucy Fairchild had learned?
7. Is there a connection between this morality and that put forward by Samuel Smiles (see p. 238)?

CHAPTER XXII

THE REVOLUTIONS OF 1848

THE YEAR 1848 was one of revolution throughout Western and Central Europe. The real signal for these widespread uprisings was the French February revolution (147) which swept away the rule of Louis Philippe and the government of Guizot (148). The Republic, established under a provisional government, decreed the "right to work" which Louis Blanc had advocated (149) and instituted the "national workshops." However, the National Assembly, elected by universal suffrage, proved to be more conservative than the provisional government, and after the first upsurge of revolution and republicanism, France was well on the road to the second Empire (see p. 275).

In Germany, Italy, and the Austrian Empire the revolutions involved national as well as social aspirations. National independence and unity was demanded by the minorities in the Austrian Empire, by men like Mazzini in Italy (p. 334), and by the Federal Parliament in Germany. That Parliament was composed, after the revolution, of liberal elements who wanted to unify Germany on the basis of a constitution. The king of Prussia, however, to whom the crown was offered, refused it (150). This put an end to the liberal plan for unification, a plan opposed both to absolutism and to the republican left (151). The Parliament of Frankfurt failed, and re-unification of Germany came about not through liberalism but through "blood and iron" (see p. 326). Although the revolutions of 1848 had failed in their immediate objectives, they foreshadowed future events and problems.

The French historian Alexis de Tocqueville, writing in 1852, looked back at the outbreak of the Revolution of 1848 in France. Here he describes how that outbreak affected him.

147 . . . The next morning was the 24th of February. On leaving my bed-room, I met the cook, who had been out; the good woman was quite beside herself, and poured out a sorrowing rigmarole of which I failed to understand a word except that the Government was massacring the poor people. I went downstairs at once, and had no sooner set foot in the street than I breathed for the first time the atmosphere of revolution. The roadway was empty; the shops were not open; there were no carriages or pedestrians to be seen; none of the ordinary hawkers' cries were heard; neighbours stood talking in little groups at their doors, with subdued voices, with a frightened air; every face seemed distorted with fear or anger. I met a National Guard hurrying along, gun in hand, with a tragic gait; I accosted him, but could learn nothing from him save that the Government was massacring the people (to which he added that the National Guard would know how to put that right). . . .

The boulevards . . . presented a strange spectacle. There was hardly a soul to be seen, although it was nearly nine o'clock in the morning, and one heard not the slightest sound of a human voice; but all the little sentry-boxes which stand along this endless avenue seemed to move about and totter on their base, and from time to time one of them would fall with a crash, while the great trees along the curb came tumbling down into the roadway as though of their own accord. These acts of destruction were the work of isolated individuals, who went about their business silently, regu-larly and hurriedly, preparing in this way the materials for the barricades which others were to erect. Nothing ever seemed to me more to resemble the carrying on of an industry, and as a matter of fact for the greater num-ber of these men it was nothing less. The instinct of disorder had given them the taste for it, and their experience of so many former insurrections the practice. I do not know that during the whole course of the day I was more keenly struck than in passing through this solitude in which one saw, so to speak, the worst passions of mankind at play, without the good ones appearing. I would rather have met in the same place a furious crowd; and I remember that in calling Languinais' attention to these tottering edifices and falling trees, I gave vent to the phrase which had long been on my lips, and said: "Believe me, this time it is no longer a riot: it is a revolution." . . . I had some difficulty in forcing my way through them. One of them, a short thickset man, who seemed to belong to the lower class of workman, asked me where I was going.

I replied, "To the Chamber," adding, to show that I was a member of the Opposition, "Reform for ever! You know the Guizot ministry has been dismissed?"

"Yes, Sir, I know," replied the man jeeringly, and pointing to the Tuileries, "but we want more than that." . . .

[Inside the Chamber of Deputies, later the same day.]

The people did not yet come into the Chamber in streams, but entered little by little, one by one; each moment there appeared a new face; the Chamber grew flooded, as it were by drops. Most of the newcomers belonged to the lowest classes; many of them were armed. . . .

At that moment, the crowd filling the semicircle was driven back by a stream from outside towards the center benches. . . . Of the few deputies who still occupied them, some slipped away and left the House, while others retreated from bench to bench, like victims surprised by the tide who retreat from rock to rock always pursued by the rising waters. All the commotion was produced by two troops of men, for the most part armed, who marched through the two lobbies, each with officers of the National Guard and flags at its head. The two officers who carried the flags . . . ascended the tribune with a theatrical air, waved their standards, and with much skipping about and great melodramatic gestures, bawled out some revolutionary balderdash or other. The President declared the sitting suspended, and proceeded to put on his hat, as is customary; but . . . in his precipitation he seized the hat of a secretary instead of his own, and pulled it down over his eyes and ears. . . .

Until then, all the galleries except the one reserved for the Press had remained empty and closed; but while Lamartine was speaking, loud blows were heard at the door of one of them, and yielding to the strain, the door burst into atoms. In a moment the gallery was invaded by an armed mob of men who noisily filled it, and soon afterwards, all the others. A man of the lower orders, placing one foot on the cornice, pointed his gun at the

President and the speaker. . . . The President muttered a few words to the
effect that the sitting was adjourned, and stepped, or rather slid, off the platform on which the chair was placed. . . . All who had remained of
the Conservative members then dispersed, and the populace sprawled over the
center benches, crying, "Let us take the place of the corrupt crew!"

The Recollections of Alexis de Tocqueville, trans. Alexander Teixeira de Mattos (New York:
The Macmillan Co., 1869), pp. 44, 46–47, 55, 62, 64, 65, 66, 67. (Reprinted by permission
of the publisher.)

Among those whose power was ended in the revolutions of 1848
was François Guizot, the long-time and last prime minister in the
bourgeois "system" of King Louis Philippe of France. Both men
were toppled and driven from the country by the victorious forces of
republicanism which had rejected Guizot's "liberalism"—the theory
that middle-class rule represented the safe and ideal mean between
the autocracy of the middle ages on the one hand and the democracy
of the mob on the other. Guizot had hardly arrived in exile in England before he published the fresh and forceful restatement of his
views from which the following excerpts are taken.

148   . . . Now it is the glory of man to be ambitious. He alone, of all created
beings, does not passively resign himself to evil; he alone incessantly aspires
after good; not only for himself, but for his fellow-creatures. He respects
and loves the race to which he belongs; he wishes to find a remedy for their
miseries, and redress for their wrongs.

But man is no less imperfect than he is ambitious. Amidst his ardent and
unceasing struggles to eradicate evil and to achieve good, every one of his
virtuous inclinations is accompanied by an evil inclination which treads
closely on its heels, or strives with it for precedence. The desire for justice and
the desire for vengeance—the spirit of liberty and the spirit of tyranny—the
wish to rise and the wish to abase what has risen—the ardent love of truth
and the presumptuous temerity of fancied knowledge;—we may fathom
all the depths of human nature; we shall find throughout the same mingled yet conflicting qualities, the same danger from their close and easy
approximation.

To all these instincts, at once contrary and parallel—to all indiscriminately,
the bad as well as the good—the word *Democracy* holds out an interminable
vista and infinite promises. It fosters every propensity, it speaks to every
passion, of the heart of man; to the most generous and the most shameful,
the most moral, and the most immoral, the gentlest and the harshest, the

most beneficent and the most destructive: to the former it loudly offers, to the latter it secretly and dimly promises, satisfaction.

Such is the secret of its power. . . .

There are men whom this fearful struggle does not alarm: they have full confidence in human nature. According to them, if left to itself, its progress is towards good: all the evils of society arise from governments which debase men by violence or corrupt them by fraud: liberty—liberty for everybody and everything—liberty will almost always suffice to enlighten or to control the wills of men, to prevent evil or to cure it: a little government—the least possible—may be allowed for the repression of extreme disorder and the control of brute force. . . .

Let any man dive into his own heart and observe himself with attention. If he have the power to look, and the will to see, he will behold, with a sort of terror, the incessant war waged by the good and evil dispositions within him—reason and caprice, duty and passion; in short, to call them all by their comprehensive names, good and evil. We contemplate with anxiety the outward troubles and vicissitudes of human life; but what should we feel if we could behold the inward vicissitudes, the troubles of the human soul?—if we could see how many dangers, snares, enemies, combats, victories, and defeats can be crowded into a day—an hour? I do not say this to discourage man, nor to humble or undervalue his free will. He is called upon to conquer in the battle of life, and the honour of the conquest belongs to his free will. But victory is impossible, and defeat certain, if he has not a just conception and a profound feeling of his dangers, his weaknesses, and his need of assistance. To believe that the free will of man tends to good, and is of itself sufficient to accomplish good, betrays an immeasurable ignorance of his nature. It is the error of pride; an error which tends to destroy both moral and political order; which enfeebles the government of communities no less than the government of the inward man. . . .

. . . Which of us has not shuddered at the sudden discovery of the abyss over which we live—the frail barriers which separate us from it, and the destructive legions ready to rush forth upon society as soon as its jaws are unclosed? For my own part, I was a spectator, day by day, hour by hour, of the purest, the wisest, the gentlest, and the shortest of these formidable convulsions; in July 1830, I saw, in the streets and the palaces, at the gate of the national councils and in the midst of popular assemblies, society abandoned to itself, an actor or spectator of the revolution. And at the same time that I admired the generous sentiments, the proofs of strong intelligence and disinterested virtue and heroic moderation which I witnessed, I shuddered as I saw a mighty torrent of insensate ideas, brutal passions, perverse inclinations, and terrible chimeras, rise and swell, minute by minute, ready to overflow and submerge a land where all the dikes that had contained it were broken down. Society had gloriously repulsed the violation of its laws and its honour, and now it was on the point of falling into ruins in the midst of its glory. Here it was that I learned the vital conditions of social order, and the necessity of resistance to ensure the safety of the social fabric.

Resistance not only to evil, but to the principle of evil; not only to disorder, but to the passions and the ideas which engender disorder—this is the paramount and peremptory duty of every government. And the greater the empire of Democracy, the more important is it that government should hold fast to its true character, and act its true part in the struggle which agitates society. Why is it that so many democracies—some of them very brilliant—have so rapidly perished? Because they would not suffer their governments to do their duty, and fulfill the objects for which governments are instituted. . . .

The history of France is filled with the struggle between the different classes of society, of which the Revolution of 1789 was the most general and mighty explosion. The contests between nobility and commonalty, aristocracy and democracy, masters and workmen, those possessing property and those dependent on wages, are all different forms and phases of the social struggle which has so long agitated France. And it is at the very moment when we are boasting of having reached the summit of civilization—it is while the most humane words that can issue from the lips of man are ringing in our ears, that this struggle is revived more violently, more fiercely than ever!

This is a curse and a shame, of which we, and the age we live in, must rid ourselves. Internal peace, peace among all classes of citizens, is the paramount want, the only chance for the salvation of France. . . .

The United States of America are universally admitted to be the model of a Republic and a Democracy. Did it ever enter the head of the American people to call the United States a Democratic Republic?

No; nor is this astonishing. In that country there was no struggle between Aristocracy and Democracy; between an ancient aristocratical society and a new democratic society; on the contrary, the leaders of society in the United States, the descendants of the first colonists, the majority of the principal planters in the country and the principal merchants in the towns, who constituted the natural aristocracy of the country, placed themselves at the head of the revolution and the republic. The devotion, energy, and constancy which they showed in the cause, were greater than those displayed by the people. The conquest of their independence, and the foundation of the republic, was not, then, the work and the victory of certain classes over certain other classes; it was the joint work of all, led by the highest, the wealthiest, and the most enlightened, who had often great difficulty in rallying the spirit and sustaining the courage of the mass of the population. . . .

The United States of America enjoyed this singular good fortune, but it is denied to the French Republic. Indeed this is not only admitted, but proclaimed and vaunted by its authors. What is the meaning of the words *Democratic Republic* now current amongst us, and adopted as the official name, the symbol of the government? It is the echo of an ancient social war cry—a cry which is still raised, still repeated in every class of society; still angrily uttered against one class by another, which, in its turn, hears it with terror directed against itself. All are in turn democrats as against those above them, aristocrats as against those below; threatening and threatened, envious or envied, and exhibiting continual and revolting changes of position, attitude, and language, and a deplorable confusion of conflicting ideas and passions. It is war in the midst of chaos. . . .

François Guizot, *Democracy in France* (London, 1849), pp. 4–5, 7, 8–10, 16, 17–18, 19.

One of the classics of "pre-scientific" evolutionary socialism was the *Organization of Work* by Louis Blanc, the eminent French social theorist and historian. It was in this pamphlet that he introduced his concept of the "national workshops." First published in 1840, it went through nine editions in the next ten years, and it produced so great a following among members of the working class, notably in Paris, that both the man and the idea became indispensable in the opening days of the Revolution of 1848 in France. Both were soon disposed of by a combination of impracticability and conservatism.

The government ought to be considered as the supreme regulator of pro- **149** duction and endowed for this duty with great power.

This task would consist of fighting competition and of finally overcoming it.

The government ought to float a loan with the proceeds of which it should erect *social workshops* in the most important branches of national industry.

As these establishments would demand considerable investments, the number of these workshops at the start ought to be carefully limited, still they would possess, by virtue of their organization—as we shall see later—an unlimited expansion.

The government, considered as the only founder of the workshops, must determine the status regulating them. This code, deliberated and voted for by the representatives of the people, ought to have the power and force of a law.

All workmen who can give guarantee of morality shall be called to work in these social workshops up to the limit of the original capital gathered together for the purchase of tools. . . .

For the first years after the workshops are established, the government ought to regulate the scale of employment. After the first year it is no longer necessary, the laborers would then have time enough to truly estimate their respective work, and, all being equally interested as we will soon see, the success of the association would eventually depend on the elective principle.

Every year an account would be made of the net profit, which should be divided into three parts: one to be meted out equally to the members of the association; the other to be assigned (1) for the maintenance of the aged, the sick and infirm (2) for meeting a crisis that oppresses other industries, in which case all industries must give help and succour; the third part to be laid aside to furnish implements of work to those who may enter into the association later. In such a way it could be expanded indefinitely.

In every one of those associations for industries which permit a wholesale trade, those could be admitted who belong to those trades whose nature forces them to work apart and individually. Thus every workshop could be composed of different trades grouped about a greater industry obeying the same laws and partaking of the same privileges.

Every member of the social workshops would have the right to use, according to his discretion, the profits of his labor; but it would not be long before the evident economy and the incontestable excellence of this communal life would call forth other voluntary associations among the workmen according to their needs and pleasures.

Capitalists can also be taken into the association and would draw interest on their invested money, which would be guaranteed by the budget; but in the profits they would participate only if they were laborers at the same time.

If the social workshops were once established according to these principles, you could easily understand what the results would be. In every great industry, in machinery, for example, or the silk or cotton industry, or in printing establishments, the social workshops would be in competition with private industries. Would the fight be a long one? No, for the social workshops would have advantages over the others, the results of the cheaper communal life and through the organization by which all laborers, without exception, are interested in producing good and quick work. Would the fight be subversive? No, for the government would always endeavor to prevent the prices of the products of the social workshops from dropping to too low a level. If today an extremely rich man were to enter into a contest with another less wealthy, this unequal fight would be only disastrous, for the private man looks only to his personal interest; if he can sell goods as cheap as his competitors, he will do so, in order to ruin them and be master of the situation. But when the power itself steps into the place of a private individual, the question develops a different phase.

The government of which we are speaking, has it any interest in upsetting industry and destroying its existence? Is it not rather by the virtue of its position the born protector even of those against whom, in its effort to transform society, it is waging a righteous competition? Therefore a comparison is not possible between the industrial war which the great capitalist today declares against the smaller capitalist, and the war which the government would declare in our system against an individual. The first necessarily consecrates fraud, violence and all evil which iniquity carries in its wake; the second would be conducted without brutality, without wreckage, and in a manner to obtain only its aim: its peaceful and successive absorption of private workshops through social ones. In this manner, instead of being, as every great capitalist is today, the master and tyrant of the market, the government would be its regulator. It would use competition as a weapon, not to destroy private industries without consideration, which would be to its own interest to avoid, but to guide them imperceptibly into the new system. Soon, indeed, workmen and capitalists would crowd to every industrial sphere where social workshops are opened, on account of the privileges they offer to their members. After a certain time we could see how production takes place, without usurpation, without injustice, without irreparable disasters, and for the profit of the principle of association, a phenomenon which is today so deplorably brought forth and only by force of tyranny for the profit of individual egotism. Today a rich manufacturer can strike a heavy blow at his rivals, leave them dead on the spot, and monopolize a whole branch of industry; in our system, the State would constitute itself, by and by, as master of industry and in place of monopoly we have obtained, as the result of success, the subversion of competition: association.

Suppose that this aim is reached in any particular branch of industry; suppose that the manufacturers of machinery, for instance, place themselves at the service of the State; that means, submit themselves to the principles of communal management. As one and the same industry is not always carried on in one place but in different centers, it would be more just to introduce into all workshops which belong to the same industry the system of association. For, after having killed competition among individuals, it would be absurd to let it subsist among corporations. Therefore, in each sphere of work which is placed under the dominion of the government, a central workshop must be established to which all others would be in the position of supplementary workshops. Just as Rothschild possesses not only business houses in France, but in all different countries of the world, which correspond to the home office; in the same way each industry should have its central establishment and its affiliated branches. This would be the end of competition. The different centers of production would be bound together by the same common interest, and the ruinous hostility of effort would be replaced by their union. . . .

From the common interest of all the laborers in the same workshop, we infer the common interest of all workshops in the same industry. In order to complete the system, we must establish the solidarity of the various industries. Therefore, from the profit yielded by each industry, we must set aside a sum by means of which the State could give aid to every industry which has suffered through extraordinary and unforeseen circumstances. Besides, in the system which we propose, crises would become rare. What causes them most frequently today? The veritable murderous contest between the interests, a contest from which no victor can come forth without leaving conquered ones on the field of battle; a combat that like all wars, chains slaves to the chariot of the victor. In destroying competition, we strangle at the same time the evils which it brings forth. No more victories and no more defeats! . . .

It is clear that this absence of solidarity among interests robs the State of all possibility of being precautious and enchains it in all relations to the foreign powers. Soldiers on the outside, police on the inside; the present State has no means of action and its whole activity is necessarily limited in checking destruction on one hand and in exercising it on the other. The State should place itself resolutely at the head of industry by rallying around one principle all those forces, all those interests, which today struggle against each other; then its external activity will be more prudent, more fertile, more fortunate and more decisive! Thus the reorganization of labor will not only obviate crises which originate in our midst, but also most of those which the wind that blows the sail of our ships conveys to us from outside!

Is it necessary that I should continue to enumerate the advantages which the new system brings about? In the industrial world in which we live, all the discoveries of science are a calamity, first because the machines supplant the laborers who need work to live, and then, because they are also murderous weapons, furnished to industry which has the right and faculty to use them against all those who have not this right and power. What does *"new machines"* mean in the system of competition? It means monopoly; we have proven it. However, in the new system of association and solidarity there are no patents for inventors, no individual exploitation. The inventor will be recompensed by the State and his discovery is then placed at the service of all. What is today a means of extermination becomes an instrument of universal progress; what today reduces the laborer to hunger, to despair and drives him to revolt, will serve only to render his task lighter and to produce a sufficient leisure to live a life of intelligence and happiness; in one word, that which has tolerated tyranny will aid in the triumph of fraternity.

In the inconceivable confusion into which we are plunged today, commerce does not and cannot depend on production. Production is forced to find among consumers all those producers who are striving to wrest consumers from each other, just as the brokers and curbstone brokers, the great merchants and the small merchants do. Commerce thus becomes the open sore of production. Placed between the laborer who works and him who consumes, commerce rules the one as well as the other. . . .

What place has credit in this system? To furnish tools to the laborer. Today credit is, as we have already proven, something quite different. Banks do not loan except to the rich. Even if they would loan to the poor, they could not do it without ruining themselves. The banks, established only from the viewpoint of individualism, could not be anything else than an admirably conceived means to make the rich wealthier and the mighty more powerful. Everywhere monopoly under the guise of freedom, everywhere tyranny under the appearance of progress! The proposed organization would make short process with such crimes. That part of the profit which is especially and invariably laid aside for the increase of the social workshops through recruitment of laborers, this furnishes the means of credit. Of what need would banks be now? Suppress them. . . .

What we have just said of the industrial reform will suffice to show according to what fundamental principles and bases the agricultural reform has been working. The abuse of collateral succession is universally recognized. These successions should be abolished and the property represented by them should be made communal property. Each community will in this way build up a domain which will be inalienable and, not being capable of being extended, will bring about without division and usurpation a great agricultural revolution. The exploitation of the communal domain, however, will take place necessarily on a much larger scale and in accordance with these laws which regulate industry. . . .

Let us sum up the whole. An economic revolution must be attempted:

1. Because the present social conditions are too full of misery, iniquity, and turpitude to last much longer.

2. Because everybody, irrespective of position, rank or fortune, is interested in the creation of a new social order.

3. Finally, because it is possible, even easy, to produce this necessary revolution in a peaceful way. . . .

Louis Blanc, *Organization of Work,* trans. by M. P. Dickoré, *University of Cincinnati Studies* (Cincinnati, 1911), VII, No. 1, 51–54, 55–56, 57, 58, 59. (Reprinted by permission of Marie Dickoré.)

After much debate, the Frankfurt Parliament offered the crown of a united Germany to King Frederick William IV of Prussia. The King, however, rejected the crown (April 3, 1849). In a letter to his ambassador in London, written five months before, Frederick William gave the reasons why he could never accept the Imperial crown at the hands of the Frankfurt Parliament.

150   You say "you want the consent of the ruling princes; very well, that you shall have." But, my dearest friend, you are whipping a dead dog. I want neither the consent of the princes to the election nor the crown itself. Do you understand the words underlined?

I will enlighten you on the subject as briefly and as clearly as possible. Firstly, the crown is no crown. The crown which a Hohenzollern could accept, if circumstances rendered such a thing possible, is not one created by an Assembly born of revolutionary seed, even if offered with princely approval (in the manner of the "crown of the streets" of Louis Philippe). Instead it must be a crown set with the seal of the Almighty, one which makes him who assumes it, after the sacred anointment, King by the "Grace of God," just as it has created more than thirty-four princes Kings of the Germans by the Grace of God, and the latest wearer will be numbered in this ancient lineage. The crown which was borne by the Ottos, the Hohenstaufen and the Hapsburgs, a Hohenzollern can, of course, wear; it honours him inexpressibly with a thousand years of glory. That [crown], however, which you unfortunately mean, dishonours one inexpressibly with its stench of the Revolution of 1848, the silliest, stupidest, wickedest—if not, thank God, the most disastrous of the century. Such a fictitious coronet baked out of mire and clay should never be worn by a legitimate King of God's Grace, and, especially, by the King of Prussia, who has the happiness of wearing, if not the most ancient, at any rate the noblest crown, and one which has not been stolen from anyone. . . . I tell you roundly: if ever that thousand year old crown of the German Nation, which has rested unworn for forty-two years, should gain by being conferred on someone, *then it is I and my peers who are going to confer it*. And woe to anyone who arrogates to himself a right which is not his due.

Briefwechsel Friedrich Wilhelm IV mit Bunsen, Hrsg. Leopold von Ranke, in *Das Jahr 48* (C. Bertelsmann Verlag Gütersloh, 1948), pp. 471–72. (Trans. George L. Mosse.)

There was keen disappointment when the King of Prussia rejected the Imperial crown. Especially the moderate, liberal members of the Frankfurt Assembly felt betrayed. Here one of them tells the story of the rejection (1849) and, incidentally, throws some light upon the internal struggles of the Assembly.

. . . There followed on the morning of the 3 April, in solemn audience, **151** that answer which not only treated the offer of the National Assembly as insufficient, needing the assent of the princes, but which also treated the constitution finally agreed upon as a mere proposal about whose future the governments would have to decide.

That was the practical aspect of those words which eight months before the King addressed to us from Cologne: "Gentlemen, do not forget that there are still princes in Germany, and that I am one of them." What sounded then like a half-hearted warning, sounded now like an angry and portentous "I told you so." Did we really forget that there were princes in Germany and that the King of Prussia was one of them? O, no! On the contrary, we had always taken the princes into account—too much, as some thought. For a full year we survived the most ardent battles with the republicans because we maintained that the preservation of the throne was necessary for the maintenance of order and for internal peace. Already in the preparatory Parliament we had squashed the attempts to make Germany a republic and saved the thrones—which at that time were shaken to their very foundations. . . . Did we not, on account of such adherence to the monarchical principle sacrifice our popularity, and the reputation of the Assembly, before a great part of the people? Were we not for that reason called traitors to the masses, put on lists of people to be purged, threatened, treated with contempt, and insulted? And for all this, such ingratitude, such misconception of our patriotic intentions, and, what was worse, of the necessities which forced us to act as we did!

Such thoughts and sensibilities moved us as we returned to the lodgings of our President from the castle. All were depressed, sorrowful and, partly, embittered. What was to happen now?

Ibid., pp. 465–66. (Trans. George L. Mosse.)

QUESTIONS

1. What does Guizot mean by "democracy"?
2. What is the "curse and shame" of which, according to Guizot, the age must rid itself? What connection does this have with the Revolution of 1848?
3. What evils were Louis Blanc's national workshops intended to combat? How does his organization of work differ from capitalism?
4. Contrast Guizot's and Louis Blanc's view of society.
5. To what previous period of history would you link the ideas on kingship of Frederick William IV?
6. Whom did the moderate member of the Frankfurt Assembly regard as the enemies he had fought (extract 151)? Contrast his ideas about the future government of Germany with that which Karl Marx entertained in 1848 (see p. 304).

CHAPTER XXIII

NAPOLEON III (1808–1873)

THE RESTORATION of the Bourbons in France in 1815 soon demonstrated the failure of reaction as a practical social philosophy. The Orleanist monarchy which replaced the Bourbons in 1830 proved that an artificial compromise between the old and the new was fated to moral complacency and political jobbery. As Frenchmen increasingly cast about looking for some system that would solve their public problems, make them great again, and once more give them high ideals to live by, some recalled the republic of the Revolution, while others remembered the reign of Napoleon. In the new revolution which came in 1848, it was the republican ideal which at the moment dominated the scene.

By the first elections under the Second Republic, however, Prince Louis Napoleon became president, and before long the Napoleonic empire was restored. This nephew and heir of the first Napoleon was the principal beneficiary of the Napoleonic legend, the growing myth that all good fruits of the Great Revolution had been saved and consolidated only by the genius of Napoleon (152), while all the misfortunes of that era were largely the responsibilities of a belligerent England. Time had dulled the recollection of the evils of Bonapartism and sharpened the memory of its glories—a process to which Napoleon himself greatly contributed by the *apologia* he dictated at St. Helena, (see p. 187) before his death in 1821, and to which others, like the statesman-historian Thiers, also added.

Unique in the literature of the legend was *Napoleonic Ideas,* written by Prince Louis Napoleon in 1839 while in exile in England. It was unique because within its text a fascinating restatement of the presumed Bonapartist ideals was harmoniously and subtly combined with the half-veiled suggestion that the one person who might success-fully inaugurate them was Prince Louis Napoleon himself. The mantle of the uncle could be worn by the nephew.

152   If the destiny which my birth presaged had not been changed by events, I, a nephew of the Emperor, should have been one of the defenders of his throne, and a propagator of his ideas; I should have enjoyed the glory of being a pillar of his edifice, or of dying in one of the squares of his guard, while fighting for France. The Emperor is no more! but his spirit still lives. Prevented from defending his shielding power with arms, I can at least at-tempt to defend his memory with the pen. To enlighten public opinion by searching out the thought which presided over his high conceptions, to recall to mind his vast plans, is a task which yet smiles upon my heart, and consoles my exile! Fear of offending contrary opinions will not restrain me: ideas which are under the aegis of the greatest genius of modern times may be avowed without reserve; nor do they need to adapt themselves to the varying caprices of the political atmosphere. Enemy of all absolute theories, and of all moral dependence, I have no engagement with any party, any sect, or any government. My voice is free,—as my thought;—and I love freedom! Carlton Terrace, July, 1839.

When the fortune of arms had rendered Napoleon master of the greater part of the continent, he desired to use his conquests for the establishment of a European confederation.

Prompt to apprehend the tendency of civilization, the Emperor hastened its march by executing, without delay, that which otherwise had been en-folded in the distant decrees of Providence. His genius foresaw that the rivalry which separates the different nations of Europe would disappear be-fore a general interest well understood.

The more the world improves itself, the more are the barriers which sepa-rate men lowered, and the greater is the number of countries which reciprocal interests tend to unite. . . .

Napoleonic Europe once founded, the Emperor would have proceeded in France to the establishment of his institutions of peace. He would have consolidated liberty; he had only to let loose the cords of the network he had prepared.

The government of Napoleon, better than any other, could have sustained liberty, for the simple reason that liberty would have strengthened his throne, though it overthrows such thrones as have not a solid foundation.

Liberty would have fortified his power, because Napoleon had established in France all that ought to precede liberty; because his power reposed upon the whole mass of the nation; because his interests were the same as those of the people; because, finally, the most perfect confidence reigned between the ruler and the governed. . . .

To the Emperor Napoleon . . . possessing the confidence of the people, all was easy. He had at the beginning surmounted the greatest difficulty and laid the principal foundations of a solid establishment by reconciling among themselves all the members of the French family. All agreed as to the fundamental basis of the constitution. The interests of the majority were mingled to such a degree with those of his dynasty, that in 1811, on the very spot where, a few years before, implacable hatred to royalty had been sworn, all Paris and all France were seen to salute with their acclamations the birth of a child, because that child appeared to be a pledge of the duration and stability of the imperial government.

Beloved especially by the people, could Napoleon fear to grant political rights to all the citizens? After being chosen consul for life, he reestablished the principle of the right of election, and used these significant words: "For the sake of the *stability* of the government, it is necessary that the people should have a share in the elections!" Thus already in 1803, Napoleon foresaw that liberty would fortify his power. His warmest partisans being among the people, the more he lowered the electoral qualification, the better chances had his natural friends of arriving at the legislative assembly; the more power he gave to the masses, the more he strengthened his own.

Nor would liberty of discussion in the Chambers have endangered the imperial government; for, all being agreed upon the fundamental questions, an opposition would only have had the effect of giving birth to a noble emulation, and instead of expending its energies in attempting the overthrow of government, it would have confined its efforts to endeavoring to improve it.

Finally, the liberty of the press would have served only to exhibit in better light the grandeur of the plans of Napoleon, to proclaim the benefits attending his reign. As General, Consul, Emperor, having done everything for the people, would he have feared being reproached with making conquests which had resulted in the prosperity and glory of France, and in the peace of the world? Would he have feared that a more brilliant glory would have been contrasted with his own? No, a government glorious with laurels both civil and military could not have feared the light! The more moral power an authority has, the less necessity does it feel to employ material force; and the more power public opinion confers upon it, the better able it is to dispense with using it. . . .

The Emperor fell because he completed his work too hastily—because, events pressing too rapidly, he conquered too promptly. Anticipating, by his genius, both time and men, when fortunate, he was regarded as a god; when unfortunate, nothing was perceived but his rashness. Borne along by the current of victory, his rapid course could not be followed by the philosophers, who, restricting their ideas to the narrow circle of the domestic hearth, on account of a gleam of liberty, aided in quenching the very fire of civilization.

At the same time foreign nations, impatient of the temporary evils of war, forgot the benefits which Napoleon brought them, and on account of a transient ill, rejected a whole future of independence. It was not within the power of even the greatest genius of modern times in so few years to destroy in foreign countries all prejudices and convince all consciences.

France had become too great, in consequence of the Revolution, not to awaken rivalries and hatreds; in order to appease them it would have been necessary to descend in the scale from the time of the commencement of the Empire. But these very rivalries caused Napoleon to mount to the climax of his power; when afterwards he was obliged to descend, he could not stop in his downward course. . . .

Not then in consequence of impotence did the Emperor succumb, but in consequence of exhaustion. And in spite of his terrible reverses and innumerable calamities, the French people always supported him by their suffrages, sustained him by their efforts, and encouraged him by their attachment.

It is a consolation to those who feel the blood of a great man flowing through their veins to think of the regrets which accompanied his removal. It is a great and proud thought that it required all the efforts of allied Europe to tear Napoleon from France, which he had rendered so glorious. It was not the French people, in their wrath, who overturned his throne; it required twice twelve hundred thousand foreign swords to break his imperial sceptre! . . .

The period of the Empire was a war of life and death, waged by England against France. England triumphed; but, thanks to the creative genius of Napoleon, France, although vanquished, has lost, substantially, less than

England. The finances of France are still the most prosperous in Europe; England bends under the weight of debt. The impulse given to industry and to commerce has not been stopped in spite of our reverses; and at this time the European continent supplies itself with the greater part of the products which England formerly supplied.

Now, we ask, who are the greatest statesmen, those who have ruled over countries which have gained, in spite of defeat, or those who have governed countries which have lost, in spite of victory?

The period of the Empire was a war of life and death against the old European system. The old system has triumphed; but in spite of the fall of Napoleon, the Napoleonic Ideas have germinated everywhere. The victors have even adopted the ideas of the vanquished, and the people consume themselves in efforts to rebuild what Napoleon had established among them.

In France the realization of the ideas of the Emperor, under other names or other forms, is demanded without cessation. If a great measure or a great work is put in execution, it is generally a project of Napoleon which is proceeded with or finished. Every act of power, every proposition of the Chambers, places itself under the aegis of Napoleon, in order to secure popularity; and upon a word fallen from his lips, a whole system is built. . . .

The Napoleonic Ideas have then the character of ideas which control the movement of society, since they advance by their own force, although deprived of their author; like a body which, launched into space, arrives by its own momentum and weight at the end designed.

There is no longer any necessity to reconstruct the system of the Emperor; it will reconstruct itself. Sovereigns and nations will concur in reestablishing it; because each one will see in it a guaranty of order, of peace, and of prosperity.

Besides, where can we find, at this day, the extraordinary man who can command the attention of the world by the respect due to the superiority of his conceptions and ideas?

The genius of our epoch has need only of simple reason. Thirty years ago it was necessary to foresee and prepare; now it is a question only of correct appreciation, and of careful collection and arrangement.

"In contemporary, as in historical facts," Napoleon has said, "lessons may be found, but rarely models." It is impossible to copy that which has been done because imitations do not always produce resemblances.

In fact, to copy in the details, instead of copying in the spirit, a past government, would be to act like a general, who, finding himself upon the same field of battle where Napoleon or Frederic had conquered, should undertake to secure victory by repeating the same maneuvers.

In reading the history of nations, as the history of battles, it is necessary to draw general principles, without confining one's self to follow servilely, step by step, vestiges which are imprinted, not upon sand, but upon a more elevated ground—the interests of humanity.

In conclusion, let us repeat it, the Napoleonic Idea is not one of war, but a social, industrial, commercial idea, and one which concerns all mankind. If to some it appears always surrounded by the thunder of combats, that is because it was in fact for too long a time veiled by the smoke of cannon and the dust of battles. But now the clouds are dispersed, and we can see, beyond the glory of arms, a civil glory greater and more enduring.

May the shade of the Emperor repose, then, in peace! His memory grows greater every day. Every surge that breaks upon the rock of Saint Helena, responding to a whisper of Europe, brings a homage to his memory, a regret to his ashes, and the echo of Longwood repeats over his tomb: THE EN-FRANCHIZED NATIONS ARE OCCUPIED EVERYWHERE IN RE-ESTABLISHING THY WORK!

Napoleon-Louis Bonaparte, *Napoleonic Ideas,* trans. James A. Dorr (New York: D. Appleton & Co., 1859), pp. 11–12, 136–37, 140–41, 142–44, 147–48, 149, 150–51, 152–54.

QUESTIONS

1. What evidence do you find of the impact of the industrial revolution upon the thought of Louis Napoleon?
2. What aspects of the reign of Napoleon I does Louis Napoleon seem to wish never to see repeated?
3. How are Napoleon's errors explained without criticizing him?
4. What falsehoods are contained in the quoted passages? (Look at the documents in the section on Napoleon, p. 176.)
5. Why could the *Napoleonic Ideas* be appealing?

CHAPTER XXIV

THE THIRD REPUBLIC

THE THIRD REPUBLIC was born in blood. First came the quick and humiliating defeat of Napoleon III's France in 1870 at the hands of a uniting Germany; then followed the fratricidal struggle in Paris of April and May, 1871, known as the Commune (153). The new national government was representative, but it was also monarchist in sentiment. Republicanism had won out partly by default, the monarchists being badly divided among themselves (154). Slowly the forces of republicanism gathered strength, and after republicanizing the institutions of a republic that was such originally only in name, they went on to defend it against an authoritarian threat (155). There followed a vaguer though much deeper attack upon the principles of democracy (156), but republicanism was so secure during the opening decades of this century that parliamentary differences seemed easily confined within its bounds (157).

The Commune has been widely misunderstood because of the popular confusion between the French word for township, *commune,* and *communism*—a misunderstanding purposely exploited at the time by Karl Marx. The movement was essentially a republican one, with only moderate socialist and anarchist overtones, and it sought in municipal autonomy a bridge over the wide gulf between the revolutionary, democratic traditions of Paris and the conservative, promonarchist sentiments of the provisional national government seated outside the city at Versailles. However, there never should have been any confusion about what the Communards had in mind, for they clearly set forth their objectives in their official journal (April 20, 1871), from which the following quotation is taken. Nevertheless, the gulf was unbridgeable and violence took place. No quarter was given and none was asked, as the national government used the army to enforce its authority over the insurgent city of Paris. During the final "Week of Bloodshed" a terrifying carnage took place, as hostages on one side and prisoners on the other were ruthlessly slaughtered by the hundreds, and the expiring Communards put to the flame a city they no longer could rule. In the years that followed it has become quite apparent that the meaning of the event was symbolized less by the white basilica of Sacré-Cœur, built in expiation on Montmartre, than by the heritage of proletarian hatred embodied in the heavy Communist vote today in the working class districts encircling Paris.

153   In the sad and terrible conflict which again imposes upon Paris the horrors of siege and bombardment, when shot and shell spill French blood and cut down our brothers, our wives, and our children, it is essential that public opinion be not divided and the national conscience not troubled.

It is necessary that Paris, and the entire country know what is the nature, the cause and the objective of the Revolution now in progress. . . .

. . . The Commune has the duty of affirming and determining the aspirations and wishes of the people of Paris; to explain the true character of the movement of March 18th—a movement which has been up to this time misunderstood, misconstrued, and calumniated by the politicians sitting at Versailles. Once more Paris labors and suffers for the whole of France, for whom she is preparing, by her battles and her sacrifices, an intellectual, moral, administrative, and economic regeneration, to win a glorious prosperity.

What does she demand?

The recognition and consolidation of the Republic as the only form of government compatible with the rights of the people and the regular and free development of society.

The absolute autonomy of the Commune and its extension to all localities in France, and the assurance by this means to each person of the integrity of his rights, to every Frenchman the full exercise of his faculties and capacities as a man, a citizen, and a worker.

The autonomy of the Commune will be limited only by the equal right of autonomy to be enjoyed by the other Communes which adhere to the contract, from which association will come the unity of France.

The inherent rights of the Commune are:

The right of voting the Communal budget of receipts and expenditure; of fixing and apportioning the taxation; of directing local services; of organizing its own magistracy, internal police and public education; of administering the property belonging to the Commune.

The right of choosing by election or competition, with responsibility and a permanent right of control and recall, the communal magistrates and officials of all ranks.

The right of individual liberty under an absolute guarantee, and of liberty of conscience and of labor.

The right of permanent participation by the citizens in communal affairs by means of the free manifestation of their ideals, and a free defense of their own interests, guarantees being given for such manifestations by the Commune, which is alone charged with the duty of guarding and securing the free and just right of meeting and of publicity.

The right of organizing the urban defenses and the national guard, which is to elect its own officers, and alone provide for the maintenance of order in the city.

Paris desires no more guarantee than this, with the condition, of course, that she shall find in the grand central administration, composed of delegates from the Federal Communes, the realization and practice of the same principles.

To insure, however, her own independence, and her own freedom of action, Paris reserves to herself the liberty of effecting as she may think fit, in her own sphere, those administrative and economic reforms which her population shall demand, of creating such institutions as are proper for developing and extending education, production, commerce, and credit; and of extending the enjoyment of power and property in accordance with the necessities of the moment, the wish of the persons interested, and the data furnished by experience.

Our enemies deceive themselves or deceive the country when they accuse Paris of desiring to impose its will or its supremacy upon the rest of the nation, and of aspiring to a dictatorship which would amount to a veritable attack against the independence and sovereignty of other communes.

They deceive themselves or the country when they accuse Paris of seeking the destruction of French unity as established by the Revolution and sworn by our fathers when they came to the festival of the Federation from all parts of the old France.

The unity which was hitherto imposed upon us by the Empire, the Monarchy, and the Parliamentary Government was nothing but a centralization, despotic, unintelligent, arbitrary, and burdensome.

Political unity as desired by Paris is a voluntary association of each local initiative, a free and spontaneous coöperation of all individual energies with one common object—the well-being, liberty, and security of all.

The Communal Revolution initiated by the people on the 18th of March inaugurated a new political principle, experimental, positive, and scientific.

It was the end of the old official and clerical world, of militarism and bureaucracy, of exploitation, stock-jobbing, monopolies and privileges, to which the working class owed its state of servitude, and the country its misfortunes and disasters. . . .

Réimpression du journal officiel de la république française sous la commune (Paris, 1871), pp. 323–24. (Trans. H. B. Hill.)

After the quick defeat of France in the fall of 1870 by the Germans, the Emperor Napoleon III was overthrown. The provisional republican government in Paris was shortly replaced by the popularly elected National Assembly, which met first at Bordeaux and then at Versailles. It was to be the unwilling task of this predominantly monarchist body to establish the Third Republic. As their chief of state and, as it proved to be, first president of that republic, they chose Louis Adolphe Thiers, widely venerated historian and liberal monarchist elder statesman who had served as minister under King Louis Philippe. By 1873, and contrary to the views of a majority of the Assembly, he had come to feel that a democracy would "divide Frenchmen least." His views, which led to his forced resignation, are given in the following paragraphs from a letter written some four years later (1877).

154   . . . Every nation has a right to the form of government that pleases it, and when this government has been established, it has the right to require that this government be served loyally. Nobody is forced to serve a government that he does not like, but if he accept it, and especially if he take office under it, he is bound to perform his duties faithfully, with a desire for the success, not for the overthrow of the form of government. Everybody, of course, has the right to aspire to office, whatever may be his party or his origin; in fact, it is to be desired that men of experience—old public servants—continue to serve the State, but always on condition that they serve it loyally.

It will be remembered that at Bordeaux we, who served the Republic, were formerly monarchists. This, however, was not true of all. But we were demanded; we did not step forward without being called, and we took office purely through goodwill, because our presence re-assured the alarmed nation. And at last we were convinced of the necessity of the Republic. I wish the Republic many similar servitors, and from whatever quarter they may come, they will always be welcomed if they are honestly determined to help on the common cause, which, if it succeed, will be a blessing and not a detriment to France.

The question, therefore, raised by the proceeding of May 16th, may be summed up as follows: Is the Republic needed, and, if so, should it be firmly established by men who wish its success? Herein lies the whole question at issue.

Now, I ask every honest man, to whatever party he may belong, if the Count de Chambord could be placed on the throne with the opinions that he professes and with the flag that he unfurls, or if it is hoped that he may some day be acceptable after he has modified his views? We respect him too much to believe it. I will say nothing of the Orleans princes, who wish to be mentioned only after the Count de Chambord, according to their hereditary rank; but I ask if the country is ready to receive the Prince Imperial, who, though innocent of the misfortunes of France, suggests them so keenly, that the nation still shudders at the bare mention of his name? Nobody dare answer me yes; and, in fact, all the friends of these candidates postpone, until a future time, the day when their claims may be put forward. The truth of this statement is seen in the fact that they make no move, though the greatest indulgence has been shown all the monarchical parties.

Now, until this day—more or less distant—arrives, what will France do? France will wait until her future masters are ready: until one is brought over to other ways of thinking, until another has made an advance in his right of succession, and until a third has finished his education. In the meanwhile everything will be in suspense, commerce, industry, finances, State affairs. How can business men be asked to engage in great industrial enterprises, and financiers to negotiate loans, when the future threatens fresh political troubles? And how can foreign Cabinets be expected to strengthen their relations and form alliances with us, when French policy is liable to be directed by new chiefs and influenced by new ideas? Dare anybody ask such sacrifices of a great nation, that Europe has admired in its prosperity and also in its misfortunes, on seeing it restored once more, on seeing it revive again, displaying a rare wisdom in the midst of provocations, which it endures with such *sang-froid* and calm firmness?

Some men who, because they call themselves monarchists, believe that they know the secrets of the crowned heads, pretend that their reign is desired, and that then France will regain its prestige and alliances. But we would say to these men who think they understand Europe, but who, in reality, know nothing about it, and attribute to it their own ignorance and prejudices, that Europe looks with pity on their pretensions and hopes, and blames them for having got their country into the present trouble, instead of giving it the only form of government possible to-day. This Europe was formerly under absolute princes, but, recognizing the march of time, it is now ruled by constitutional princes, and is satisfied with the change. Europe understands that France, after the fall of three dynasties, has gone over to the Republic, which, during the last six years, has lifted the country out of the abyss into which the monarchists precipitated it. Europe has seen our military prestige destroyed and a new prestige take its place, that of the inexhaustible vitality of a prostrate country, suddenly rising up and furnishing the world an unheard of example of resources of every kind, so that France, even after Wörth, Sedan and Metz, has shown herself to be great still. It was under the Monarchy that she fell, but under the Republic that she arose again. And once more on the road to prosperity, it was the monarchists again that threw obstacles in the way of her reconstruction. If it be the esteem of Europe that is sought, listen to Europe, hearken to its opinion!

For this it is, that we persistently ask if there be any other alternative than the following: Either the Monarchy, which is impossible, because there are three claimants and but one throne; or the Republic, difficult to establish without doubt, not because of itself, but because of the opposition of the monarchical parties, and, nevertheless, possible, for it is supported by an immense majority of the people.

It is the duty, therefore, of this immense majority of the people to consult together, to unite and to vote against those who resist the establishment of the only government possible. The Monarchy to-day, after the three revolutions that have overthrown it, is immediate civil war, if it be established now; and if put off for two years, or three years, the civil war is only postponed until that epoch. The Republic is an equitable participation of all the children of France in the government of their country, according to their abilities, their importance, and their callings,—a possible and practical participation, excluding nobody except those who announce that they will govern only by revolution. . . .

François le Goff, *The Life of Louis Adolphe Thiers*, trans. T. Stanton (New York: G. P. Putnam & Sons, 1879), pp. 342–45.

The first decisive test to which the new French Republic was put came when General Georges Boulanger was made minister of war in 1886. Boulanger possessed demagogic attractions translatable into political action, and, strongly backed by nationalist, monarchist, and Catholic leaders, he played upon the fears, resentments, and frustrations of Frenchmen from all parts of the social spectrum. Forced out of office, he began to run for election to the Chamber of Deputies in constituency after constituency, by which means he won a sort of piecemeal plebescite for his dictatorial program of "revising" the constitution and pushing a warlike foreign policy. His peak was reached in January, 1889, when the extent and the fervor of his following in both Paris and the provinces might have made a *coup d'état* possible. He failed to turn the trick, however, and the gathering republican opposition soon resulted in his total eclipse. The following passages are taken from an article by one of his ardent followers written for a contemporary English magazine (1888). Notice both its fervid tone and its poorly disguised appeal to what we now call authoritarianism.

The Boulangist movement has in reality a twofold character: it is at once **155** patriotic and anti-parliamentary. France understands perfectly well the necessity incumbent upon her at present of fortifying herself against all attacks from the outside, and also the impossibility of continuing to keep alive a Republic founded upon monarchical institutions. It has been said repeatedly— and no insinuation or suggestion, however vile, has been neglected which might press the statement home—that General Boulanger was the representative in France of the desire for an immediate revenge upon Germany, and that he was eager for war at all risks. That is simply a calumny borrowed from the German prints, which Prince Bismarck keeps alive out of his "Reptile Fund." Even when he was Minister of War General Boulanger put forward the following declaration, which those who know him, know to be his real and characteristic opinion: "If I wished war I would be a fool; if I did not prepare for war I should be a currish traitor." And those who saw him at work as Minister of War are able to testify that he did prepare for war with a well-directed energy of which, unfortunately, none of his predecessors had set the example, and of which his successors seem to have lost the secret. . . .

Actually there is more than a chance, there is a probability that the new German Emperor will attack us without warning; it is with the prospect of this aggression before our eyes—an aggression continually held over us as a threat—that all Frenchmen who desire the safety of their country desire to see at the head of the army the one man who possesses their confidence, and whose qualities of resolute energy and patriotism constitute a guarantee which no other Minister of War within the last ten years has been capable of giving. The opponents of General Boulanger ought to have understood at once that there was no other way open to them of triumphing over him than by surpassing him in activity on his own line. . . .

It never seems to occur to General Boulanger's opponents that all the methods they are using to undermine his popularity must of necessity increase it. Libellous statements and shameful caricatures, paid journals, and hybrid leagues do little more than keep public attention directed to a man who only needs to be known in order to be appreciated. . . . What his friends demand for him is surely not unreasonable—they simply require that he should be reinstated in his position as Minister of War, from which he was driven in order to put in his place mere nobodies who did not even know how to continue the work of arming the French army properly, which was inaugurated and pushed with such energy by General Boulanger. What General Boulanger himself demands is . . . the revision of the constitution by means of an assembly especially elected for that purpose. And yet the Radicals, Opportunists, and followers of M. Ferry who make this demand a pretext for attacking General Boulanger, were themselves the first to start the cry for revision. . . .

Properly speaking, the constitution of 1875 is nothing more or less than organised anarchy. One cannot expect those who profit by an abuse to abolish it; the present Senate, it is evident, will never commit suicide. Yet the constitution must be changed; our institutions must evidently be made as democratic as is public opinion in France. From 1875 to 1885 the Republican party in the Chamber was unanimous in recognizing the abuses inherent in our constitution. Why, then, do these men accuse General Boulanger of aiming at a dictatorship because he sees what they saw and advocates the change which they themselves were the first to propose? The explanation is simple. They know well that General Boulanger is earnest in his demand, whereas in the last ten years they have got a liking for the spoils of office, and are now content with the abuses of an institution which they have learnt how to turn to their own personal profit.

But it may be asked, admitting that the desire of General Boulanger is laudable enough, what are the methods by which he and his friends hope to achieve their end in presence of the bitter opposition of a majority of the representatives of France? The method advocated by General Boulanger and his friends is as simple as it is legal. We propose to educate public opinion on the matter, and show the French electorate, which is disgusted with the inefficacy of the present Chamber, that the faults of the existing Republic in France are inherent in the monarchist constitution of 1875. We shall advise them, in season and out of season, to democratise their institutions, and we shall pray them, in order to bring this about, to elect a new Chamber, three-fourths of which shall be made up of deputies pledged to revision. . . . General Boulanger may have personal views on many political subjects which differ from those of his friends. He undoubtedly has strong personal opinions upon the way in which the powers confided in a new Chamber should be organised, and this fact explains the reserved and sometimes enigmatic speech with which his enemies reproach him; but it must not be forgotten that it is the national assembly and not General Boulanger who will revise the constitution. . . . In the assembly chosen to revise the constitution General Boulanger will only have his seat as deputy and his single voting paper. . . .

In fine, the Boulangist movement is the product of a twofold current of opinion. It resumes in itself on the one hand the dissatisfaction which all thinking Frenchmen feel in view of the stupid inefficiency of the present Chambers, and on the other hand that love of country, that desire for the security and greatness of France, which is the deepest passion in the French nature. . . . I have a wild hope and a profound belief that if within our time the French flag shall float again over Strasbourg and Metz it will be planted there by the patriotic officer who was turned out of the active army by politicians who can do nothing but talk.

Henri Rochefort, "The Boulangist Movement," *The Fortnightly Review*, XLIV² (1888), 11–12, 14, 19–21, 22–23.

The most significant domestic event in the history of the Third Republic was the Dreyfus Affair. Captain Alfred Dreyfus, an Alsatian Jew, was falsely accused in 1894 of having committed treason, the incriminating document being a list (the *bordereau*) of army secrets given to the Germans. Quite quickly after Dreyfus was condemned, the high command learned that the real culprit was a Major Esterhazy, but to save the face of the general staff he was protected. The issues involved rocked France to its foundations and divided the country from end to end—between those who supported Dreyfus (republicans and liberals) and those who did not (monarchists, militant nationalists, many prominent Roman Catholics). The turning point in the struggle came on January 13, 1898, when the great French novelist Emile Zola published the dramatically moving letter from which the following paragraphs were taken. It led to the ultimate exoneration of Dreyfus in 1906, but not until Zola had falsely been found guilty of defamation and had died in exile, and the victorious republicans had radically reformed both the army command and the relations between church and state.

156   I ACCUSE . . . . . !

Letter to M. Félix Faure, President of the Republic.

Monsieur le Président:

Will you permit me, in my gratitude for the kindly welcome that you once extended to me, to have a care for the glory that belongs to you, and to say to you that your star, so lucky hitherto, is threatened with the most shameful, the most ineffaceable, of stains? . . .

And to you, *Monsieur le Président,* will I cry this truth, with all the force of an honest man's revolt. Because of your honor I am convinced that you are ignorant of it. And to whom then shall I denounce the malevolent gang of the really guilty, if not to you, the first magistrate of the country?

First, the truth as to the trial and conviction of Dreyfus.

A calamitous man has managed it all, has done it all—Colonel du Paty de Clam, then a simple major. He is the entire Dreyfus case; it will be fully known only when a sincere investigation shall have clearly established his acts and his responsibilities. He appears as the most heady, the most intricate, of minds, haunted with romantic intrigues, delighting in the methods of the newspaper novel, stolen papers, anonymous letters, meetings in deserted spots, mysterious women who peddle overwhelming proofs by night. It is he who conceived the idea of dictating the *bordereau* to Dreyfus; it is he who dreamed of studying it in a room completely lined with mirrors. . . .

But here is Dreyfus before the council of war. The most absolute secrecy is demanded. Had a traitor opened the frontier to the enemy in order to lead the German emperor to Notre Dame, they would not have taken stricter measures of silence and mystery. The nation is awe-struck; there are whisperings of terrible doings, of those monstrous treasons that excite the indignation of History, and naturally the nation bows. There is no punishment severe enough; it will applaud even public degradation; it will wish the guilty man to remain upon his rock of infamy, eaten by remorse. Are they real then,—these unspeakable things, these dangerous things, capable of setting Europe aflame, which they have had to bury carefully behind closed doors? No, there was nothing behind them save the romantic and mad fancies of Major du Paty de Clam. All this was done only to conceal the most ridiculous of newspaper novels. And, to assure one's self of it, one need only study attentively the indictment read before the council of war. . . .

And we come to the Esterhazy case. Three years have passed; many consciences remain profoundly disturbed, are anxiously seeking, and finally become convinced of the innocence of Dreyfus.

I shall not give the history of M. Scheurer-Kestner's doubts, which later became convictions. But, while he was investigating for himself, serious things were happening to the staff. Colonel Sandherr was dead, and Lieutenant-Colonel Picquart had succeeded him as chief of the bureau of information. And it is in this capacity that the latter, in the exercise of his functions, came one day into possession of a letter-telegram addressed to Major Esterhazy by an agent of a foreign power. His plain duty was to open an investigation. It is certain that he never acted except at the command of his superiors. So he submitted his suspicions to his hierarchical superiors, first to General Gonse, then to General de Boisdeffre, then to General Billot, who had succeeded General Mercier as minister of war. The famous Picquart documents, of which we have heard so much, were never anything but the Billot documents,—I mean, the documents collected by a subordinate for his minister, the documents which must be still in existence in the war department. The inquiries lasted from May to September, 1896, and here it must be squarely affirmed that General Gonse was convinced of Esterhazy's guilt, and that General de Boisdeffre and General Billot had no doubt that the famous *bordereau* was in Esterhazy's handwriting. Lieutenant-Colonel Picquart's investigation had ended in the certain establishment of this fact. But the emotion thereat was great, for Esterhazy's conviction inevitably involved a revision of the Dreyfus trial; and this the staff was determined to avoid at any cost. . . .

Colonel Picquart had done his duty as an honest man. He insisted in the presence of his superiors, in the name of justice; he even begged of them; he told them how impolitic were their delays, in view of the terrible storm which was gathering, and which would surely burst as soon as the truth should be known. . . .

Such, then, is the simple truth, *Monsieur le Président,* and it is frightful.

It will remain a stain upon your presidency. I suspect that you are power-less in this matter,—that you are the prisoner of the constitution and of your environment. You have none the less a man's duty, upon which you will reflect, and which you will fulfill. Not indeed that I despair, the least in the world, of triumph. I repeat with more vehement certainty; truth is on the march, and nothing can stop it. To-day sees the real beginning of the affair, since not until to-day have the positions been clear: on one hand, the guilty, who do not want the light; on the other, the doers of justice, who will give their lives to get it. When truth is buried in the earth, it accumu-lates there, and assumes so mighty an explosive power that, on the day when it bursts forth, it hurls everything into the air. We shall see if they have not just made preparations for the most resounding of disasters, yet to come.

But this letter is long, *Monsieur le Président,* and it is time to finish.

I accuse Lieutenant-Colonel du Paty de Clam of having been the dia-bolical workman of judicial error,—unconsciously, I am willing to believe,— and of having then defended his calamitous work, for three years, by the most guilty machinations.

I accuse General Mercier of having made himself an accomplice, at least through weakness of mind, in one of the greatest iniquities of the century.

I accuse General Billot of having had in his hands certain proofs of the innocence of Dreyfus, and of having stifled them; of having rendered him-self guilty of this crime of *lèse-humanité* and *lèse-justice* for a political pur-pose, and to save the compromised staff.

I accuse General de Boisdeffre and General Gonse of having made them-selves accomplices in the same crime, one undoubtedly through clerical pas-sion, the other perhaps through that *esprit de corps* which makes of the war offices the Holy Ark, unassailable.

I accuse General de Pellieux and Major Ravary of having conducted a rascally inquiry,—I mean by that a monstrously partial inquiry, of which we have, in the report of the latter, an imperishable monument of naive audacity.

I accuse the three experts in handwriting, Belhomme, Varinard, and Couard, of having made lying and fraudulent reports, unless a medical examination should declare them afflicted with diseases of the eye and of the mind.

I accuse the war offices of having carried on in the press, particularly in "L'Eclair" and in "L'Echo de Paris," an abominable campaign, to mislead opinion and cover up their faults.

I accuse, finally, the first council of war of having violated the law by condemning an accused person on the strength of a secret document, and I accuse the second council of war of having covered this illegality, in obedience to orders, in committing in its turn the judicial crime of knowingly acquitting a guilty man.

In preferring these charges, I am not unaware that I lay myself liable under Articles 30 and 31 of the press law of July 29, 1881, which punishes defamation. And it is willfully that I expose myself thereto.

As for the people whom I accuse, I do not know them, I have never seen them, I entertain against them no feeling of revenge or hatred. They are to me simple entities, spirits of social ill-doing. And the act that I perform here is nothing but a revolutionary measure to hasten the explosion of truth and justice.

I have but one passion, the passion for the light, in the name of humanity which has suffered so much, and which is entitled to happiness. My fiery protest is simply the cry of my soul. Let them dare, then, to bring me into the assize court, and let the investigation take place in the open day.

I await it.

Accept, *Monsieur le Président,* the assurance of my profound respect.

Emile Zola.

The Trial of Emile Zola (New York: Ben R. Tucker, 1898), pp. 3, 4, 6, 7-8, 9, 13-14.

Among the republican elements which in the 1880's and '90's struggled to make republicanism real in France, the most dynamic group were known as the Radicals, the ancestors of the Radical Socialist party of the twentieth century, of whom it so often has been said that they were neither radical nor socialist. In any recent sense they were not, and having fulfilled a democratizing rôle in the nineteenth century they were, like their English counterpart, the Liberals, left with no program to follow in later years. Before their decline set in, however, they struggled hard to keep anything to the left of them from looking attractive to the voters, because revolutionary radicalism has long had great popular appeal in France. In 1905 the widely followed French Socialist leader Jean Jaurès had succeeded in effectively uniting most of the theretofore quarreling Socialists. To this serious threat from the left the brilliantly clever Radical deputy Georges Clemenceau, the later wartime premier, replied. The following quotations are taken from this reply, which gives an insight into the social thought of the day, as well as into French parliamentary tactics.

157   The Socialist party has issued a programme for the use of all its candidates. Nothing could be more natural. This programme contains two sections: a declaration of principles, and a statement of immediate reforms
which may and ought to be demanded from this present legislature. . . . It
would be well if each one in this assembly should set himself to inquire what
are the topics which it is his duty first to bring before this tribunal. I find in
this manifesto, in the first place, a statement of doctrine: "There is only one
way of emancipating yourselves; it is to substitute collective property for
capitalist property." I find no explanation of the consequences of this statement, no suggestion of the means of carrying it out. But at least it contains
an affirmation of principle. What reforms, then, are to follow from it? Here
they are:

"Limitation of the working day to eight hours.

"Extension to all employees of the State, the Department, and the Commune of the right to form unions.

"General insurance against sickness and unemployment.

"Progressive income tax and death duties.

"Restoration to the nation of the monopolies in which capital has its
strongest fortresses.

"General election tickets, with proportional representation."

What a terribly *bourgeois* programme. When M. Jaurès, after expounding
his programme, challenged me to produce my own, I had great difficulty in
resisting the temptation to reply: "You know my programme very well; you
have it in your pocket, you stole it from me." I am in principle for the eight-
hour day. I do not suppose that any of you would run the risk of an economic
crisis by suddenly changing the eleven-hour day to eight. I could not; but I
am ready to put things in action as quickly as possible for an ultimate eight-
hour day. I am in favor of a progressive income tax. But M. Jaurès, you
voted against it in 1885; and it is in the name of this shifting infallibility of
yours that you are surprised at my remaining true to my convictions! Truly
that will not bear examination. I affirm, then, that this practical programme
is ours; I am for the restoration to the nation of the great monopolies which
are now in the hands of private industry. But we must understand each
other. I do not want you to put into my words a sense they do not bear. If
you think I mean to say that I am prepared to bring in a bill to-morrow for
the restoration of all these monopolies, you deceive yourselves; that is not
my idea. What I mean is, that I am quite ready to begin the work this very
day, for example, by the repurchase of certain of the railways. I have no
authority from the Cabinet to make that statement. I must avow it in loyalty
to the Chamber; but you must not make much of it; only I know the opinion
of most of my colleagues, and I know that they will not contradict me. . . .

Having said so much, I am bound to recognize that you have set up an organization from the principle of which my bourgeois soul recoils. I mean what you call *unification*. Unification to my eyes is nothing but a kind of *catholicization* of socialism. It is the heavy hand of a governing oligarchy laid on a democracy of workmen who are struggling for freedom. It is the introduction of that ancient state of mind, which, in order to secure the triumph of the gospel, has turned a message of liberty into a most terrible instrument of authority over the free expansion of the individual. But it is not only the Pope of Catholicism who was beaten at the last election; it was the spirit of oppression, the dogmatic spirit, in all fields of human activity. The dogmatic spirit has been banished from the purely intellectual sphere, and we will have nothing to do with reëstablishing it in the sphere of economics. We are for liberty everywhere and in everything; and we will allow no organization to set up an authority which, according to a saying of Ernest Renan, aptly quoted this morning by M. Gerault-Richard, would put us into the position of doing our thinking through an agent. . . .

M. Jaurès, there are only two hypotheses before the Chamber,—the existing form of society and the one you propose; but between these two extremes there are an infinite number of social schemes which might come to pass. You make the task too easy. Even if we were to admit that . . . the society you describe is really possible, still you have left out the one point which is worthy of consideration. We are not obliged to choose between the society you promise and the society we have. There are countless other hypotheses; presently when I come to speak of the schemes of social order which this Republican bourgeoisie of which you speak so ill has succeeded in bringing about, I can easily show you that the social régime of to-day is not that of twenty years ago, and that it rests in fact upon quite different principles. I cannot, therefore, permit you to limit us to a choice between these two plans and to wind up with the challenge, "Beware of not accepting my plan, for otherwise the human mind is bankrupt." . . .

After all, is this type of an ideal society which you offer us really so new? Who has not dreamed of a society of the future? I myself am not incapable of dreaming of it along with you whenever you like. Only it is not yet proved —the demonstration is for you to effect by and by—that this dream is as yet in a condition to occupy the attention of a deliberative assembly. It was the everlasting object of the dreams of all Asia. Jesus, the last of a long line of prophets, proposed to renovate all mankind by his words; but his disciples reëstablished under his name the society of violence and bloodshed against which he had protested. Your victory will not be greater than his. I do not think the day will come when you will have your temples throughout the civilized world, and that your words will be daily rehearsed to crowded audiences eager to hear them. You will have no greater success; and when you remember that the material success of Christianity has only ended in the moral bankruptcy of the words of Christ,—that is, in a state of things which has only reproduced the ancient conditions which he proposed to destroy,— you will permit me not to wish you a triumph of that kind. America is full of mystical societies which are endeavoring to realize the City of God on earth. I have heard in forests of New England predictions not appreciably different from yours. In 1848 the Republic thought itself on the eve of the Great Day, and we have seen many a builder of the cities of the future. Do you recall the sittings of the Constituent and Legislative Assemblies in which Pierre Leroux or Victor Considérant or Proudhon developed, as you are presently going to do, his plans of the new society? A great many people pronounced in favor of the suppression of private property. Even before them Sir Thomas More, at the beginning of the sixteenth century, condemned private property in terms more definite than you can employ. These men were not inferior to you. Where are they now? Look for them. You have taken their place, and others will by and by take yours. . . .

The Radical party will baffle your tactics by remaining true to itself,—to the Radical policy of action. You need not remind us of our programme, or ask whether we are prepared to carry it out. Our only right to sit here lies in action,—action which clears up ambiguities, which carries forward the weak, which regulates and disciplines the will of the strong. It is by action that we have overcome the Church, by action that we shall put down economic oppression, the oppression of the existing privileged class. We have set free the mind, we shall set free the body.

Have confidence, man of little faith, you who distrust the work of the Revolution of which you were a good workman. If we do not think alike, is that a reason for enmity? That is a survival of religious animosity. So far as I am concerned, I have no condemnation to pronounce against you, and it matters little that you have this or that ideal conception of the future. If we understand one another, which is a necessary condition of common action in this assembly, we can work together, if only your aid be sincere and complete.

Contemporary Review, XC (1906), 197 ff., as quoted in J. H. Robinson and C. A. Beard, *Readings in Modern European History* (Boston: Ginn & Co., 1908–9), II, 233–37.

QUESTIONS

1. What kind of a political system did the Commune seek to establish?
2. Why was monarchy impractical in the France of the 1870's?

3. What evidence do you find in the article on Boulanger that makes you suspicious of the General's intentions?
4. Why would *J'Accuse* stir its readers?
5. What is clever about Clemenceau's attack upon the Socialist program?

CHAPTER XXV

SOCIALISM

PROPOSALS for the abolition of private property and the equal sharing of wealth are as old as the earliest organized societies, but the modern socialist movement dates from the end of the eighteenth century. To some, socialism seemed to be the logical outcome of the great French Revolution, with its slogan of "Liberty, Equality, Fraternity" (158). Contemporaneously, the industrial revolution in England provided the material basis for a socialist society by the mechanization of labor and the creation of a large urban working class (159). By the first half of the nineteenth century a number of proposals for a socialist reorganization of society were proposed by idealistic visionaries who were subsequently dubbed "Utopians" by Marx (160). However, the only actual attempts to realize socialist aims in practice, apart from the founding of a few "Utopian" communities in the wilderness of America, were the "national workshops" of Louis Blanc in the French Revolution of 1848 (see p. 267) and the Chartist movement in England (see p. 253).

"Scientific socialism"—another of Marx's phrases—dates from the publication of the *Communist Manifesto* in 1848 (162). This, the Marxist variety of socialism, dominated most socialist movements either directly or indirectly down to 1914; it was adopted as the official program of the German Social Democratic party and trade unions, which together constituted the largest and most effective socialist movement before World War I. It did not, however, have the field to itself. Anarchism and syndicalism, related forms of socialist doctrine which, unlike most other varieties of socialism, advocated the outright abolition of organized political states, had large followings in France, Italy, Spain, and even Russia (161). In England the Fabian Society and other socialist groups sought to bring about a socialist state by tried and true "British" methods—that is, gradual, peaceable, political reform (164). The close connection between socialist doctrine and moral and ethical questions led religious groups to participate— *pro* or *con*—in the discussion. In England there was a "Christian Socialist" movement (165); the pope himself entered the discussion with the publication in 1891 of his encyclical *On the Condition of Labor* (166). Finally, at the beginning of the twentieth century, Marxism itself was transformed in two directions: on the one hand, Lenin argued that changed conditions dictated that the socialist revolution must take place first in the underdeveloped countries, like Russia, instead of in the most capitalistic countries as Marx had said (see p. 412); on the other hand, the German "Revisionist" movement argued that socialism might, after all, be achieved by peaceful means, and the revolution would be unnecessary (163).

I. SOCIALIST FORERUNNERS

Socialism in the French Revolution

Following the fall of Robespierre in 1794, a "Conspiracy of Equals" was organized by a devoted admirer of Robespierre, one "Graccus" Babeuf (1760-1797), who hoped to keep the Revolution on the right track by overthrowing the "counter-revolutionary" Directory. The aims of the "Conspiracy of Equals" are set forth in the following extract, taken from the "Manifesto of Equals" and a letter published by Babeuf in his newspaper, *La Tribune du Peuple* (1796).

. . . The French Revolution is but the forerunner of another revolution **158** far more grand, far more solemn, and which will be the last. . . .

It was due to the French Revolution to put in practical execution the conceptions of philosophy, hitherto regarded as chimerical. We have commenced the great work: let us finish it. Were we to stop at the point where we now are, humanity and posterity would have little to thank us for.

In order to pass from our present vicious state to the one I advocate, it is necessary:

1. To place all the existing wealth of the country in the hands of the Republic.

2. To make all the valid citizens work, each according to his capacity and actual habits.

3. To utilize the objects of labor by bringing together those which mutually aid one another, and by giving a new direction to such as are only the effect of the existing stagnant masses of riches.

4. To bring together (so as to have a continued supply) into the public depots all the productions of the land and of industry.

5. To effect an equal distribution of productions and enjoyments.

6. To dry up the source of all property, of all individual or private commerce, and to substitute for them a wise distribution confided to the public authority.

7. To establish common halls of education in which each individual should be trained to the employment or work most suitable to his strength and inclinations.

Thus egoism would be no longer the spring of action or the stimulus to labor for individuals, who, whatever the variety and use of their productions, would receive the same retribution in food, clothing, etc., etc. . . .

Bronterre [James Bronterre O'Brien], ed. and trans., *Buonarroti's History of Babeuf's Conspiracy for Equality* (London, 1836), pp. 315, 369.

Socialism in the Industrial Revolution

Robert Owen (1771–1858) went to work in a cotton mill at the age of nine; before he was twenty-one he was manager of the mill, and within a few years he became part owner of a large cotton factory at New Lanark, Scotland. The latter establishment, which included a "company town," schools, churches, a hospital, etc., was a model of paternalistic endeavor. Having amassed a fortune while still a young man, Owen spent the remainder of his long life in agitating for social reform, establishing model communities on communal lines (New Harmony, Indiana), attempting to create a working-class political movement, and in promulgating the virtues of his pantheistic religion. His personality was a curious combination of the realistic traits of a "practical" businessman and the visionary schemes of a Utopian reformer. He was almost unique among the men of his generation in foreseeing the limitless possibilities for material progress which the mechanization of industry provided, as well as the social adjustments which this progress would require. The following selection is from one of his newspapers (1840).

The present position of what is termed, by courtesy, "the civilized world," is pregnant with matter for grave reflection. The discoveries of science, and their practical application to the production of wealth by means of machinery and other inventions, have, within the last half century, totally changed the aspect of society. The legislator and philanthropist are bound to take into their consideration these new, and hitherto unparalleled elements; and disregarding the petty, unimportant, local questions which generally occupy the attention of mankind to look forward to the effects which they are calculated to produce in their further progress and development. Hitherto all has been chance work, and the direction of these mighty revolutionizers has been left to ignorant and avaricious selfishness, which, intent upon securing its individual benefit, and seeing nothing beyond the circumscribed field of its own vision, has caused them to become a general evil, in its endeavour to realise a personal and partial good.

The workings of this spirit of short-sighted individualism have, however, produced a state of things which must, ere long, compel even the most thoughtless and prejudiced to pause, and take a more comprehensive view of the subject. Failing profits, frequent panics, gluts and bankruptcies in the midst of a superabundance of means to ensure general well-being and prosperity are admonitions of the erroneous nature of our present manufacturing and commercial policy, which cannot fail to produce reflection and amendment. In our use of the gigantic powers of modern science, we have, as is usual with humanity, done wrong before we have learned how to do right; but the very errors we have committed will become, in the course of time, our best instructors as to the nature of our future course. . . .

The benevolent and far-sighted philosopher of New Lanark [Owen] discerned this even in the infancy of the new powers, and predicted the conclusion at their commencement, if the measures he proposed were not adopted by the governments to whose consideration they were submitted. He says, in a preliminary memorial addressed to the Governments of Europe and America, and dated Frankfort, 20th April, 1818: "To this day the means of consumption or of obtaining the necessaries of life by the working classes, have been acquired solely through the medium of their labour, the value of which the new [scientific] power has already much diminished; *and the certain consequences of the misdirected progress of this power will be to reduce the exchangeable value of manual labour, until it falls below the means of procuring a wretched subsistence for any large portion of the working classes; while the remainder of them must be starved out of existence.*" Read the prediction, and mark its partial fulfillment and approaching completion in the present state of our manufacturing population, and the coming destruction of the entire system, by the appearance of new and superior rivals. No sectional reformers can grapple with this question, or avert the evils wherewith we are threatened; the only remedy is a philosophic, comprehensive, scientific, and well-digested reconstruction of society, in accordance with the new truths and powers which time and experience have evolved: and that remedy is the "Rational System of Society" as advocated by Owen and his disciples.

New Moral World, Vol. I, No. 21, 3rd Enlarged Series (London), November 21, 1840, pp. 321, 322.

Utopian Socialism in France

Count Claude Henri de Saint-Simon (1760–1825), a contemporary of Robert Owen and a descendant of French nobility, fought against England during the American Revolution, abdicated his heritage during the French Revolution, won and lost a fortune by speculation, and then settled down for the last twenty-five years of his life to serious study, meditation, and writing. He imagined a hierarchical socialist society which would do away with "social parasites" and economic inequality, and which would be ruled by an "aristocracy of talent"— philosophers, scientists, engineers, etc. After his death his disciples formed a "school" and even a "religion" based on his ideas; this group had no practical influence and soon dissolved as a formal organization, but many of its members went on to become leading businessmen, bankers, and engineers in capitalistic French society. Like Owen, Saint-Simon caught a vision of the immense possibilities of modern industry and the necessity for social adjustments, but his blueprint for the new society was even more Utopian than Owen's. The following selection is from his "Political Catechism of the Industrialists" (1824).

160   Q. What is an industrialist?

A. An industrialist is a man who works to produce or to make available to the different members of society one or more material means for the satisfaction of their needs or physical wants: thus, a cultivator who sows wheat, who raises poultry or cattle, is an industrialist; a wheelwright, a blacksmith, a metalworker, a carpenter are industrialists; a maker of shoes, of hats, of cloth is also an industrialist; a merchant, a carter, a merchant sailor are industrialists. All the industrialists together work to produce and to make available to the members of society all the material means for the satisfaction of their needs and physical wants, and they form three great classes that one may call cultivators, manufacturers, and merchants.

Q. What rank in society should the industrialists occupy?

A. The industrial class should occupy the first rank, because they are the most important of all; because they can get along without the others, but the others cannot get along without them; because they exist by their own means, by their personal labor. The other classes should work for it, because they are its creatures, and it supports their existence; in a word, everything is created by industry, everything should be done for it.

Q. What rank in society do the industrialists [actually] occupy?

A. The industrial class is, according to the present organization of society, the last of all. The social order accords greater consideration and power to secondary works and even to idleness than to the most important of all works, those of the greatest direct utility. . . .

Oeuvres complètes de Saint-Simon (Paris, 1832), II, 1-3. (Trans. R. E. Cameron.)

II. ANARCHISM AND SYNDICALISM

P. J. Proudhon (1809-1865), a French contemporary of Karl Marx, was the founder of anarchism. Although anarchism, like other varieties of socialism, does not consist of a single, consistent body of doctrine, there is one principle which is common to all anarchist thought. Anarchists are opposed to any form of compulsory social organization, such as the national state, preferring to place their trust in purely voluntary associations. Private property, which permits an individual to exist without work, is, in the opinion of most anarchists, the result of artificial inequalities produced by compulsory social organization. In his book entitled *Qu'est-ce que la propriété?* (*What is Property?*), Proudhon startled the French society of his time with the answer, "Property is theft." The following selection is an extract from this work (1840). (The term "property," as used by Proudhon, should be understood as the equivalent of "capitalism.")

. . . [The system of private] property and communism have been considered always the only possible forms of society. This deplorable error has been the life of property. The disadvantages of communism are so obvious that its critics never have needed to employ much eloquence to thoroughly disgust men with it. . . .

Singularly enough, systematic communism—the deliberate negation of [private] property—is conceived under the direct influence of the proprietary prejudice; and property is the basis of all communistic theories.

The members of a community, it is true, have no private property; but the community is proprietor, and proprietor not only of the goods, but of the persons and wills. . . .

Communism is inequality, but not as property is. Property is the exploitation of the weak by the strong. Communism is the exploitation of the strong by the weak. In property, inequality of conditions is the result of force, under whatever name it be disguised: physical and mental force; force of events, chance, *fortune*; force of accumulated property, etc. In communism, inequality springs from placing mediocrity on a level with excellence. . . .

Communism seeks *equality* and *law*. Property, born of the sovereignty of the reason and the sense of personal merit, wishes above all things *independence* and *proportionality*.

But communism, mistaking uniformity for law, and levelism for equality, becomes tyrannical and unjust. Property, by its despotism and encroachments, soon proves itself oppressive and antisocial.

The objects of communism and property are good—their results are bad. And why? Because both are exclusive, and each disregards two elements of society. Communism rejects independence and proportionality; property does not satisfy equality and law.

Now, if we imagine a society based upon these four principles—equality, law, independence, and proportionality—we find:

1. That *equality,* consisting only in *equality of conditions,* that is, *of means,* and not in *equality of comfort*—which it is the business of the laborers to achieve for themselves, when provided with equal means—in no way violates justice and *équité.*

2. That *law,* resulting from the knowledge of facts, and consequently based upon necessity itself, never clashes with independence.

3. That individual *independence,* or the autonomy of the private reason, originating in the difference in talents and capacities, can exist without danger within the limits of the law.

4. That *proportionality,* being admitted only in the sphere of intelligence and sentiment, and not as regards material objects, may be observed without violating justice or social equality.

This third form of society, the synthesis of communism and property, we will call *liberty* [anarchism]. . . .

P. J. Proudhon, *What is Property?,* trans. Benjamin R. Tucker (Princeton, Massachusetts, 1876), I, 259, 260, 261, 280.

III. MARXIAN SOCIALISM

Karl Marx (1818-1883) and Friedrich Engels (1820-1895), authors of the *Communist Manifesto,* were products of German bourgeois radicalism. Marx studied at the universities of Bonn and Berlin, was greatly influenced by Hegelian philosophy, and took a doctorate in philosophy. He edited a radical bourgeois newspaper in Germany, was exiled for criticizing the absolutist government of Russia, and studied political economy and socialism in Paris. Engels, the son of a wealthy textile manufacturer, was sent to England to learn the cotton trade in his father's firm in Manchester, but he wrote a book describing the condition of the masses and vilifying capitalism (see p. 208). In 1847 he and Marx were invited by the Communist League, a weak international revolutionary group, to draw up a program of action; thus resulted the *Communist Manifesto,* published in German in February, 1848, on the eve of the revolutions which broke out in that year throughout Europe (see p. 261). But the immediate influence of the *Manifesto* was not great; it was scarcely heard of during the revolutions of 1848; only gradually, as it was translated into several languages and as Marx's reputation grew with his other writings, did it assume a prominent place in socialist literature. However, by 1881, when its ideas were fully adopted as the program of the German Social Democratic party, it had become the "Bible" of the socialist movement. Meanwhile, Marx had published in 1867 the first volume— the only one to appear in his lifetime—of his greatest work, *Das Kapital,* a theoretical and historical analysis of capitalist society. Nevertheless, the *Communist Manifesto* has remained the most popular, the most influential—and the most readable—of all his numerous writings. The extract presented below is a drastically condensed version of the original.

. . . A spectre is haunting Europe—the spectre of Communism. All the **162** powers of old Europe have entered into a holy alliance to exorcise this spectre: Pope and Czar, Metternich and Guizot, French Radicals and German police-spies.

Where is the party in opposition that has not been decried as communistic by its opponents in power? Where the Opposition that has not hurled back the branding reproach of Communism, against the more advanced opposition parties, as well as against its reactionary adversaries?

Two things result from this fact:

I. Communism is already acknowledged by all European powers to be itself a power.

II. It is high time that Communists should openly, in the face of the whole world, publish their views, their aims, their tendencies, and meet this nursery tale of the spectre of Communism with a manifesto of the party itself.

To this end, Communists of various nationalities have assembled in London, and sketched the following manifesto, to be published in the English, French, German, Italian, Flemish and Danish languages.

BOURGEOIS AND PROLETARIANS

The history of all hitherto existing society is the history of class struggles.

Freeman and slave, patrician and plebeian, lord and serf, guild-master and journeyman, in a word, oppressor and oppressed, stood in constant opposition to one another, carried on an uninterrupted, now hidden, now open fight, a fight that each time ended, either in a revolutionary reconstitution of society at large, or in the common ruin of the contending classes.

In the earlier epochs of history, we find almost everywhere a complicated arrangement of society into various orders, a manifold gradation of social rank. In ancient Rome we have patricians, knights, plebeians, slaves; in the Middle Ages, feudal lords, vassals, guild-masters, journeymen, apprentices, serfs; in almost all of these classes, again, subordinate gradations.

The modern bourgeois society that has sprouted from the ruins of feudal society, has not done away with class antagonisms. Society as a whole is more and more splitting up into two great hostile camps, into two great classes directly facing each other—bourgeoisie and proletariat. . . .

The bourgeoisie has played a most revolutionary rôle in history.

The bourgeoisie, wherever it has got the upper hand, has put an end to all feudal, patriarchal, idyllic relations. It has pitilessly torn asunder the motley feudal ties that bound man to his "natural superiors," and has left no other bond between man and man than naked self-interest, than callous "cash payment." It has drowned the most heavenly ecstasies of religious fervour, of chivalrous enthusiasm, of philistine sentimentalism, in the icy water of egotistical calculation. It has resolved personal worth into exchange value, and in place of the numberless indefeasible chartered freedoms, has set up that single, unconscionable freedom—Free Trade. In one word, for exploitation, veiled by religious and political illusions, it has substituted naked, shameless, direct, brutal exploitation.

The bourgeoisie has stripped of its halo every occupation hitherto honoured and looked up to with reverent awe. It has converted the physician, the lawyer, the priest, the poet, the man of science, into its paid wage-labourers.

The bourgeoisie has torn away from the family its sentimental veil, and has reduced the family relation to a mere money relation. . . .

The bourgeoisie cannot exist without constantly revolutionising the instruments of production, and thereby the relations of production, and with them the whole relations of society. . . .

The bourgeoisie has subjected the country to the rule of the towns. It has created enormous cities, has greatly increased the urban population as compared with the rural, and has thus rescued a considerable part of the population from the idiocy of rural life. Just as it has made the country dependent on the towns, so it has made barbarian and semibarbarian countries dependent on the civilised ones, nations of peasants on nations of bourgeois, the East on the West.

More and more the bourgeoisie keeps doing away with the scattered state of the population, of the means of production, and of property. It has agglomerated population, centralised means of production, and has concentrated property in a few hands. The necessary consequence of this was political centralisation. Independent, or but loosely connected provinces, with separate interests, laws, governments and systems of taxation, became lumped together into one nation, with one government, one code of laws, one national class interest, one frontier and one customs tariff.

The bourgeoisie, during its rule of scarce one hundred years, has created more massive and more colossal productive forces than have all preceding generations together. Subjection of nature's forces to man, machinery, application of chemistry to industry and agriculture, steam-navigation, railways, electric telegraphs, clearing of whole continents for cultivation, canalisation of rivers, whole populations conjured out of the ground—what earlier century had even a presentiment that such productive forces slumbered in the lap of social labour? . . .

. . . Modern bourgeois society with its relations of production, of exchange and of property, a society that has conjured up such gigantic means of production and of exchange, is like the sorcerer who is no longer able to control the powers of the nether world whom he has called up by his spells. . . .

The weapons with which the bourgeoisie felled feudalism to the ground are now turned against the bourgeoisie itself.

But not only has the bourgeoisie forged the weapons that bring death to itself; it has also called into existence the men who are to wield those weapons—the modern working class—the proletarians.

In proportion as the bourgeoisie, *i.e.,* capital, is developed, in the same proportion is the proletariat, the modern working class, developed—a class of labourers, who live only so long as they find work, and who find work only so long as their labour increases capital. These labourers, who must sell themselves piecemeal, are a commodity, like every other article of commerce, and are consequently exposed to all the vicissitudes of competition, to all the fluctuations of the market. . . .

But with the development of industry the proletariat not only increases in number; it becomes concentrated in greater masses, its strength grows, and it feels that strength more. The various interests and conditions of life within the ranks of the proletariat are more and more equalised, in proportion as machinery obliterates all distinctions of labour and nearly everywhere reduces wages to the same low level. The growing competition among the bourgeois, and the resulting commercial crises, make the wages of the workers ever more fluctuating. The unceasing improvement of machinery, ever more rapidly developing, makes their livelihood more and more precarious; the collisions between individual workmen and individual bourgeois take more and more the character of collisions between two classes. Thereupon the workers begin to form combinations [trade unions] against the bourgeoisie; they club together in order to keep up the rate of wages; they found permanent associations in order to make provision beforehand for these occasional revolts. Here and there the contest breaks out into riots. . . .

Of all the classes that stand face to face with the bourgeoisie today, the proletariat alone is a really revolutionary class. The other classes decay and finally disappear in the face of modern industry; the proletariat is its special and essential product. . . .

All the preceding classes that got the upper hand, sought to fortify their already acquired status by subjecting society at large to their conditions of appropriation. The proletarians cannot become masters of the productive forces of society, except by abolishing their own previous mode of appropriation, and thereby also every other previous mode of appropriation. They have nothing of their own to secure and to fortify; their mission is to destroy all previous securities for, and insurances of, individual property.

All previous historical movements were movements of minorities, or in the interest of minorities. The proletarian movement is the self-conscious, independent movement of the immense majority, in the interest of the immense majority. The proletariat, the lowest stratum of our present society, cannot stir, cannot raise itself up, without the whole superincumbent strata of official society being sprung into the air. . . .

PROLETARIANS AND COMMUNISTS

In what relation do the Communists stand to the proletarians as a whole?

The Communists do not form a separate party opposed to other working class parties.

They have no interests separate and apart from those of the proletariat as a whole.

They do not set up any sectarian principles of their own, by which to shape and mould the proletarian movement.

The Communists are distinguished from the other working class parties by this only: 1. In the national struggles of the proletarians of the different countries, they point out and bring to the front the common interests of the entire proletariat, independently of all nationality. 2. In the various stages of development which the struggle of the working class against the bourgeoisie has to pass through, they always and everywhere represent the interests of the movement as a whole. . . .

The distinguishing feature of Communism is not the abolition of property generally, but the abolition of bourgeois property. But modern bourgeois private property is the final and most complete expression of the system of producing and appropriating products that is based on class antagonisms, on the exploitation of the many by the few. . . .

In this sense, the theory of the Communists may be summed up in the single sentence: Abolition of private property. . . .

Communism deprives no man of the power to appropriate the products of society; all that it does is to deprive him of the power to subjugate the labour of others by means of such appropriation. . . .

We have seen above, that the first step in the revolution by the working class, is to raise the proletariat to the position of ruling class, to establish democracy.

The proletariat will use its political supremacy to wrest, by degrees, all capital from the bourgeoisie, to centralise all instruments of production in the hands of the state, *i.e.,* of the proletariat organised as the ruling class; and to increase the total of productive forces as rapidly as possible.

Of course, in the beginning, this cannot be effected except by means of despotic inroads on the rights of property, and on the conditions of bourgeois production; by means of measures, therefore, which appear economically insufficient and untenable, but which, in the course of the movement, outstrip themselves, necessitate further inroads upon the old social order, and are unavoidable as a means of entirely revolutionising the mode of production.

These measures will of course be different in different countries.

Nevertheless in the most advanced countries, the following will be pretty generally applicable.

1. Abolition of property in land and application of all rents of land to public purposes.

2. A heavy progressive or graduated income tax.

3. Abolition of all right of inheritance.

4. Confiscation of the property of all emigrants and rebels.

5. Centralisation of credit in the hands of the state, by means of a national bank with state capital and an exclusive monopoly.

6. Centralisation of the means of communication and transport in the hands of the state.

7. Extension of factories and instruments of production owned by the state; the bringing into cultivation of waste lands, and the improvement of the soil generally in accordance with a common plan.

8. Equal obligation of all to work. Establishment of industrial armies, especially for agriculture.

9. Combination of agriculture with manufacturing industries; gradual abolition of the distinction between town and country, by a more equable distribution of the population over the country.

10. Free education for all children in public schools. Abolition of child factory labour in its present form. Combination of education with industrial production, etc.

When, in the course of development, class distinctions have disappeared, and all production has been concentrated in the hands of a vast association of the whole nation, the public power will lose its political character. Political power, properly so called, is merely the organised power of one class for oppressing another. If the proletariat during its contest with the bourgeoisie is compelled, by the force of circumstances, to organise itself as a class; if, by means of a revolution, it makes itself the ruling class, and, as such sweeps away by force the old conditions of production, then it will, along with these conditions, have swept away the conditions for the existence of class antagonisms, and of classes generally, and will thereby have abolished its own supremacy as a class.

In place of the old bourgeois society, with its classes and class antagonisms, we shall have an association, in which the free development of each is the condition for the free development of all.

POSITION OF THE COMMUNISTS IN RELATION TO THE VARIOUS EXISTING OPPOSITION PARTIES

The Communists disdain to conceal their views and aims. They openly declare that their ends can be attained only by the forcible overthrow of all existing social conditions. Let the ruling classes tremble at a Communist revolution. The proletarians have nothing to lose but their chains. They have a world to win.

Workingmen of all countries, unite!

Karl Marx and Friedrich Engels, *Manifesto of the Communist Party,* ed. Friedrich Engels (New York, 1932), pp. 8, 9, 11, 12–23, 25, 30–31, 44.

IV. EVOLUTIONARY SOCIALISM

German Revisionism

The German Social Democratic party adopted Marxism as its official program, but, especially after 1890, it acted less and less like a truly revolutionary conspiracy, more and more like a reformist political party. Eduard Bernstein (1850-1932), a devoted official of the Social Democratic party who had been exiled from Germany for his services to it, spent several years in England where he observed the gradual democratization of English political life and fell under the influence of the Fabian Socialists (164). In 1899 he published his *Voraussetzungen des Sozialismus und die Aufgaben der Sozialdemokratie,* subsequently translated into English as *Evolutionary Socialism,* in which he set forth his doubts concerning the necessity for the violent overthrow of capitalist society. His thesis was granted the honor of a formal debate in the convention of the German Social Democratic party, and although it was rejected as a program in favor of the "orthodox" version of Marxism, it became in actual fact the guide book of socialist practice in Germany and several other countries.

. . . I am opposed to the view that we can shortly expect a collapse of **163** bourgeois society, and that Social Democracy should base its tactics on the assumption of such a great social cataclysm. . . .

The holders of this cataclysmic theory rely principally on the conclusions of the *Communist Manifesto*—erroneously, in every respect.

The prognosis of the development of modern society which is found in the *Communist Manifesto* is correct insofar as the general tendencies of this development are concerned. It errs, however, in several special deductions, above all in the estimate of the time which the development will require. This has been acknowledged without reservation by Friedrich Engels, the joint author of the *Manifesto,* in his preface to *The Class Struggles in France.* It is obvious, therefore, that if economic development requires a greater span of time than was assumed, it must also take forms and lead to patterns which were not and could not be foreseen in the *Communist Manifesto.*

The intensification of social relations has not taken place in the manner described in the *Manifesto*. It is not only useless, it is also the greatest folly to conceal this from ourselves. The number of the propertied class has not become smaller, but larger. The enormous increase in social wealth does not belong to a shrinking number of capitalist magnates, but to a growing number of capitalists of all degrees. The middle classes change their character, but they do not disappear from the social scale. . . .

Politically, we see the privileges of the capitalist bourgeoisie giving way step by step to democratic arrangements in all advanced countries. Under this influence and driven on by the ever stronger working class movement, a social reaction has set in against the exploiting tendencies of capital, which, although it is still timid and groping its way, is bringing more and more areas of economic life under its influence. Factory legislation, the democratization of local government and the extension of its functions, the freeing of trade unions and cooperatives from all legal restrictions, consideration of workers organizations in all work undertaken by the public authorities—this is descriptive of the present phase of development. That it is possible in Germany to think of gagging the trade unions is descriptive, not of the height, but of the backwardness of its political development.

But the more the political arrangements of modern nations are democratized, the more the necessities and opportunities of political catastrophes are diminished. Whoever holds to the cataclysmic theory must, as a logical consequence, struggle to prevent and hinder the developments I have just described. . . . But is it true that the conquest of political power by the proletariat can take place only as the result of a political cataclysm? Is it to be the appropriation and utilization by the proletariat of the power of the state against the whole nonproletarian world? . . .

No one has questioned the necessity of the working class struggle for democracy. What is in doubt is the cataclysmic theory and the question whether, given the present level of economic development of Germany and the degree of maturity of its working class, in city and country, a sudden catastrophe would be opportune for Social Democracy. I have denied it, and I deny it still, because in my opinion a greater opportunity for lasting success lies in steady advance than in the possibilities presented by such a social upheaval.

Eduard Bernstein, *Die Voraussetzungen des Sozialismus und die Aufgaben der Sozialdemokratie* (Stuttgart, 1899), pp. v-vi, vii. (Trans. R. E. Cameron.)

English Fabianism

The English Fabian Society, which took its name from Fabius Cunctator, a famous Roman general who won wars by not engaging his troops in pitched battle, was an organization of middle-class intellectuals devoted to social reform and the gradual socialization of industry. Its list of luminaries included George Bernard Shaw, H. G. Wells, and Sidney and Beatrice Webb. Its aims and methods are fully set forth in the following official statement (1896).

The object of the Fabian Society is to persuade the English people to **164** make their political constitution thoroughly democratic and to socialise their industries sufficiently to make the livelihood of the people entirely independent of private Capitalism.

The Fabian Society endeavours to pursue its Socialist and Democratic objects with complete singleness of aim. For example:

It does not ask the English people to join the Fabian Society.

It does not propose that the practical steps towards Social-Democracy should be carried out by itself, or by any other specially organised Socialist society or party.

It brings all the pressure and persuasion in its power to bear, not on the imaginary forces of the future, but on the existing forces of to-day, caring nothing by what name any party calls itself, or what principles, Socialist or other, it professes, but having regard solely to the tendency of its actions, supporting those which make for Socialism and Democracy, and opposing those which are reactionary. . . .

The Fabian Society does not claim to be the people of England, or even the Socialist party, and therefore does not seek direct political representation by putting forward Fabian candidates at elections. But it loses no opportunity of influencing elections and inducing constituencies to select Socialists as their candidates. No person, however, can obtain the support of the Fabian Society, or escape its opposition, by merely repeating a few shibboleths and calling himself a Socialist or Social-Democrat. . . .

The Fabian Society is perfectly constitutional in its attitude, and its methods are those usual in political life in England.

The Fabian Society accepts the conditions imposed on it by human nature and by the national character and political circumstances of the English people. It sympathises with the ordinary man's preference for gradual, peaceful changes, to revolution, conflict with the army and police, and martyrdom. It recognises the fact that Social-Democracy is not the whole of the working-class programme, and that every separate measure towards the socialisation of industry will have to compete for precedence with numbers of other reforms. It therefore does not believe that the moment will ever come when the whole of Socialism will be staked on the issue of a single General Election or a single Bill in the House of Commons as between the proletariat on one side and the proprietariat on the other. Each instalment of Social-Democracy will only be a measure among other measures, and will have to be kept to the front by an energetic Fabian section of the working-class party. The Fabian Society therefore begs those Socialists who are looking forward to a sensational historical crisis to join some other Society. . . .

Socialism, as understood by the Fabian Society, means the organisation and conduct of the necessary industries of the country and the appropriation of all forms of economic rent of land and capital, by the nation as a whole, through the co-ordinate agency of the most suitable public authorities. . . .

The Fabian Society strenuously maintains its freedom of thought and speech with regard to the errors of Socialist authors, economists, leaders, and parties, no less than to those of its opponents. It insists on the necessity of maintaining as critical an attitude towards Marx and Lassalle, some of whose views must by this time be discarded as erroneous or obsolete, as these eminent Socialists themselves maintained towards their predecessors, St. Simon and Robert Owen. . . .

In view of the fact that the Socialist movement has been hitherto inspired, instructed, led, and suffered for by members of the middle class or "bourgeoisie," the Fabian Society, though not at all surprised to find these middle-class leaders attacking with much bitterness the narrow social ideals current in their own class, protests against the absurdity of Socialists representing the very class from which Socialism has sprung as specially hostile to it. The Fabian Society has no romantic illusions as to the freedom of the proletariat from these same narrow ideals. Like all other Socialist societies, it can only educate the people in Socialism by making them conversant with the conclusions of the most enlightened members of the middle classes and their pupils. The Fabian Society therefore cannot reasonably use the words "bourgeois" or "middle class" as terms of reproach, more especially as it would thereby condemn a large proportion of its own members.

The Fabian Society endeavours to rouse social compunction by making the public conscious of the evil condition of society under the present system. This it does by the collection and publication of authentic and impartial statistical tracts, compiled, not from the works of Socialists, but from official sources. The first volume of Karl Marx's "Das Kapital," which contains an immense mass of carefully verified facts concerning modern capitalistic civilisation, and practically nothing at all about Socialism, is probably the most successful propagandist work ever published. The Fabian Society, in its endeavours to continue the work of Marx in this direction, has found that the guesses made by Socialists at the condition of the people almost invariably flatter the existing system instead of, as might be suspected, exaggerating its evils. The Fabian Society therefore concluded that in the natural philosophy of Socialism, light is a more important factor than heat.

The Fabian Society is fully alive to the social value of what is called "brain work," and deeply regrets that it cannot include under that description many of the speeches and articles produced at present in England either for or against Socialism. . . .

The Fabian Society does not put Socialism forward as a panacea for all the ills of human society, but only for those produced by defective organisation of industry and radically bad distribution of wealth.

The Fabian Society, by steadfastly refusing to sacrifice the interests of Socialism either to the mistakes of Socialists on the one hand, or the political convenience of the established political parties on the other, has been violently denounced from both sides, the Liberal and Socialist newspapers often vying with one another in their efforts to discredit the Fabian Society. The only compliments which the Fabian Society receives or expects from non-Fabian Socialists, are the applications for advice, speakers, and money, which are invariably made to it in all emergencies, and to which it always responds to the best of its ability.

Full Report of the Proceedings of the International Workers' Congress, London, July and August, 1896 ([London, 1896]), pp. 45–49.

V. SOCIALISM AND RELIGION

Christian Socialism

The movement known as Christian Socialism, which was confined mainly to England but had slight manifestations in continental Western Europe and the United States, grew out of the feeling on the part of a few clergymen and other devoted Christians that organized religion should practice what it preached on the subject of the brotherhood of man. Its roots are to be found even before 1848, but it reached its high point—not a very high one—in the 1880's. The following statement by a clergyman of the Church of England indicates its general tendency (1888).

. . . . The distinguishing mark of Christian Socialism is its firm faith in **165** the power of Christian ethics to bring about a complete transformation of industrial economy. Hence its main efforts are directed towards bringing about a reconcilation of classes with the fuller development of the passive virtues of Christianity, and with it ultimately a regeneration of society as the result of a previous improvement in the industrial [sphere]. From the growth of the active virtues of Christianity above all, it expects important social reforms, founded on Christian principle; and these are to remove the causes of social discontent, and so bring about social peace; in short, Christian Socialism works by means of spiritual *dynamics,* or religious influence, whereas Socialism proper (at least, in its most recent forms) aims at a *mechanical* reconstruction, or governmental regulation, of society on purely materialistic principles. Yet, notwithstanding their essential differences, both have much in common, and are frequently met in company in the historical development of European society. . . .

M. Kaufmann, *Christian Socialism* (London: Kegan Paul, 1888), p. xiii. (Reprinted by permission of the publisher.)

Catholicism and Socialism

The inroads made by the various socialist movements on the working class members of the Catholic Church finally forced the church to take an official stand on the question of capitalism and socialism. Pope Leo XIII, more tolerant and enlightened than his predecessor, did this with his encyclical *De Rerum Novarum* (*On the Condition of Labor*) in 1891. The encyclical, which treated the problems of both capitalism and socialism, has been variously interpreted as expressing a "plague-on-both-your-houses" attitude, and as bidding the lion (employer) and lamb (labor) to lie down together. It has also been viewed as a philosophical predecessor of Mussolini's Fascism (see p. 454). Following is a brief extract from an English translation.

166   . . . The great mistake that is made in the matter now under consideration is to possess oneself of the idea that class is naturally hostile to class; that rich and poor are intended by Nature to live at war with one another. So irrational and so false is this view that the exact contrary is the truth. Just as the symmetry of the human body is the result of the disposition of the members of the body, so in a State it is ordained by Nature that these two classes should exist in harmony and agreement, and should, as it were, fit into one another, so as to maintain the equilibrium of the body politic. Each requires the other; capital cannot do without labour, nor labour without capital. Mutual agreement results in pleasantness and good order; perpetual conflict necessarily produces confusion and outrage. Now, in preventing such strife as this, and in making it possible, the efficacy of Christianity is marvellous and manifold. First of all, there is nothing more powerful than Religion (of which the Church is the interpreter and guardian) in drawing rich and poor together, by reminding each class of its duties to the other, and especially of the duties of justice. Thus Religion teaches the labouring man and the workman to carry out honestly and well all equitable agreements freely made; never to injure capital, or to outrage the person of an employer; never to employ violence in representing his own cause, or to engage in riot or disorder; and to have nothing to do with men of evil principles, who work upon the people with artful promises and raise foolish hopes which usually end in disaster and in repentance when too late. Religion teaches the rich man and the employer that their working people are not their slaves; that they must respect in every man his dignity as a man and as a Christian; that labour is nothing to be ashamed of, if we listen to right reason and to Christian philosophy, but is an honourable employment, enabling a man to sustain his life in an upright and creditable way; and that it is shameful and inhuman to treat men like chattels to make money by, or to look upon them merely as so much muscle or physical power. . . .

Pope Leo XIII, *De Rerum Novarum,* as reprinted in Francesco S. Nitti, *Catholic Socialism,* trans. Mary Mackintosh (London, 1895), p. 409.

QUESTIONS

1. What features of French Revolutionary doctrine might give rise to socialist expectations?
2. Why did Robert Owen think that a socialist reorganization of society was necessary?
3. According to Saint-Simon, was a ditch-digger an "industrialist"? An engineer? A banker? An army officer? The King?
4. What reasoning led Proudhon to identify property with theft?
5. What, according to Marx, was the "historic" role of the bourgeoisie? Marx has been interpreted as saying the bourgeoisie was "digging its own grave"; explain.
6. What specific course of action did Marx advocate for the destruction of capitalist society? Marx stated that the demise of capitalist society was inevitable, but at the same time he exhorted workingmen to unite to achieve its forcible overthrow; how can this contradiction be reconciled?
7. What was the "revised" element in Bernstein's revision of Marxism?
8. What was the goal of the Fabian Society? What were its methods?
9. What was the goal of Christian Socialism? What were its methods?
10. What, according to Pope Leo XIII, was the proper attitude of workmen toward their employers? Of employers toward their workmen?

CHAPTER XXVI

THE PROGRESS OF SCIENCE

SCIENTIFIC ADVANCE in the nineteenth century was rapid, varied, and striking. Ever since the seventeenth century, scientific progress has influenced human thought (see p. 93), and the nineteenth century was no exception in this. Perhaps the most influential doctrine of nineteenth-century science was the idea of evolution. Charles Darwin's *Origin of the Species by Means of Natural Selection* (1859) (167) had repercussions far beyond his own field of research. Men like Herbert Spencer (see p. 234) and others applied Darwinism to the political and social fields. Darwin's *Descent of Man* (1871) (168), emphasizing man's descent from the lower animals, came into conflict with many traditional religious beliefs.

Where early science had tended toward deism (see p. 95) and thus toward a reconciliation of the "new" knowledge with traditional beliefs, the nineteenth century saw the use of scientific advancement in an attack on religious fundamentals. "Scientific" methods were adopted by some in the task of denying the historical truth of biblical revelation. David Friedrich Strauss's *Life of Jesus* (1835) was the first of these attempts to use science to prove that most of Scripture was mythical, legendary, and unhistorical (169). Just as Darwinism influenced political and social thought, this kind of biblical criticism had great effect on nineteenth-century religious thought.

Charles Darwin (1809-1882) in his *Origin of the Species* (1859) explains his doctrines of natural selection and the survival of the fittest.

. . . Before entering on the subject of this chapter I must make a few **167** preliminary remarks to show how the struggle for existence bears on natural selection. It has been seen in the last chapter that among organic beings in a state of nature there is some individual variability: indeed, I am not aware that this has ever been disputed. It is immaterial for us whether a multitude of doubtful forms be called species or subspecies or varieties; what rank, for instance, the two or three hundred doubtful forms of British plants are entitled to hold, if the existence of any well-marked varieties be admitted. But the mere existence of individual variability and of some few well-marked varieties, though necessary as the foundation for the work, helps us but little in understanding how species arise in nature. How have all those exquisite adaptations of one part of the organization to another part, and to the conditions of life and of one organic being to another being, been perfected? We see these beautiful co-adaptations most plainly in the woodpecker and the mistletoe; and only a little less plainly in the humblest parasite which clings to the hairs of a quadruped or feathers of a bird; in the structure of the beetle which dives through the water; in the plumed seed which is wafted by the gentlest breeze; in short, we see beautiful adaptations everywhere and in every part of the organic world.

Again, it may be asked, how is it that varieties, which I have called incipient species, become ultimately converted into good and distinct species, which in most cases obviously differ from each other more than do the species of the same genus, arise? All these results, as we shall more fully see in the next chapter, follow from the struggle for life. Owing to this struggle, variations, however slight and from whatever cause proceeding, if they be in any degree profitable to the individuals of a species, in their infinitely complex relations to other organic beings and to their physical conditions of life, will tend to the preservation of such individuals, and will generally be inherited by the offspring. The offspring, also, will thus have a better chance of surviving, for, of the many individuals of any species which are periodically born, but a small number can survive. I have called this principle, by which each slight variation, if useful, is preserved, by the term natural selection, in order to mark its relation to man's power of selection. But the expression often used by Mr. Herbert Spencer, of the Survival of the Fittest, is more accurate, and is sometimes equally convenient. We have seen that man by selection can certainly produce great results, and can adapt organic beings to his own uses, through the accumulation of slight but useful variations, given to him by the hand of Nature. But Natural Selection, we shall hereafter see, is a power incessantly ready for action, and is as immeasurably superior to man's feeble efforts as the works of Nature are to those of Art. . . .

How will the struggle for existence, briefly discussed in the last chapter, act in regard to variation? Can the principle of selection, which we have seen is so potent in the hands of man, apply under nature? I think we shall see that it can act most efficiently. Let the endless number of slight variations and individual differences occurring in our domestic production, and, in a lesser degree, in those under nature, be borne in mind; as well as the strength of the hereditary tendency. Under domestication, it may truly be said that the whole organization becomes in some degree plastic. But the variability which we almost universally meet with in our domestic productions is not directly produced, as Hooker and Asa Gray have well remarked, by man; he can neither originate varieties nor prevent their occurrence; he can only preserve and accumulate such as do occur. Unintentionally he exposes organic beings to new and changing conditions of life, and variability ensues; but similar changes of conditions might and do occur under nature. Let it also be borne in mind how infinitely complex and close-fitting are the mutual relations of all organic beings to each other and to their physical conditions of life; and consequently what infinitely varied diversities of structure might be of use to each being under changing conditions of life. Can it then be thought improbable, seeing that variations useful to man have undoubtedly occurred, that other variations useful in some way to each being in the great and complex battle of life, should occur in the course of many successive generations? If such do occur, can we doubt (remembering that many more individuals are born than can possibly survive) that individuals having any advantage, however slight, over others, would have the best chance of surviving and procreating their kind? On the other hand, we may feel sure that any variation in the least degree injurious would be rigidly destroyed. This preservation of favorable individual differences and variations, and the destruction of those which are injurious, I have called Natural Selection, or the Survival of the Fittest. Variations neither useful nor injurious would not be affected by natural selection, and would be left either a fluctuating element, as perhaps we see in certain polymorphic species, or would ultimately become fixed, owing to the nature of the organism and the nature of the conditions. . . .

We shall best understand the probable course of natural selection by taking the case of a country undergoing some slight physical change, for instance, of climate. The proportional numbers of its inhabitants will almost immediately undergo a change, and some species will probably become extinct. We may conclude, from what we have seen of the intimate and complex manner in which the inhabitants of each country are bound together, that any change in the numerical proportions of the inhabitants, independently of the change of climate itself, would seriously affect the others. If the country were open on its borders, new forms would certainly immigrate, and this would likewise seriously disturb the relations of some of the former inhabitants. Let it be remembered how powerful the influence of a single introduced tree or mammal has been shown to be. . . .

As man can produce, and certainly has produced, a great result by his methodical and unconscious means of selection, what may not natural selection effect? Man can act only on external and visible characters; Nature, if I may be allowed to personify the natural preservation or survival of the fittest, cares nothing for appearances, except in so far as they are useful to any being. She can act on every internal organ, on every shade of constitutional difference on the whole machinery of life. Man selects only for his own good; Nature only for that of the being which she tends. Every selected character is fully exercised by her, as is implied by the fact of their selection. Man keeps the natives of many climates in the same country. He seldom exercises each selected character in some peculiar and fitting manner; he feeds a long and a short-beaked pigeon on the same food; he does not exercise a long-backed or long-legged quadruped in any peculiar manner; he exposes sheep with long and short wool to the same climate; does not allow the most vigorous males to struggle for the females; he does not rigidly destroy all inferior animals, but protects during each varying season, as far as lies in his power, all his productions. He often begins his selection by some half-monstrous form, or at least by some modification prominent enough to catch the eye or to be plainly useful to him. Under nature, the slightest differences of structure or constitution may well turn the nicely balanced scale in the struggle for life, and so be preserved. How fleeting are the wishes and efforts of man! How short his time, and consequently how poor will be his results, compared with those accumulated by Nature during whole geological periods! Can we wonder, then, that Nature's production should be far "truer" in character than man's productions; that they should be infinitely better adapted to the most complex conditions of life, and should plainly bear the stamp of far higher workmanship? . . .

If under changing conditions of life organic beings present individual differences in almost every part of their structure, and this cannot be disputed; if there be, owing to their geometrical rate of increase, a severe struggle for life at some age, season or year, and this certainly cannot be disputed; then, considering the infinite complexity of the relations of all organic beings to each other and to their conditions of life, causing an infinite diversity in structure, constitution and habits, to be advantageous to them, it would be a most extraordinary fact if no variations had ever occurred useful to each being's own welfare, in the same manner as so many variations have occurred useful to man. But if variations useful to any organic being ever do occur, assuredly individuals thus characterized will have the best chance of being preserved in the struggle for life; and from the strong principle of inheritance, these will tend to produce offspring similarly characterized. This principle of preservation, or the survival of the fittest, I have called natural selection. It leads to the improvement of each creature in relation to its organic and inorganic conditions of life; and consequently, in most cases, to what must be regarded as an advance in organization. . . .

The affinities of all the beings of the same class have sometimes been represented by a great tree. I believe this simile largely speaks the truth. The green and budding twigs may represent existing species; and those produced during former years may represent the long succession of extinct species. At each period of growth all the growing twigs have tried to branch out on all sides, and to overtop and kill the surrounding twigs and branches, in the same manner as species and groups of species have at all times overmastered other species in the great battle for life. The limbs divided into great branches, and these into lesser and lesser branches, were themselves once, when the tree was young, budding twigs; and this connection of the former and present buds by ramifying branches may well represent the classification of all extinct and living species in groups subordinate to groups. Of the many twigs which flourished when the tree was a mere bush, only two or three, now grown into great branches, yet survive and bear the other branches; so with the species which lived during long past geological periods, very few have left living and modified descendants. From the first growth of the tree, many a limb and branch has decayed and dropped off; and these fallen branches of various sizes may represent those whole orders, families and genera which have now no living representatives, and which are known to us only in a fossil stage. . . . As buds give rise by growth to fresh buds, and these, if vigorous, branch out and overtop on all sides many a feebler branch, so by generation I believe it has been with the great Tree of Life, which fills with its dead and broken branches the crust of the earth, and covers the surface with its ever-branching and beautiful ramifications.

Charles Darwin, *The Origin of the Species by Means of Natural Selection* (New York: The Macmillan Co., 1934), pp. 57–58, 74–75, 76, 77–78, 125, 127, 128. (Reprinted by permission of the publisher.)

In the last chapter of *The Descent of Man* (1871) Charles Darwin summarizes his findings:

The first chapter of this book is a summary of the evidence for the **168** view that man is descended from the brutes. We have pointed out his bodily similarity to the lower animals, the striking analogies in his embryonic development, and the overwhelming evidence of his rudimentary or vestigial organs. The second chapter takes up various important aspects of the evolutionary process, and considers the general topic of natural selection. In the third chapter we discuss man's mental faculties, and compare them with those of the lower animals, showing that the differences between them are differences of degree, not of kind.

The fourth chapter deals with the so-called moral sense, or conscience, and defends the idea that this faculty is only a development of the social instincts, which are common to many of the lower animals. In the fifth chapter we follow the intellectual growth of the various races of men, from the ape-like beings of the prehistoric period to the civilized men of modern Europe. In chapter six there is a brief discussion of man's proper zoological classification, and some speculations about his antiquity and his probable birthplace. The seventh chapter offers a general introduction to the subject of sexual selection, and a discussion of the rôle which this force has played in the evolution of the human race.

The main conclusion of the whole work is simply that *man is descended body and mind from the lower animals.* I regret to think that this conclusion will be highly distasteful to many people, who will regard it as inimical to both morality and religion. But we scientists are not concerned with hopes or fears—only with the truth as far as we are able to discover it. Having considered the evidence, it seems to me that we must acknowledge that man still bears indelible and unmistakable traces of his lowly origin. His body is still the body of an animal, and the mark of the beast is still clearly discernible in all his mental and moral faculties.

Charles Darwin, *The Substance of the Descent of Man,* summarized by Newell R. Tripp (New York: Vanguard Press, 1926), pp. 128–29. (Reprinted by permission of the publisher.)

David Friedrich Strauss (1808–1874) used scientific methods to deny the reality of God either in history or in directly influencing individuals. This led him to view the Bible largely in terms of myths and legends. In his *Life of Jesus* (1834), he explains the criterion for his judgement. The book created a furor on its appearance and produced a whole school of such biblical criticism.

169 If we have hitherto explained through external and internal reasons the legendary and mythical in the evangelical books [of the Bible] . . . so we must finally ask ourselves how we can recognize its actual presence in each individual case? . . .

That an account is unhistorical, that something which is narrated could not have happened that way, can above all be recognized if it is:

1. Incompatible with the otherwise universally valid laws of action.

Now it is above all a property of these laws that, according to both correct philosophic concepts and proven experience, absolute causality never interferes, through single acts, in the chain of necessary causes; instead it reveals itself in the creation of a totality of causes and their varying effects. Thus where an account tells us of an occurrence or an event with the express or implied statement that it has been caused by God himself (. . . heavenly choruses etc.) or that it has been caused by human beings in consequence of supernatural powers given by God (miracles, prophecies); in such cases we cannot recognize the narrative as historical. . . .

2. However, such an account may not conflict with the laws of action only, but it must also not be in contradiction with itself, or with other narratives, if it is to have historical validity.

Most decidedly such an account is self-contradictory when one relation of events says what the other denies, as when one account makes Jesus appear definitely only after the arrest of the Baptists in Galilee, but the other after he had already worked for some time in Galilee as well as in Judea. . . .

David Friedrich Strauss, *Das Leben Jesu* (1838), pp. 115, 116, 117–18. (Trans. George L. Mosse.)

QUESTIONS

1. What is the relationship between natural selection and the survival of the fittest?
2. How does the struggle for existence act in regard to variation?
3. How does Darwin make the transition from plant life to human individuals?

4. How important is environment to Darwin's thought?

5. Compare the readings on Darwin with the extract from Herbert Spencer (see p. 234). What are the similarities?

6. What would you call "scientific" about Strauss's biblical criticism?

7. What factors about man's nature do you think both Darwin and Strauss failed to take into account?

CHAPTER XXVII

GERMANY FINDS UNITY

THE REVOLUTION OF 1848 (p. 261) had failed to herald German unity on the basis of liberalism. Bismarck had attended the Frankfurt Diet and had reached the conclusion that Germany must find its unity under Prussian leadership and that where liberalism had failed, force might have to be used. The new Germany was unified by external war and by Prussian domination within the Confederation itself, a confederation which now excluded Austria. Once he had achieved his objective of unification (170), Bismarck worked for a peaceful Germany on a conservative, monarchical, basis.

Though Bismarck outlawed the Social Democratic party in the name of conservatism, he had little sympathy for doctrines of aggressive and racially-oriented nationalism (171). Nevertheless, the process of national unification provided the impetus for a more aggressive nationalism such as that of the historian Heinrich von Treitschke (172). At the same time, national unification also meant a stepped-up economic development, and here Friedrich List (173) foreshadows what was to happen as Germany became the most important industrial nation on the continent of Europe.

Here Bismarck defends himself against the accusation of not being a conservative and in so doing gives his interpretation of the process of German unification (1891).

. . . There is a good old saying, *quieta non movere;* that is to say, do not **170** disturb what lies quietly, and this is typically conservative: not to take part in the making of laws which might disturb matters where there is no need for a change. . . . A government which stands for unnecessary innovations gives an anticonservative impression by changing through legislation matters which have proved useful, without any pressure from those affected by such a change.

I am accused of not having been conservative as Chancellor and Prime Minister, for I destroyed many of the old forms and created new ones. Well, here you have to weigh the old which was destroyed against the new which was to be attained. I realized when I entered my ministry, and before that at Frankfurt (1848), that we could only achieve the ability to breathe and live freely among the peoples of Europe through the reawakening of the German nationality, and through the unity of the German tribes. As soon as I saw the possibility of extending our unity beyond the borders of Prussia, I put aside all else to achieve this. We have had, after all, and still have, a special feeling of nationality in Prussia, originally a branch of the greater German feeling. Basically, this has no more justification than the specific patriotism of the individual German states. It was for me a matter of course that I felt vividly this Prussian consciousness in which I had been reared; but as soon as I became convinced that the Prussian national feeling was the anvil to hammer out the others, I ceased to follow lopsided Prussian aims.

In those days the tasks of a governing minister were different from what they are today when we have been called by God to be *one* of the first—as I say politely, instead of *the* first—nations in Europe. Thus it was my task above all to develop our feeling of nationality. My share in the beginning and in the course of the German civil war—I mean in the year 1866—and in the destruction of old forms was basically more conservative than keeping the old disunity would have been. For this would have led to dissolution or even to foreign domination: but for me the task was to shore up the remainder of German national feeling, which was still glowing among the ashes; thus to conserve something of great antiquity. This old possession was conserved and strengthened, mainly through war—it is regrettable that it could not be done peacefully—but it is grounded the more firmly for all that.

The accusation of being a renegade made against me by contemporary conservatives, who themselves follow no clearly recognizable goal, is unjust. The unification of Germany was a conservative deed. . . .

Otto von Bismarck, *Die gesammelten Werke* (Berlin, 1924–35), XIII, 420–21. (Trans. George L. Mosse.)

The following extracts, taken from a variety of Bismarck's speeches, mirror some of his political thought.

171   The question is this: are we a great power or merely a member of the German federation; are we to be ruled monarchically like a great power, or, as conceivable for a mere small state, ruled by professors, judges, and small town politicians? . . . Our strength cannot spring from cabinet or newspaper politics, but only from the actions of a great, armed power. . . . I am not afraid of a war, on the contrary. I am also indifferent towards [being called] Revolutionary or Conservative, as I am towards all mere slogans . . . if one were to apply the standards of morality and justice to European politics, such standards would have to be abolished. . . .

I have never in my life asserted that I am an enemy of the freedom of the people, but have only qualified it according to the state of affairs: my interest in foreign policy is not only stronger, but at the moment the only decisive one—so that, as much as lies in my power, I will overcome any obstacle which stands in the way of the arrival at the goal, which, as I believe, must be reached for the good of the fatherland. This does not exclude . . . that it is the duty of every honest government to work for that highest degree of freedom for the people, and the individual, which is compatible with the safety of the state. . . .

The proposed law [banning the Social Democrats] seems to me a logical result of the behavior of men who negate in principle our national and social institutions, seeing in their overthrow the principal political task, and who openly say so. Against such currents, the state can protect and insure itself when it excludes these elements, incompatible as they are with its existence. He who negates the state and its law rejects therewith his claim on their protection, whose precondition is the recognition of the authority of the state. . . . He who denies freedom and obedience to the totality of his fellow citizens, is put under the ban of outlawry as the logical consequence of his enmity to the state. . . .

Man cannot himself create or guide the flow of destiny, he can only ride upon it and steer himself with more or less experience and ability. One can suffer shipwreck and be cast upon the shores, or land in good harbors. Political development is as slow as geological formations, layers form on top of each other and produce new hills and mountains. Do not succumb too much to the German love for criticism, accept what God has given you, and what we have with much labor brought into safe harbor under the threat of war from all other Europeans. . . . I try to be satisfied with God's will, and the passage "thy will be done" in the Lord's Prayer is always decisive for me.

Der Kanzler, Otto von Bismarck in seinen Briefen, Reden und Erinnerungen (Ebenhausen, 1915), pp. 173, 211, 384, 273 ff. (Trans. George L. Mosse.)

Heinrich von Treitschke (1834-1896), historian and publicist, was one of the intellectual leaders of German nationalism. His nationalism was much more extreme than that of Bismarck. The following passages, written during the Franco-Prussian War of 1870, show how this nationalism was combined with hostility toward France.

We are not callous about the terrible woe which this war will bring **172** to hundreds of thousands: who could feel indifferent amidst our armed people, where each household has pledged its best and most loved ones for the great decision? Nevertheless, it must be said: it is a blessed necessity which forces us Germans to construct our nation in two big wars. The task of stilling the quarrels of many centuries cannot be solved without the existence of idealistic and moral forces which can only be released through a just war. It is not fit for Germans to repeat the prayers of the ordinary apostles of peace, or of the priests of Mammon, nor to close their eyes to the grim truth that we live in an age of wars. What terrific wars have swept over the world in a short fifteen years: in the Crimea, in East India, in Italy, in America, in Bohemia and now on the Rhine! If this time is one of iron, then it is necessary for the morality of the world that there exist one nation which, besides the idealism of learning, guards the idealism of war. . . .

We, however, begin this war in the belief that it cannot end differently than with a victory of Germany, and with the decision to square the terribly sinful account which has accrued since the rape of Lorraine. We do not lament that fate has given us the task to lead this fight for Europe all alone. The arrogance of France, which sits on Europe like an oppressive nightmare, feeds on the memory that hitherto only European coalitions could beat that nation on its own soil. Such overconfidence will not bow until one single, politically not yet wholly united people, brandishes the arms of victory over France. . . .

At a time when Alsace fell to the rule of France, our Reich lay disunited; the flame of the German spirit which once gave light to Europe seemed extinguished; Germany bent before the more mighty state and the superior culture of the French. Nevertheless, the French did not succeed in destroying the characteristics of the German folk on the Upper Rhine. Since that time the life of our people has been a steady gaining of strength. We are superior today to the French in number and density of population. How often have their war mongers asked for new conquests on the Rhine, because France could not remain in step with the growth of our population— as if we Germans had the duty to help the Latin lack of morals, and weakness of body, through periodical deliveries of fresh German blood. We have destroyed the rules of their art and can safely put the free development of our scholarly and religious life side by side with theirs. We have developed our richer and more grandiose language to a point of freedom and *finesse* which does not have to fear comparison with the French language. Yes, even the advantages of their older culture, the fine tone and manners of daily intercourse, are vanishing since the impudent cheekiness of the Parisian *demimonde* has almost blotted out the distinction between the good and the debased society. . . .

The powerful stream of strength of the German folk which once before broke out in the Middle Ages, and rolled over the Slavic lands of the Northeast, rolls today back, towards the West, in order to fructify anew its old and sanded bed, the beautiful homelands of German stock. In those same countries of the West where the old Reich once suffered its deepest humiliation, the new victory today completes the new Reich; and this Prussia, abused so often in the German tongue, builds us the nation which, full of arms and thoughts, shall proudly walk from century to century.

Heinrich von Treitschke, *Zehn Jahre deutscher Kämpfe* (Berlin, 1897), pp. 309-10, 315-16, 327-28, 369. (Trans. George L. Mosse.)

In the first half of the nineteenth century Germany was as backward economically as she was politically, and for some of the same reasons— political fragmentation, mutual petty jealousies, and an exaggerated spirit of provincialism. In the 1830's the first railways were built, and within two decades all the principal cities were connected by this modern form of transportation. Simultaneously the Zollverein (customs union), which became effective on January 1, 1834, made of Germany a single free trade area. The combined effect of these two institutions was to create a unified German economy and to promote rapid industrialization. By 1870, Germany had surpassed France, until then the most important industrial nation on the continent, in its output of industrial products.

In the following selection Friedrich List, a publicist and promoter of both railways and the customs union, expounds on the relationship between economic development and political unity (1841).

. . . we have proved that national unity is an essential condition of **173** durable prosperity; we have shown that only where private interest has been subordinate to public interest, and where a succession of generations has pursued one object, have nations attained an harmonious development of their productive power, that without the collective labors of the individuals of not merely one generation, but even of successive generations, towards a common end, private industry cannot flourish.

If there be any country destined to manufacturing industry, it is undoubtedly Germany. The high rank she occupies in science, in the fine arts, and in literature, as well as in reference to education, public administration, and institutions of public utility; her moral and religious sense, her love of labor and economy, her dogged perseverance, her inventive genius, her great and powerful population, the extent and the nature of her territory, the development of her agriculture, her national, social, and intellectual resources, all these circumstances, and many more, indicate her special vocation to manufacturing industry.

If any country has a right to expect from the protective system, appropriate to its position, advantageous results in the development of its manufactures, in the increase of its foreign trade and shipping, for the improvement of its ways of communication, in the prosperity of its agriculture, as well as in the consolidation of its power, in the guarantees of its independence, and in the increase of its influence abroad, that country is Germany.

We fear not to affirm that on the perfecting of the protective system depends the active life, the independence, and the duration of German nationality. The national mind cannot take deep root, cannot bear beautiful flowers and abundant fruits, but on the soil of general competency. From the unity of material interests only can moral unity issue; from both united, flow the power of the nation. What signifies all our efforts, whatever we may be, governors or governed, nobles, citizens, learned or illiterate, men of war, or men of state, manufacturers, agriculturists, or tradesmen, if we have no nationality; if we want a security for the duration of our nationality?

But the German protective system will have but imperfectly performed its mission, so long as the thread of cotton and flax which Germany uses or weaves shall not be of her own spinning; so long as she imports not directly the tropical commodities she consumes, paying for them with the productions of her own manufactories; so long as she shall not accomplish all this by the aid of her own ships, making her flag everywhere respected; so long as she shall not possess a complete system of internal communications, by rivers, canals, and railroads; so long as the Customs-Union shall not extend to her whole sea-coast, as well as to Holland and Belgium.

Friedrich List, *National System of Political Economy* (Philadelphia, 1856), pp. 243, 488–89.

QUESTIONS

1. In what sense did Bismarck believe German unification to be a conservative enterprise?
2. Can you arrive at a definition of what Bismarck means by "freedom"?
3. Why does Treitschke think that war is a good thing?
4. What are the accusations which Treitschke levels against France? Do you think that these accusations have any foundations in fact?
5. Do you see any difference between Bismarck's thoughts, as put forth in these documents, and those of Treitschke?
6. How does Friedrich List justify a protective system for the German economy?

CHAPTER XXVIII

THE UNIFICATION OF ITALY

THE VIENNA SETTLEMENT of 1815 had left Italy divided into small nation states, with Austrian influence preponderant in the north. The system of government was arbitrary, and the situation contained an affront both to liberalism and to nationalism.

Apart from certain ideas of home rule for Lombardy and Venetia (as put forward by Manin just before the 1848 revolution), opinion easily crystallized on expulsion of the Austrians and overthrow of other tyrannical governments. What was not so easy to decide was what to put in their place.

Three main solutions were put forward. The first was a federation of liberal states under the presidency of the pope. Although somewhat attractive due to Italy's peculiar conditions, this proposal never attained any practical importance. The second was a single Republic, appealing to youth, and centering upon the Roman tradition, a Rome of the Italian people to succeed the Rome of the emperors and the popes (174). This idea of Mazzini had two great defects: it frightened all moderate men, and it ignored the special position of the pope as a temporal ruler. The third was to base unification upon the kingdom of Piedmont. This would be practicable, since it would have a nucleus of political, administrative, and military organization. It would conciliate the more conservative elements. It would make possible diplomatic maneuvers with other powers.

It was this third solution which came to be adopted. Italy was unified as the result of: the strengthening of Piedmont by Cavour (175); the temporary alliance with France against Austria in 1859; the unofficial expedition of Garibaldi, and Piedmontese intervention in his support in 1860; the Austro-Prussian and Franco-Prussian wars, which diverted from Italy the attention of interested and hostile European powers. By 1870, Italy was completely unified under Piedmontese leadership, and the papacy had ceased to be a temporal power.

Mazzini (1805–1872) was the catalyst of Italian unity. His "Young Italy" was a group designed to propagandize the cause. These extracts illustrate aspects of Mazzini's thought.

174   Young Italy is a brotherhood of Italians who believe in the law of *Progress* and *Duty,* and are convinced that Italy is destined to become one nation. . . . They join this association in the firm intent of consecrating both thought and action to the great aim of reconstituting Italy as one independent sovereign nation of free men and equals. . . .

Young Italy is Republican and . . . dedicated to a United Italy.

The means by which Young Italy proposes to reach its aim are: education and insurrection, to be adopted simultaneously. . . .

The priesthood preach ignorance in the name of the God of truth; and abject submission in the name of the God of battles. They storm against the irreligion, incredulity and wickedness of an epoch which, like all great revolutionary epochs, is essentially religious; against those who, strong in virtue and self-sacrifice, seek to elevate the creature from the dust in the name of the Creator, and restore to man the consciousness of his origin and of his mission; and against enterprises having for their aim the destruction of the anarchy produced by tyranny, and the union of humanity in the name of the spirit of love. . . . Humanity will not stop short because unaccompanied by the depositaries of the ancient creed. The religious idea exists in and for humanity. . . .

You are citizens, you have a country, in order that in a given and limited sphere of action the assistance of a certain number of men, already related to you by language, tendencies and customs, may enable you to labor more effectually for the good of all men. . . .

Never deny your sister Nations. Be it yours to evolve the life of your country in loveliness and strength, free from all servile fears and skeptical doubts, maintaining as its basis the People; as its guide the consequences of the principles of its Religious Faith, logically and energetically applied; its strength the united strength of all; its aim the fulfillment of the mission given to it by God.

And so long as you are ready to die for Humanity, the life of your Country will be immortal. . . .

Sacred in the hand of Judith was the sword that took the life of Holofernes; sacred was the dagger which Harmodius encircled with roses; sacred the dagger of Brutus; sacred the stiletto of the Sicilian who began the Vespers; sacred the arrow of Tell. Whenever justice is extinct, and the terror of a single tyrant cancels and denies the conscience of a people, and the God who willed them free—if a man, pure from hatred and of every bitter passion—arises in the religion of Country, and in the name of the Eternal Right incarnate within him, and says to him: "You torture millions of my brothers; you withhold from them that which God has decreed theirs; you destroy their bodies and corrupt their souls; through you my Country dies a lingering death; you are the keystone of an entire edifice of slavery, dishonour and wrong; I overthrow that edifice by destroying you," I recognize in that manifestation of tremendous equality between the tyrant of millions and a single individual, the finger of God. Most men feel in their hearts as I do. I express it. . . .

The Life and Writings of Joseph Mazzini (London: Smith, Elder & Co., 1890–91), I, 96, 106, 253, 254; IV, 280; VI, 276, 277.

Count Camillo Benso di Cavour (1810–1861), prime minister of Piedmont, was the political architect of Italian unity. In his correspondence with the Countess of Circourt, he reflects on the problems faced by Italy in the crucial year of 1860 and gives his philosophy of government.

Italy finds herself in a most critical position. It is not very convenient to **175** work with diplomacy on one side of the street and to have Garibaldi on the other. I still hope that we will be able to draw ourselves out of this dilemma, and that we will be able to found our Nation on the solid principles of order and liberty; despite the defiance of the absolutists and the follies of the Republicans. . . .

For my part, I have no confidence in dictatorships, and above all in civilian dictatorships. I believe that one can do things with a Parliament which are impossible with absolute power. Experience of thirteen years has convinced me that a ministry which is honest and energetic, which has nothing to fear from demagogic revelations, and which is not in the mood to be intimidated by the violence of parties, has everything to gain from Parliamentary battles. I have never felt myself weak, except when Parliament was closed. Moreover, I am not able to betray my background or to deny the principles of my whole life. If a veil has to be drawn over the statue [of Liberty] it is not for me to do so. If one could persuade the Italians that they were in need of a dictatorship, they would choose Garibaldi and not myself. And they would have reason to make that choice. The Parliamentary way is the longer path, but it is the surer one. . . .

The majority of the nation is monarchical, the army is free of all Garibaldian taint, the Capitalists are ultraconservative. If with these ingredients we do not tide over our difficulties, we are great imbeciles.

Le Comte de Cavour et La Comtesse de Circourt, Letters inédites, publiées par Le Comte Nigra (Turin-Rome: L. Roux & Cie, 1894), pp. 106–9. (Trans. George L. Mosse.)

QUESTIONS

1. List the main points of Mazzini's idea on nationalism and contrast these with Bismarck's ideas (see p. 328).
2. How does Mazzini combine humanitarianism and the idea of a holy war?
3. Why did Cavour think Italy in a critical position in 1860? How did he, in fact, emerge from this position?

CHAPTER XXIX

RUSSIA IN THE NINETEENTH CENTURY

THE NAPOLEONIC WARS brought Russia directly into contact with both Western liberalism and conservatism (176, 177). They also brought into sharper focus the perennial question: What is Russia's place and mission in the world? This question involved more specifically Russia's relations with the West. It was inevitable that these colliding cross-currents should have brought turmoil to Russia in the nineteenth century. As royal absolutism led to increasing oppression in the reigns of Alexander I and Nicholas I (177, 178), sensitive Russians, who were highly aware of liberal movements in the West, were bound to react. The Decembrist revolt of 1825 clearly shows that the rise of a revolutionary movement against royal absolutism was a theme in Russian history long before the importation of Marxian socialism (179).

On the other hand, the growth of Russian nationalism and imperialism, which was the result of the traditional Russian desire to compete on a par with the Western powers and to secure Russia's position in the world, brought Russia into conflict with the West. Foreign wars and domestic crises had an intimate connection in modern Russian history (180, 181). In the middle of the nineteenth century Russia's defeat in the Crimean War forced Alexander II's government to inaugurate the Great Reforms, especially the abolition of serfdom. However, instead of heeding the advice of liberal elements to continue his father's reforms (182), Alexander III preferred the counsel of reactionaries (183, 184). This choice eventually contributed to the double crisis of 1905—defeat by the Japanese and a revolution at home, and the double crisis of 1917—defeat in the World War and the downfall of the Russian monarchy.

I. THE REIGN OF ALEXANDER I (1801–25)

The following is a description of Napoleon's entry into Moscow in 1812 and his retreat from the southern Russian capital. This episode marked the beginning of Napoleon's terrible flight from Russia and his eventual defeat in Europe. Moreover, it marked a high point in the development of modern Russian nationalism. It is noteworthy that the Russian name for the War of 1812—"the Great Fatherland War" —is also the name used by the Soviet Union for the second World War. The following account, based largely on French sources, was written by the Russian historian Eugene Tarle.

176   At two o'clock in the afternoon Napoleon with his suite ascended Poklonnaya Hill, and Moscow unfolded before their eyes. A bright sun shone down on the vast city sparkling with innumerable golden domes. The Old Guard, following Napoleon's suite, suddenly forgot discipline. They broke ranks and rushed upon the hill. Thousands of voices cried: 'Moscow! Moscow! Long live the Emperor!' And again: 'Moscow! Moscow!' On the peak of the hill, Napoleon stopped and, unable to restrain his joy, also exclaimed: 'Moscow!' Count Ségur, who was present, tells us that the marshals promptly forgot their resentment and, 'drunken with the enthusiasm of glory,' rushed towards the Emperor with congratulations: 'Here, at last, is the famous city!' Napoleon said: 'It was time!' Even in this moment of triumph Napoleon did not forget what it had cost him to win the great Eurasian beauty.

Not Milan, or Venice, or Alexandria and Cairo, or Jaffa, or Berlin, or Lisbon, or Madrid, or Warsaw, or Amsterdam, or Rome, or Antwerp— not a single capital his troops had entered as victors—had in his eyes and in the eyes of his army such a tremendous political significance as Moscow, the connecting link between Europe and Asia, the key to world domination. In Moscow the Emperor expected that Alexander would sue for peace; the army expected warm apartments, plentiful provisions, all the comforts and indulgences of a big city after an agonizing campaign marked by starvation rations, absence of drinking water, sultry heat, and constant clashes with a brave and stubborn foe.

Persons who experienced these hours on Poklonnaya Hill, generals of the suite and the Old Guard, the guards themselves, said later that for them this was the culminating point of the campaign of 1812; they were then ready to believe that the resistance of the Russian people was broken, and that the signing of a truce, followed by peace, was but a matter of days.

The sun began to set in the west. Murat with his cavalry had already entered the city, and, in a parallel stream, somewhat to the left, the corps of Beauharnais. Napoleon wished to receive a deputation from the city here, on Poklonnaya Hill, and he knew that the first thing Murat and Eugène would do on entering the city would be to get in touch with the Moscow authorities and Moscow population, who would be directed to send this deputation with the keys of the city.

But no deputation appeared. Suddenly an incredible report began to spread, first among the Guard, then among the suite, till it reached Napoleon: there would be no deputation from the inhabitants in Moscow. Moscow had been abandoned by the entire population. This news seemed to Napoleon so preposterous that at first he simply refused to believe it. Finally he decided to abandon Poklonnaya Hill and he rode up to Dorogomilov Gate. There he summoned Count Daru: 'Moscow is empty! Incredible! We must enter. Go and bring me some of the Boyars!' Napoleon, apparently, had received the impression from his spies that the higher aristocrats in Russia bore the formal title of 'Boyars,' as those in England were called Lords.

Daru rode into the city but soon returned without any 'Boyars.' He merely confirmed that the city was empty, that its inhabitants had vanished. 'But such was Napoleon's stubbornness, that he insisted on waiting,' wrote Ségur, the most truthful of Napoleon's worshippers. 'Finally, an officer, either anxious to please or convinced that everything desired by the Emperor must take place, penetrated the city, caught five or six vagrants, and, pushing them forward with his horse, brought them into the presence of the Emperor, imagining that he had brought a deputation. From the very first answer of these unfortunates, Napoleon saw that he had before him but a few pitiful day-labourers.' . . .

Everything was quiet, silent, dead. Here and there, at street intersections, a few persons lounged about. Later, the French spoke of their uncanny feeling as they moved past the vacant windows and doors of the great city.

They realized that the people were not hiding, that these houses and yards were empty, that no one was in the city. Actually, a few thousand persons of all sorts remained—no exact count was possible. There were those who just hadn't managed to get away; there were foreigners—Frenchmen, Swiss, Italians, Poles, Germans—who hoped that the conqueror would show himself kind; and there were a few Russian soldiers who had deserted or who just happened to stray into the city. But these few thousand persons were lost in the vast emptiness. . . .

Before sunset, Napoleon was informed by Murat, Poniatowski, and Eugène that the city had been occupied without opposition. Napoleon decided not to spend his first night (14-15 September) in the Kremlin, but in one of the abandoned houses near Dorogomilov Gate, where he had stopped with his suite after leaving Poklonnaya Hill. He was very gloomy. 'What a terrible desert!' he exclaimed, surveying the desolate streets. This was quite different from his entrance into the European capitals, or Alexandria.

Even before he retired for the night several adjutants and orderlies came to report from various parts of the city. Each had one and the same story to tell: fires were breaking out everywhere.

Napoleon did not at once realize the full significance of this fact. At first he assumed that the soldiers of his army were looting the abandoned houses and that their carelessness was responsible for the fires. Actual reports of looting were coming in. He summoned Marshal Mortier, whom he had just appointed Military Governor of Moscow, and sternly commanded him to stop the pillaging. 'You will answer with your head for this!' the Emperor added.

He had not yet fallen asleep, when, at three o'clock in the morning, he was informed that the heart of the city was on fire. Gostinny Dvor, the centre of Moscow trade, was aflame; houses never entered by a French soldier, and situated in districts to which no French soldier had penetrated, were burning. The wind blew furiously, the sparks fell like a dense rain of fire and ignited the neighbouring buildings. The sun rose, and in the daylight dense clouds of smoke floated over the city. . . .

But by the morning of 15 September, the full weight of the catastrophe was clear. The fires begun the night before had spread over half of the city and were increasing.

First of all, the Wine Arcade burned down, with the New Arcades and the Market Stalls, and a powder magazine blew up. Then, in several places simultaneously, houses and churches began to burn, 'in particular, all the factories . . .'—'These fires continued for six days on end, so that it was difficult to distinguish between night and day. During all this time, looting continued.' . . .

That night Napoleon was awakened by the bright light which suddenly illumined his windows. Half awakened by the glow, the officers of his suite thought that morning had come. The Emperor went to one window, then to another; he looked out on all sides, and everywhere the spectacle was the same: an unendurably bright light, immense sheets of flame, streets transformed into rivers of fire, palaces and large houses all burning like vast bonfires. A powerful gale fanned the flames and drove them straight on the Kremlin; the moan of the wind was so strong that at times it interrupted and drowned the crash of collapsing buildings and the howl of the raging flames.

Napoleon, his suite, and the Old Guard were staying in the Kremlin. The previous day the French artillery stores had been brought there, and the powder magazine, abandoned by the Russian garrison because of the lack of facilities to transport it, was still in the fortress. A raging wind bore the flames towards the Kremlin. One of its towers was already on fire. It was necessary to leave at once, without wasting a minute. Napoleon was very pale but had recovered self-possession. He gazed silently through the window of the palace and said: 'They themselves are setting it afire. What a people! They are Scythians!' Later he said: 'What resoluteness! The barbarians! What a terrible spectacle!' . . .

He left the fortress accompanied by his suite and the Old Guard, but all of them nearly perished in this effort to save themselves. The Viceroy, Ségur, Berthier, and Murat walked with the Emperor. They never forgot this exit from the Kremlin. Count Ségur's well-known description follows:

'We were besieged by an ocean of flames: flames closed all our exits from the fortress before us and repulsed our first attempts to leave. We finally found a narrow path between the stone walls leading to the Moskva River. By this narrow passage, Napoleon, his officers, and his Guard managed to escape from the Kremlin. But what had they gained? Being closer to the fire, they could neither retreat nor remain where they were. But how could they advance, how plunge into the waves of this fiery sea? Those who ran about in the streets, stupefied by the gale, blinded by the ashes, could not recognize where they were, because the streets vanished in smoke and ruins. But haste was imperative. Every instant the roar of the flames grew louder. The only street, winding and all in flames, seemed more like an entrance into the inferno than an exit from it. Without wavering, the Emperor, on foot, dashed into the dangerous passage. He strode forward through the flaming bonfires, to the crash of collapsing arches, falling rafters, and melting iron roofs. The ruins hindered his footsteps . . . We walked upon burning ground, between two walls of fire. The piercing heat burned our eyes, but we had to keep them open and alert to the danger. The stifling air, the flying sparks, and tongues of flame scorched the air we breathed; our breath grew dry, short, gasping and we almost choked from the smoke . . .'

Napoleon and his suite were saved by marauding soldiers who happened to be in the neighbourhood.

The Emperor moved to the Petrovsky Palace. For two days longer, the seventeenth and eighteenth, the fire raged, destroying three fourths of the city. Sporadic fires continued after that, and during the entire stay of the French in Moscow there was scarcely any day without its fire. Napoleon was in the gloomiest state of mind. 'This presages great misfortunes for us,' he said, looking at the ruins and smoking debris into which the wealthiest parts of the city had been turned. What mattered was not merely the unexpected loss of the conquered booty. The Emperor clearly realized that peace with Alexander would now be even more difficult than before. He did not yet understand that a peace with Russia was not only difficult but impossible, that for the Russian people the war which he considered ended by the capture of Moscow was only beginning. . . .

Peace! Immediate peace with Alexander—this became Napoleon's first and chief aim after the Moscow fire. And in this he was to meet the greatest disappointment of his entire career.

Eugene Tarle, *Napoleon's Invasion of Russia, 1812* (New York: Oxford University Press, 1942), pp. 229–31, 232–33, 235, 237–38, 239–40, 244. (Reprinted by permission of the publisher.)

Though a liberal in the first half of his reign, Alexander I turned to conservatism after the Napoleonic invasion. In foreign policy this meant an adherence to Metternich's principle of "legitimacy," the defense of thrones against popular sovereignty. In domestic affairs it meant stifling liberal thought through conformism. The following excerpts are from instructions to the director of the University of Kazan which were written by M. L. Magnitskii and confirmed by Alexander I on January 17, 1820.

177 1. The aim of the government in educating students is to bring up faithful sons of the Orthodox Church, faithful subjects of the sovereign, and good and useful citizens of the fatherland.

2. The soul of education and the prime virtue of the citizen is—obedience. Obedience is the most important virtue of the young: only in youth,

through the exercise of obedience, does the will receive that pliancy which will remain for life and which is so necessary to the social welfare. Therefore it is the obligation of the director to see to it at all times that religious lessons on love and obedience be carried out in practise; that the university students might always observe around them examples of the most strict respect for authority on the part of instructors and superintendents, and that the slightest violation always be punished, regardless of the offender's position.

3. Inasmuch as religion binds obligation to the will . . . , the director is required above all to see to it, under the strictest personal responsibility and by all the means of authority granted to him, that the university students be instilled with respect and love for the teachings of the Holy Gospel. For this he is required to take care:

a) That the spirit of free thought, whether openly or secretly, not be permitted to weaken the teachings of the Church in lectures dealing with philosophy, history or literature. The director is required to obtain reliable information concerning the outlook of university instructors, to attend their lectures frequently, to inspect at intervals the notebooks of students, to see to it that nothing harmful might escape censorship, and to take diligent care that all employees of the university fulfill the duties of their respective religion (the Christian, of course) in regularly attending church services and in receiving the sacraments.

b) That no harmful or seductive literature or speeches in any form whatever be permitted to spread through the university. . . .

III. *Regarding Courses of Instruction in the Department of Natural Philosophy*

In order to avoid that confusion of ideas which is so frequently observed in education as the result of the nonconformity of various philosophical systems, the professor is required to bring them together under one principle and to show how limited truth, which serves as the subject of speculative philosophy, could substitute for the truth of Christianity before the advent of the Savior of the world; and how it is now permitted to be a part of our education only as a useful exercise of the mind, for sharpening the mental faculties so as to apprehend other humane studies which are founded on philosophical principles. . . . Students must be convinced that all which is not in accord with Holy Writ is error and falsehood and should be rejected without any pity; that only those philosophical theories are fundamental and true which agree with the teachings of the Gospel; for the truth is one, while error is legion.

IV. *Regarding the Department of Political Science*

Beneficial instruction in the political sciences should demonstrate that the monarchical form of government is the most ancient and established by God Himself, that the divine right of monarchs, exercised in lawful succession and within those limits which are peculiar to the development and the spirit of each people, emanates from God, and that the laws established by such an order are the expression of the will of the Highest. . . . The morality of this subject should be pure, and thus the instructor is required to show repugnance at the deceptions of Machiavelli and of Hobbes. . . .

V. *Regarding the Department of Physics and Mathematics*

1) The professor of theoretical and experimental physics is required, throughout his course, to refer to God's wisdom and to the limited nature of our senses and means which we use in apprehending the wonders which constantly surround us.

2) The professor of natural history will show how the vast realm of nature, no matter how wise it may seem to us or how inconceivable, is but a pale reflection of that higher order to which, after a short life, we are all destined.

S. S. Dmitriev and M. V. Nechkina, *Khrestomatiia po istorii SSSR* (2nd ed.; Moscow, 1949), II, 524–26. (Trans. Michael Petrovich.)

II. THE REIGN OF NICHOLAS I (1825–55)

Alexander I's brother Nicholas came to the throne of Russia amid the turbulence of a revolt led by liberal army officers in December, 1825. The following selections, written by leaders of the Decembrist uprising while under arrest after the failure of their *coup,* show that this was not just another palace revolution in Russian history but a genuine, though abortive, attempt to gain liberal reforms.

Extract from Pestel's Testimony

178   QUESTION 6: How did the revolutionary ideas gradually develop and become implanted in men's minds? Who first conceived these ideas and continued to preach and spread them throughout the State?

ANSWER 6: This question is very difficult to answer, for it must go beyond the realm of discussion about the secret Society. However, in order to fulfill the demand of the Committee I shall try so far as I can to explain it.

Political books are in the hands of everyone; political science is taught and political news spread everywhere. These teach all to discuss the activities and conduct of the Government, to praise one thing and assail another. A survey of the events of 1812, 1813, 1814, and 1815, likewise of the preceding and following periods, will show how many thrones were toppled over, how many others were established, how many kingdoms were destroyed, and how many new ones were created; how many Sovereigns were expelled, how many returned or were invited to return and were then again driven out; how many revolutions were accomplished; how many *coups d'état* carried out—all these events familiarized the minds of men with the idea of revolutions, with their possibilities, and with the favorable occasions on which to execute them. Besides that, every century has its peculiar characteristic: ours is marked by revolutionary ideas. From one end of Europe to the other, the same thing is observed, from Portugal to Russia, without the exception of a single state, not even England or Turkey, those two opposites. The same spectacle is presented also in the whole of America. The spirit of reform causes mental fermentation (*faire bouillir les esprits*). Here are the causes, I think, which gave rise to revolutionary ideas and which have implanted them in the minds of the people. As to the cause of the spread of the spirit of reform through the country, it could not be ascribed to the Society, for the organization was still too small to have any popular influence.

Extract from a Letter of Kakhovsky to General Levashev

Your Excellency,
Dear Sir!

The uprising of December 14 is a result of causes related above. I see, Your Excellency, that the Committee established by His Majesty is making a great effort to discover all the members of the secret Society. But the government will not derive any notable benefit from that. We were not trained within the Society but were already ready to work when we joined it. The origin and the root of the Society one must seek in the spirit of the time and in our state of mind. I know a few belonging to the secret Society but am inclined to think the membership is not very large. Among my many acquaintances who do not adhere to secret societies very few are opposed to my opinions. Frankly I state that among thousands of young men there are hardly a hundred who do not passionately long for freedom. These youths, striving with pure and strong love for the welfare of their Fatherland, toward true enlightenment, are growing mature.

The people have conceived a sacred truth—that they do not exist for governments, but that governments must be organized for them. This is the cause of struggle in all countries; peoples, after tasting the sweetness of enlightenment and freedom, strive toward them; and governments, surrounded by millions of bayonets, make efforts to repel these peoples back into the darkness of ignorance. But all these efforts will prove in vain; impressions once received can never be erased. Liberty, that torch of intellect and warmth of life, was always and everywhere the attribute of peoples emerged from primitive ignorance. We are unable to live like our ancestors, like barbarians or slaves.

But even our ancestors, though less educated, enjoyed civil liberty. During the time of Tsar Aleksei Mikhailovich the National Assembly, including representatives of various classes of the people, still functioned and participated in important affairs of the State. In his reign, five such Assemblies were summoned. Peter I, who killed everything national in the State, also stamped out our feeble liberty. This liberty disappeared outwardly but lived within the hearts of true citizens; its advancement was slow in our country. Wise Catherine II expanded it a little; Her Majesty inquired from the Petersburg Free Economic Society concerning the value and consequences of the emancipation of peasants in Russia. This great beneficial thought lived in the heart of the Empress, whom the people loved. Who among Russians of her day and time could have read her INSTRUCTION without emotion? The INSTRUCTION alone redeems all the shortcoming of that time, characteristic of that century.

Emperor Alexander promised us much; he, it could be said, enormously stirred the minds of the people toward the sacred rights of humanity. Later he changed his principles and intentions. The people became frightened, but the seed had sprouted and the roots grew deep. So rich with various revolutions are the latter half of the past century and the events of our own time that we have no need to refer to distant ones. We are witnesses of great events. The discovery of the New World and the United States, by virtue of its form of government, have forced Europe into rivalry with her. The United States will shine as an example even to distant generations. The name of Washington, the friend and benefactor of the people, will pass from generation to generation; the memory of his devotion to the welfare of the Fatherland will stir the hearts of citizens. In France the revolution which began so auspiciously turned, alas, at the end from a lawful into a criminal one. However, not the people but court intrigues and politics were responsible for that. The revolution in France shook all the thrones of Europe and had a greater influence upon the governments and peoples than the establishment of the United States.

The dominance of Napoleon and the war of 1813 and 1814 united all the European nations, summoned by their monarchs and fired by the call to freedom and citizenship. By what means were countless sums collected among citizens? What guided the armies? They preached freedom to us in Manifestoes, Appeals, and in Orders! We were lured and, kindly by nature, we believed, sparing neither blood nor property. Napoleon was overthrown! The Bourbons were called back to the throne of France and, submitting to circumstances, gave that brave, magnanimous nation a constitution, pledging themselves to forget the past. The Monarchs united into a Holy Alliance; congresses sprang into existence, informing the nations that they were assembled to reconcile all classes and introduce political freedom. But the aim of these congresses was soon revealed; the nations learned how greatly they had been deceived. The Monarchs thought only of how to retain their unlimited power, to support their shattered thrones, and to extinguish the last spark of freedom and enlightenment. . . .

The story told to Your Excellency that, in the uprising of December 14 the rebels were shouting "Long live the Constitution!" and that the people were asking "What is Constitution, the wife of His Highness the Grand Duke?" is not true. It is an amusing invention. We knew too well the meaning of a constitution and we had a word that would equally stir the hearts of all classes—LIBERTY! . . .

The events of December are calamitous for us and, of course, must be distressing to the Emperor. Yet the events of this date should be fortunate for His Imperial Highness. After all, it was necessary sometime for the Society to begin its activities, but hardly could it have been so precipitate as in this instance. I swear to God, I wish the kind Sovereign prosperity! May God aid him in healing the wounds of our Fatherland and to become a friend and benefactor of the people. . . .

Most obedient and devoted servant of Your Excellency,

1826, February, 24th day   *Peter Kakhovsky*

Anatole G. Mazour, *The First Russian Revolution, 1825* (Berkeley: University of California Press, 1937), pp. 273–77. (Reprinted by permission of the publisher.)

Instead of liberal reform Nicholas I inaugurated a reign of such oppression that it disgusted even as enthusiastic an adherent of absolute monarchy as the French Marquis de Custine, who visited Russia in 1839. "I went to Russia in search of arguments against representative government," he wrote in his memoirs. "I returned from Russia a partisan of constitutions. . . ." The French aristocrat's memoirs, from which the following extracts are taken, were first published in 1846. A century later they were recommended reading for members of the United States Embassy in Stalin's Moscow. As a recent American Ambassador to the Soviet Union, Walter Bedell Smith, has said of Custine's memoirs, "I could have taken many pages verbatim from his journal and, after substituting present-day names and dates for those of a century ago, have sent them to the State Department as my own official reports."

179   What an extraordinary country this must be to produce only slaves receiving on bended knee opinion that has been made for them, spies who have no opinion—the better to grasp that of others, or scoffers who exaggerate the evil—another shrewd way of avoiding the observant eye of foreigners; but even this finesse becomes a confession, for what other people has ever believed it necessary to have recourse to this? The practice of mystifying foreigners is unknown except in Russia, and it serves to make us divine and understand the condition of society in this extraordinary land. . . .

. . . all foreigners are treated as criminals upon arrival at the Russian frontier. . . .

. . . everything was dismal, regulated as in a barracks or a camp; it was like war—but with less enthusiasm and less life. Military discipline dominates Russia. . . .

The Russian government is the discipline of the camp substituted for the civic order—it is a state of siege become the normal state of society. . . .

The more I see of Russia, the more I agree with the Emperor when he forbids Russians to travel and makes access to his own country difficult to foreigners. The political system of Russia could not withstand twenty years of free communication with Western Europe. . . .

The diplomatic corps and Westerners in general have always been considered by this government, with its Byzantine spirit, and by Russia as a whole, as malevolent and jealous spies. . . .

. . . In Russia, fear replaces, that is to say paralyzes, thought. . . .

I never cease to be astonished in seeing that there exists a people indifferent to the point of calmly living and dying in the dim light granted to it by its masters' police. Up to now, I believed that man could no more do without truth for the spirit than air and sun for the body; my journey to Russia disabuses me. Here, to lie is to protect the social order, to speak the truth is to destroy the State. . . .

Russia is a nation of mutes; some magician has changed sixty million men into automatons who await the wand of another magician to be reborn and to live. Nothing is lacking in Russia . . . except liberty, that is to say life. . . .

With this obedient people, the influence of social institutions is so great in all classes, the involuntary formation of habits dominates character to such a point that even the recent outbursts of vengeance seem to be regulated by a certain discipline. Calculated murder is executed in cadence; men kill other men militarily, religiously, without anger, without emotion, without words, with a calm more terrible than the delirium of hatred. They clash together; they are overturned; they are crushed; they run over each others' bodies, as machines turn regularly on their pivots. This physical impassiveness in the midst of the most violent actions, this monstrous audacity in conception, this coldness in execution, this silence of fury, this mute fanaticism, is, if one may so express himself, conscientious crime. A certain order contrary to nature presides in this astonishing country of the most unprecedented excesses; tyranny and revolt march in time, each regulating its step to that of the other. . . .

If better diplomats are found among the Russians than among highly civilized peoples, it is because our papers warn them of everything that happens and everything that is contemplated in our countries. Instead of disguising our weaknesses with prudence, we reveal them with vehemence every morning; whereas, the Russians' Byzantine policy, working in the shadow, carefully conceals from us all that is thought, done, and feared in their country. We proceed in broad daylight; they advance under cover; the game is one-sided. The ignorance in which they leave us blinds us; our sincerity enlightens them; we have the weakness of loquacity; they have the strength of secrecy. There, above all, is the cause of their cleverness. . . .

. . . But in a nation governed like this one passions boil a long time before breaking out; while the danger approaches from hour to hour, the evil is prolonged, and the crisis delayed. Even our grandchildren may not see the explosion; but we can say today that explosion is inevitable, while we cannot predict the time. . . .

In Russia, everything that meets your eye, everything that goes on around you is of a frightening regularity, and the first thought that comes to the mind of a traveler when he contemplates this symmetry is that such complete uniformity, such regularity, so contrary to the natural inclinations of man, could not have been achieved and cannot subsist without violence. Under such a régime man can know, and does know, from the first day of his life what he will see and what he will do to the last day of his life.

In Russia, the government dominates everything and gives life to nothing. In this vast Empire, the people, if they are not tranquil, are silent; death hovers over all heads and strikes them capriciously—this serves to create doubt of the supreme justice; there man has two coffins—the cradle and the tomb. . . .

A so-called strong government which pitilessly demands respect on all occasions must necessarily produce wretched men. Everything in a social order can serve the purposes of despotism, whether that social order be called a monarchy or a democracy. Wherever the operation of the political machine is rigorously exact, there is despotism. . . .

It would be necessary to stop and start over. Is such an effort possible? Can one take away the underpinnings of such a vast edifice? The too recent civilization of the Russian Empire, entirely artificial as it is, has already produced some real results that no human power would be able to annul. . . .

Peter I and Catherine II have given the world a great and useful lesson, for which Russia has paid. They have shown us that despotism is never so redoubtable as when it pretends to do good; for then it believes its most revolting deeds are exculpated by its professed intentions and the evil that is given as a remedy has no bounds. . . .

Russia sees Europe as a prey which our dissensions will sooner or later deliver up to her; she foments anarchy among us in the hope of profiting by a corruption she promotes because it is favorable to her views. . . .

. . . One word of truth hurled into Russia is like a spark landing in a keg of powder. . . .

When your son is discontented in France, use my formula; say to him: "Go to Russia." It is a journey that would be beneficial to every foreigner; for whoever has really seen Russia will find himself content to live anywhere else. It is always good to know that a society exists where no happiness is possible because, by a law of his nature, man cannot be happy unless he is free. . . .

Journey for Our Time, ed. Phyllis Penn Kohler (New York: Farrar, Straus & Cudahy, 1951), pp. 21, 42, 56, 74, 98, 145, 159–60, 179, 181, 217, 319, 320, 325, 330, 338. (Reprinted by permission of the publisher.)

III. THE REIGN OF ALEXANDER II (1855–81)

Russian defeats abroad have always had a profound effect on Russia's shaky structure at home. When Russia suffered a bad defeat in the Crimean War, the government of Alexander II tried to soften the blow by issuing an evasive Imperial Manifesto on March 19, 1856.

The stubborn sanguinary struggle which has convulsed Europe in the course of nearly three years has come to an end. It was not provoked by Russia, and even before its beginning our ever-memorable parent, who now rests in God, solemnly declared to all his faithful subjects and to all foreign lands that the only aim of his quest and desire was the protection of rights and a surcease of the oppression of our coreligionists in the East.

. . . Providence, in its inexplicable but always beneficent ways, has brought to pass the event which our ever-memorable and most beloved parent, and we, and with us all of Russia, desired so zealously and unanimously, that which was the prime aim of the war. The future lot and the rights of all Christians in the East have been made secure. The Sultan solemnly recognizes them, and as a result of this act of justice, the Ottoman Empire enters the community of European states. Russians! Your labors and sacrifices have not been in vain. A great deed has been accomplished, though by other, unforeseen means, and we can now with calm consciences put an end to these sacrifices and efforts, restoring precious peace to our beloved fatherland. In order to hasten the negotiation of the peace terms and to prevent, even for the future, the very thought of any show of vainglory or belligerence on our part, we have agreed to the establishment of certain special precautions against contact between our war vessels and those of the Turks in the Black Sea, and to the drawing of new boundary lines in the southern part of Bessarabia which is closest to the Danube. These concessions are not important in comparison with the burdens of a prolonged war and with the benefits which are promised by the pacification of the state which God has placed in our care.

May these benefits be fully achieved by the common efforts of ourselves and all our faithful subjects. With the help of Divine Providence, which has always been gracious to Russia, may her domestic welfare be established and perfected; may justice and mercy reign in her courts; may the desire for education and for every beneficial activity be developed everywhere and with a new intensity; and may all abide under the shadow of laws equally just for all, equally protecting all; may the fruits of the labor of the innocent find enjoyment in peace. Finally, and this is our prime and most fervent desire, may the light of the saving faith, which enlightens minds and strengthens hearts, preserve and ever increase social morality, that surest pledge of order and felicity.

S. S. Dmitriev and M. V. Nechkina, *op. cit.,* II, 789–90. (Trans. Michael Petrovich.)

Quick to see through the hypocrisy of the Imperial Manifesto of March 19, 1856, an underground student organization published an incisive parody which it distributed on the streets of Kharkov on April 15, 1856.

181   The stubborn sanguinary struggle, which began so happily, and which has been distinguished by the repeated defeats of our armies, has shaken the state and has endangered its security; meanwhile the forces of our enemies have increased through the adherence to their alliance of states which have till now maintained neutrality. Thus we are forced to sue for peace and to accept conditions dictated to us by the allied states, conditions which, though unfavorable and an insult to the honor of our people, are imposed by the game of fate, but for whose acceptance by us hymns of praise are sung to us in the foreign press.

These conditions are as follows: 1) Protection of the Eastern Christian is assumed by the five great powers; according to this provision Russia loses the rights which it had gained in the treaties of Küchük-Kainardji, Jassy, Bucharest and Adrianople, which gave Russia the sole right of a protectorate over the Eastern Christians. 2) Our fleet in the Black Sea is to be destroyed, except for a few small vessels; though Turkey is bound by a similar provision, she keeps the right to maintain in the Archipelago any kind of fleet she may desire, thus being in a position at the first opportunity to attack the southern regions of our empire, which remain unprotected as a result of the third provision. 3) All fortresses along the shores of the Black Sea which have not been demolished are to be demolished, and those already demolished are not to be rebuilt; the docks, arsenal and fortifications of Nikolaev are to be destroyed. 4) In order to prevent any hope in the recovery of the loser, the concert of powers has recognized the necessity of establishing between Russia and Turkey a new independent state, which we are obliged to recognize and which is to receive from our own cherished possessions the mouths of the Danube and a part of Bessarabia from the Danubian lakes to Khotin. 5) Kars, with all its towns, which we took from the Turks in the present war, is to be returned to Turkey.

. . . And so, Russians, your generous zeal for the glory of the fatherland, your sacrifices, your blood have been in vain. The people and the army have done all they could, but the inability and rapacity of the generals, the plundering by the high officials, engineers and contractors, our own unpreparedness, carelessness and negligence were the cause of our failure. Our parent, who is remembered by all Russians, persecuted and suppressed every development of the intellect, every impulse of true love for the fatherland. This is why in a moment so decisive for the fatherland there were found no worthy leaders, honorable engineers and officials.

Having presented the conditions of the present peace, we wish to express to our beloved Russian people our true gratitude. We thank you, good Russians, for your blindness, in which you cannot see all our abuses. We thank you for the truly bovine patience with which you endure all misery, all injustice, all the dark evils which emanate from our despotic government. We thank you for so zealously helping us parasites to destroy you, to use government funds, gained through your sweat and blood, for our own pleasure. We thank you for not desiring true education but rather trusting in our servants and your despoilers—the bishops and priests, who traffic in the Gospel truth and your consciences as you sleep in the darkness of ignorance. Sleep on, good Russians, until your last shirt falls from you in tatters, until your last drop of blood is drunk. Sleep on, faithful servants of the bishops and the priests who have sold and crucified Christ, the eternal truth incarnate. Take comfort in our promises of change in which there was not and will not be a word of truth! Be always as you are now! We are inexpressibly pleased with you!

S. S. Dmitriev and M. V. Nechkina, *op. cit.,* II, 807–9. (Trans. Michael Petrovich.)

IV. THE REIGN OF ALEXANDER III (1881–94)

On March 1, 1881, Alexander II signed an edict authorizing still another in a series of basic reforms for Russia—this time in the direction of parliamentary government. This edict did not, however, go into effect. The Tsar-Liberator was assassinated a few hours later by a member of a terrorist organization called the People's Will. For the Tsar's son and heir Alexander III came the moment to decide— whether to continue his father's reforms or whether to take the road of reaction. The following excerpts are from a letter sent to him nine days after the assassination of his father. It was written by members of the Executive Committee of the People's Will.

March 10, 1881. **182**

Your Majesty:

Although the Executive Committee understands fully the grievous oppression that you must experience at this moment, it believes that it has no right to yield to the feeling of natural delicacy which would perhaps dictate the postponement of the following explanation to another time. There is something higher than the most legitimate human feeling, and that is duty to one's country—the duty for which a citizen must sacrifice himself and his own feelings, and even the feelings of others. In obedience to this all-powerful duty we have decided to address you at once, waiting for nothing, as will wait for nothing the historical process that threatens us with rivers of blood and the most terrible convulsions.

The tragedy enacted on the Ekaterinski canal was not a mere casualty, nor was it unexpected. After all that had happened in the course of the previous decade it was absolutely inevitable; and in that fact consists its deep significance for a man who has been placed by fate at the head of governmental authority. Such occurrences can be explained as the results of individual malignity, or even of the evil disposition of "gangs," only by one who is wholly incapable of analyzing the life of a nation. For ten whole years—notwithstanding the strictest prosecution; notwithstanding the sacrifice by the late Emperor's Government of liberty, the interests of all classes, the interests of industry and commerce, and even its own dignity; notwithstanding the absolute sacrifice of everything in the attempt to suppress the revolutionary movement—that movement has obstinately extended, attracting to itself the best elements of the country,—the most energetic and self-sacrificing people of Russia,—and the revolutionists have carried on, for three years, a desperate partizan warfare with the administration.

You are aware, your Majesty, that the Government of the late Emperor could not be accused of a lack of energy. It hanged the innocent and the guilty, and filled prisons and remote provinces with exiles. Tens of so-called "leaders" were captured and hanged, and died with the courage and tranquillity of martyrs; but the movement did not cease—on the contrary it grew and strengthened. The revolutionary movement, your Majesty, is not dependent upon any particular individuals; it is a process of the social organism; and the scaffolds raised for its more energetic exponents are as powerless to save the out-grown order of things as the cross that was erected for the Redeemer was powerless to save the ancient world from the triumph of Christianity. The Government, of course, may yet capture and hang an immense number of separate individuals, it may break up a great number of separate revolutionary groups, it may even destroy the most important of existing revolutionary organizations; but all this will not change, in the slightest degree, the condition of affairs. Revolutionists are the creation of circumstances; of the general discontent of the people; of the striving of Russia after a new social framework. It is impossible to exterminate the whole people; it is impossible, by means of repression, to stifle its discontent. Discontent only grows the more when it is repressed. . . .

A dispassionate glance at the grievous decade through which we have just passed will enable us to forecast accurately the future progress of the revolutionary movement, provided the policy of the Government does not change. The movement will continue to grow and extend; deeds of a terroristic nature will increase in frequency and intensity, and the revolutionary organization will constantly set forth, in the places of destroyed groups, stronger and more perfect forms. Meanwhile the number of the discontented in the country will grow larger and larger; confidence in the Government, on the part of the people, will decline; and the idea of revolution—of its possibility and inevitability—will establish itself in Russia more and more firmly. A terrible explosion, a bloody hurly-burly, a revolutionary earthquake throughout Russia will complete the destruction of the old order of things. Upon what depends this terrible prospect? Yes, your Majesty, "terrible" and lamentable! Do not take this for a mere phrase. We understand, better than any one else can, how lamentable is the waste of so much talent and energy, the loss, in bloody skirmishes and in the work of destruction, of so much strength that, under other conditions, might have been expended in creative labor and in the development of the intelligence, the welfare, and the civil life of the Russian people. Whence proceeds this lamentable necessity for bloody conflict? It arises, your Majesty, from the lack in Russia of a real government in the true sense of that word. A government, in the very nature of things, should only give outward form to the aspirations of the people and effect to the people's will. But with us—excuse the expression—the Government has degenerated into a mere camarilla, and deserves the name of a usurping "gang" much more than does the Executive Committee.

Whatever may be the *intentions* of the Tsar, the *actions* of the Government have nothing in common with the popular welfare, or popular aspirations. The Imperial Government subjected the people to serfdom, put the masses into the power of the nobility, and is now openly creating the most injurious class of speculators and jobbers. All of its reforms result merely in a more perfect enslavement and a more complete exploitation of the people. It has brought Russia to such a pass that, at the present time, the masses of the people are in a state of pauperism and ruin; are subjected to the most humiliating surveillance, even at their own domestic hearths; and are powerless even to regulate their own communal and social affairs. The protection of the law and of the Government is enjoyed only by the extortionist and the exploiter, and the most exasperating robbery goes unpunished. But, on the other hand, what a terrible fate awaits the man who sincerely considers the general good! You know very well, your Majesty, that it is not only socialists who are exiled and prosecuted. Can it be possible that the *Government* is the guardian of such "order"? Is it not rather probable that this is the work of a "gang"—the evidence of a complete usurpation?

These are the reasons why the Russian Government exerts no moral influence, and has no support among the people. These are the reasons why Russia brings forth so many revolutionists. These are the reasons why even such a deed as Tsaricide excites in the minds of a majority of the people only gladness and sympathy. Yes, your Majesty! Do not be deceived by the reports of flatterers and sycophants—Tsaricide, in Russia, is popular.

From such a state of affairs there can be only two exits: either a revolution, absolutely inevitable and not to be averted by any punishments, or a voluntary turning of the Supreme Power to the people. In the interest of our native land, in the hope of preventing the useless waste of energy, in the hope of averting the terrible miseries that always accompany revolution, the Executive Committee approaches your Majesty with the advice to take the second course. Be assured, so soon as the Supreme Power ceases to rule arbitrarily, so soon as it firmly resolves to accede to the demands of the people's conscience and consciousness, you may, without fear, discharge the spies that disgrace the administration, send your guards back to their barracks, and burn the scaffolds that are demoralizing the people. The Executive Committee will voluntarily terminate its own existence, and the organizations formed about it will disperse, in order that their members may devote themselves to the work of culture among the people of their native land.

We address your Majesty as those who have discarded all prejudices, and who have suppressed the distrust created by the actions of the Government throughout a century. We forget that you are the representative of the authority that has so often deceived and that has so injured the people. We address you as a citizen and as an honest man. We hope that the feeling of personal exasperation will not extinguish in your mind your consciousness of your duties and your desire to know the truth. *We* also might feel exasperation. You have lost your father. We have lost not only our fathers, but our brothers, our wives, our children and our dearest friends. But we are ready to suppress personal feeling if it be demanded by the welfare of Russia. We expect the same from you.

We set no conditions for you—do not let our proposition irritate you. The conditions that are prerequisite to a change from revolutionary activity to peaceful labor are created, not by us, but by history. These conditions, in our opinion, are two.

1. A general amnesty to cover all past political crimes; for the reason that they were not crimes but fulfillments of civil duty.

2. The summoning of representatives of the whole Russian people to examine the existing framework of social and governmental life, and to remodel it in accordance with the people's wishes.

We regard it as necessary, however, to remind you that the legalization of the Supreme Power, by the representatives of the people, can be valid only in case the elections are perfectly free. For this reason such elections must be held under the following conditions.

1. Delegates are to be sent from all classes, without distinction, and in number are to be proportionate to the number of inhabitants.

2. There shall be no limitations, either for voters or delegates.

3. The canvass and the elections shall be absolutely unrestricted, and therefore the Government, pending the organization of the National Assembly, shall authorize, in the form of temporary measures,

a. Complete freedom of the press.

b. Complete freedom of speech.

c. Complete freedom of public meeting.

d. Complete freedom of election program.

This is the only way in which Russia can return to the path of normal and peaceful development.

We declare solemnly, before the people of our native land and before the whole world, that our party will submit unconditionally to the decisions of a National Assembly elected in the manner above indicated, and that we will not allow ourselves, in future, to offer violent resistance to any Government that the National Assembly may sanction.

And now, your Majesty, decide! Before you are two courses, and you are to make your choice between them. We can only trust that your intelligence and conscience may suggest to you the only decision that is compatible with the welfare of Russia, with your own dignity, and with your duty to your native land.

The Executive Committee.

George Kennan, *Siberia and the Exile System* (London: James R. Osgood, McIlvaine & Co., 1891) II, 499–503.

The following excerpts are taken from an address made by K. P. Pobedonostsev before the meeting of March 8, 1881, of the Russian Council of Ministers. This meeting had been called by Alexander III to consider whether or not to continue reforms. It was Pobedonostsev's speech which decided Alexander III against reform.

Your Majesty, I am bound by oath and conscience to express to you all **183** that is in my soul. I find myself not only agitated, but desperate. Just as in earlier times, before the destruction of Poland, they said "Finis Poloniae," so now one can almost say to us "Finis Russiae." In considering the draft law which is being submitted for your confirmation, the heart shrinks. There is something about this draft law which does not ring true; nay more, it is steeped in falsehood. . . .

We are told that it is necessary for a better discussion of draft laws to invite men who are acquainted with the national life, to listen to experts. I would say nothing against this if this was our only purpose. Experts have been called upon in times past too, but not in the manner proposed now. No, they want to introduce into Russia a constitution, and if not exactly that, then at least the first step toward that. . . . And what exactly is a constitution? Western Europe gives us the answer to that question. The constitutions which exist there are the instruments of every injustice, the instruments of all intrigues. . . .

. . . And this is the fraud, according to a foreign model unsuited to ourselves, which they wish to introduce among us, to our misfortune, to our destruction. Russia has been powerful thanks to autocracy, thanks to the unlimited mutual trust and close bond between the people and their tsar. Such a bond between the Russian tsar and people is an inestimable treasure. The people are the defenders of all our virtues and our good qualities; one can learn much from them. The so-called representatives of the land only separate the tsar from the people. On the other hand, the government should care for the people; it must recognize their true needs and help them to cope with their frequently critical needs. Here is the task toward whose accomplishment we must strive. Here is the true task of the new reign.

Instead of this, however, we are advised to set up a debating society, something in the manner of the French Estates General. We suffer as it is from debating societies which, under the influence of malcontented and worthless newspapers only incite popular passions. Thanks to idle chatterboxes, what has become of the lofty plans of our ever-memorable late sovereign, who took upon himself the martyr's crown at the end of his reign? To what has the great sacred idea of the emancipation of the peasants brought us? . . . To this: that they were given freedom but there were not established over them superior authorities, without whom the dark masses cannot get along. Not only that, but taverns have been opened everywhere, and the poor people, abandoned to their own devices and left without any care, have begun to drink and to grow indolent, and have thus become the unhappy victims of barkeepers, skinflints, Jews, and all kinds of loansharks.

Then there were inaugurated certain country and municipal social in-stitutions—debating societies which do not occupy themselves with real work but which jabber at length about the most important questions of state which do not fall at all within the competence of the discussants. And who are they that jabber, that lead these debating societies? Men who are worthless, immoral, among them persons with high posts who are not living with their families, who have given themselves over to debauchery, men who think only of their own advantage, who seek popularity and incite others to every kind of sedition.

Then there were inaugurated new legal institutions—new debating so-cieties, debating societies of lawyers, thanks to whom the most horrible crimes, undoubted murders and other grave misdeeds, go unpunished.

Finally, they granted freedom of the press, that most horrible of the debating societies, which spreads blasphemy and censure of the govern-ment throughout all corners of the vast Russian land, for thousands and tens of thousands of miles, sowing the seeds of dissension and dissatisfaction among peaceful and honorable people, inflaming passions, and inciting people to the most heinous crimes.

And when, Sire, do they propose that you establish, according to a foreign model, a new *supreme* debating society? . . . Now, when but a few days have elapsed since the most horrible crime ever to take place in Russia, when on this side of the Neva River, but a stone's throw away, there lies in the Cathedral of Saints Peter and Paul the still unburied dust of the magnanimous tsar who was torn to bits in the middle of the day by Russians. I shall not speak of the guilt of the criminals who carried out that horrible crime without parallel in history. All of us, however, from the first to the last, should repent for having looked so lightly upon events occurring about us. All of us are guilty for not having succeeded in our inactivity and apathy, in protecting a righteous man despite repeated at-tempts on the life of our common benefactor. On us all lies the blot of the ineradicable shame which has fallen over the Russian land. We should all repent! . . .

In such a terrible hour, Sire, one should not think about the establish-ment of more debating societies in which still other corrupting speeches will be held, but about work. It is necessary to act!

S. S. Dmitriev, *op. cit.,* III, 396–99. (Trans. Michael Petrovich.)

The Imperial Manifesto of April 26, 1881, represents Alexander III's decision to set aside his father's liberalism and to rule with an iron hand. Though signed by him, the Manifesto was actually written by Pobedonostsev.

184   I declare to all our faithful subjects:

It has pleased God, in His inscrutable ways, to end with a martyr's death the glorious reign of our beloved parent, and to charge us with the sacred obligation of autocratic rule.

Submitting to the will of Providence and to the State law of inheritance, we have taken upon ourselves this yoke in a terrible moment of national sorrow and horror, before the face of almighty God, in the belief that, having foreordained us to assume the affairs of government in such a grievous and difficult time, He will not deprive us of His all-powerful help. We believe also that the fervent prayers of our pious people, who are known throughout the whole world for the love and the loyalty which they have for their sovereign, will draw God's blessing on us and on the task of government which lies before us.

Having received from God the autocratic power for the good of the people entrusted to him, our parent, who now rests in God, remained true unto death to the vow which he took, and he sealed his service in his blood. Not so much by strict commands of power as by mercy and goodness, he carried out the greatest act of his reign—the emancipation of the enserfed peasants, succeeding in attracting the cooperation in this of the noble landowners, who have ever been attentive to the voice of goodness and honor; he established courts in the land, and he called his subjects, whom he had made free forever and without distinction, to take up the task of local government and social economy. May his memory be blessed unto all ages!

The base and criminal murder of the Russian sovereign in the midst of his faithful people, who were ready to lay down their lives for him, by the unworthy outcasts of the people is a terrible infamous deed unheard of in Russia and which has darkened the whole land with our sorrow and horror.

Yet in the midst of our great sorrow, God's voice does command us to stand firm in the task of government, hoping in divine Providence, with faith in the force and truth of the autocratic power which we have been called to strengthen and to protect for the advancement of the public welfare against all evil desires.

Let our faithful subjects, who love the fatherland and who have been loyal from generation to generation to the hereditary monarchical power, take courage, take courage into their hearts, which have been smitten by anxiety and horror. Under the shade of the monarchy and in indissoluble unity with it our land has often survived great troubles and has achieved strength and glory in the midst of grave trials and calamities, following its own destinies with faith in God.

Dedicating myself to our great service, we call all our faithful subjects to serve us and the state with faith and justice, in order to uproot the vile sedition which has besmirched the Russian land, to defend faith and morals, to educate our children properly, to wipe out injustice and rapacity, and to establish order and justice in the affairs of those institutions which have been granted to Russia by its benefactor, our beloved parent.

S. S. Dmitriev, *op. cit.*, III, 400–402. (Trans. Michael Petrovich.)

QUESTIONS

1. On the basis of Tarle's description of Napoleon's retreat from Moscow, and especially after reading between the lines, what reasons can you find for Napoleon's defeat in Russia?
2. Judging by Alexander I's instructions to the director of the University of Kazan in 1820, what role was assigned to religion by the state in Tsarist Russia?
3. What reasons did the Decembrist leaders give for their discontent?
4. Does the apparent parallel between the Russia which Custine described in 1839 and Stalin's Russia strengthen the contention that "history repeats itself," or is this an invalid conclusion?
5. Wherein lie the specific differences between the Imperial Manifesto of March 19, 1856, and the parody of that Manifesto in their evaluation of the causes and consequences of Russia's defeat in the Crimea?
6. How do you judge Alexander III for not following the advice of his father's murderers?
7. Assuming that you are republican-minded constitutionalists, try to overcome your antipathy for Pobedonostsev's views long enough to summarize why he sincerely believed that constitutional government was not as well suited to Russia as absolute monarchy.

CHAPTER XXX

IMPERIALISM

MODERN IMPERIALISM, particularly as manifested in the period from 1870 to 1914, is an extremely complex social phenomenon. Millions of man-hours have been devoted to study and research on it, and tons of paper to the exposition of its history, principles, and purpose; but from all of this there has resulted no general agreement as to its true nature. The superficial facts of the historical record are relatively simple and obvious: for example, in the period 1884–1900 alone, Great Britain acquired 3,700,000 square miles of territory with a population of 57,000,000; France, 3,600,000 square miles with a population of 36,500,000; Germany, one million square miles with 16,700,000 inhabitants; Belgium, 800,000 square miles and thirty million people; Portugal, 800,000 square miles and nine million souls; the United States took possession of the Hawaiian and Philippine Islands, Guam, Samoa, etc.; Japan took Korea and Formosa; and so on, to lesser annexations and attempts at annexation. The ease with which the superficial facts can be established is matched by the extreme difficulty of understanding and explaining the causes and ultimate consequences of imperialism—especially the former.

Many explanations of imperialism have been offered, some as rationalizations, others as serious attempts at understanding. They have been couched in terms of inevitable natural law (185–87), of economic necessity and/or pecuniary greed (188, 189), of an atavistic (anachronistic) expression of militarism and autocracy (190), and of the moral obligation of "superior" or "civilized" people to "protect" and develop "backward" nations (191). In this chapter we can do no more than present a brief sampling of representative explanations.

I. SOCIAL DARWINISM AND THE IDEOLOGY OF IMPERIALISM

"Social Darwinism" designates in terms of an analogy with the Darwinian theory of biological evolution (see p. 319) the predominant social philosophy of the second half of the nineteenth century. It was an outgrowth—an extreme version, or perhaps a perversion—of the "Manchester School" of economic liberalism which was supreme in mid-nineteenth-century England (p. 230), but it also reflected the influence of Central European nationalism—the *Realpolitik* of Bismarck (p. 328)—and borrowed heavily from developments in natural science, notably, of course, from the Darwinian theory of evolution. Its basic tenet was that competition—of individuals, business firms, and nations—would insure the "survival of the fittest" and the subjugation and/or elimination of the "unfit." Its application to imperialist expansion is obvious: whether one viewed imperialism primarily in economic, political, or moral terms, the conquests and annexations of the European powers were at once proof and justification of their superiority over "the lesser breeds without the law."

The most popular and influential exponent of Social Darwinism was the British philosopher Herbert Spencer (1820–1903). Spencer himself did not apply his philosophy to the case of imperialism—he was, in fact, an ardent anti-imperialist—but his writings, especially of his earlier period, helped to set the climate of opinion which made imperialist expansion acceptable to middle-class Europeans (see also p. 234). The following selections, taken from Spencer's writings at different dates, show not so much the "evolution" of his thought—for an exponent of the theory of evolution, his own mind was peculiarly rigid and doctrinaire—as his increasing astonishment, bordering on shocked surprise, that his doctrines were being accepted and applied literally in an area for which he had not intended them.

Spencer on the Nature of Social Progress (1857)

In the following selection, written shortly before the publication of Darwin's *Origin of Species* (see p. 319), Spencer applies the theory of "organic" evolution to his own concept of social evolution and identifies the result with "progress." Without realizing or intending it, Spencer supplied a rationale for the political conquest of "backward" areas by the "civilized" Europeans.

185   . . . It is settled beyond dispute that organic progress consists in a change from the homogeneous to the heterogeneous.

Now, we propose in the first place to show that this law of organic progress is the law of all progress. Whether it be in the development of the Earth, in the development of Life upon its surface, in the development of Society, of Government, of Manufactures, of Commerce, of Language, Literature, Science, Art, this same evolution of the simple into the complex, through successive differentiations, holds throughout. From the earliest traceable cosmical changes down to the latest results of civilization, we shall find that the transformation of the homogeneous into the heterogeneous, is that in which Progress essentially consists. . . .

Among the vertebrata in general, progress is marked by an increasing heterogeneity in the vertebral column, and more especially in the vertebrae constituting the skull: the higher forms being distinguished by the relatively larger size of the bones which cover the brain, and the relatively smaller size of those which form the jaw, etc. Now, this characteristic, which is stronger in Man than in any other creature, is stronger in the European than in the savage. Moreover, judging from the greater extent and variety of faculty he exhibits, we may infer that the civilized man has also a more complex or heterogeneous nervous system than the uncivilized man: and indeed the fact is in part visible in the increased ratio which his cerebrum bears to the subjacent ganglia.

If further elucidation be needed, we may find it in every nursery. The infant European has sundry marked points of resemblance to the lower human races; as in the flatness of the alae of the nose, the depression of its bridge, the divergence and forward opening of the nostrils, the form of the lips, the absence of a frontal sinus, the width between the eyes, the smallness of the legs. Now, as the developmental process by which these traits are turned into those of the adult European, is a continuation of that change from the homogeneous to the heterogeneous displayed during the previous evolution of the embryo, which every physiologist will admit; it follows that the parallel developmental process by which the like traits of the barbarous races have been turned into those of the civilized races, has also been a continuation of the change from the homogeneous to the heterogeneous. . . .

On passing from Humanity under its individual form to Humanity as socially embodied, we find the general law still more variously exemplified. The change from the homogeneous to the heterogeneous is displayed equally in the progress of civilization as a whole, and in the progress of every tribe or nation; and is still going on with increasing rapidity. As we see in existing barbarous tribes, society in its first and lowest form is a homogeneous aggregation of individuals having like powers and like functions: the only marked difference of function being that which accompanies difference of sex. Every man is warrior, hunter, fisherman, toolmaker, builder; every woman performs the same drudgeries; every family is self-sufficing, and save for purposes of aggression and defence, might as well live apart from the rest. Very early, however, in the process of social evolution we find an incipient differentiation between the governing and the governed. Some kind of chieftainship seems coeval with the first advance from the state of separate wandering families to that of a nomadic tribe. The authority of the strongest makes itself felt among a body of savages as in a herd of animals, or a posse of schoolboys. . . .

In the course of ages, there arises, as among ourselves, a highly complex political organization of monarch, ministers, lords and commons, with their subordinate administrative departments, courts of justice, revenue offices, etc., supplemented in the provinces by municipal governments, county governments, parish or union governments—all of them more or less elaborated. . . .

Simultaneously there has been going on a second differentiation of a more familiar kind; that, namely, by which the mass of the community has been segregated into distinct classes and orders of workers. While the governing part has undergone the complex development above detailed, the governed part has undergone an equally complex development, which has resulted in that minute division of labour characterizing advanced nations. It is needless to trace out this progress from its first stages, up through the caste divisions of the East and the incorporated guilds of Europe, to the elaborate producing and distributing organization existing among ourselves. . . . But there are yet other and higher phases of this advance from the homogeneous to the heterogeneous in the industrial organization of society.

Long after considerable progress has been made in the division of labour among different classes of workers, there is still little or no division of labour among the widely separated parts of the community; the nation continues comparatively homogeneous in the respect that in each district the same occupations are pursued. But when roads and others means of transit become numerous and good, the different districts begin to assume different functions, and to become mutually dependent. . . . Nay, more, this subdivision of functions shows itself not only among the different parts of the same nation, but among different nations. . . . So that beginning with a barbarous tribe, almost if not quite homogeneous in the functions of its members, the progress has been and still is, towards an economic aggregation of the whole human race.

Herbert Spencer, *Illustrations of Universal Progress* (New York, 1865), pp. 3, 11, 12, 14, 15–16.

Spencer on the End of Social Evolution (1885)

In this selection, written on the eve of the greatest imperialist expansion in history, Spencer "admits" that in the past social progress has resulted from conflict, conquest, and militarism; now, he says, "no further benefits are to be looked for" as a result of military conquest. But the floodgates of rampant nationalism, once opened, could not easily be closed again.

186   . . . That under its primary aspect political development is a process of integration, is clear. By it individuals originally separate are united into a whole; and the union of them into a whole is variously shown. In the earliest stages the groups of men are small, they are loose, they are not unified by subordination to a centre. But with political progress comes the compounding, the re-compounding, and re-re-compounding of groups until great nations are produced. . . .

From war has been gained all that it had to give. The peopling of the Earth by the more powerful and intelligent races is a benefit in great measure achieved; and what remains to be done calls for no other agency than the quiet pressure of a spreading industrial civilization on a barbarism which slowly dwindles. That integration of simple groups into compound ones, and of these into doubly compound ones, which war has effected, until at length great nations have been produced, is a process already carried as far as seems either practicable or desirable. Empires formed of alien peoples habitually fall to pieces when the coercive power which holds them together fails; and even could they be held together, would not form harmoniously working wholes: peaceful federation is the only further consolidation to be looked for. . . .

Thus, that social evolution which had to be achieved through the conflicts of societies with one another, has already been achieved; and no further benefits are to be looked for.

Only further evils are to be looked for from the continuance of militancy in civilized nations. The general lesson taught by all the foregoing chapters is that, indispensable as has been this process by which nations have been consolidated, organized, and disciplined, and requisite as has been the implied coercion to develop certain traits of individual human nature, yet that, beyond the unimaginable amount of suffering directly involved by the process, there has been an unimaginable amount of suffering indirectly involved; alike by the forms of political institutions necessitated, and by the accompanying type of individual nature fostered. . . .

Herbert Spencer, *The Principles of Sociology* (New York and London, 1885), II, 2, 643, 664, 665.

Spencer on Imperialism and Liberty (1902)

Within his lifetime Spencer witnessed the fulfillment, the logical conclusion of his theory of social evolution—the virtually complete subjugation of the non-European world by the "civilized," "superior" Europeans. Without abandoning his theory—it was psychologically impossible for him to do so—Spencer sought to show that imperialism involved not merely the political subordination of the conquered nations, but also the loss of liberty by the conquerors.

   . . . The coincidence in time between the South African war [1899– **187** 1902] and the recent outburst of Imperialism, illustrates the general truth that militancy and Imperialism are closely allied—are, in fact, different manifestations of the same social condition. It could not, indeed, be otherwise. Subject races or subject societies, do not voluntarily submit themselves to a ruling race or a ruling society: their subjection is nearly always the effect of coercion. An army is the agency which achieved it, and an army must be kept ever ready to maintain it. Unless the supremacy has actual or potential force behind it there is only federation, not Imperialism. Here, however, as above implied, the purpose is not so much to show that an imperial society is necessarily a militant society, as to show that in proportion as liberty is diminished in the societies over which it rules, liberty is diminished within its own organization. . . .

And now what is the lesson? Is it that in our own case imperialism and slavery, everywhere else and at all times united, are not to be united? Most will say Yes. Nay they will join, as our Poet Laureate [Rudyard Kipling; see 191 on p. 377] lately did in the title to some rhymes, the words

"Imperialism and Liberty"; mistaking names for things as of old. Gibbon writes:

> "Augustus was sensible that mankind is governed by names; nor was he deceived in his expectation, that the senate and people would submit to slavery, provided they were respectfully assured that they still enjoyed their ancient freedom." . . .

Even were it possible to bring home to men the extent to which their lives are, and presently will be still more, subordinated to State requirements, so as to leave them less and less owned by themselves, little effect would be produced. So long as the passion for mastery overrides all others the slavery that goes along with Imperialism will be tolerated. Among men who do not pride themselves on the possession of purely human traits, but on the possession of traits which they have in common with brutes, and in whose mouths "bulldog courage" is equivalent to manhood—among people who take their point of honour from the prize-ring, in which the combatant submits to pain, injury, and risk of death, in the determination to prove himself "the better man," no deterrent considerations like the above will have any weight. So long as they continue to conquer other peoples and to hold them in subjection, they will readily merge their personal liberties in the power of the State, and hereafter as heretofore accept the slavery that goes along with Imperialism. . . .

Herbert Spencer, *Facts and Comments* (New York, 1902), pp. 159–160, 165, 170–71.

II. IMPERIALISM AS AN ECONOMIC PHENOMENON

Probably the most popular of all explanations of imperialism are those which identify it as an economic phenomenon. There are two broad classifications of economic explanations. The first, and simplest, runs in purely pecuniary terms: imperialism results from the actions of greedy men who grasp at every opportunity to make more and larger profits.

The more complicated and sophisticated explanation views imperialism as a manifestation of economic necessity: capitalism must expand, or die. Specific reasons given to justify or show why capitalistic nations must extend political dominion over underdeveloped or undeveloped areas include the necessity for sources of raw materials for manufacture, markets for surplus manufactured goods, and opportunities for the investment of surplus capital. It was sometimes argued that colonies offered an outlet for surplus population, as well, but this argument was little used in view of the obvious fact that most emigrants preferred to go to countries that were politically independent, or semi-independent, of the motherland.

The argument of economic necessity was used alike by the advocates and opponents of capitalism and imperialism. The following extracts present a representative view of each.

A Capitalist Advocate of Economic Imperialism

Jules F. C. Ferry (1832–1893) was the architect of the modern French empire. During his tenure as prime minister, in 1880–81 and 1883–85, France acquired Tunisia, French Congo, parts of French Sudan and French Somaliland, Annam and Tonkin, several archipelagos in the Pacific, and gained a foothold in Madagascar. On each occasion as prime minister, Ferry's opponents forced him out of office precisely on the issue of his imperial exploits. In justifying French occupation of Tunisia in 1881, Ferry scarcely mentioned economic factors; in his second term of office he made greater use of economic arguments, but not until he was permanently retired from office did he elaborate the full-blown explanation of economic imperialism presented below (1890). Ferry's arguments are typical of those of statesmen, journalists, and military men in all imperialist nations—Great Britain, Germany, the United States, Italy, etc.

. . . An irresistible movement forces the great European nations to **188** the conquest of new lands. . . . In a phenomenon so general, so characteristic, is it possible to see only ambitious caprice, the false conceptions of men or peoples, or, on the contrary, the imperious manifestation, the fatal law of an economic condition common to all Europe?

Colonial policy is a daughter of industrial policy. For rich nations, where capital is abundant and accumulates rapidly, where manufactures constantly increase . . . exportation is an essential factor of public prosperity, and the field for the investment of capital, as the demand for labor, is measured by the extent of the foreign market. If it had been possible to establish among manufacturing nations something like the industrial division of labor, a methodical and rational division of industries according to aptitudes and the natural and social economic conditions of the different producing nations, placing the cotton industry here, metallurgy there, reserving for one sugar and spirits, for another silk and wool, perhaps Europe would not have had to search outside its own boundaries for markets for its wares. That was the ideal which led to the treaties of 1860. But today the whole world wants to spin and weave, to forge and distill. All Europe is making sugar as fast as it can, and is trying to export it. . . .

On the other side of the Vosges [Germany] as well as across the Atlantic, the protective system has multiplied manufactures, closed former markets, and thrown on the European market strong new competitors. To defend oneself by raising one's own [tariff] barriers is something, but it is not enough. Mr. Torrens has thoroughly demonstrated, in his fine book on the colonization of Australia, that an increase in manufacturing capital, if it is not accompanied by a proportional extension of foreign markets, tends to produce solely through internal competition a general lowering of prices, profits, and wages.

The protective system is a steam engine without a safety valve if it does not have as a corrective and auxiliary a serious and sensible colonial policy. The plethora of capital in industry does not tend merely to diminish profits, but it also halts the increase in wages, which is the natural and beneficent law of modern societies. And this is not just an abstract law, but a phenomenon of flesh and bone, of passion and the will, which agitates, complains, and protects itself. Social peace is, in the industrial age of humanity, a question of markets. . . . The European market is saturated; it is necessary to discover new groups of consumers in other parts of the world, or to put modern society in bankruptcy and to prepare for a cataclysmic social liquidation in the dawn of the twentieth century, the consequences of which are impossible to foretell. . . .

Jules Ferry, *Le Tonkin et la Mère-Patrie* (Paris, 1890), pp. 37, 40–43. (Trans. R. E. Cameron.)

A Marxist Critic of Economic Imperialism

V. I. Lenin (1870–1924) was the architect of the Bolshevik Revolution in Russia (see Chapter XXXIII). He made two major "contributions" to, or modifications of, Marxist doctrine. One was the idea that the socialist revolution must take place first in the backward nation of Russia, instead of in the most highly industrialized nations, as Marx had implied (see p. 305). The other was his theory of imperialism, "capitalism in the age of monopolies." The following extracts are from his famous work on the subject, *Imperialism, the Highest Stage of Capitalism* (1916). The student will note the similarity between Lenin's ideas and Ferry's.

. . . The enormous growth of industry and the remarkably rapid process of concentration of production in ever-larger enterprises represent one of the most characteristic features of capitalism. . . . This transformation of competition into monopoly is one of the most important—if not the most important—phenomena of modern capitalist economy. . . .

The principal stages in the history of monopolies are the following: 1) 1860–1870, the highest stage, the apex of development of free competition; monopoly is in the barely discernible, embryonic stage. 2) After the crisis of 1873, a wide zone of development of cartels; but they are still the exception. They are not yet durable. They are still a transitory phenomenon. 3) The boom at the end of the nineteenth century and the crisis of 1900–03. Cartels become one of the foundations of the whole economic life. Capitalism has been transformed into imperialism. . . .

The beginning of the twentieth century marks the turning point, not only in regard to the growth of monopolies . . . but also in regard to the development of finance capital. . . . It is particularly important to examine the part which export of capital plays in creating the international network of dependence and ties of finance capital.

Under the old capitalism, when free competition prevailed, the export of *goods* was the most typical feature. Under modern capitalism, when monopolies prevail, the export of *capital* has become the typical feature. . . .

As long as capitalism remains what it is, surplus capital will never be utilized for the purpose of raising the standard of living of the masses in a given country, for this would mean a decline in profits for the capitalists; it will be used for the purpose of increasing those profits by exporting capital abroad to the backward countries. In these backward countries profits are usually high, for capital is scarce, the price of land is relatively low, wages are low, raw materials are cheap. . . . The necessity for exporting capital arises from the fact that in a few countries capitalism has become "over-ripe" and . . . cannot find "profitable" investment. . . .

We saw above that the apex of pre-monopoly capitalist development, of capitalism in which free competition was predominant, was reached in the 'sixties and 'seventies of the last century. We now see that it is *precisely after that period* that the "boom" in colonial annexations begins, and that the struggle for the territorial division of the world becomes extraordinarily keen. It is beyond doubt, therefore, that capitalism's transition to the stage of monopoly capitalism, to finance capitalism, is *bound up* with the intensification of the struggle for the partition of the world. . . .

V. I. Lenin, *Imperialism, the Highest Stage of Capitalism* (new, revised trans.; New York: International Publishers, 1939), pp. 16, 17, 21–22, 61, 62, 63, 64, 77–78. (Reprinted by permission of the publisher.)

III. IMPERIALISM AS A SOCIOLOGICAL PHENOMENON

Joseph A. Schumpeter (1883–1950) was one of the most distinguished social scientists of the first half of the twentieth century. A native of the old Austrian Empire, he had already achieved worldwide eminence as an economist before World War I. After the war and the breakup of the empire, he served briefly as minister of finance in the Austrian government; subsequently he migrated to Germany, and then to the United States. His work on "The Sociology of Imperialisms," from which the following is extracted, was written during the latter years of World War I and first published in 1919.

"The Sociology of Imperialisms"

190   . . . Our problem arises from the fact that aggressive attitudes on the part of states—or of such earlier organizational structures as history may record—can be explained, directly and unequivocally, only in part by the real and concrete interests of the people. Examples will best illustrate what we mean. When two tribes come into conflict over essential salt deposits or hunting grounds; or when a state, hemmed in on all sides by customs and communication barriers, resorts to aggression in order to gain access to the sea, we have a case in which aggression is explained by interests. It is true that there are many methodological difficulties in speaking of the interests of a people as such. Here, however, reference to "concrete" interest explains everything that would seem to stand in need of explanation. A concrete interest need not be economic in character. When a state resorts to aggression in order to unite its citizens politically, as was the case with Piedmont in 1848 and 1859, this likewise betokens a real, concrete interest, explaining its conduct. The interest, moreover, need not necessarily extend to the *entire* population of the state. When a planter aristocracy prevails upon its government to seize some foreign base of operations for the slave trade, this too is explained by a real, concrete interest. The interest that actually explains a warlike act need not, finally, be openly admitted—or of the kind that *can* be openly admitted; it need not, to use our own term, be an *avowed* interest. Such cases nevertheless come under the present heading, if the concrete interests of a sufficiently powerful class are accessible to scientific consideration. There are, on the other hand, certain cases that do *not* belong here, such as that of a group of people who contrive to have a declaration of war issued because they gain financially from the waging of war, or because they need a war as a diversion from domestic political difficulties. Here there is no concrete interest, in the sense that applies to the aforementioned cases. True, there must be *some* concrete interest. There must be a reason for the declaration of war. But that *reason* is not the *cause*. The true cause, of course, must also lie in an interest. But that interest is not in the concrete war aims. It is not a question of the advantages offered by the attainment of those aims, but of an interest in the waging of war as such. The questions that then arise are how the people came to acquire such a generally belligerent disposition and why they happened to choose this particular occasion for war. Thus mere reference to a concrete interest is satisfactory under only three conditions: In the first place, such a concrete interest *must be present,* in the sense that has now been made clear—an interest which the observer can grasp as such, of course taking into account the social structure, mentality, and situation of the people in question. In the second place, the conduct of the state which is under study must be calculated to *promote* this interest, with the sum total of predictable sacrifices and risks in some proportion to the anticipated gains. In the third place, it must be possible to *prove* that this interest, whether avowed or not, is actually the *political driving force* behind the action.

In the individual case it may often become difficult to establish whether these conditions obtain. The fabric of social interests is so closely woven that scarcely ever can there be any action on the part of a state that is not in keeping with the concrete interest of someone, an interest to which that action can be reduced without manifest absurdity. To this must be added the belief, inculcated into the people, especially in the present age, that concrete interests of the people dictate the behavior of the state and that concrete advantages for all classes are to be expected. Government policies are always officially justified in this way, and often, without the slightest doubt, in perfect good faith. Finally, current fallacies, especially of an economic character, may serve to create the semblance of an adequate, concrete interest in the mind of the people—and occasionally even in the mind of the scientific observer, especially the historian. In such cases the true background is laid bare only by an inquiry into the manner in which the people came to their belief. But the individual case does not concern us. We are concerned only with the fact, which is beyond doubt, that the three above-mentioned conditions are frequently not fulfilled. Whenever such is the case, a problem arises. And among the problems of this nature is the problem of imperialism.

No one calls it imperialism when a state, no matter how brutally and vigorously, pursues concrete interests of its own; and when it can be expected to abandon its aggressive attitude as soon as it has attained what it was after. The word "imperialism" has been abused as a slogan to the point where it threatens to lose all meaning, but up to this point our definition is quite in keeping with common usage, even in the press. For whenever the word imperialism is used, there is always the implication—whether sincere or not—of an aggressiveness, the true reasons for which do not lie in the aims which are temporarily being pursued; of an aggressiveness that is only kindled anew by each success; of an aggressiveness for its own sake, as reflected in such terms as "hegemony," "world dominion," and so forth. And history, in truth, shows us nations and classes—most nations furnish an example at some time or other—that seek expansion for the sake of expanding, war for the sake of fighting, victory for the sake of winning, dominion for the sake of ruling. This determination cannot be explained by any of the pretexts that bring it into action, by any of the aims for which it seems to be struggling at the time. It confronts us, independent of all concrete purpose or occasion, as an enduring disposition, seizing upon one opportunity as eagerly as the next. It shines through all the arguments put forward on behalf of present aims. It values conquest not so much on account of the immediate advantages—advantages that more often than not are more than dubious, or that are heedlessly cast away with the same frequency—as because it *is* conquest, success, action. Here the theory of concrete interest in our sense fails. What needs to be explained is how the will to victory itself came into being.

Expansion for its own sake always requires, among other things, concrete objects if it is to reach the action stage and maintain itself, but this does not constitute its meaning. Such expansion is in a sense its own "object," and the truth is that it has no adequate object beyond itself. Let us therefore, in the absence of a better term, call it "objectless." It follows for that very reason that, just as such expansion cannot be explained by concrete interest, so too it is never satisfied by the fulfillment of a concrete interest, as would be the case if fulfillment were the motive, and the struggle for it merely a necessary evil—a counterargument, in fact. Hence the tendency of such expansion to transcend all bounds and tangible limits, to the point of utter exhaustion. This, then, is our definition: imperialism is the objectless disposition on the part of a state to unlimited forcible expansion. . . .

Our analysis of the historical evidence has shown, first, the unquestionable fact that "objectless" tendencies toward forcible expansion, without definite, utilitarian limits—that is, non-rational and irrational, purely instinctual inclinations toward war and conquest—play a very large role in the history of mankind. It may sound paradoxical, but numberless wars —perhaps the majority of all wars—have been waged without adequate "reason"—not so much from the moral viewpoint as from that of reasoned and reasonable interest. The most herculean efforts of the nations, in other words, have faded into the empty air. Our analysis, in the second place, provides an explanation for this drive to action, this will to war—a theory by no means exhausted by mere references to an "urge" or an "instinct." The explanation lies, instead, in the vital needs of situations that molded peoples and classes into warriors—if they wanted to avoid extinction—and in the fact that psychological dispositions and social structures acquired in the dim past in such situations, once firmly established, tend to maintain themselves and to continue in effect long after they have lost their meaning and their life-preserving function. Our analysis, in the third place, has shown the existence of subsidiary factors that facilitate the survival of such dispositions and structures—factors that may be divided into two groups. The orientation toward war is mainly fostered by the domestic interests of ruling classes, but also by the influence of all those who stand to gain individually from a war policy, whether economically or socially. Both groups of factors are generally overgrown by elements of an altogether different character, not only in terms of political phraseology, but also of psychological motivation. Imperialisms differ greatly in detail, but they all have at least these traits in common, turning them into a single phenomenon in the field of sociology, as we noted in the introduction.

Imperialism thus is atavistic in character. It falls into that large group of surviving features from earlier ages that play such an important part in every concrete social situation. In other words, it is an element that stems from the living conditions, not of the present, but of the past—or, put in terms of the economic interpretation of history, from past rather than present relations of production. It is an atavism in the social structure, in individual, psychological habits of emotional reaction. . . .

It is from absolute autocracy that the present age has taken over what imperialist tendencies it displays. And the imperialism of absolute autocracy flourished before the Industrial Revolution that created the modern world, or rather, before the consequences of that revolution began to be felt in all their respects. . . .

Among all capitalist economies, that of the United States is least burdened with precapitalist elements, survivals, reminiscences, and power factors. Certainly we cannot expect to find imperialist tendencies altogether lacking even in the United States, for the immigrants came from Europe with their convictions fully formed, and the environment certainly favored the revival of instincts of pugnacity. But we can conjecture that among all countries the United States is likely to exhibit the weakest imperialist trend. . . . Even in the United States, of course, politicians need slogans —especially slogans calculated to divert attention from domestic issues. Theodore Roosevelt and certain magnates of the press actually resorted to imperialism—and the result, in that world of high capitalism, was utter defeat, a defeat that would have been even more abject, if other slogans, notably those appealing to anti-trust sentiment, had not met with better success. . . .

. . . Thus the gain of the capitalists as a class cannot be a motive for war. . . . There remain the entrepreneurs in the war industries, in the broader sense, possibly also the large landowner—a small but powerful minority. Their war profits are always sure to be an important supporting element. But few will go so far as to assert that this element alone is sufficient to orient the people of the capitalist world along imperialist lines. At most, an interest in expansion may make the capitalists allies of those who stand for imperialist trends. . . .

. . . It is a basic fallacy to describe imperialism as a necessary phase of capitalism, or even to speak of the development of capitalism into imperialism. We have seen before that the mode of life of the capitalist world does not favor imperialist attitudes. We now see that the alignment of interests in a capitalist economy—even the interests of its upper strata —by no means points unequivocally in the direction of imperialism. . . .

. . . In the capitalist world it is actually not big business and industry at all that are the carriers of nationalist trends, but the intellectual, and the content of his ideology is explained not so much from definite class interests as from chance emotion and individual interest. . . .

. . . Nationalism and militarism, while not creatures of capitalism, become "capitalized" and in the end draw their best energies from capitalism. Capitalism involves them in its workings and thereby keeps them alive, politically as well as economically. And they, in turn, affect capitalism, cause it to deviate from the course it might have followed alone, support many of its interests.

Here we find that we have penetrated to the historical as well as the sociological sources of modern imperialism. It does not coincide with nationalism and militarism, though it fuses with them by supporting them as it is supported by them. It too is—not only historically, but also sociologically—a heritage of the autocratic state, of its structural elements, organizational forms, interest alignments, and human attitudes, the outcome of precapitalist forces which the autocratic state has reorganized, in part by the methods of early capitalism. It would never have been evolved by the "inner logic" of capitalism itself. . . .

Joseph A. Schumpeter, *Imperialism and Social Classes,* trans. Heinz Norden (New York: Augustus M. Kelley, Inc., 1951), pp. 3–7, 83–86, 94–96, 98–99, 118, 126, 128. (Copyright 1951 by the trustees of Elizabeth B. Schumpeter. Quotations by permission of the estate.)

IV. IMPERIALISM AS A MORAL OBLIGATION OF WESTERN CIVILIZATION

In the intellectual cross-currents of the late nineteenth century, confusion was bound to arise concerning the motives for which imperial expansion was undertaken. While some proclaimed such expansion to be a necessity—for good or evil—of Western nations, others demanded the expansion on behalf of the colonial areas themselves. Missionary activity—the desire to bring the comforts of Christianity to "heathen races"—and the belief of well-intentioned humanitarians that non-Europeans would benefit from Western legal institutions, technology, etc.—even if imposed by force—were advanced as reasons for dispatching expeditionary forces to distant lands. In the United States, Theodore Roosevelt spoke grandly of "manifest destiny," and in England Rudyard Kipling (1865–1936), poet laureate of the British Empire, extolled the nobility, the heroism, and the "suffering" of those who went forth to bring civilization to the sullen savage. The closing lines of his famous poem, written on the occasion of the annexation of the Philippine Islands by the United States, contain a profound, prophetic message for the world of the mid-twentieth century.

The White Man's Burden (*1899*)   **191**

Take up the White Man's burden—
    Send forth the best ye breed—
Go bind your sons to exile
    To serve your captives' need;
To wait in heavy harness
    On fluttered folk and wild—
Your new-caught, sullen peoples,
    Half devil and half child.

. . . .

Take up the White Man's burden—
    And reap his old reward:

The blame of those ye better,
The hate of those ye guard—
The cry of hosts ye humour
(Ah, slowly!) toward the light:
"Why brought ye us from bondage,
"Our loved Egyptian night?"

Take up the White Man's burden—
Ye dare not stoop to less—
Nor call too loud on Freedom
To cloak your weariness;
By all ye cry or whisper,
By all ye leave or do,
The silent, sullen peoples
Shall weigh your Gods and you.

Rudyard Kipling's Verse (Garden City, N. Y.: Doubleday & Co., 1946), pp. 321, 322. (Reprinted by permission of the publisher.)

QUESTIONS

1. What did Spencer mean by "the change from the homogeneous to the heterogeneous"? Give illustrations from organic life and social life. How did he think the change came about?
2. What function did Spencer think war performed in the past? What effect did he expect it to have in the future?
3. What are the points of similarity and difference in Ferry's and Lenin's analysis of imperialism? Are there any flaws in their arguments?
4. How did Schumpeter distinguish between "concrete interests" and "the objectless disposition on the part of a state to unlimited forcible expansion"? What is the significance of each for his theory of imperialism? What, according to Schumpeter, are the historical and sociological roots of modern imperialism?
5. What is the "white man's burden"? Why should he assume it? What are its rewards?

CHAPTER XXXI

THE FIRST WORLD WAR

THE ORIGINS of the first World War are still a matter of considerable controversy. The long-range causes which produced this disaster go far back into history, but we can list four causes which, though also long range, lie in the more immediate past. They are the armament race, the spirit of nationalism, the imperial and economic rivalries and the system of alliances which took shape during the decades before 1914. The table illustrating the changing war potential of the major nations which were to be involved in the conflict is an indication of both the armaments race and the economic rivalries between nations (193). It also throws some light upon the strength of those nations which were involved in the alliance systems which grew up before 1914 (192).

The immediate origins of the war lie in the events precipitated by the assassination of the Austrian Archduke Francis Ferdinand at Sarajevo. It resulted in an Austrian ultimatum to Serbia (194) and in the reply (195) which Austria, however, did not deem satisfactory. These documents are, in part, reprinted here and will enable you to form your own picture as to the "guilt" of either Austria or Serbia in the outbreak of the war. To these considerations of power and prestige, the United States, with its entrance into the war, added a strong ideological note which culminated in 1918 in the famous Fourteen Points. President Wilson's Declaration of War illustrates this (197).

The diagram on page 380 illustrates the European alliance system as it grew up after 1879.

THE EUROPEAN ALLIANCE SYSTEM, 1879–1914

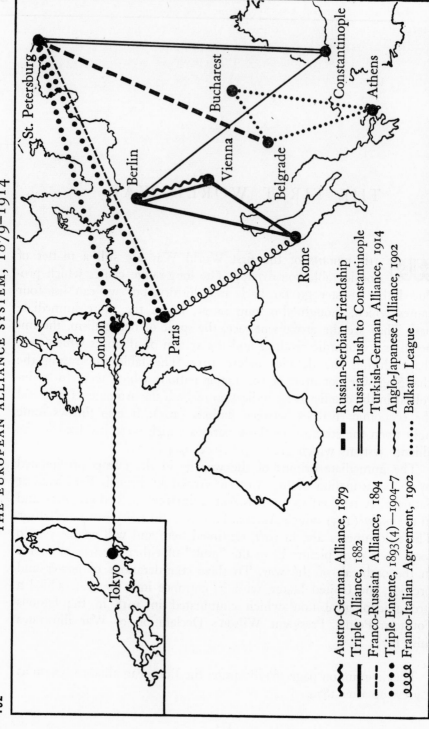

⌇⌇⌇ Austro-German Alliance, 1879	▬▬ Russian-Serbian Friendship
━━━ Triple Alliance, 1882	══ Russian Push to Constantinople
┅┅┅ Franco-Russian Alliance, 1894	─── Turkish-German Alliance, 1914
•••• Triple Entente, 1893(4)—1904-7	ℓℓℓ Anglo-Japanese Alliance, 1902
ℓℓℓ Franco-Italian Agreement, 1902	⋯⋯ Balkan League

Modern warfare is largely a question of men, material, and machinery. The following tables are designed to illustrate the changes in the war potential of some of the principal nations between 1850 and 1914. They may, incidentally, throw light on some of the underlying causes of World War I.

POPULATION **193**

(*millions*)

Year	Germany	United Kingdom	France	United States	Austria-Hungary	European Russia
1850	35.3	27.2	35.6	23.2	35.5	60.
1870	40.8	31.8	36.1	39.8	35.9	72.
1880	45.2	34.6	37.7	50.2	37.8	85.2
1890	49.4	37.5	38.3	62.9	41.3	93.7
1900	56.4	41.5	39.0	76.0	45.4	99.7
1910	64.9	44.9	39.6	92.0	49.2	115.6
1914	67.8	46.2	39.8	99.1	50.8	124.2

PERCENTAGE DISTRIBUTION OF WORLD'S MANUFACTURING

Year	Germany	United Kingdom	France	United States
1870	13.2	31.8	10.3	23.3
1896-1900	16.6	19.5	7.1	30.1
1913	15.7	14.0	6.4	35.8

PRODUCTION OF COAL (INCLUDING LIGNITE)

(*annual averages, millions of metric tons*)

Year	Germany	United Kingdom	France	United States
1850	5.8	40.	4.4	6.5
1870-74	42.	123.	15.	44.
1880-84	66.	159.	20.	85.
1890-94	94.	183.	26.	156.
1900-04	157.	230.	33.	286.
1910-14	247.	274.	40.	474.
1915-18	250.	247.	20.	545.

PRODUCTION OF PIG IRON AND STEEL
(millions of metric tons)

Year	Germany Iron	Germany Steel	United Kingdom Iron	United Kingdom Steel	France Iron	France Steel	United States Iron	United States Steel
1850	.2	...	3.0	...	.4	...	.6	...
1870	1.4	.2	6.1	.2	1.2	.2	1.8	.1
1880	2.7	.7	7.9	1.3	1.7	.4	3.9	1.3
1890	4.6	2.2	8.0	3.6	2.0	.7	9.4	4.3
1900	8.5	6.6	9.1	5.0	2.7	1.6	14.0	10.4
1910	14.8	13.7	10.2	6.5	4.0	3.4	27.7	26.5
1913	19.3	18.9	10.4	7.8	5.2	4.7	31.5	31.8
1918	11.9	15.0	9.2	9.7	1.3	1.8	39.7	45.2

FOREIGN TRADE: EXPORTS OF DOMESTIC PRODUCTION ONLY
(millions of dollars, current prices)

Year	Germany	United Kingdom	France	United States
1850	...	357	200	135
1870	500	998	560	377
1880	765	1,115	694	824
1890	885	1,317	750	845
1900	1,150	1,455	825	1,370
1910	1,870	2,150	1,240	1,710
1913	2,410	2,625	1,360	2,428

(per cent of world total)

Year	Germany	United Kingdom	France	United States
1913	13.1	13.9	7.2	13.3

MERCHANT SHIPPING: TOTAL TONNAGE AND STEAM TONNAGE
(thousands of gross tons; steam tonnage in parentheses)

Year	Germany	United Kingdom	France	United States
1850	...	3,565	688	1,586
		(168)	(14)	(45)
1870	982	5,691	1,072	1,517
	(82)	(1,113)	(154)	(193)
1900	1,942	9,304	1,038	827
	(1,348)	(7,208)	(528)	(341)
1910-12	3,000	11,700	1,463	928
	(2,500)	(10,700)	(838)	(618)

Compiled by Rondo E. Cameron

The following is the note sent by the Austro-Hungarian government to Serbia after the assassination of Archduke Francis Ferdinand at Sarajevo, the chief city of Bosnia, on June 28, 1914.

The Austro-Hungarian Note to Serbia　　　　　　　　　**194**

The Austro-Hungarian Minister for Foreign Affairs to the Minister at
　Belgrade,　　　　　　　　　　　　　　*Vienna, July 22, 1914*
Your Excellency will present the following note to the Royal Government on the afternoon of Thursday, July 23:

On the 31st of March, 1909, the Royal Serbian Minister at the Court of Vienna made, in the name of his Government, the following declaration to the Imperial and Royal Government:

Serbia recognizes that her rights were not affected by the state of affairs created in Bosnia, and states that she will accordingly accommodate herself to the decisions to be reached by the Powers in connection with Article 25 of the Treaty of Berlin. Serbia, in accepting the advice of the Great Powers, binds herself to desist from the attitude of protest and opposition which she has assumed with regard to the annexation since October last, and she furthermore binds herself to alter the tendency of her present policy toward Austria-Hungary, and to live on the footing of friendly and neighborly relations with the latter in the future.

Now the history of the past few years, and particularly the painful events of the 28th of June, have proved the existence of a subversive movement in Serbia, whose object it is to separate certain portions of its territory from the Austro-Hungarian Monarchy. This movement, which came into being under the very eyes of the Serbian Government, subsequently found expression outside of the territory of the Kingdom in acts of terrorism, in a number of attempts at assassination, and in murders.

Far from fulfilling the formal obligations contained in its declaration of the 31st of March, 1909, the Royal Serbian Government has done nothing to suppress this movement. It has tolerated the criminal activities of the various unions and associations directed against the Monarchy, the unchecked utterances of the press, the glorification of the authors of assassinations, the participation of officers and officials in subversive intrigues; it has tolerated an unhealthy propaganda in its public instruction; and it has tolerated, finally, every manifestation which could betray the people of Serbia into hatred of the Monarchy and contempt for its institutions.

This toleration of which the Royal Serbian Government was guilty, was still in evidence at that moment when the events of the 28th of June exhibited to the whole world the dreadful consequences of such tolerance.

It is clear from the statements and confessions of the criminal authors of the assassination of the 28th of June, that the murder at Serajevo was conceived at Belgrade, that the murderers received the weapons and the bombs with which they were equipped from Serbian officers and officials who belonged to the *Narodna Odbrana* [black hand], and, finally, that the dispatch of the criminals and of their weapons to Bosnia was arranged and effected under the conduct of Serbian frontier authorities.

The results brought out by the inquiry no longer permit the Imperial and Royal Government to maintain the attitude of patient tolerance which it has observed for years toward those agitations which center at Belgrade and are spread thence into the territories of the Monarchy. Instead, these results impose upon the Imperial and Royal Government the obligation to put an end to those intrigues, which constitute a standing menace to the peace of the Monarchy.

In order to attain this end, the Imperial and Royal Government finds itself compelled to demand that the Serbian Government give official assurance that it will condemn the propaganda directed against Austria-Hungary, that is to say, the whole body of the efforts whose ultimate object it is to separate from the Monarchy territories that belong to it; and that it will obligate itself to suppress with all the means at its command this criminal and terroristic propaganda.

In order to give these assurances a character of solemnity, the Royal Serbian Government will publish on the first page of its official organ of July 26/13 [old and new style date] the following declaration:

> The Royal Serbian Government condemns the propaganda directed against Austria-Hungary, that is to say, the whole body of the efforts whose ultimate object it is to separate from the Austro-Hungarian Monarchy territories that belong to it, and it most sincerely regrets the dreadful consequences of these criminal transactions.
>
> The Royal Serbian Government regrets that Serbian officers and officials should have taken part in the above-mentioned propaganda and thus have endangered the friendly and neighborly relations, to the cultivation of which the Royal Government had most solemnly pledged itself by its declaration of March 31, 1909.
>
> The Royal Government, which disapproves and repels every idea and every attempt to interfere in the destinies of the population of whatever portion of Austria-Hungary, regards it as its duty most expressly to

call the attention of the officers, officials, and the whole population of the Kingdom to the fact that for the future it will proceed with the utmost rigor against any persons who shall become guilty of any such activities, activities to prevent and to suppress which, the Government will bend every effort.

This declaration shall be brought to the attention of the Royal army simultaneously by an order of the day from His Majesty the King, and by publication in the official organ of the army.

The Royal Serbian Government will furthermore pledge itself:

1. to suppress every publication which shall incite to hatred and contempt of the Monarchy, and the general tendency of which shall be directed against the territorial integrity of the latter;

2. to proceed at once to the dissolution of the *Narodna Odbrana,* to confiscate all of its means of propaganda, and in the same manner to proceed against the other unions and associations in Serbia which occupy themselves with propaganda against Austria-Hungary; the Royal Government will take such measures as are necessary to make sure that the dissolved associations may not continue their activities under other names or in other forms;

3. to eliminate without delay from public instruction in Serbia, everything, whether connected with the teaching corps or with the methods of teaching, that serves or may serve to nourish the propaganda against Austria-Hungary;

4. to remove from the military and administrative service in general all officers and officials who have been guilty of carrying on the propaganda against Austria-Hungary, whose names the Imperial and Royal Government reserves the right to make known to the Royal Government when communicating the material evidence now in its possession;

5. to agree to the co-operation in Serbia of the organs of the Imperial and Royal Government in the suppression of the subversive movement directed against the integrity of the Monarchy;

6. to institute a judicial inquiry against every participant in the conspiracy of the 28th of June who may be found in Serbian territory; the organs of the Imperial and Royal Government delegated for this purpose will take part in the proceedings held for this purpose;

7. to undertake with all haste the arrest of Major Voislav Tankositch and of one Milan Ciganovitch, a Serbian official, who have been compromised by the results of the inquiry;

8. by efficient measures to prevent the participation of Serbian authorities

in the smuggling of weapons and explosives across the frontier; to dismiss from the service and to punish severely those members of the Frontier Service at Schabats and Losnitza who assisted the authors of the crime of Serajevo to cross the frontier;

9. to make explanations to the Imperial and Royal Government concerning the unjustifiable utterances of high Serbian functionaries in Serbia and abroad who, without regard for their official position, have not hesitated to express themselves in a manner hostile toward Austria-Hungary since the assassination of the 28th of June;

10. to inform the Imperial and Royal Government without delay of the execution of the measures comprised in the foregoing points.

The Imperial and Royal Government awaits the reply of the Royal Government by Saturday, the twenty-fifth instant, at 6 p.m., at the latest.

A mémoire concerning the results of the inquiry at Serajevo, as far as they concern the functionaries referred to in Points 7 and 8, is appended to this note.

> *Outbreak of the World War,* German documents collected by Karl Kautsky (New York, 1924), pp. 603–5. (Reprinted by permission of the Carnegie Endowment for International Peace.)

The reply of the Serbian Government to the demands made in the Austrian note (194) follows. The Austrian government deemed the reply unsatisfactory and ordered its troops to mobilize against Serbia. This is the immediate cause for the outbreak of the war.

195   *Reply of Servian Government to Austro-Hungarian Note (Communicated by the Servian Minister, July 27)*

The Royal Servian Government have received the communication of the Imperial and Royal Government of the 10th instant [old style date], and are convinced that their reply will remove any misunderstanding which may threaten to impair the good neighbourly relations between the Austro-Hungarian Monarchy and the Kingdom of Servia. . . .

The Royal Government cannot be held responsible for manifestations of a private character, such as articles in the press and the peaceable work of societies—manifestations which take place in nearly all countries in the ordinary course of events, and which, as a general rule, escape official control. The Royal Government are all the less responsible in view of the fact that at the time of the solution of a series of questions which arose between Servia and Austria-Hungary they gave proof of a great readiness to oblige, and thus succeeded in settling the majority of these questions to the advantage of the two neighbouring countries.

For these reasons, the Royal Government have been pained and surprised at the statements, according to which members of the kingdom of Servia are supposed to have participated in the preparations for the crime committed at Serajevo; the Royal Government expected to be invited to collaborate in an investigation of all that concerns this crime and they were ready, in order to prove the entire correctness of their attitude, to take measures against any persons concerning whom representations were made to them. Falling in, therefore, with the desire of the Imperial and Royal Government, they are prepared to hand over for trial any Servian subject, without regard to his situation or rank, of whose complicity in the crime of Serajevo proofs are forthcoming, and more especially they undertake to cause to be published on the first page of the "Journal officiel," on the date of the 13th (26th) [old and new style date] July, the following declaration:

"The Royal Government of Servia condemn all propaganda which may be directed against Austria-Hungary, that is to say, all such tendencies as aim at ultimately detaching from the Austro-Hungarian Monarchy territories which form part thereof, and they sincerely deplore the baneful consequences of these criminal movements. The Royal Government regret that, according to the communication from the Imperial and Royal Government, certain Servian officers and officials should have taken part in the above-mentioned propaganda, and thus compromised the good neighbourly relations to which the Royal Servian Government was solemnly engaged by the declaration of the 31st March, 1909, which declaration disapproves and repudiates all idea or attempt at interference with the destiny of the inhabitants of any part whatsoever of Austria-Hungary, and they consider it their duty formally to warn the officers, officials and entire population of the kingdom that henceforth they will take the most rigorous steps against all such persons as are guilty of such acts, to prevent and to repress which they will use their utmost endeavor."

This declaration will be brought to the knowledge of the Royal Army in an order of the day, in the name of His Majesty the King, by his Royal Highness the Crown Prince Alexander, and will be published in the next official army bulletin.

The Royal Government further undertake:

1. To introduce at the first regular convocation of the Skuptchina [diet] a provision into the press law providing for the most severe punishment of incitement to hatred or contempt of the Austro-Hungarian Monarchy, and for taking action against any publication the general tendency of which is

directed against the territorial integrity of Austria-Hungary. The Government engage at the approaching revision of the Constitution to cause an amendment to be introduced into article 22 of the Constitution of such a nature that such publication may be confiscated, a proceeding at present impossible under the categorical terms of article 22 of the Constitution.

2. The Government possess no proof, nor does the note of the Imperial and Royal Government furnish them with any, that the "Narodna Odbrana" and other similar societies have committed up to the present any criminal act of this nature through the proceedings of any of their members. Nevertheless, the Royal Government will accept the demand of the Imperial and Royal Government, and will dissolve the "Narodna Odbrana" Society and every other society which may be directing its efforts against Austria-Hungary.

3. The Royal Servian Government undertake to remove without delay from their public educational establishments in Servia all that serves or could serve to foment propaganda against Austria-Hungary whenever the Imperial and Royal Government furnish them with facts and proofs of this propaganda.

4. The Royal Government also agree to remove from military service all such persons as the judicial enquiry may have proved to be guilty of acts directed against the integrity of the territory of the Austro-Hungarian Monarchy, and they expect the Imperial and Royal Government to communicate to them at a later date the names and the acts of these officers and officials for the purposes of the proceedings which are to be taken against them.

5. The Royal Government must confess that they do not clearly grasp the meaning or the scope of the demand made by the Imperial and Royal Government that Servia shall undertake to accept the collaboration or the organs of the Imperial and Royal Government upon their territory, but they declare that they will admit such collaboration as agrees with the principle of international law, with criminal procedure, and with good neighbourly relations.

6. It goes without saying that the Royal Government consider it their duty to open an enquiry against all such persons as are, or eventually may be, implicated in the plot of the 15th June [old style date], and who happen to be within the territory of the kingdom. As regards the participation in this enquiry of Austro-Hungarian agents or authorities appointed for this purpose by the Imperial and Royal Government, the Royal Government cannot accept such an arrangement as it would be a violation of the Constitution and of the law of criminal procedure; nevertheless, in concrete cases communi-

cations as to the results of the investigation in question might be given to the Austro-Hungarian agents.

7. The Royal Government proceeded, on the very evening of the delivery of the note, to arrest Commandant Voislav Tankossitch. As regards Milan Ziganovitch, who is a subject of the Austro-Hungarian Monarchy and who up to the 15th of June was employed (on probation) by the directorate of railways, it has not yet been possible to arrest him.

The Austro-Hungarian Government are requested to be so good as to supply as soon as possible, in the customary form, the presumptive evidence of guilt, as well as the eventual proofs of guilt which have been collected up to the present, at the enquiry at Serajevo for the purposes of the later enquiry.

8. The Servian Government will reinforce and extend the measures which have been taken for preventing the illicit traffic of arms and explosives across the frontier. It goes without saying that they will immediately order an enquiry and will severely punish the frontier officials on the Schabatz-Loznitza line who have failed in their duty and allowed the authors of the crime of Serajevo to pass.

9. The Royal Government will gladly give explanations of the remarks made by their officials whether in Servia or abroad, in interviews after the crime which according to the statement of the Imperial and Royal Government were hostile towards the Monarchy, as soon as the Imperial and Royal Government have communicated to them the passages in question in these remarks, and as soon as they have shown that the remarks were actually made by the said officials, although the Royal Government will itself take steps to collect evidence and proofs.

10. The Royal Government will inform the Imperial and Royal Government of the execution of the measures comprised under the above heads, in so far as this has not already been done by the present note, as soon as each measure has been ordered and carried out.

If the Imperial and Royal Government are not satisfied with this reply, the Servian Government, considering that it is not to the common interest to precipitate the solution of this question, are ready, as always, to accept a pacific understanding, either by referring this question to the decision of the International Tribunal of The Hague, or to the Great Powers which took part in the drawing up of the declaration made by the Servian Government on the 18th (31st) [old and new style date] March 1909.

Belgrade, July 12 (25), 1914.

Collected Diplomatic Documents Relating to the Outbreak of the European War (London: His Majesty's Stationery Office, 1915), pp. 31–37.

One day after receiving the preceding note, Austria declared war on Serbia. Serbia appealed to Russia, and that nation mobilized in order to go to Serbia's defense, thus setting off a chain reaction which was to make the war a Europe-wide conflict.

196   *Dr. M. Spalaikovitch, Minister at Petrograd, to M. Sazonof,*
        Russian Minister for Foreign Affairs

Petrograd, July 15/28, 1914

Your Excellency,

I have the honor to inform Your Excellency that I have received from M. Pashitch the following urgent telegram despatched from Nish at 2:10 p.m.

"The Austro-Hungarian Government declared war on Serbia today at noon by an open telegram to the Serbian Government."

I have the honor to inform Your Excellency of this regrettable act, which a Great Power had the courage to commit against a small Slav country which only recently emerged from a long series of heroic but exhausting battles, and I beg leave on this occasion of deep gravity for my country, to express the hope that this act, which disturbs the peace of Europe and revolts her conscience, will be condemned by the whole civilized world and severely punished by Russia, the protector of Serbia.

I beg Your Excellency to be so kind as to lay this petition from the whole Serbian nation before the throne of His Majesty.

I take this opportunity to assure Your Excellency of my loyalty and respect.

I have, &c.

Ibid., p. 392. (From the *Serbian Blue Book*.)

President Woodrow Wilson's speech on the Declaration of War against Germany stressed his view of the issues involved in the conflict.

197   . . . let us be very clear, and make very clear to all the world what our motives and our objects are. . . . Our object now, as then, is to vindicate the principles of peace and justice in the life of the world as against selfish and autocratic power and to set up amongst the really free and self-governed peoples of the world such a concert of purpose and of action as will henceforth insure the observance of these principles. Neutrality is no longer feasible or desirable where the peace of the world is involved and the freedom lies in the existence of autocratic governments backed by organized force which is controlled wholly by their will, not by the will of their people. We have seen the last of neutrality in such circumstances. We are at the beginning of an age in which it will be insisted that the same standards of conduct and of responsibility for wrong done shall be observed among nations and their governments that are observed among the individual citizens of civilized states.

We have no quarrel with the German people. We have no feeling towards them but one of sympathy and friendship. It was not upon their impulse that their government acted in entering this war. It was not with their previous knowledge or approval. It was a war determined upon as wars used to be determined upon in the old unhappy days when peoples were nowhere consulted by their rulers and wars were provoked and waged in the interest of dynasties or of little groups of ambitious men who were accustomed to use their fellow men as pawns and tools. . . .

We are accepting this challenge of hostile purpose because we know that in such a Government, following such methods, we can never have a friend; and that in the presence of its organized power, always lying in wait to accomplish we know not what purpose, there can be no assured security for the democratic Governments of the world. We are now about to accept gauge of battle with this natural foe to liberty and shall, if necessary, spend the whole force of the nation to check and nullify its pretensions and its power. We are glad, now that we see the facts with no veil of false pretense about them, to fight thus for the ultimate peace of the world and for the liberation of its peoples, the German peoples included: for the rights of nations great and small and the privilege of men everywhere to choose their way of life and of obedience. The world must be made safe for democracy. Its peace must be planted upon the tested foundations of political liberty. We have no selfish ends to serve. We desire no conquest, no dominion. We seek no indemnities for ourselves, no material compensation for the sacrifices we shall freely make. We are but one of the champions of the rights of mankind. We shall be satisfied when those rights have been made as secure as the faith and the freedom of nations can make them.

Sixty-fifth Congress, first session (*Senate Document 5*), *passim.*

QUESTIONS

1. Looking at the table of men and materials, can you determine the relative strength of the powers at the beginning of the war? How does this strength influence the course of the war?

2. Do you think the Serbian reply to the Austrian note meets all the points demanded by Austria?

3. Comparing the Austrian and Serbian notes, can you come to any conclusion about "guilt" in the immediate outbreak of hostilities?

4. Can you see in President Wilson's statement a foreshadowing of the Fourteen Points?

5. Why does Wilson support the side of the Triple Entente?

CHAPTER XXXII

PEACE AT VERSAILLES

IN VIEW of subsequent developments, the Peace of Versailles has been described as a "lost peace." It was a peace settlement which attempted to deal with the problem of balance-of-power politics through the creation of a League of Nations (198), and which was, on the whole, lenient toward Germany, if not toward the other vanquished nations. The principle of the self-determination of peoples was seriously discussed for the first time and even put into practice in some parts of Europe, such as Yugoslavia. The high hopes which the treaty inspired can be seen in Clemenceau's speech to the French Chamber of Deputies (199). Two decades after the peace conference, another chief architect of the treaty, David Lloyd George, once more came to its defense (200). Lloyd George by then realized that the hopes which had been put upon the treaty had not been fulfilled, and he gives us his opinion of the reasons for that failure. You can compare them with the documents on the international scene from 1919 to 1939, and, in particular, with Maxim Litvinov's arguments for collective security (see p. 510).

The following is an extract from the Covenant of the League of Nations, concentrating on those articles which envisaged sanctions against aggressors (1919).

198   The High Contracting Parties,

In order to promote international co-operation, and to achieve international peace and security,

by the acceptance of obligations not to resort to war,

by the prescription of open, just and honourable dealings between nations,

by the firm establishment of the understandings of international law as the actual rule of conduct among governments, and

by the maintenance of justice and a scrupulous respect for all treaty obligations in the dealings of organized peoples with one another,

Agree to this Covenant of the League of Nations. . . .

(Article 12) The members of the League agree that if there should arise between them any dispute likely to lead to a rupture, they will submit the matter either to arbitration or to inquiry by the Council. . . .

(Article 16) Should any member of the League resort to war in disregard of its covenants under Articles 12, 13, or 15, it shall *ipso facto* be deemed to have committed an act of war against all other members of the League, which hereby undertake immediately to subject it to severance of all trade or financial relations. . . . It shall be the duty of the Council in such case to recommend to all the several governments what effective military, naval, or air forces the members of the League shall severally contribute to the armed forces to be used to protect the covenants of the League. . . .

(Article 18) Every treaty or international engagement entered into hereafter by any member of the League shall be forthwith registered with the Secretariat and published as soon as possible. . . .

(Article 20) The members of the League severally agree that this Covenant is accepted as abrogating all obligations or understandings *inter se* (among themselves) which are inconsistent with the terms thereof.

The Treaties of Peace, 1919–23 (New York: Carnegie Endowment for International Peace, 1924), I, 10, 14, 17, 18, 19. (Reprinted by permission of the publisher.)

On Monday, June 30, 1919, two days after the Treaty of Versailles was signed, Clemenceau, as head of the cabinet, presented the document to the French Chamber of Deputies. He used the occasion to deliver the following address, which was received with great emotion.

Note the references to France's revolutionary ideals, to her sacrifices, and to the treatment accorded to France in 1871 by the then victorious Germany and its chancellor, Bismarck. Perhaps even more significant is Clemenceau's repeated preoccupation with the deep underlying social tensions in France.

Gentlemen. I have the honor of placing before the Chamber . . . the **199** treaty of peace concluded at Versailles on June 28, 1919, between France [and her allies] on the one hand, and Germany on the other, accompanied by complementary acts, including . . . the treaties signed at Versailles on June 28, 1919, between France and the United States of America and be-tween France and Great Britain concerning the support to be given to France in the case of unprovoked German aggression.

I do not wish to anticipate the discussion which will take place here of the specific provisions of the treaty itself or of the spirit which inspired it. At the very moment, however, when the greatest drama in history is drawing to a close, and while we are still trembling from the supreme effort so magnificently accomplished, the first thought in our minds ought to be for the future of France and of all mankind. France's ideal, the ideal of humanity itself, we can—indeed we must—publicly acclaim as in har-mony with the thoughts of our great ancestors under whose guidance it is our hope to keep the nation.

What an unbounded joy it is to be able to stand on this rostrum and speak the definitive word: because of the sacrifices of France and her allies, the world has at last been rescued from the deadly peril in which it stood.

Now our sole responsibility is the duty of seeing to it that the old spirit of military domination remains forever crushed. The day has come when force and right, the one dangerous, the other in danger wherever separated, must be joined together to establish the kind of peace in which men may pursue their appointed tasks. Then humanity may rise to its full stature.

This peace, we shall achieve it as we did in battle, with a will nothing can make deviate. This peace, we will defend it as we fought the war, without weakness or theatrical arrogance, but with the inflexible resolve of remaining faithful to our glorious dead whose desire it was to push forward ever farther, ever higher in pursuit of France's historic mission.

Since France stands at the frontier of events, it was inevitable that first against her would be directed that abominable effort to establish universal oppression which has just been annihilated. In order to crush the right of free peoples in the fullness of the enjoyment of life, it was necessary above everything else that the France of the Revolution be defeated. All was demanded of us; we gave all.

This peace, it is proper to say here and now, must be a peace among friends, as well as one containing the sanctions of justice. General peace, in fact, will one day become a false mirage if we are not above all capable of living in peace among ourselves, that is to say, of contributing as profoundly to the internal peace of our own country as to peace abroad.

In order to achieve that, it is essential that old conflicts be settled, and settled by compromise, for if the spirit of warfare persists in any form, civil peace will be betrayed at the very moment we wish to secure it.

External peace has been won in a sublime moment by the sacrifice of everything that makes life worth while and valuable. Internal peace can be obtained only by a continuous effort in a spirit of equity transcending the impulses, ambitions, beliefs, and thoughts of the traditionally opposed, even occasionally contradictory, interests involved.

An unsung, frequently thankless, heroism of voluntary self-denial is necessary to the determined preservation of the rational order, which, if it does not immediately produce all that is desired, can bring their gradual realization by whatever degree we are able to implant in party activity that idealism so easily expressed but so slowly embodied into living reality.

Is this not the real objective of the Republic, the one it has had ever since the day it was born in the struggles of the Revolution? Is this not the history of France we find traced here? If our victory in war is to become our victory in peace, there are several victories over ourselves we must first win.

At Bordeaux, at Versailles in 1871, I had the sad experience of witnessing with my own eyes and heart the inflicting of a deep wound which has never healed. Military revenge and moral revenge thereupon became synonymous. The first has come. Earlier, in defeat, we had begun the other. In victory, we shall complete it.

For far too long have we dissipated our strength in political and social conflict, the fate of all peoples of all times, and which, despite their fecundity, has in the end always sapped their energy, this is the universal history of all mankind. Every great conquest has cost a tumultuous effort. The outcome this time is victory in the noblest sense of the word, victory not only in deed but also of an idea, victory not just of men but of France, of the Republic itself, victory of all our parliaments which labored toward the common goal of rebuilding France so she might regain her rightful place in the world; victory of all our governments which, since the dismemberment of the nation, have borne the perilous honor of confronting the riddle posed by the German sphinx: victory or death. We have chosen. The enigma has been resolved.

The man who, after 1871, was responsible for organizing the final savage onslaught aimed at establishing universal servitude, stupidly boasted that in allowing, nay, encouraging, our reborn Republic, he was supporting a regime which would bring weakness, discord, and national ruin. That is all he knew about liberty!

Ah, well, the experiment he wished to try went on unhampered for half a century. His people, whom he chained to the chariot of the lord of war and whose necks were yoked for the abasement of the human species, can now verify the full results of the proof. History has spoken clearly.

It is true our fields are ravaged, our towns and cities razed, the cream of our youth buried in consecrated soil in shrouds of glory—our most precious treasure. All of these costs have been prodigious beyond measure. Our best blood has been shed, tears have creased all our faces, all our hearts have trembled with an indescribable horror, but the tears of our anguish and the blood of our wounds have left us better, nobler, greater, more completely French. France is erect, alive, and strong, as strong in her desires for justice as in the military virtues of her great soldiers, of whom the greater part have already returned to civilian life, without forgetting our constant need for vigilance.

And now all the work for the fulfillment of the duties of tomorrow succeeds that of yesterday and today—for the completion, before all, of the necessary reparations. No less indispensable in peace than in war, social harmony remains that fundamental basis of our country which we could hardly have saved from barbarians only to destroy with our own hands. . . . Let us begin, all of us. The hour is pressing.

The government, for its part, will try as best it can to replace progressively the chaotic expediencies of the war with a rational peacetime system. Do not expect miracles. No people have been known to pass suddenly from the upsetting conditions of a desperate defense to the orderly existence we all want without serious difficulty.

Gentlemen, you are the representatives of the people. No one would doubt but that you are inspired with a deep sense of your duty. In agreement with you, we have collaborated in a task for which your support was never lacking. That task will be completed in the way you know best how to determine, and you will decide in full independence. The law of democracies establishes that the people are the ultimate voice of the nation.

Annales de la Chambre des Députés, session ordinaire de 1919, deuxième partie (Paris, 1920), pp. 2726–27. (Trans. H. B. Hill.)

David Lloyd George, who had been British prime minister during and after the war (1916–22), was one of the chief architects of the Treaty of Versailles. Writing twenty years later (1939), he asked whether the treaty had achieved its object.

200   Let us examine whether or not the Treaties have achieved the aims which their framers strove and hoped to attain. To do this it is necessary to summarize the objects which they had in view:

(1). The vindication of international right.

Under this heading the aggressors were beaten. By the Armistice they were obliged to give up territory they had forcibly occupied, and by the Peace Treaties to pay heavy compensation for damage inflicted on the invaded countries owing to their lawlessness.

(2) The liberation of oppressed nations which had for centuries been victimized by the rapine of greedy and tyrannical Empires.

No peace ever signed emancipated as many subject races. The treaties constitute a charter of freedom for Poland, Alsace-Lorraine, Czechoslovakia, Transylvania, Croatia, Slovenia, Bosnia, Herzegovina, and the many lands where dwell the Arabs of the Turkish Empire. From the estuary of the Vistula to the mouth of the Euphrates the despotisms of generations were overthrown and cleared off the map. For the first time boundaries were fixed on the principle of government with the consent of the governed, and after taking evidence as to the wishes of inhabitants, shifted from one allegiance to another.

(3) The breaking up of the huge armaments that were responsible for the War, and especially for its unparalleled destructiveness in human life and property. The Treaties stipulated that the aggressors were to set an example and that then the victorious countries were to follow.

The first part of this was achieved to the complete satisfaction of the Allies. As to the second part, with the exception of Britain, the victors were guilty of an outrageous breach of faith. In effect and in practice they repudiated the undertaking they had given.

(4) War was treated as a crime against society for which redress was to be made in respect of all damage inflicted on the victims of the aggressor, and for which the guilty were to be tried and punished by a tribunal responsible to the nations. Those who had transgressed the laws of war were to be tried and punished as criminals.

For this stipulation we found that the public attitude was not ripe for action. When war was denounced in pulpit, on platform and in the Press, as a crime we discovered that the expression was rhetorical and had no ethical foundation in the conscience of mankind.

(5) The framers of the Treaties placed in the forefront of all the Peace Treaties the establishment of a Society of Nations for the settlement of international disputes by peaceable methods and secured the adhesion of 42 nations, great and small, to a Covenant that would bind them to combine their forces against any transgressors who violated international right. They aimed at the substitution of the reign of law amongst nations for the endless national conflicts which had drenched continents with blood.

The weakness and the vacillation displayed in the direction of the affairs of the League of Nations have frustrated the purpose which the authors of the Treaty had in view in setting up this great and beneficent organization.

(6) A new international organization was created in order to humanize the conditions of labour throughout the world.

This organization has been one of the unchallengeable triumphs of the Treaty.

(7) The treatment of the German Colonies as an international trust administered for the benefit of the uncivilized peoples of these vast regions.

This has been achieved and fairly administered.

(8) The conferring upon the League of Nations of full powers to revise any part of the Treaties where experience revealed that it was unjust or unworkable.

Up to the present the League has not exercised these powers, and most of the trouble in Europe to-day is due to its complete neglect of this important function which was cast upon it.

These are the essential aims and actual provisions of the Treaties. In what respect have any of these enactments contravened the principles of equity and wise statesmanship? Such crudities and injustices as were revealed by experience in the Treaties, and which in their operation irritated and embittered nations, must inevitably creep into any arrangements which are patched up in a hurry on so vast a scale. They could have been removed under the revisionary provisions of the Treaty enacted for that purpose, provided these had been honestly applied. . . .

Where there has been failure it has been attributable to two causes. The first is the way in which the victorious nations who dictated the Treaties have broken the pledges they gave when the Treaties were signed:

(1) They refused to carry out the solemn undertaking they gave to Germany that once she were disarmed they would follow her example.

(2) In one case after another of wanton aggression against weak countries who were members of the League, the Great Powers have failed to come to their aid and to check aggression.

(3) Undertakings given as an integral part of the Peace Settlement that the rights of minority races in a country would be respected have been shamelessly disregarded.

(4) The revisionary provisions of the Treaty have been ignored.

The Treaties are not to be blamed for these events, but the dishonourable infraction of them. The permanence of a peace settlement depends not only on the justice of its provisions, but also on the wisdom and integrity of its interpreters. Vision, breadth of sympathy and outlook, restraint, honest dealing, courage and magnanimity were essential to the successful working of the Peace Treaties. These attributes were conspicuously absent amongst the men to whose lot fell the application and execution of the Treaties. Fate played a shattering part in the working of the healing and appeasing measures projected by the scheme of the Settlement.

David Lloyd George, *Memoirs of the Peace Conference* (New Haven: Yale University Press, 1939), II, 907–11. (Reprinted by permission of the publishers and of the holders of copyright.)

QUESTIONS

1. How does Clemenceau tie the past history of the Republic to the present peace settlement?
2. Is there any evidence in this extract that Clemenceau thought of the treaty as one of "revenge"?
3. On what factors does Lloyd George blame the failure of the treaty? Do you think they are justified and can you think of any concrete instances which would prove his point?
4. Do you think his good opinion of the treaty has justification? Compare this with Stresemann's opinions (p. 505).

CHAPTER XXXIII

THE RUSSIAN REVOLUTION

RUSSIA experienced three revolutions in the first two decades of the twentieth century: the Revolution of 1905, the March Revolution of 1917, and the November Revolution of 1917. The first of these explosions was set off by Bloody Sunday (January 22), 1905, when an unarmed procession led by an Orthodox priest, Father George Gapon, came peaceably to Tsar Nicholas II's Winter Palace bearing a petition, only to be shot down (201). The decade which followed provided the Russian Old Regime with its last chance. Despite weak attempts at semi-parliamentary government, land reform, and social legislation, the Russian monarchy could not withstand the pressures which were heightened and then released by the first World War. In March, 1917 (February by the old Julian calendar used by the Russians), a spontaneous revolt (202) led to the Tsar's abdication and the formation of a Provisional Government (203).

However, side by side with that middle-class government was an extra-legal body, the Council (Soviet) of Workers' and Soldiers' Deputies, which represented various parties of the Left, including the small but well-organized Bolshevik minority. It was this Soviet which issued the famous Order No. I (204), which showed that while the Provisional Government had legal recognition, the Soviet wielded the real power. It was with his arrival from exile in April, 1917, that Lenin, the Bolshevik leader, began to urge an end to this dual power (205, 206) and the establishment of a Communist-led dictatorship of the proletariat. Lenin's theses triumphed with the success of the Communist coup against the middle-class government of Russia in November, 1917 (207, 208). Not even a Constituent Assembly on January 9, 1918, was able to restore parliamentary government to Russia (209).

I. THE REVOLUTION OF 1905

Here is the text of Father George Gapon's petition to Tsar Nicholas II which an unarmed procession of workers and their families bore to the Winter Palace on January 22, 1905. The letter which follows the petition reflects the Orthodox priest's horror at the massacre which took place on that Bloody Sunday.

201   Sire: We, working men and inhabitants of St. Petersburg of various classes, our wives and our children and our helpless old parents, come to Thee, Sire, to seek for truth and defence. We have become beggars; we have been oppressed; we are burdened by toil beyond our powers; we are scoffed at; we are not recognized as human beings; we are treated as slaves who must suffer their bitter fate and who must keep silence. We suffered, but we are pushed farther into the den of beggary, lawlessness, and ignorance. We are choked by despotism and irresponsibility, and we are breathless. We have no more power, Sire, the limit of patience has been reached. There has arrived for us that tremendous moment when death is better than the continuation of intolerable tortures. We have left off working, and we have declared to the masters that we shall not begin to work until they comply with our demands. We beg but little; we desire only that without which life is not life, but hard labor and eternal torture. The first request which we made was that our masters should discuss our needs with us; but this they refused, on the ground that no right to make this request is recognized by law. They also declared to be illegal our requests to diminish the working hours to eight hours daily, to agree with us about the prices for our work, to consider our misunderstandings with the inferior administration of the mills, to increase the wages for the labor of women and of general laborers, so that the minimum daily wage should be one ruble per day, to abolish overtime work, to give us medical attention without insulting us, to arrange the workshops so that it might be possible to work there, and not find in them death from awful drafts and from rain and snow. All these requests appeared to be, in the opinion of our masters and of the factory and mill administrations, illegal. Every one of our requests was a crime, and the desire to improve our condition was regarded by them as impertinence, and as offensive to them.

Sire, here are many thousands of us, and all are human beings only in appearance. In reality in us, as in all Russian people, there is not recognized any human right, not even the right of speaking, thinking, meeting, discussing our needs, taking measures for the improvement of our condition. We have been enslaved, and enslaved under the auspices of Thy officials, with their assistance, and with their co-operation. Every one of us who dares to raise a voice in defence of working-class and popular interests is thrown into jail or is sent into banishment. For the possession of good hearts and sensitive souls we are punished as for crimes. Even to pity a beaten man—a man tortured and without rights—means to commit a heavy crime. All the people—working men as well as peasants—are handed over to the discretion of the officials of the Government, who are thieves of the property of the State—robbers who not only take no care of the interests of the people, but who trample these interests under their feet. The Government officials have brought the country to complete destruction, have involved it in a detestable war, and have further and further led it to ruin. We working men have no voice in the expenditure of the enormous amounts raised from us in taxes. We do not know even where and for what is spent the money collected from a beggared people. The people are deprived of the possibility of expressing their desires, and they now demand that they be allowed to take part in the introduction of taxes and in the expenditure of them.

The working men are deprived of the possibility of organizing themselves in unions for the defence of their interests.

Sire, is it in accordance with divine law, by grace of which Thou reignest? Is it not better to die, better for all of us toiling people of Russia, and to let the capitalist exploiters of the working class, officials, "grafters," and robbers of the Russian people live? This is before us, Sire, and this has brought us to the walls of Thy Palace. We are seeking here the last salvation. Do not refuse assistance to Thy people. Bring them from the grave of rightlessness, beggary, and ignorance. Give their destiny into their own hands. Cast away from them the intolerable oppression of officials. Destroy the wall between Thyself and Thy people, and let them rule the country together with Thyself. Art Thou not placed there for the happiness of Thy people? But this happiness the officials snatch from our hands. It does not come to us. We get only distress and humiliation. Look without anger, attentively upon our requests. They are directed, not to evil, but to good for us as well as for Thee. Sire! not impudence, but consciousness of needs, of emerging from a situation intolerable for us all, becomes articulate in us.

Russia is too great. Its necessities are too various and numerous for officials alone to rule it. National representation is indispensable. It is indispensable that people should assist and rule themselves. To them only are known their real necessities. Do not reject their assistance, accept it, order immediately the convocation of representatives of the Russian land from all ranks, including representatives from the working men. Let there be capitalists as well as working men—official and priest, doctor and teacher —let all, whatever they may be, elect their representatives. Let everyone be equal and free in the right of election, and for this purpose order that the elections for the Constitutional Assembly be carried on under the condition of universal, equal, and secret voting. This is the most capital of our requests. In it and upon it everything is based. This is the principal and only plaster for our painful wounds, without which our wounds will fester and will bring us rapidly near to death. Yet one measure alone cannot heal our wounds. Other measures are also indispensable. Directly and openly as to a Father, we speak to Thee, Sire, about them in person, for all the toiling classes of Russia. The following are indispensable:

I. Measures against the ignorance and rightlessness of the Russian people:

1. The immediate release and return of all who have suffered for political and religious convictions, for strikes, and national peasant disorders.

2. The immediate declaration of freedom and of the inviolability of the person—freedom of speech and press, freedom of meetings, and freedom of conscience in religion.

3. Universal and compulsory elementary education of the people at the charge of the State.

4. Responsibility of the Ministers before the people and guarantee that the Government will be law abiding.

5. Equality before the law of all without exception.

6. Separation of the Church from the State.

II. Measures against the poverty of the people:

1. Abolition of indirect taxes and the substitution of a progressive income tax.

2. Abolition of the Redemption Instalments, cheap credit, and gradual transference of the land to the people.

3. The orders for the military and naval ministries should be fulfilled in Russia, and not abroad.

4. The cessation of the war by the will of the people.

III. Measures against the oppression of labor:

1. Abolition of the factory inspectorships.

2. Institution at factories and mills of permanent committees of elected workers, which, together with the administration (of the factories) would consider the complaints of individual workers. Discharge of working men should not take place otherwise than by resolution of this committee.

3. Freedom of organization of co-operative societies of consumers and of labor trade unions immediately.

4. Eight hours working day and regulation of overtime working.

5. Freedom of the struggle of labor against capital immediately.

6. Normal wages immediately.

7. Participation of working-class representatives in the working out of projects of law upon workmen's State insurance immediately.

Here, Sire, are our principal necessities with which we come to Thee! Only by the satisfaction of these the release of our native land from slavery and beggary is possible; only by this means is possible the flourishing of our native land, and is it possible for working men to organize themselves for the defence of their interests against impudent exploitation of capitalists and of the officials' government which is plundering and choking the people. Order and take an oath to comply with these requests, and Thou wilt make Russia happy and famous and Thou wilt impress Thy name in our hearts and in the hearts of our posterity to all eternity. If Thou wilt not order and wilt not answer our prayers—we shall die here on this Place before Thy Palace.

We have nowhere to go farther and nothing for which to go. We have only two ways—either towards liberty and happiness or into the grave. . . . Let our life be a sacrifice for Russia which has suffered to the extreme limit. We do not regret this sacrifice. We willingly offer it.

Letter to Nicholas Romanov, formerly Tsar and at present soul destroyer of the Russian Empire

With naïve belief in thee as father of thy people, I was going peacefully to thee with the children of these very people. Thou must have known, thou didst know, this. The innocent blood of workers, their wives and children, lies forever between thee, O soul destroyer, and the Russian people.

Moral connection between thee and them may never be any more. The mighty river during its overflowing thou art already unable to stem by any half measures, even by a Zemsky Sobor [Popular Assembly]. Bombs and dynamite, the terror by individuals and by masses, against thy breed and against the robbers of rightless people—all this must be and shall absolutely be. A sea of blood—unexampled—will be shed. Because of thee, because of thy whole family, Russia may perish. Once for all, understand this and remember, better soon with all thy family abdicate the throne of Russia and give thyself up to the Russian people for trial. Pity thy children and the Russian lands, O thou offerer of peace for other countries and blood drunkard for thine own!

Otherwise let all blood which has to be shed fall upon thee, Hangman, and thy kindred!

George Gapon

Postscriptum. Know that this letter is the justifying document of the coming revolutionary terroristic occurrences in Russia.

20th March—7th February 1905.   *G.G.*

Supplement to *Revolutionary Russia,* No. 59, 10th February 1905. [Printed in Geneva.]

James Mavor, *An Economic History of Russia* (New York: E. P. Dutton & Co., 1914), II, 469–73. (Reprinted by permission of the publisher.)

II. THE MARCH REVOLUTION OF 1917

The following eyewitness account of the March Revolution in Petrograd and Moscow comes from a letter by an American which was published in the New York *Evening Post* on May 5, 1917.

202   Moscow, Russia, March 15.—This letter, I am fairly sure, will eventually fall into your hands, for some one is kind enough to take it to America for me. The last three days have been historical and every one declares that to-day, the 15th of March, is going to be an annual holiday in Russia to celebrate this marvelously successful Revolution.

On Thursday last, the 8th of March, H. was in Petrograd, and, as far as I can gather, there was a strike among the workmen for bread. This strike was put down with a little bloodshed by the soldiers. Now, this strike was the final bubbling over of a kettle that had been long in the boiling. All over Russia there had been the desperate feeling of being betrayed to the Germans, that no matter how great their courage and sacrifice might be, in the end, the fruit of their sacrifices would be denied them and everything handed over to the Germans. Whole regiments have been wiped out at the front, sent there without arms. Brusilov, every one, has been hindered in every possible way while the German officials were nullifying all Russia's gigantic sacrifices. They all say, 'If we had only a chance, we would have beaten the Germans long ago.' The chance has never been given them, and they were being driven crazy by the thought.

I have just come back from Kazan; there, steaks are being sold for fifty kopeks and bread and compote for fifty kopeks. Two hundred versts [a measurement] from Moscow there were masses of white bread going begging; in Moscow, bread lines were everywhere and, of course, there was great suffering. The Russians are all convinced that the Germans are responsible for this, and I imagine that they are. Every one despised the Tzar, hated the Empress as a traitress, and all agreed that Russia was in as bad a way as she well could be, and that the war could not go on under such conditions very much longer.

To return to the sequence of events. On Friday, March the ninth, in Petrograd, crowds began gathering and on Saturday afternoon the storm broke. There was no mob rioting in the streets. All was too well organized. It was a battle between the regiments on the people's side and those on the Tzar's. All Friday, the people had been mingling with patrolling infantry and cavalry, arguing with them and explaining the causes of their revolt; they only wanted bread. 'Dear little soldiers, don't shoot us, all we want is bread'; and in this business the women were as active as the men. The Pavlovsk regiment went over first, killed its colonel and joined the people. Then one by one, the people gained company after company and, finally, on Saturday only one regiment remained loyal. This regiment took up its quarters across the Liteinaya with machine guns and waited. Meanwhile all the officers had had their swords taken away and those who resisted were killed. The policemen were locked up in a big building and burned alive. That seems to have been the only really bloody slaughter. . . .

When H. arrived in Moscow on Monday morning I was having my breakfast and he told me the news. I was fairly knocked out, for it was indeed news to me. Of course, the same news came down with him on the train, and, as we were talking, a crowd of students went by the hotel singing. I shall never forget the thrill. The Revolution was on here, too. There were crowds of people in front of the Duma [city council] which is situated opposite the Sacred Yellow Gate which leads to the Red Square. On the Duma itself the red flag was flying. We mingled with the crowds and watched. Troops began marching. The soldiers grimly enough and the people wheedling them as they walked alongside, begging them not to shoot and saying that all they wanted was bread; and the appeals to refrain from shooting were not made from fear. As we watched, a squadron of cavalry galloped in formation of fours through the gate, formed in a long line, two deep, and charged the crowd, and the crowd did not move an inch, did not even sway. Once in a while, one of the marching soldiers would wave his hat and the crowd would cheer wildly. It seemed to dread bloodshed, but to be ready to stand anything if the test should come. The soldiers lined the Red Square, both infantry and cavalry, and a crowd of, perhaps, ten thousand people stood around, mostly students, arguing with the soldiers. So the situation remained through Monday night.

On Tuesday morning things were stirring early. The streets leading to the Duma Square were filled with masses of strangely silent people; students everywhere kept marvellous order. The roadway was kept open. No one was allowed in the Red Square or in the path of the troops or in the Duma Square. They realized well that, if a great mob collected in the squares, and become entangled with the soldiers, great disturbances would follow. This must be avoided, and the students controlled the crowd in a good-humored, cheerful way, and no one was angry as yet. One angry word from an officer, a stray shot, or a drunken brawler would at that stage have meant a bloody riot. Thanks to the students' wonderful organization, however, it never occurred. They were everywhere. Some linking arms and holding back the crowd; others walking through the crowd urging temperance and patience; others talking with the soldiers. During all of Tuesday, detachments deserted and came over to the crowd, and, as they marched along shouting their wonderful marching songs, the crowd cheered them wildly. All day this went on, and by night-time the Duma Square was packed with men. Perfect discipline had been maintained all day. The crowd was kept in the streets, not allowed to mass in the squares, while the garrison was slowly coming over.

On Wednesday morning the first company of Cossacks rode in. They were wildly cheered. All felt now that the Revolution had nothing to fear if the hated Cossacks were on their side. During the morning they acquired three field-guns and much cavalry. At five o'clock they pointed a field-gun at the Kremlin Gate, massed their soldiers, and gave the regulars five minutes to surrender. The Kremlin surrendered, then the Manege, and now, without a single shot being fired, the Revolution was in control of Moscow. As fast as the old Government brought in outside regiments, they went over to the people. The sight on Wednesday night can never be forgotten—the vast, cheering crowds, the deep-throated singing of the marching soldiers, the stacked arms and bivouac fires in the Duma Square, the artillery commanding the approaches. There were now about fifteen guns in the Square, with their caissons. All the streets as far as the eye could see were packed with crowds, and then more crowds cheering, cheering, almost ready to cry with joy, laughing and talking quietly together, as Russians do. All through, there had been no loud yelling—either cheering or quiet talking. No uproariousness, no hooliganism, and this you could understand when you looked at the crowd. They all seemed prosperous and well-to-do. All in furs. No roughs or toughs. All either good old mujiks [peasants] or the intelligentsia. And all so very happy. Every one went home at night. When I went out this morning, the Revolution was over. Constitutional government was assured, and the whole people began to make holiday.

If there had been masses yesterday, what were there today? The squares were a solid mass, and the streets also. I made my way through it to a small hill looking down on the square of the Great Theatre, and the streets leading to it. A vast river of people was flowing down the hill with a band at its head, playing the Marseillaise; the cheering was one solid roar, and, as far as the eye could see, was a vast mass of men and women, all carrying red flags. Various lanes were kept open by the students, and down these marched the soldiers, also processions of all kinds, some of women, usually singing the Marseillaise, some of the auto-trucks filled with officers and students waving red flags, some of fire engines. It was all a great holiday. I did not hear an angry voice or see an angry face all day. Gradually they began to disperse, and by six o'clock they were all quiet again. Perfect order had been maintained. One or two men had tried to start a pogrom. They were immediately arrested. A little boy near me yelled out 'Oorah!' An officer turned round and said 'Nye kreetchi, maltchik' [don't scream, little boy]; that is the motto of the Revolution; noise and disturbance were frowned upon.

Such has been the chronological sequence of events in Petrograd and Moscow. . . .

It seems to me as if a great weight were lifted off Russia. No more Germans in control; no more secret police; no more passports; freedom of the press. At last, they say, our country is going to develop; no longer are we under the thumb of Germany; as a united people and nation we are going to fulfill our destiny, and we are going to make an end to the war by throwing the whole of Russia's strength into it, unhampered by Germans. The last few years have seemed a horrid nightmare as they struggled under the thumb of Germany; now they have shaken themselves free and breathe again. How proud they are of their Revolution! 'Look how cleverly we did it! No bloodshed! No disagreeableness!' Even as I write a great chorus bursts out, as soldiers go marching by, a wonderful chorus that dies in the distance. It is more than I can write about. It is so great and magnificent a sight that we are both of us knocked out and speechless.

A. J. Sack, *The Birth of the Russian Democracy* (New York: Russian Information Service, 1918), pp. 228–33, 234–37. (Reprinted by permission of the publisher.)

This document, dated March 16, 1917, represents the first public act of the middle-class Provisional Government of Russia and outlines that government's program.

203   Citizens, the Provisional Executive Committee of the members of the Duma, with the aid and support of the garrison of the capital and its inhabitants, has triumphed over the dark forces of the Old Régime to such an extent as to enable it to organize a more stable executive power. With this idea in mind, the Provisional Committee has appointed as ministers of the first Cabinet representing the public, men whose past political and public life assures them the confidence of the country.

PRINCE GEORGE E. LVOV, *Prime Minister and Minister of the Interior*
P. N. MILIUKOV, *Minister of Foreign Affairs*
A. I. GUCHKOV, *Minister of War and Marine*
M. I. TERESCHENKO, *Minister of Finance*
A. A. MANUILOV, *Minister of Education*
A. I. SHINGAREV, *Minister of Agriculture*
N. V. NEKRASOV, *Minister of Transportation*
A. I. KONOVALOV, *Minister of Commerce and Industry*
A. F. KERENSKI, *Minister of Justice*
Vl. LVOV, *Holy Synod*

The Cabinet will be guided in its actions by the following principles:
1. An immediate general amnesty for all political and religious offenses, including terrorist acts, military revolts, agrarian offenses, etc.
2. Freedom of speech and press; freedom to form labor unions and to strike. These political liberties should be extended to the army in so far as war conditions permit.
3. The abolition of all social, religious and national restrictions.
4. Immediate preparation for the calling of a Constituent Assembly,

elected by universal and secret vote, which shall determine the form of government and draw up the Constitution for the country.

5. In place of the police, to organize a national militia with elective officers, and subject to the local self-governing body.

6. Elections to be carried out on the basis of universal, direct, equal, and secret suffrage.

7. The troops that have taken part in the revolutionary movement shall not be disarmed or removed from Petrograd.

8. On duty and in war service, strict military discipline should be maintained, but when off duty, soldiers should have the same public rights as are enjoyed by other citizens.

The Provisional Government wishes to add that it has no intention of taking advantage of the existence of war conditions to delay the realization of the above-mentioned measures of reform.

President of the Duma, M. RODZIANKO

President of the Council of Ministers, PRINCE LVOV

Ministers MILIUKOV, NEKRASOV, MANUILOV, KONOVALOV, TERESCHENKO, Vl. LVOV, SHINGAREV, KERENSKI.

Documents of Russian History, 1914–1917, ed. Frank Alfred Golder, trans. Emanuel Aronsberg (New York: Appleton-Century-Crofts, 1927), pp. 308–9. (Reprinted by permission of the publisher.)

Order No. I, issued by the Petrograd Soviet on March 14, 1917, not only virtually ended military discipline in the Russian armed forces but also proved that the real power lay not with the middle-class Provisional Government but with the left-wing Soviet of Workers' and Soldiers' Deputies.

Order No. I   **204**

March 14, 1917

To the garrison of the Petrograd District, to all the soldiers of the guard, army, artillery, and navy, for immediate and strict execution, and to the workers of Petrograd for their information:

The Soviet of Workers' and Soldiers' Deputies has resolved:

1. In all companies, battalions, regiments, parks, batteries, squadrons, in the special services of the various military administrations, and on the vessels of the navy, committees from the elected representatives of the lower ranks of the above-mentioned military units shall be chosen immediately.

2. In all those military units which have not yet chosen their representatives to the Soviet of Workers' Deputies, one representative from each company shall be selected, to report with written credentials at the building

of the State Duma by ten o'clock on the morning of the fifteenth of this March.

3. In all its political actions, the military branch is subordinated to the Soviet of Workers' and Soldiers' Deputies and to its own committees.

4. The orders of the military commission of the State Duma shall be executed only in such cases as do not conflict with the orders and resolutions of the Soviet of Workers' and Soldiers' Deputies.

5. All kinds of arms, such as rifles, machine guns, armoured automobiles, and others, must be kept at the disposal and under the control of the company and battalion committees, and in no case be turned over to officers, even at their demand.

6. In the ranks and during their performance of the duties of the service, soldiers must observe the strictest military discipline, but outside the service and the ranks, in their political, general civic, and private life, soldiers cannot in any way be deprived of those rights which all citizens enjoy. In particular, standing at attention and compulsory saluting, when not on duty, is abolished.

7. Also, the addressing of the officers with the title, "Your Excellency," "Your Honor," etc., is abolished, and these titles are replaced by the address of "Mister General," "Mister Colonel," etc. Rudeness towards soldiers of any rank, and, especially, addressing them as "Thou," is prohibited, and soldiers are required to bring to the attention of the company committees every infraction of this rule, as well as all misunderstandings occurring between officers and privates.

The present order is to be read to all companies, battalions, regiments, ships' crews, batteries, and other combatant and noncombatant commands.

Materials for the Study of the Soviet System, State and Party Constitutions, Laws, Decrees, Decisions and Official Statements of the Leaders in Translation, ed. James H. Meisel and Edward S. Kozera (Ann Arbor: Wahr's Bookstore, 1953), pp. 2–3. (Reprinted by permission of the publisher.)

Lenin returned to Russia from exile—in the famous "sealed car" across Germany—only in April, 1917. As soon as he arrived, he wrote these so-called April Theses, in which he outlined Bolshevik aims.

205   I arrived in Petrograd only on the night of April 2, and I could therefore, of course, deliver a report at the meeting on April 4 on the tasks of the revolutionary proletariat only upon my own responsibility, and with reservations as to insufficient preparation.

The only thing I could do to facilitate matters for myself and for *honest* opponents was to prepare *written* theses. I read them, and gave the text to

Comrade Tsereteli. I read them very slowly, twice: first at a meeting of Bolsheviks and then at a meeting of Bolsheviks and Mensheviks.

I publish these personal theses with only the briefest explanatory comments, which were developed in far greater detail in the report.

Theses

1. In our attitude towards the war, which also under the new government of Lvov and Co. unquestionably remains on Russia's part a predatory imperialist war owing to the capitalist nature of that government, not the slightest concession must be made to "revolutionary defencism."

The class-conscious proletariat could consent to a revolutionary war, which would really justify revolutionary defencism, only on condition: a) that the power of government pass to the proletariat and the poorest sections of the peasantry bordering on the proletariat; b) that all annexations be renounced in deed and not only in word; c) that a complete and real break be made with all capitalist interests.

In view of the undoubted honesty of the broad strata of the mass believers in revolutionary defencism, who accept the war as a necessity only, and not as a means of conquest, in view of the fact that they are being deceived by the bourgeoisie, it is necessary very thoroughly, persistently and patiently to explain their error to them, to explain the inseparable connection between capital and the imperialist war, and to prove that *it is impossible* to end the war by a truly democratic, non-coercive peace without the overthrow of capital.

The most widespread propaganda of this view among the army on active service must be organized.

Fraternization.

2. The specific feature of the present situation in Russia is that it represents a *transition* from the first stage of the revolution—which, owing to the insufficient class-consciousness and organization of the proletariat, placed the power in the hands of the bourgeoisie—*to the second* stage, which must place the power in the hands of the proletariat and the poorest strata of the peasantry.

This transition is characterized, on the one hand, by a maximum of freedom (Russia is *now* the freest of all the belligerent countries in the world); on the other, by the absence of violence in relation to the masses, and, finally, by the unreasoning confidence of the masses in the government of capitalists, the worst enemies of peace and Socialism.

This specific situation demands of us an ability to adapt ourselves to the *specific* requirements of Party work among unprecedentedly large masses of proletarians who have just awakened to political life.

3. No support must be given to the Provisional Government; the utter falsity of all its promises must be explained, particularly those relating to the renunciation of annexations. Exposure, and not the unpardonable illusion-breeding "demand" that *this* government, a government of capitalists, should *cease* to be an imperialist government.

4. The fact must be recognized that in most of the Soviets of Workers' Deputies our Party is in a minority, and so far in a small minority, as against *a bloc of all* the petty-bourgeois opportunist elements, who have yielded to the influence of the bourgeoisie and convey its influence to the proletariat, from the Popular Socialists and the Socialist-Revolutionaries down to the Organization Committee (Chkheidze, Tsereteli, etc.), Steklov, etc., etc.

It must be explained to the masses that the Soviets of Workers' Deputies are the *only possible* form of revolutionary government, and that therefore our task is, as long as *this* government yields to the influence of the bourgeoisie, to present a patient, systematic, and persistent *explanation* of the errors of their tactics, an explanation especially adapted to the practical needs of the masses.

As long as we are in the minority we carry on the work of criticizing and explaining errors and at the same time we preach the necessity of transferring the entire power of state to the Soviets of Workers' Deputies, so that the masses may by experience overcome their mistakes.

5. Not a parliamentary republic—to return to a parliamentary republic from the Soviets of Workers' Deputies would be a retrograde step—but a republic of Soviets of Workers', Agricultural Labourers' and Peasants' Deputies throughout the country, from top to bottom.

Abolition of the police, the army and the bureaucracy.

The salaries of all officials, who are to be elected and to be subject to recall at any time, not to exceed the average wage of a competent worker.

6. In the agrarian program the emphasis must be laid on the Soviets of Agricultural Labourers' Deputies.

Confiscation of all landed estates.

Nationalization of *all* lands in the country, the disposal of the land to be put in the charge of the local Soviets of Agricultural Labourers' and Peasants' Deputies. The organization of separate Soviets of Deputies of Poor Peasants. The creation of model farms on each of the large estates (varying from 100 to 300 dessiatins, in accordance with local and other conditions, at the discretion of the local institutions) under the control of the Soviets of Agricultural Labourers' Deputies and for the public account.

7. The immediate amalgamation of all banks in the country into a single national bank, control over which shall be exercised by the Soviets of Workers' Deputies.

8. Our *immediate* task is not to "introduce" Socialism, but only to bring social production and distribution of products at once under the *control* of the Soviets of Workers' Deputies.

9. Party tasks:
   a) Immediate summoning of a Party congress;
   b) Alteration of the Party program, mainly:
      1) On the question of imperialism and the imperialist war;
      2) On the question of our attitude towards the state and *our* demand for a "commune state";
      3) Amendment of our antiquated minimum program.
   c) A new name for the Party.

10. A new International.

The Essentials of Lenin (London: Lawrence and Wishart, 1947), II, 17–19. (Reprinted by permission of the publisher.)

For many months the left-wing Soviet hesitated, largely for ideological reasons, to assume sole power by overthrowing the Provisional Government; Marxist theory envisaged a period of bourgeois government before conditions would be ripe for a proletarian revolution. In this famous article, written in *Pravda,* April 22, 1917, Lenin urged immediate overthrow of the Provisional Government by depriving it of the support of the Soviets.

The basic question in any revolution is that of state power. Unless this **206** question is understood, there can be no intelligent participation in the revolution, let alone guidance of the revolution.

The highly remarkable feature of our revolution is that it has established a *dual power.* This fact must be grasped first and foremost; unless it is understood, we cannot advance. We must know, for instance, how to supplement and amend old "formulas," for example those of Bolshevism, for, as it proved, they were sound in general, but their concrete realization *turned out to be* different. *Nobody* hitherto thought, or could have thought, of dual power.

In what does this dual power consist? In the fact that side by side with the Provisional Government, the government of the *bourgeoisie,* there has developed *another government,* weak and embryonic as yet, but undoubtedly an actually existing and growing government—the Soviets of Workers' and Soldiers' Deputies.

What is the class composition of this other government? It consists of the proletariat and the peasantry (clad in army uniform). What is the political character of this government? It is a revolutionary dictatorship, i.e., a power directly based on revolutionary seizure, on the direct initiative of the masses from below, and *not on* a *law* passed by a centralized government. It is an entirely different power from that of the general type of parliamentary bourgeois-democratic republic which has hitherto usually prevailed in the advanced countries of Europe and America. This circumstance is often forgotten, often not reflected upon, yet it is the crux of the matter. *This* power is of exactly *the same type* as the Paris Commune of 1871. The fundamental characteristics of this type are: (1) The source of power is not a law previously discussed and passed by parliament, but the direct initiative of the masses from below, in their localities—outright "seizure," to use a current expression; (2) the direct arming of the whole people in place of the police and the army, which are institutions separated from the people and opposed to the people; order in the state under such power is maintained by the armed workers and peasants *themselves,* by the armed people *itself;* (3) officials and bureaucrats are either displaced by the direct rule of the people itself or at least placed under special control; they not only become elected officials, but are also *subject to recall* at the first demand of the people; they are reduced to the position of simple agents; from a privileged stratum occupying highly remunerative "posts," remunerated on a bourgeois scale, they become workers handling a special "kind of weapon," and remunerated at a salary not *exceeding* the ordinary pay of a competent worker.

This, and this alone constitutes the essence of the Paris Commune as a specific type of state. This essence was forgotten and perverted by . . . all those Social-Democrats, Socialist Revolutionaries, etc. etc., who are now in control.

Should the Provisional Government be overthrown immediately?

My answer is: (1) It should be overthrown, for it is an oligarchical, bourgeois, and not a people's government, and *cannot* provide peace, or bread, or full freedom; (2) it cannot be overthrown now, for it is being maintained by a direct and indirect, a formal and actual *agreement* with the Soviets of Workers' Deputies, and particularly with the chief Soviet, the Petrograd Soviet; (3) generally, it cannot be "overthrown" by any ordinary method, for it rests on the *"support"* given to the bourgeoisie by the *second* government—the Soviet of Workers' Deputies, and this government is the only possible revolutionary government, which directly expresses the mind and the will of the majority of the workers and peasants.

Humanity has not yet evolved and we do not as yet know a type of government superior to and better than the Soviets of Workers', Agricultural Workers', Peasants' and Soldiers' Deputies.

Meisel and Kozera, eds., *op. cit.*, pp. 7–9.

III. THE NOVEMBER REVOLUTION OF 1917

The following description of the crucial days of the November Revolution of 1917 is taken from the daily dispatches and memoirs of the British Ambassador to Russia in 1917, Sir George Buchanan.

November 6.   **207**

Tereschenko tells me that there were troubles last night in the suburbs and other quarters of the town; that the Bolsheviks had intended organizing an armed demonstration; that their courage failed them at the last moment and that it had been countermanded. They had, moreover, formed a revolutionary military committee, which has issued an injunction to the troops forbidding them to obey any orders which are not countersigned by themselves.

At three o'clock this morning the printing presses of several Bolshevik papers, which the Government had decided to suppress, were seized, and Tereschenko expects that this will provoke a Bolshevik rising. He is urging Kerensky to arrest the members of the revolutionary military committee, and will not in any case leave for London till the situation has been cleared up.

November 7.

Yesterday evening the executive committee of the Soviet decided to arrest the Ministers and to form a Government themselves. On telephoning this morning to the Ministry I was informed that Tereschenko had given up all idea of going to London and that he could not see me. A little later I heard that all the troops of the garrison had obeyed the summons of the Bolsheviks and that the whole town, including the State bank, stations, post and telegraph offices, were in their hands.

All the Ministers are in the Winter Palace, and their motors, which had been left unguarded in the adjoining square, have been either damaged or seized by the soldiers. About ten in the morning Kerensky sent out an officer to try to get him another motor. The officer found Whitehouse, one of the secretaries of the United States Embassy, and persuaded him to lend Kerensky his car with the American flag. They drove back together to the Winter Palace. After telling Whitehouse that he proposed driving to Luga to join the troops which had been summoned from the front, he begged him to ask the Allied Ambassadors not to recognize the Bolshevik Government, as he hopes to return on the 12th with sufficient troops to re-establish the situation.

At 4 A.M. this morning the Provisional Government called out the Cossacks, but the latter refused to act alone, as they had never forgiven Kerensky for having, after the July rising in which some of their comrades had been killed, prevented them putting down the Bolsheviks, as well as for having proclaimed their chosen leader, Korniloff, a traitor. About 8 A.M. the cruiser *Aurora* and three other ships arrived from Cronstadt and landed sailors; while sections of the armoured car detachments, which had originally declared for the Government, now joined the Bolsheviks. Though a certain amount of firing went on during the day, the Bolsheviks practically met with no resistance, as the Government had neglected to organize any force for their own protection. In the afternoon I walked down the quay to the Winter Palace Square and watched from a distance the troops surrounding one of the Government buildings, whose evacuation had been demanded. The aspect of the quay itself was more or less normal except for the groups of armed soldiers stationed near the bridges.

November 8.

At six o'clock yesterday evening armoured cars took up positions at all points commanding the approaches to the Winter Palace, and shortly afterwards delegates from the revolutionary committee came and demanded its unconditional surrender. As no answer was returned the signal for attack was given by the firing at 9 P.M. of a few blank rounds by the guns of the fortress and of the cruiser *Aurora*. The bombardment which followed was kept up continually till ten o'clock, when there was a lull for about an hour. At eleven o'clock it began again, while all the time, as we watched it from the Embassy windows, the trams were running as usual over the Troitski Bridge. The garrison of the palace consisted mainly of cadets from the military school and of a company of the women's battalion—for Russian women had been fighting at the front, and had by their courage and patriotism set a bright example that ought to have shamed the men. There was, however, no organized defence, and the casualties on either side were but few in number. The Ministers meanwhile must have passed through a terrible ordeal as they moved about from room to room, not knowing what fate was in store for them. By half-past two in the morning parties of the attacking force had penetrated into the palace by side entrances and disarmed the garrison. The Ministers were then arrested and marched off through hostile crowds to the fortress. They seem to have been well treated by the commandant, who apparently thought it prudent to make friends with the mammon of unrighteousness for fear, as he remarked to someone, that the tables might be one day turned and that he might find himself an occupant of one of their cells.

I walked out this afternoon to see the damage that had been done to the Winter Palace by the prolonged bombardment of the previous evening, and to my surprise found that, in spite of the near range, there were on the river side but three marks where the shrapnel had struck. On the town side the walls were riddled with thousands of bullets from machine guns, but not one shot from a field gun that had been fired from the opposite side of the Palace Square had struck the building. In the interior very considerable damage was done by the soldiers and workmen, who looted or smashed whatever they could lay hands on.

In the evening two officer instructors of the women's battalion came to my wife and beseeched her to try and save the women defenders of the Winter Palace, who, after they had surrendered, had been sent to one of the barracks, where they were being most brutally treated by the soldiers. General Knox at once drove to the Bolshevik headquarters at the Smolny Institute. His demands for their immediate release were at first refused on the ground that they had resisted desperately, fighting to the last with bombs and revolvers. Thanks, however, to his firmness and persistency, the order for their release was eventually signed, and the women were saved from the fate that would inevitably have befallen them had they spent the night in the barracks.

November 9.

Aksentieff, the president of the Provisional Council, who came to see me to-day, assured me that, though the Bolsheviks had succeeded in overthrowing the Government owing to the latter's criminal want of foresight, they would not hold out many days. At last night's meeting of the Congress of All Russian Soviets they had found themselves completely isolated, as all the other Socialist groups had denounced their methods and had refused to take any further part in the proceedings. The Council of Peasants had also pronounced against them. The Municipal Council, he went on to say, was forming a Committee of Public Safety composed of representatives of the Provisional Council, the Central Committee of the Soviet, the Peasants' Council, and the Committee of Delegates from the front; while the troops, which were expected from Pskov, would probably arrive in a couple of days. I told him that I did not share his confidence. . . .

November 10.

The Bolsheviks have formed a Government, with Lenin as First Commissary and Trotzky as Commissary for Foreign Affairs. It is to be called 'The Council of the People's Commissaries,' and is to act under the immediate control of the Central Committee of the All-Russian Congress of Soviets. . . .

Sir George Buchanan, *My Mission to Russia and Other Diplomatic Memories* (Boston: Little, Brown & Co., 1923), II, 204–9. (Reprinted by permission of Brandt & Brandt.)

Here John Reed, an American journalist and supporter of the Bolshevik Revolution, gives an eyewitness account of the events of November 7, 1917, just after the fall of the Provisional Government. The scene is the Second All-Russian Congress of Soviets of Workers' and Soldiers' Deputies in the building of the Smolny Institute. Included in this account are two of the first public documents of the Bolshevik government—the Proclamation to the Peoples and Governments of All the Belligerent Nations, and the Decree on Land.

208   It was just 8:40 when a thundering wave of cheers announced the entrance of the presidium, with Lenin—great Lenin—among them. A short, stocky figure, with a big head set down in his shoulders, bald and bulging. Little eyes, a snubbish nose, wide, generous mouth, and heavy chin; clean-shaven now, but already beginning to bristle with the well-known beard of his past and future. Dressed in shabby clothes, his trousers much too long for him. Unimpressive, to be the idol of a mob, loved and revered as perhaps few leaders in history have been. A strange popular leader—a leader purely by virtue of intellect; colourless, humourless, uncompromising and detached, without picturesque idiosyncrasies—but with the power of explaining profound ideas in simple terms, of analysing a concrete situation. And combined with shrewdness, the greatest intellectual audacity.

Kameniev was reading the report of the actions of the Military Revolutionary Committee; abolition of capital punishment in the Army, restoration of the free right of propaganda, release of officers and soldiers arrested for political crimes, orders to arrest Kerensky and confiscation of food supplies in private store-houses. . . . Tremendous applause. . . .

. . . Now Lenin, gripping the edge of the reading stand, letting his little winking eyes travel over the crowd as he stood there waiting, apparently oblivious to the long-rolling ovation, which lasted several minutes. When it finished, he said simply, "We shall now proceed to construct the Socialist order!" Again that overwhelming human roar.

"The first thing is the adoption of practical measures to realise peace. . . . We shall offer peace to the peoples of all the belligerent countries upon the basis of the Soviet terms—no annexations, no indemnities, and the right of self-determination of peoples. At the same time, according to our promise, we shall publish and repudiate the secret treaties. . . . The question of War and Peace is so clear that I think that I may, without preamble, read the project of a Proclamation to the Peoples of All the Belligerent Countries. . . ."

His great mouth, seeming to smile, opened wide as he spoke; his voice was hoarse—not unpleasantly so, but as if it had hardened that way after years and years of speaking—and went on monotonously, with the effect of being able to go on forever. . . . For emphasis he bent forward slightly. No gestures. And before him, a thousand simple faces looking up in intent adoration.

PROCLAMATION TO THE PEOPLES AND GOVERNMENTS OF ALL THE BELLIGERENT NATIONS.

The Workers' and Peasants' Government, created by the revolution of November 6th and 7th and based on the Soviets of Workers', Soldiers' and Peasants' Deputies, proposes to all the belligerent peoples and to their Governments to begin immediately negotiations for a just and democratic peace.

The Government means by a just and democratic peace, which is desired by the immense majority of the workers and the labouring classes, exhausted and depleted by the war—that peace which the Russian workers and peasants, after having struck down the Tsarist monarchy, have not ceased to demand categorically—immediate peace without annexations (that is to say, without conquest of foreign territory, without forcible annexation of other nationalities), and without indemnities.

The Government of Russia proposes to all the belligerent peoples immediately to conclude such a peace, by showing themselves willing to enter upon the decisive steps of negotiations aiming at such a peace, at once, without the slightest delay, before the definitive ratification of all the conditions of such a peace by the authorised assemblies of the people of all countries and of all nationalities.

By annexation or conquest of foreign territory, the Government means—conformably to the conception of democratic rights in general, and the rights of the working-class in particular—all union to a great and strong State of a small or weak nationality, without the voluntary, clear and precise expression of its consent and desire; whatever be the moment when such an annexation by force was accomplished, whatever be the degree of civilisation of the nation annexed by force or maintained outside the frontiers of another State, no matter if that nation be in Europe or in the far countries across the sea.

If any nation is retained by force within the limits of another State; if, in spite of the desire expressed by it, (it matters little if that desire be expressed by the press, by popular meetings, decisions of political parties, or by disorders and riots against national oppression), that nation is not given the right of deciding by free vote—without the slightest constraint, after the complete departure of the armed forces of the nation which has annexed it or wishes to annex it or is stronger in general—the form of its national and political organisation, such a union constitutes an annexation —that is to say, conquest and an act of violence.

To continue this war in order to permit the strong and rich nations to divide among themselves the weak and conquered nationalities is considered by the Government the greatest possible crime against humanity; and the Government solemnly proclaims its decision to sign a treaty of peace which will put an end to this war upon the above conditions, equally fair for all nationalities without exception.

The Government abolishes secret diplomacy, expressing before the whole country its firm decision to conduct all the negotiations in the light of day before the people, and will proceed immediately to the full publication of all secret treaties confirmed or concluded by the Government of land-owners and capitalists, from March until November 7th, 1917. All the clauses of the secret treaties which, as occur in a majority of cases, have for their object to procure advantages and privileges for Russian capitalists, to maintain or augment the annexations of the Russian imperialists, are denounced by the Government immediately and without discussion.

In proposing to all Governments and all peoples to engage in public negotiations for peace, the Government declares itself ready to carry on these negotiations by telegraph, by post, or by pourparlers [talks] between the representatives of the different countries, or at a conference of these representatives. To facilitate these pourparlers, the Government appoints its authorised representatives in the neutral countries. . . .

When the grave thunder of applause had died away, Lenin spoke again: "We propose to the Congress to ratify this declaration. We address ourselves to the Governments as well as to the peoples, for a declaration which would be addressed only to the peoples of the belligerent countries might delay the conclusion of peace. The conditions of peace, drawn up during the armistice, will be ratified by the Constituent Assembly. In fixing the duration of the armistice at three months, we desire to give to the peoples as long a rest as possible after this bloody extermination, and ample time for them to elect their representatives. This proposal of peace will meet with resistance on the part of the imperialist governments—we don't fool ourselves on that score. But we hope that revolution will soon break out in all the belligerent countries; that is why we address ourselves especially to the workers of France, England and Germany. . . .

"The revolution of November 6th and 7th," he ended, "has opened the era of the Social Revolution. . . . The labour movement, in the name of peace and Socialism, shall win, and fulfil its destiny. . . ."

There was something quiet and powerful in all this, which stirred the souls of men. It was understandable why people believed when Lenin spoke. . . .

It was exactly 10:35 when Kameniev asked all in favour of the proclamation to hold up their cards. One delegate dared to raise his hand against, but the sudden sharp outburst around him brought it swiftly down. . . . Unanimous.

Suddenly, by common impulse, we found ourselves on our feet, mumbling together into the smooth lifting unison of the *Internationale*. A grizzled old soldier was sobbing like a child. Alexandra Killontai rapidly winked the tears back. The immense sound rolled through the hall, burst windows and doors and seared into the quiet sky. "The war is ended! The war is ended!" said a young workman near me, his face shining. And when it was over, as we stood there in a kind of awkward hush, some one in the back of the room shouted, "Comrades! Let us remember those who have died for liberty!" The *Internationale* is an alien air, after all. The Funeral March seemed the very soul of those dark masses whose delegates sat in this hall, building from their obscure visions a new Russia—and perhaps more.

You fell in the fatal fight
For the liberty of the people, for the honour of the people . . .
You gave up your lives and everything dear to you,
You suffered in horrible prisons,
You went to exile in chains. . . .

Without a word you carried your chains because you could not ignore your suffering brothers,

Because you believed that justice is stronger than the sword. . .

The time will come when your surrendered life will count.

That time is near; when tyranny falls the people will rise, great and free!

Farewell, brothers, you chose a noble path,

You are followed by the new and fresh army ready to die and to suffer. . . .

Farewell, brothers, you chose a noble path,

At your grave we swear to fight, to work for freedom and the people's happiness. . . .

For this did they lie there, the martyrs of March, in their cold Brotherhood Grave on Mars Field; for this thousands and tens of thousands had died in the prisons, in exile, in Siberian mines. It had not come as they expected it would come, nor as the *intelligentzia* desire it; but it had come —rough, strong, impatient of formulas, contemptuous of sentimentalism; *real*. . . .

Lenin was reading the Decree on Land:

(1.) All private ownership of land is abolished immediately without compensation.

(2.) All land-owners' estates, and all lands belonging to the Crown, to monasteries, church lands with all their live stock and inventoried property, buildings and all appurtenances, are transferred to the disposition of the township Land Committees and the district Soviets of Peasants' Deputies until the Constituent Assembly meets.

(3.) Any damage whatever done to the confiscated property which from now on belongs to the whole People, is regarded as a serious crime, punishable by the revolutionary tribunals. The district Soviets of Peasants' Deputies shall take all necessary measures for the observance of the strictest order during the taking over of the land-owners' estates, for the determination of the dimensions of the plots of land and which of them are subject to confiscation, for the drawing up of an inventory of the entire confiscated property, and for the strictest revolutionary protection of all the farming property on the land, with all buildings, implements, cattle, supplies of products, etc., passing into the hands of the People.

(4.) For guidance during the realisation of the great land reforms until their final resolution by the Constituent Assembly, shall serve the following peasant *nakaz* [instructions], drawn up on the basis of 242 local peasant *nakazi* by the editorial board of the "*Izviestia* of the All-Russian Soviet of

Peasants' Deputies," and published in No. 88 of said *"Izviestia"* (Petrograd, No. 88, August 19th, 1917).

The lands of peasants and of Cossacks serving in the Army shall not be confiscated. . . .

At two o'clock the Land Decree was put to vote, with only one against and the peasant delegates wild with joy. . . . So plunged the Bolsheviki ahead, irresistible, over-riding hesitation and opposition—the only people in Russia who had a definite programme of action while the others talked for eight long months. . . .

At 2:30 A.M. fell a tense hush. Kameniev was reading the decree of the Constitution of Power:

Until the meeting of the Constituent Assembly, a provisional Workers' and Peasants' Government is formed, which shall be named the Council of People's Commissars.

The administration of the different branches of state activity shall be intrusted to commissions, whose composition shall be regulated to ensure the carrying out of the programme of the Congress, in close unison with the mass-organisations of working-men, working-women, sailors, soldiers, peasants and clerical employees. The governmental power is vested in a *collegium* made up of the chairmen of these commissions, that is to say, the Council of People's Commissars.

Control over the activities of the People's Commissars, and the right to replace them, shall belong to the All-Russian Congress of Soviets of Workers', Peasants' and Soldiers' Deputies, and its Central Executive Committee.

Still silence; as he read the list of Commissars, bursts of applause after each name, Lenin's and Trotzky's especially.

President of the Council: Vladimir Ulianov (*Lenin*)
Interior: A. E. Rykov
Agriculture: V. P. Miliutin
Labor: A. G. Shliapnikov
Military and Naval Affairs—a committee composed of V. A. Avseenko (*Antonov*), N. V. Krylenko, and F. M. Dybenko.
Commerce and Industry: V. P. Nogin
Popular Education: A. V. Lunatcharsky
Finance: E. E. Skvortsov (*Stepanov*)
Foreign Affairs: L. D. Bronstein (*Trotzky*)
Justice: G. E. Oppokov (*Lomov*)

Supplies: E. A. Teodorovitch
Post and Telegraph: N. P. Avilov (*Gliebov*)
Chairman for Nationalities: I. V. Djougashvili (*Stalin*)
Railroads: To be filled later. . . .

Then came the vote on the Constitution of Power, which carried the Council of People's Commissars into office by an enormous majority. . . .

The election of the new *Tsay-ee-kah,* the new parliament of the Russian Republic, took barely fifteen minutes. Trotzky announced its composition: 100 members, of which 70 Bolsheviki. . . . As for the peasants, and the seceding factions, places were to be reserved for them. "We welcome into the Government all parties and groups which will adopt our programme," ended Trotzky.

And thereupon the Second All-Russian Congress of Soviets was dissolved, so that the members might hurry to their homes in the four corners of Russia and tell of the great happenings. . . .

John Reed, *Ten Days That Shook the World* (New York: International Publishers, 1919), pp. 125–26, 126–29, 130, 132–34, 137, 138–39, 144–45. (Reprinted by permission of the publisher.)

Like the other revolutionary parties, Lenin's Bolsheviks had supported calling a Constituent Assembly which would chart Russia's future course. Therefore, they could not easily prevent its meeting on January 9, 1918, after they came to power. However, the Bolsheviks were not willing to grant parliamentary freedoms. How they got rid of the Constituent Assembly is told by its president, Victor Chernov. He was also leader of the Social Revolutionaries, the party which had received the largest number of votes in the elections for the Constituent Assembly, in which the Bolsheviks received only some twenty-five per cent of the votes.

209   When we, the newly elected members of the Constituent Assembly, entered the Tauric Palace, the seat of the Assembly in Petrograd, on January 9, 1918, we found that the corridors were full of armed guards. They were masters of the building, crude and brazen. At first they did not address us directly, and only exchanged casual observations to the effect that "This guy should get a bayonet between his ribs" or "It wouldn't be bad to put some lead into this one." When we entered the large hall, it was still empty. The Bolshevik deputies had not yet appeared.

A tank division billeted in Petrograd remained faithful to the Assembly. It intended to demonstrate this faithfulness by participating in the march to the Palace which was to pass on its way the barracks of the Preobrazhenski and Semionovski Regiments, the two best units of the Petrograd garrison.

At the meetings held by these regiments, resolutions were invariably adopted demanding the transfer of state power to the Constituent Assembly. Thus a prospect was open for the consolidation of democratic forces.

But the Bolsheviks were not caught off guard. They attacked the columns of demonstrators converging on the Tauric Palace from various parts of Petrograd. Whenever the unarmed crowd could not be dispersed immediately, the street was blocked by troops or Bolshevik units would shoot into the crowd. The demonstrators threw themselves on the pavement and waited until the rattle of machine guns quieted down; then they would jump up and continue their march, leaving behind the dead and wounded until they were stopped by a new volley. Or the crowd would be bayoneted by enraged Bolshevik outfits, which would get hold of the banners and placards carried by the demonstrators and tear them into scraps.

The Assembly hall was gradually filled by the deputies. Near the dais were placed armed guards. The public gallery was crowded to overflowing. Here and there glittered rifle muzzles. Admission tickets for the public were distributed by the notorious Uritski. He did his job well. . . .

At last all the deputies had gathered in a tense atmosphere. The left sector was evidently waiting for something. From our benches rose Deputy Lordkapanidze and said in a calm, business-like voice that, according to an old parliamentary custom, the first sitting should be presided over by the senior deputy. The senior was S. P. Shvetsov, an old Socialist Revolutionary (SR).

As soon as Shvetsov's imposing figure appeared on the dais, somebody gave a signal, and a deafening uproar broke out. The stamping of feet, hammering on the desks and howling made an infernal noise. The public in the gallery and the Bolshevik allies, the Left Socialist Revolutionaries, joined in the tumult. The guards clapped their rifle butts on the floor. From various sides guns were trained on Shvetsov. He took the President's bell, but the tinkling was drowned in the noise. He put it back on the table, and somebody immediately grabbed it and handed it over, like a trophy, to the representative of the Sovnarkom (Soviet of Commissars), Sverdlov. Taking advantage of a moment of comparative silence, Shvetsov managed to pronounce the sacramental phrase: "The session of the Constituent Assembly is open." These words evoked a new din of protest. Shvetsov slowly left the dais and joined us. He was replaced by Sverdlov, who opened the session for the second time, but now in the name of the Soviets, and presented its "platform." This was an ultimatum: we had just to vote Aye or No.

In the election of the Assembly's President, the Bolsheviks presented no candidate of their own. They voted for Maria Spiridonova, nominated by the Left SRs. Later they threw Spiridonova into jail and tormented her until she was on the verge of insanity. But at this moment they wanted to take full advantage of her popularity and reputation as a martyr in the struggle against Tzarism. My nomination as candidate for the Presidency received even greater support than had been expected. Some leftist peasants evidently could not bring themselves to oppose their own "muzhik minister." I obtained 244 votes against 150.

I delivered my inauguration address, making vigorous efforts to keep self-control. Every sentence of my speech was met with outcries, some ironical, others spiteful, often buttressed by the brandishing of guns. Bolshevik deputies surged forward to the dais. Conscious that the stronger nerves would win, I was determined not to yield to provocation. I said that the nation had made its choice, that the composition of the Assembly was a living testimony to the people's yearning for Socialism, and that its convention marked the end of the hazy transition period. Land reform, I went on, was a foregone conclusion: the land would be equally accessible to all who wished to till it. The Assembly, I said, would inaugurate an era of active foreign policy directed toward peace. . . .

I finished my speech amidst a cross-fire of interruptions and cries. It was now the turn of the Bolshevik speakers—Skvortsov and Bukharin. During their delivery, our sector was a model of restraint and self-discipline. We maintained a cold, dignified silence. The Bolshevik speeches, as usual, were shrill, clamorous, provocative and rude, but they could not break the icy silence of our majority. As President, I was bound in duty to call them to order for abusive statements. But I knew that this was precisely what they expected. Since the armed guards were under their orders, they wanted clashes, incidents and perhaps a brawl. So I remained silent.

The Social Democrat Tseretelli rose to answer the Bolsheviks. They tried to "scare" him by levelling at him a rifle from the gallery and brandishing a gun in front of his face. I had to restore order—but how? Appeals to maintain the dignity of the Constituent Assembly evoked an even greater noise, at times turning into a raving fury. Dybenko and other demagogues called for more and more assaults. Lenin, in the government box, demonstrated his contempt for the Assembly by lounging in his chair and putting on the air of a man who was bored to death. I threatened to clear the gallery of the yelling public. Though this was an empty threat, since the guards were only waiting for the order to "clear" us out of the hall, it proved temporarily effective. Tseretelli's calm and dignified manner helped to restore peace.

There was a grim significance in the outburst that broke loose when a middle-of-the-road deputy, Severtsov-Odoievski, started to speak Ukrainian. In the Assembly the Bolsheviks did not want to hear any language except Russian. I was compelled to state emphatically that in the new Russia, each nationality had the right to use its own language whenever it pleased.

When it appeared that we refused to vote the Soviet "platform" without discussion, the Bolsheviks walked out of the sitting in a body. They returned to read a declaration charging us with counter-revolution and stating that our fate would be decided by organs which were in charge of such things. Soon after that the Left SRs also made up their minds. Just before the discussion of the land reform started, their representative, I. Z. Steinberg, declared that they were in disagreement with the majority, and left the Assembly. . . .

We knew that the Bolsheviks were in conference, discussing what to do next. I felt sure that we would be arrested. But it was of utmost importance for us to have a chance to say the last word. I declared that the next point on the agenda was the land reform. At this moment somebody pulled at my sleeve.

"You have to finish now. These are orders from the People's Commissar."

Behind me stood a stocky sailor, accompanied by his armed comrades.

"What People's Commissar?"

"We have orders. Anyway, you cannot stay here any longer. The lights will be turned out in a minute. And the guards are tired."

"The members of the Assembly are also tired but cannot rest until they have fulfilled the task entrusted to them by the people—to decide on the land reform and the future form of government."

And leaving the guards no time to collect themselves, I proceeded to read the main paragraphs of the Land Bill, which our party had prepared long ago. But time was running short. Reports and debates had to be omitted. Upon my proposal, the Assembly voted six basic points of the bill. It provided that all land was to be turned into common property, with every tiller possessing equal rights to use it. Amidst incessant shouts: "That's enough! Stop it now! Clear the hall!" the other points of the bill were voted.

Fearing that the lights would be extinguished, somebody managed to procure candles. It was essential that the future form of government be voted upon immediately. Otherwise the Bolsheviks would not fail to charge the Assembly with having left the door open for the restoration of the monarchy. The motion for a republican form of government was carried unanimously.

In the dawn of a foggy and murky morning I declared a recess until noon.

At the exit a palefaced man pushed his way to me and beseeched me in a trembling voice not to use my official car. A bunch of murderers, he said, was waiting for me. He admitted that he was a Bolshevik, but his conscience revolted against this plot.

I left the building, surrounded by a few friends. We saw several men in sailor's uniforms loitering near my car. We decided to walk. We had a long distance to go, and when I arrived home I learned that rumors were in circulation that the Constituent Assembly had been dispersed, and that Chernov and Tseretelli had been shot.

At noon several members of the Assembly were sent on reconnaissance. They reported that the door of the Tauric Palace was sealed and guarded by a patrol with machine guns and two pieces of field artillery. Later in the day, a decree of the Sovnarkom was published by which the Constituent Assembly was "dissolved."

Thus ended Russia's first and last democratic parliament.

Victor M. Chernov, "The 1918 Dissolution of the Constituent Assembly: Russia's One Day Parliament," *The New Leader*, January 31, 1948, p. 8. (Reprinted by permission of the publisher.)

QUESTIONS

1. On the basis of specific comparison with the situation in other European countries at the time, how "revolutionary" were the demands contained in Father Gapon's petition?
2. What immediate reasons did the American eyewitness of the March Revolution give for the outbreak of the revolt?
3. To what extent did the program of the Provisional Government in 1917 correspond with Father Gapon's demands in 1905?
4. What were the practical consequences of Order No. 1 in the struggle for power which took place in Russia in 1917?
5. How did Lenin's April Theses bring Russia closer to another revolution?
6. What did Lenin mean by "dual power," and what had this to do with the Paris Commune of 1871?
7. What is the significance of the two decrees contained in John Reed's description of the Second All-Russian Congress of Soviets of Workers' and Soldiers' Deputies?
8. What parallel can you find in the history of the French Revolution with the Bolshevik dissolution of the Russian Constituent Assembly?
9. What other specific parallels are there between the French and the Russian revolutions as a whole? What are the main differences?

CHAPTER XXXIV

THE UNION OF SOVIET
SOCIALIST REPUBLICS

LENIN BROUGHT Russia a communist government but not communism. It was Stalin who, during three turbulent decades (1923-53), forced upon the Soviet Union his brand of communism, minus democracy, though Lenin had rejected him as a successor (210). Stalin's main weapon was fear. Giving as his excuse fear of the non-communist powers—the "capitalist encirclement," to use his famous phrase—Stalin purged his opponents, sometimes in staged public trials (211), which his successors have since openly denounced as mockeries of justice. Stalin used fear of the capitalist world to propel the Five-Year Plans which brought industrialization to the Soviet Union (212, 213). Terrorism was openly used to collectivize the peasantry (214). Stalin sowed fear of the Soviet Union throughout the world by advocating a war on capitalism and social democracy alike (215). Terror and arbitrariness became so much a part of Stalin's rule that it reduced to a sham much of the constitution which once bore his name (216). Even as he talked of peace, as in his last work (217), Stalin predicted the inevitability of war and the overthrow of capitalism. Stalin's successors have repudiated some of his methods, but none of his goals.

These excerpts from what has since become known as Lenin's Testament were written by Lenin on January 4, 1923, shortly before his death. Never made officially public during Stalin's lifetime because of its warning against Stalin, this testament was finally officially publicized by Stalin's successors.

210   Comrade Stalin, having become general secretary, has concentrated enormous power in his hands, and I am not sure that he always knows how to use that power with sufficient caution. On the other hand, Comrade Trotsky, as was proved by his struggle against the Central Committee in connection with the question of the People's Commissariat of Ways and Communication, is distinguished not only by his exceptional ability—personally, he is, to be sure, the most able man in the present Central Committee—but also by his too far-reaching self-confidence and a disposition to be far too much attracted by the purely administrative side of affairs.

These two qualities of the two most able leaders of the present Central Committee might, quite innocently, lead to a split. If our Party does not take measures to prevent it, a split may occur unexpectedly.

I will not further characterize the other members of the present Central Committee as to their personal qualities. I will only remind you that the October episode of Zinoviev and Kamenev was not, of course, accidental, but that it ought as little to be used against them as the "non-Bolshevism" of Trotsky.

Of the younger members of the Central Committee, I want to say a few words about Piatakov and Bukharin. They are, in my opinion, the most able forces (amongst the youngest). In regard to them it is necessary to bear in mind the following: Bukharin is not only the most valuable theoretician of the Party, as he is the biggest, but he also may be considered the favorite of the whole Party. But his theoretical views can with only the greatest reservations be regarded as fully Marxist, for there is something scholastic in him. (He never has learned, and I think never fully understood, the dialectic.)

And then Piatakov—a man undoubtedly distinguished in will and ability, but too much given over to the administrative side of affairs to be relied upon in serious political questions.

Of course both these remarks are made by me merely with regard to the present time, or on the supposition that these two able and loyal workers may not find occasion to supplement their knowledge and correct their one-sidedness.

December 25, 1922.

Postscript: Stalin is too rude, and this fault, entirely supportable in relation to us Communists, becomes insupportable in the office of General Secretary. Therefore I propose to the comrades to find a way to remove Stalin from that position and appoint to it another man who in all respects differs from Stalin only in superiority—namely, more patient, more loyal, more polite, and more attentive to comrades, less capricious, et cetera. This circumstance may seem an insignificant trifle, but I think that from the point of view of preventing a split and from the point of view of the relation between Stalin and Trotsky, which I discussed above, it is not a trifle, or it is such a trifle as may acquire a decisive significance.

January 4, 1923.   *Lenin*

David Shub, *Lenin* (New York: Doubleday & Co., 1948), pp. 381–82. (Reprinted by permission of the publisher.)

The trial on March 2–13, 1938, of Bukharin and others accused not only of opposition to Stalin but of "espionage on behalf of foreign states" was but one of several spectacular public trials in the late 1930's. Stalin was not satisfied with liquidating his victims; he compelled them publicly to confess to crimes which they never committed. No such confession was as elaborate as Bukharin's. It is given here as it was recorded by the Military Collegium of the Supreme Court of the U.S.S.R. Yet Stalin's successors have since officially declared such confessions to have been staged.

EVENING SESSION, MARCH 12, 1938   **211**

THE COMMANDANT OF THE COURT: The Court is coming, please rise.

THE PRESIDENT: Please be seated. The session is resumed. Accused Bukharin, you may make your last plea.

BUKHARIN: Citizen President and Citizen Judges, I fully agree with Citizen the Procurator regarding the significance of the trial, at which were exposed our dastardly crimes, the crimes committed by the "bloc of Rights and Trotskyites," one of whose leaders I was, and for all the activities of which I bear responsibility.

This trial, which is the concluding one of a series of trials, has exposed all the crimes and the treasonable activities, it has exposed the historical significance and the roots of our struggle against the Party and the Soviet government.

I have been in prison for over a year, and I therefore do not know what is going on in the world. But, judging from those fragments of real life that sometimes reached me by chance, I see, feel and understand that the interests which we so criminally betrayed are entering a new phase of gigantic development, are now appearing in the international arena as a great and mighty factor of the international proletarian phase.

We, the accused, are sitting on the other side of the barrier, and this barrier separates us from you, Citizen Judges. We found ourselves in the accursed ranks of the counter-revolution, became traitors to the Socialist fatherland.

At the very beginning of the trial, in answer to the question of Citizen the President, whether I pleaded guilty, I replied by a confession.

In answer to the question of Citizen the President whether I confirmed the testimony I had given, I replied that I confirmed it fully and entirely.

When, at the end of the preliminary investigation, I was summoned for interrogation to the State Prosecutor, who controlled the sum total of the materials of the investigation, he summarized them as follows (Vol. V, p. 114, December 1, 1937):

Question: Were you a member of the centre of the counter-revolutionary organization of the Rights? I answered: Yes, I admit it.

Second question: Do you admit that the centre of the anti-Soviet organization, of which you are a member, engaged in counter-revolutionary activities and set itself the aim of violently overthrowing the leadership of the Party and the government? I answered: Yes, I admit it.

Third question: Do you admit that this centre engaged in terrorist activities, organized kulak uprisings and prepared for White-guard kulak uprisings against members of the Political Bureau, against the leadership of the Party and the Soviet power? I answered: It is true.

Fourth question: Do you admit that you are guilty of treasonable activities, as expressed in preparations for a conspiracy aiming at a coup d'état? I answered: Yes, that is also true.

In court I admitted and still admit my guilt in respect to the crimes which I committed and of which I was accused by Citizen the State Prosecutor at the end of the Court investigation and on the basis of the materials of the investigation in the possession of the Procurator. I declared also in Court, and I stress and repeat it now, that I regard myself politically responsible for the sum total of the crimes committed by the "bloc of Rights and Trotskyites."

I have merited the most severe punishment, and I agree with Citizen the Procurator, who several times repeated that I stand on the threshold of my hour of death. . . .

It seems to me that when some of the West European and American intellectuals begin to entertain doubts and vacillations in connection with the trials taking place in the U.S.S.R., this is primarily due to the fact that these people do not understand the radical distinction, namely, that in our country the antagonist, the enemy, has at the same time a divided, a dual mind. And I think that this is the first thing to be understood.

I take the liberty of dwelling on these questions because I had considerable contacts with these upper intellectuals abroad, especially among scientists, and I must explain to them what every Young Pioneer in the Soviet Union knows.

Repentance is often attributed to diverse and absolutely absurd things like Thibetan powders and the like. I must say of myself that in prison, where I was confined for over a year, I worked, studied, and retained my clarity of mind. This will serve to refute by facts all fables and absurd counter-revolutionary tales.

Hypnotism is suggested. But I conducted by own defense in Court from the legal standpoint too, orientated myself on the spot, argued with the State Prosecutor; and anybody, even a man who has little experience in this branch of medicine, must admit that hypnotism of this kind is altogether impossible.

This repentance is often attributed to the Dostoyevsky mind, to the specific properties of the soul ("l'âme slave" as it is called), and this can be said of types like Alyosha Karamazov, the heroes of *The Idiot* and other Dostoyevsky characters, who are prepared to stand up in the public square and cry: "Beat me, Orthodox Christians, I am a villain!"

But that is not the case here at all. "L'âme slave" and the psychology of Dostoyevsky characters are a thing of the remote past in our country, the pluperfect tense. Such types do not exist in our country, or exist perhaps only on the outskirts of small provincial towns, if they do even there. On the contrary, such a psychology is to be found in Western Europe.

I shall now speak of myself, of the reasons for my repentance. Of course, it must be admitted that incriminating evidence plays a very important part. For three months I refused to say anything. Then I began to testify. Why? Because while in prison I made a revaluation of my entire past. For when you ask yourself: "If you must die, what are you dying for?"—an absolutely black vacuity suddenly rises before you with startling vividness. There was nothing to die for, if one wanted to die unrepented. And, on the contrary, everything positive that glistens in the Soviet Union acquires new dimensions in a man's mind. This in the end disarmed me completely and led me to bend my knees before the Party and the country. And when you ask yourself: "Very well, suppose you do not die; suppose by some miracle you remain alive, again what for? Isolated from everybody, an enemy of the people, in an inhuman position, completely isolated from everything that constitutes the essence of life. . . ." And at once the same reply arises. And at such moments, Citizen Judges, everything personal, all the personal incrustation, all the rancour, pride, and a number of other things, fall away, disappear. And, in addition, when the reverberations of the broad international struggle reach your ear, all this in its entirety does its work, and the result is the complete internal moral victory of the U.S.S.R. over its kneeling opponents. I happened by chance to get Feucht-wanger's book from the prison library. There he refers to the trials of Trotskyites. It produced a profound impression on me; but I must say that Feuchtwanger did not get at the core of the matter. He stopped half way, not everything was clear to him; when, as a matter of fact, everything is clear. World history is a world court of judgement: A number of groups of Trotskyite leaders went bankrupt and have been cast into the pit. That is true. But you cannot do what Feuchtwanger does in relation to Trotsky in particular, when he places him on the same plane as Stalin. Here his arguments are absolutely false. For in reality the whole country stands behind Stalin; he is the hope of the world; he is a creator. Napoleon once said that fate is politics. The fate of Trotsky is counter-revolutionary politics.

I am about to finish. I am perhaps speaking for the last time in my life.

I am explaining how I came to realize the necessity of capitulating to the investigating authorities and to you, Citizen Judges. We came out against the joy of the new life with the most criminal methods of struggle. I refute the accusation of having plotted against the life of Vladimir Ilyich, but my counter-revolutionary confederates, and I at their head, endeavoured to murder Lenin's cause, which is being carried on with such tremendous success by Stalin. The logic of this struggle led us step by step into the blackest quagmire. And it has once more been proved that departure from the position of Bolshevism means siding with political counter-revolutionary banditry. Counter-revolutionary banditry has now been smashed, we have been smashed, and we repent our frightful crimes.

The point, of course, is not this repentance, or my personal repentance in particular. The Court can pass its verdict without it. The confession of the accused is not essential. The confession of the accused is a medieval principle of jurisprudence. But here we also have the internal demolition of the forces of counter-revolution. And one must be a Trotsky not to lay down one's arms.

I feel it my duty to say here that in the parallelogram of forces which went to make up the counter-revolutionary tactics, Trotsky was the principal motive force. And the most acute methods—terrorism, espionage, the dismemberment of the U.S.S.R. and wrecking—proceeded primarily from this source.

I may infer a priori that Trotsky and my other allies in crime, as well as the Second International, all the more since I discussed this with Nikolayevsky, will endeavour to defend us, especially and particularly myself. I reject this defence, because I am kneeling before the country, before the Party, before the whole people. The monstrousness of my crimes is immeasurable especially in the new stage of the struggle of the U.S.S.R. May this trial be the last severe lesson, and may the great might of the U.S.S.R. become clear to all. Let it be clear to all that the counter-revolutionary thesis of the national limitedness of the U.S.S.R. has remained suspended in the air like a wretched rag. Everybody perceives the wise leadership of the country that is ensured by Stalin.

It is in the consciousness of this that I await the verdict. What matters is not the personal feelings of a repentant enemy, but the flourishing progress of the U.S.S.R. and its international importance.

People's Commissariat of Justice of the U.S.S.R., *Report of Court Proceedings in the Case of the Anti-Soviet "Bloc of Rights and Trotskyites" Heard before the Military Collegium of the Supreme Court of the U.S.S.R., Moscow, March 2–13, 1938* (Moscow, 1938), pp. 767–68, 776–79.

The following statement was made by Stalin on February 4, 1931, to the First All-Union Conference of Managers of Socialist Industry. Here Stalin advances fear of the "capitalist encirclement" as a prime mover behind the first Five-Year Plan.

It is sometimes asked whether it is not possible to slow down the tempo **212** a bit, to put a check on the movement. No, comrades, it is not possible! The tempo must not be reduced! On the contrary, we must increase it as much as is within our powers and possibilities. This is dictated to us by our obligations to the workers and peasants of the U.S.S.R. This is dictated to us by our obligations to the working class of the whole world.

To slacken the tempo would mean falling behind. And those who fall behind get beaten. But we do not want to be beaten. No, we refuse to be beaten! One feature of the history of old Russia was the continual beatings she suffered for falling behind, for her backwardness. She was beaten by the Mongol khans. She was beaten by the Turkish beys. She was beaten by the Swedish feudal lords. She was beaten by the Polish and Lithuanian gentry. She was beaten by the British and French capitalists. She was beaten by the Japanese barons. All beat her—for her backwardness: for military backwardness, for cultural backwardness, for political backwardness, for industrial backwardness, for agricultural backwardness. She was beaten because to do so was profitable and could be done with impunity. Do you remember the words of the pre-revolutionary poet: "You are poor and abundant, mighty and impotent, Mother Russia." These words of the old poet were well learned by those gentlemen. They beat her, saying: "You are abundant," so one can enrich oneself at your expense. They beat her, saying: "You are poor and impotent," so you can be beaten and plundered with impunity. Such is the law of the exploiters—to beat the backward and the weak. It is the jungle law of capitalism. You are backward, you are weak— therefore you are wrong; hence, you can be beaten and enslaved. You are mighty—therefore you are right; hence, we must be wary of you.

That is why we must no longer lag behind.

In the past we had no fatherland, nor could we have one. But now that we have overthrown capitalism and power is in the hands of the working class, we have a fatherland, and we will defend its independence. Do you want our Socialist fatherland to be beaten and to lose its independence? If you do not want this you must put an end to its backwardness in the shortest possible time and develop genuine Bolshevik tempo in building up its Socialist system of economy. There is no other way. That is why Lenin said during the October Revolution: "Either perish, or overtake and outstrip the advanced capitalist countries."

We are fifty or a hundred years behind the advanced countries. We must make good this distance in ten years. Either we do it, or they crush us.

J. Stalin, *Problems of Leninism* (Moscow, 1947), pp. 355–56.

The industrialization of the Soviet Union was a prime aim of the Five-Year Plans. How heavy industry was brought to the barren steppes east of the Ural Mountains is told here by an American, John Scott, who helped build the steel plants of Magnitogorsk in the early 1930's.

213   In 1940, Winston Churchill told the British people that they could expect nothing but blood, sweat, and tears. The country was at war. The British people did not like it, but most of them accepted it.

Ever since 1931 or thereabouts the Soviet Union has been at war, and the people have been sweating, shedding blood and tears. People were wounded and killed, women and children froze to death, millions starved, thousands were court-martialed and shot in the campaigns of collectivization and industrialization. I would wager that Russia's battle of ferrous metallurgy alone involved more casualties than the battle of the Marne. All during the thirties the Russian people were at war.

It did not take me long to realize that they ate black bread principally because there was no other to be had, wore rags because they could not be replaced.

In Magnitogorsk I was precipitated into a battle. I was deployed on the iron and steel front. Tens of thousands of people were enduring the most intense hardships in order to build blast furnaces, and many of them did it willingly, with boundless enthusiasm, which infected me from the day of my arrival. . . .

The 'Magnetic Mountain,' iron heart of Magnitogorsk, is situated on the eastern slopes of the Ural Mountains, some seventy miles east of the watershed which separates Europe from Asia. The surrounding countryside is barren steppe—rolling hills so smooth they remind one of a desert. The summers are hot and dusty, and only about three months long. The winters are long, cold, and windy. There is very little rainfall. . . .

In 1924 the general industrial production of Russia was between ten and fifteen per cent of the level of 1913. For the next four years the country struggled back to its feet with the help of the New Economic Policy. Foreign concessions and the partial development of private enterprise in industry and commerce facilitated this recovery.

During this period, while old capitalist forms were successfully utilized to strengthen Soviet economy, a bitter struggle was in progress between various factions among the leading groups of the Soviet Union. Stalin emerged victorious, annihilated his enemies, and proceeded to force the realization of those measures which he considered necessary.

Stalin's program was essentially nationalistic. It was dedicated to the proposition that Socialism could and would be constructed in one country, in the Soviet Union. Whereas Lenin had counted on revolutions in Central Europe to aid backward Russia on its difficult road to Socialism, Stalin counted on the ability of the Soviet Union to equip and defend itself.

In order to construct Socialism and defend it against the attacks which Stalin felt sure were coming, it was necessary to build Russian heavy industry, to collectivize and mechanize agriculture. These monumental tasks were undertaken in the late twenties. The first Five Year Plan provided for the reconstruction of the national economy and the creation of whole new industries, new industrial bases. One of its most important projects was the creation of a heavy industry base in the Urals and Siberia out of reach of any invader, and capable of supplying the country with arms and machines in immense quantities.

This project had several very outstanding advantages. In the first place, the iron deposit of Magnitogorsk had been known for years as one of the richest in the world. The ore was right on the surface and tested up to sixty per cent iron. The coal deposits in the Kuzbas in Central Siberia were almost unique. In some places the coal lay in strata three hundred feet thick. By connecting these two great untouched sources of raw material into one immense metallurgical combine, the country would be ensured of an iron and steel base, not inferior to that of the United States, to supply the growing needs of the country for decades to come. In the second place, both Magnitogorsk and Kuznetsk were in the center of the country, some two thousand miles from any frontier, so that new interventionists, which, Stalin felt, were bound to come sooner or later, would be unable to reach them, even with their best airplanes.

So great were the expenses and so enormous the technical difficulties that no one in the pre-revolutionary days had ever undertaken to project a Ural-Kuznetsk metallurgical base. The capital investment necessary was much more than any firm, or even the Czarist government itself, could afford. 'Too large and difficult for the capitalists, the task was left to the workers,' as the doctor said.

It was necessary to start from scratch. There were no supply bases, no railroads, no other mills in or near Magnitogorsk or Kuznetsk. But Stalin and his Political Bureau decided that the job must be done, and so in 1928 the first serious attempt was made to project the Ural-Kuznetsk Combine and a powerful, modern metallurgical plant in Magnitogorsk.

Stalin was probably one of the few men in the Soviet Union who realized how catastrophically expensive it was going to be. But he was convinced that it was just a matter of time until the Soviet Union would again be invaded by hostile capitalist powers seeking to dismember and destroy the first Socialist State. Stalin considered it his sacred obligation to see to it that when the time came the attackers would not be able to accomplish this. The fulfillment of this task justified all means.

As the doctor told me, there had been many discussions among scientists and economists about the desirability of going headlong into the construction of the Ural-Kuznetsk Combinat with its galaxy of machine-building and armament plants. Initial costs stood twice as high as those in similar units built in the Ukrainian or Donbass industrial regions already equipped with railroads and power lines, and near bases of industrial and agricultural supplies. The regions around Magnitogorsk and Kuznetsk were as yet little known, geological surveys had been superficial. Would it not be better to build in the Ukraine, and wait with the Ural-Kuznetsk Combine until more thorough surveys had been made?

At many times during the late twenties and the early thirties such objections were raised. The tempo of construction was such that millions of men and women starved, froze, and were brutalized by inhuman labor and incredible living conditions. Many individuals questioned whether or not it was worth it.

Stalin suppressed such ideas with his usual vigor. The Ukraine had been invaded by the Germans in 1918. It might be invaded again. The Soviet Union must have an uninvadable heavy industry base, and must have it immediately, said the Georgian Bolshevik. His word was law.

In January, 1931, Stalin made an historic speech to a conference of business managers. In his inimitable, simple vernacular Stalin insisted on the necessity of increasing the tempo of industrialization. He warned the Russian people that they must make their country as strong as the surrounding capitalist states within ten years or Russia would be invaded and annihilated. . . .

The history of the actual construction of Magnitogorsk was fascinating. Within several years, half a billion cubic feet of excavation work was done, forty-two million cubic feet of reinforced concrete poured, five million cubic feet of fire bricks laid, a quarter of a million tons of structural steel erected.

This was done without sufficient labor, without necessary quantities of the most elementary supplies and materials. Brigades of young enthusiasts from every corner of the Soviet Union arrived in the summer of 1930 and did the groundwork of railroad and dam construction necessary before work could be begun on the plant itself. Later, groups of local peasants and herdsmen came to Magnitogorsk because of bad conditions in the villages, due to collectivization. Many of these peasants were completely unfamiliar with industrial tools and processes. They had to start at the very beginning and learn how to work in groups. Nevertheless they learned so well that the first dam across the Ural River was finished the sixth of April, 1931, and the lake began to fill up. Within two years it was five miles long and assured an adequate water supply to the city and plant for the first half of the construction work.

The first quarter of 1931 saw the ground broken for excavation and foundation work for the basic departments of the plant, while the iron mine went into production. A colony of several hundred foreign engineers and specialists, some of whom made as high as one hundred dollars a day and expenses, arrived to advise and direct the work. Money was spent by the millions (170,000,000 roubles in 1931).

Despite difficulties the work went on much faster than the most optimistic foreigners anticipated, although much more slowly than the chimeric plans of the Soviet government demanded. By the end of 1931 the first battery of coke ovens and Blast Furnace No. 1 were ready to be put into operation. The first of February, 1932, saw the first melting of Magnitogorsk pig iron. . . .

This was the Magnitogorsk of 1933. A quarter of a million souls— Communists, kulaks, foreigners, Tartars, convicted saboteurs and a mass of blue-eyed Russian peasants—making the biggest steel combinat in Europe in the middle of the barren Ural steppe. Money was spent like water, men froze, hungered, and suffered, but the construction work went on with a disregard for individuals and a mass heroism seldom paralleled in history.

John Scott, *Behind the Urals: An American Worker in Russia's City of Steel* (Boston: Houghton Mifflin Co., 1942), pp. 5–6, 56, 62–65, 70–71, 91–92. (Reprinted by permission of John Scott.)

Collectivization of agriculture was another of Stalin's principal aims. This program affected so many millions of farmers that it is sometimes called the Second Bolshevik Revolution. The brutal methods used to force the farmers to collectivize were so effective that even Stalin, somewhat belatedly, grew fearful and warned Communist party members in an article published in *Pravda* on March 2, 1930, against being "dizzy with success."

214   Everybody is now talking about the successes achieved by the Soviet government in the sphere of the collective-farm movement. Even our enemies are compelled to admit that important successes have been achieved. And these successes are great indeed.

It is a fact that by February 20, this year, 50 per cent of the peasant farms of the U.S.S.R. have been collectivized. This means that by February 20, 1930, we had *fulfilled* the estimates of the Five-Year Plan *more than twice over*.

It is a fact that by February 28, this year, the collective farms had *already* stored more than 3,600,000 tons of seed for the spring sowing, *i.e.,* more than 90 per cent of the plan, or about 220,000,000 poods. It cannot but be admitted that the storing of 220,000,000 poods of seed by the collective farms alone—after the grain purchasing plan had been successfully fulfilled—is a tremendous achievement.

What does all this show?

It shows that *the radical turn of the rural districts towards Socialism may already be regarded as guaranteed.*

There is no need to prove that these successes are of tremendous importance for the fate of our country, for the whole working class as the leading force of our country, and, finally, for the Party itself. Apart from the direct practical results, these successes are of tremendous importance for the internal life of the Party itself, for the education of our Party. They imbue the Party with a spirit of cheerfulness and confidence in its strength. They arm the working class with confidence in the triumph of our cause. They bring to our Party new millions of reserves.

Hence, the task of our Party: to *consolidate* the successes achieved and to *utilize* them systematically for the purpose of advancing further.

But successes also have their seamy side; especially when they are achieved with comparative "ease," "unexpectedly," so to speak. Such successes sometimes induce a spirit of conceit and arrogance: "We can do anything!" "We can win hands down!" People are often intoxicated by such successes, they become dizzy with success, they lose all sense of proportion, they lose the faculty of understanding realities, they reveal a tendency to overestimate their own strength and to underestimate the strength of the enemy; reckless attempts are made to settle all the problems of Socialist construction "in two ticks." In such cases care is not taken to *consolidate* the successes achieved and systematically to *utilize* them for the purpose of advancing further. Why should we consolidate successes? We shall anyhow reach the complete victory of Socialism in "two ticks," "We can do anything!" "We can win hands down!" . . .

The art of leadership is a serious matter. One must not lag behind the movement, because to do so is to become isolated from the masses. But neither must one rush ahead, for to rush ahead is to lose contact with the masses. He who wants to lead a movement and at the same time keep in touch with the vast masses must wage a fight on two fronts—against those who lag behind and against those who rush on ahead.

Our Party is strong and invincible because, while leading the movement, it knows how to maintain and multiply its contacts with the vast masses of the workers and peasants.

Stalin, *op. cit.,* pp. 326–27, 331.

Stalin repudiated Trotsky's definition of "Permanent Revolution." He nevertheless believed no less in the world mission of communism, as he made clear in the following address, printed in *Pravda* on November 6–7, 1927, on the occasion of the tenth anniversary of the Bolshevik Revolution.

215   The October Revolution cannot be regarded merely as a revolution "within national bounds." It is, primarily, a revolution of an international, world order; for it signifies a radical turn in the world history of mankind, a turn from the old, capitalist world to the new, socialist world.

Revolutions in the past usually ended by one group of exploiters at the helm of government being replaced by another group of exploiters. The exploiters changed, exploitation remained. Such was the case during the liberation movements of the slaves. Such was the case during the period of the uprisings of the serfs. Such was the case during the period of the well-known "great" revolutions in England, France and Germany. I am not speaking of the Paris Commune, which was the first glorious, heroic, yet unsuccessful attempt on the part of the proletariat to run history against capitalism.

The October Revolution differs from these revolutions *in principle*. Its aim is not to replace one form of exploitation by another form of exploitation, one group of exploiters by another group of exploiters, but to abolish all exploitation of man by man, to abolish all groups of exploiters, to establish the dictatorship of the proletariat, to establish the power of the most revolutionary class of all the oppressed classes that have ever existed, to organise a new, classless, socialist society.

It is precisely for this reason that the *victory* of the October Revolution signifies a radical change in the history of mankind, a radical change in the historical destiny of world capitalism, a radical change in the liberation movement of the world proletariat, a radical change in the methods of struggle and the forms of organisation, in the manner of life and traditions, in the culture and ideology of the exploited masses throughout the world.

That is the basic reason why the October Revolution is a revolution of an international, world order.

That also is the source of the profound sympathy which the oppressed classes in all countries entertain for the October Revolution, which they regard as a pledge of their own emancipation.

A number of fundamental issues could be noted on which the October Revolution influences the development of the revolutionary movement throughout the world.

1. The October Revolution is noteworthy primarily for having breached the front of world imperialism, for having overthrown the imperialist bourgeoisie in one of the biggest capitalist countries and put the socialist proletariat in power.

The class of wage-workers, the class of the persecuted, the class of the oppressed and exploited has *for the first time* in the history of mankind risen to the position of the *ruling* class, setting a contagious example to the proletarians of all countries. . . .

2. The October Revolution has shaken imperialism not only in the centres of its domination, not only in the "metropolises." It has also struck at the rear of imperialism, its periphery, having undermined the rule of imperialism in the colonial and dependent countries.

Having overthrown the landlords and the capitalists, the October Revolution broke the chains of national and colonial oppression and freed from it, without exception, all the oppressed peoples of a vast state. The proletariat cannot emancipate itself unless it emancipates the oppressed peoples. It is a characteristic feature of the October Revolution that it accomplished these national-colonial revolutions in the U.S.S.R. not under the flag of national enmity and conflicts among nations, but under the flag of mutual confidence and fraternal rapprochement of the workers and peasants of the various peoples in the U.S.S.R., not in the name of *nationalism,* but in the name of *internationalism.* . . .

3. Having sown the seeds of revolution both in the centres of imperialism and in its rear, having weakened the might of imperialism in the "metropolises" and having shaken its domination in the colonies, the October Revolution has thereby put in jeopardy the very existence of world capitalism *as a whole.* . . .

Capitalism may become partly stabilised, it may rationalise its production, turn over the administration of the country to fascism, temporarily hold down the working class; but it will never recover the "tranquillity," the "assurance," the "equilibrium" and the "stability" that it flaunted before; for the crisis of world capitalism has reached the stage of development when the flames of revolution must inevitably break out, now in the centres of imperialism, now in the periphery, reducing to naught the capitalist patchwork and daily bringing nearer the fall of capitalism. Exactly as in the well-known fable, "when it pulled its tail out of the mud, its beak got stuck; when it pulled its beak out, its tail got stuck." . . .

4. The October Revolution cannot be regarded merely as a revolution in the sphere of economic and social-political relations. It is at the same time a revolution in the minds, a revolution in the ideology, of the working class. . . .

It is impossible to put an end to capitalism without putting an end to Social-Democratism in the labour movement. That is why the era of dying capitalism is also the era of dying Social-Democratism in the labour movement.

The great significance of the October Revolution consists, among other things, in the fact that it marks the inevitable victory of Leninism over Social-Democratism in the world labour movement.

The era of the domination of the Second International and of Social-Democratism in the labour movement *has ended.*

The era of the domination of Leninism and of the Third International *has begun.*

Pravda, No. 255,
November 6-7, 1927   Signed: *J. Stalin*

J. V. Stalin, *Works* (Moscow, 1954), X, 244-45, 247-48, 250, 251, 253, 255.

The Soviet Constitution of 1936 was hailed as a great achievement of the Stalin epoch, even though it embodied basically the same one-party dictatorship which marked the Constitution of 1924. It is true that Chapter X on the Fundamental Rights and Duties of Citizens, given below in full, contains admirable provisions. Yet most of these remained but unkept promises.

ARTICLE 118

216   Citizens of the U.S.S.R. have the right to work, that is, the right to guaranteed employment and payment for their work in accordance with its quantity and quality.

The right to work is ensured by the socialist organization of the national economy, the steady growth of the productive forces of Soviet society, the elimination of the possibility of economic crises, and the abolition of unemployment.

ARTICLE 119

Citizens of the U.S.S.R. have the right to rest and leisure.

The right to rest and leisure is ensured by the establishment of an eight-hour day for factory and office workers, the reduction of the working day to seven or six hours for arduous trades and to four hours in shops where conditions of work are particularly arduous, by the institution of annual vacations with full pay for factory and office workers, and by the provision of a wide network of sanatoria, rest homes and clubs for the accommodation of the working people.

ARTICLE 120

Citizens of the U.S.S.R. have the right to maintenance in old age and also in case of sickness or disability.

This right is ensured by the extensive development of social insurance of factory and office workers at state expense, free medical service for the working people, and the provision of a wide network of health resorts for the use of the working people.

ARTICLE 121

Citizens of the U.S.S.R. have the right to education.

This right is ensured by universal and compulsory elementary education; by free education up to and including the seventh grade; by a system of state stipends for students of higher educational establishments who excel in their studies; by instruction in schools being conducted in the native language, and by the organization in the factories, state farms, machine and tractor stations, and collective farms of free vocational, technical and agronomic training for the working people.

ARTICLE 122

Women in the U.S.S.R. are accorded equal rights with men in all spheres of economic, government, cultural, political and other public activity.

The possibility of exercising these rights is ensured by women being accorded an equal right with men to work, payment for work, rest and leisure, social insurance and education, and by state protection of the interests of mother and child, state aid to mothers of large families and unmarried mothers, maternity leave with full pay, and the provision of a wide network of maternity homes, nurseries and kindergartens.

ARTICLE 123

Equality of rights of citizens of the U.S.S.R., irrespective of their nationality or race, in all spheres of economic, government, cultural, political and other public activity, is an indefeasible law.

Any direct or indirect restriction of the rights of, or, conversely, the establishment of any direct or indirect privileges for, citizens on account of their race or nationality, as well as any advocacy of racial or national exclusiveness or hatred and contempt, is punishable by law.

ARTICLE 124

In order to ensure to citizens freedom of conscience, the church in the U.S.S.R. is separated from the state, and the school from the church. Freedom of religious worship and freedom of anti-religious propaganda is recognized for all citizens.

ARTICLE 125

In conformity with the interests of the working people, and in order to strengthen the socialist system, the citizens of the U.S.S.R. are guaranteed by law:

a) freedom of speech;
b) freedom of the press;
c) freedom of assembly, including the holding of mass meetings;
d) freedom of street processions and demonstrations.

These civil rights are ensured by placing at the disposal of the working people and their organizations printing presses, stocks of paper, public buildings, the streets, communications facilities and other material requisites for the exercise of these rights.

ARTICLE 126

In conformity with the interests of the working people, and in order to develop the organizational initiative and political activity of the masses of the people, citizens of the U.S.S.R. are guaranteed the right to unite in public organizations: trade unions, cooperative societies, youth organizations, sport and defence organizations, cultural, technical and scientific societies; and the most active and politically-conscious citizens in the ranks of the working class and other sections of the working people unite in the Communist Party of the Soviet Union (Bolsheviks), which is the vanguard of the working people in their struggle to strengthen and develop the socialist system and is the leading core of all organizations of the working people, both public and state.

ARTICLE 127

Citizens of the U.S.S.R. are guaranteed inviolability of the person. No person may be placed under arrest except by decision of a court or with the sanction of a procurator.

ARTICLE 128

The inviolability of the homes of citizens and privacy of correspondence are protected by law.

ARTICLE 129

The U.S.S.R. affords the right of asylum to foreign citizens persecuted for defending the interests of the working people, or for scientific activities, or for struggling for national liberation.

ARTICLE 130

It is the duty of every citizen of the U.S.S.R. to abide by the Constitution of the Union of Soviet Socialist Republics, to observe the laws, to maintain labour discipline, honestly to perform public duties, and to respect the rules of socialist intercourse.

ARTICLE 131

It is the duty of every citizen of the U.S.S.R. to safeguard and fortify public, socialist property as the sacred and inviolable foundation of the Soviet system, as the source of the wealth and might of the country, as the source of the prosperity and culture of all the working people.

Persons committing offences against public, socialist property are enemies of the people.

ARTICLE 132

Universal military service is law.

Military service in the Armed Forces of the U.S.S.R. is an honourable duty of the citizens of the U.S.S.R.

ARTICLE 133

To defend the country is the sacred duty of every citizen of the U.S.S.R. Treason to the motherland—violation of the oath of allegiance, desertion to the enemy, impairing the military power of the state, espionage—is punishable with all the severity of the law as the most heinous of crimes.

Constitution (Fundamental Law) of the Union of Soviet Socialist Republics (Moscow, 1947), pp. 89–99.

The following statement by Stalin on the inevitability of wars among capitalist states was taken from his last published work. It provides a noteworthy definition of what Soviet official policy means by "peace."

ECONOMIC PROBLEMS OF SOCIALISM IN THE U.S.S.R. 217

To Participants in the Economics Discussion: Remarks on Economic Questions Connected with the November Discussion of 1951. (By J. V. Stalin. Bolshevik, No. 18, September [published in October], 1952, pp. 1–50. Reprinted in Pravda, Oct. 3, pp. 2–5, and Oct. 4, pp. 2–4. Complete text:) I have received all the documents on the economic discussion held in connection with the evaluation of the draft of the textbook of political economy.

Among these I have received the "proposals for improving the draft text-book of political economy," "proposals for eliminating mistakes and in-accuracies" in the draft and "memorandum on disputable questions."

I consider it necessary to make the following observations on all these documents and on the draft of the textbook. . . .

6. THE QUESTION OF THE INEVITABILITY OF WARS AMONG CAPITALIST COUNTRIES

Some comrades affirm that, in consequence of the development of inter-national conditions after the second world war, wars among capitalist countries have ceased to be inevitable. They consider that the contradictions between the camp of socialism and the camp of capitalism are greater than the contradictions among capitalist countries, that the U.S.A. has made other capitalist countries sufficiently subservient to itself to prevent them from going to war with one another and weakening one another, that forward-looking people of capitalism have learned enough from two world wars which inflicted serious damage on the whole capitalist world not to permit themselves again to draw the capitalist countries into war among themselves, that, in view of all this, wars among capitalist countries have ceased to be inevitable.

These comrades are mistaken. They see the external appearances which glitter on the surface but they fail to see those profound forces which, though at present operating imperceptibly, will nevertheless determine the course of events.

Outwardly everything appears to be "all right:" The U.S.A. has placed Western Europe, Japan and other capitalist countries on a dole; Germany (Western), Britain, France, Italy and Japan, having fallen into the clutches of the U.S.A., are obediently carrying out the U.S. commands. But it would be wrong to think that things can go on well forever and ever, that these countries will tolerate without end the domination and oppression of the U.S.A., that they will not seek to free themselves from American bondage and set out on a course of independent development.

Let us first take Britain and France. There is no doubt that these coun-tries are imperialist. Undoubtedly cheap raw materials and guaranteed markets for their goods are of primary importance to them. Is it to be as-sumed that they will endlessly tolerate the present stage of affairs, in which the Americans, using the stratagem of Marshall Plan aid, are penetrating the economy of Britain and France, seeking to turn them into appendages of the U.S. economy, in which American capital is seizing the raw material sources and export markets in the Anglo-French colonies and thereby preparing a catastrophe for the high profits of Anglo-French capitalists? Would it not be more correct to say that first capitalist Britain and then capitalist France will ultimately be forced to wrest themselves from the embraces of the U.S.A. and enter into conflict with the U.S.A. in order to assure themselves an independent position and of course high profits?

Let us now proceed to the chief vanquished countries, Germany (Western) and Japan. These countries are now leading a sorry existence under the heel of American imperialism. Their industry and agriculture, their trade, their domestic and foreign policies, all their way of life, are shackled by the American occupation "regime." But it was only yesterday that these countries were still great imperialist powers which shook the foundations of British, U.S. and French domination in Europe and Asia. To think that these countries will not attempt to rise to their feet again, smash the U.S. "regime" and break away on a path of independent development is to believe in miracles.

It is said that the contradictions between capitalism and socialism are greater than the contradictions between the capitalist countries. Theoretically this is of course true. It is true not only now, at the present time, but it was also true before the second world war. And this the leaders of the capitalist countries did, more or less, understand. Yet the second world war began not with a war against the U.S.S.R., but with a war among the capitalist countries. Why?

First, because war with the U.S.S.R., as a socialist country, is more dangerous to capitalism than a war between capitalist countries, for if a war between capitalist countries raises only the question of the supremacy of certain capitalist countries over other capitalist countries, war with the U.S.S.R. must necessarily raise the question of the existence of capitalism itself. Second, because the capitalists, although for propaganda purposes they raise a hubbub about the aggressive nature of the Soviet Union, do not themselves believe in its aggressive nature, since they take into consideration the peaceful policy of the Soviet Union and know that the Soviet Union will not itself attack the capitalist countries.

After the first world war it was believed that Germany had been finally put out of action, just as certain comrades now think that Japan and Germany have been finally put out of action. Then, too, it was also said—the press dinned forth—that the U.S.A. had placed Europe on a dole, that Germany could no longer rise to her feet, that from now on there could be no war among the capitalist countries. Yet in spite of this Germany revived and rose to her feet as a great power within some 15 to 20 years after her defeat, having broken out of bondage and set out upon a course of independent development. It is typical in this regard that none other than Britain and the U.S.A. should have helped Germany to revive economically and to raise her economic war potential. Of course, the U.S.A. and Britain, though helping Germany to revive economically, in so doing intended to direct the revived Germany against the Soviet Union, to use her against the country of socialism. However, Germany directed her forces in the first place against the Anglo-French-American bloc. And when Hitler Germany declared war on the Soviet Union, the Anglo-French-American bloc not only failed to join with Hitler Germany, but, on the contrary, was obliged to enter into a coalition with the U.S.S.R. against Hitler Germany.

Consequently, the capitalist countries' struggle for markets and the desire to crush their competitors turned out in actuality to be stronger than the contradictions between the camp of capitalism and the camp of socialism.

The question is, what guarantee is there that Germany and Japan will not again rise to their feet, that they will not try to wrest themselves from American bondage and to live their own independent lives? I think there are no such guarantees.

But it follows from this that the inevitability of wars among the capitalist countries remains.

It is said that Lenin's thesis that imperialism inevitably gives birth to wars should be considered obsolete since powerful peoples' forces have now grown up which are taking a stand in defense of peace, against a new world war. This is not correct.

The aim of the present movement for peace is to arouse the masses of the people for the struggle to preserve peace and to avert a new world war. Consequently, it does not pursue the aim of overthrowing capitalism and establishing socialism. It limits itself to the democratic aims of the struggle to preserve peace. In this respect the present movement for the preservation of peace differs from the movement during the first world war to turn the imperialist war into a civil war, since this latter movement went further and pursued socialist ends.

Under a certain confluence of circumstances, the struggle for peace may possibly develop in one place or another into a struggle for socialism. This, however, would no longer be the present peace movement but a movement for the overthrow of capitalism.

It is most probable that the present peace movement, as a movement for the preservation of peace, will, should it be successful, result in prevention of a *particular* war, in its postponement, a temporary preservation of a *particular* peace, to the resignation of a bellicose government and its replacement by another government, ready to preserve peace for the time being. This is good, of course. Even very good. But this, however, is still insufficient to eliminate altogether the inevitability of wars among capitalist countries. It is insufficient since with all these successes of the peace movement imperialism still remains and retains power, and consequently the inevitability of wars also remains.

In order to eliminate the inevitability of wars imperialism must be destroyed.

Current Soviet Policies: The Documentary Record of the 19th Communist Party Congress and the Reorganization after Stalin's Death, ed. Leo Gruliow (New York: The Current Digest of the Soviet Press, 1953), pp. 1, 7–8. (Reprinted by permission of the publisher.)

QUESTIONS

1. In the light of later history, how accurate were Lenin's appraisal of Stalin and his prediction of a split in the Communist Party of the Soviet Union?
2. How convincing was Bukharin's confession? Why do you think he made it?
3. What justification, both historical and contemporary, do you think there was for Stalin's fear of an attack on the Soviet Union?
4. What specific comparisons can you draw between Stalin's industrialization program and the reforms of Peter the Great (p. 113)?
5. How well do you think Stalin fulfilled his own definition of "the art of leadership" in the *Pravda* article of March 2, 1930?
6. What, in Stalin's opinion, were the international consequences of the Bolshevik Revolution? What arguments can you give for and against Stalin's appraisal?
7. Which articles in the Soviet "Bill of Rights" do you think have been kept, and which do you know have been violated by the Soviet government? Give examples.
8. According to Stalin's last published work, how do Communists look upon "peace" and the campaign for peace?

CHAPTER XXXV

FASCISM

FASCISM prided itself upon being a practical faith born out of the need for action in the time of chaos that followed the first World War. In Italy the fascist program (218) was at first vague and opportunistic, centered upon patriotism. Not until Mussolini had arrived in power (1922) did he try to find a more definite ideological basis for fascism (219). Fascism, however, was to be more than merely an Italian phenomenon. In the 1930's, nations like Austria, Portugal, and Spain also set up fascist regimes. These governments differed from Italian fascism above all in their stress on the Christian nature of the dictatorship (220).

I. ITALIAN FASCISM

This extract from an article by Mussolini describing the early program of the Italian "Fascists" (Fasci di combattimento) appeared in *Il Popolo d'Italia* (March 24, 1919), a daily paper founded and edited by Mussolini.

218   *First declaration:*

The meeting of March 23rd addresses its first salute and its enduring, reverent thought to the sons of Italy who fell for the country's greatness and for the freedom of the world; to the disabled and invalids, to all combatants, and ex-prisoners who did their duty; and declares itself ready to support vigorously the vindications of a material and moral order which the associations of combatants shall put forth.

Since we don't want to found a combatant's party, for something like this is already being formed in several Italian cities, we cannot be precise concerning the program of these vindications. That will be done by those interested; we declare that we will support it. We don't want to divide up the dead, to go through their pockets in order to find out their party affiliation; we leave this dirty business to the official socialists. We will embrace all the dead in a single affectionate thought, from the general to the last infantryman, from the cleverest among them to those who were rough and uneducated. . . . When one speaks today of the country's greatness and the world's freedom, there are, of course, those who sneer and display an ironical smile since it is now fashionable to question the war. Well, one either accepts or rejects the war as a whole. If there is to be any questioning, we will do it and not the others. And besides, examining the situation in its factual aspects, let us say immediately that the assets and liabilities of such a great exploit cannot be determined according to the rules of bookkeeping. One can't put the "quantum" of what was done and what was not done on one side, but must take the "qualitative" element into account. From this point of view we can affirm with full confidence that the country is greater today, not only because it reaches to the Brenner Pass . . . not only because it stretches to Dalmatia . . . it is greater because we feel greater inasmuch as we have the experience of this war; in that we desired it, that it was not forced upon us, and we could have avoided it. If we have chosen this path it is a sign that there are in our history, in our blood, elements and emotions of greatness, for were it otherwise we would today be the last people in the world. The war has given what we asked; it has given its negative and positive advantages; negative inasmuch as it prevented the Hohenzollern, Hapsburg and other houses from dominating the world, and this is a result obvious to all and enough to justify the war. It has also had its positive results, for in no victorious nation do we see the triumph of reaction. In all these the trend is towards greater political and economic democracy. . . .

Second declaration:

The meeting of March 23rd declares its opposition to the imperialism of other peoples at Italy's expense and to possible Italian imperialism at the expense of other peoples; it accepts the supreme postulate of the League of Nations which requires the integration of each of them, an integration which in Italy's case must be realized at the Alps and on the Adriatic with the vindication and annexation of Fiume and Dalmatia.

We have forty million inhabitants in an area of 287,000 square kilometers divided by the Appennines, which reduce even more the availability of our workable territory. Within ten or twenty years we will be sixty millions and we possess scarcely a million and a half square kilometers of colony, in great part sandy, towards which we will certainly not be able to send most of our population. But if we look about us we see England which, with forty-seven million inhabitants, has a colonial empire of fifty-five million square kilometers and France, which with a population of thirty-eight million inhabitants, has a colonial empire of fifteen million square kilometers. And I could show you by available figures that all nations of the world, Portugal, Holland and Belgium not excluded, have all of them a colonial empire which they maintain and which they are in no ways disposed to weaken in accordance with all the ideologies which may come from across the ocean. Lloyd George speaks frankly of the English empire. Imperialism is the basis of life for any people which tends to expand in economy and in spirit. What distinguishes imperialisms are the means. Now the means which we will be able to choose, and which we will choose, will never be means of barbaric penetration, like those the Germans adopted. Let's say it now: either let all be idealists, or none. Let each take care of his own interests. That those who are fortunate should preach idealism to those who suffer is hard to understand, for that would be too easy. We want our place in the world because we have a right to it.

In this order of the day we reaffirm the societal postulate of the League of Nations. All in all, it is ours as well, but let us make this clear: if the League of Nations is to be a solemn swindle of the proletariat nations by the rich nations through setting forever what are to be the conditions of world equilibrium, let's have no illusions. I understand perfectly that successful nations may fix premiums to insure their wealth and ruling position. But this is not idealism; it is self-interest. . . .

It is inevitable that majorities are static, while minorities are dynamic. We want to be an active minority; we want to split the Official Socialist Party from the proletariat, but if the bourgeoisie thinks we will serve as lightning rods, it is mistaken. We must go towards labor. Already at the time of the armistice I wrote that it was necessary to greet labor returning from the trenches, because it would be hateful and bolshevik to deny recognition of the rights of those who had fought. It is therefore necessary to accept the postulates of the laboring classes. Do they want the eight-hour day? Won't the miners and nighttime laborers later demand a six-hour day? What of invalid and old-age pensions? And the control of industry? We will support these demands, and do so because we also wish to accustom the working classes to managerial skills in business in order as well to convince the workers that it is not easy to run industry and commerce.

These are our postulates, ours for the reasons I have already spoken of and because there are inevitable cycles in history when everything is renewed, transformed. If syndicalist doctrine holds that the necessary directors capable of assuming the management of labor can be drawn from the masses, we cannot oppose it, and particularly if this movement takes two realities into account: the reality of production and that of the nation. . . .

I have the impression that there will be a succession to Italy's present regime. There is a crisis which strikes everyone. During the war we all felt the insufficiency of those who govern us, and we know that the war was won only due to the virtues of the Italian people and not because of the wisdom and capability of its leaders. . . .

If the regime is to be surpassed, we are the ones who must take its place. It is for this that we are forming the *Fasci,* those organs of creation and agitation capable of going into the squares and crying out: "We are the ones who have the right of succession because it was we who thrust the country into war and led it to victory."

From the political point of view, our program has some reforms: the Senate must be abolished. However, while drawing up this death certificate, I must add that the Senate has shown itself of late far superior to the Chamber. . . .

We want, then, the abolition of this feudal body; we demand universal suffrage for men and women; voting by list on a regional basis; proportional representation. Out of the new elections a national assembly will come which we will ask to pass on the form of government of the Italian state. It will call for a republic or a monarchy, and we, who have always tended to be republicans, from this moment say: republic! . . .

But we can't stop at details. Among all the present problems, what most interests us is the creation of the managerial class and providing it with the necessary powers.

It is useless to pose more or less urgent problems if the leaders capable of solving them are not created.

In examining our program some analogies with other programs will be found: postulates in common with the official socialists will be found, but they are not therefore identical in spirit, for we stand for the war and the victory, and it is in establishing this position that we can be all-daring. I would like to see the socialists try to run the country today, for it is easy to promise paradise but difficult to achieve it. No government could demobilize all the troops tomorrow within a few days, or increase the food supplies, because there aren't any. But we can't permit this trial since the official socialists would like to bring into Italy a counterfeit of the Russian phenomenon to which all thinking minds of Socialism are opposed, from Branting and Thomas to Bernstein, since the bolshevik phenomenon does not abolish classes but is a savagely applied dictatorship. We are decidedly opposed to all forms of dictatorship, from that of the saber to that of the three-cornered hat; from that of money to that of numbers. We recognize only the dictatorship of will and intelligence. . . .

Having thus set our course, our activity will soon produce the *Fasci di combattimento*. Tomorrow we will simultaneously direct their action in all centers of Italy. We are not the sort that stands still; we are dynamic, and we want to take our place which must always be at the vanguard.

Opera omnia di Benito Mussolini, a cura di Edoardo e Duilo Susmel (Florence, 1953), XII, 321, 322–23, 325, 326–27. (Trans. John Thayer.)

By 1932, Mussolini had worked out a more consistent basis for the ideology of fascism. Here, greatly reduced, is the article on fascism by Mussolini (1932) from the *Enciclopedia Italiana.*

219   Fascism was not the nursling of a doctrine worked out beforehand with detailed elaboration. It was born of the need for action and from the beginning it was practical rather than theoretical. It was not merely another political party, but even in the first two years, . . . in opposition to all political parties as such, it was a living movement.

It [fascism] repudiates the doctrine of Pacifism—born of a renunciation of struggle, and an act of cowardice in the face of sacrifice. War alone brings up to its highest tension all human energy and puts the stamp of nobility upon the peoples who have the courage to meet it. . . .

This anti-pacifist spirit is carried by Fascism even into the life of the individual. The proud motto of the *Squadrista,* "Me ne frego" [never mind], written on the bandage of a wound, is an act of philosophy not only stoic, the summary of a doctrine not only political—it *is* the education to combat, the acceptance of the risks which combat implies, and a new way of life for Italy. Thus the Fascist accepts life and loves it, knowing nothing of and despising suicide: he conceives of life as duty and struggle and conquest, life which should be high and full, lived for oneself, but above all for others—those who are near and those who are far distant, those of the present and those who will come after. . . .

Such a conception of life makes Fascism the complete opposite of that basic doctrine of so-called scientific and Marxian Socialism, the materialist conception of history. . . . Fascism now and always believes in holiness and heroism; that is to say, in actions influenced by no economic motive, direct or indirect. . . . And above all, Fascism denies that class-war can be the preponderant force in the transformation of society. . . .

After Socialism, Fascism combats the whole complex system of democratic ideology and repudiates it, whether in its theoretical promises or in its practical application. Fascism denies that the majority, by the simple fact that it is a majority, can direct human society. . . . Fascism denies, in democracy, the absurd conventional untruth of political equality dressed out in the garb of collective irresponsibility and the myth of "happiness" and indefinite progress. But, if democracy may be conceived in diverse forms —that is to say, taking democracy to mean a state of society in which the populace are not reduced to impotence in the State—Fascism may write itself down as "an organized, centralized, and authoritative democracy." . . .

But the Fascist negation of Socialism and Liberal Democracy must not be taken to mean that Fascism desires to lead the world back to the state of affairs before 1789. A party which governs a nation is a fact entirely new to history. . . .

The foundation of Fascism is the conception of the State. . . . The Fascist State is itself conscious, and has itself a will and a personality— thus it may be called the "ethic" state. . . . The individual in the Fascist State is not annulled but rather multiplied, just as a soldier in a regiment is not diminished but rather increased by the number of his comrades. The Fascist State organizes the nation, but leaves a sufficient margin of liberty to the individual. The latter is deprived of all useless and possibly harmful freedom but retains what is essential. The deciding power in this question cannot be the individual, but the State alone.

The Fascist State is not indifferent to the fact of religion in general, or to that particular and positive faith, Italian Catholicism. The State professes no theology, but a morality. . . .

The Fascist State is an embodied will to power and government: the Roman tradition is here an ideal of force in action. . . . For Fascism, the growth of empire, that is to say the expansion of the nation, is an essential manifestation of vitality, and its opposite a sign of decadence. . . . Fascism is the doctrine best adapted to represent the tendencies and aspirations of a people, like the people of Italy, who are rising again after many centuries of abasement and foreign servitude. . . .

Benito Mussolini, in the *Enciclopedia Italiana*, 1932. Authorized English translation printed in *International Conciliation*, No. 306, January, 1935, pp. 5 ff. (Reprinted by permission of the publisher.)

II. TOTALITARIANISM OUTSIDE ITALY

The following extracts are meant to illustrate totalitarianism as it grew up outside Italy. Austria was one of the principal nations which, in 1934, changed from a democratic to an authoritarian state. In that year Chancellor Engelbert Dollfuss had defeated the Social Democratic workers of Vienna in a three-day battle. It was Mussolini who urged Dollfuss to make the change, though the Austrian corporatist state was to differ from Italy in its strong emphasis upon the Christian nature of the state. Only one political organization was allowed, the "Patriotic Front." This combination of totalitarianism and Christian emphasis is also typical of Portuguese and Spanish fascism. An Austrian minister, Otto Ender, explains the Constitution of 1934:

220   . . . In the meantime there arose plans to strip the [old] Constitution of its democratic character and to clothe it in different forms; to build it, in a return to the past, upon an estate [corporatist] basis. Furthermore, there appeared on the 15th of May, 1931, the papal Encyclical *Quadregesimo anno* which advocates the self-government of each individual occupational group as taking from the shoulders of the state those tasks which it cannot fulfill. This papal Encyclical found a strong echo in Austria. It also found a willing ear with the Austrian government, which soon began to make preparations in order to make possible a corporatist organization of the people, with self-government of the occupational groups; and which in addition should make it possible to transfer tasks of public administration to the autonomous corporatist bodies. It followed naturally that the law-making body in the federation should principally emerge from the occupational groups. . . .

If we add to this that there can be no doubt about the purely germanic character and Christian way of life of our overwhelmingly German and Catholic people, one can understand the preamble to the new Constitution, which reads: "In the name of God the Almighty from whom all law flows, the Austrian people receives for its Christian, German federation this Constitution on a corporatist basis." . . .

Die Neue Oesterreichische Verfassung, etc. Eingeleitet und Erleutert von Bundesminister Dr. O. Ender (Oesterreichischer Bundesverlag, 1935), pp. 4, 5. (Trans. George L. Mosse.)

On the same day that the constitution was ratified, the so-called "Patriotic Front" received official recognition as the one official political party. Here are excerpts from this law:

1. The totality of the juridical and physical persons who belong to the **221** Patriotic Front, constitutes a community at law built upon authoritarian foundations.
2. The Patriotic Front is called to be the carrier of the Austrian concept of the State. Its goal is to gather together politically all the citizens who stand for an independent, Christian, German, corporately organized Austrian federation; and who will be subject to the present leader of the Patriotic Front or of his designated successor. . . .

Ibid., p. 131.

QUESTIONS

1. From Mussolini's ideas in 1919 (extract 218), can you list the points which would make up a definite program for early fascism? When you have listed these points, does the program still seem vague to you?
2. To what classes of the population do you think Mussolini's programs would appeal?
3. Contrast the program of 1919 with that of 1932. What changes do you detect? What do you think is the significance of these changes?
4. List the main characteristics of the kind of fascism symbolized in Austria. In what respects does this differ from Italian fascism and what are its similarities?
5. Can you arrive at a definition of "fascism" from these sources?

CHAPTER XXXVI

THE GERMAN REPUBLIC

GERMANY'S REQUEST for an armistice was preceded by revolution at home. The Emperor fled to Holland, and for the first time in her history Germany became a Republic. On the 11th of November, 1918, the armistice was signed, but restoration of peace in the world did not mean the restoration of peace within Germany. The Revolution had brought power to the socialists, but now a definite split within the party threatened to throw the new Republic into chaos. The "left socialists" wanted a dictatorship of proletarians after the Russian model, while the majority socialists wanted a democratic Republic. Calling themselves "Spartacists," the left socialists rose up against the government. On the same day that the armistice was signed, the revolutionaries issued their proclamation (222). This could have been part of the Communist uprisings which took place in the years 1918–19 over much of Europe: in Hungary, Poland, and Bavaria. But the majority socialists, now called Social Democrats, won the day, while the Spartacists became the powerful German Communist party. The Social Democrats wholeheartedly supported the Republic (223).

But Germany was not to find repose, for to the menace from the left was added the equally dangerous menace from the right. After a period of relative stability, associated with the policies of Stresemann in the international field (see p. 505), the great depression brought the republican government to a complete standstill. Since no party in the Diet could form a majority coalition, the political power fell into the hand of the President, according to Article 48 of the Weimar Constitution (224). Field Marshal Paul von Hindenburg thus became the real repository of political power from 1931 to 1933. In those twilight years of the Republic, it moved away from democratic government in a parliamentary sense and toward the idea of a "Presidential Cabinet" governing by decree.

But as this attempt to solve the deadlocked political situation failed (225), Hindenburg turned to Adolf Hitler, the leader of the largest political party. In the so-called Enabling Act (226) Hitler, as Chancellor, got powers even more sweeping than the President possessed under Article 48, and this with the consent of a large majority of the Diet. Thus the German Republic had moved from government by Presidential decree to outright dictatorship.

On the 11th of November, 1918, the revolutionaries issued the following manifesto. They were at that time in partial control of Berlin, and it was still well over a month before the Social-Democratic government was able to contain the revolt. The Russian model is very marked in this manifesto, from the forming of soldiers' and workers' councils down to its phraseology.

To the working people! The old Germany no longer exists. The German **222** people have recognized that they have been engulfed for years by deception and lies.

The much criticized militarism, hitherto recommended to the regard of the whole people, has collapsed. The Revolution has started its march of victory from Kiel, and has succeeded victoriously.

The Dynasties have forfeited their existence. The bearers of crowns have been stripped of their power.

Germany has become a Republic, a socialist Republic. Immediately, the gates of prisons, jails and penitentiaries have opened for those who had been condemned or arrested for political and military crimes. The repositories of political power are the councils of workers and soldiers. In all garrisons and towns in which as yet no soldiers' and workers' council exists, the formation of such councils will be undertaken with dispatch.

The task of the provisional government, elected by the workers' and soldiers' council of Berlin, will be, above all, to negotiate an armistice and to stop the bloody massacre.

Immediate peace is the slogan of the revolution. Whatever peace will be made, it will be preferable to the continuation of tremendous mass slaughters.

The quick and consequent nationalization of the capitalist means of production can be carried out without great upheaval, given Germany's social structure and the degree of development of her economic and political organizations. This is necessary in order to build a new economy from the ruins drenched with blood, in order to prevent the economic enslavement of the masses of the people and the collapse of culture. All workers, workers of the mind and intellect, who stand for this are called upon to co-operate.

The workers' and soldiers' council is penetrated with the conviction that in the whole world an upheaval leading to the same goal is in preparation. It expects confidently that the proletariate in other countries will use all their force in order to prevent the rape of the German people at the end of the war.

It remembers with admiration the Russian workers and soldiers who have marched ahead on the road to Revolution; it is proud that the German soldiers and workers followed suit, and thus preserved their ancient fame of being in the vanguard of the International. It sends fraternal greetings to the Russian workers' and soldiers' government.

It resolves that the German Republican government establish at once international legal relations with the Russian government, and receive a mission of that government in Berlin.

Through the terrible war, which lasted over four years, Germany is ruined in a most frightful way. Immeasurable material and moral goods have been destroyed. It is a gigantic task to create new life out of this ruination and destruction.

The workers' and soldiers' council knows that the revolutionary power cannot at one sweep rectify the crimes and mistakes of the old regime and of the propertied classes, that it cannot, at once, create an excellent condition for the masses. But this revolutionary power is the only one which can still save what is to be saved. Only the Socialist Republic is capable of releasing the power of international socialism for the achieving of a democratic perpetual peace in the world.

Long live the German Socialist Republic!

Vossische Zeitung (November 11, 1918), Eberhard Buchner, *Revolutionsdokumente* (Berlin: Deutsche Verlagsgesellschaft fuer Politik und Geschichte, 1921), I, 157–58 (Trans. George L. Mosse.)

Hugo Preuss was one of the principal architects of the Constitution of the German Republic. Here he writes, in 1923, about the hopes and the dangers of the new Republic. Notice the great importance which he assigns to the Social Democratic party as the mainstay of the democratic state.

The constitution of the German Republic had to be democratic and **223** parliamentary at the same time.

. . . The rule by the Divine Right of kings, of a monarchy ruling by its own right and dominating national life from the top down, accepted uncritically (in Germany) for longer than anywhere else, had broken down. Under this rule no ruling class, recognized as such by the people, had been able to develop. There was no political nobility, no politically independent and leading bourgeoisie. If the political development had thus, on the one hand, lagged behind the social and economic developments, the position of the Social Democrats, on the other hand, was much stronger (in Germany) than elsewhere. They had constituted the only effective opposition to the authoritarian regime. Thus, when the latter collapsed, they took up the reins of leadership. But within the breast of the Social Democrats there lurked two souls: that of political democracy and that of the proletarian class struggle. . . . But as the collapse of the authoritarian regime suddenly called this opposition to the place of power, the cause of political democracy came to the fore as far as the majority of the thinking and responsible element [of the Social Democratic party] was concerned. They recognized that the class struggle and the dictatorship of the proletariat would not be able to accomplish Germany's rise from its hopeless position; but instead would mean the accomplishment of external and internal ruin. That they recognized this, that they separated themselves from the blind advocates of the proletarian revolution and were willing to collaborate in the making of the constitution with those bourgeois parties which also advocated political democracy, this fact has, at least momentarily, saved Germany from chaos. . . .

But [the old habits] are too deeply seated within the German people to lead easily toward a parliamentary view of things: a view which sees in the cabinet minister the natural parliamentary leader—on the contrary now such a leader is regarded with mistrust as soon as he gains leadership in Parliament. The task of the representatives of the people, as long as they confronted an independent authority [i.e., the Emperor] was limited to mere verbal criticism. The role of an opposition is the most comfortable and gratifying: it can always proclaim the unsullied principles of the party without being constrained by the necessity of putting them into practice through responsible political action. . . . The consequences of this for our own time are an exaggeration and magnifying of the theoretical and dogmatic differences between our parties, differences which are alien to countries ruled by a parliamentary regime, and which hinder the development toward a parliamentary State. Moreover, on the basis of the conditions under which we have hitherto lived, we can explain our great lack of personalities which are suited to both parliamentary and practical political leadership and which [at the same time] are universally recognized. . . .

In addition to all this there is the circumstance that even the Social Democrats, though in the great crisis [i.e., revolutionaries' revolt] they had stood on the principles of a political democracy, have not been able to get away from their concept of class struggle. This injects a very detrimental insecurity and additional division into the grouping of majority and minority parties which are necessary to parliamentary government, for instead of this one division we now have two groupings of parties running across and contradicting the logical grouping of majority and minority parties. The consolidation of our parliamentary government, and therefore of our political future in general, depends on the firm union of those parties which abide by the constitution against the opposition of the proletarian dictatorship from the left, and the political reaction from the right. . . .

The indispensability of parliamentary democracy for Germany's future brings with it the obligation to release all those forces which can overcome all these obstacles and dangers, great though they may be.

Hugo Preuss, *Deutschlands republikanische Reichsverfassung* (Berlin, 1923), pp. 12 ff. (Trans. George L. Mosse.)

Article 48 of the Constitution of 1919 granted emergency powers to the President. Against the abuse of this power it was believed that there were three safeguards. The President was popularly elected and thus would not govern in an anti-parliamentary sense; any measure so promulgated could be cancelled by simple Reichstag majority; and the Reichstag could regulate further details of this Article. However, in the crisis of 1931–33 these safeguards proved inadequate as President Hindenburg, through his "Presidential Cabinet," governed by decree, basing his actions on the powers set forth in this Article.

ARTICLE 48. If a Land fails to fulfill the duties incumbent upon it **224** according to the Constitution or the laws of the Reich, the Reichspresident can force it to do so with the help of the armed forces.

The Reichspresident may, if the public safety and order in the German Reich are considerably disturbed or endangered, take such measures as are necessary to restore public safety and order. If necessary he may intervene with the help of the armed forces. For this purpose he may temporarily suspend, either partially or wholly, the Fundamental Rights established in Articles 114, 115, 117, 118, 123, 124 and 153.[1]

The Reichspresident shall inform the Reichstag without delay of all measures taken under Paragraph 1 or Paragraph 2 of this Article. On demand by the Reichstag the measures shall be repealed. . . .

Die Verfassung des deutschen Reiches (Leipzig, 1930). (Trans. George L. Mosse.)

When Adolf Hitler was first requested to form a government, in November, 1932, he asked the President to explain the difference between a "Presidential Cabinet" and parliamentary government. Hindenburg's Secretary of State replied to Hitler and is quoted in part below. Not only does he give us the definitions which had been requested, but he also gives the President's views on the nature of the governments of Heinrich Bruening (1930–32) and of Franz von Papen (1932). As yet Hindenburg did not believe that Hitler could remedy the faults of the Papen cabinet (see 225) and asked him to form a purely parliamentary government. This Hitler rejected. Thus it was not until January, 1933, that, after the failure of yet one more "Presidential Cabinet" (Schleicher), Hindenburg asked Hitler to form the government and was willing to concede to him extraordinary powers. Hitler accepted and gained powers beyond those of Article 48 in the Enabling Act (226).

[1] Article 114 (freedom of the individual), Article 115 (freedom of residence), Article 117 (secrecy of postal communications), Article 118 (freedom of expression), Article 123 (freedom of assembly), Article 124 (freedom of organization), Article 153 (guarantee of personal property).

225   The Reichspresident sees the difference between a Presidential Cabinet and a Parliamentary government as consisting in the following characteristics:

1. The Presidential Cabinet—born out of the difficulties of the times and the failure of the Parliament—will as a rule put into force the necessary governmental measures without prior Parliamentary approval, on the basis of Article 48 of the Reichsconstitution. Therefore it derives its powers in the first place from the Reichspresident, and as a rule needs the Parliament only to sanction or to tolerate such measures. It follows from this that the leader of the Presidential Cabinet must be a man who has the special confidence of the Reichspresident.

2. The Presidential Cabinet must be above parties in its leadership and composition, and must follow a program which is above parties and sanctioned by the Reichspresident. A Parliamentary government is as a rule led by the leader of one of the parties which come into consideration for the formation of a majority or a coalition, and essentially follows goals upon which the Reichspresident has only small and indirect influence. . . .

3. Reichschancellor Bruening, upon his first call to office, formed a distinctly Parliamentary Cabinet, supported by the parties, which only gradually evolved into a kind of Presidential Cabinet after the Reichstag had failed in its legal functions and Herr Bruening had attained, in the greatest measure, the confidence of the Reichspresident. . . .

4. The Papen cabinet was a purely Presidential Cabinet which resigned only because it could not find in Parliament a majority to sanction or to tolerate its measures. . . . A new Presidential Cabinet would only then be an improvement, if it could get rid of this fault while at the same time possessing the qualities of the Papen cabinet.

Ernst Forsthoff, *Deutsche geschichte seit 1918 in Dokumenten* (Stuttgart, 1938), pp. 189-90. (Trans. George L. Mosse.)

It was the Enabling Act of March 23, 1933, which in a legal way conferred dictatorial powers on Adolf Hitler. Only 94 Social Democratic votes were cast against it. The date for its abrogation (see Article 5) was never kept. Indeed, the Enabling Act is the last measure which the Reichstag passed under the republican and democratic Constitution of the Republic. It spelled its end and the beginning of National Socialist dictatorship.

226   Article 1. Laws of the Reich can also be promulgated by the Reich government apart from the method prescribed by the Constitution.

Article 2. Laws decided upon by the government of the Reich can depart from the Constitution of the Reich, in so far as they do not touch the existence as such, of such institutions as the Reichstag and the Reichsrat. The rights of the Reichspresident remain untouched. . . .

Article 4. Treaties of the Reich with foreign powers which have reference to matters concerning the laws of the Reich, do not need the consent of the bodies which had part in the making of such laws, as long as this present law is valid.

Article 5. This law is in force on the day of its promulgation. It is abrogated on April 1, 1937; it is further abrogated if the present government of the Reich is replaced by another.

Ibid., pp. 289–90. (Trans. George L. Mosse.)

QUESTIONS

1. To what extent is the revolutionary manifesto based upon models of the Russian Revolution? Compare it with the ideas and phrasing of the documents on page 411.
2. To what extent did the subsequent history of the Republic validate the dangers which Hugo Preuss foresaw?
3. Can we call the idea of the "Presidential Cabinet" a legalized dictatorship under Article 48 of the Constitution? What were the limits of such Presidential action as they emerge from documents 224 and 225?
4. Compare the Enabling Act with Article 48 of the Constitution. Who now had wider powers, Adolf Hitler or the President?

CHAPTER XXXVII

NATIONAL SOCIALISM

NAZISM was not some terrible accident which fell upon the German people out of a blue sky. One historian has called it the *reductio ad absurdum* of the German tradition of nationalism, militarism, worship of success, and force, as well as the exaltation of state. Yet the conditions which Hitler exploited were not confined to one country, although they were stronger in Germany than anywhere else. Adolf Hitler's own thought was a mixture of racism, anti-Marxism, and the idea of struggle (which we also found in Italian fascism; see p. 454) (227). His own effectiveness depended to a large degree upon the party organization. Here, in the duties and principles of party membership and in the relationship between the party and state, the ideas of National Socialism are spelled out in concrete terms (228). Finally, the racial doctrine upon which this ideology rested in large part can be seen through the eyes of the party's "ideologist" —Alfred Rosenberg (229).

The following extracts illustrate some of the political ideas of Adolf Hitler (1889–1945). (See also p. 508 for another Hitler speech.)

227   In that we deny the principle of parliamentary democracy we strike the strongest blow for the right of the nation to the self-determination

of its own life. For in the parliamentary system we see no genuine expression of the nation's will—a will which cannot logically be anything else than a will to the maintenance of the nation—but we do see a distortion, if not a perversion, of that will. The will of a nation to the self-determination of its being manifests itself most clearly and is of most use when its most capable minds are brought forth. They form the representative leaders of a nation, they alone can be the pride of a nation—certainly never the parliamentary politician who is the product of the ballot box and thinks only in terms of votes. The constructive development of the future leadership of the nation through its most able men will take years; the intelligent education of the German people will take decades. (Nürnberg, September 1, 1933; *Voelkischer Beobachter,* September 2, 1933.)

Internationalism is weakness in the life of nations. What is there that is born of internationalism? Nothing. The real values of human culture were not born of internationalism, but they were created by the whole heritage and tradition of the people [das Volkstum]. When peoples no longer possess creative power they become international. Wherever there is weakness in regard to spiritual matters in the life of nations, internationalism makes its appearance. It is no coincidence that a people, namely the Jews, which does not have any real creative ability, is the carrier of this internationalism. It is the people with the least creative power and talent. It dominates only in the field of crooked and speculative economy.

The Jew, as a race, has a remarkable instinct of self-preservation, but as an individual he has no cultural abilities at all. He is the demon of the disintegration of nations—the symbol of continual destruction of peoples. If the first of May, therefore, is to have any meaning in the life of peoples, it can be only a glorification of the national, creative idea as against the international idea of decay. (Munich, May 1, 1923; *Voelkischer Beobachter,* May 3, 1923.)

I do not want even to speak of the Jews. They are simply our old enemies, their plans have suffered shipwreck through us, and they rightly hate us, just as we hate them. We realize that this war can end only either in the wiping out of the Germanic nations, or by the disappearance of Jewry from Europe. On September 3rd I spoke in the Reichstag—and I dislike premature prophecies—and I said that this war would not end the way the Jews imagine, that is, in the extinction of the European Aryan nations, but that the result of this war would be the destruction of Jewry. For the first time, it will not be the others who will bleed to death, but for the first time the genuine ancient Jewish law, "an eye for an eye, a tooth for a tooth," is being applied. The more this struggle spreads, the more anti-Semitism will spread—and world Jewry may rely on this. It will find nourishment in every prison camp, it will find nourishment in every family which is being enlightened as to why it is being called upon to make such sacrifices, and the hour will come when the worst enemy of the world, of all time, will have finished his part for at least one thousand years to come. (Berlin, January 30, 1942; B.B.C.)

For fourteen or fifteen years I have continually proclaimed to the German nation that I regard it as my task before posterity to destroy Marxism, and that is no empty phrase but a solemn oath which I shall follow as long as I live. I have made this confession of faith, the confession of faith of a single man, that of a mighty organization. I know now that even if fate were to remove me, the fight would be fought to the end; this movement is the guarantee for that. This for us is not a fight which can be finished by compromise. We see in Marxism the enemy of our people which we will root out and destroy without mercy. . . .

We must then fight to the very end those tendencies which have eaten into the soul of the German nation in the last seventeen years, which have done us such incalculable damage and which, if they had not been van-quished, would have destroyed Germany. Bismarck told us that liberalism was the pace-maker of Social Democracy. I need not say here that Social Democracy is the pace-maker of Communism. And Communism is the forerunner of death, of national destruction, and extinction. We have joined battle with it and will fight it to the death. (Berlin, May 10, 1933; *Voelkischer Beobachter*, May 11, 1933.)

We are enemies of cowardly pacifism because we recognize that according to the laws of nature, struggle is the father of all things. We are enemies of democracy because we recognize that an individual genius represents at all times the best in his people and that he should be the leader. Numbers can never direct the destiny of a people. Only genius can do this. We are the deadly enemies of internationalism because nature teaches us that the purity of race and the authority of the leader alone are able to lead a nation to victory. (Kulmbach, February 5, 1928; *Voelkischer Beobachter*, February 9, 1928.)

. . . Thus I am standing for exactly the same principles that I stood for already a year ago. We are convinced that a final showdown will come in this fight against Marxism. We are convinced that it must come, for two *Weltanschauungen* are fighting each other and there can be only one outcome! One will be destroyed and the other will win. . . . It is the great mission of the National Socialist Movement, to give this epoch a new faith and to see to it that millions will swear by this faith, so that, when some day the hour for the showdown comes, the German people will not meet the Jewish international murderers completely unarmed. (Munich, May 23, 1926; *Voelkischer Beobachter,* May 26, 1926.)

Hitler's Words, ed. Gordon W. Prange (Washington: American Council of Public Affairs, 1944), pp. 38, 43, 83, 254, *passim.* (Reprinted by permission of the publisher.)

The following extracts are taken from the *Nazi Party Organization Book* (1940) and illustrate the duties of party members, as well as the National Socialist concept of the State:

6. Duties of the Party Comrade   **228**

   The National Socialist commandments:

   The Führer is always right!

   Never go against discipline!

   Don't waste your time in idle chatter or in self-satisfying criticism, but take hold and do your work!

   Be proud but not arrogant!

   Let the program be your dogma. It demands of you the greatest devotion to the movement.

   You are a representative of the party; control your bearing and your manner accordingly!

   Let loyalty and unselfishness be your highest precepts!

   Practice true comradeship and you will be a true socialist!

   Treat your racial comrades as you wish to be treated by them!

   In battle be hard and silent!

   Spirit is not unruliness!

   That which promotes the movement, Germany, and your people, is right!

   If you act according to these commandments, you are a true soldier of your Führer.

7. Guiding Principles for Members of the *Ortsgruppen* [local groups]

   The following guiding principles are to be made known to all members, and all men and women of the party should impress them upon themselves:

Lighten the work of the political leaders by the punctual performance of your duties.

Women of the party should participate in the activities of the NS Association of Women; there they will find work to do.

Don't buy from Jews!

Spare the health of the party comrades and speakers and refrain voluntarily from smoking at the meetings.

Don't make yourself a mouthpiece for our political opponents by spreading false reports.

To be a National Socialist is to set an example.

I. The State

The state is born out of the necessity of ordering the community of the *Volk* in accordance with certain laws. Its characteristic attribute is *power* over *every* branch of the community. The state has the right to demand of every racial comrade [*Volksgenosse*] that he live according to the law. Whoever violates the laws of the state will be punished. The state has officials to execute its laws and regulations. The constitution of the state is the basis for its legislation. *The state embodies power!* In the state men of *different* opinions and different outlook *can* live beside each other. The state cannot demand that all men be of the same opinion. It can, however, demand that all men observe its laws.

II. The Party

In contrast to the state, the party is the community of men *of like opinion.* It is born out of the struggle for an ideology. In order to survive this struggle, it gathered together all men who were prepared to fight for this ideology. The ideology is the basis of the order in accordance with which men live within the party. While in the state laws are considered as pressure, obstacles, and difficulties by many citizens, the laws of the party are no burden but rather signify the will of the community. In the state the characteristic is the *must;* in the party the *I will.*

III. The Functions of the Party and the State

(a) It is conceivable that party and state are one and the same thing. This is the case when all racial comrades are converted to the ideology of the party and the laws of the state are the clear expression of the will of the ideology. Then the *state* becomes the great community of men of like opinion. This ideal situation will only seldom be attained in history. It is, in fact, only conceivable if *this* ideology is the only basis for the inner attitude and takes complete possession of the people. . . .

(c) If the *Volk* in all its branches is not impregnated by the party and its ideology, party and state must remain separated. The party will then be an order in which a select group of leaders and fighters is found. The ideology will be carried to the *Volk* by these fighters. The party shall prepare public opinion and public desire so that the spiritual condition of the *Volk* shall be in accord with the actual legislation of the state.

Therefore it does not suffice for the party to be an elite, a minority which is bound together in unity. The party has rather the task of accomplishing the political education and the political unification of the German *Volk*. It accordingly is charged also with the leadership of its associated organizations. In the course of this leadership the party fulfils its primary task: the ideological conquest of the German *Volk* and the creation of the "Organization of the *Volk*." The state is a technical instrument to assist in the creation of this community of the people. It is the instrument for the realization of the ideology. The *party* is, therefore, *the primary* which constantly refills dead material with life and the will to life. . . .

The state administrative apparatus functioned before the war and functioned also after the war. Notwithstanding, the German *Volk* experienced the Black Day of November 9, 1918; notwithstanding, it experienced the terrible collapse of the post-war period in all fields of political, cultural, and economic life. Germany could only be saved from sinking into Communistic chaos through the spirit, will, and readiness to sacrifice of the German freedom movement. Its forces of will and spirit alone made reconstruction possible. The party now has the right and the task of again pumping streams of its spirit and will into the state apparatus.

National Socialism (Washington: United States Government Printing Office, 1943), pp. 195, 198 ff.

Alfred Rosenberg discusses the relationship between the state and the "Volk" in his *Myth of the Twentieth Century* (1935).

The state is nowadays no longer an independent idol, before which 229 everything must bow down; the state is not even an end but is only a means for the preservation of the "Volk". . . . Forms of the state change, and the laws of the state pass away; the folk remains. From this alone follows that the nation is the first and *last*, that to which everything else has to be subordinated.

The new thought puts folk and race higher than the state and its forms. It declares protection of the folk more important than protection of a religious denomination, a class, the monarchy, or the republic; it sees in treason against the folk a greater crime than high treason against the state.

No "Volk" of Europe is racially unified, including Germany. In accordance with the newest researches, we recognize five races, which exhibit noticeably different types. Now it is beyond question true that the Nordic race primarily has borne the genuine cultural fruits of Europe. The great heroes, artists, founders of states have come from this race. . . . Nordic blood created *German* life above all others. Even those sections, in which only a small part today is pure Nordic, have their basic stock from the Nordic race. Nordic is German and has functioned so as to shape the culture and human types of the *westisch, dinarisch,* and *ostisch-Baltisch* races. Also a type which is predominantly *dinarisch* has often been innerly formed in a Nordic mode. This emphasis on the Nordic race does not mean a sowing of "race-hatred" in Germany, but on the contrary, the conscious acknowledgment of a kind of racial cement within our nationality. . . . On the day when Nordic blood should completely dry up, Germany would fall to ruin, would decline into a characterless chaos. That many forces are consciously working toward this, has been discussed in detail. For this they rely primarily on the Alpine lower stratum, which, without any value of its own, has remained essentially superstitious and slavish despite all Germanization. Now that the external bond of the old idea of the Reich has fallen away, this blood is active, together with other bastard phenomena, in order to put itself in the service of a magic faith or in the service of the democratic chaos, which finds its herald in the parasitic but energetic Judaism.

The foundation for the arising of a *new aristocracy* lies in those men who have stood—in a spiritual, political, and military sense—in the foremost positions in the struggle for the coming Reich. It will appear thereby with inner necessity that up to 80 per cent of these men will also externally approach the Nordic type, since the fulfilment of the demanded values lies on a line with the highest values of this blood. With the others the inheritance, which exhibits itself in actions, outweighs personal appearance.

Europe's states have all been founded and preserved by the Nordic man. This Nordic man through alcohol, the World War, and Marxism has partially degenerated, partially been uprooted. . . . In order to preserve Europe, the Nordic energies of Europe must first be revitalized, strengthened. That means then Germany, Scandinavia with Finland, and England. . . . Nordic Europe is the fated future, with a *German* central Europe.

Germany as racial and national state, as central power of the continent, safe-guarding the south and southeast; the Scandinavian states with Finland as a second group, safe-guarding the northeast; and Great Britain, safe-guarding the west and overseas at those places where required in the interest of the Nordic man.

Ibid., pp. 176–77.

QUESTIONS

1. What was Hitler's ideology? Can you reconstruct it by listing all the ideas which he attacks in his thought?
2. What was the relationship between the state and the National Socialist party?
3. From your reading, do you think it is true to say that Hitler and his party thought of peace as merely a state of inactive war?
4. What exactly does Rosenberg mean by the term "Volk"?
5. What are the forces which are endangering the German race, according to Rosenberg and Hitler? What consequences did National Socialism draw from this?
6. Do you see anywhere in these extracts a justification for Hitler's expansionist policies?

CHAPTER XXXVIII

BRITAIN BETWEEN THE WARS

THE FIRST World War imposed a severe strain on Britain. The country lost a million men, had much of her merchant fleet sunk, and converted a large portion of her industry to military purposes. Meanwhile other countries, stimulated by war conditions, moved to free themselves of British economic dominance. No serious attempt was made in Britain, however, to adjust the economic system to this new situation. Free trade survived and the gold standard was restored, and this at a time when over a million persons were normally unemployed. Under such conditions, labor unrest was bound to be considerable. The General Strike of 1926 was only its most dramatic manifestation (230).

But Britain did not drift into a dictatorship of either the right or the left. Stanley Baldwin's confidence in the moderateness of British labor leadership was justified (230). Ramsay MacDonald, the leader of the Labor party, was a socialist who believed in parliamentary government and extreme gradualism (231). As a result, no fundamental changes were made, even when Labor was in power (1924, 1929-31). The great depression, which hit Britain as it did the rest of Europe, meant the end of the gold standard and of free trade. The Statute of Westminster legalized the status of the Dominions in return for a larger share of the Empire market (232). But Britain had weathered the crisis without profound economic or constitutional alterations.

Yet many problems remained. Unemployment was an issue throughout the 1930's. The Labor opposition tried to prevent the government's attempt to cut social benefits for the sake of economy (233). The abdication crisis of 1936 threatened to add a constitutional problem in the midst of economic difficulties. That crisis also passed, and the monarchy continued to be a stabilizing factor in Britain's increasingly difficult domestic and foreign situation (234).

Stanley Baldwin headed the Conservative governments in power (1923, 1924-29) at a time of great labor unrest, culminating in the General Strike (1926). In a speech subsequent to the strike, he looks back over the event and expresses his hopes for the future of the British labor movement. Notice that in tune with the new conservatism (see p. 254) he does not reject the labor movement itself.

There was no doubt in my mind—and I am going to give you my **230** own views—that there were responsible and respected trade union leaders who assented with reluctance and with anxiety to the telegrams ordering the General Strike, and in the hope that somehow or other the consequences of their action would be avoided. Some of them saw and believed, without reason in my view, but also genuinely from their point of view, that if the miners had to concede anything in wages or in hours the industries which they represented would be, in their own language, attacked next, and they were determined to ward off that attack. Let us give those leaders the most generous interpretation that we can of how they came to authorise that strike. But there were other leaders who, if you may judge by the speeches they have made in the past, regarded any such attempt as a chance of bringing off or of aiding what is called the social revolution. It is certain, too, that however much you may call or believe the General Strike to be industrial, the results are political and social. It is a great tribute to the good qualities of the strikers, who are our own people, that they showed that sense of discipline and restraint in obedience to their instructions. Many of them obeyed their orders from their sense of loyalty, orders of which they disapproved themselves, but if that strike had been successful it would have meant industrial ruin, not only to the miners, but to the whole country, and you do not alter that fact by using long words.

It may have been a magnificent demonstration of the solidarity of labour, but it was at the same time a most pathetic evidence of the failure of all of us to live and work together for the good of all. I recognise the courage that it took on the part of the leaders who had taken a false step to recede from that position unconditionally, as they did on 12th May. It took a good deal more courage than it takes their critics now, who are blaming them for not going straight on, whatever happened. But if that strike showed solidarity, sympathy with the miners—whatever you like —it showed something else far greater. It proved the stability of the whole fabric of our own country, and to the amazement of the world not a shot was fired. We were saved by common sense and the good temper of our own people. We have been called a stupid people; but the moment the public grasped that what was at stake was not the solidarity of labour nor the fate of the miners, but the life of the State, then there was a response to the country's need deep and irresistible. And mark this: in my view there was that feeling in the country because the leaders of the strike and the men who were on strike felt it in their innermost hearts, too. They felt a conflict of loyalties. They knew that that same conflict was raging in the breasts of thousands of men who had fought for their country ten years ago. Many of the strikers were uneasy in their minds and their consciences, because the British workman, as I know him, does not like breaking contracts, as so many of them did. I do not think many of them like stopping food supplies and shutting down the Press. I sometimes amuse myself with wondering what their language would have been like if these things had been done by the Government. And, after all, when all has been said about England, about the mistakes we make, and about our stupidity, and about how much better they do things in Russia, yet how many of those men, or any of us, would prefer to have been born and brought up in any country in the world but this, or to send our children to be brought up there. In these post-war years, in spite of all the depression, in spite of all our troubles, never before has the wealth of this country, through the taxes and the rates, been so distributed to those less fortunate and for the provision of those thrown out of work.

We carry in our hearts what is the innermost core of the British Constitution. We have the widest franchise. We have a party system highly susceptible to public opinion in the country, and we legislate in accordance with that opinion. We have these things, and we know in our hearts that no revolutionary change can give us a more democratic freedom. The historians of English law taught us a profound truth when they wrote, "In England the law for the great men has become the law for all men." The nobles and merchants centuries ago established their rights against the arbitrary authority of the Crown and the divine right of kings ceased to be acknowledged. Our people are not going to throw over Parliament to set up divine right either of the capitalist or of the trade unionist, and we are not going to bow down to a dictatorship of either. In no country in the world is there less need to do so, and in no country in the world is there less justification politically for a general strike.

I have tried to give you as briefly as I can—though, I fear, at some length—how I regard the situation through which we are passing, and some of its causes. I want to see our British Labour movement free from alien and foreign heresy. I want to see it pursued and developed on English lines, led by English men. The temptations that beset the growth of these vast organisations, in many respects as they are today outside the law, controlling multitudes of men and large sums of money—the temptation to set such a machine in motion and make people follow it is great indeed.

Stanley Baldwin, *Our Inheritance* (New York: Doubleday Doran & Co., 1928), pp. 231–35. (Reprinted by permission of A. P. Watt & Son.)

Ramsay MacDonald was one of the founders of the Labor party and its leader until 1931. Here he gives his ideas on the nature of socialism in Britain (1920). It was this kind of "gradualism" which dominated his thinking when he was prime minister (1924, 1929–31) and which deeply influenced the more conservative wing of the English Labor party. It is not too far removed from the kind of orientation which Stanley Baldwin wanted to see for British labor (230).

I cannot conceive that the end of good government is to make Society **231** stagnant by its excellence and to lull the individual into quiescence by the security he feels under it. Nor can I conceive of any rational theory of progress that depends upon periodic and violent revolution as a means. Every day comes with its own revolution in a progressive society just as a series of explosions produces motion and a series of impacts produces harmony. The individual, energetic in mind and in action, is too valuable to his community to be lulled to sleep or to be condemned if he occasionally produces trouble and inconvenience. The revolutionary and exploring spirit will always be necessary to keep Society from stagnating. It is not a menace to Society; it is the life of Society. Therefore, whilst the Socialist conception of Society remains fixed, its creeds and methods must never sink into infallible dogma and its gospels become closed books. It is said of Marx that he was once overheard muttering to himself, "Thank God, I am no Marxist," and his great protagonist, Clara Zetkin, has written, "When the pen fell from Marx's hand, the last word on Socialism had not been written." . . .

The Russian Revolution has been one of the greatest events in the history of the world, and the attacks that have been made upon it by frightened ruling classes and hostile capitalism should rally to its defence everyone who cares for political liberty and freedom of thought. But it is Russian. Its historical setting and parentage is Russia; the economic State in which it is is Russia. Moreover, it is still in its eruptive stage, and has hardly passed under the moulding hand of evolution. What it is to become, who can say? All we can do is to see that it has a chance of becoming something, and not die away like the Peace Night flares that are gleaming in the sky as I write this. To cry as flare after flare goes up: "This is the permanent pillar of fire which is to light us to Canaan," is certainly not common sense. We know that some expedients have been purely temporary; we know that others cannot bear close and detailed examination. For them the comprehensive excuse, which is a justification under the circumstances, can be made that they belong to the stress of revolution. History may justify their authors, but it certainly will not their copyers. Lenin in this respect is too big a man to be a Leninite, as he told Bela Kun when Hungary passed under Soviet Government.

Political action remains the normal method of transforming the structure of communities, both politically and socially. . . .

If this is said to be slow, I reply that it need not be so, but that, if it is, it is so by the nature of Society, and no revolutionary action can be planned to avoid the slowness. All short cuts swing round in a circuit to where they started. The footpath is for the individual, the high road for the crowd. It is hard for Socialists to fight capitalism; it is much harder for them to fight Nature. Whether by revolution or without it, the transformation of the economic structure of Society is no easy undertaking, as Lenin is now confessing, and the success of the venture must depend in a very great measure upon the spirit in which it is undertaken. One kind of spirit which appeals to the impatience of the time is, I believe, to lead Socialism into disaster proportionate to the simplicity with which it presents our problems and the dogmatic logic with which it supports them.

To such minds force and authority are the characteristic modes of thought and expedients for action. They deal with book logic, and not with Society; they begin their researches by writing their conclusions; and their political method is at enmity with liberty. . . .

The Socialist spirit is that of liberty, of discussion. It is historical and not cataclysmic. . . .

Above all, it discards lightning changes as the way to realise itself. It knows that no system of government or of society can rest upon anything but common consent—the consent of passive minds, or the consent of active minds. The latter kind of consent is the only one it values. The idea of a revolution transforming the structure of Society by the will of a minority must seem as Utopian to it as the ideas of the Owenites and of all who sought to create an oasis of peace in the wilderness of the capitalist system. It believes in democracy, not only as a moral creed which alone is consistent with its views of humanity, but because it is the only practical creed. It knows that, revolutions or no revolutions, public consent is the basis of all social order and that the good builder makes his foundations sound before he puts up his storeys.

The Independent Labour Party is a product of British history and British conditions. . . . It knows that opinion must always precede reconstruction, but it also knows that the harvest of Socialism does not ripen in a night and has therefore to be gathered at one cutting, but that every day brings something to fruition, that the moments as they go bring us nearer to Socialism by their products of Socialist thought and experiment which have to be seized and embodied in the transforming structure of Society, not in a bunch, but bit by bit. It believes in the class conflict as a descriptive fact, but it does not regard it as supplying a political method. It strives to transform through education, through raising the standards of mental and moral qualities, through the acceptance of programmes by reason of their justice, rationality, and wisdom. It trusts to no regeneration by trick or force. Founding itself on the common sense of every day experience, it knows that, come enthusiasm or depression, impatience or lethargy, the enlightened State can be built up and maintained only by enlightened citizens. It walks with the map of Socialism in front of it and guides its steps by the compass of democracy.

J. Ramsay MacDonald, *Parliament and Revolution* (New York: Scott & Seltzer, 1920), pp. 147–48, 149–50, 154, 155–57.

The Statute of Westminster (1931) put the approval of statute law on the dominion status of a great part of the former British

Empire. It formalized what had been worked out by the Imperial Conference of 1926.

232   Whereas the delegates of His Majesty's Governments in the United Kingdom, the Dominion of Canada, the Commonwealth of Australia, the Dominion of New Zealand, the Union of South Africa, the Irish Free State, and Newfoundland, at Imperial Conferences holden at Westminster in the years of our Lord nineteen hundred and twenty-six and nineteen hundred and thirty did concur in making the declarations and resolutions set forth in the Reports of the said Conferences:

And whereas it is meet and proper to set out by way of preamble to this Act that, inasmuch as the Crown is the symbol of the free association of the members of the British Commonwealth of Nations, and as they are united by a common allegiance to the Crown, it would be in accord with the established constitutional position of all the members of the Commonwealth in relation to one another that any alteration in the law touching the Succession to the Throne or the Royal Style and Titles shall hereafter require the assent as well of the Parliaments of all the Dominions as of the Parliament of the United Kingdom:

And whereas it is in accord with the established constitutional position that no law hereafter made by the Parliament of the United Kingdom shall extend to any of the said Dominions as part of the law of that Dominion otherwise than at the request and with the consent of that Dominion:

And whereas it is necessary for the ratifying, confirming and establishing of certain of the said declarations and resolutions of the said Conferences that a law be made and enacted in due form by authority of the United Kingdom:

And whereas the Dominion of Canada, the Commonwealth of Australia . . . have severally requested and consented to the submission of a measure to the Parliament of the United Kingdom for making such provision with regard to the matters aforesaid as is hereafter in this Act contained:

Now, therefore, be it enacted by the King's most Excellent Majesty by and with the advice and consent of the Lords Spiritual and Temporal, and Commons, in this present Parliament assembled, and by the authority of the same, as follows:—

1. In this Act the expression "Dominion" means any of the following Dominions, that is to say, the Dominion of Canada, the Commonwealth of Australia, the Dominion of New Zealand, the Union of South Africa, the Irish Free State and Newfoundland. . . .

(2) No law and no provision of any law made after commencement

of this Act by the Parliament of a Dominion shall be void or inoperative on the ground that it is repugnant to the law of England, or to the provisions of any existing or future Act of Parliament of the United Kingdom, or to any order, rule or regulation made under any such Act, and the powers of the Parliament of a Dominion shall include the power to repeal or amend any such Act, order, rule or regulation in so far as the same is part of the law of the Dominion.

3. It is hereby declared and enacted that the Parliament of a Dominion has full power to make laws having extra-territorial operation. . . .

7.—(1) Nothing in this Act shall be deemed to apply to the repeal, amendment, or alteration of the British North American Acts, 1867 to 1930, or any order, rule or regulation made thereunder.

(2) The provisions of section two of this Act shall extend to laws made by any of the Provinces of Canada and to the powers of the legislatures of such Provinces.

(3) The powers conferred by this Act upon the Parliament of Canada or upon the legislatures of the Provinces shall be restricted to the enactment of laws in relation to matters within the competence of the Parliament of Canada or of any of the legislatures of the Provinces respectively. . . .

11. Notwithstanding anything in the Interpretation Act, 1889, the expression "Colony" shall not, in any Act of the Parliament of the United Kingdom passed after the commencement of this Act, include a Dominion or any Province or State forming part of a Dominion.

12. This Act may be cited as the Statute of Westminster, 1931.

Statutes of the Realm, 17 George V.

The slow decline in unemployment, after 1933, hardly affected the "distressed areas" of the English midlands, Scotland, and, above all, Wales. In the following extract from a Parliamentary debate (December 17, 1936), a member of Parliament is opposing two policies of an economy-minded government: firstly, the reduction in unemployment benefits, and, secondly, the so-called "means test," which inquired into the actual financial status of the unemployed and adjusted his relief accordingly. The motion lost, but it is typical of Britain's internal difficulties.

"That, being opposed to any action calculated to intensify the appalling **233** distress prevailing in many parts of the country, this House is of opinion that the Unemployment Assistance (Determination of Need) Regulations, in so far as they will involve reductions in existing allowances, should be suspended."

The purpose of this Motion is to prevail upon the Government to refrain from reducing the allowances to the unemployed under the new Regulations. In moving the Motion in this form we on this side of the House have not in any way withdrawn our hostility to the Regulations as a whole, and especially to the means test. . . .

It can be truly said that the Special Areas of this country are in the melting pot, all of them similar to South Wales, where whole districts are being driven to destruction, where families are broken up, where homes are scattered and the people, young and old, are driven to despair. Among the mass of the people, resident in those areas, stricken people, more damage has been wrought than among those who suffered during the four years of the Great War. On top of the already deplorable conditions now existing in those areas the new Regulations and the means test are to be imposed by the Government, and they will create new records of havoc and distress amongst the people, for their application will not only drive the unemployed still further into the depths of starvation, but will impose new cuts on the already low wages of the employed workers, will further destroy home life, will so reduce the purchasing power of the people that small traders and shopkeepers will be driven into bankruptcy, and the already difficult task of the local authorities in those areas will be made impossible.

I put it to the Minister and to the Unemployment Assistance Board, which is so far removed from this problem, that they are responsible for the moral, physical and even the spiritual welfare of these millions of people. These men and their families have committed no crime. They are out of work through no fault of their own. Why should they be punished? These are the men who along the years have made a great contribution to the material wealth of this nation and to the domestic comfort of its people. They, with others, are responsible for the place that this nation holds in the industrial world—men who are absolutely indispensable, coal miners, steel workers, shipbuilders, engineers and so on, all in the productive industries. They were the real backbone of the nation. They were a proud people, maintaining their families, independent in every way, and good citizens.

To-day they are suffering the agony of idleness; they are living a life of hopelessness. The homes of which they were so proud are being destroyed; families are being separated; their wives, the bravest women in the world, have suffered indignity for the last five, six or seven years. Some of them

have not been able to purchase a single new garment in that period. . . .
I have here a statement which appeared in a London newspaper. It is
from a lady who has done considerable charitable work in the worst areas
in South Wales. She asked those who live in the prosperous south-east
England and in London to have some idea as to the extent of the suffering
in the districts where these new Regulations will make conditions very
much worse—in Durham, in South Wales and other areas. She says:

"Theoretically the Regulations regarding unemployment relief may
sound fair, even generous. But in practice their working leaves room for
numerous cases of acute poverty equal to any of the horrors of the last
century." . . .

[Another social worker] concludes his report with these words:

"In this Area we are already doing as much as it is possible to do,
but it is still far from adequate for the needs of the growing child and
the pregnant mother. I am of opinion that the whole of the community
of this Area is slowly but insidiously deteriorating owing to lack of nourishment."

That is the statement by the medical officer of health for Mountain Ash,
a district where we have had between 40 per cent. and 45 per cent. of the
insured persons unemployed. Eighty per cent. of these men have come
under the operation of the Unemployment Assistance Board, and that is
their condition. . . .

Hansard's Parliamentary Debates, 5th series, CCCXVIII, 2661, 2663–64, 2665–66.

Stanley Baldwin, as prime minister, had a key part in the abdication
crisis of King Edward VIII. Here he tells the House of Commons
about the crisis and, at the same time, analyzes the function of the
Monarchy in the kingdom (December 10, 1936).

The Prime Minister: **234**

. . . And then I reminded him of what I had often told him and
his brothers in years past. The British Monarchy is a unique institution.
The Crown in this country through the centuries has been deprived of
many of its prerogatives, but to-day, while that is true, it stands for far
more than it ever has done in its history. The importance of its integrity
is, beyond all question, far greater than it has ever been, being as it is
not only the last link of Empire that is left, but the guarantee in this
country so long as it exists in that integrity, against many evils that have

affected and afflicted other countries. There is no man in this country, to whatever party he may belong, who would not subscribe to that. But while this feeling largely depends on the respect that has grown up in the last three generations for the Monarchy, it might not take so long, in face of the kind of criticisms to which it was being exposed, to lose that power far more rapidly than it was built up, and once lost I doubt if anything could restore it.

That was the basis of my talk on that aspect, and I expressed my anxiety and desire, that such criticism should not have cause to go on. I said that in my view no popularity in the long run would weigh against the effect of such criticism. . . .

I then pointed out the danger of the divorce proceedings, that if a verdict was given in that case that left the matter in suspense for some time, that period of suspense might be dangerous, because then everyone would be talking, and when once the Press began, as it must begin some time in this country, a most difficult situation would arise for me, for him, and there might well be a danger which both he and I had seen all through this—I shall come to that later—and it was one of the reasons why he wanted to take this action quickly—that is, that there might be sides taken and factions grow up in this country in a matter where no faction ought ever to exist. . . .

I would say a word or two on the King's position. The King cannot speak for himself. The King has told us that he cannot carry, and does not see his way to carry, these almost intolerable burdens of Kingship without a woman at his side, and we know that. This crisis, if I may use the word, has arisen now rather than later from that very frankness of His Majesty's character which is one of his many attractions. It would have been perfectly possible for His Majesty not to have told me of this at the date when he did, and not to have told me for some months to come. But he realised the damage that might be done in the interval by gossip, rumours and talk, and he made that declaration to me when he did, on purpose to avoid what he felt might be dangerous, not only here but throughout the Empire, to the moral force of the Crown which we are all determined to sustain.

Ibid., pp. 2179–80, 2183.

QUESTIONS

1. What does Stanley Baldwin mean when he says he wants to see the British labor movement free from alien heresies?

2. What is Ramsay MacDonald's attitude toward Russia? Compare this attitude with that of the German revolutionaries (see p. 463).
3. Compare the attitudes of Stanley Baldwin with Ramsay MacDonald toward labor. How far apart are they?
4. What are the ties between the Dominions and Britain according to the Statute of Westminster?
5. What is the objection to the means test? How does the description of the unemployed in Wales in the 1930's compare with the description of labor in the nineteenth century (see p. 208)?

CHAPTER XXXIX

FRANCE BETWEEN THE WARS

FRANCE made a heroic effort to defend herself during World War I, and she never fully recovered from the toll of this effort—physically, economically, politically, or morally. The tremendous expenses involved forced an inflation her conservative business elements could neither accept nor prevent. In stabilizing the franc, Premier Poincaré showed how France's problems might be met (235), but even the popular and persuasive Premier Herriot could not keep the French from being short-sighted (236). Lack of effective leadership generally resulted in middle-of-the-road drift, apathy, and half measures. Not even the revolutionary elements on the Right and the Left could generate successful leadership, as the former demonstrated in the February Riots of 1934 (237), and the latter in the later days of the Popular Front (238). It was a badly divided, politically stalemated, distraught, and bewildered country, poorly prepared in almost every respect, which came up to the Polish crisis of 1939 (239).

Between the wars there was only one political leader in France in whom the people were willing to vest sufficient authority to carry through a decisive program. He was the conservative wartime president, Raymond Poincaré, a member of the Chamber of Deputies.

On July 27, 1926, during the crisis of the skyrocketing franc, he was called upon to be premier for the second time since the end of the war. His program was a rigid one of economy and more taxes, but he stated it, as the Cabinet declaration which follows indicates, with a blunt and commanding forthrightness rare in the annals of the Republic. It worked, and Poincaré saved the franc while partially repudiating the public debt, but with his passing two years later, no similar man of strength emerged.

The Cabinet which presents itself before you has been formed in a **235** spirit of national reconciliation to meet the danger which threatens the value of our money, the liberty of our treasury and the equilibrium of our finances.

Each of the men who have joined thus to work with the same heart in this task of public safety has considered that it was his duty at this moment to consecrate to it all of his mind and strength.

There may arise later questions on which these men may differ, but today they are entirely in accord on the necessity, on the urgency and on the means of financial salvation. They ask you to give them your confidence and permit them to accomplish the task to which they have been called by the President of the Republic.

After a careful and conscientious review of the situation we have the profound conviction that it is possible rapidly to better the situation of the French finances and increase the value of the franc. This result depends entirely on immediate and real collaboration between the Government and the Chamber.

We will submit to you in a moment a bill intended to cover the present insufficiency of our resources as compared with our commitments. To avoid for all time new risks of inflation we ask you to vote indispensable increased taxation along with the principle of important economies. If the unavoidable obligation to collect them without delay obliges us, as the experts suggested, to increase certain indirect taxes we will ask at the same time by direct taxes for participation of acquired wealth, which it is all ready to furnish, and of which part will serve to feed the annual sinking fund for bond defense.

We appeal to your foresight and patriotism to avoid debates, which, if prolonged, would increase the evil instead of remedying it.

The application of this first remedy will relieve us of the duty of watching continually the condition of finances and of completing our initial effort by measures to maintain public confidence, and it will permit us to fulfil promptly all the engagements of the State, to stimulate production at home and in our colonies, and to develop the vitality of the country.

We do not pretend to solve in several weeks, nor even several months the totality of the economic and financial problems which almost universal uneasiness has erected before us. The essential is to get started quickly and without deviation.

As well as ourselves, the nations which are our creditors and toward which France has the firm intention to acquit herself to the extent of her ability have an interest that before everything else we put an end to the monetary crisis, which has many causes, but which it is not impossible to calm and to remove its perilous influence.

France has known hours graver and sadder than these. She saved herself by union and energy. Today victory depends on the same conditions. For the Republic and for the country let us shoulder our heavy task immediately.

New York Times, July 28, 1926, pp. 1, 4. (Reprinted by permission.)

The leader of the moderate Radical Socialist party for well over a generation was Edouard Herriot. On December 15, 1932, he was premier when the Chamber of Deputies voted to default on its then due semi-annual payment on war debts owed to the United States— the world depression, the Hoover moratorium and the Lausanne Agreement (to say nothing of American tariff policy) having already made a shambles of both reparations and war debts. Herriot chose to make the issue one of confidence, and although his ministry fell in the accompanying defeat, he was thought by many to have made his most brilliant public performance. The debate involved was too complicated and interrupted to do justice to here, but the substance of it Herriot repeated ten days later in an address, quoted here in part, to his constituents in Lyons, where he simultaneously was mayor for many years. This is a very different, although thoroughly characteristic, Herriot—the fatherly, provincial bourgeois speaking familiarly to his friends. This, with the moral tone of his stand, will be the remembered Herriot.

236   . . . The head of a government should have the duty of trying to obtain delays, but the due date having come, common honesty required payment. The Americans, we should not forget, loaned us great sums during and after the war. I well remember—I was, after all, then Minister of Supplies—that in 1917 it was due to them that we had at our disposal, during those tragic hours, wheat, coal, ships, and money. And there is something else involved which transcends all questions of money: 75,000 Americans sleep forever in the soil of France which they defended. I firmly hope that we never again witness parallel events, but if we refuse to pay our debts and such things do happen again where are we going to find any credit? As the guardian of the future of France I had to think of such matters, and I did.

That due date was established by law. What, then, could be done to make non-payment seem legitimate? It is undebatable that there are factors of great moral weight involved, but none of them with any legal worth. Some opponents have invoked the Hoover moratorium. I only have to recall for you how at the time I protested against the way that move would destroy the Young Plan—but no one listened to me then. President Hoover had not foreseen how the moratorium would weaken the whole structure of war debts. On that subject I had also spoken. And, ironically enough, as head of the government I found myself in the paradoxical situation of having to honor the signatures of those very men who refused to honor their own signatures in order to overthrow me. . . .

I should add that in all truth this was a poorly chosen occasion to carry out such a business. Can we expect the two American presidents [Roosevelt had been elected, but Hoover was still in office] now to see any necessity in revising the debts? There is no question but that this will prove to be a tactical error in its effect on American politics. I think it is grossly imprudent, for a mere 480,000,000 francs, to have compromised our friendship with the United States, especially when we have been able to find 300,000,000 francs to loan to Hungary and almost 2,000,000,000 to devote to underwriting tottering banks. The English, whose pound has not been stabilized, have said, "We will pay." They have, by so doing, protected at one and the same time both their moral credit and their material interests. We, with our franc already stabilized, have refused to pay in the very same year in which we have indulged in such squandering. Again, I only repeat, one must pay if he wishes assurance of the possibility of future borrowing. And beyond that, more important than the political aspect is the moral one. I am completely taken aback by the specious reasoning of so many, and I cannot get away from the fact that for the first time the French Republic has refused to respect its signed word. Those who have tried to uphold it, however, remember that it was to honor its signature that England entered the war on our side, and that it was on the other side that one spoke of "scraps of paper." Do we want to be over there? What will Germany say to us tomorrow?

No, the public irritation should not have been allowed to sway responsible representatives at the very moment Chancellor von Papen himself was pronouncing important words on the respect of contracts. Those who refused to pay should also have remembered that they were the very ones who earlier, when Germany refused to pay, counselled the occupation of the Ruhr, establishing the theory of sanctions for the non-payment of debts. Can we now reproach Japan for being in Manchuria, and the Austro-Germans who hope to realize the Anschluss? Truly I have been stupefied at seeing the Right and the Center in rebellion against traditional morality and in support of a Bolshevist trick, while at the same time those parties which hold that contracts are a better defense of international morality than force is have committed an act of force in refusing to pay.

Le Temps (Paris), December 26, 1932, p. 1. (Trans. H. B. Hill.)

In no way involving Herriot, it was out of the same Radical Socialist party, which had largely fulfilled its mission in the nineteenth century and ideologically had no appealingly positive program in the twentieth, that came the scandals and governmental connivance dramatized by the operations of the crooked financier Alexandre Stavisky in the winter of 1933–34. The public reaction was widespread and decisive, centered in those two areas of opinion which advocated action on a moral basis—the Right and the Left—each, needless to say, on different grounds. The first to move was the Right, and how determined it was may be seen from the vivid eyewitness account of the February 6 riots by a highly skilled *New York Times* reporter given below.

237 The disturbances began much earlier than had been expected. From 5 o'clock until after 8 the Place de la Concorde was the scene of incessant battles, which began with a fusillade of missiles from among the trees in the Champs-Élysées gardens. Broken pieces of pavement, branches of trees and scraps of iron grating all served as ammunition and mounted guards had to charge repeatedly.

Almost immediately the crowds threw barricades across the Champs-Élysées, using everything that could be found. Trees were torn down, lamp-posts were smashed and paving stones were ripped up. Within a few minutes the barricades were sufficient to prevent any cavalry charge. As soon as the guards cleared one side of the square they had to turn to the other. Among the crowd were some who stabbed the horses with knives. Half a dozen policemen and guards were knocked unconscious by paving stones and for more than two hours this kind of fighting continued.

Then near 7:30 o'clock reinforcements arrived to deal with the rioters, who were mostly men between the ages of 17 and 25 years who carried in front of them small tricolor flags. Just before they reached the Madeleine a cordon of police had tried to stop them, but almost immediately from every direction hundreds more of them gathered, swamping the police lines and shouting "Vive Chiappe!" [Jean Chiappe, fascist in sympathy, had just been removed as prefect of police in Paris.] It was only two weeks ago that much the same crowd shouted "Down with Chiappe!" but today he was the hero of all the unruly elements.

The police lines were completely swamped and the victorious columns, growing larger and larger at each step, went across the Place de la Concorde, where the ancestors of this same people 150 years ago beheaded King Louis XVI and Marie Antoinette. The republican flag was a rallying point for all in the square and from every side came two cries: "Vive Chiappe!" and "Resignation!" [Of Premier Daladier.]

The police were outnumbered nearly ten to one. There was no way to stop that moving mass in the wide square. When police charges broke the center the wings swept around, enveloping the police. Everybody was singing the "Marseillaise," and in front of the moving mass the tricolored flag still went bravely on, slowly at first, then breaking into a run, and the police retreated, reforming at the bridgehead.

The crowds now were not more than a hundred yards from the chamber gates. Firemen's hose was brought into action and it sprayed and deluged the crowd, but the mass behind pushed forward those in front. In a few seconds forty or fifty had won their way right to the hose fighting line and, seizing it, turned it on the police themselves.

Many on both sides were knocked down and injured in the mêlée that followed, but still the tricolored flags were waving in the van. It looked for an instant as if the police must give way. Halfway across the bridge they formed triple lines and warning was given that they were going to fire.

But those in front could not turn, even if they had wanted to, so great was the crush behind them.

The first shots rang out, but nobody was hurt. Immediately the crowd began yelling that the police were firing blank cartridges and surged forward again.

Then the pistol shots again were heard. But this time they had not used blanks. Most of the police had fired high, but some half-dozen of the front-rank rioters fell. This time the crowd broke, as mounted guards with drawn swords came on, and there was a stampede across the square.

Women's voices were raised piercing above the din in cries of "Assassins! Assassins!"

Who began the shooting will, of course, never be definitely established, but it is clear that some of the demonstrators were armed. Two police inspectors were shot and more than ninety policemen were admitted to hospitals and some of them were said to be suffering from bullet wounds.

While the battle was in progress in the Place de la Concorde and the Boulevard St. Germain, rioting had broken out all over the city.

Three motor buses were overturned and set afire. In the Champs-Élysées railings torn from the Tuileries Gardens were used for ammunition and barricades. Stragglers from all parties, mostly youths, wandered away from where the fighting was taking place and broke street lamps. With whatever missiles they could obtain they broke nearly every lamp in the Rue de la Paix. Near the Tuileries Gardens several private motor cars were overturned and set afire. Traffic signals were broken all over town and gas jets flared violently.

Hundreds of thousands paraded along the boulevards yelling and shouting. Many carried banners. Most of the paraders were well dressed, but on the fringes of each procession there were many hooligans.

From 9 o'clock until 11 the mob was master of the center of Paris, except in the streets immediately around the Chamber. Because of the taxi strike there was scarcely any traffic on the streets, which permitted the rioters more freedom.

There were fights in the boulevards and the opera district and near the Hotel de Ville. Two columns of demonstrators were driven back and dispersed near the Gare Saint Lazare. At times one could hear the "Marseillaise" being sung by one crowd and "The Internationale" by another.

Just before 10 o'clock a battalion of the twenty-first colonial infantry was brought in from a suburban garrison and posted around the Chamber of Deputies. They had full field equipment, and cartridges were issued to them. Near midnight, although the Chamber had long been closed, crowds from the Champs-Élysées and the boulevards again gathered in the Place de la Concorde and tried once more to reach the bridge. The police and troops had to fire again, and a lively fusillade was needed before the square could again be cleared.

Several police, among them the Directeur Judicial of Police, were wounded. . . .

The second battle for the Concorde bridgehead was more carefully planned and more determinedly carried out than the earlier affray. Ten thousand rioters surged out of the Champs-Élysées and, rushing along the quays, drove back the police under a hail of stones. Several guards were isolated around the obelisk in the Place de la Concorde and had to fight their way through the mob, leaving a score of injured in their wake.

P. J. Philip in the *New York Times*, February 7, 1934, p. 2. (Reprinted by permission.)

The Left, also specifically set in motion by the February riots but gathering its forces somewhat more slowly, gave expression to its drive for action in the organization of the Popular Front. The Communists, Socialists, and what might be called the better elements among the Radical Socialists, united tactically at the polls behind an extensive program in the 1936 elections and put through a sweeping victory. The new premier was the Socialist leader, Léon Blum, and his inaugural ministerial declaration delivered on June 6, 1936, held out much promise. The program was never fully carried out, however, for Blum was, although a great man, too much the intellectual and too little the politician with the common touch, and he was faced with the growing intransigence of the Right—to say nothing of the increasing menace from across the Rhine.

The government comes before you following the general elections at **238** which the sentence of universal suffrage, which is the judge and master of all of us, has been rendered with more power and clarity than at any time in the history of the republic.

The French people have shown a steadfast decision to preserve the democratic liberties which they created and which remain in their possession against all attempts of violence or of cunning. They have confirmed their resolution to seek by new ways remedies for the crisis that is crushing them, for relief from sufferings and torment, and a return to active, healthy and confident life.

Finally they have proclaimed the will for peace that animates the whole nation.

The task of the government that comes before you, therefore, has been laid down from the outset.

It does not need to seek a majority. Its majority is established. Its majority is that which the country has returned. It is an expression of that mass of voters assembled under the banner of the Popular Front. It has the confidence of that majority, and the only problem confronting it will be to deserve and keep that confidence.

It does not need to formulate a program. Its program is that common program signed by all the parties who compose the majority, and all that has to be done is to translate that program into laws.

These laws will be rapidly put in force successively, for it is by the convergence of their effect that the government will reach the moral and material changes demanded by the country.

At the beginning of next week we shall lay before the House a number of bills that we shall ask both assemblies to vote before their vacations.

These bills will deal with political amnesty; a 40-hour week; collective contracts; paid holidays; a large public works program for improved economic, sanitary, scientific, sport and tourist equipment; nationalization of the manufacture of arms of war; creation of a wheat board, which will serve as an example for the revalorization of other agricultural products, like wine, meat and milk; extension of the school age; reform of the statutes of the Bank of France guaranteeing a preponderance of national interests in its direction; partial revision of the decree laws in favor of the public servants and war veterans who are most severely affected.

As soon as these measures are voted we shall present in Parliament a second series of bills concerning national funds for unemployment, insurance against agricultural calamities, management of the agricultural debt system, and pensions guaranteeing aged workers in the cities and country against misery.

Shortly afterward we shall lay before you a large system of fiscal simplification and relief, which will ease production and commerce and call for no new revenues except out of the accumulated fortunes of repression and fraud and, above all, out of a return of general activity.

While we shall be seeking in full collaboration with you to reanimate French economy, to absorb the unemployed, to increase the mass of incomes and to furnish some happiness and security to all those who create the real wealth by their labor, we shall have to govern the country.

We shall govern as republicans. We shall assure republican order. We shall apply with quiet firmness the laws in defense of the Republic. We shall show that we intend to animate the whole administration and all public services with the republican spirit. If democratic institutions are attacked we shall assure to them inviolable respect with a vigor equal to any threats or resistance.

The government does not under-estimate either the character or gravity of the difficulties that await it. It will not conceal them from the country. Within a few days it will publish a balance sheet of the economic and financial situation as it is at the commencement of the present Legislature.

It knows that to a country like France, ripened by the long use of political liberty, it can speak the truth without fear, and that by frankness the government will reassure, instead of diminish, the necessary confidence of the nation in itself.

As for ourselves the immensity of the task that confronts us, instead of discouraging us, only increases our ardor for work.

It is in the same spirit and with the same resolution that we shall undertake the conduct of international affairs. The desire of the country is plain. It wants peace. It wants it unanimously. It wants peace with all the nations of the world and for all the nations of the world.

It identifies peace with respect for international law and international contracts and with fidelity of engagements and to the given word. It desires ardently that the organization of collective security should permit the end of the unbridled armaments race in which Europe is involved and should lead to an international agreement for the publication, progressive reduction and effective control of national armaments.

For its guidance the government will take this unanimous desire, which is not an evidence of weakness. The will for peace of a nation like France —when it is sure of itself, when it is based on morality and on honor, on fidelity to proved friendship, on the profound sincerity of the appeal that it addresses to all peoples—can be proclaimed with pride and honor.

Such is our program of action. To accomplish it we ask no other authority than that which is fully compatible with the principles of democracy. But we need that in full.

What creates authority in a democracy is the rapidity and energy of methodically concerted action—the conformity of this action with the decision of universal suffrage, the fidelity to public engagements toward the electoral body, the firm determination to put an end to all forms of corruption. What makes it legitimate is the double confidence of Parliament and of the country.

We need both. The republican Parliament, the delegate of the sovereign people, will understand with what impatience great accomplishments are awaited and how perilous it would be to disappoint the eager hope of relief, of change and of renewal, which is not special to any political majority or to any social class but which spreads throughout the whole nation.

It will thus show once more the partiality and vanity of attempts made to discredit it in public opinion.

On its side the country will understand that the task which it has given to the new chamber, and which in turn the majority has given to us, cannot be accomplished unless the government has free direction, as it has responsibility, unless the maintenance of concord and public security provides the indispensable conditions for the efficacy of its work and unless political parties and cooperative organizations all help in its efforts.

We have an ardent desire that the first results of the measures that we are going to set in operation with your collaboration should be promptly effective. We do not expect from them only the appeasement of present miseries. We shall hope to reanimate in the heart of the nation its faith in itself, in its future, in its destiny.

Closely bound to the majority from which we spring, we are convinced that our action should and can reply to all generous aspirations and benefit all legitimate interests.

Fidelity to our engagements will be our rule. Public welfare will be our aim.

As France's pressing domestic and foreign problems remained unsolved there was a growing frustration, given evidence in the form of discouragement, growing class hostility, and spreading apathy. Like an ever-thickening pall, they hung over the country. One of the most vivid descriptions of both the nature and the effect of this condition is in the memoirs of General Charles de Gaulle, the leader about whom Frenchmen later rallied after their initial defeat in World War II.

239   . . . At this period I was detailed to the Secrétariat Général de la Défense Nationale, a permanent body at the disposal of the Premier for preparing the state and the nation for war. From 1932 to 1937, under fourteen governments, I found myself involved, in a planning capacity, in the whole range of political, technical, and administrative activity concerning the country's defense. I had, in particular, to be familiar with the plans for security and for limitation of armaments presented by André Tardieu and Paul-Boncour, respectively, at Geneva; to supply the Doumergue Cabinet with the elements for its decisions when it chose to adopt a different course after the arrival of the Führer; to weave the Penelope-web of the bill for the wartime organization of the nation; and to go into the measures involved by the mobilization of the civil departments, of industry, and of public services. The work I had to do, the discussions at which I was present, the contacts I was obliged to make, showed me the extent of our resources, but also the feebleness of the state.

For the disjointedness of government was rife all over this field. Not —certainly—that the men who figured there lacked intelligence or patriotism; on the contrary, I saw men of incontestable value and sometimes of great talent come to the head of the ministries. But the political game consumed them and paralysed them. As a reserved but passionate witness of public affairs, I watched the constant repetition of the same scenario. Hardly had a Premier taken office when he was at grips with innumerable demands, criticisms, and bids for favour, which all his energy was absorbed in warding off without ever contriving to master them. Parliament, far from supporting him, offered him nothing but ambushes and desertions. His Ministers were his rivals. Opinion, the press, and sectional interests regarded him as the proper target for all complaints. Everyone, indeed—and he first of all—knew that he was there for only a short time; in fact, after a few months, he had to give place to another. As regards national defence, such conditions prevented those responsible from achieving that organic whole of continuous plans, matured decisions, and measures carried to their conclusion, which we call a policy.

For these reasons the military, who received from the state no more than spasmodic and contradictory impulses, continued to defer to doctrine. The Army became stuck in a set of ideas which had had their heyday before the end of the First World War. It was all the more inclined that way because its leaders were growing old at their posts, wedded to errors that had once constituted their glory.

Hence the concept of the fixed and continuous front dominated the strategy envisaged for a future action. Organization, doctrine, training, and armament derived from it directly. It was understood that, in case of war, France would mobilize the mass of her reserves and would build up the largest possible number of divisions, designed not for manoeuvring, attacking, and exploiting, but for holding sectors. They would be placed in position all along the French and Belgian frontiers—Belgium being then explicitly our ally—and would there await the enemy's offensive.

As for the means: tanks, aircraft, mobile and revolving guns—which the last battles of the First World War had already shown to be capable of effecting surprise and the breakthrough, and whose power had since been growing without cease—were to be used only for reinforcing the line and, at need, restoring it by local counterattacks. The types of weapons were established with this in mind: heavy tanks armed with light, short pieces and intended for escorting infantry, not for rapid, independent action; interceptor aircraft designed for defending areas of sky, beside which the Air Force could muster few bombers and no dive-bombers;

artillery designed to fire from fixed positions with a narrow horizontal field of action, not to push ahead through all sorts of country and fire at all angles. Besides, the front was traced in advance by the works of the Maginot Line, prolonged by the Belgian fortifications. Thus the nation in arms would hold a barrier, behind which it would wait—so it was thought—for the blockade to wear the enemy down and the pressure of the free world to drive him to collapse.

Such a conception of war suited the spirit of the regime. Condemned by governmental weakness and political cleavages to stagnation, it was bound to espouse a static system of this kind. But, in addition, this reassuring panacea corresponded too well to the country's state of mind for anyone desirous of being elected, applauded, or given space in print not to be tempted to approve it. Public opinion did not care for offensives, yielding to the illusion that by making war against war the bellicose would be prevented from making war, remembering many ruinous attacks, and failing to discern the revolution in military strength produced since then by the internal-combustion engine. In short, everything converged to make passivity the very principle of our national defense.

To my mind, such an orientation was as dangerous as could be. I considered that, from the strategic point of view, it handed the initiative over to the enemy, lock, stock, and barrel. From the political point of view, I believe that by proclaiming our intention to keep our armies at the frontier, Germany was being egged on to act against the weak, who were from that moment isolated: the Saar, the Rhineland, Austria, Czechoslovakia, the Baltic states, Poland, and so on; that Russia was being discouraged from forming any bond with us; and that Italy was being assured that, whatever she might do, we would not impose any limit to her malevolence. Lastly, from the moral point of view, it seemed to me deplorable to make the country believe that war, if it came, ought to consist, for it, in fighting as little as possible.

Charles de Gaulle, *The Call to Honour* (New York: The Viking Press, 1955), pp. 6–8. (Reprinted by permission of the publisher.)

QUESTIONS

1. What elements in Poincaré's statement demonstrate that he was a strong-minded leader?
2. On what points did Herriot rest his argument in favor of paying the war debts?

3. What evidence can you find in Philip's report on the February Riots to indicate that it was largely a Rightist affair? Did the Left take any part?

4. What were the main features of the Popular Front program? What would you call the social order it sought to establish?

5. To what factors within France does General de Gaulle attribute his country's weakness on the eve of World War II?

CHAPTER XL

THE INTERNATIONAL SCENE, 1919-39

INTERNATIONAL RELATIONS between the first and the second World Wars can be divided into two periods. In the 1920's there was hope for a peaceful settlement of the outstanding differences among the European powers. Germany, under the guidance of her foreign minister, Gustav Stresemann (1923-29), pursued a policy of fulfilling her obligations under the Versailles Treaty (240). The treaties of Locarno between the great powers (1924) climaxed this policy of peace. As Stresemann saw it, the idea of "conciliation" was to be substituted for the harsher terms of the Versailles Treaty (241). The "Spirit of Locarno" was to have inaugurated a new era of international co-operation.

These hopes were destroyed during the 1930's by the policies of the dictatorships. This decade was marked by three approaches to international relations: aggression, collective security, and appeasement. The German-Czechoslovakian crisis of 1938 brought all three viewpoints into play. Adolf Hitler justified his aggressive actions by recalling, once again, the "betrayed" principles of Versailles (242).

To counter this attitude, the Soviet foreign minister, Maxim Litvinov, called for collective security through the League of Nations (243). The British prime minister, Neville Chamberlain, advocated appeasement (244) and carried out this policy in his talks with Hitler at Munich in September of 1938 following the Czech crisis (245). By the Munich agreement (246), Chamberlain obtained Hitler's personal assurance of peace (247). By March of the next year, however, the German Führer had broken this understanding, taking over all of Czechoslovakia (248).

The stage was now set for the last major diplomatic act leading to the outbreak of the second World War: the German-Soviet alliance (1939). Germany, whose next design was on Poland, executed a remarkable about-face by proposing this alliance with a communist nation which, up to this point, had figured as her chief enemy (249). The Soviet Union on its side rejected a Western alliance and signed the Nonaggression Pact (250) with the nation that had been its foremost rival (see Litvinov's speech, 243). How the two new allies viewed the world situation, less than a month before the beginning of the war, is seen in the transcript of the conversation between Joachim von Ribbentrop, the German foreign minister, and Stalin (251).

I. THE PERIOD OF "FULFILLMENT" AND "CONCILIATION"

In a speech to the Reichstag, March 6, 1924, Gustav Stresemann, as foreign minister, stated the policy of "fulfillment."

... A great many people are inclined to believe that our sole aim **240** under existing circumstances must be to tear up the Treaty of Versailles. I am convinced that no 'German National' Foreign Minister would talk like that if he was occupying the post I now hold. I am firmly convinced that he would realize that at present, unfortunately, the only course open to us is to compel the other Powers to acknowledge the obligations they have contracted towards us under the Treaty of Versailles. Even if we were able at the present time to enforce the Rhineland agreement for the benefit of the population and to restore the conditions which prevailed in the Palatinate before the reign of violence began and had got the French out of the Ruhr, we should not have escaped from the Treaty of Versailles; we should however have done a very great deal for millions of our fellow countrymen. We cannot do anything for the present but admit the obligations that were imposed upon us by the Treaty of Versailles, which also stipulates that we have the right to demand the reinvestigation of our capacity to make reparations; we have got, however, to compel the others to admit their obligations under this treaty. . . .

Gustav Stresemann, *Essays and Speeches on Various Subjects* (London: Thornton Butterworth, 1930), pp. 183–84.

In a broadcast address, after his return from Locarno, Stresemann explained the meaning of the treaties (November 3, 1925).

241   . . . Europe is gradually coming to understand that nothing is to be gained by war or the continued application of the methods of Versailles. Other ways must be found, and the most important feature of the Treaty of Locarno to my thinking, when all is said and done, is the indication it affords of a general resolve to steer a different course and substitute methods of conciliation for those in vogue at Versailles. The negotiations that we have been engaged in at Locarno were a proof of the earnestness and sincerity of the Allied statesmen in this respect. The era of dictation and ultimatums is said to be over. If the history of the world goes for anything, solutions must be found which will allow for the satisfaction of the vital needs of all the nations concerned. . . .

Let me explain to you shortly the principal features of the work we have accomplished at Locarno. The Western pact, the pact of security, upon which the various treaties of Locarno turn, contains the undertaking on the part of the countries adjacent to our Western frontier neither to attack nor invade each other. This undertaking, of course, is of a mutual character and applies just as much to France and Belgium as to ourselves. The treaty, however, distinctly entails no further obligation upon us beyond the undertaking not to pursue aggressive ends by forcible methods. We have not renounced morally or otherwise any of our claims to German territory or its inhabitants. The right of the nations to settle their own destinies in a peaceable manner has not in any way been impaired. It must be borne in mind, in judging of the value of this undertaking not to wage a war of aggression, that as matters now stand it is just as great a sacrifice, to say the least of it, upon the part of the French statesmen as for us; for whereas they have a strong army we are without the means of defence, and there have been plenty of people in their country who were anxious to make the Rhine their frontier. I need only remind you of Marshal Foch's famous note of the 10th of January 1919, in which he demanded that the Rhine should form the Western boundary of Germany. His demand was adopted by Clemenceau who was then Prime Minister, for the gist of the memorandum issued by the French Government upon the 15th of February was contained in the sentence: "The Rhine must be the Western frontier of Germany." The conclusion of the pact of security means that France has finally abandoned this policy. She declares that our territory shall never again be violated by her military forces, and, further, that she is quite willing that England as guarantor should come to the help of Germany in the event of the non-observance by France of the conditions laid down in the Western pact. The value of this guarantee of the German Western frontier must not be underestimated. If doubts are felt as to whether England would really carry out her duties as guarantor, I can only repeat to-night that we have no reason to doubt her good faith with regard to the treaty. But quite apart from any actual danger of war, the very fact that England, who has hitherto been the ally of France, should solemnly undertake to protect Germany with all her land and sea forces against an attack on the part of the French, is a matter of the very greatest political importance. . . .

Should the German Government decide to give its signature in London on the 1st of December to the treaties which have been initialled at Locarno, we shall be willing to join the League of Nations. We have already declared our willingness to do so on a previous occasion and circulated a memorandum to the powers concerned in September 1924 which contained a frank exposition of our views on the subject. A dispute had arisen as to the interpretation of Article 16 of the Statutes of the League of Nations, which was only settled at Locarno. In the course of these negotiations the Powers concerned undertook to communicate to us a note in which Article 16 would be interpreted in a manner which would not conflict with our vital needs. No State can compel Germany against its will to take part, for instance, in a war against Russia. No State can claim the right to march through German territory without her consent. We are not demanding a privileged position in the League of Nations. We are, however, peculiarly situated in consequence of our having been disarmed, and in view of this fact, for which we are not responsible, we were bound to insist upon a strict definition of any obligations we might incur under Article 16. We were bound also, owing to the peculiarity of our military and geographical situation, to reserve to ourselves the right of deciding as to the extent to which we would join in taking action against a disturber of the peace, even when a State was obviously and unmistakably in the wrong. This concession has now been made, and nobody can blame us if we decide not to take part in any collective action by the League of Nations against a disturber of the peace.

Our relations with Russia are therefore not compromised by our entry into the League of Nations. We are anxious to improve our friendly relations with Russia to the advantage of both nations, for we quite realize the importance of their being on good terms with one another. I am glad to have the opportunity of saying this. The commercial treaty which we have just concluded with Russia is a proof of the friendliness of our attitude towards that great Empire. . . .

Locarno may be interpreted as signifying that the States of Europe at last realize that they cannot go on making war upon each other without being involved in common ruin. The distress which prevails on all sides is a serious warning to us to come to our senses. The elation of Versailles has passed away, and we have got to look at things nowadays from another point of view. The attempt to create a new and better Europe by methods of compulsion, dictation and violence has been a failure. Let us try to achieve this object on the basis of peace and of equal rights and liberty for Germany.

Ibid., pp. 232–34, 236–37, 238.

II. AGGRESSION, COLLECTIVE SECURITY, AND APPEASEMENT, ILLUSTRATED THROUGH DOCUMENTS RELATING TO THE GERMAN-CZECHOSLOVAKIAN CRISIS OF 1938

In a speech in Berlin, September 26, 1938, Adolf Hitler justified his demands for the German-speaking part of Czechoslovakia (the *Sudetenland*). He threatened President Beneš with war in case the German demands were rejected.

242 You know that at one time the German people too, thanks to the slogan "self-determination of peoples," were imbued with a belief in super-political assistance and accordingly renounced to the utmost the utilization of its own strength. You know that this trust of those days was most shamefully betrayed. The result was the Versailles Treaty, and you all remember its frightful consequences. You remember how our people first were robbed of their weapons and how, disarmed then, they were later mistreated. You know the terrible fate that befell us for a decade and a half. . . .

In 1918 under the slogan "the right of self-determination of nations," Central Europe was torn up and reshaped by some insane so-called statesmen. Without regard for the origin of peoples, for their national wishes, or their economic necessities, they smashed up Europe and arbitrarily set up so-called new states. To this procedure Czechoslovakia owes its existence. This Czech state began with one single lie, and the father of this erstwhile lie is Benes. This Mr. Benes at that time turned up at Versailles and assured them, to begin with, that there was a Czechoslovak nation. He had to invent this lie to give the insignificant number of his own nationals somewhat larger and thereby more legitimate dimensions. And those Anglo-Saxon statesmen, not very adequately versed in geographical and national aspects, did not think it necessary at that time to put Mr. Benes' assertions to a test. Otherwise they would have been able to determine at once that there is no Czechoslovak nation, but that there are only Czechs and Slovaks, and that the Slovaks prefer to have nothing to do with the Czechs. . . .

So at last the Czechs through Mr. Benes annexed Slovakia. As this state did not appear capable of survival, 3,500,000 Germans were simply unceremoniously taken over against their right of self-determination and their will to self-determination. Since this did not suffice, over 1,000,000 Magyars had to be added, then the Carpatho-Russians and at last several hundred thousand Poles. This is the state, then, which later called itself Czechoslovakia—in contradiction to the right of self-determination of nations and in contradiction to the clear wish and will of the violated nations. As I here talk to you, I naturally feel sympathy for the fate of all these oppressed; I feel sympathy for the fate of the Slovaks, the Poles, the Hungarians, the Ukrainians; naturally, however, I am spokesman only for the fate of my Germans. . . .

Accordingly I made my demand at Nuremberg. It was quite clear. There, for the first time, I said that at last, nearly twenty years after the declarations of President Wilson, the right of self-determination for these 3,500,000 must be enforced. Again Mr. Benes replied with new victims, new imprisonments, new arrests. The German element had to flee. . . . I am spokesman for the Germans, and for those Germans I have now spoken and given assurance that I am no longer willing to watch quietly and passively while this lunatic in Prague goes on believing that he can mishandle 3,500,000 human beings. I left no doubt about it that a characteristic of our German mentality is to accept things for a long time and with increasing patience, but that a moment comes when we have had enough. . . .

I want now to declare before the German people that as regards the Sudeten German problem my patience is at last exhausted. I have made an offer to Mr. Benes that is nothing else than a realization of what he himself has already conceded. He now holds the decision in his hand. Peace or war! Either he will now accept this offer and at last give the Germans their freedom, or we will take this freedom for ourselves! (*Voelkischer Beobachter,* Sept. 27, 1938).

Hitler's Words, ed. Gordon W. Prange (Washington: American Council on Public Affairs, 1944), pp. 239–40. (Reprinted by permission of the publisher.)

Soviet foreign minister Maxim Litvinov urged a policy of collective security, through the League of Nations, in reply to the German threat to Czechoslovakia (September 21, 1938).

243   Unfortunately, our discussion has not been limited to the recording and explanation of the League's blunders and mistakes, but has included attempts retrospectively to justify them, and even to legalize them for the future. Various arguments have been used, among them the most favoured being a reference to the absence of universality. The shallowness of this argument has been pointed out more than once. The League of Nations was not any more universal during the first twelve years of its existence than it is today. From the outset it lacked three of the largest Powers and a multitude of smaller States. Furthermore, some States left it: others joined it: and up to the time of the first case of aggression it never crossed anyone's mind—or, at all events, no one expressed such views in the League— that the League could not fulfil its principal functions, and that therefore its Constitution should be altered and those functions, the functions of guardianship of peace, withdrawn.

No one has yet proved, and no one can prove, that the League of Nations refused to apply sanctions to the aggressor in this case or in that because States were absent from its ranks, and that this was the reason why sanctions, applied in one case [i.e., Italy] were prematurely brought to an end. Even composed as it is today, the League of Nations is still strong enough by its collective action to avert or arrest aggression. All that is necessary is that the obligatory character of such actions be confirmed, and that the machinery of the League of Nations be at least once brought into action in conformity with the Covenant. This requires only the goodwill of the States Members, for there are no objective reasons of such a character as to prevent the normal functioning of the League: at any rate, no such reasons as could not be foreseen by the founders of the League and by those States which later joined it. . . .

Careful study of the case presented by the opponents of sanctions will reveal yet another argument. Aggression has raised its head too high;

its forces have been multiplied and are growing daily. The exponents of aggression today are several, and fairly powerful; moreover, they have joined forces in mutual defence (true, so far principally with the help of printing ink and radio). These facts cannot be contested. The aggressor States have grown immensely during the last three years. They have formed a *bloc* in order to defend the principle of aggression. For the triumph of that principle they defend and justify one another, even when one of them is infringing the vital interests of another. There are cases, too, of their joint aggression.

But the responsibility for this regrettable fact lies with those States which restrained the League from resistance to the aggressors when they were still weak and divided, and were still making only their first timid attempts to break the peace. They have grown stronger thanks to the fact that these attempts were allowed to reach a successful conclusion: thanks to the tolerance, and indeed impunity, of one breach of international treaties after another, and of the propaganda of aggression; thanks to the policy of concessions, fruitless negotiations and backstairs intrigues with them. They are still weaker, even yet, than the possible *bloc* of peaceable States. But the policy of non-resistance to evil and of humouring the aggressors which we are being recommended to adopt by the opponents of sanctions will have no other end than the further strengthening and expansion of the forces of aggression, the further extension of the scope of their activities. Then the moment may really arrive at which they have grown so strong that the League of Nations—or what remains of the League of Nations—will be unable to deal with them, even should it desire to do so.

There are inside and outside the League two tendencies, two conceptions of how best to preserve peace. There exists an opinion that when some State announces a foreign policy based on aggression, on the violation of other people's frontiers, on the violent annexation of other people's possessions, on the enslavement of other nations, on domination over entire continents, the League of Nations has not only the right, but also the duty of declaring, loudly and clearly, that it has been set up to preserve universal peace; that it will not permit the realization of such a programme; and that it will fight that programme by every means at its disposal. Within the framework of such declarations, individual Members of the League can and must constitute special groups for the joint defence of individual sectors of the threatened peace front.

It is presumed that States which openly denounce the principles underlying the League Covenant and the Briand-Kellogg Pact, which extol aggression and ridicule international obligations, are inaccessible to persuasion or argument—save the argument of force—and that there is no room for bargaining or compromise with them. They can be restrained from carrying their evil designs into effect only by a demonstration of the force which they will encounter, should they make the attempt.

Naturally, at the least attempt to carry out aggression in practice, there should be brought into play in appropriate measure, and according to the capacities of each Member of the League, the collective action provided by Article 16 of the Covenant. In other words, the aggressor should be met with the programme laid down by the League Covenant, resolutely, consistently and without hesitation. Then the aggressor himself will not be led into temptation, and peace will be preserved by peaceful means.

There is, however, another conception, which recommends as the height of human wisdom, under cover of imaginary pacifism, that the aggressor be treated with consideration, and his vanity be not wounded. It recommends that conversations and negotiations be carried on with him, that he be assured that no collective action will be undertaken against him, and no groups or *blocs* formed against him—even though he himself enters into aggressive *blocs* with other aggressors—that compromise agreements be concluded with him, and breaches of those very agreements overlooked; that his demands, even the most illegal, be fulfilled; that journeys be undertaken, if necessary, to receive his dictates and ultimatums; that the vital interests of one State or another be sacrificed to him; and that, if possible, no question of his activity be raised at the League of Nations—because the aggressor does not like that, takes offence, sulks. Unfortunately, this is just the policy that so far has been pursued towards the aggressors; and it has had as its consequence three wars, and threatens to bring down on us a fourth. Four nations have already been sacrificed, and a fifth is next on the list.

In view of such lamentable results of this policy, we had the right to expect that there would be recognition of its mistaken character, and of the necessity of replacing it by some other policy. Instead we have heard proposals here to make the old policy permanent. Hitherto the aggressor reckoned with the possible reaction of the League of Nations, and showed a certain hesitation in preparing his aggression, carrying it out gradually and in proportion to his growing certainty that there would be no reaction at all. But now we are asked to reassure him beforehand that he need fear nothing at the hands of the League, and that the League henceforward will not apply to him either military or even economic and financial sanctions. At the very worst, he is threatened with moral condemnation, and that, in all probability, clothed in appropriately courteous diplomatic forms. . . .

At the moment when the mines are being laid to blow up the organization on which were fixed the great hopes of our generation and which stamped a definite character on the international relations of our epoch; at a moment when, by no accidental coincidence, decisions are being taken outside the League [i.e., between Hitler and Chamberlain] which recall to us the international transactions of pre-war days, and which are bound to overturn all present conceptions of international morality and treaty obligations; at a moment when there is being drawn up a further list of sacrifices to the god of aggression, and a line is being drawn under the annals of all post-war international history, with the sole conclusion that nothing succeeds like aggression—at such a moment, every State must define its role and its responsibility before its contemporaries and before history. That is why I must plainly declare here that the Soviet Government bears no responsibility whatsoever for the events now taking place, and for the fatal consequences which may inexorably ensue. . . .

To avoid a problematic war today and receive in return a certain and large-scale war tomorrow—moreover, at the price of assuaging the appetites of insatiable aggressors and of the destruction or mutilation of sovereign States—is not to act in the spirit of the Covenant of the League of Nations. To grant bonuses for sabre-rattling and recourse to arms for the solution of international problems—in other words, to reward and encourage aggressive super-imperialism—is not to act in the spirit of the Briand-Kellogg Pact.

The Soviet Government takes pride in the fact that it has no part in such a policy, and has invariably pursued the principles of the two pacts I have mentioned, which were approved by nearly every nation in the world. Nor has it any intention of abandoning them for the future, being convinced that in present conditions it is impossible otherwise to safeguard a genuine peace and international justice. It calls upon other Governments likewise to return to this path.

Soviet Documents on Foreign Policy, ed. Jane Degras (London: Oxford University Press, 1953), III, 299–302, 304. (Reprinted by permission of the publisher and the Royal Institute of International Affairs.)

Before the House of Commons Prime Minister Neville Chamberlain explained his policy of appeasement (1938).

. . . On a former occasion I described [English] foreign policy as being **244** based upon three principles—first upon the protection of British interests

... secondly on the maintenance of peace, and, as far as we can influence it, the settlement of differences by peaceful means and not by force; and thirdly the promotion of friendly relations with other nations who are willing to reciprocate our friendly feelings and who will keep those rules of international conduct without which there can be neither security nor stability. ...

If we truly desire peace it is necessary to make a sustained effort to ascertain, and if possible to remove the causes which threaten peace. ... We are now engaged upon a gigantic scheme of rearmament ... indeed, we were the last of the nations to rearm; but this process of general re-armament has been forced upon us all, because every country is afraid to disarm lest it should fall a victim of some armed neighbor. I recognize the force of that hard fact, but have never publicly ceased to deplore what seems to me a senseless waste of money. ... I cannot believe that, with a little good will and determination, it is not possible to remove genuine grievances and to clear away suspicions which may be entirely unfounded.

For these reasons, then, my colleagues and I have been anxious to find some opportunity of entering upon conversations with the two European countries with which we have been at variance, namely Germany and Italy, in order that we might find out whether there was any common ground on which we might build up a general scheme of appeasement in Europe. ... The peace of Europe must depend upon the attitude of the four major powers, Germany, Italy, France and ourselves. For ourselves, we are linked to France by common ideals of democracy, of liberty and Parliamentary government. ... On the other side we find Italy and Germany linked by affinity of outlook and in the forms of their government. The question that we have to think of is this: Are we to allow these two pairs of nations to go on glowering at one another across the frontier, allowing the feeling between the two sides to become more and more embittered, until at last the barriers are broken down and the conflict begins which many think would mark the end of civilization? Or can we bring them to an understanding of one another's aims and objects, and to such discussion as may lead to a final settlement? If we can do that, if we can bring these four nations into friendly discussion, into a settling of their differences, we shall have saved the peace of Europe for a generation.

Hansard's Parliamentary Debates (1938), pp. 53, 54, 64, 332.

On returning from his first meeting with Adolf Hitler, Chamberlain gave a radio address (September 27, 1938) about the accomplishments of their talks. Here, once again, we can see some of the ideas which underlay the policy of appeasement.

... First of all I must say something to those who have written to **245** my wife or myself in these last weeks to tell us of their gratitude for my efforts and to assure us of their prayers for my success. ... If I felt my responsibility heavy before, to read such letters has made it seem almost overwhelming. How horrible, fantastic, incredible it is that we should be digging trenches and trying on gas-masks here because of a quarrel in a far away country between peoples of whom we know nothing. It seems still more impossible that a quarrel which has already been settled in principle should be the subject of war.

I can well understand the reasons why the Czech Government have felt unable to accept the terms which have been put before them in the German memorandum. Yet I believe after my talks with Herr Hitler that, if only time were allowed, it ought to be possible for the arrangements for transferring the territory that the Czech Government has agreed to give to Germany to be settled by agreement under conditions which would assure fair treatment to the population concerned.

You know already that I have done all that one man can do to compose this quarrel. After my visits to Germany I have realized vividly how Herr Hitler feels that he must champion other Germans, and his indignation that grievances have not been met before this. He told me privately, and last night he repeated publicly, that after this Sudeten German question is settled, that is the end of Germany's territorial claims in Europe.

After my first visit to Berchtesgaden I did get the assent of the Czech Government to proposals which gave the substance of what Herr Hitler wanted, and I was taken completely by surprise when I got back to Germany and found that he insisted that the territory should be handed over to him immediately, and immediately occupied by German troops without previous arrangements for safeguarding the people within the territory who were not Germans or did not want to join the German Reich.

I must say that I find this attitude unreasonable. If it arises out of any doubts that Herr Hitler feels about the intentions of the Czech Government to carry out their promises, and hand over the territory, I have offered on the part of the British Government to guarantee their words, and I am sure the value of our promise will not be underrated anywhere.

I shall not give up the hope of a peaceful solution, or abandon my efforts for peace, as long as any chance for peace remains. I would not hesitate to pay even a third visit to Germany if I thought it would do any good. But at this moment I see nothing further that I can usefully do in the way of mediation.

Meanwhile there are certain things we can and shall do at home. Volunteers are still wanted for air raid precautions, for fire brigades and police services, and for the Territorial units . . . . I ask you all to offer your services. . . . Do not be alarmed if you hear of men being called up to man the anti-aircraft defences of ships. These are only precautionary measures . . . they do not necessarily mean that we have determined on war or that war is imminent.

However much we may sympathize with a small nation confronted by a big and powerful neighbor, we cannot in all circumstances undertake to involve the whole British Empire in war simply on her account. If we have to fight it must be on larger issues than that. I am myself a man of peace to the depths of my soul. Armed conflict between nations is a nightmare to me; but if I were convinced that any nation had made up its mind to dominate the world by fear of its force, I should feel that it must be resisted. Under such a domination life for people who believe in liberty would not be worth living; but war is a fearful thing, and we must be very clear, before we embark on it, that it is really the great issues which are at stake, and that the call to risk everything in their defence, when all the consequences are weighed, is irresistible.

For the present I ask you to await as calmly as you can the events of the next few days. As long as war has not begun, there is always hope that it may be prevented, and you know that I am going to work for peace to the last moment. Good night.

Times (London), September 28, 1938, p. 21.

The Munich agreement was signed on September 29, 1938.

246 Germany, the United Kingdom, France, and Italy, taking into consideration the agreement, which has been already reached in principle for the cession to Germany of the Sudeten German territory, have agreed on the following terms and conditions governing the said cession and the measures consequent thereon, and by this agreement they each hold themselves responsible for the steps necessary to secure its fulfilment:

1. The evacuation will begin on the 1st October.

2. The United Kingdom, France, and Italy agree that the evacuation of the territory shall be completed by the 10th October, without any existing

installations having been destroyed and that the Czechoslovak Government will be held responsible for carrying out the evacuation without damage to the said installations.

3. The conditions governing the evacuation will be laid down in detail by an international commission composed of representatives of Germany, the United Kingdom, France, Italy, and Czechoslovakia.

4. The occupation by stages of the predominantly German territory by German troops will begin on the 1st October. The four territories marked on the attached map will be occupied by German troops in the following order: the territory marked No. I on the 1st and 2nd of October, the territory marked No. II on the 2nd and 3rd of October, the territory marked No. III on the 3rd, 4th and 5th of October, the territory marked No. IV on the 6th and 7th of October. The remaining territory of preponderantly German character will be ascertained by the aforesaid international commission forthwith and be occupied by German troops by the 10th of October.

5. The international commission referred to in paragraph 3 will determine the territories in which a plebiscite is to be held. These territories will be occupied by international bodies until the plebiscite has been completed. The same commission will fix the conditions in which the plebiscite is to be held, taking as a basis the conditions of the Saar plebiscite. The commission will also fix a date, not later than the end of November, on which the plebiscite will be held.

6. The final determination of the frontiers will be carried out by the international commission. This commission will also be entitled to recommend to the four Powers, Germany, the United Kingdom, France and Italy, in certain exceptional cases minor modifications in the strictly ethnographical determination of the zones which are to be transferred without plebiscite.

7. There will be a right of option into and out of the transferred territories, the option to be exercised within six months from the date of this agreement. A German-Czechoslovak commission shall determine the details of the option, consider ways of facilitating the transfer of population and settle questions of principle arising out of the said transfer.

8. The Czechoslovak Government will within a period of four weeks from the date of this agreement release from their military and police forces

any Sudeten Germans who may wish to be released, and the Czechoslovak Government will within the same period release Sudeten German prisoners who are serving terms of imprisonment for political offences.

Adolf Hitler
Neville Chamberlain
Édouard Daladier
Benito Mussolini

Great Britain, *House of Commons,* XXX (1937–38), *Accounts and Papers,* XV. Cmd. 5848, "Further Documents Respecting Czechoslovakia, Including the Agreement Concluded at Munich on September 29, 1938," Miscellaneous No. 8 (1938), pp. 3–4.

Chamberlain brought back from Munich not only an agreement concerning the partition of Czechoslovakia, but also a personal reassurance from Hitler of his peaceful intentions. The precious "scrap of paper" Chamberlain read in the course of a radio address from the airport where he had landed (September 30, 1938).

247   . . . This morning I had another talk with the German Chancellor, Herr Hitler, and here is a paper which bears his name upon it as well as mine. Some of you perhaps have already heard what it contains, but I would just like to read it to you.

"We, the German Führer and Chancellor and the British Prime Minister, have had a further meeting today and are agreed in recognizing that the question of Anglo-German relations is of the first importance for the two countries and for Europe.

"We regard the agreement signed last night and the Anglo-German Naval Agreement as symbolic of the desire of our two peoples never to go to war with one another again.

"We are resolved that the method of consultation shall be the method adopted to deal with any other questions that may concern our two countries, and we are determined to continue our efforts to remove possible sources of difference and thus to assure the peace of Europe."

Neville Chamberlain, *In Search of Peace* (New York: G. P. Putnam's Sons, 1939), p. 200. (Reprinted by permission of the publisher.)

Four months after the Munich treaty and Hitler's personal assurances of peaceful intentions, both were reduced to meaningless scraps of paper. In March Germany took possession of all Czechoslovakia, and in a proclamation of March 16, 1939, quoted here, in part, Hitler told why he took this action. This step marked the end of the policy of appeasement. On March 31st, the British government pledged Anglo-French aid to the Poles in the event of German aggression, thus drawing a line beyond which they were willing to fight the aggressors.

For a millennium the territories of Bohemia and Moravia belonged to **248** the living-space (*Lebensraum*) of the German people. Violence and stupidity (*Unverstand*) tore them arbitrarily from their ancient historic setting and at last through their inclusion in the artificial construction of Czechoslovakia created a hotbed of continual unrest. Year by year the danger grew ever greater that from this area, as had already happened once in the past, there might arise a new, vast menace to the peace of Europe. For the Czechoslovak State and its authorities had not been able to organize on a reasonable basis the common life of the groups of peoples arbitrarily united within it and thus to awaken and maintain the interest of all concerned in the preservation of the State of which they all were members. The Czechoslovak State has thus proved its inability to live its own internal life and in consequence has now in fact fallen into dissolution.

But the German Reich cannot tolerate permanent disturbances in these territories which are of such decisive importance, alike for its own calm and security, as well as for the general welfare and the general peace.

Sooner or later the Power which through its history and its geographical position is most intimately interested and affected would be bound to suffer the most serious consequences. It is therefore but to obey the dictate of self-preservation if the German Reich is resolved decisively to intervene in order to restore the foundations of a reasonable Central European order and to issue such regulations as are the natural result of such a decision, for through the history of its millennial past the Reich has already proved that thanks to the greatness and also to the characteristics of the German people it alone is qualified to solve these problems. . . .

The Speeches of Adolf Hitler, April 1922–August 1939, ed. Norman H. Baynes (London: Oxford University Press, 1942), II, 1586–87. (Reprinted by permission of the publisher.)

III. THE GERMAN-SOVIET ALLIANCE OF 1939

In a telegram to the German ambassador in the Soviet Union, German foreign minister Ribbentrop argues for an alliance between the two countries.

249 MOST URGENT   *BERLIN, August 14, 1939—10:53 p.m.*
                                  Received Moscow, August 15, 1939—4:40 a.m.
For the Ambassador personally.

I request that you call upon Herr Molotov personally and communicate to him the following:

1) The ideological contradictions between National Socialist Germany and the Soviet Union were in past years the sole reason why Germany and the U.S.S.R. stood opposed to each other in two separate and hostile camps. The developments of the recent period seem to show that differing world outlooks do not prohibit a reasonable relationship between the two states, and the restoration of cooperation of a new and friendly type. The period of opposition in foreign policy can be brought to an end once and for all and the way lies open for a new sort of future for both countries.

2) There exist no real conflicts of interest between Germany and the U.S.S.R. The living spaces of Germany and the U.S.S.R. touch each other, but in their natural requirements they do not conflict. Thus there is lacking all cause for an aggressive attitude on the part of one country against the other. Germany has no aggressive intentions against the U.S.S.R. The Reich Government is of the opinion that there is no question between the Baltic and the Black Seas which cannot be settled to the complete satisfaction of both countries. Among these are such questions as: the Baltic Sea, the Baltic area, Poland, Southeastern questions, etc. In such matters political cooperation between the two countries can have only a beneficial effect. The same applies to German and Soviet economy, which can be expanded in any direction.

3) There is no doubt that German-Soviet policy today has come to an historic turning point. The decisions with respect to policy to be made in the immediate future in Berlin and Moscow will be of decisive importance for the aspect of relationships between the German people and the peoples of the U.S.S.R. for generations. On those decisions will depend whether the two peoples will some day again and without any compelling reason take up arms against each other or whether they pass again into a friendly relationship. It has gone well with both countries previously when they were friends and badly when they were enemies.

4) It is true that Germany and the U.S.S.R., as a result of years of hostility in their respective world outlooks, today look at each other in a distrustful fashion. A great deal of rubbish which has accumulated will

have to be cleared away. It must be said, however, that even during this period the natural sympathy of the Germans for the Russians never disappeared. The policy of both states can be built anew on that basis.

5) The Reich Government and the Soviet Government must, judging from all experience, count it as certain that the capitalistic Western democracies are the unforgiving enemies of both National Socialist Germany and of the U.S.S.R. They are today trying again, by the conclusion of a military alliance, to drive the U.S.S.R. into the war against Germany. In 1914 this policy had disastrous results for Russia. It is the compelling interest of both countries to avoid for all future time the destruction of Germany and of the U.S.S.R., which would profit only the Western democracies.

6) The crisis which has been produced in German-Polish relations by English policy, as well as English agitation for war and the attempts at an alliance which are bound up with that policy, make a speedy clarification of German-Russian relations desirable. Otherwise these matters, without any German initiative, might take a turn which would deprive both Governments of the possibility of restoring German-Soviet friendship and possibly of clearing up jointly the territorial questions of eastern Europe. The leadership in both countries should, therefore, not allow the situation to drift, but should take action at the proper time. It would be fatal if, through mutual lack of knowledge of views and intentions, our peoples should be finally driven asunder. . . .

Nazi-Soviet Relations, 1939–1941, ed. Raymond Sontag and James Beddie (Washington: Department of State, 1948), pp. 50–51.

The treaty between Germany and the Soviet Union was signed on August 23, 1939. The secret protocol of the treaty divided the eastern European spheres of influence between the two powers.

The Government of the German Reich and   **250**
the Government of the Union of Soviet Socialist Republics
desirous of strengthening the cause of peace between Germany and the U.S.S.R., and proceeding from the fundamental provisions of the Neutrality Agreement concluded in April 1926 between Germany and the U.S.S.R., have reached the following agreement:

ARTICLE I

Both High Contracting Parties obligate themselves to desist from any act of violence, any aggressive action, and any attack on each other, either individually or jointly with other powers. . . .

Secret Additional Protocol

On the occasion of the signature of the Nonaggression Pact between the German Reich and the Union of Socialist Soviet Republics the undersigned plenipotentiaries of each of the two parties discussed in strictly confidential conversations the question of the boundary of their respective spheres of influence in Eastern Europe. These conversations led to the following conclusions:

1. In the event of a territorial and political rearrangement in the areas belonging to the Baltic States (Finland, Estonia, Latvia, Lithuania), the northern boundary of Lithuania shall represent the boundary of the spheres of influence of Germany and the U.S.S.R. In this connection the interest of Lithuania in the Vilna area is recognized by each party.

2. In the event of a territorial and political rearrangement of the areas belonging to the Polish state the spheres of influence of Germany and the U.S.S.R. shall be bounded approximately by the line of the rivers Narew, Vistula, and San.

The question of whether the interests of both parties make desirable the maintenance of an independent Polish state and how such a state should be bounded can only be definitely determined in the course of further political developments.

In any event both Governments will resolve this question by means of a friendly agreement.

3. With regard to Southeastern Europe attention is called by the Soviet side to its interest in Bessarabia. The German side declares its complete political disinterestedness in these areas.

4. This protocol shall be treated by both parties as strictly secret.
Moscow, August 23, 1939.

<table>
<tr><td>For the Government
of the German Reich:
V. Ribbentrop</td><td>Plenipotentiary of the
Government of the U.S.S.R.
V. Molotov</td></tr>
</table>

Ibid., pp. 76, 78.

The following is a report of the conversation between Ribbentrop and Stalin after the signing of the treaty (August 23, 1939). Here, shortly before the outbreak of the war, both powers gave their views on some of the major issues of European politics.

Memorandum of a Conversation Held on the Night of August 23rd to 24th, **251** between the Reich Foreign Minister, on the One Hand, and Herr Stalin and the Chairman of the Council of People's Commissars Molotov, on the Other Hand.

VERY SECRET!

STATE SECRET

The following problems were discussed:

1) *Japan*:

The REICH FOREIGN MINISTER stated that the German-Japanese friendship was in no wise directed against the Soviet Union. We were, rather, in a position, owing to our good relations with Japan, to make an effective contribution to an adjustment of the differences between the Soviet Union and Japan. Should Herr Stalin and the Soviet Government desire it, the Reich Foreign Minister was prepared to work in this direction. He would use his influence with the Japanese Government accordingly and keep in touch with the Soviet representative in Berlin in this matter.

HERR STALIN replied that the Soviet Union indeed desired an improvement in its relations with Japan, but that there were limits to its patience with regard to Japanese provocations. If Japan desired war, it could have it. The Soviet Union was not afraid of it and was prepared for it. If Japan desired peace—so much the better! Herr Stalin considered the assistance of Germany in bringing about an improvement in Soviet-Japanese relations as useful, but he did not want the Japanese to get the impression that the initiative in this direction had been taken by the Soviet Union.

The REICH FOREIGN MINISTER assented to this and stressed the fact that his cooperation would mean merely the continuation of talks that he had for months been holding with the Japanese Ambassador in Berlin in the sense of an improvement in Soviet-Japanese relations. Accordingly, there would be no new initiative on the German side in this matter.

2) *Italy*:

HERR STALIN inquired of the Reich Foreign Minister as to Italian aims. Did not Italy have aspirations beyond the annexation of Albania—perhaps for Greek territory? Small, mountainous, and thinly populated Albania was, in his estimation, of no particular use to Italy.

The REICH FOREIGN MINISTER replied that Albania was important to Italy for strategic reasons. Moreover, Mussolini was a strong man who could not be intimidated.

This he had demonstrated in the Abyssinian conflict, in which Italy had asserted its aims by its own strength against a hostile coalition. Even Germany was not yet in a position at that time to give Italy appreciable support.

Mussolini welcomed warmly the restoration of friendly relations between Germany and the Soviet Union. He had expressed himself as gratified with the conclusion of the Nonaggression Pact.

3) Turkey:

HERR STALIN asked the Reich Foreign Minister what Germany thought about Turkey.

The REICH FOREIGN MINISTER expressed himself as follows in this matter: he had months ago declared to the Turkish Government that Germany desired friendly relations with Turkey. The Reich Foreign Minister had himself done everything to achieve this goal. The answer had been that Turkey became one of the first countries to join the encirclement pact against Germany and had not even considered it necessary to notify the Reich Government of the fact.

HERREN STALIN and MOLOTOV hereupon observed that the Soviet Union had also had a similar experience with the vacillating policy of the Turks.

The REICH FOREIGN MINISTER mentioned further that England had spent five million pounds in Turkey in order to disseminate propaganda against Germany.

HERR STALIN said that according to his information the amount which England had spent in buying Turkish politicians was considerably more than five million pounds.

4) England:

HERREN STALIN and MOLOTOV commented adversely on the British Military Mission in Moscow, which had never told the Soviet Government what it really wanted.

The REICH FOREIGN MINISTER stated in this connection that England had always been trying and was still trying to disrupt the development of good relations between Germany and the Soviet Union. England was weak and wanted to let others fight for its presumptuous claim to world domination.

HERR STALIN eagerly concurred and observed as follows: the British Army was weak; the British Navy no longer deserved its previous reputation. England's air arm was being increased, to be sure, but there was a lack of pilots. If England dominates the world in spite of this, this was due to the stupidity of the other countries that always let themselves be bluffed. It was ridiculous, for example, that a few hundred British should dominate India.

The REICH FOREIGN MINISTER concurred and informed Herr Stalin confidentially that England had recently put out a new feeler which was connected with certain allusions to 1914. It was a matter of a typically English, stupid maneuver. The Reich Foreign Minister had proposed to the Führer to inform the British that every hostile British act, in case of a German-Polish conflict, would be answered by a bombing attack on London.

HERR STALIN remarked that the feeler was evidently Chamberlain's letter to the Führer, which Ambassador Henderson delivered on August 23 at the Obersalzberg. Stalin further expressed the opinion that England, despite its weakness, would wage war craftily and stubbornly.

5) *France:*

HERR STALIN expressed the opinion that France, nevertheless, had an army worthy of consideration.

The REICH FOREIGN MINISTER, on his part, pointed out to Herren Stalin and Molotov the numerical inferiority of France. While Germany had available an annual class of more than 300,000 soldiers, France could muster only 150,000 recruits annually. The West Wall was five times as strong as the Maginot Line. If France attempted to wage war with Germany, she would certainly be conquered.

6) *Anti-Comintern Pact:*

The REICH FOREIGN MINISTER observed that the Anti-Comintern Pact was basically directed not against the Soviet Union but against the Western democracies. He knew, and was able to infer from the tone of the Russian press, that the Soviet Government fully recognized this fact.

HERR STALIN interposed that the Anti-Comintern Pact had in fact frightened principally the City of London and the small British merchants.

The REICH FOREIGN MINISTER concurred and remarked jokingly that Herr Stalin was surely less frightened by the Anti-Comintern Pact than the City of London and the small British merchants. What the German people thought of this matter is evident from a joke which had originated with the Berliners, well known for their wit and humor, and which had been going the rounds for several months, namely, "Stalin will yet join the Anti-Comintern Pact." . . .

9) When they took their leave, HERR STALIN addressed to the Reich Foreign Ministers words to this effect:

The Soviet Government takes the new Pact very seriously. He could guarantee on his word of honor that the Soviet Union would not betray its partner.

Moscow, August 24, 1939.   *Hencke*

Ibid., pp. 72–75, 76.

QUESTIONS

1. Why did Stresemann believe that Germany should not tear up the Versailles Treaty?
2. What did Germany gain by the treaties of Locarno?
3. How, for Stresemann, does Locarno differ from the "methods of Versailles"?
4. How does Adolf Hitler use the idea of "self-determination" to justify his aggression against Czechoslovakia?
5. What, for Litvinov, were the basic obstacles to collective security?
6. Compare Litvinov's arguments with those of Neville Chamberlain in the attempt to remove the causes which oppose peace.
7. How did Chamberlain justify his hope that with good will and determination it was possible to remove grievances?
8. To what extent does Chamberlain's radio address of September foreshadow the actual settlement reached at Munich?
9. Compare Hitler's speech of the 26th of September, 1938, with his Prague Proclamation of March 16, 1939. Are there any contradictions between the demands expressed in them? What new arguments are added in Prague?
10. How does Ribbentrop explain away the differences between Germany and the Soviet Union?

11. From the secret protocol of the treaty between Germany and the Soviet Union, delineate the spheres of influence between the two countries. Can you determine where the areas of friction between the two powers were likely to occur in the future?

12. From the conversation between Stalin and Ribbentrop, can you determine those issues which Stalin seems particularly interested in and anxious about?

CHAPTER XLI

THE SECOND WORLD WAR

AT THE OUTSET of the second World War the Germans took the offensive. Within one year most of Western Europe was conquered. The climax of the German march to victory came with the invasion of France. It was then that Italy abandoned her neutrality and entered the conflict on the side of her Axis partners. France surrendered on June 13, 1940. An armistice was signed on June 22, following which the defeated nation, under the leadership of Marshal Pétain (252), began a period of collaboration with Germany. France now became one of the fascist states. With the fall of France, only England still resisted Germany in the West. The United States, however, was by then ready to aid England and to oppose the predominance of the Axis in Europe. The Lend-Lease Act of March, 1941 (253), empowered the President to send arms and other necessities of war to countries fighting the Axis. It proved to be a most effective support. The waning of the Axis initiative in the war came, first, with the invasion of Russia on July 22, 1941, and then with the attack at Pearl Harbor and the entrance of the United States into the European as well as the Far Eastern war (December 10, 1941). War means the rapid development of new weapons, yet it was not until after the European war had ended that the United States announced the most portentous weapon to come out of the conflict: the atom bomb (254).

Times of war, however, are also periods of preparation for the coming peace. There were a number of conferences between the leaders of the Allies, the most important of which was the meeting at Yalta, in the Crimea (255). Here, in February 1945, Roosevelt, Stalin, and Churchill—the Big Three—believed that they had reached general agreement on the outstanding issues which would confront a liberated Europe. To see what went wrong after Yalta it is instructive to compare the passage on free elections (p. 537) with the later (1950) definition of party coalition politics by the East German (communist) government (p. 555). The groundwork was also laid at Yalta for an international organization which would replace the old League of Nations. The basis for this organization was to be the wartime alliance against Axis aggression, an alliance in which some forty-seven nations eventually joined. The function of the Security Council had been an early obstacle to the formation of the United Nations. A formula giving the major powers a veto was agreed upon at the Crimean meeting. The Charter of the United Nations was signed on July 26, 1945, at San Francisco (256).

I. THE WAR

When the defeated French concluded an armistice with Hitler's Germany on June 22, 1940, France was divided into two zones. The northern and western sector was occupied by the Germans. The rest, with its seat of government at Vichy, was ruled by the aging hero of Verdun, Marshal Henri Philippe Pétain. The following passages from a radio address he delivered on August 12, 1941, over a year after the fall of France and when it seemed most likely that Germany would dominate the continent for some years to come, reflect the pattern of the Marshal's views: a willingness to collaborate in some degree, his sympathy for fascism in Spain and elsewhere, his distrust of middle-class businessmen as well as organized labor, his opposition to democracy and yet his desire to hold American friendship, his inherent authoritarianism, and, finally, his hope of getting Frenchmen to rationalize their acceptance of the new order by inducing them to wallow in a feeling of guilt for their national "sins."

252   FRENCHMEN!

I have grave things to tell you!

For the last several weeks I have felt an ill wind rising in many regions of France. Disquiet is overtaking minds; doubt is gaining control of spirits. The authority of my government is made the subject of discussion; orders are often being ill executed.

In an atmosphere of false rumors and intrigues, the forces of reconstruction are growing discouraged. Others are trying to take their place without their nobleness or disinterestedness. My sponsorship is too often invoked, even against the government, to justify self-styled undertakings of salvation which, in fact, amount to nothing more than appeals for indiscipline. . . .

Is this, indeed, the fate France has deserved after thirteen months of calm, of work, of incontestable revival?

Frenchmen, I put this question to you. I ask you to measure its scope and answer it in the confines of your consciences.

Our relations with Germany have been defined by an armistice convention the character of which could be only provisional. Dragging out this situation makes it that much harder to support insofar as it governs relations between two great nations.

As for collaboration—offered in the month of October, 1940, by the chancellor of the Reich under conditions that made me appreciate their deference—it was a long-term labor and has not yet been able to bear all its fruits.

We must be able to overcome a heavy heritage of distrust handed down by centuries of dissensions and quarrels and to turn ourselves toward broad perspectives that can open up a reconciled continent to our activity. . . .

I would also recall to the great American republic the reasons why it has no cause to fear a decline of French ideals. Certainly our parliamentary democracy is dead, but it never had more than a few traits in common with the democracy of the United States. As for the instinct of liberty, it still lives within us, proud and strong. . . .

The troops of the old regime are legion. I rank among them without exception all who place their personal interests ahead of the permanent interests of the State—Freemasonry, political parties deprived of clientele but thirsting for a comeback, officials attached to an order of which they were beneficiaries and masters—or those who have subordinated the interests of the Fatherland to foreign interests.

A long wait will be needed to overcome the resistance of all those opponents of the new order, but we must start in now to smash their undertakings by decimating their leaders.

If France did not understand that she was condemned by the impact of events to change her regime, then she would see open up before her the abyss in which Spain of 1936 just missed being swallowed and from which she was saved only by faith, youth and sacrifice. . . .

As for the power of the trusts, it is trying to reassert itself, using for its own ends the institution of Committees of Economic Organizations. These committees were created, however, to rectify the errors of capitalism. They had in addition the purpose of entrusting responsible men with necessary authority to negotiate with Germany and assure equitable distribution of raw materials indispensable to our factories. . . .

In the light of experience, I shall correct the work I have undertaken, and I shall renew against a selfish and blind capitalism that struggle which the sovereigns of France waged and won against feudalism. I shall see to it that France is rid of the most despicable tutelage, that of money. . . .

Authority no longer emanates from below. The only authority is that which I entrust or delegate. . . .

To my government I shall leave the necessary initiative, but in various fields I intend to trace for it a very clear line. This is what I have decided:

1. Activity of political parties and groups of political origin is suspended until further notice. . . .

2. Payment of members of Parliament is suppressed as of September 30. . . .

4. The Legion of War Veterans remains the best instrument . . . of the National Revolution. But it is able to carry out its civil task only by remaining in all ranks subordinate to the government.

5. I will double the means of police protection, whose discipline and loyalty should guarantee public order. . . .

8. The labor charter designed to regulate . . . relations among workers, artisans, technicians and employers in an agreement reached with mutual understanding, has resulted in a solemn accord. It will be published shortly. . . .

12. . . . all Ministers and high officials must swear an oath of fealty to me. . . .

I know by my calling what victory is; I see today what defeat is. I have rescued the heritage of a wounded France. It is my duty to defend that heritage by maintaining your aspirations and your rights.

In 1917 I put an end to mutiny [i.e., at Verdun]. In 1940 I put an end to rout. Today I wish to save you from yourselves.

New York Times, August 13, 1941, p. 4. (Reprinted by permission.)

In March, 1941, the Congress of the United States passed the Lend-Lease Act which marked the effective end of American neutrality in the war. It empowered President Roosevelt to send arms and other war materials to any nation opposing the Axis. This Act was in force during the entire war.

253 AN ACT Further to promote the defense of the United States, and for other purposes. . . .

Notwithstanding the provisions of any other law, the President may, from time to time, when he deems it in the interest of national defense, authorize the Secretary of War, the Secretary of the Navy, or the head of any other department or agency of the Government—

(1) To manufacture in arsenals, factories, and shipyards under their jurisdiction, or otherwise procure . . . any defense article for the government of any country whose defense the President deems vital to the defense of the United States.

(2) To sell, transfer title to, exchange, lease, lend, or otherwise dispose of, to any such government any defense article . . . .

The terms and conditions upon which any such foreign government receives any aid . . . shall be those which the President deems satisfactory. . . .

Nothing in this Act shall be construed to change existing law relating to the use of the land and naval forces of the United States. . . .

Approved, March 11, 1941.

United States Statutes at Large, Seventy-seventh Congress, First Session, chap. 11.

Early in August, 1945, the United States dropped two atom bombs on Japan. This bomb was undoubtedly the most awesome weapon to be developed during the war. On August 6, 1945, President Harry S. Truman made the first public statement about the atom bomb.

254 Sixteen hours ago an American airplane dropped one bomb on Hiroshima, an important Japanese Army base. That bomb had more power than 20,000 tons of TNT. . . .

The Japanese began the war from the air at Pearl Harbor. They have been repaid manyfold. And the end is not yet. With this bomb we have now added a new and revolutionary increase in destruction to supplement the growing power of our armed forces. In their present form these bombs are now in production and even more powerful forms are in development.

It is an atomic bomb. It is a harnessing of the basic power of the universe. The force from which the sun draws its powers has been loosed against those who brought war to the Far East.

Before 1939, it was the accepted belief of scientists that it was theoretically possible to release atomic energy. But no one knew any practical method of doing it. By 1942, however, we knew that the Germans were working feverishly to find a way to add atomic energy to the other engines of war with which they hoped to enslave the world. But they failed. We may be grateful to Providence that the Germans got the V-1's and the V-2's late and in limited quantities and even more grateful that they did not get the atomic bomb at all.

The battle of the laboratories held fateful risks for us as well as the battles of the air, land, and sea, and we have now won the battle of the laboratories as we have won the other battles.

Beginning in 1940 . . . scientific knowledge useful in war was pooled between the United States and Great Britain, and many priceless helps to our victory have come from that arrangement. . . . With American and British scientists working together, we entered the race of discovery against the Germans.

The United States had available a large number of scientists of distinction. . . . It had the tremendous industrial and financial resources necessary for the project. . . . In the United States the laboratory work and the production plants, on which a substantial start had already been made, would be out of the reach of enemy bombing, while at the time Britain was exposed to constant air attack and was still threatened with the possibility of invasion.

For these reasons Prime Minister Churchill and President Roosevelt agreed that it would be wise to carry on the project here. We now have two great plants and many lesser works devoted to the production of atomic power. Employment during peak construction numbered 125,000. . . . Few know what they have been producing. . . . We have spent two billion dollars on the greatest scientific gamble in history—and won. . . .

We are now prepared to obliterate more rapidly and completely every productive enterprise the Japanese have above ground in any city. . . .

Let there be no mistake; we shall completely destroy Japan's power to make war.

It was to spare the Japanese people from destruction that the ultimatum of July 26 was issued at Potsdam. Their leaders promptly rejected that ultimatum. If they do not now accept our terms they may expect a rain of ruin from the air, the like of which has never been seen on this earth. . . .

The fact that we can release atomic energy ushers in a new age in man's understanding of nature's forces. . . . It has never been the habit of the scientists of this country or the policy of the Government to withhold from the world scientific knowledge. Normally, therefore, everything about the work with atomic energy would be made public.

But under present circumstances it is not intended to divulge the terminal processes of production of all the military applications pending further examination of possible methods of protecting us and the rest of the world from the danger of sudden destruction.

I shall recommend that the Congress of the United States consider promptly the establishment of an appropriate commission to control the production and use of atomic power within the United States. . . .

New York Times, August 7, 1945, p. 4. (Reprinted by permission.)

II. PREPARING FOR PEACE

In February, 1945, the Big Three met at Yalta in the Crimea. There they issued various declarations on the future state of Europe. This was a pressing necessity, for victory in Europe was within reach. These declarations mirror the compromises between East and West (especially in the case of Poland), as well as the resentment against Germany. Free elections were promised in the liberated countries, and Germany was to be dismembered. At Potsdam (p. 543) Germany was dealt with at greater length, and dismemberment was abandoned; free elections never took place in the East, as the East German communist government defined them differently from the West (see p. 555). Here are extracts from the Yalta conference protocols.

255   II. DECLARATION ON LIBERATED EUROPE

The following declaration has been approved:

"The Premier of the Union of Soviet Socialist Republics, the Prime Minister of the United Kingdom and the President of the United States of America have consulted with each other in the common interests of the peoples of their countries and those of liberated Europe. They jointly declare their mutual agreement to concert during the temporary period of instability in liberated Europe the policies of their three governments in assisting the peoples liberated from the domination of Nazi Germany and the peoples of the former Axis satellite states of Europe to solve by democratic means their pressing political and economic problems.

"The establishment of order in Europe and the re-building of national economic life must be achieved by processes which will enable the liberated peoples to destroy the last vestiges of Nazism and Fascism and to create democratic institutions of their own choice. This is a principle of the Atlantic Charter—the right of all peoples to choose the form of government under which they will live—the restoration of sovereign rights and self-government to those peoples who have been forcibly deprived of them by the aggressor nations.

"To foster the conditions in which the liberated peoples may exercise these rights, the three governments will jointly assist the people in any European liberated state or former Axis satellite state in Europe where in their judgment conditions require (a) to establish conditions of internal peace; (b) to carry out emergency measures for the relief of distressed peoples; (c) to form interim governmental authorities broadly representative of all democratic elements in the population and pledged to the earliest possible establishment through free elections of governments responsive to the will of the people; and (d) to facilitate where necessary the holding of such elections.

"The three governments will consult the other United Nations and provisional authorities or other governments in Europe when matters of direct interest to them are under consideration.

"When, in the opinion of the three governments, conditions in any European liberated state or any former Axis satellite state in Europe make such action necessary, they will immediately consult together on the measures necessary to discharge the joint responsibilities set forth in this declaration.

"By this declaration we reaffirm our faith in the principles of the Atlantic Charter, our pledge in the Declaration by the United Nations, and our determination to build in co-operation with other peace-loving nations world order under law, dedicated to peace, security, freedom and general well-being of all mankind.

"In issuing this declaration, the Three Powers express the hope that the Provisional Government of the French Republic may be associated with them in the procedure suggested."

III. Dismemberment of Germany

"The United Kingdom, the United States of America and the Union of Soviet Socialist Republics shall possess supreme authority with respect to Germany. In the exercise of such authority they will take such steps, including the complete disarmament, demilitarisation and the dismemberment of Germany as they deem requisite for future peace and security."

V. Reparation

The following protocol has been approved:

1. Germany must pay in kind for the losses caused by her to the Allied nations in the course of the war. Reparations are to be received in the first instance by those countries which have borne the main burden of the war, have suffered the heaviest losses and have organised victory over the enemy.

2. Reparation in kind is to be exacted from Germany in three following forms:

a) Removals within 2 years from the surrender of Germany or the cessation of organised resistance from the national wealth of Germany located on the territory of Germany herself as well as outside her territory (equipment, machine-tools, ships, rolling stock, German investments abroad, shares of industrial, transport and other enterprises in Germany etc.), these removals to be carried out chiefly for purpose of destroying the war potential of Germany.

b) Annual deliveries of goods from current production for a period to be fixed.

c) Use of German labour.

3. For the working out on the above principles of a detailed plan for exaction of reparation from Germany an Allied Reparation Commission will be set up in Moscow. It will consist of three representatives—one from the Union of Soviet Socialist Republics, one from the United Kingdom, and one from the United States of America.

4. With regard to the fixing of the total sum of the reparation as well as the distribution of it among the countries which suffered from the German aggression the Soviet and American delegations agreed as follows:

"The Moscow Reparation Commission should take in its initial studies as a basis for discussion the suggestion of the Soviet Government that the total sum of the reparation in accordance with the points (a) and (b) of the paragraph 2 should be 20 billion dollars and that 50% of it should go to the Union of Soviet Socialist Republics."

The British delegation was of the opinion that pending consideration of the reparation question by the Moscow Reparation Commission no figures of reparation should be mentioned.

The above Soviet-American proposal has been passed to the Moscow Reparation Commission as one of the proposals to be considered by the Commission.

VII. POLAND

The following Declaration on Poland was agreed by the Conference:

"A new situation has been created in Poland as a result of her complete liberation by the Red Army. This calls for the establishment of a Polish Provisional Government which can be more broadly based than was possible before the recent liberation of the Western part of Poland. The Provisional Government which is now functioning in Poland should therefore be re-organised on a broader democratic basis with the inclusion of democratic leaders from Poland itself and from Poles abroad. This new Government should then be called the Polish Provisional Government of National Unity.

"M. Molotov, Mr. Harriman and Sir A. Clark Kerr are authorised as a commission to consult in the first instance in Moscow with members of the present Provisional Government and with other Polish democratic leaders from within Poland and from abroad, with a view to the reorganisation of the present Government along the above lines. This Polish Provisional Government of National Unity shall be pledged to the holding of free and unfettered elections as soon as possible on the basis of universal suffrage and secret ballot. In these elections all democratic and anti-Nazi parties shall have the right to take part and to put forward candidates.

"When a Polish Provisional Government of National Unity has been properly formed in conformity with the above, the Government of the U.S.S.R., which now maintains diplomatic relations with the United Kingdom and the Government of the U. S. A. will establish diplomatic relations with the new Polish Provisional Government of National Unity, and will exchange Ambassadors by whose reports the respective Governments will be kept informed about the situation in Poland.

"The three Heads of Government consider that the Eastern frontier of Poland should follow the Curzon Line with digressions from it in some regions of five to eight kilometres in favour of Poland. They recognise that Poland must receive substantial accessions of territory in the North and West. They feel that the opinion of the new Polish Provisional Government of National Unity should be sought in due course on the extent of these accessions and that the final delimitation of the Western frontier of Poland should thereafter await the Peace Conference."

Foreign Relations of the United States, "The Conferences at Malta and Yalta" (Washington: Department of State, 1955), pp. 977–81.

The Charter of the United Nations was signed by the member nations in San Francisco on July 26, 1945, and came into force on October 24 of that same year. You can compare these extracts with those reprinted from the Covenant of the League of Nations (see p. 394).

256 ARTICLE 1—Purposes and Principles

The Purposes of the United Nations are:

1. To maintain international peace and security, and to that end: to take effective collective measures for the prevention and removal of threats to the peace, and for the suppression of acts of aggression or other breaches of the peace, and to bring about by peaceful means, and in conformity with the principles of justice and international law, adjustment or settlement of international disputes or situations which might lead to a breach of the peace;

2. To develop friendly relations among nations based on respect for the principle of equal rights and self-determination of peoples, and to take other appropriate measures to strengthen universal peace;

3. To achieve international cooperation in solving international problems of an economic, social, cultural, or humanitarian character, and in promoting and encouraging respect for human rights and for fundamental freedoms for all without distinction as to race, sex, language, or religion; and

4. To be a center for harmonizing the actions of nations in the attainment of these common ends.

ARTICLE 25—Security Council

The Members of the United Nations agree to accept and carry out the decisions of the Security Council in accordance with the present Charter.

ARTICLE 27—Security Council

1. Each member of the Security Council shall have one vote.

2. Decisions of the Security Council on procedural matters shall be made by an affirmative vote of seven members.

3. Decisions of the Security Council on all other matters shall be made by an affirmative vote of seven members including the *concurring votes*

of the permanent members; provided that, in decisions under Chapter VI, and under paragraph 3 of Article 52, a party to a dispute shall abstain from voting.

ARTICLE 41—Breaches of the Peace

The Security Council may decide what measures not involving the use of armed force are to be employed to give effect to its decisions, and it may call upon the Members of the United Nations to apply such measures. These may include complete or partial interruption of economic relations and of rail, sea, air, postal, telegraphic, radio, and other means of communication, and the severance of diplomatic relations.

ARTICLE 42—Breaches of the Peace

Should the Security Council consider that measures provided for in Article 41 would be inadequate or have proved to be inadequate, it may take such action by air, sea, or land forces as may be necessary to maintain or restore international peace and security. Such action may include demonstrations, blockade, and other operations by air, sea, or land forces of Members of the United Nations.

ARTICLE 43—Breaches of the Peace

1. All Members of the United Nations, in order to contribute to the maintenance of international peace and security, undertake to make available to the Security Council, on its call and in accordance with a special agreement or agreements, armed forces, assistance, and facilities, including rights of passage, necessary for the purpose of maintaining international peace and security.

ARTICLE 62—Economic and Social Council

1. The Economic and Social Council may make or initiate studies and reports with respect to international economic, social, cultural, educational, health, and related matters to the General Assembly, to the Members of the United Nations, and to the specialized agencies concerned.

2. It may make recommendations for the purpose of promoting respect for, and observance of, human rights and fundamental freedoms for all.

3. It may prepare draft conventions for submission to the General Assembly, with respect to matters falling within its competence.

4. It may call, in accordance with the rules prescribed by the United Nations, international conferences on matters falling within its competence.

ARTICLE 76—International Trusteeship System

The basic objectives of the trusteeship system, in accordance with the Purposes of the United Nations laid down in Article 1 of the present Charter, shall be:

a. to further international peace and security;

b. to promote the political, economic, social, and educational advancement of the inhabitants of the trust territories, and their progressive development towards self-government or independence as may be appropriate to the particular circumstances of each territory and its peoples and the freely expressed wishes of the peoples concerned, and as may be provided by the terms of each trusteeship agreement;

c. to encourage respect for human rights and for fundamental freedoms for all without distinction as to race, sex, language, or religion, and to encourage recognition of the interdependence of the peoples of the world; and

d. to ensure equal treatment in social, economic, and commercial matters for all Members of the United Nations and their nationals, and also equal treatment for the latter in the administration of justice, without prejudice to the attainment of the foregoing objectives and subject to the provisions of Article 80.

L. M. Goodrich and E. Hambro, *Charter of the United Nations, Commentary and Documents* (Boston: World Peace Foundation, 1946), pp. 339, 345–46, 348–49, 353, 356–57.

QUESTIONS

1. What does Marshal Pétain mean by the "new order"?
2. Is it a fascist state which Pétain is advocating? Compare his speech with the extracts on page 454.
3. List the basic principles underlying the Yalta declarations.
4. Compare Yalta on Germany with the regulations for Germany arrived at in the Potsdam conference (p. 543). Do you think Potsdam supplemented the Yalta ideas on Germany, or are there modifications of the harsh Yalta declaration?
5. Compare Yalta on free elections with the excerpt on communist coalition politics (p. 555).
6. Compare the relevant part of the United Nations Charter with the excerpts from the League of Nations Covenant (p. 394).
7. What is the function, composition, and voting method of the security council of the United Nations?

CHAPTER XLII

THE POSTWAR WORLD

ON MAY 9, 1945, hostilities in Europe came to an end. The Allies now faced the problem of dealing with the defeated Axis powers and, still more important, of putting Europe on its feet again. The work begun in wartime conferences, such as Yalta (see p. 534), had now to be translated into reality. Two months after Germany's defeat, the Big Three met at Potsdam to draw up more detailed terms for that country's future (257). Stalin was the only one left of the Big Three who had made the Yalta decisions. Harry S. Truman had replaced Roosevelt as President of the United States and, partway through the conference, Clement Attlee replaced Churchill as English prime minister. The decision to go ahead with the war-crimes trials of the Nazi leaders was upheld at the meeting, and these trials began in Nürnberg in October of 1945 (258).

With the end of the war, Europe faced economic ruin. It was more denuded of its resources than at any time in modern history; industry and agriculture were in a state of disorganization, while many cities were in ruins. In 1943 the United Nations Relief and Rehabilitation Administration (UNRRA) was created in order to put Europe back on its economic feet. For all of UNRRA's accomplishments, Europe's trade deficit kept growing and a new cure seemed called for if economic recovery were to be achieved. On June 5, 1947, Secretary of State Marshall put forward the plan which bears his name (259). It was the Marshall Plan which, in the end, made possible the economic recovery of those countries which joined in the system of economic co-operation set up under its auspices (260).

The reconstruction of Europe soon brought about tensions between the Soviet Union and the West. It was Winston Churchill who alerted the West to the new situation which had developed in its relations with the Soviet Union (261). His "iron curtain" speech in March, 1946, can be taken as the beginning of the cold-war period. The result of the East-West split was the closer co-operation between the countries of Western Europe which had its climax in the North Atlantic Pact, signed on April 4, 1949 (262). This pact established the North Atlantic Treaty Organization (NATO) which was a military as well as a political alliance.

Meanwhile, the Soviet Union had organized Eastern Europe. At first, a show of democratic procedure was made through the establishment of governments along united-front lines (see p. 555) with the Communists in the lead. Soon the Communist parties became dominant. They used the slogan of national unity in order to keep the other coalition parties in line and, indeed, to put an end to their independence (263). However, there were strains within the communist block which came into the open with the Soviet-Yugoslav dispute in June, 1948 (264, 265). Yugoslavia's successful defiance of Moscow, without abandoning its communist orientation, was a serious blow to Russia's prestige. Yet, no other country in the Soviet block followed the Yugoslav example. With Stalin's death a new leadership emerged in the Soviet Union. There now seemed a faint hope of liquidating the cold war, as President Eisenhower, Prime Minister Eden, and the French premier met with Khrushchev and Bulganin at Geneva in July, 1955 (266). One year later Khrushchev made a sensational speech repudiating many of the policies and methods of the Stalin era, including the handling of the Yugoslav dispute (267). The effects of these events on the cold war remain to be seen.

I. THE RECONSTRUCTION OF EUROPE

After the Axis defeat the Big Three met in the city of Potsdam to deal with defeated Germany (July 17, 1945). The following excerpts from the protocol of the conference concern the occupation of Germany and the kind of governmental organization which the great powers wanted to enforce.

GERMANY

257

The Allied Armies are in occupation of the whole of Germany and the German people have begun to atone for the terrible crimes committed under the leadership of those whom in the hour of their success, they openly approved and blindly obeyed.

Agreement has been reached at this conference on the political and economic principles of a co-ordinated Allied policy toward defeated Germany during the period of Allied control.

The purpose of this agreement is to carry out the Crimea [i.e., Yalta] Declaration on Germany. German militarism and Nazism will be extirpated and the Allies will take in agreement together, now and in the future, the other measures necessary to assure that Germany never again will threaten her neighbors or the peace of the world.

It is not the intention of the Allies to destroy or enslave the German people. It is the intention of the Allies that the German people be given the opportunity to prepare for the eventual reconstruction of their life on a democratic and peaceful basis. If their own efforts are steadily directed to this end, it will be possible for them in due course to take their place among the free and peaceful peoples of the world.

The text of the agreement is as follows:

THE POLITICAL AND ECONOMIC PRINCIPLES TO GOVERN THE TREATMENT OF GERMANY IN THE INITIAL CONTROL PERIOD

A. *Political Principles*

1. In accordance with the agreement on control machinery in Germany, supreme authority in Germany is exercised on instructions from their respective governments, by the Commanders-in-Chief of the armed forces of the United States of America, the United Kingdom, the Union of Soviet Socialist Republics, and the French Republic, each in his own zone of occupation, and also jointly, in matters affecting Germany as a whole, in their capacity as members of the Control Council.

2. So far as is practicable, there shall be uniformity of treatment of the German population throughout Germany.

3. The purposes of the occupation of Germany by which the Control Council shall be guided are:

(i) The complete disarmament and demilitarization of Germany and the elimination or control of all German industry that could be used for military production. To these ends:

(a) All German land, naval and air forces, the S.S., S.A., S.D., and Gestapo, with all their organizations, staffs and institutions, including the General Staff, the Officers' Corps, Reserve Corps, military schools, war veterans' organizations and all other military and quasi-military organizations, together with all clubs and associations which serve to keep alive the military tradition in Germany, shall be completely and finally abolished in such manner as permanently to prevent the revival or reorganization of German militarism and Nazism.

(b) All arms, ammunition and implements of war and all specialized facilities for their production shall be held at the disposal of the Allies or destroyed. The maintenance and production of all aircraft and all arms, ammunition and implements of war shall be prevented.

(ii) To convince the German people that they have suffered a total military defeat and that they cannot escape responsibility for what they have brought upon themselves, since their own ruthless warfare and the fanatical Nazi resistance have destroyed German economy and made chaos and suffering inevitable.

(iii) To destroy the National Socialist Party and its affiliated and supervised organizations, to dissolve all Nazi institutions, to ensure that they are not revived in any form, and to prevent all Nazi and militarist activity or propaganda.

(iv) To prepare for the eventual reconstruction of German political life on a democratic basis and for eventual peaceful cooperation in international life by Germany.

4. All Nazi laws which provided the basis of the Hitler regime or established discrimination on grounds of race, creed, or political opinion shall be abolished. No such discrimination, whether legal, administrative or otherwise, shall be tolerated.

5. War criminals and those who have participated in planning or carrying out Nazi enterprises involving or resulting in atrocities or war crimes shall be arrested and brought to judgment. Nazi leaders, influential Nazi supporters and high officials of Nazi organizations and institutions and any other persons dangerous to the occupation or its objectives shall be arrested and interned.

6. All members of the Nazi party who have been more than nominal participants in its activities and all other persons hostile to allied purposes shall be removed from public and semi-public office, and from positions of

responsibility in important private undertakings. Such persons shall be replaced by persons who, by their political and moral qualities, are deemed capable of assisting in developing genuine democratic institutions in Germany.

7. German education shall be so controlled as completely to eliminate Nazi militarist doctrines and to make possible the successful development of democratic ideas.

8. The judicial system will be reorganized in accordance with the principles of democracy, of justice under law, and of equal rights for all citizens without distinction of race, nationality or religion.

9. The administration of affairs in Germany should be directed towards the decentralization of the political structure and the development of local responsibility. To this end:

(i) Local self-government shall be restored throughout Germany on democratic principles and in particular through elective councils as rapidly as is consistent with military security and the purposes of military occupation;

(ii) All democratic political parties with rights of assembly and of public discussion shall be allowed and encouraged throughout Germany;

(iii) Representative and elective principles shall be introduced into regional, provincial and state (land) administration as rapidly as may be justified by the successful application of these principles in local self-government;

(iv) For the time being no central German government shall be established. Notwithstanding this, however, certain essential central German administrative departments, headed by state secretaries, shall be established, particularly in the fields of finance, transport, communications, foreign trade and industry. Such departments will act under the direction of the Control Council.

10. Subject to the necessity for maintaining military security, freedom of speech, press and religion shall be permitted, and religious institutions shall be respected. Subject likewise to the maintenance of military security, the formation of free trade unions shall be permitted.

B. *Economic Principles*

11. In order to eliminate Germany's war potential, the production of arms, ammunition and implements of war as well as all types of aircraft and sea-going ships shall be prohibited and prevented. Production of metals, chemicals, machinery and other items that are directly necessary to a war economy shall be rigidly controlled and restricted to Germany's approved post-war peacetime needs to meet the objectives stated in paragraph 15. Productive capacity not needed for permitted production shall be removed in accordance with the reparations plan recommended by the Allied Com-

mission on reparations and approved by the governments concerned or if not removed shall be destroyed.

12. At the earliest practicable date, the German economy shall be decentralized for the purpose of eliminating the present excessive concentration of economic power as exemplified in particular by cartels, syndicates, trusts and other monopolistic arrangements.

13. In organizing the German economy, primary emphasis shall be given to the development of agriculture and peaceful domestic industries.

14. During the period of occupation Germany shall be treated as a single economic unit. . . .

U.S. Department of State, *Bulletin*, XIII, No. 319 (August 5, 1945), pp. 154-56.

One paragraph of the Potsdam protocol dealt with the trial of war criminals. The following is an excerpt of the Charter of the Nürnberg tribunal under which the indictments were drawn up by October, 1945. The verdict was brought in on October 1, 1946. Twelve Nazi leaders were condemned to death, three to life imprisonment, four to various prison terms, and three were acquitted. The trials were an attempt to establish crimes against humanity as punishable, and it has caused much dispute in Germany as well as elsewhere.

258   II. JURISDICTION AND GENERAL PRINCIPLES

Article 6. The Tribunal established by the agreement referred to in article 1 hereof for the trial and punishment of the major war criminals of the European Axis countries shall have the power to try and punish persons who, acting in the interests of the European Axis countries, whether as individuals or as members of organizations committed any of the following crimes.

The following acts, or any of them, are crimes coming within the jurisdiction of the Tribunal for which there shall be individual responsibility:

(a) Crimes against peace. Namely, planning, preparation, initiation, or waging of a war of aggression or a war in violation of international treaties, agreements, or assurances, or participation in a common plan or conspiracy for the accomplishment of any of the foregoing.

(b) War Crimes. Namely, violations of the laws or customs of war. Such violations shall include, but not be limited to, murder, ill treatment, or deportation to slave labor or for any other purpose of civilian population of or in occupied territory, murder or ill treatment of prisoners of war or persons on the seas, killing of hostages, plunder of public or private property, wanton destruction of cities, towns, or villages, or devastation not justified by military necessity.

(c) Crimes against humanity. Namely, murder, extermination, enslavement, deportation, and other inhumane acts committed against any civilian population before or during the war or persecutions on political, racial, or religious grounds in execution of or in connection with any crime within the jurisdiction of the Tribunal, whether or not in violation of the domestic law of the country where perpetrated.

Leaders, organizers, instigators, and accomplices participating in the formulation or execution of a common plan or conspiracy to commit any of the foregoing crimes are responsible for all acts performed by any persons in execution of such plan.

Article 7. The official position of defendants, whether as heads of state or responsible officials in government departments, shall not be considered as freeing them from responsibility or mitigating punishment.

Article 8. The fact that the defendant acted pursuant to order of his government or of a superior shall not free him from responsibility but may be considered in mitigation of punishment if the Tribunal determines that justice so requires.

Article 9. At the trial of any individual member of any group or organization the Tribunal may declare (in connection with any act of which the individual may be convicted) that the group or organization of which the individual was a member was a criminal organization. . . .

U.S. Department of State, *Bulletin*, XIII, No. 320 (August 12, 1945), p. 224.

In his commencement address at Harvard University on June 5, 1947, Secretary of State Marshall set out the program of aid to European economic recovery which was to be known as the Marshall Plan.

I need not tell you, gentlemen, that the world situation is very serious. **259** . . . I think one difficulty is that the problem is one of such enormous complexity and that the very mass of facts . . . make it exceedingly difficult for the man in the street to reach a clear appraisement of the situation. Furthermore, the people in this country are distant from the troubled areas . . . and it is hard for them to comprehend the plight and consequent reactions of the long-suffering peoples, and the effect of those reactions on their governments in connection with our efforts to promote peace in the world.

In considering the requirements for the rehabilitation of Europe the physical loss . . . was correctly estimated, but it has become obvious during recent months that this visible destruction was probably less serious than the dislocation of the entire fabric of European economy. For the past ten years conditions have been highly abnormal. . . . The breakdown of the business structure of Europe during the war was complete. Recovery has been seriously retarded by the fact that two years after the close of hostilities a peace settlement with Germany and Austria has not been agreed upon. But even given a more prompt solution of these difficult problems, the rehabilitation of the economic structure of Europe quite evidently will require a much longer time and greater effort than had been foreseen.

There is a phase of this matter which is both interesting and serious. The farmer has always produced the foodstuffs to exchange with the city dweller for the other necessities of life. This division of labor is the basis of modern civilization. At the present time it is threatened with breakdown. The town and city industries are not producing adequate goods to exchange with the food producing farmers. . . . The farmer or peasant cannot find the goods for sale which he desires to purchase. So the sale of his farm produce for the money which he cannot use seems to him an unprofitable transaction. He, therefore, has withdrawn many fields from crop cultivation and is using them for grazing. He feeds more grain to stock. . . Meanwhile people in the cities are short of food and fuel. So the governments are forced to use their foreign money and credits to procure these necessities abroad. This process exhausts funds which are urgently needed for reconstruction. Thus a very serious situation is rapidly developing which bodes no good for the world. The modern system of the division of labor upon which the exchange of products is based is in danger of breaking down.

The truth of the matter is that Europe's requirements for the next three or four years of foreign food and other essential products—principally from America—are so much greater than her present ability to pay that she must have substantial additional help, or face economic, social and political deterioration of a very grave character.

The remedy lies in breaking the vicious circle and restoring the confidence of the European people in the economic future of their own countries and of Europe as a whole. The manufacturer and the farmer throughout wide areas must be able and willing to exchange their products for currencies, the continuing value of which is not open to question.

Aside from the demoralizing effect on the world at large and the possibilities of disturbances arising as a result of the desperation of the people concerned, the consequences to the economy of the United States should be apparent to all. It is logical that the United States should do whatever it is able to do to assist in the return of normal economic health in the world, without which there can be no political stability and no assured peace.

Our policy is directed not against any country or doctrine but against hunger, poverty, desperation and chaos. Its purpose should be the revival of a working economy in the world so as to permit the emergence of political and social conditions in which free institutions can exist. Such assistance, I am convinced, must not be on a piecemeal basis as various crises develop. Any assistance that this government may render in the future should provide a cure rather than a mere palliative.

Any government which is willing to assist in the work of recovery will find full cooperation, I am sure, on the part of the United States Government. Any government which maneuvers to block the recovery of other countries cannot expect help from us. Furthermore, governments, political parties and groups which seek to perpetuate human misery in order to profit therefrom politically or otherwise will encounter the opposition of the United States.

It is already evident that before the United States Government can proceed much further in its efforts to alleviate the situation . . . there must be some agreement among the countries of Europe as to the requirements of the situation and the part those countries themselves will take in order to give proper effect to whatever action might be undertaken by this Government. It would be neither fitting nor efficacious for this Government to undertake to draw up unilaterally a program designed to place Europe on its feet economically. This is the business of the Europeans. The initiative, I think, must come from Europe. The role of this country should consist of friendly aid in the drafting of a European program and of later support of such a program so far as it may be practical for us to do so. The program should be a joint one, agreed to by a number, if not all European nations.

An essential part of any successful action on the part of the United States is an understanding on the part of the people of America of the character of the problem and the remedies to be applied. Political passion and prejudice should have no part. With foresight, and a willingness on the part of our people to face up to the vast responsibility which history has clearly placed upon our country, the difficulties I have outlined can and will be overcome.

New York Times, June 6, 1947, p. 2. (Reprinted by permission.)

The Marshall Plan had encouraged economic co-operation among the West European powers. Under the leadership of France, several nations went one step further, pooling their coal and steel resources. This European Coal and Steel Community is sometimes called the Schuman Plan, after the French foreign minister who advocated it. The following is the preamble to the draft treaty which was initialed, at Paris, on March 19, 1951, by representatives of France, Italy, West Germany, Belgium, the Netherlands, and Luxemburg.

260 THE HIGH CONTRACTING PARTIES:

Considering that world peace may be safeguarded only by creative efforts which measure up to the dangers which menace it;

Convinced that the contribution which an organized and vital Europe can bring to civilization is indispensable to the maintenance of peaceful relations;

Conscious of the fact that Europe can be built only by concrete actions which create a real solidarity and by the establishment of common bases of economic development;

Desirous of assisting through the expansion of their basic production in raising the standard of living and in furthering the works of peace;

Resolved to substitute for historic rivalries a fusion of their essential interests; to establish, by creating an economic community, the foundation of a broad and independent community among peoples long divided by bloody conflicts; and to lay the bases of institutions capable of giving direction to their future common destiny;

Have decided to create a European Coal and Steel Community and have agreed to the following provisions. . . .

Draft Treaty Constituting the European Coal and Steel Community (Washington, 1951), p. 7.

II. THE COLD WAR

In March, 1946, Winston Churchill and President Truman visited Westminster College in Fulton, Missouri. It was on this occasion that Churchill delivered his famous "iron curtain" speech, of which excerpts are given below.

261   . . . A shadow has fallen upon the scenes so lately lightened, lighted by the Allied victory. Nobody knows what Soviet Russia and its Communist international organization intends to do in the immediate future, or what are the limits, if any, to their expansive and proselytizing tendencies.

I have a strong admiration and regard for the valiant Russian people and for my wartime comrade, Marshal Stalin. There is deep sympathy and good will in Britain—and I doubt not here also—toward the peoples of all the Russias. . . . We understand the Russian need to be secure on her western frontiers . . . by the removal of all possibility of German aggression. We welcome Russia to her rightful place among the leading nations of the world. . . .

It is my duty, however, and I am sure that you would not wish me not to state the facts as I see them to you, it is my duty to place before you certain facts about the present position in Europe.

From Stettin in the Baltic to Trieste in the Adriatic, an iron curtain has descended across the Continent. Behind that line lie all the capitals of the ancient states of central and eastern Europe . . . all these famous cities and the populations around them lie in what I might call the Soviet sphere. . . . Police governments are pervading from Moscow. . . . The Russian-dominated Polish government has been encouraged to make enormous and wrongful inroads upon Germany. . . . The Communist parties, which were very small in all these eastern states of Europe, have been raised to preeminence and power far beyond their numbers and are seeking everywhere to obtain totalitarian control. Police governments are prevailing in nearly every case, and so far, except in Czechoslovakia, there is no true democracy. . . .

An attempt is being made by the Russians, in Berlin, to build up a quasi-Communist party in their zone of occupied Germany. . . . At the end of the fighting last June the American and British armies withdrew westward, in accordance with an earlier agreement . . . in order to allow our Russian allies to occupy this vast expanse of territory which the western democracies had conquered.

If now the Soviet Government tries, by separate action, to build up a pro-Communist Germany in their areas this will cause new serious difficulties in the American and British zones and will give the defeated Germans the power of putting themselves up to auction between the Soviets and the Western democracies. Whatever conclusions may be drawn from these facts . . . this is certainly not the liberated Europe we fought to build up. Nor is it one which contains the essentials of permanent peace.

The safety of the world, ladies and gentlemen, requires a unity in Europe from which no nation should be permanently outcast. It is from the strong parent races in Europe that world wars . . . have sprung. . . . Surely we should work with conscious purpose for a grand pacification of Europe within the structure of the United Nations and in accordance with our charter. . . .

In front of the iron curtain which lies across Europe are other causes for anxiety. In Italy the Communist party is seriously hampered by having to support the Communist-trained Marshal Tito's claims to former Italian territory at the head of the Adriatic. Nevertheless the future of Italy hangs in the balance. Again one cannot imagine a regenerated Europe without a strong France. . . .

However, in a great number of countries, far from the Russian frontiers and throughout the world, Communist fifth columns are established and work in complete unity and absolute obedience to directions they receive from the Communist center. Except in the British Commonwealth and in the United States, where communism is in its infancy, the Communist parties or fifth columns constitute a growing challenge and peril to Christian civilization. These are somber facts for anyone to have to recite on the morrow of a victory gained by so much splendid comradeship in arms and in the cause of freedom and democracy, but we should be most unwise not to face them squarely while time remains.

The outlook is also anxious in the Far East and especially in Manchuria. The agreement which was made at Yalta, to which I was party, was extremely favorable to Soviet Russia, but it was made at a time when no one could say that the German war might not extend all through the summer and autumn of 1945 and when the Japanese war was expected by the best judges to last for a further eighteen months from the end of the German war. . . .

I was a Minister at the time of the Versailles treaty. . . . In those days there were high hopes and unbounded confidence that the wars were over, and that the League of Nations would become all-powerful. I do not see or feel that same confidence or even the same hopes in the haggard world at the present time.

On the other hand, ladies and gentlemen, I repulse the idea that a new war is inevitable; still more that it is imminent. It is because I am sure that our fortunes are still in our hands, in our own hands, and that we hold the power to save the future, that I feel the duty to speak out now that I have the occasion and opportunity to do so.

I do not believe that Soviet Russia desires war. What they desire is the fruits of war and the indefinite expansion of their power and doctrines. . . .

From what I have seen of our Russian friends and allies during the war, I am convinced that there is nothing they admire so much as strength, and there is nothing for which they have less respect than for weakness, especially military weakness.

For that, for that reason the old doctrine of a balance of power is unsound. We can not afford, if we can help it, to work on narrow margins offering temptations to a trial of strength.

If the Western democracies stand together in strict adherence to the principles of the United Nations Charter, their influence for furthering those principles will be immense and no one is likely to molest them. If, however, they become divided or falter in their duty, and if these all-important years are allowed to slip away, then indeed catastrophe may overwhelm us all.

Last time I saw it all coming and cried aloud to my own fellow-countrymen and to the world, but no one paid any attention. Up to the year 1933 or even 1935, Germany might have been saved from the awful fate which has overtaken her. . . . There never was a war easier to prevent by timely action than the one which has just desolated such great areas of the globe. It could have been prevented, in my belief, without the firing of a single shot, and Germany might be powerful, prosperous and honored today. . . .

We surely, ladies and gentlemen, I put it to you, but surely we must not let that happen again. This can only be achieved by reaching now, in 1946 . . . a good understanding on all points with Russia under the general authority of the United Nations Organization and by the maintenance of that good understanding through many peaceful years, by the world instrument, supported by the whole strength of the English-speaking world and all its connections. . . .

Let no man underrate the abiding power of the British Empire and Commonwealth. . . . If the population of the English-speaking Commonwealth be added to that of the United States . . . there will be no quivering, precarious balance of power to offer its temptation to ambition and adventure. On the contrary there would be an overwhelming assurance of security. . . .

New York Times, March 6, 1946, p. 4. (Reprinted by permission.)

The North Atlantic Pact was signed on April 4, 1949. The original member nations were Denmark, Portugal, Iceland, Britain, France, Italy, the Netherlands, Norway, Belgium, Luxemburg, Canada, and the United States. In 1951 Greece and Turkey were added, and Germany entered the pact in 1955. In this speech, Secretary of State Dean Acheson explained the meaning of the North Atlantic Pact a few weeks before it was actually signed (March 18, 1949).

. . . It is important to keep in mind that the really successful national **262** and international institutions are those that recognize and express underlying realities. The North Atlantic community of nations is such a reality. It is based on the affinity and natural identity of interests of the North Atlantic powers.

The North Atlantic treaty, which now formally unites them, is the product of at least three hundred and fifty years of history, perhaps more. There developed on our Atlantic coast a community, which has spread across the continent, connected with Western Europe by common institutions and moral and ethical beliefs. Similarities of this kind are not superficial, but fundamental. They are the strongest kind of ties, because they are based on moral conviction, on acceptance of the same values in life.

The very basis of western civilization, which we share with the other nations bordering the North Atlantic, and which all of us share with many other nations, is the ingrained spirit of restraint and tolerance. This is the opposite of the Communist belief that coercion by force is a proper method of hastening the inevitable. Western civilization has lived by mutual restraint and tolerance. This civilization permits and stimulates free inquiry and bold experimentation. It creates the environment of freedom, from which flows the greatest amount of ingenuity, enterprise, and accomplishment.

These principles of democracy, individual liberty, and the rule of law have flourished in this Atlantic community. They have universal validity. They are shared by other free nations and find expression on a universal basis in the Charter of the United Nations; they are the standards by which its members have solemnly agreed to be judged. They are the elements out of which are forged the peace and welfare of mankind.

Added to this profoundly important basis of understanding is another unifying influence—the effect of living on the sea. The sea does not separate people as much as it joins them, through trade, travel, mutual understanding, and common interests.

For this second reason, as well as the first, North America and Western Europe have formed the two halves of what is in reality one community, and have maintained an abiding interest in each other.

It is clear that the North Atlantic pact is not an improvisation. It is the statement of the facts and lessons of history. We have learned our history lesson from two world wars in less than half a century. That experience has taught us that the control of Europe by a single aggressive, unfriendly power would constitute an intolerable threat to the national security of the United States. We participated in those two great wars to preserve the integrity and independence of the European half of the Atlantic community in order to preserve the integrity and independence of the American half. It is a simple fact, proved by experience, that an outside attack on one member of this community is an attack upon all members.

We have also learned that if the free nations do not stand together, they will fall one by one. The stratagem of the aggressor is to keep his intended victims divided, or, better still, set them to quarreling among themselves. Then they can be picked off one by one without arousing unified resistance. We and the free nations of Europe are determined that history shall not repeat itself in that melancholy particular. . . .

U.S. Department of State, *Bulletin,* XX, No. 508 (March 27, 1949), pp. 385–86.

In Eastern Europe the Communist parties at first entered into united-front governments with other political parties. They formed coalition governments rather than taking over power directly. However, very soon the other parties found themselves without any real power—mere window dressing for the communist leadership. In this article a professor from the East German "Peoples' Republic" explains the importance and development of coalition politics in the German Democratic Republic. It is taken from a periodical called *History in the School* and is intended for high-school teachers and students (1950).

. . . The necessities of coalition politics came, for one thing, from the **263** lessons of the German past, out of the realisation that Fascism could only succeed in Germany because the democratic forces were disunited, because it proved impossible to unite all progressive forces in the fight against the Fascist threat, and for peace and order. Its necessity sprang, secondly, from the fact that in face of the huge difficulties which had to be overcome in the fight for the rebuilding and democratisation of Germany, it was only possible to conduct this fight successfully when all anti-fascist-democratic forces were mobilised in its behalf; when all loss of effort in party strife was avoided as long as the existence of the German people was at stake. The basis for such coalition politics was solely the initiative of the working classes, and the basic solidity of the coalition lay in the unity of the working classes, which developed from the unity of action of July 1945, to the organisational fusion of the working class parties which was carried through at the party day of unity of the Social Democrats and Communists on the 21st and 22nd of April 1946. . . .

This coalition politics made it possible to realise the aims which were already contained in the program of action of the German Communist party of June 11, 1945. Such coalition politics enabled the unanimous execution of agrarian reform, to make sure of the expropriation of war and Nazi criminals, the successful creation of a nationalised sector of the economy, school and cultural reform. . . .

Every disturbance of the unanimity and unity of the Democratic coalition must signify a weakening of the forces of democracy, peace, reconstruction and unity of Germany. It is evident that every splitting of the democratic coalition plays into the hands of the war mongers and the advocates of an imperialistic enslavement of Germany, that it is nothing less than direct national treason.

Clearly recognising the significance of such attempts at dissension, the democratic coalition already in June, 1949 arrived at a decision which bound all constituent parties and organisations:

". . . to face with decision unteachable and unregenerate elements in their own ranks and not to shy away from using organisational cleansing processes. There is no room in the parties of the coalition, or the allied organisation, for unfruitful critics, professional disturbers of the peace, and political reactionaries, who cannot tear themselves away from yesteryear and who hinder our work consciously or systematically. Successful common work presupposes, for tasks undertaken communally and of free will, mutual trust."

This unity must be endangered by no one. Therefore the coalition of the anti-fascist-democratic parties have decided to fight the elections . . . on the basis of a common program and with common proposals.

Herbert Krueger, "Die Entwicklung und die Bedeutung der Blockpolitik in der Deutschen Demokratischen Republik," *Geschichte in der Schule,* 3. Jahrgang, October, 1950, pp. 5, 12. (Trans. George L. Mosse.)

On June 28, 1948, the Comintern made its attack against the leadership of the Communist party of Yugoslavia. It accused that leadership, and specifically Tito, of deviations from Soviet orthodoxy. (See Khrushchev's account of this action, p. 570.) The following is an excerpt from the "Resolution of the Information Bureau Concerning the Situation in the Communist party of Yugoslavia" (June 28, 1948).

264   The Information Bureau, composed of the representatives of the Bulgarian Workers' Party (Communists), Rumanian Workers' Party, Hungarian Workers' Party, Polish Workers' Party, The Communist Party of the Soviet Union (Bolsheviks), Communist Party of France, Communist Party of Czechoslovakia and the Communist Party of Italy, upon discussing the situation in the Communist Party of Yugoslavia and announcing that the representatives of the Communist Party of Yugoslavia had refused to attend the meeting of the Information Bureau, unanimously reached the following conclusions:

1. The Information Bureau notes that recently the leadership of the Communist Party of Yugoslavia has pursued an incorrect line on the main questions of home and foreign policy, a line which represents a departure from Marxism-Leninism. . . .

2. The Information Bureau declares the leadership of the Yugoslav Communist Party is pursuing an unfriendly policy toward the Soviet Union and the CPSU. An undignified policy of defaming Soviet military experts and discrediting the Soviet Union, has been carried out in Yugoslavia. A special régime was instituted for Soviet civilian experts in Yugoslavia, whereby they were under surveillance of Yugoslav state security organs and were continually followed. . . .

All these and similar facts show that the leaders of the Communist Party of Yugoslavia have taken a stand unworthy of Communists, and have begun to identify the foreign policy of the Soviet Union with the foreign policy of the imperialist powers, behaving toward the Soviet Union in the same manner as they behave to the bourgeois states. . . .

3. In home policy, the leaders of the Communist Party of Yugoslavia are departing from the positions of the working class and are breaking with the Marxist theory of classes and class struggle. They deny that there is a growth of capitalist elements in their country, and consequently, a sharpening of the class struggle in the countryside. This denial is the direct result of the opportunist tenet that the class struggle does not become sharper during the period of transition from capitalism to socialism, as Marxism-Leninism teaches, but dies down, as was affirmed by opportunists of the Bukharin type, who propagated the theory of the peaceful growing over of capitalism into socialism. . . .

In Yugoslavia, however, the People's Front, and not the Communist Party, is considered to be the main leading force in the country. The Yugoslav leaders belittle the role of the Communist Party and actually dissolve the Party in the nonparty People's Front, which is composed of the most varied class elements (workers, peasants engaged in individual farming, kulaks, traders, small manufacturers, bourgeois intelligentsia, etc.) as well as mixed political groups which include certain bourgeois parties. The Yugoslav leaders stubbornly refuse to recognize the falseness of their tenet that the Communist Party of Yugoslavia allegedly cannot and should not have its own specific programme and that it should be satisfied with the programme of the People's Front. . . .

5. The Information Bureau considers that the bureaucratic régime created inside the Party by its leaders is disastrous for the life and development of the Yugoslav Communist Party. There is no inner Party democracy, no elections, and no criticism and self-criticism in the Party. . . .

6. The Information Bureau considers that the criticism made by the Central Committee of the Communist Party of the Soviet Union and Central Committees of the other Communist Parties of the mistakes of the Central Committee of the Communist Party of Yugoslavia, and who in this way rendered fraternal assistance to the Yugoslav Communist Party, provides the Communist Party of Yugoslavia with all the conditions necessary to speedily correct the mistakes committed.

However, instead of honestly accepting this criticism and taking the Bolshevik path of correcting these mistakes, the leaders of the Communist Party of Yugoslavia, suffering from boundless ambition, arrogance and conceit, met this criticism with belligerence and hostility. They took the anti-Party path of indiscriminately denying all their mistakes, violated the doctrine of Marxism-Leninism regarding the attitude of a political party to its mistakes and thus aggravated their anti-Party mistakes. . . .

7. Taking into account the situation in the Communist Party of Yugoslavia, and seeking to show the leaders of the Party the way out of this situation, the Central Committee of the Communist Party of the Soviet Union and the Central Committees of other fraternal parties, suggested that the matter of the Yugoslav Communist Party should be discussed at a meeting of the Information Bureau, on the same, normal party footing as that on which the activities of other Communist Parties were discussed at the first meeting of the Information Bureau. . . .

The refusal of the Yugoslav Party to report to the Information Bureau on its actions and to listen to criticism by other Communist Parties means, in practice, a violation of the equality of the Communist Parties and is, in fact, tantamount to a demand for a privileged position for the Communist Party of Yugoslavia in the Information Bureau.

8. In view of this, the Information Bureau expresses complete agreement with the estimation of the situation in the Yugoslav Communist Party, with the criticism of the mistakes of the Central Committee of the Party, and with the political analysis of these mistakes contained in letters from the Central Committee of the Communist Party of the Soviet Union to the Central Committee of the Communist Party of Yugoslavia between March and May 1948.

The Information Bureau unanimously concludes that by their anti-Party and anti-Soviet views, incompatible with Marxism-Leninism, by their whole attitude and their refusal to attend the meeting of the Information Bureau, the leaders of the Communist Party of Yugoslavia have placed themselves in opposition to the Communist Parties affiliated to the Information Bureau, have taken the path of seceding from the united socialist front against imperialism, have taken the path of betraying the cause of the international solidarity of the working people, and have taken up a position of nationalism.

The Information Bureau condemns this anti-Party policy and attitude of the Central Committee of the Communist Party of Yugoslavia.

The Information Bureau considers that, in view of all this, the Central Committee of the Communist Party of Yugoslavia has placed itself and the Yugoslav Party outside the family of the fraternal Communist Parties, outside the united Communist front and consequently outside the ranks of the Information Bureau. . . .

The Information Bureau considers that the basis of these mistakes made by the leadership of the Communist Party of Yugoslavia lies in the undoubted fact that nationalist elements, which previously existed in a disguised form, managed in the course of the past five or six months to reach a dominant position in the leadership of the Communist Party of Yugoslavia, and that consequently the leadership of the Yugoslav Communist Party has broken with the international traditions of the Communist Party of Yugoslavia and has taken the road of nationalism. . . .

The Information Bureau does not doubt that inside the Communist Party of Yugoslavia there are sufficient healthy elements, loyal to Marxism-Leninism, to the international traditions of the Yugoslav Communist Party and to the united socialist front.

Their task is to compel their present leaders to recognize their mistakes openly and honestly and to rectify them; to break with nationalism, return to internationalism; and in every way to consolidate the united socialist front against imperialism.

Should the present leaders of the Yugoslav Communist Party prove incapable of doing this, their job is to replace them and to advance a new internationalist leadership of the Party.

The Information Bureau does not doubt that the Communist Party of Yugoslavia will be able to fulfill this honourable task.

The Soviet-Yugoslav Dispute (London: Royal Institute of International Affairs, 1948), pp. 61–70.

Instead of purging their leadership, as the Comintern expected, the Yugoslav Communist party rejected the charges as unfounded.

This meant a breach between Tito and the Soviet Union which gave rise to the hope that other Communist parties might cut loose from Moscow and become "Titoists." This was prevented in the Eastern nations by purges, and in the West the Communist parties remained loyal to the Soviet Union. The following is part of the statement of the Central Committee of the Communist Party of Yugoslavia (June 29, 1948).

265   In connection with the publication of the Resolution of the Information Bureau, the Central Committee of the Communist Party of Yugoslavia makes the following statement:

1. The criticism contained in the Resolution is based on inaccurate and unfounded assertions and represents an attempt to destroy the prestige of the CPY both abroad and in the country, to arouse confusion amongst the masses in the country and in the international workers' movement, to weaken the unity within the CPY and its leading role. . . .

2. The Resolution maintains, without citing any proof, that the leadership of the CPY carried out a hostile policy towards the USSR. The statement that Soviet military specialists in Yugoslavia have been treated with scant respect, and that Soviet civilian citizens have been under the surveillance of state security agents does not in the least correspond to the truth. . . .

On the contrary, it is correct, as stated in the letter to the CC of the CPSU of 13 April, and based on numerous reports of members of the CPY to their Party organizations as well as on statements of other citizens of our country, that from the liberation up to date the Soviet intelligence service sought to enroll them. The CC of the CPY considered and considers that such an attitude towards a country where the communists are the ruling party and which is advancing toward socialism is impermissible—and that it leads towards the demoralization of the citizens of the Federated People's Republic of Yugoslavia and towards the weakening and undermining of the governmental and Party leadership. . . .

3. The Resolution criticized the policy of the CPY in regard to the conduct of the class struggle and particularly the policy of the CPY in the village. In connection with this, well-known passages from Lenin are quoted. The CC of the CPY points out that in its policy of restricting the capitalist elements in the village, it is guided by the mentioned and similar passages from Lenin, which the authors of the Resolution—had they taken the trouble—might have read in the published Party documents and articles, and

might have convinced themselves concerning the practical execution of this policy. . . .

4. The CC of the CPY cannot but reject with deep indignation the assertion that the leading ranks in the CPY are deviating to the course of a kulak party, to the path of the liquidation of the Communist Party of Yugoslavia, that there is no democracy in the Party, that methods of military leadership are fostered within the Party, that the most basic rights of Party members are trampled upon in the Party and that the mildest criticism of irregularities in the Party is answered by sharp reprisals, etc. Could the members of the Party who dauntlessly faced death in thousands of battles, tolerate in the Party a state of affairs unworthy of both men and communists? The assertion that criticism is not allowed in the Party and similar statements are a terrible insult to every member of our Party, a degradation of the heroic and glorious past of the Party and its present heroic struggle for the reconstruction and development of the country. The CC of the CPY emphasizes that because certain Party organizations have not yet held elections it cannot be maintained that there is no democracy within the Party. These are the remnants of the war period and the tempestuous postwar development through which the CPY passed and in their time they were to be found in other Parties and in the CPSU as well.

As regards the assertion that the Party is losing itself in the Front . . . the facts, as well as numerous declarations made throughout the war and after it—not only by communists but by non-communists in the Front— show, first, that the CP is the leading force in the Front; second, that the CP does not lose itself in the Front but that on the contrary the Party ideologically and politically is raising the masses of Front members, educating them in the spirit of its policy of Marxism-Leninism; third, that the People's Front of Yugoslavia is in practice fighting for socialism, which surely could not be the case if motley political groups played any important role in it—the bourgeois parties, kulaks, merchants, small industrialists and the like, as is said in the Resolution, or if it were a coalition between the CP and other parties or a form of agreement of the proletariat with the bourgeoisie; fourth, that the Party does not take over the Front programme but that rather the Front gets its basic direction and its programme from the CP, which is natural in view of its leading role in the Front. . . .

5. The CC of the CPY rejects as unworthy the accusation that a Turkish régime reigns in the CP. . . .

6. The CC of the CPY rejects as absurd the assertion that recently the Yugoslav leaders took measures for the nationalization of small-scale industry and small shops in a great hurry and for demagogical reasons. These

measures as a matter of fact were prepared six months before the charges made by the CC of the CPSU against the CC of the CPY and are the result of the strengthening and development of the socialist sector. . . .

8. The CC of the CPY does not consider that by refusing to discuss the mistakes of which it is not guilty, it has in any way injured the unity of the communist front. The unity of this front is not based on the admission of invented or fabricated errors and slanders, but on the fact of whether or not the policy of a Party is actually internationalist. One cannot, however, ignore the fact that the Information Bureau has committed a breach of the principles on which it was based and which provide for the voluntary adoption of conclusions by every Party. The Informbureau, however, not only forces the leaders of the CPY to admit errors which they did not commit but also calls members of the CPY to rebellion within the Party, to shatter the unity of the Party. The CC of the CPY can never agree to a discussion about its policy on the basis of inventions and uncomradely behaviour without mutual confidence. . . .

The CC of the CPY calls upon the Party membership to close their ranks in the struggle for the realization of the Party line and for even greater strengthening of Party unity, while it calls upon the working class and other working masses, gathered in the People's Front, to continue to work even more persistently on the building of our socialist homeland. This is the only way, the only method to prove in full and by deeds the unjustness of the above-mentioned charges.

The Plenum of the CC of the CPY

Belgrade,
29 June 1948

Ibid., pp. 71–79.

QUESTIONS

1. How did the Big Three hope to prevent Germany's resurgence as a great power?
2. In what manner did the Potsdam protocol attempt to democratize Germany?
3. What in the Charter of the Nürnberg tribunal could cause controversy?
4. What is the vicious circle which Secretary Marshall wanted to break?
5. How did he want to restore the European economy?
6. How did Winston Churchill want to prevent a new war? What lessons from the past were important to him?
7. What were Churchill's accusations against the Soviet Union?

8. Do you think that Secretary Acheson's analysis of Western history is valid?

9. What do the Communists understand by coalition politics? How does their view differ from that of the West as to the role of political parties?

10. Make a point by point comparison between the attack of the Comintern on the Yugoslav Communist party, and that party's reply. What can the different viewpoints tell you about the problems faced by postwar communism in running a nation?

CHAPTER XLIII

THE LONG TWILIGHT STRUGGLE

BOTH the cold war and the reconstruction of Europe continued after 1950. In the Soviet Union a new era started with the death of Stalin and the emergence of Nikita Khrushchev. In 1956 the new Soviet prime minister made a sensational speech repudiating many of the policies and methods of the Stalinist era, including the handling of the dispute with Yugoslavia (267). However, by the 1960's Khrushchev himself faced a controversy much more serious than that with Yugoslavia had been. The exchanges between the Soviet Union and The People's Republic of China touch not only problems of national rivalry but also involve more basic differences in Communist outlook and strategy (268, 269).

Meanwhile efforts continued to lessen the tensions of the cold war. The most important of these was the plan put forward by the Polish foreign minister Rapacki (270). Though it proved attractive to many statesmen outside the Communist block, the German Federal Republic offered strong opposition to the Rapacki Plan which eventually doomed the proposal (271). Instead Chancellor Adenauer advocated a policy of Western unity and military preparedness (272). Such unity was based not only upon the North Atlantic Treaty Organization, but also upon closer economic ties within the Common Market (273). Britain, excluded from this market, attempted to form her own European trade block (274). The unity of Western Europe did not include all non-Communist nations. In its turn, the Communist block formed a common market of its own, though it proved to be much less successful than the Western Common Market (276). The attempted unity of the West was further bedevilled by rivalries for leadership—a position claimed by General Charles de Gaulle (277). However much he may have damaged the cause of unity, the French president succeeded in restoring his nation to a central place in the West.

The 1960's opened with a more hopeful note in East-West relations. No progress had been made on disarmament which had been a topic for discussion at the Geneva meeting of 1955 (266). However, nearly ten years later, a test ban agreement was signed (278). None of the plans put forward by Rapacki or by Chancellor Adenauer had succeeded in liquidating the cold war but here a beginning was made, however slight. The effect of all these events upon the 1960's remains to be seen. At the moment Europe as a whole seems more deeply divided than during much of its previous history, while the unity of Western Europe, though started with much hope, still has a long way to go.

With the death of Stalin it looked as if there might now come a loosening of the cold war. President Eisenhower and Prime Minister Anthony Eden, as well as the French premier, met with the Soviet leaders Khrushchev and Bulganin at Geneva on July 20, 1955. After the meetings they issued the following directives to their foreign ministers (July 23, 1955).

The Heads of the Government of France, the United Kingdom, the **266** U.S.S.R. and the U.S.A., guided by the desire to contribute to the relaxation of international tension and to the consolidation of confidence between states, instruct their Foreign Ministers to continue the consideration of the following questions with regard to which an exchange of views has taken place at the Geneva Conference, and to propose effective means for their solution, taking account of the close link between the reunification of Germany and the problems of European security and the fact that the successful settlement of each of these problems would serve the interests of consolidating peace.

1. *European Security and Germany*

For the purpose of establishing European security with due regard to the legitimate interests of all nations and their inherent right to individual and collective self-defense, the Ministers are instructed to consider various proposals to this end, including the following: A security pact for Europe or for a part of Europe, including the provision for assumption by member nations of an obligation not to resort to force and to deny assistance to an aggressor; limitation, control and inspection in regard to armed forces and armaments; establishment between East and West of a zone in which the disposition of armed forces will be subject to mutual agreement; and also to consider other possible proposals pertaining to the solution of the problem.

The Heads of Government, recognizing their common responsibility for the settlement of the German question and the reunification of Germany, have agreed the settlement of the German question and the reunification of Germany by means of free elections shall be carried out in conformity with the national interests of the German people and the interests of European security. The Foreign Ministers will make whatever arrangements they may consider desirable for the participation of, or for the consultation with, other interested parties.

2. *Disarmament*

The Four Heads of Government,

Desirous of removing the threat of war and lessening the burden of armaments,

Convinced of the necessity, for secure peace and for the welfare of mankind, of achieving a system for the control and reduction of all armaments and armed forces under effective safeguard,

Recognizing that achievements in this field would release vast material resources to be devoted to the peaceful economic development of nations, for raising their well-being, as well as for assistance to underdeveloped countries,

Agree:

(1) for these purposes to work together to develop an acceptable system for disarmament through the Sub-Committee of the United Nations Disarmament Commission;

(2) to instruct their representatives in the Sub-Committee in the discharge of their mandate from the United Nations to take account in their work of the views and proposals advanced by the Heads of Government at this Conference;

(3) to propose that the next meeting of the Sub-Committee be held on August 29, 1955, at New York;

(4) to instruct the Foreign Ministers to take note of the proceedings in the Disarmament Commission, to take account of the views and proposals advanced by the Heads of Government at this Conference and to consider whether the four Governments can take any further useful initiative in the field of disarmament.

3. *Development of Contacts between East and West*

The Foreign Ministers should by means of experts study measures, including those possible in organs and agencies of the United Nations, which could (a) bring about a progressive elimination of barriers which interfere with free communications and peaceful trade between people and (b) bring about such freer contacts and exchanges as are to the mutual advantage of the countries and peoples concerned.

4. *The Foreign Ministers of the Four Powers will meet at Geneva during October to initiate the consideration of these questions and to determine the organisation of their work.*

U.S. Department of State, *Bulletin*, XXXIII, No. 840 (August 1, 1955), pp. 176–77.

At a secret session of the Communist party's twentieth congress in Moscow (February 24–25, 1956), Nikita S. Khrushchev made an attack upon Stalin which caused a sensation. This version, from which we have taken the extracts, was obtained by the State Department. It is not an official release by the Soviet government, though there is every reason to think it authentic.

. . . After Stalin's death the Central Committee of the party began to **267** implement a policy of explaining concisely and consistently that it is impermissible and foreign to the spirit of Marxism-Leninism to elevate one person, to transform him into a superman possessing supernatural characteristics akin to those of a god. Such a man supposedly knows everything, sees everything, thinks for everyone, can do anything, is infallible in his behavior. . . .

At the present we are concerned with a question which has immense importance for the party now and for the future—[we are concerned] with how the cult of the person of Stalin has been gradually growing, the cult which became at a certain specific stage the source of a whole series of exceedingly serious and grave perversions of party principles, of party democracy, of revolutionary legality. . . .

Allow me first of all to remind you how severely the classics of Marxism-Leninism denounced every manifestation of the cult of the individual. . . .

Marxism does not negate the role of the leaders of the workers' class in directing the revolutionary liberation movement.

While ascribing great importance to the role of the leaders and organizers of the masses, Lenin at the same time mercilessly stigmatized every manifestation of the cult of the individual, inexorably combated the foreign-to-Marxism views about a "hero" and a "crowd" and countered all efforts to oppose a "hero" to the masses and to the people.

Lenin taught that the Party's strength depends on its indissoluble unity with the masses, on the fact that behind the Party follow the people—workers, peasants and intelligentsia. "Only he will win and retain the power," said Lenin, "who believes in the people, who submerges himself in the fountain of the living creativeness of the people." . . .

In addition to the great accomplishments of V. I. Lenin for the victory of the working class and of the working peasants, for the victory of our party and for the application of the ideas of scientific communism to life, his acute mind expressed itself also in this that he detected in Stalin in time those negative characteristics which resulted later in grave consequences. . . .

In December, 1922, in a letter to the party congress Vladimir Ilyich [Lenin] wrote: "After taking over the position of Secretary General, Comrade Stalin accumulated in his hands immeasurable power and I am not certain whether he will be always able to use this power with the required care." . . .

Vladimir Ilyich said: "Stalin is excessively rude, and this defect, which can be freely tolerated in our midst and in contacts among us Communists, becomes a defect which cannot be tolerated in one holding the position of the Secretary General. Because of this, I propose that the comrades consider the method by which Stalin would be removed from this position and by which another man would be selected for it; a man who, above all, would differ from Stalin in only one quality, namely, greater tolerance, greater loyalty, greater kindness and more considerate attitude towards the comrades, a less capricious temper, etc." . . .

As later events have proven, Lenin's anxiety was justified: in the first period after Lenin's death Stalin still paid attention to his [Lenin's] advice, but later he began to disregard the serious admonitions of Vladimir Ilyich.

When we analyze the practice of Stalin in regard to the direction of the party and of the country, when we pause to consider everything which Stalin perpetrated, we must be convinced that Lenin's fears were justified. The negative characteristics of Stalin, which, in Lenin's time, were only incipient, transformed themselves during the last years into a grave abuse of power by Stalin, which caused untold harm to our party. . . .

Stalin acted not through persuasion, explanation, and patient cooperation with people, but by imposing his concepts and demanding absolute submission to his opinion. Whoever opposed this concept or tried to prove his viewpoint and the correctness of his position was doomed to removal from the leading collective and to subsequent moral and physical annihilation. This was especially true during the period following the seventeenth party congress, when many prominent party leaders and rank-and-file party workers, honest and dedicated to the cause of communism, fell victim to Stalin's despotism. . . .

It was precisely during this period (1935–1937–1938) that the practice of mass repression through the Government apparatus was born, first against the enemies of Leninism—Trotskyites, Zinovievites, Bukharinites, long since politically defeated by the party, and subsequently also against many honest Communists, against those party cadres who had borne the heavy load of the Civil War and the first and most difficult years of industrialization and collectivization, who actively fought against the Trotskyites and the rightists for the Leninist party line.

Stalin originated the concept "enemy of the people." This term automatically rendered it unnecessary that the ideological errors of a man or men engaged in a controversy be proven; this term made possible the usage of the most cruel repression, violating all norms of revolutionary legality, against anyone who in any way disagreed with Stalin, against those who were only suspected of hostile intent, against those who had bad reputations.

This concept "enemy of the people" actually eliminated the possibility of any kind of ideological fight or the making of one's views known on this or that issue, even those of a practical character. In the main, and in actuality, the only proof of guilt used, against all norms of current legal science, was the "confession" of the accused himself; and, as subsequent probing proved, "confessions" were acquired through physical pressures against the accused. . . .

Lenin used severe methods only in the most necessary cases, when the exploiting classes were still in existence and were vigorously opposing the revolution, when the struggle for survival was decidedly assuming the sharpest forms, even including a civil war.

Stalin, on the other hand, used extreme methods and mass repressions at a time when the revolution was already victorious, when the Soviet state was strengthened, when the exploiting classes were already liquidated and Socialist relations were rooted solidly in all phases of national economy, when our party was politically consolidated and had strengthened itself both numerically and ideologically. It is clear that here Stalin showed in a whole series of cases his intolerance, his brutality and his abuse of power. Instead of proving his political correctness and mobilizing the masses, he often chose the path of repression and physical annihilation, not only against actual enemies, but also against individuals who had not committed any crimes against the party and the Soviet Government. Here we see no wisdom but only a demonstration of the brutal force which had once so alarmed V. I. Lenin. . . .

. . . It became apparent that many party, Government and economic activists who were branded in 1937–38 as "enemies," were actually never enemies, spies, wreckers, etc., but were always honest Communists.

They were only so stigmatized and often, no longer able to hear barbaric tortures, they charged themselves (at the order of the investigative judges—falsifiers) with all kinds of grave and unlikely crimes. . . .

The same fate met not only the Central Committee members but also the majority of the delegates to the seventeenth party congress. Of 1,966 delegates with either voting or advisory rights, 1,108 persons were arrested on charges of anti-revolutionary crimes, i.e., decidedly more than a majority. This very fact shows how absurd, wild and contrary to common sense were the charges of counter-revolutionary crimes made, as we now see, against a majority of participants at the seventeenth party congress. (Indignation in the hall.) . . .

The mass repressions at this time were made under the slogan of a fight against the Trotskyites. Did the Trotskyites at this time actually constitute such a danger to our party and to the Soviet State? We should recall that in 1927 on the eve of the Fifteenth Party Congress only about 4,000 votes were cast for the Trotskyite-Zinovievite opposition, while there were 724,000 for the party line. During the ten years that passed between the Fifteenth Party Congress and the February-March Central Committee Plenum, Trotskyism was completely disarmed; many former Trotskyites had changed their former views and worked in the various sectors building socialism. It is clear that in the situation of Socialist victory there was no basis for mass terror in the country. . . .

This terror was actually directed not at the remnants of the defeated exploiting classes but against the honest workers of the party and of the Soviet state; against them were made lying, slanderous and absurd accusations concerning "two-facedness," "espionage," "sabotage," preparation of fictitious "plots," etc. . . .

Facts prove that many abuses were made on Stalin's orders without reckoning with any norms of party and Soviet legality. Stalin was a very distrustful man, sickly suspicious; we knew this from our work with him. He could look at a man and say: "Why are your eyes so shifty today," or "Why are you turning so much today and avoiding to look me directly in the eyes?" The sickly suspicion created in him a general distrust even toward eminent party workers whom he had known for years. Everywhere and in everything he saw "enemies," "two-facers" and "spies."

Possessing unlimited power, he indulged in great willfulness and choked a person morally and physically. A situation was created where one could not express one's own will.

When Stalin said that one or another should be arrested, it was necessary to accept on faith that he was an "enemy of the people." Meanwhile, Beria's gang, which ran the organs of state security, outdid itself in proving the guilt of the arrested and the truth of materials which it falsified.

And what proofs were offered? The confessions of the arrested, and the investigative judges accepted these "confessions." And how is it possible that a person confesses to crimes which he has not committed? Only in one way—because of application of physical methods of pressuring him, tortures, bringing him to a state of unconsciousness, deprivation of his judgment, taking away of his human dignity. In this manner were "confessions" acquired. . . .

The power accumulated in the hands of one person, Stalin, led to serious consequences during the Great Patriotic War. . . .

What are the facts of this matter? . . .

During the war and after the war Stalin put forward the thesis that the tragedy which our nation experienced in the first part of the war was the result of the "unexpected" attack of the Germans against the Soviet Union. But, Comrades, this is completely untrue.

As soon as Hitler came to power in Germany he assigned to himself the task of liquidating communism. The Fascists were saying this openly; they did not hide their plans. . . .

Documents which have now been published show that by April 3, 1941 [Sir Winston] Churchill, through his Ambassador to the U.S.S.R. [Sir Stafford] Cripps, personally warned Stalin that the Germans had begun regrouping their armed units with the intent of attacking the Soviet Union. It is self-evident that Churchill did not do this at all because of his friendly feeling toward the Soviet nation.

He had in this his own imperialistic goals—to bring Germany and the

U.S.S.R. into a bloody war and thereby to strengthen the position of the British Empire. Just the same, Churchill affirmed in his writings that he sought to "warn Stalin and call his attention to the danger which threatened him." . . .

Despite these particularly grave warnings, the necessary steps were not taken to prepare the country properly for defense and to prevent it from being caught unawares.

Did we have time and the capabilities for such preparations? Yes, we had the time and capabilities. Our industry was already so developed that it was capable of supplying fully the Soviet Army with everything that it needed. This is proven by the fact that although during the war we lost almost half of our industry and important industrial and food production areas as the result of enemy occupation of the Ukraine, Northern Caucasus and other western parts of the country, the Soviet nation was still able to organize the production of military equipment in the eastern parts of the country, install there equipment taken from the Western industrial areas, and to supply our armed forces with everything which was necessary to destroy the enemy.

Had our industry been mobilized properly and in time to supply the army with the necessary *matériel,* our wartime losses would have been decidedly smaller. Such mobilization had not been, however, started in time. And already in the first days of the war it became evident that our army was badly armed, that we did not have enough artillery, tanks and planes to throw the enemy back. . . .

Such was the armament situation. . . .

Stalin was very far from an understanding of the real situation that was developing at the front. That was natural because during the whole patriotic war he never visited any section of the front or any liberated city except for one short ride on the Mozhaisk Highway during a stabilized situation at the front. . . .

All the more shameful was the fact that after our great victory over the enemy which cost us so much, Stalin began to down-grade many of the commanders who contributed so much to the victory over the enemy, because Stalin excluded every possibility that services rendered at the front should be credited to anyone but himself. . . .

All the more monstrous are the acts whose initiator was Stalin and which are rude violations of the basic Leninist principles of the nationality policy of the Soviet State. We refer to the mass deportations from their native places of whole nations, together with all Communists and Komsomols [communist youth groups] without any exception; this deportation action was not dictated by any military considerations. . . .

Not only a Marxist-Leninist but also no man of common sense can grasp how it is possible to make whole nations responsible for inimical activity, including women, children, old people, Communists and Komsomols, to use mass repression against them, and to expose them to misery and suffering for the hostile acts of individual persons or groups of persons. . . .

The July Plenum of the Central Committee studies in detail the reasons for the development of conflict with Yugoslavia. It was a shameful role which Stalin played here. The "Yugoslav Affair" contained no problems that could not have been solved through Party discussions among comrades.

There was no significant basis for the development of this "affair," it was completely possible to have prevented the rupture of relations with that country. This does not mean, however, that the Yugoslav leaders did not make mistakes or did not have shortcomings. But these mistakes and shortcomings were magnified in a monstrous manner by Stalin, which resulted in a break of relations with a friendly country.

I recall the first days when the conflict between the Soviet Union and Yugoslavia began artificially to be blown up. Once, when I came from Kiev to Moscow, I was invited to visit Stalin who, pointing to the copy of a letter lately sent to Tito, asked me, "Have you read this?"

Not waiting for my reply he answered: "I will shake my little finger—and there will be no more Tito. He will fall."

We have dearly paid for this "shaking of the little finger." This statement reflected Stalin's mania for greatness, but he acted just that way: "I will shake my little finger—and there will be no Kosior"; "I will shake my little finger once more and Postyshev and Chubar will be no more"; "I will shake my little finger again—and Voznesensky, Kuznetsov and many others will disappear."

But this did not happen to Tito. No matter how much or how little Stalin shook, not only his little finger but everything else that he could shake, Tito did not fall. Why? The reason was that, in this case of disagreement with the Yugoslav comrades, Tito had behind him a state and a people who had gone through a severe school of fighting for liberty and independence, a people which gave support to its leaders.

You see to what Stalin's mania for greatness led. He had completely lost consciousness of reality; he demonstrated his suspicion and haughtiness not only in relation to individuals in the U.S.S.R., but in relation to whole parties and nations. . . .

Stalin's reluctance to consider life's realities and the fact that he was not aware of the real state of affairs in the provinces can be illustrated by his direction of agriculture.

All those who interested themselves even a little in the national situation saw the difficult situation in agriculture, but Stalin never even noted it. Did we tell Stalin about this? Yes, we told him, but he did not support us. Why? Because Stalin never traveled anywhere, did not meet city and collective workers; he did not know the actual situation in the provinces.

He knew the country and agriculture only from films. And these films had dressed up and beautified the existing situation in agriculture. . . .

Some comrades may ask us: Where were the members of the Political Bureau of the Central Committee? Why did they not assert themselves against the cult of the individual in time? And why is this being done only now? . . .

Stalin evidently had plans to finish off the old members of the Political Bureau. He often stated that Political Bureau members should be replaced by new ones. . . .

Comrades! In order not to repeat errors of the past, the Central Committee has declared itself resolutely against the cult of the indivdual. We consider that Stalin was excessively extolled. However, in the past Stalin doubtlessly performed great services to the party, to the working class and to the international workers' movement.

This question is complicated by the fact that all this that we have just discussed was done during Stalin's life under his leadership and with his concurrence; here Stalin was convinced that this was necessary for the defense of the interests of the working classes against the plotters of the enemies and against the attack of the imperialist camp.

He saw this from the position of the interest of the working class, of the interest of the laboring people, of the interest of the victory of socialism and communism. We cannot say that these were the deeds of a giddy despot. He considered that this should be done in the interest of the party; of the working masses, in the name of the defense of the revolution's gains. In this lies the whole tragedy! . . .

Comrades: We must abolish the cult of the individual decisively, once and for all; we must draw the proper conclusions concerning both ideological-theoretical and practical work. . . .

[We must] continue systematically and consistently the work done by the party's Central Committee during the last years, a work characterized by minute observation in all party organizations, from the bottom to the top, of the Leninist principles of party leadership, characterized, above all, by the main principle of collective leadership, characterized by the observation of the norms of party life described in the statutes of our party, and finally, characterized by the wide practice of criticism and self-criticism.

Thirdly, to restore completely the Leninist principles of Soviet Socialist democracy, expressed in the Constitution of the Soviet Union, to fight willfulness of individuals abusing their power. The evil caused by acts violating revolutionary Socialist legality which have accumulated during a long time as a result of the negative influence of the cult of the individual has to be completely corrected.

Comrades! The twentieth congress of the Communist Party of the Soviet Union has manifested with a new strength the unshakable unity of our party, its cohesiveness around the Central Committee, its resolute will to accomplish the great task of building communism. (Tumultuous applause.) . . .

New York Times, June 5, 1956, pp. 13–16.

Even more serious than the Yugoslav-Soviet rift has been the more recent quarrel between Communist China and the Soviet Union. The two giants of world communism have clashed over some very fundamental issues involving their attitudes toward war and peace, revolutions, nuclear weapons and disarmament, and the mutual relations of Communist parties. We first present the Chinese Communist side of the debate, in the form of extracts from a letter sent June 14, 1963, by the Central Committee of the Chinese Communist party to the Central Committee of the Communist party of the Soviet Union. Bear in mind that references to "certain persons," "anybody," etc. are all aimed at the Soviet Communist leaders.

It is true that for several years there have been differences within the **268** international Communist movement in the understanding of, and the attitude toward, the declaration of 1957 and the statement of 1960. The central issue here is whether or not to accept the revolutionary principles of the declaration and the statement. In the last analysis, it is a question of whether or not to accept the universal truth of Marxism-Leninism, whether or not to recognize the universal significance of the road of the October Revolution, whether or not to accept the fact that the people still living under the imperialist and capitalist system, who comprise two-thirds of the world's population, need to make revolution, and whether or not to accept the fact that the people already on the Socialist road, who comprise one-third of the world's population, need to carry their revolution forward to the end. . . .

What are the revolutionary principles of the declaration and the statement? They may be summarized as follows:

Workers of all countries, unite; workers of the world, unite with the oppressed peoples and oppressed nations; oppose imperialism and reaction in all countries; strive for world peace, national liberation, people's democracy and Socialism; consolidate and expand the Socialist camp; bring the proletarian world revolution step by step to complete victory; and establish a new world without imperialism, without capitalism and without the exploitation of man by man. . . .

This general line is one of forming a broad united front, with the Socialist camp and the international proletariat as its nucleus, to oppose the imperialists and reactionaries headed by the United States; it is a line of boldly arousing the masses, expanding the revolutionary forces, winning over the middle forces and isolating the reactionary forces. . . .

If the general line of the international Communist movement is onesidedly reduced to "peaceful coexistence," "peaceful competition" and "peaceful transition," this is to violate the revolutionary principles of the 1957 declaration and the 1960 statement, to discard the historical mission of proletarian world revolution, and to depart from the revolutionary teachings of Marxism-Leninism. . . .

What are the fundamental contradictions in the contemporary world? Marxist-Leninists consistently hold that they are:

The contradiction between the Socialist camp and the imperialist camp;

The contradiction between the proletariat and the bourgeoisie in the capitalist countries;

The contradiction between the oppressed nations and imperialism; and

The contradictions among imperialist countries and among monopoly capitalist groups. . . .

These contradictions and the struggles to which they give rise are interrelated and influence each other. Nobody can obliterate any of these fundamental contradictions or subjectively substitute one for all the rest.

It is inevitable that these contradictions will give rise to popular revolutions, which alone can resolve them. . . .

The balance of forces between imperialism and socialism has undergone a fundamental change since World War II. The main indication of this change is that the world now has not just one Socialist country but a number of Socialist countries forming the mighty Socialist camp, and that the people who have taken the Socialist road now number not two hundred million but a thousand million, or a third of the world's population. . . .

It is under new historical conditions that the Communist and Workers' parties are now carrying on the task of proletarian internationalist unity and struggle. When only one Socialist country existed and when this country was faced with hostility and jeopardized by all the imperialists and reactionaries because it firmly pursued the correct Marxist-Leninist line and policies, the touchstone of proletarian internationalism for every Communist party was whether or not it resolutely defended the only Socialist country. Now there is a Socialist camp consisting of 13 countries, Albania, Bulgaria, China, Cuba, Czechoslovakia, the German Democratic Republic, Hungary, the Democratic People's Republic of Korea, Mongolia, Poland, Rumania, the Soviet Union and the Democratic Republic of Vietnam. Under these circumstances, the touchstone of proletarian internationalism for every Communist party is whether or not it resolutely defends the whole of the Socialist camp, whether or not it defends the unity of all the countries in the camp on the basis of Marxism-Leninism and whether or not it defends the Marxist-Leninist line and policies which the Socialist countries ought to pursue. . . .

Taking advantage of the situation after World War II, the United States imperialists stepped into the shoes of the German, Italian and Japanese Fascists, and have been trying to erect a huge world empire such as has never been known before. The strategic objectives of United States imperialism have been to grab and dominate the intermediate zone lying between the United States and the Socialist camp, put down the revolutions of the oppressed peoples and nations, proceed to destroy the Socialist countries, and thus to subject all the peoples and countries of the world, including its allies to domination and enslavement by United States monopoly capital. . . .

The 1960 statement points out:

"U.S. imperialism has become the biggest international exploiter."

"The United States is the mainstay of colonialism today."

"U.S. imperialism is the main force of aggression and war."

"International developments in recent years have furnished many new proofs of the fact that U.S. imperialism is the chief bulwark of world reaction and an international gendarme, that it has become an enemy of the peoples of the whole world."

United States imperialism is pressing its policies of aggression and war all over the world, but the outcome is bound to be the opposite of that intended—it will only be to hasten the awakening of the people in all countries and to hasten their revolutions.

The United States imperialists have thus placed themselves in opposition to the people of the whole world and have become encircled by them. The international proletariat must and can unite all the forces that can be united, make use of the internal contradictions in the enemy camp and establish the broadest united front against the United States imperialists and their lackeys.

The realistic and correct course is to entrust the fate of the people and of mankind to the unity and struggle of the world proletariat and to the unity and struggle of the people in all countries.

Conversely, to make no distinction between enemies, friends and ourselves and to entrust the fate of the people and of mankind to collaboration with United States imperialism is to lead people astray. The events of the last few years have exploded this illusion. . . .

The anti-imperialist revolutionary struggles of the people in Asia, Africa and Latin America are pounding and undermining the foundations of the rule of imperialism and colonialism, old and new, and are now a mighty force in defense of world peace.

In a sense, therefore, the whole cause of the international proletarian revolution hinges on the outcome of the revolutionary struggles of the people of these areas, who constitute the overwhelming majority of the world's population. . . .

Certain persons in the international Communist movement are now taking a passive or scornful or negative attitude toward the struggles of the oppressed nations for liberation. They are in fact protecting the interests of monopoly capital, betraying those of the proletariat, and degenerating into Social Democrats. . . .

Communists would always prefer to bring about the transition to Socialism by peaceful means. But can peaceful transition be made into a new world-wide strategic principle for the international Communist movement? Absolutely not.

Marxism-Leninism consistently holds that the fundamental question in all revolutions is that of state power. The 1957 declaration and the 1960 statement both clearly point out, "Leninism teaches, and experience confirms, that the ruling classes never relinquish power voluntarily." The old government never topples even in a period of crisis, unless it is pushed. This is a universal law of class struggle.

In specific historical conditions, Marx and Lenin did raise the possibility that revolution may develop peacefully. But, as Lenin pointed out, the peaceful development of revolution is an opportunity "very seldom to be met with in the history of revolution."

As a matter of fact, there is no historical precedent for peaceful transition from capitalism to Socialism. . . .

Certain persons say that revolutions are entirely possible without war. Now which type of war are they referring to—is it a war of national liberation or a revolutionary civil war, or is it a world war?

If they are referring to a war of national liberation or a revolutionary civil war, then this formulation is, in effect, opposed to revolutionary wars and to revolution.

If they are referring to a world war, then they are shooting at a non-existent target. Although Marxist-Leninists have pointed out, on the basis of the history of the two world wars, that world wars inevitably lead to revolution, no Marxist-Leninist ever has held or ever will hold that revolution must be made through world war. . . .

However, certain persons now actually hold that it is possible to bring about "a world without weapons, without armed forces and without wars." Through "general and complete disarmament" while the system of imperialism and of the exploitation of man by man still exists. This is sheer illusion. . . .

The question then is, what is the way to secure world peace? According to the Leninist viewpoint, world peace can be won only by the struggles of the people in all countries and not by begging the imperialists for it. World peace can only be effectively defended by relying on the development of the forces of the Socialist camp, on the revolutionary struggles of the proletariat and working people of all countries, on the liberation struggles of the oppressed nations and on the struggles of all peace-loving peoples and countries. . . .

In recent years, certain persons have been spreading the argument that a single spark from a war of national liberation or from a revolutionary people's war will lead to a world conflagration destroying the whole of mankind. What are the facts? Contrary to what these persons say, the wars of national liberation and the revolutionary peoples' wars that have occurred since World War II have not led to world war. The victory of these revolutionary wars has directly weakened the forces of imperialism and greatly strengthened the forces which prevent the imperialists from launching a world war and which defend world peace. Do not the facts demonstrate the absurdity of this argument? . . .

. . . However, a few years ago certain persons suddenly claimed Lenin's policy of peaceful coexistence as their own "great discovery." They maintain that they have a monopoly on the interpretation of this policy. They treat "peaceful coexistence" as if it were an all-inclusive, mystical book from heaven and attribute to it every success the people of the world achieve by struggle. What is more, they label all who disagree with their distortions of Lenin's views as opponents of peaceful coexistence, as people completely ignorant of Lenin and Leninism, and as heretics deserving to be burned at the stake.

How can the Chinese Communists agree with this view and practice? They cannot; it is impossible.

Lenin's principle of peaceful coexistence is very clear and readily comprehensible by ordinary people. Peaceful coexistence designates a relationship between countries with different social systems, and must not be interpreted as one pleases. It should never be extended to apply to the relations between oppressed and oppressor nations, between oppressed and oppressor countries or between oppressed and oppressor classes, and never be described as the main content of the transition from capitalism to Socialism, still less should it be asserted that peaceful coexistence is mankind's road to Socialism. The reason is that it is one thing to practise peaceful coexistence between countries with different social systems. It is absolutely impermissible and impossible for countries practicing peaceful coexistence to touch even a hair of each other's social system. The class struggle, the struggle for national liberation and the transition from capitalism to Socialism in various countries are quite another thing. They are all bitter, life-and-death revolutionary struggles which aim at changing the social system. Peaceful coexistence cannot replace the revolutionary struggles of the people. The transition from capitalism to Socialism in any country can only be brought about through the proletarian revolution and the dictatorship of the proletariat in that country.

In the application of the policy of peaceful coexistence, struggles between the Socialist and imperialist countries are unavoidable in the political, economic and ideological spheres, and it is absolutely impossible to have "all-round cooperation."

It is necessary for the Socialist countries to engage in negotiations of one kind or another with the imperialist countries. It is possible to reach certain agreements through negotiation by relying on the correct policies of the Socialist countries and on the pressure of the people of all countries. But necessary compromises between the Socialist countries and the imperialist countries do not require the oppressed peoples and nations to follow suit and compromise with imperialism and its lackeys. No one should ever demand in the name of peaceful coexistence that the oppressed peoples and nations should give up their revolutionary struggles. . . .

We note that in its letter of March 30 the Central Committee of the C.P.S.U. says that there are no "superior" and "subordinate" parties in the Communist movement; that all Communist parties are independent and equal, and that they should all build their relations on the basis of proletarian internationalism and mutual assistance. . . .

If the principle of independence and equality is accepted in relations among fraternal parties, then it is impermissible for any party to place itself above others, to interfere in their internal affairs, and to adopt patriarchal ways in relations with them.

If it is accepted that there are no "superiors" and "subordinates" in relations among fraternal parties, then it is impermissible to impose the program, resolutions and line of one's own party on other fraternal parties as the "common program" of the international Communist movement. . . .

A most important lesson from the experience of the international Communist movement is that the development and victory of a revolution depend on the existence of a revolutionary proletarian party.

There must be a revolutionary party.

There must be a revolutionary party built according to the revolutionary theory and revolutionary style of Marxism-Leninism.

There must be a revolutionary party able to integrate the universal truth of Marxism-Leninism with the concrete practice of the revolution in its own country.

There must be a revolutionary party able to link the leadership closely with the broad masses of the people.

There must be a revolutionary party that perseveres in the truth, corrects its errors and knows how to conduct criticism and self-criticism.

Only such a revolutionary party can lead the proletariat and the broad masses of the people in defeating imperialism and its lackeys, winning a thorough victory in the national democratic revolution and winning the Socialist revolution.

If a party is not a proletarian revolutionary party but a bourgeois reformist party;

If it is not a Marxist-Leninist party but a revisionist party;

If it is not a vanguard party of the proletariat but a party tailing after the bourgeoisie;

If it is not a party representing the interests of the proletariat and all the working people but a party representing the interests of the labor aristocracy;

If it is not an international party but a nationalist party;

If it is not a party that can use its brains to think for itself and acquire an accurate knowledge of the trends of the different classes in its own country through serious investigation and study, and knows how to apply the universal truth of Marxism-Leninism and integrate it with the concrete practice of its own country, but instead is a party that parrots the words of others, copies foreign experience without analysis, runs hither and thither in response to the baton of certain persons abroad, and has become a hodge-podge of revisionism, dogmatism and everything but Marxist-Leninist principle;

Then such a party is absolutely incapable of leading the proletariat and the masses in revolutionary struggle, absolutely incapable of winning the revolution and absolutely incapable of fulfilling the great historical mission of the proletariat. . . .

Printed in English in the Chinese weekly *Peking Review* and reprinted by the *New York Times*, July 5, 1963, pp. 6–9.

One month after the Chinese Communist party published its indictment, the Soviet Communist party addressed an Open Letter to all Communist organizations in the Soviet Union, in which it presented its reply to the Chinese Communist charges. This statement summarizes the policy of Khrushchev and his supporters which is known by the Soviet phrase "peaceful coexistence."

269   Dear Comrades,

The CPSU Central Committee deems it necessary to address an open letter to you in order to set out its position on fundamental questions of the international communist movement in connection with the letter of the Central Committee of the Communist Party of China of June 14, 1963.

The Soviet people are well aware that our Party and Government, expressing the will of the entire Soviet people, spare no efforts to strengthen fraternal friendship with the peoples of all socialist countries, with the Chinese people. We are united by common struggle for the victory of communism; we have the same aim, the same aspirations and hopes. . . .

All who read the letter of the CPC Central Committee will see—behind the fine phrases about unity and cohesion—unfriendly, slanderous attacks on our Party and the Soviet country, a striving to play down the historic significance of our people's struggle for the victory of communism in the USSR, for the triumph of peace and socialism throughout the world. This document is full of charges, overt and covert, against the CPSU and the Soviet Union. . . .

What is the essence of the difficulties between the CPC, on the one hand, and the CPSU and the international communist movement on the other? This question will undoubtedly be asked by anyone who familiarizes himself with the June 14 letter of the CPC Central Committee. . . .

The CPSU Central Committee considers it its duty to tell the Party and the people, with all frankness, that on questions of war and peace the CPC leadership has cardinal differences, based on principle, with us, with the world communist movement. The essence of these differences lies in the diametrically opposite approach to such vital problems as the possibility of averting a world thermonuclear war, peaceful coexistence of states with different social systems, the interconnection between the struggle for peace and the development of the world revolutionary movement.

Our Party—in the decisions of the 20th and 22nd Congresses—and the world communist movement—in the Declaration and Statement—placed before Communists as a task of extreme importance that of struggling for peace, for averting a world thermonuclear catastrophe. We appraise the world balance of forces realistically and hence draw the conclusion that although the nature of imperialism has not changed and the danger of beginning a war has not been averted, the forces of peace, of which the mighty community of socialist states is the main bulwark, can—under modern conditions—avert a new world war through their joint efforts.

We also soberly appraise the radical, qualitative change of the means of waging war and, consequently, its potential consequences. Nuclear rocket weapons, created in the middle of our century, changed old concepts about war. These weapons possess an unheard-of devastating force. Suffice it to say that the explosion of only one powerful thermonuclear bomb surpasses the explosive force of all ammunition used during all previous wars, including World Wars I and II. And many thousands of such bombs have been accumulated. . . .

The historic task of Communists is to organize and be in the forefront of the struggle of the peoples for averting a world thermonuclear war.

To prevent a new world war is quite a realistic and feasible task. The 20th Congress of our Party came to the extremely important conclusion that in our time there is no fatal inevitability of war between states. This conclusion is not the fruit of good intentions but the result of a realistic, strictly scientific analysis of the balance of class forces in the world arena; it is based on the gigantic might of world socialism. Our views on this question are shared by the whole world communist movement. "A world war can be averted"; "a real possibility of excluding world war from the life of society will emerge even before the complete victory of socialism on earth, while capitalism remains in part of the world," the Statement stresses.

Under this Statement there also stands the signature of the Chinese comrades.

And what is the position of the CPC leadership? What can the propositions they disseminate mean: an end cannot be put to wars as long as imperialism exists; peaceful coexistence is an illusion, it is not the general principle of foreign policy of the socialist countries; struggle for peace hinders revolutionary struggle?

These propositions mean that the Chinese comrades are acting contrary to the general course of the world communist movement on questions of war and peace. They do not believe in the possibility of preventing a new world war; they underestimate the forces of peace and socialism and over-estimate the forces of imperialism, and actually ignore the mobilization of the masses in the struggle against the war danger. . . .

The Chinese comrades obviously underestimate all of the danger of a thermonuclear war. "The atomic bomb is a paper tiger," it "is not terrible at all," they contend. The main thing, they say, is to put an end to imperialism as quickly as possible, but how and with what losses this will be achieved seems to be a secondary question. For whom, it may be asked, is it a secondary question? Is it for the hundreds of millions of people who are doomed to death in the event a thermonuclear war is unleashed? Is it for the states that will be razed from the face of the earth in the very first hours of such a war?

No one, not even the big states, has the right to play with the destinies of millions of people. Those who do not want to exert efforts so as to exclude world war from the life of the peoples, to avert the mass annihilation of people and the destruction of the values of human civilization, deserve condemnation. . . .

Apparently, the people who refer to the thermonuclear weapon as a "paper tiger" are not fully aware of the destructive force of this weapon. . . .

. . .If both the exploiters and the exploited are buried under the ruins of the old world, who will build the "wonderful future"? . . .

The CPSU Central Committee declares that we have pursued and will continue to pursue the Leninist policy of peaceful coexistence. In this our Party sees its duty both to the Soviet people and to the peoples of all other countries. To ensure peace means to contribute most effectively to the consolidation of the socialist system and, consequently, to the growth of its influence on the entire course of the liberation struggle, on the world revolutionary process.

The profound difference in the views of the CPSU and other Marxist-Leninist Parties, on the one hand, and the CPC leaders on the other hand, on the questions of war, peace and peaceful coexistence, was manifested with particular clarity during the 1962 crisis in the Caribbean Sea. It was a sharp international crisis; never before did mankind come so close to the brink of a thermonuclear war as it did last October.

The Chinese comrades claim that in the period of the Caribbean crisis we made an "adventurist" mistake by supplying rockets to Cuba and then, allegedly, "capitulated" to American imperialism when we withdrew the rockets from Cuba. (Such allegations were made in the leading article in Jenmin Jihpao on March 8, 1963, "On the Statement of the Communist Party of the USA.")

Such assertions utterly contradict the facts.

What was the actual state of affairs? The CPSU Central Committee and the Soviet Government possessed trustworthy information that an armed aggression by United States imperialism against Cuba was to start shortly. We realized, with sufficient clarity, that to rebuff aggression, to defend the Cuban Revolution effectively, we had to take the most resolute measures. Curses and warnings—even if they are called "serious warnings" and are repeated two hundred fifty times—have no effect on the imperialists. . . .

Inasmuch as the point at issue was not simply a conflict between the United States and Cuba but a clash between two major nuclear powers, the crisis in the area of the Caribbean Sea would have turned from a local into a world clash. A real danger of a world thermonuclear war arose.

In the prevailing situation there were two alternatives: either to follow in the wake of the "madmen" (that is what the most aggressive and reactionary representatives of American imperialism are called) and embark upon the road of unleashing a world thermonuclear war or, using the opportunities afforded by the delivery of missiles, to take all measures to reach agreement on the peaceful solution of the crisis and to prevent aggression against the Cuban Republic.

We chose, as is known, the second road and we are convinced that we did the right thing. . . .

We live in an epoch when there are two worlds, two systems—socialism and imperialism. It would be absurd to think that all questions inevitably arising in relations between the countries of these two systems must be solved only by force of arms, ruling out all talks and agreements. Wars would never end then. We are against such an approach.

The Chinese comrades argue that the imperialists cannot be trusted in anything, that they will definitely deceive. But this is not a case of faith, but rather of sober calculation. Eight months have elapsed since the liquidation of the crisis in the Caribbean area, and the United States Government is keeping its word—there is no invasion of Cuba. We too assumed a commitment to remove our missiles from Cuba, and we have fulfilled it.

But it should also not be forgotten that we have also made a commitment to the Cuban people: if the U.S. imperialists do not keep their promise and invade Cuba, we shall come to the assistance of the Cuban people. Every sober-minded person well understands that in the event of an aggression by American imperialists we shall come to the assistance of the Cuban people from Soviet territory, just as we would have helped them from Cuban territory, too. True, in this case the rockets would be in flight slightly longer, but this would not impair their precision. . . .

The struggle for peace, for peaceful coexistence, is organically linked with the revolutionary struggle against imperialism. "In conditions of peaceful coexistence," the 81 Communist Parties stated, "favorable opportunities are created for the development of class struggle in capitalist countries and of the national liberation movement of the peoples in colonial and dependent countries. In turn, the successes of the revolutionary class struggle and national liberation struggle help strengthen peaceful coexistence." . . .

The next important question on which we differ is that of the ways and methods of the revolutionary struggle of the working class in the countries of capitalism, the struggle for national liberation, and the paths of transition by all mankind to socialism.

As depicted by the Chinese comrades, the differences on this question are manifested as follows: one side—they themselves—stands for a world revolution, while the other side—the CPSU, the Marxist-Leninist parties— has forgotten the revolution, even "fears" it and, instead of revolutionary struggle, displays concern for such things "unworthy" of a genuine revolutionary as peace, the economic development of socialist countries and improvement of the living standards of their peoples, struggle for the democratic rights and vital interests of the working people of capitalist countries. . . .

Everyone who has pondered the meaning of the present struggle for peace, against a thermonuclear war, realizes that by their policy of peace the Soviet Communists, and the fraternal parties of the other socialist countries, are giving inestimable aid to the working class, to the working people of capitalist countries. And this is not only because prevention of a nuclear war means saving from death the working class, the peoples of whole countries and even continents, although this alone is enough to justify our policy.

The other reason is that this policy is the best way of helping the international revolutionary working-class movement achieve its principal class aims. Is it not a tremendous contribution to the working-class struggle when, in conditions of peace they themselves have achieved, the socialist countries score brilliant successes in economic development, attain ever new achievements in science and technology, constantly improve the living and working conditions of the people, and develop and improve socialist democracy? . . .

V. I. Lenin taught that "we exert our main influence on the international revolution by our economic policy. In this field the struggle is waged on a world-wide scale. If we accomplish this task, we shall win on an international scale, finally and forever" (Works, Vol. 32, page 413, Russian edition).

This behest of the great Lenin has been firmly mastered by Soviet Communists. It is followed by Communists of other socialist countries. But now it turns out that there are comrades who have decided that Lenin was wrong.

What is this—lack of faith in the ability of the countries of socialism to defeat capitalism in economic competition? Or is this the position of people who, having encountered difficulties in building socialism, have become disappointed, fail to see the possibility of exerting the main influence on the international revolutionary movement by their economic successes, by the example of the successful building of socialism in their countries? They want to achieve the revolution sooner by other ways they regard as shorter. But a victorious revolution can consolidate its successes and prove the superiority of socialism over capitalism by the work of the people, and only by this. True, this is not easy, especially if the revolutions are accomplished in countries that have inherited an underdeveloped economy. But the example of the Soviet Union and of many other socialist countries proves convincingly that under these conditions, too, if correct leadership is given, it is possible to score great successes and demonstrate to the entire world the superiority of socialism over capitalism.

Furthermore, what situation is more propitious for the revolutionary struggle of the working class in capitalist countries—a situation of peace and peaceful coexistence, or a situation of constant international tension and the cold war?

There is no doubt as to the answer to this question. Who is not aware of the fact that the ruling circles of imperialist states use the cold war situation to fan chauvinism, war hysteria, unbridled anti-communism, to put in power the most rabid reactionaries and profascists, abolish democracy, do away with political parties, trade unions and other mass organizations of the working class. . . .

The Chinese comrades haughtily and humiliatingly accuse the Communist Parties of France, Italy, the United States and other countries of nothing less than opportunism and reformism, of "parliamentary cretinism," and even of sliding back to "bourgeois socialism." On what grounds? On the ground that these Communist Parties do not advance the slogan for an immediate proletarian revolution, although the Chinese leaders too must realize that this cannot be done without the existence of a revolutionary situation.

Every well-versed Marxist-Leninist knows that to advance a slogan for an armed uprising, when there is no revolutionary situation in the country, means to doom the working class to defeat. . . .

The Marxist-Leninist parties have determined their common line, the main provisions of which amount to the following:

The nature and substance of the world revolutionary process in the present epoch is determined by the merging into struggle against imperialism of the peoples building socialism and communism, the revolutionary movement of the working class in the capitalist countries, the national liberation struggle of the oppressed peoples, the general democratic movements; in the alliance of the anti-imperialist revolutionary forces, the decisive role belongs to the international working class and its main offspring— the world system of socialism, which exerts its principal influence on the development of the world socialist system by force of its example, by its economic construction;

Due to prevailing objective historical conditions (extreme growth of the aggressiveness of imperialism, emergence of weapons of tremendous destructive power, etc.) the central place among all tasks facing the anti-imperialist forces in the present epoch is held by the struggle to prevent a thermonuclear war. The primary task of the Communist Parties is to rally all peaceloving forces to the defense of peace, to save mankind from a nuclear catastrophe;

The socialist revolution is effected as a result of the internal development of class struggle in every country, and its forms and roads are determined by the concrete conditions of each given country. The general law is the revolutionary overthrow of the power of capital and establishment of the dictatorship of the proletariat in one or another form. It is the task of the working class and the Communist Parties to make maximum use of the opportunities now available for a peaceful road of the socialist revolution, not connected with civil war, and at the same time to be ready for a non-peaceful method, for the armed suppression of the resistance of the bour-geoisie; the general democratic struggle is an indispensable part of the struggle for socialism; . . .

The Chinese leaders are undermining the unity not only of the socialist camp but of the entire world communist movement as well, trampling under foot the principles of proletarian internationalism and grossly violating the norms of relations between fraternal parties. . . .

Open Letter of CPSU Central Committee to All Party Organizations and All Communists of the Soviet Union, July 14, 1963 (New York: Crosscurrents Press, 1963).

On February 14, 1958, the Polish government circulated a memorandum concerning the creation of an atom free zone in Central Europe. This memorandum became known as the Rapacki plan, named after the Polish foreign minister. It did attract much attention in the West, especially in England, and has remained a goal of the foreign policy of the Communist block.

On October 2, 1957, the Government of the Polish People's Republic **270** presented to the General Assembly of the United Nations a proposal concerning the establishment of a denuclearised zone in Central Europe. The Governments of Czechoslovakia and of the German Democratic Republic declared their readiness to accede to that zone.

The Government of the Polish People's Republic proceeded with the conviction that the establishment of the proposed denuclearised zone could lead to an improvement in the international atmosphere and facilitate broader discussions on disarmament as well as the solution of other controversial international issues, while the continuation of nuclear armaments and making them universal could only lead to a further solidifying of the division of Europe into opposing blocs and to a further complication of the situation, especially in Central Europe.

In December 1957, the Government of the Polish People's Republic renewed their proposal through diplomatic channels.

Considering the wide repercussions which the Polish initiative has evoked and taking into account the proposition emerging from the discussion which has developed on this proposal, the Government of the Polish People's Republic hereby present a more detailed elaboration of their proposal, which may facilitate the opening of negotiations and reaching of an agreement on this subject.

I. The proposed zone should include the territory of: Poland, Czechoslovakia, German Democratic Republic and German Federal Republic. In this territory nuclear weapons would neither be manufactured nor stockpiled, the equipment and installations designed for their servicing would not be located there, the use of nuclear weapons against the territory of this zone would be prohibited.

II. The contents of the obligations arising from the establishment of the denuclearised zone would be based upon the following premises:

1. The States included in this zone would undertake the obligation not to manufacture, maintain or import for their own use and not to permit the location on their territories of nuclear weapons of any type, as well as not to install on or to admit to their territories of installations and equipment designed for servicing nuclear weapons, including missile-launching equipment.

2. The four Powers (France, United States, Great Britain and U.S.S.R.) would undertake the following obligations:

a) Not to maintain nuclear weapons in the armaments of their forces stationed on the territories of States included in this zone; neither to maintain nor to install on the territories of these States any installations or equipment designed for servicing nuclear weapons, including missile-launching equipment.

b) Not to transfer in any manner and under any reason whatsoever, nuclear weapons or installations and equipment designed for servicing nuclear weapons, to governments or other organs in this area.

3. The Powers which have at their disposal nuclear weapons should undertake the obligation not to use these weapons against the territory of the zone or against any targets situated in this zone.

Thus the Powers would undertake the obligation to respect the status of the zone as an area in which there should be no nuclear weapons and against which nuclear weapons should not be used.

4. Other States, whose forces are stationed on the territory of any state included in the zone, would also undertake the obligation not to maintain nuclear weapons in the armaments of these forces and not to transfer such weapons to Governments or to other organs in this area. Neither will they install equipment or installations designed for the servicing of nuclear weapons, including missiles-launching equipment, on the territories of States in the zone nor will they transfer them to Governments or other organs in this area.

The manner and procedure for the implementation of these obligations could be the subject of detailed mutual stipulations.

III. 1. In order to ensure the effectiveness and the implementation of the obligations contained in part II, para 1–2 and 4, the States concerned would undertake to create a system of broad and effective control in the area of the proposed zone and submit themselves to its functioning.

The system could comprise ground as well as aerial control. Adequate control posts, with rights and possibilities of action which would ensure the effectiveness of inspection, could also be established.

The details and forms of the implementation of control can be agreed upon on the basis of the experience acquired up to the present time in this field, as well as on the basis of proposals submitted by various States in the course of the disarmament negotiations, in the form and to the extent in which they can be adapted to the area of the zone.

The system of control established for the denuclearised zone could provide useful experiences for the realization of broader disarmament agreement.

2. For the purpose of supervising the implementation of the proposed obligations an adequate control machinery should be established. There could participate in it, for example, representatives appointed (not excluding *ad personam* appointments) by organs of the North Atlantic Treaty Organization and of the Warsaw Treaty. Nationals or representatives of States, which do not belong to any military grouping in Europe, could also participate in it.

IV. The procedure of the establishment, operation and reporting of the control organs can be the subject of further mutual stipulations.

The most simple form of embodying the obligations of States included in the zone would be the conclusion of an appropriate international convention. To avoid, however, complications, which some States might find in such a solution, it can be arranged that:

1. These obligations be embodied in the form of four unilateral declarations, bearing the character of an international obligation, deposited with a mutually agreed upon depository State;

2. The obligations of Great Powers be embodied in the form of a mutual document or unilateral declarations (as mentioned above in para 1);

3. The obligations of other States, whose armed forces are stationed in the area of the zone, be embodied in the form of unilateral declarations (as mentioned above in para 1).

On the basis of the above proposals the Government of the Polish People's Republic suggest to initiate negotiations for the purpose of a further detailed elaboration of the plan for the establishment of the denuclearised zone, of the documents and guarantees related to it as well as of the means of implementation of the undertaken obligations. . . .

Polish Information Service.

On behalf of the German Federal Republic foreign minister Von Brentano replied to the Rapacki plan. He did this in a speech before the Bundestag, the Federal parliament (January 24, 1958).

271   In the opinion of the Federal Government, this sort of isolated move would not diminish world tension and would not increase the chances of genuine, broadly designed and controlled disarmament.

Quite to the contrary: first, a step of this kind could be taken at all only under the condition of the recognition of the Soviet occupation zone as a partner in negotiations and agreement; it may even be assumed that the project has been put forth precisely in order to achieve this aim for which the Soviet Union has been insistently striving for a long time. Besides, this proposal is neither new, nor surprising. . . . What is more, the adoption of this proposal would be bound to lead, and such is precisely the aim of the proposal, to the withdrawal of the troops of our allies from Germany. I have already mentioned that probably no one believes seriously that we could maintain these troops on German territory and on the threatened frontier if we wanted to forbid them to possess adequate defense means. To this should be added that by such partial solution of the question we would decisively weaken the defence potential of the West in comparison with the aggressive potential of the East. As concerns the Soviet Union which boasts of the fact that it possesses long range rockets, the realization of this proposal not only would not prevent it from carrying out an attack, but would rather encourage it to do so, for then the U.S.S.R. would not have to fear to the same degree as at present a direct reaction. One would have to do all this despite the fact that in doing so we would not make one step forward in the direction of alleviating tension, of disarmament, of solving the German problem. Neither would it diminish the danger to which we are exposed in connection with the possibility of a recourse to weapons of mass annihilation.

Bulletin des Presse—und Informationsdienstes der Bundesregierung, 24, I, 1958.

Five years before the Rapacki plan the Federal Chancellor, Konrad Adenauer, had rejected the neutralization of Germany and based his policy upon the European Defense Community (EDC). Though the EDC never came about, the general guidelines of this policy remained in tact. Thus this speech made in Paris (December 11, 1953) still fixes the position of the German Federal Republic.

A necessary precondition of European integration is the European Defence Community. Why? Because it is thereby made impossible for one partner of the Community to wage war against another. None of the partners will have it in its power any longer to destroy the Community when there are not more national armies but only one European army.

This is the main object of the EDC: to render impossible for all time war among European states, especially any war between France and Germany. Speaking as German Federal Chancellor, I solemnly and formally declare: it is the most ardent desire of all of us to create a lasting partnership between Germany and France, to render forever impossible a war between these two countries which are and will continue to be neighbours. I emphasize and repeat: the most ardent desire of us all.

Owing to the development in foreign policy the talk is, unfortunately, too often only of the 12 German divisions which are needed for the defence against the East, while much too little is said of the far greater objectives of the EDC, reaching far into the future, to which I have just referred.

You know, ladies and gentlemen, that Soviet Russia has proposed the neutralization of Germany. This proposal has met with the approval of some politicians, of politicians who look upon a rearmed Germany as a threat to her neighbours. I shall discuss the question of the neutralization of Germany with all candour but also with requisite thoroughness.

Neutralization is not the same thing as neutrality. A neutral country like Switzerland of its own free will wants to be neutral, and it puts itself in a position to defend this neutrality against any third party. A neutralized country, on the other hand, is forcibly deprived of its right to arm itself. Neutralization can only be based on compulsion and therefore bears in it the germ of transience. In due course it will fail because of two factors: for one thing because of the resolution and the resistance of the coerced people, and for another because of the gradually weakening interest or the disagreement of the states enforcing neutralization.

And now, look at the situation which would in fact arise if Germany were to be neutralized. I do not want to go into details, but I must say two sentences. I do not think that the United States will keep forces in Germany permanently in order to maintain Germany's neutralization. Nor do I think that the United Kingdom would do so. But then it will be Soviet Russia which takes over the lead in the control of Germany. Does anyone in the world doubt that in this case Germany would be turned into a Russian satellite state within the shortest time by means of subversion, bribery and coercion? And this in turn would spell such an increase of power for Soviet Russia as would be dangerous and therefore intolerable to the free nations.

If Germany should succumb to Communism, this would naturally give an impulse to Communism in the other Western European countries sufficient to seal the fate of the countries neighbouring on Germany. No, ladies and gentlemen, the neutralization of Germany means the victory of Communism, the victory of Soviet Russia over Western Europe. The policy constantly pursued by Soviet Russia, namely, to secure preponderance in war potential over the remaining nations of the free world, particularly the United States and the United Kingdom, would thus have attained its object.

But the people do want peace, all the nations want peace, all would be glad if they could use the huge sums they now have to spend on armaments for raising the standard of living, for works of culture. In view of the deeply rooted distrust of one nation for another, will it ever be possible to obtain disarmament and a lasting peace? I am firmly convinced that it is possible.

It may be that one day the Soviet Union will yet become convinced that she is not threatened by others and thus it would therefore be wiser and better not to devote her efforts and resources to the preparation of war on such a scale as to cause scarcity of consumer goods and farm produce and to become too heavy a burden on her population. The Soviet Union knows that she must provide new arable land on a large scale in order to feed her constantly growing population. She realizes that it is impossible for her to create an optimum of armaments and at the same time to increase agricultural production, the output of consumer goods and her arable surface. We are fully justified in making these factors the basis of our hope that the Soviet Union—once she is freed from fear of aggression—will be ready for negotiations promising success, concerning the establishment of peace. You have read the harrowing statements made by President Eisenhower when he addressed the General Assembly of the United Nations on 8 December 1953 on the dangers of atomic warfare. You have also read the magnificent proposals which he made to preserve mankind from utter annihilation through atomic warfare.

We all can only wish and hope that Soviet Russia, to whom these proposals are addressed in the first place, will give them serious consideration, and that agreement and disarmament will be brought about on the basis of these or similar proposals. If this can be achieved, peace will be secured.

For Europe—Peace and Freedom (German Government Information Service).

The first five years after the war had been a period of economic recovery and reconstruction. In the 1950's the European economies, both capitalist and socialist, experienced rapid growth, and in each bloc plans were put forward for economic integration to promote further development.

In the West, the Schuman Plan (260) had set the pattern and enunciated the goals for programs of economic co-operation. In 1957 the same six nations joined in a more ambitious effort, the formation of the European Economic Community, or Common Market. The essential feature of the EEC was to be a customs union among the six, with free trade inside the union and a common tariff for trade with countries outside it. The hope of the founders was that the Common Market would be the first step toward full economic co-operation and the eventual achievement of a united Europe.

The treaty initiating the Common Market, part of which is given here, was signed at Rome on March 25, 1957.

Article 1

By the present Treaty, the HIGH CONTRACTING PARTIES establish **273** among themselves a EUROPEAN ECONOMIC COMMUNITY.

Article 2

It shall be the aim of the Community, by establishing a Common Market and progressively approximating the economic policies of Member States, to promote throughout the Community a harmonious development of economic activities, a continuous and balanced expansion, an increased stability, an accelerated raising of the standard of living and closer relations between its Member States.

Article 3

For the purposes set out in the preceding Article, the activities of the Community shall include, under the conditions and with the timing provided for in this Treaty:

(a) the elimination, as between Member States, of customs duties and of quantitative restrictions in regard to the importation and exportation of goods, as well as of all other measures with equivalent effect;

(b) the establishment of a common customs tariff and a common commercial policy towards third countries;

(c) the abolition, as between Member States, of the obstacles to the free movement of persons, services and capital. . . .

Article 8

1. The Common Market shall be progressively established in the course of a transitional period of twelve years.

The transitional period shall be divided into three stages of four years each. . . .

Article 38

1. The Common Market shall extend to agriculture and trade in agricultural products. . . .

Article 110

By establishing a customs union between themselves the Member States intend to contribute, in conformity with the common interest, to the harmonious development of world trade, the progressive abolition of restrictions on international exchanges and the lowering of customs barriers. . . .

Article 240

This Treaty shall be concluded for an unlimited period.

Intergovernmental Conference on the Common Market and EURATOM, *Treaty establishing the European Economic Community* . . . (Brussels, 1957).

The proponents of the Common Market had originally conceived it as a broad union including all the members of the Organization for European Economic Co-operation (to which nearly every country in Western Europe belonged). As it actually emerged, the EEC was a much narrower grouping. After it was formed, there was a period of negotiation concerning a possible trade link between it and the non-member states, chiefly the United Kingdom; but the problems raised by Britain's economic ties with the Commonwealth nations, and the opposition of the new French government of President de Gaulle, brought these talks to an end in November, 1958. The British responded by creating a second organization, a looser and more limited trade association of a number of nations not participating in the Common Market—the "outer seven." Unlike the EEC, the new European Free Trade Association covered only trade in industrial products, established no common external tariff, and was not regarded as the basis of any permanent or far-reaching set of institutions. Its character is indicated by these extracts from the documents which established it, signed at Stockholm on November 20, 1959.

I. *Communique Issued at Stockholm, 20th November, 1959.*

On behalf of their Governments, Ministers from Austria, Denmark, **274** Norway, Portugal, Sweden, Switzerland and the United Kingdom have today initialled at Stockholm the text of a Convention establishing the European Free Trade Association, to consist of the seven founding members together with any other countries which may accede to it.

The purposes of the Association are economic expansion, full employment, the rational use of resources, financial stability and a higher standard of living.

The convention will establish a free market between the members of the Association. This will be achieved by the abolition of tariffs and other obstacles to trade in the industrial products of members over a period of ten years, or earlier if so decided. Each country will be free to decide its own external tariffs.

Freer trade between the participating countries will stimulate competition and economic expansion. . . .

II. *Resolution.*

. . . The existence of two groups, the European Free Trade Association and the European Economic Community, inspired by different but not incompatible principles, implies the risk that further progress along these lines be hampered, if such a danger could not be avoided by an agreement to which all countries interested in European economic co-operation could subscribe. . . .

. . . [T]he seven Governments who will sign the Convention establishing the European Free Trade Association, declare their determination to do all in their power to avoid a new division in Europe. They regard their Association as a step toward an agreement between all member countries of E.E.C.

To this end the seven Governments are ready to initiate negotiations with the members of the E.E.C. as soon as they are prepared to do so. . . .

Parliamentary Papers (House of Commons and Command), Session 1959–1960, XXXIV; Cmnd. 906.

The hope expressed at Stockholm of a *rapprochement* between the EEC and the EFTA blocs had not, by 1963, been fulfilled. A round of negotiations in which Britain sought membership in the EEC broke down, in late January, 1963, for essentially the same reasons that had led to the failure of the earlier discussions. In the remarks below, which were made by Dr. Walter Hallstein, President of the EEC's Commission, in the months following the rejection of British entry, the ideals of the Common Market are reiterated, and its political and economic character as a federation of competitive, capitalist nations is outlined.

275   . . . Today, the European Community is very much in the news, simply because it has . . . had to face a crisis in its development.

. . . I need not remind you that on January 29, 1963, the negotiations for Great Britain's membership in the European Economic Community had to be suspended . . . .

The crisis . . . is something that will pass. It is not the first setback that the European cause has encountered, nor will it be the last. What I wish to speak about is something more concrete, something that must and will endure. That is—European unification itself, in the real and concrete form of the European Community, which is and remains its only true expression.

. . . [T]he negotiations helped shed the light upon what the Community is. This was true in both the economic and the political sense. . . .

Let us take the economic questions first. It has been said more than once that a customs union—which is the basis of the Community's Common Market—logically involves economic union also. To enjoy the full benefits of a customs union, one must abolish not only the classical barriers to trade among its members, but also less obvious distortions and restrictions of competition. If the movement of goods is to be freed, so must current payments; if the result is to be the more economic relocation of resources, investment capital and manpower must be liberalized, too. With free movement of goods and of the factors of production, common rules of competition must be applied, and separate national policies in many fields—social, economic, and monetary—begin to make less and less sense. Branches of the economy where competition alone is insufficient must likewise be subject to common policies—to coordinate transportation, to aid and modernize farming, or to develop backward areas.

Economically, therefore, the Common Market involves a customs union and an economic union. . . .

In [the] second, . . . political sense, too, the negotiation helped shed light upon the nature of the Community. Already it is clear that with such a degree of economic union as the Common Market involves, what is really being achieved is political union in the economic field; for what is being integrated is not the action of businessmen or trade unionists, but the role of national governments in fixing the framework within which such action takes place. The acceptance of this process requires a high degree of political commitment. It requires a commitment to a whole new system in European politics, a system which has turned its back resolutely upon the past.

At the end of World War II, the peoples of Europe, victors and vanquished alike, faced two essential and parallel tasks. The first was to recover from the economic bankruptcy into which war had plunged them; the second, even more fundamental, was to find a way out of the calamitous political bankruptcy of the old order in Europe—the order based upon the balance of power. . . . [T]he bankruptcy of this balance of power system, for the second time in a generation, had involved the world in war. Europeans of every shade of political opinion were determined that it must never happen again. . . .

The turning point came on May 9, 1950, with the famous Declaration made by the French Foreign Minister, Robert Schuman. . . .

What Schuman proposed, in brief, was to substitute for the balance of power the progressive fusion of interests. This would enable Europe once more to stand on its own feet, both economically and politically. It would meet the challenge of size that faces all of us in the present stage of modern technology. It would give Europe the power to act and to play its part in the building of a better world. Above all, it would be a decisive rejection of an old, precarious, and unstable system which had led to such destruction and misery. . . .

From what I have already said it follows that we must not regard the European Community as simply a new power bloc or a new coalition. It is not, in my view, just the magnification of nineteenth-century nationalism to a more than national scale. It is the embodiment of a new method and a new approach to the relations between states. This method is not merely international, nor yet fully federal; but, while it is not some brand of "Instant Federalism," it is an attempt to build on a federal pattern a democratically constituted Europe. Essentially, the Community may be described as a federation in the making.

. . . It should be clear from what I have said that I cannot regard the suspension of the negotiations as the end of a chapter, or, at least, as the end of the book.

... [J]ust as the British government has pledged itself not to turn its back on Europe, so our own ideals and principles demand that we should not turn our backs on Great Britain. ...

... I know that our work will be very much harder in the months to come. What I am pleading for is the gradual, dogged, determined accomplishment of our original aims: the transformation of the old nationalist Europe, the fusion of interests, the creation of solidarity, the end of hegemony, the submergence of selfish ambitions, the death of suspicion and fear. To these goals there is one route already mapped out, although others may follow. That route is the Treaty of Rome. In pleading that we respect both its letter and its spirit, I am pleading for the European idea. ...

Reprinted from the *Political Science Quarterly*, Volume 78, No. 2, June 1963, pp. 162, 163, 165, 166, 168, 174, 175, 176.

... Another point I should like to mention ... is that of longer-term forecasting. ... [O]ur Community has a federal structure. Not even the most enthusiastic Europeans ever aimed at a centralist European State. ... Nobody is thinking of using these longer-term forecasts to introduce a kind of planned economy or centrally administered economy such as Eucken had in mind, or an economy on the eastern model. To put it in other words: nobody intends to let *"dirigisme"* triumph in the Community. Nobody is thinking of making such programmes binding upon the individual entrepreneur. Where such programmes are elaborated they bind only those who draw them up, in the same way as a Government declaration of policy or a party programme binds that Government or that party. ...

"1963—Year of Trial," speech given in Frankfurt/Main, at the annual meeting of the Federal Association of German Newspaper Publishers, July 4, 1963.

Meanwhile, in the very different economies of Eastern Europe, efforts toward economic co-operation were also underway. In 1949, the Soviet Union and the newly socialist nations of Eastern Europe had formed the Council for Mutual Economic Assistance (often referred to as COMECON). During its first years, when intensive industrialization was just getting started in some of the member countries and there were substantial differences in their respective levels of development, the role of this body was largely limited to technical assistance and minimal coordination of trade. But by the early 1960's COMECON was being viewed increasingly as a medium for economic integration, leading ultimately to a unified communist economy embracing all these nations and operating under a single plan. At the same time, the original program of comprehensive industrialization of each country was giving way to the goal of specialization within the bloc, although this met some resistance from members such as Rumania, where heavy industry received less emphasis than previously. In the resolution adopted by the June, 1962, conference of COMECON, the new policy was set forth; this document, while still asserting the primacy of heavy industry in each economy, stresses the principle of regional specialization.

BASIC PRINCIPLES OF INTERNATIONAL SOCIALIST DIVISION OF **276** LABOUR

The world socialist system is a social, economic and political community of free, sovereign nations following the path of socialism and communism, united by common interests and goals and by indestructible ties of international socialist solidarity. . . .

The community of the socialist countries is based on the existence in all of them of an identical economic foundation—public ownership of the means of production; an identical political system—the power of the people headed by the working class; and an identical ideology—Marxism-Leninism. . . .

The main road to still higher socialist economic levels lies through each socialist country combining its economic development efforts with the joint effort to consolidate and expand economic co-operation and mutual assistance between all the members of the socialist camp.

There exist and are being perfected a variety of forms of economic co-operation and mutual assistance between the socialist countries: co-ordination of national economic plans, production specialization and co-operation, international socialist trade, credits, technical assistance, scientific and technical co-operation, co-operation in economic projects, development of natural resources, etc. . . .

Stronger and broader economic ties between the socialist countries will promote the objective trend, noted by V. I. Lenin, towards a future world communist economy regulated by the victorious working people according to a single plan.

A new type of international division of labour is being born out of the economic, scientific and technical co-operation between the socialist countries. . . .

The objectives of international socialist division of labour are more efficient social production, a higher rate of economic growth, higher living standards for the working people in all the socialist countries, industrialization and gradual removal of historical differences in the economic development levels of the socialist countries, and the creation of a material basis for their more or less simultaneous transition to communism, within one and the same historical era. . . .

The experience of the world socialist economic system has shown that at the present stage co-ordination of national economic plans is the principal means for extending international socialist division of labour and pooling the productive efforts of the socialist countries. . . .

Further improvement of international socialist division of labour on the basis of plan co-ordination calls for accelerated development of such advanced forms as specialization and co-operation of production within the socialist camp. Interstate specialization implies concentrating production of similar products in one or several socialists countries so as to meet the needs of all interested countries, thus improving industrial techniques and management, and establishing stable economic ties and co-operation. International specialization should serve to expand production, reduce costs, raise productivity and improve quality and technical standards. . . .

International specialization and co-operation are potent economic factors in the development of all industries, especially engineering, chemicals, ferrous and non-ferrous metallurgy. . . .

New Times (Moscow), July 4, 1962.

The recovery of France from the disasters of the war was quick and real, except in the political field. There, both at home and in the colonies, the ineptitude which had characterized the Third Republic pervaded the Fourth. From the uncertainties and frustrations entailed, General de Gaulle rose to the top in May of 1958, by way of a legalized *coup d'état*. Constitutionally he was not long thereafter elected president of the Fifth Republic; in actuality he became a sort of uncrowned king with few limits on his authority. Out of an artful use of a combination of circumstances—business prosperity in France, liquidation of costly and humiliating colonial ties abroad, establishment of a friendly *modus vivendi* with Germany, continuing lethargy in Britain, embarrassing disputes in the Communist world, and indirection in America—General de Gaulle found the elements for an attempted reassertion of French leadership in Europe. The following sections from his remarks at a press conference are not in the flowing and dramatic prose which mark his public addresses, nor do they so clearly reveal the asperity of his longer statements about the presumed unreliability of the United States and Britain from the continental position. They do, however, contain a tight and lucid summary of his views. Should he have his way, the destiny of Europe west of the Iron Curtain, through the loosest of associations, would be directed by his hand.

From President de Gaulle's press conference of July 29, 1963   **277**

French-American Relations

Question: Would you tell us, in your opinion, what are the effects of the recent international agreements which have just been signed in Moscow on the evolution of French-American relations?

Answer: There has been much agitation, particularly in the American press, in the last few months. I can tell you after my personal experience of nearly 25 years of public reactions in the United States, I am hardly surprised by the ups and downs of what it is customary there to call opinion. But, all the same, I must confess that recently the tone and the song, as regards France, have seemed rather excessive to me.

It is true that to judge this one has to take into account a certain tension which exists there and which is naturally caused by pressing domestic and foreign concerns, as well as by an electoral situation which is continually recurring. Needless to say I myself many times noted how this pounding was as useless as it was exaggerated. . . .

But I believe it useful to stress right away that this agitation by the press, political circles and more or less semiofficial bodies, which rages on the other side of the Atlantic and which naturally finds a ready echo in the various sorts of unconditional opponents, all this agitation, I say, cannot alter in France what is fundamental as regards America. For us, the fundamental factors of French-American relations are friendship and alliance.

This friendship has existed for close on 200 years as an outstanding psychological reality in keeping with the nature of the two countries, special and reciprocal bonds maintained by the fact that among all the world powers France is the only one, with the exception, I should say, of Russia, with which the United States never exchanged a single cannon shot, while it is the only power without exception which fought at its side in three wars— the War of Independence and the First and Second World Wars—under conditions forever unforgettable. . . .

As regards the French-American alliance, if, since the days of Washington and Franklin, of Lafayette, of de Grasse, of Rochambeau, it was forged only during the First World War, in 1917 and 1918, and during the Second after December 1941, it is a fact that it now exists and that everything makes it vital for the two countries to maintain it. Indeed, so long as the free world is faced with the Soviet bloc, which is capable of suddenly submerging this or that territory, and which is moved by a dominating and detestable ideology, it will be essential that the peoples on both sides of the ocean, if they wish to defend themselves, be linked together to do so.

The Atlantic Alliance is an elemental necessity, and it is obvious that in this respect the United States and France have a capital responsibility, the United States because it disposes of a nuclear armament without which the fate of the world would be rapidly settled and France because, whatever the present inferiority of its means, it is politically, geographically, morally, militarily essential to the coalition. . . .

To my mind, these present differences are purely and simply the result of the intrinsic changes which took place in the last few years and which are continuing with regard to the absolute and relative situation of the United States and France. France had been materially and morally destroyed by the collapse of 1940 and by the capitulation of the Vichy people. Doubtless, the recovery achieved by the Resistance, at the sides of the Allies, gave it back, as though by a miracle, its integrity, its sovereignty and is dignity. But France came out of the ordeal greatly weakened in every respect.

In addition, the inconsistency of the régime which it fell back upon prevented it from achieving its growth within and its rank without. Moreover, failing to adopt and to apply the decisions necessary with a view to decolonization, France's national development and international action were hampered by distant and fruitless struggles.

That is why, with regard to the United States—rich, active and powerful —it found itself in a position of dependence. France constantly needed its assistance in order to avoid monetary collapse. It was from America that it received the weapons for its soldiers. France's security was dependent entirely on its protection. With regard to the international undertakings in which its leaders at that time were taking part, it was often with a view to dissolving France in them, as if self-renouncement were henceforth its sole possibility and even its only ambition, while these undertakings in the guise of integration were automatically taking American authority as a postulate. This was the case with regard to the project for a so-called supranational Europe, in which France as such would have disappeared, except to pay and to orate; a Europe governed in appearance by anonymous, technocratic and stateless committees; in other words, a Europe without political reality, without economic drive, without a capacity for defense, and therefore doomed, in the face of the Soviet bloc, to being nothing more than a dependent of that great Western power, which itself had a policy, an economy and a defense—the United States of America.

But it happens that, since then, France's position has considerably changed. Its new institutions put it in a position to wish and to act. Its internal development brings it prosperity and gives it access to the means of power. It has restored its currency, its finances, its balance of trade, to such an extent that, from this standpoint, it no longer needs anyone, but to the contrary it finds itself receiving requests from many sides, and so, far from borrowing from others, particularly from the Americans, it is paying back its debts to them and even on occasion is granting them certain facilities. It has transformed into cooperation between States the system of colonization which it once applied to its African territories and, for the first time in a quarter of a century, it is living in complete peace. France is modernizing its armed forces, is equipping them itself with *matériel* and is undertaking to endow itself with its own atomic force. It has cleared away the clouds which were surrounding and paralyzing the construction of Europe and is undertaking this great task on the basis of realities, beginning with the setting up of the economic community by giving, together with Germany, an example of the beginnings of political cooperation and by indicating that it wishes to be France within a Europe which must be European. Once again the national and international condition of our country resembles less and less what it used to be. How could the terms and conditions of its relations with the United States fail to be altered thereby? All the more so since the United States, on its side, as regards its own problems, is undergoing great changes which modify the character of hegemonic solidarity which, since the last World War, has marked its relations with France.

From the political standpoint it is true that the Soviet bloc holds to its totalitarian and threatening ideology and again recently the Berlin wall, the scandal of the Berlin wall, or the installation of nuclear arms in Cuba have shown that, because of the Soviet bloc, peace remained precarious. On the other hand, human evolution in Russia and its satellites, considerable economic and social difficulties in the life of those countries, and above all the beginnings of an opposition which is appearing between a European empire possessing immense Asiatic territories which make it the greatest colonial power of our times, and the empire of China, its neighbor for 6,000 miles, inhabited by 700 million men, an empire that is indestructible, ambitious and deprived of everything—all that can, in effect, introduce some new elements into the concerns of the Kremlin and lead it to insert a note of sincerity in the couplets that it devotes to peaceful coexistence. And, thus, the

United States which, since Yalta and Potsdam, has nothing, after all, to ask from the Soviets, the United States sees tempting prospects opening up before it. Hence, for instance, all the separate negotiations between the Anglo-Saxons and the Soviets, which, starting with the limited agreement on nuclear testing, seem likely to be extended to other questions, notably European ones, until now in the absence of the Europeans, which clearly goes against the views of France.

France, in effect, has for a long time believed that the day might come when a real *détente,* and even a sincere *entente,* will enable the relations between East and West in Europe to be completely changed and it intends, if this day comes—I have said this on other occasions—to make constructive proposals with regard to the peace, balance and destiny of Europe. But for the time being, France will not subscribe to any arrangement that would be made above its head and which would concern Europe and particularly Germany. As for a draft nonaggression pact—which, we are told, was discussed in Moscow—between the States belonging to NATO and the leaders of the countries subjected to the Kremlin's yoke, I must say right away that France does not appreciate this assimilation between the Atlantic Alliance and Communist servitude. And then, moreover, there is no need for a pact in order for France to declare that it will never be the first to attack, its being understood that it will defend itself with whatever means it may have against whomsoever would attack either it or its allies. But today France solemnly declares through the voice of the President of the Republic that there will never be any French aggression. And consequently our eventual participation in a nonaggression pact no longer has any kind of purpose.

But it remains that what happened in Moscow shows that the course followed by the policy of the United States is not identical with ours. . . . The result of this is that, as far as the French Government is concerned, important modifications are necessary with regard to the terms and conditions of our participation in the Alliance, since this organization has been built on the basis of integration, which today is no longer valid for us.

Lastly, on the economic level, the time has come when the United States, whose enormous production and trade capacity is not at all impaired, sees that of the European countries, particularly of France, rising, to the point of making them quite disturbing competitors. Furthermore, the burden represented for the United States by the financial support it grants to many States and by the military forces it maintains abroad, these burdens cannot but weigh heavily upon it, while a considerable part of its capital is being invested abroad. For these reasons the balance of payments and the dollar problem of the United States are becoming essential concerns. It is therefore perfectly understandable that its intentions are no longer those it formerly had on the subject of the organization of a European Europe and of the role that France can play in it, but it is also understandable that France, which is industrial and agricultural, cannot and does not wish to see either the nascent economy of Europe or its own dissolved in a system of a type of Atlantic community which would only be a new form of that famous integration. In sum, for France, and I believe, for the United States, the friendship that unites them and the alliance that links them are above and beyond all jeopardy, but it is true that there are differences between the two countries in the face of certain international problems. The evolution of both countries has created this state of things which, once again, is not at all surprising, however disturbing it may perhaps appear to the Americans. In any case, in the relations between the two peoples, we believe that each must accept this new situation. That being done, it will doubtless be advisable to harmonize, in each case and to the greatest extent possible, the respective policies. France for its part is cordially, very cordially disposed to this.

The Moscow Agreement

Question: What do you think about the agreement banning nuclear tests between the three powers which met in Moscow and the rupture which has taken place between China and the Soviet Union in a field which is in appearance ideological but which is in reality political?

Answer: I will speak first on the ideological rupture, then about the realities, that is the Moscow agreement. The break? Over what ideology? During my lifetime, Communist ideology has been personified by many people. There have been the eras of Lenin and Trotsky and Stalin—whom I knew personally—and of Beria and Malenkov and Khrushchev and Tito and Nagy and Mao Tse-tung. I know as many holders of the Communist ideology as there are fathers of Europe. And that makes quite a few. Each of these holders in his turn condemns, excommunicates, crushes and at times kills the others. In any event, he firmly fights against the personality cult of the others. I refuse to enter into a valid discussion on the subject of the ideological quarrel between Peking and Moscow. What I want to consider are the deep-rooted realities which are human, national and consequently international.

The banner of ideology in reality covers only ambitions. And I believe that it has been thus since the world was born.

Let's move on to the Moscow agreement.

The fact that the Soviets and the Anglo-Saxons decided directly to halt their nuclear tests in space, the air and the sea, is in itself satisfactory, and we share the joy that President Kennedy so eloquently expressed the day before yesterday on the subject of this event. . . .

However, without failing to realize that this Moscow agreement has indeed—quite the contrary—anything that can afford anyone, and in any case not us, it must be noted that it in no way alters the terrible threat that the nuclear weapons of the two rivals bring to bear on the world, and above all on the people who do not possess them.

It is a fact that both of them hold the means to annihilate the world and it is a fact that there is no question of their being ready to give them up.

In these conditions, the world situation in relation to this threat not being changed in any way whatsoever, it is quite natural for a country such as France, which is beginning to have the means of freeing itself to a certain degree from this permanent terror, continue along this course. All the more so since nothing prevents the two rivals, their tests having been halted, from continuing to manufacture missiles in increasing quantities and power and to equip themselves with increasingly advanced launch vehicles, rockets, airplanes, submarines, and satellites. The savings they could perhaps make from halting tests will enable them to strengthen even further their means of destruction. That is why the Moscow agreement, I say this frankly, has only limited practical importance. Unless, of course, it were the starting point for something else, which would extend to other very different areas, and for that reason the agreement, while having France's approval, nevertheless awakens its vigilance.

Then you ask me what France is going to do after the Moscow agreement?

I will tell you once again that if one day the Americans and the Soviets reach the point of disarmament, that is the controlled destruction and banning of their nuclear means, it is wholeheartedly that we ourselves would give up securing them. Nothing, unfortunately, indicates that we are about to reach that point. And the sad Geneva Conference, as was to be foreseen, will have interminably sat for nothing. . . .

Question: Since your last conference the French-German Treaty has been put to the test in many domains, concerning the coordination of French-German policies in the Common Market or with regard to the eventual membership of Great Britain, in the more modest Atlantic organization, in the purchase of French agricultural products by Germany, in the manufacture of a European tank, etc.—have the facts exceeded, met or disappointed your hopes?

Answer: The European economic organization is continuing to make progress and the French-German Treaty is directly contributing to it. The first meeting of the two Governments which, in accordance with the Treaty, was held in Bonn at the beginning of this month, first had the advantage of organizing and extending the contacts for the examination of problems of common interest. It is thus, for example, that I myself, independently of my talks with Chancellor Adenauer, had the opportunity, with which I am very pleased, of holding detailed discussions with Vice Chancellor Erhard. In addition, the Bonn meeting strengthened the feeling in the minds of those taking part that French-German cooperation should during the present year affirm itself in an essential area: the economic organization of Europe, the complete and effective setting up of the Common Market. It is quite clear that this is, we might say, the testing ground of the Treaty.

If, on this issue, it proves effective, we may think that it will continue to develop and grow stronger on other issues such as those which you have mentioned and on which only a start has been made as yet.

As for the Common Market, to the development of which we hope the French-German Treaty will contribute in an effective manner, it is of course the agricultural problem that the Six have still to settle. What would the very words "European Economic Community" mean if Europe did not for the most part assure its food supplies from its own agricultural products, which are amply sufficient for this? And what would France do in a system in which there would soon no longer be any customs tariffs except for its wheat, its meat, its milk, its wine and its fruit? Undoubtedly, the Rome Treaty, which is fairly well set up as regards industry, went no further than raising the question of agriculture, without settling it. But since January of last year, when France obtained a formal commitment from its partners to reach a conclusion in this domain, failing which the development of the whole would be halted, considerable progress has been made. Still greater progress remains to be accomplished, and this must take place before the end of this year.

Indeed, the date adopted for the completion of the regulations still pending is December 31st: first because the imbalance between the conditions for industrial exchanges and those for agricultural exchanges could not last any longer; then because it is under this condition that the Six, having taken note of the fact that Great Britain cannot at present enter into the organization of a European Europe, agreed upon using the WEU which already existed in order to exchange their views with those of the British on world economic problems. Finally, for the reason that the tariff negotiations between the United States and Europe are due to open next spring and that in face of the storms which will not fail to come up on that occasion, it will be necessary then that the Common Market be standing on its feet, complete and assured, or that it disappear.

Thus the year 1963 is decisive for the future of a united Europe. If, at the heart of the world, a real community is established between the Six in the economic domain, it may indeed be thought that they will be led more than they are to organize themselves in order to conduct together a policy which is European. From this point of view also, the French-German Treaty provides an example which may be followed and a framework which may be enlarged. All the more so since the events about which we spoke before, and particularly the direct contacts which are being re-established between the Anglo-Saxons and the Soviets and which once again may commit Europe's fate, should convince it that it is time for it to be itself, or that it run the risk of never being it.

Ambassade de France, Service de Presse et d'Information, New York, Speeches and Press Conferences No. 192, July 29, 1963, pp. 5–13.

The quest of disarmament paralleled the quest for other political solutions to the stalemate of the cold war. The Nuclear Test Ban Treaty (July 25, 1963) was a positive step in a quest which had already produced some general statements about disarmament at the Geneva Conference (266). The Treaty was ratified by the United States Senate and adhered to by most of the nations of the world (with the exception of France [see 277], Communist China, and Cuba). It gave some promise of peace to the 1960's.

278   TREATY BANNING NUCLEAR WEAPON TESTS IN THE ATMOSPHERE, IN OUTER SPACE AND UNDER WATER

The Governments of the United States of America, the United Kingdom of Great Britain and Northern Ireland, and the Union of Soviet Socialist Republics, hereinafter referred to as the "Original Parties",

Proclaiming as their principal aim the speediest possible achievement of an agreement on general and complete disarmament under strict international control in accordance with the objectives of the United Nations which would put an end to the armaments race and eliminate the incentive to the production and testing of all kinds of weapons, including nuclear weapons,

Seeking to achieve the discontinuance of all test explosions of nuclear weapons for all time, determined to continue negotiations to this end, and desiring to put an end to the contamination of man's environment by radioactive substances,

Have agreed as follows:

Article I

1. Each of the Parties to this Treaty undertakes to prohibit, to prevent, and not to carry out any nuclear weapon test explosion, or any other nuclear explosion, at any place under its jurisdiction or control:

(a) in the atmosphere; beyond its limits, including outer space; or underwater, including territorial waters or high seas; or

(b) in any other environment if such explosion causes radioactive debris to be present outside the territorial limits of the State under whose jurisdiction or control such explosion is conducted. It is understood in this connection that the provisions of this subparagraph are without prejudice to the conclusion of a treaty resulting in the permanent banning of all nuclear test explosions, including all such explosions underground, the conclusion of which, as the Parties have stated in the Preamble to this Treaty, they seek to achieve.

2. Each of the Parties to this Treaty undertakes furthermore to refrain from causing, encouraging, or in any way participating in, the carrying out of any nuclear weapon test explosion, or any other nuclear explosion, anywhere which would take place in any of the environments described, or have the effect referred to, in paragraph 1 of this Article.

Article II

1. Any Party may propose amendments to this Treaty. The text of any proposed amendment shall be submitted to the Depositary Governments which shall circulate it to all Parties to this Treaty. Thereafter, if requested to do so by one-third or more of the Parties, the Depositary Governments shall convene a conference, to which they shall invite all the Parties, to consider such amendment.

2. Any amendment to this Treaty must be approved by a majority of the votes of all the Parties to this Treaty, including the votes of all of the Original Parties. The amendment shall enter into force for all Parties upon the deposit of instruments of ratification by a majority of all the Parties, including the instruments of ratification of all of the Original Parties.

Article III

1. This Treaty shall be open to all States for signature. Any State which does not sign this Treaty before its entry into force in accordance with paragraph 3 of this Article may accede to it at any time.

2. This Treaty shall be subject to ratification by signatory States. Instruments of ratification and instruments of accession shall be deposited with the Governments of the Original Parties—the United States of America, the United Kingdom of Great Britain and Northern Ireland, and the Union of Soviet Socialist Republics—which are hereby designated the Depositary Governments.

3. This Treaty shall enter into force after its ratification by all the Original Parties and the deposit of their instruments of ratification.

4. For States whose instruments of ratification or accession are deposited subsequent to the entry into force of this Treaty, it shall enter into force on the date of the deposit of their instruments of ratification or accession.

5. The Depositary Governments shall promptly inform all signatory and acceding States of the date of each signature, the date of deposit of each instrument of ratification of and accession to this Treaty, the date of its entry into force, and the date of receipt of any requests for conferences or other notices.

6. This Treaty shall be registered by the Depositary Governments pursuant to Article 102 of the Charter of the United Nations.

Article IV

This Treaty shall be of unlimited duration.

Each Party shall in exercising its national sovereignty have the right to withdraw from the Treaty if it decides that extraordinary events, related to the subject matter of this Treaty, have jeopardized the supreme interests of its country. It shall give notice of such withdrawal to all other Parties to the Treaty three months in advance.

Article V

This Treaty, of which the English and Russian texts are equally authentic, shall be deposited in the archives of the Depositary Governments. Duly certified copies of this Treaty shall be transmitted by the Depositary Governments to the Governments of the signatory and acceding States.

IN WITNESS WHEREOF the undersigned, duly authorized, have signed this Treaty.

DONE in triplicate at the city of Moscow the fifth day of August, one thousand nine hundred and sixty-three.

For the Government of the United States of America:

DEAN RUSK

WAH

For the Government of the United Kingdom of Great Britain and Northern Ireland:

HOME

H

For the Government of the Union of Soviet Socialist Republics:

A. GROMYKO

A.G.

Eighty-eighth Congress, First Session, Senate, Executive M., pages 7–8.

QUESTIONS

1. How do the recommendations about Germany at Geneva (266) differ in viewpoint from the Yalta (p. 534) and Potsdam (p. 543) treatment of the German question?
2. How does Khrushchev criticize Stalin's definition of the "enemies of the people"?
3. What does Khrushchev mean by the "cult of the individual"? How would he rectify it?
4. Does Khrushchev in his speech come close to abandoning communist principles? How close is he to Lenin's ideas (see p. 412)?
5. How do the Chinese Communist and Soviet positions in 1963 agree or disagree with respect to the likelihood and the inevitability of war?
6. How do the respective Soviet and Chinese positions agree or disagree with respect to the destiny of capitalism and communism?
7. According to both statements, what should the correct Communist attitude toward armed revolution be?
8. How do the Chinese Communist leaders envisage the organisation and mutual relations of the Communist parties of the world?
9. From the Soviet statement, what conclusions do you draw concerning the Soviet definition of "peaceful existence" and the motivations behind it?
10. What controls for neutralization does the Rapacki plan offer? What criticism of these controls did the West German government make?

11. What are the bases for Chancellor Adenauer's hopes for peace, and how do they differ from Rapacki's?

12. From General de Gaulle's statements, how does he envisage the unity of Europe?

13. What are De Gaulle's views of East-West relations and how do they compare to the other views you have read?

14. Compare the goals, structure and methods of the European Economic Community on the one hand with those of the European Free Trade Association and the Council for Mutual Economic Assistance (COMECON) on the other.

A NOTE ABOUT THIS BOOK

The text is set in Linotype Granjon.
Marginal numbers are in
Gothic Condensed No. 2.
Designed by William Nicoll, Edit, Inc.
Composed, printed, and bound
by Rand McNally & Company.

PRINTED IN U.S.A.